All communications with regard to the
Society should be addressed to
THE HON. SECRETARY
English Place-name Society
University College
Gower Street
W.C. 1

ENGLISH PLACE-NAME SOCIETY.   VOLUME XVI

GENERAL EDITORS
ALLEN MAWER *and* F. M. STENTON

THE
PLACE-NAMES OF WILTSHIRE

CAMBRIDGE
UNIVERSITY PRESS
LONDON: BENTLEY HOUSE

NEW YORK, TORONTO, BOMBAY
CALCUTTA, MADRAS: MACMILLAN
TOKYO: MARUZEN COMPANY LTD

ENGLISH PLACE-NAME SOCIETY.   VOLUME XVI

THE PLACE-NAMES OF WILTSHIRE

By

J. E. B. GOVER, ALLEN MAWER
AND F. M. STENTON

CAMBRIDGE

AT THE UNIVERSITY PRESS

1939

The collection from unpublished documents of
material for this volume has been made possible
by a grant received from the British Academy

PRINTED IN GREAT BRITAIN

PREFACE

THE SURVEY of the Place-names of Wiltshire is the heaviest task which the Survey has undertaken since the completion of the volume on the Place-names of Essex by Dr P. H. Reaney. The task has, however, been rendered more than usually interesting by the large amount of help received from the county itself. From the days of Aubrey onwards Wiltshire has been fortunate in the number of scholars, antiquaries and archaeologists who have interested themselves in her history, and the volume which we are now able to present to our subscribers and to the general public owes a very great debt to men like Canon Goddard, the doyen of these studies in Wiltshire at the present time, Mr H. C. Brentnall, the President of the Wiltshire Archaeological and Natural History Society, and Mr G. M. Young, for all that they have done in helping us in its preparation.

The main responsibility for the collection of the material has been in the hands of Mr J. E. B. Gover, our sub-Editor. He it was who constructed the gazetteer which forms the basis of the survey and undertook the whole investigation of the vast mass of documents, printed and unprinted, relating to Wiltshire on which this account of its place-names rests. After that initial stage it is impossible to assign individual responsibility, even to those persons whose names appear on the title-page. The whole survey has been a co-operative effort, and at various stages it has had the advantage of the comments and criticisms of many friends of the Survey. On the more local aspects of the matter, the editors stand deeply indebted to the three persons already named who, partly in the manuscript stage, partly in the proof stage, sometimes in both, have given us the advantage of their criticism and comment. In the manuscript stage we had the further help of comments upon some of our *cruces* by Professor Ekwall, Professor Max Förster and Dr Ritter. In the proof stage we had the help of Professor Bruce Dickins, Professor Ekwall and Professor Tait. They are in no sense responsible for the volume as it now appears, but the editors are very clear that through them very many imperfections have been removed and many good new points made. Their share in the improvement of the volume is by no means fully indicated by the references to their names which are made in the text itself.

The editors stand very much indebted in their collection of material to various landowners who have given us access to documents in their possession; in particular we would desire to thank the Marquess of Ailesbury, the Marquess of Bath, the Earl of Pembroke, the Earl of Radnor, Lord Arundell of Wardour and Miss Fox Talbot. Our thanks are due also to the Dean and Chapter of Salisbury, the Dean and Chapter of Winchester, to Eton College, Winchester College, King's College, Cambridge, Brasenose College, Oxford, Corpus Christi College, Oxford, Magdalen College, Oxford, and New College, Oxford, who gave us permission to search their muniments, and to the Ecclesiastical Commissioners who gave us access to documents in their possession deposited at the Public Record Office.

In this volume once again an attempt has been made to deal not only with the names recorded on the Ordnance Survey maps but also with the field-names. The study of the field-names is based primarily upon the names as recorded in the Tithe Awards, but we owe a very great debt of gratitude for the supplementary material and comment provided for us by some ninety schools in the county. Through the kind offices of Mr Keith Innes, the Director of Education for Wiltshire, the co-operation of these schools was secured and much excellent work was done. Lists were made of the field-names of various parishes with any necessary topographical or other comment; tracings were taken from the 6-inch Ordnance Survey sheets, showing the position of the fields thus named; numerous questions were answered with regard to local topography. All this work was of great value in enabling us to record and interpret these names and also in giving us a lively picture of the rapid changes which those names are undergoing at the present time. To the teachers in the various schools we stand indebted for their untiring labour in endeavouring to carry through a very difficult task.

In relation to the field-name material the editors also desire to thank the officers of the Tithe Award Office for their great courtesy and kindness in meeting the somewhat heavy demands which our work makes upon them.

We stand indebted to many old friends of the Society in our work on this county. Mr O. G. S. Crawford of the Ordnance Survey Office gave us much help by giving us access to his own copy of the Ordnance Survey sheets for the county with many valuable notes. To him we also owe ready access to photographs of old estate maps and the like which are in the possession of the Ordnance Survey Office, and the loan of transcripts of Forest material made by him at the Public Record Office and elsewhere. To Mr F. T. S. Houghton we are indebted for much help with Gloucestershire parallels and with those parishes which have been transferred either from Wiltshire to Gloucestershire or from Gloucestershire to Wiltshire. Professor E. J. Salisbury has again given us valuable assistance in the interpretation of names involving questions of plant ecology.

Among recent writers upon our own particular theme, we should like to express our indebtedness to Dr Ekblom for his pioneer volume on the place-names of the county, and to Dr G. B. Grundy for the many valuable identifications and comments to be found in his studies of the Anglo-Saxon charters of Wiltshire as published in the *Archaeological Journal*.

For various miscellaneous services we desire to thank the following: Captain Cunnington for help in securing access to the Wiltshire Enclosure Awards and for guidance in the use of the Library of the Wiltshire Archaeological and Natural History Society at Devizes; Mr W. N. Haden for comments on the manuscript sheets dealing with the district round Trowbridge; Mr A. L. Ingpen for help with the work at an early stage; Canon A. A. Mayhew for help in Salisbury; Mr J. H. Pafford for help in the Bradford on Avon district, more especially with the parishes of Atworth and Holt; the Rev. F. H. S. Powell for the use of a collection of local names made by his predecessor, the Rev. W. B. Sykes, Vicar of Wilcot; Dr M. S. Serjeantson for the transcription of forms from unprinted charters in the Bodleian Library; Mr and Mrs Trotter of Teffont for personal help of every kind received by the Director during a long holiday in Teffont in the summer of 1937; the Rev. F. G. Walker for help in the parish of Knook; Miss Withycombe for help with Knoyle *Hodierne*. In addition, mention must be made of the useful gift of a great collection of slips, partly by way of gazetteer, partly giving early forms, which was presented to the Survey soon after its establishment. Unfortunately, the letter accompanying this gift cannot now be found, and all enquiries have failed to identify the donor. We desire none the less to express our thanks to him.

Our thanks are as always due to the staff of the Public Record Office and the British Museum for numerous services, and to the Cambridge University Press for its careful work in the production of the volume.

Finally, the editors desire to thank Miss Armstrong for all her work upon the volume alike in its manuscript and its printed stage, and more especially for her share in securing that most difficult thing, uniformity of reference and the like in a work which is so full of varied detail.

A. M.
F. M. S.

St Valentine's Day, 1939

CONTENTS

MAPS

INTRODUCTION

IF WEST SAXON tradition can be trusted, the English occupation of what is now Wiltshire can scarcely have begun before the middle of the sixth century. According to the *Anglo-Saxon Chronicle*, the campaigns which for a time made the West Saxons the strongest people in southern England began in the year 552 with a victory won by Cynric their king over the Britons on the site now familiar under the name of Old Sarum. Four years later, according to the same tradition, Cynric and Ceawlin his son fought with, and no doubt defeated, the Britons at a place called *Beranbyrg*, which can safely be identified with Barbury Hill above the Ridge Way, south of Swindon[1]. The first of these battles must have opened to the Saxons the whole series of river valleys which converge from the north and west upon Salisbury. The second presumably carried them beyond the crest of the northern downs to the fertile country along the upper course of the Bristol Avon and its tributaries. It is with the record of these two battles that the written history of Anglo-Saxon Wiltshire begins. The question of its credibility is important, not only for the date at which the Saxon settlement of this region became possible, but also for the general chronology of the English conquest of the South.

From the archaeological standpoint, there is no reason to challenge the substantial accuracy of these dates. In the aggregate, Wiltshire has yielded a comparatively small body of material for the study of heathen Saxon culture, and none of it seems to belong to the phases of this culture which were prevalent in the age of the actual migration to Britain. There are no sites within the county on which life appears to have continued without any appreciable break from the Romano-British into the Anglo-Saxon period. In a recent survey of the archaeological evidence bearing on the Anglo-Saxon conquest,[2] Mr J. N. L. Myres has observed that "the traditional date of 552 for the West Saxon victory at *Searoburh* may well be approximately

---

[1] For early forms, see *infra* 278–9.
[2] *Oxford History of England*, I, 400.

correct for the first appearance of Saxon elements at the Harnham Hill settlement" (near Salisbury). He also remarks that
the local custom of using earlier barrows for the reception of
individual interments "points far more strongly to the disposal
of casualties incurred in raiding than to the habits of a settled
population." Whatever future discoveries may be made within
the county, it is most unlikely that they will include any traces
of heathen English settlement or burial comparable to the
remains which have led some scholars to propose a fifth-century
date for the beginnings of Saxon occupation in Berkshire.

Wiltshire was undoubtedly occupied at a date when Saxon
heathenism was an active force. The name of Woden is found
in Wansdyke (*infra* 17) and the neighbouring *wodnesdenu* (BCS
734) in the bounds of West Overton and in *wodnesbeorh* (ib. 390),
a barrow now known as Adam's Grave, in the bounds of Alton
Priors. His popular name Grim is found in more than one
Grim's Ditch in the county (*infra* 15). Thunor occurs in
Thunresfeld near Hardenhuish (*infra* 341), while in Waden Hill
in Avebury (*infra* 295) and the lost *Weolond* in Tockenham we
have OE *weoh*, 'heathen temple,' 'sacred precinct,' as the first
element. Further, we may have traces of OE *hearg*, 'heathen
temple,' 'sacred grove,' in *Haradon Hill* (*infra* 359) and perhaps
in Harrow Fm (*infra* xli, 346). But the conversion of Wessex
did not begin until 634, and these names cannot be regarded as
evidence of fifth-, or early sixth-century settlement. If the name
Wodnes dic means that the Saxons believed Wansdyke to be a
supernatural work, it would seem to follow that they cannot
have become acquainted with this post-Roman earthwork until
the circumstances of its making had been forgotten.

The place-names which are the subject of the present volume
give the same impression. They show very few of the ancient
features which distinguish the local nomenclature of regions of
primary settlement, such as Sussex, Kent, and Essex. As a
whole they clearly suggest the sixth century rather than the
fifth. Apart from Cannings (*infra* 249–50), which may well have
been the name, not of a village community, but of a folk or small
tribe, the county has no place-names ending in -*ingas*. The work
undertaken for this survey has produced no certain Wiltshire
examples of the distinctive type of name in which the element

-ing, in the singular, follows a personal name, an adjective, or a common noun. There are no Wiltshire parallels to the Berkshire Balking and Lockinge, or the Hampshire Nursling and Swaythling. The copious store of words on which the men of Kent or Sussex could draw for the description of natural features of the country has been reduced in Wiltshire to a local vocabulary of much smaller range. The personal names compounded in Wiltshire place-names include few of those obvious survivals from the personal nomenclature of the pre-migration age which can be found in the eastern counties and in Sussex[1]. There are many Wiltshire place-names which cannot be explained, but as a rule their obscurity is due, not to their archaic character but to the badness of the forms in which they have been handed down by medieval copyists. Even without the definite evidence of the *Chronicle*, the character of the place-names of Wiltshire would suggest that the settlement of the county did not begin until the sixth century was well advanced.

The most interesting feature of this nomenclature is the Celtic strain by which it is diversified. Names of British origin are more prominent in Wiltshire than in any other district, except perhaps Devon, with which the Survey has so far dealt, and they occur in every part of the county. For many—perhaps for most—of them no certain explanation can be offered. Even so, the mere fact of their survival points clearly enough to a period of peaceful intercourse between the Britons who had survived the first impact of the Saxon invasion and the new lords of their country. In Wiltshire, as generally in England, the Britons seem to have transmitted few, if any, village names to their conquerors[2]. It was by handing on the names of hills, woods and rivers that they left their impress on the local nomenclature of the shire. Many of the best known place-names of Wiltshire, such as Calne, Deverill, Melchet, Savernake and Fonthill, prove under examination to be British names of streams or woods which had been adopted by Saxon settlers. The frequency of the elements *penn* (*infra* 33–4), *chet* (*infra* 12–14), *cors*

---

[1] The *Mehha* of Mannington (*infra* 275) and the *Brænci* of Brencesberge (*infra* 205) are among the few personal names in the county which have an archaic appearance.

[2] Cherhill is a possible example.

(*infra*, 7, 50, 152, 495) and the strange repetition of *idover* (*infra* 2–4) suggest that these British words may actually have been adopted into the speech of the settlers. Hybrid compounds also occur in Conkwell, Cricklade, Pertwood, Pimperleaze, Quemerford (*infra* 124, 42, 176, 180, 258), but it is impossible to make any precise estimate of the strength of this British element. In several cases, such as Chitterne and Bedwyn (*infra* 163, 332), there is no means of deciding for certain whether a particular name is of British or Saxon origin. On the whole, the number of undoubted British names which have survived is sufficiently large to support the view that the Saxon occupation of Wiltshire did not begin until the first and most devastating phase of the English invasion was over.

Possible traces of the British population are to be found in Walcot, Wallen, Wallmead and the lost *Walton* (*infra* 277, 244, 198, 394), containing OE *weala* (gen. pl.), 'Britons, serfs.' Only one of these, the lost *Walton* in Downton, is near to an important Anglo-Saxon settlement. We may also note Britford near Salisbury (*infra* 220). On the other hand, of the numerous pre-English earthworks, camps and barrows scattered throughout the county and especially in the Salisbury Plain area, hardly one example can be found of the survival of a British name, though in the case of Brokenborough (*infra* 53) the tradition of an earlier Celtic one has been preserved.

There are no means of determining the rate of the Saxon advance across the county, nor the relative density of settlement in the various river valleys by which it is intersected. But the name which it has borne since the ninth century shows that throughout what may be called historic times, the centre of its administration had lain in the south. The name *Wiltunscir*, from which the modern Wiltshire has descended, means the district dependent for purposes of local government upon Wilton, and it is clear that at least as early as the reign of Alfred, the men of the whole region between the Thames and Cranborne Chase regarded that royal village as their capital. But a name like *Wiltunscir* belongs to the language of an age in which a considerable measure of political centralisation had already come into being. It is the description of a unit of local government, and in character and significance it differs fundamentally from the tribal names which in Wessex as elsewhere were current before the primitive English kingdoms had been divided into shires[1]. By a fortunate chance, it is possible in the case of Wiltshire to get behind this official designation to the tribal name by which the men of the district were originally known. In the *Chronicle* under the years 800 and 878, they are called the *Wilsætan*, or dwellers by the Wylye[2]. In the absence of direct evidence, it is possible that this name was at first restricted to the men who lived in and around the valleys of the Wylye and the other southern rivers to which the Saxons had gained access through their victory of 552. But even if this were so, the name had certainly been extended to cover the men of the country beyond Salisbury Plain before the year 802, when the *Wilsætan*, under their ealdorman, or local ruler, met and defeated an army from the north which had just crossed the Thames at Kempsford[3]. There can be little doubt that the administrative unit which afterwards appears as Wiltshire existed, with substantially its medieval boundaries, before the end of the eighth century.

The English element in the place-names of the county contains a few elements such as *benc*, **clacc*, **clenc*, *cnugel*, *cwylle* (*infra* 404, 406) which have not been noted in any county hitherto surveyed. Other elements of interest which have been found, however, in other districts, include **bors*, *byd*, **forst*, *spræg*, *þrocc*, *wrocc* (*infra* 404–14). The frequency of *yfer* (*infra* 414) can be explained by its common application to the steep smooth slopes of the chalk downs. The element *dræg* occurs three times in combination with *cot(e)* (*infra* 69, 282, 325), but is not found with *tun*. In all three cases we have reference to a steep slope, not to a portage or the like. The element *stede* is less frequent than in the south-eastern counties, but the list includes two compounds not hitherto noted in place-names, viz. *hus-stede* and *wic-stede*, v. Hursted, Wicksted *infra* 38, 27. *tun* is, as usual,

---

[1] Few of these tribal names have been recorded in documents relating to Wessex, but in the seventh century the eastern part of the district which afterwards became Berkshire is described as the province of the *Sunningas*, whose name survives in Sonning (BCS 34).

[2] Compare similarly the Mercian *Tomsætan*, which in the ninth century denoted the people by the river Tame. See PN Wa xvii, xviii.

[3] ASC s.a. 800.

very common and continued in living use after the Norman Conquest (*v. infra* 417–18), though post-Conquest place-names of this type are much less frequent than in Dorset or Devon. No certain post-Conquest place-names compounded with *cot(e)* or *worþ* have been noted.

We have three examples of burhtun in close association with ancient boroughs and distinctive of the county are names of the type first illustrated under Haydon Wick (*infra* 25) which are common in the north and north-west of the county. We may note Badbury, Bremhill, Farleigh, Hannington, Heddington, Kemble, Kington, Potterne and Tockenham Wick and several places now called simply Wick or Wyke which earlier bore fuller names such as Rowde Wick, Melksham Wyke. Interesting too are the three examples of *Kingsbury* in ancient royal manors (*infra* 218, 256, 299).

Among the names which have reference to Old English social classes or customs there are five examples of *ceorl*, four of *cniht*, two of *gebur*, one or two of *cild* and one of *swan* (*infra* 404–14). The *cotsetla* (*infra* 427) figures prominently in the minor and field-names. *hiwisc* (*infra* 417) is rare both among the minor and among the field-names, but *hid* (ib.) is fairly common. The *hide*-names include several examples of 'five hides,' one of 'two hides' and one of 'ten hides.' The history of most of these estates can be traced in Domesday Book.

The place-names of the 'Plain' seem to have little reference to the past. Although in the Old English land boundaries of the charters there are numerous references to 'burials' or 'heathen burials,' none of these is preserved in actual name on the modern map[1]. Of place-names preserving the memory of old legends the most interesting is perhaps Drake North in Damerham (*infra* 400), while Puck Shipton (*infra* 319) and certain other minor and field-names containing the OE *puca*, 'goblin,' perhaps had reference to some haunted site or building.

The Scandinavian element is, as was to be expected, extremely meagre. Thoulstone (*infra* 156) certainly, and Haxton (*infra* 330) probably contain as first elements Scandinavian or Anglo-Scandinavian personal names, but we find such types in other

---

[1] The field-name *Burrells* (*infra* 491) with its earlier form *The Burials*, preserving the *s* of OE *byrgels*, does however almost certainly belong here.

counties also in the South and West, e.g. Swainston (Wt), Thruxton (Ha), Thurloxton (So), such places being probably named from Scandinavians of the court of Cnut or Edward the Confessor rather than from earlier settlers of the Viking period. One of these may have had St Olaf as his favourite saint and founded the chapel which gave name to *Tuley streete* in Bradford on Avon (*infra* 117).

The Norman-French element is also very slight. Devizes, a settlement which grew up around a twelfth-century castle, is the only major place-name of French origin (*infra* 242–3), but French forest terms have given rise to some minor place-names such as Brail, Clears, Lawn, Purley. Also a few other Middle English words of Norman-French origin appear in later place-names and field-names such as *causeway, close, pece, trenche, waite.*

The feudal element in Wiltshire names is on the other hand very strong, as in all the south-western counties other than Cornwall (*infra* 420). It will be seen to include a good many family names which occur but rarely in names of this type elsewhere in England.

In connection with the personal name element it will be found that the number of dithematic personal names is much smaller than that for Devon and for the west midland counties, some thirty out of a hundred and seventy in all. The number of feminine names is six and it may be noted that three of these are compounds in *ðryð*, though each has a different first theme. Of uncompounded personal names *Cada* occurs in three or four place-names, but *Bic(c)a*, so common in Devon, is not found. Occasionally it may be suspected that the same man has given name to two neighbouring places. The *Babba* of Bapton and Baverstock (*infra* 161, 212), the *Bubbe* of Bupton and Bubbeclive (*infra* 266) and the *Beocc* of Bagshot and *Beoccesheal* (*infra* 354), are probably illustrations of this practice.

NOTES ON THE DIALECT OF WILTSHIRE
AS ILLUSTRATED IN ITS PLACE-NAMES

OE *æ* usually appears as *a* in ME and ModEng as in *Ashley, Hatt, Nash, Wadswick,* with occasional *e* in ME.

OE *ǣ* usually appears as *a* but occasionally as *e* in Middle English as in *Mancombe, Manwood, Mean Wood, Stratford, Stratton.* *e*-forms are universal in ME in *Marten* and *Martin.*

OE *e* (*æ*) in *denu* (cf. PN Ess xxv, PN Herts xxiv) occasionally appears in ModEng as *a* in the form *Dane* but there is no evidence for this change in ME and it is probable that it is for the most part due to late pseudo-historical associations as in *Danes Lye.*

ME *lawe* (*lowe*) and *lewe, rawe* (*rowe*) and *rewe* from OE *hlaw, hlæw* and *raw, ræw* are common in early forms but in ModEng we usually have **low** and **row.**

OE *ĕo* appears in ME as *u(o)* or (more often) as *e.* Occasionally the *u(o)* survives in the ModEng form. Cf. *s.nn. Bedborough, Bemerton, Charlton, Chelworth, Crudwell, Dean, Deptford, Derriads, Durrington, Hartham, Melksham, Nethermore, Redlands, Rodbourne, Rodmead, Stert.*

OE *īĕ* appears in ME as *u, i* and occasionally *e* in *Biddestone, Flisteridge, Grittenham, Lipe, Lypiatt, Stype, Tinhead Tytherton.* It is the *i*-form which ultimately survives except in two examples of *Shute* which may have been influenced by initial [ʃ].

OE, ME *o* occasionally develops to ModEng *a* as in *Cra(f)t* for *Croft, Faxley* for *Foxley, Platt, Ratfyn, Splatts.*

OE *u* develops to ModEng *i* in the neighbourhood of point consonants in *Dinton, Stitchcombe, Tidpit, Tidworth* and probably also in *Dilton, Pitton* and *Wilton* (in Grafton). Cf. *s.nn.* Diddington (PN BedsHu 254), Diglis (PN Wo 162).

OE *ȳ* generally appears as *u(o)* in ME but we often have *i* and occasionally *e*-forms. Occasionally the *u*-form survives as in *Dunge, Rudge, Rudloe.* Forms such as *Burcombe, Hurst, Purton* are due, not to the survival of ME *u* but to the influence of the *r*-sound on the preceding vowel in ModEng.

OE *ceald* commonly develops to ME *chald* and retains initial [tʃ] in ModEng as in *Chalcot, Chaldicotts, Chalfield, Challymead, Chowell,* but we have also *Calcote* and *Coldcote.* So similarly cealf in *Choulden.*

OE *f* (pronounced [v] initially and medially alike) frequently retains the old voiced pronunciation and the pronunciation is often recorded in the spelling itself. We may note *Burnivale, Clanville, Twivers, Vasterne, Venn, Venny Sutton, Vernditch,* all retained on the map, and such occasional forms as *Bradvyld* for *Bradfield, Chavill* for *Chalfield, Mivord* for *Milford, Virlon* for *Furlong, Vorty* for *Forty, Voxcote* for *Foscote, Voxlee* for *Foxley.* This interchange occasionally leads to inverted spellings and forms such as Stoke *Farthing* for *Vardon* (*infra* 206).

Final *f* is lost in *Penceley* and in some forms of *Baycliff, Whitecliff.*

OE initial *s* (pronounced [z]) frequently retains the old voiced pronunciation and it is sometimes expressed in writing as in *Zeals, Zidles* for *Sidehills, Zons* for *Sands.*

Metathesis of *r* is common in the later developments of OE *brycg* as in *Reyburge* for *Reybridge, Wodburge* for *Woodbridge, Sheepen Berds* for *Sheeppen Bridge,* with further sound substitution of [dz] for [dʒ].

Metathesis of [sk] to [ks] is found in *Axford, Froxfield, Haxmore*; [sk] for OE *sc* in *Skilling infra* 454.

Confusion of [t] and [k], [g] and [d] is fairly common as in *Ditteridge, Rudloe, Tottenham, Widbrook.*

Sound substitution of [dʒ] for [dz], [tʃ] for [ts] and *vice versa* is fairly common as in *Bulidge* for *Bulhides, Sheeppen Berds* for *Sheeppen Burge, Stitchcombe* for *Stuttescombe, Tedgell* for *Tedzell, Whitsbury* for *Whichbury.*

Inflexional *n* is often preserved in ME and occasionally in ModEng as in the examples of *Newnton* and *Newton.* So also *Langham.*

The weak genitive plural inflexion is preserved in *Carternestrete, Gygornestrete* (*infra* 20).

BIBLIOGRAPHY AND ABBREVIATIONS

a.	*ante.*
A and D	J. Andrews and A. Dury, *A Topographical Map of Wiltshire*, 1773.
Abbr	*Placitorum Abbreviatio*, 1811.
AC	*Ancient Charters* (Pipe Roll Soc.), 1888.
A.C.S.	A. C. Smith, *Guide to British and Roman Antiquities of the North Wiltshire Downs*, 1884.
Act	Enclosure, Turnpike and other Acts of Parliament in Devizes Museum Library.
AD	*Catalogue of Ancient Deeds.* (In progress).
AD	Unpublished Deeds at the PRO.
Add	Additional MSS (BM), Nos. 24316, 28206, 28211, 34566, 37270.
AddCh	Additional Charters (BM), Nos. 15020, 18307, 18466, 22440–1, 24394, 26579, 26903, 37534, 37603.
AN	Anglo-Norman.
ANG	*Ungedruckte anglo-normannische Geschichtsquellen*, ed. Liebermann, 1879.
AnnMon	*Annales Monastici* (Rolls Series), 5 vols., 1864–9.
AntonItin	*Itinerarium Antonini Augusti*, ed. Parthey and Pinder, 1848.
AOMB	Augmentation Office, Miscellaneous Books (PRO), vols. 385, 398, 400, 420, 422.
Arch	*Archaeologia.* (In progress.)
ASC	Anglo-Saxon Chronicle.
Ass	*Somerset Assize Rolls* (SRS vols., 11, 36, 41, 44).
Ass	Assize Rolls for Wiltshire (PRO), Nos. 996, 997, 998, 1000, 1001, 1005, 1006, 1007, 1010, 1011, 1013, 1015, 1016, 1018 and for divers counties, rolls of various dates between 1252 and 1426.
Asser	Asser, *Life of King Alfred*, ed. W. H. Stevenson, 1904.
ASWills	*Anglo-Saxon Wills*, ed. Whitelock, 1930.
Aubrey	*The Topographical Collections of John Aubrey for Wiltshire*, ed. J. E. Jackson, 1862.
AubreyNH	John Aubrey, *Natural History of Wiltshire*, ed. Britten, 1847.
Banco	*Placita de Banco* (PRO Lists and Indexes, no. 32).
BCS	Birch, *Cartularium Saxonicum*, 3 vols., 1885–93.
B.D.	*ex inf.* Professor Bruce Dickins.
Bede	Bede, *Historica Ecclesiastica*, ed. C. Plummer, 2 vols., 1896.
Berkeley Charters	I. H. Jeayes, *Catalogue of the Charters at Berkeley Castle*, 1892.
Berks	Berkshire.
BM	British Museum.
BM	*Index to the Charters and Rolls in the British Museum*, 2 vols., 1900–12.
BM Facs	*Facsimiles of Royal and other Charters in the British Museum*, 1903.
Boarstall	*The Boarstall Cartulary* (Oxford Hist. Soc. 88), 1930.

Bodl	*Calendar of Charters and Rolls in the Bodleian*, 1898.
BodlCh	*Bodleian Charters* (unprinted, forms transcribed by Dr M. S. Serjeantson).
Boniface	*Vita Sancti Bonifatii*, ed. Jaffé (Monumenta Moguntiana), 1866.
BorRec	*Records of Chippenham, relating to the Borough*, ed. C. T. Flower and M. C. B. Davies, 1934.
Bowles	W. L. Bowles, *History of Bremhill*, 1828.
BPR	*The Register of Edward the Black Prince*, 4 vols., 1930–3.
Bracton	*Bracton's Note Book*, ed. Maitland, 3 vols., 1887.
Bradenstoke	Cartulary of Bradenstoke Priory (Cott MS Vitell A. XI) (BM).
Brasenose	Documents in the possession of Brasenose College, Oxford.
B.T.	Bosworth, *An Anglo-Saxon Dictionary*, ed. Toller, 1898.
Bülbring	*Altenglisches Elementarbuch*, ed. K. D. Bülbring, 1902.
Burghal Hidage	*The Burghal Hidage* (London Medieval Studies, 1, 63).
c.	circa.
Cambs PR	W. P. W. Phillimore, *Cambridgeshire Parish Registers* (*Marriages*), 8 vols., 1907–27.
CartMisc	*Cartæ Miscellaneæ* in Augmentation Office, Miscellaneous Books, vols. 32–54.
Cary	Cary, *Map of Wiltshire* (in Camden's *Britannia*, 1789).
Ch	*Calendar of Charter Rolls*, 6 vols., 1903–27.
Ch	Cheshire.
Chanc	*Calendar of Chancery Rolls*, 1912.
ChancP	*Chancery Proceedings in the Reign of Elizabeth*, 3 vols., 1827–32.
Chrest	J. Loth, *Chrestomathie bretonne*, 1890.
ChwAcct	*The Churchwardens Accounts of Mere*. (WM xxxv.)
Cl	*Calendar of Close Rolls*. (In progress.)
ClR	*Rotuli Litterarum Clausarum*, 2 vols., 1833–44.
Co	Cornwall.
Coins	*Catalogue of English Coins in the BM, Anglo-Saxon Series*, 2 vols., 1887–93.
Cole	Cole MSS (*Add* 5802–87).
Contributions	Ekwall, *Contributions to the History of OE Dialects*, 1917.
Cor	Coroners Rolls (PRO), Nos. 193–6, 199, 200, 203.
Corn	Cornish.
Corpus	Documents in the possession of Corpus Christi College, Oxford.
CottCh	Cotton Charters (BM).
Crawford	*Crawford Charters*, ed. Napier and Stevenson, 1895.
Ct	*Wanborough Court Rolls* (NQ iv).
Ct	Court Rolls (unpublished) at the BM, PRO and in private hands.
CtWards	Court of Wards (PRO).
Cunnington	*Annals of the Borough of Devizes*, ed. B. H. Cunnington, 1925.
Cur	*Curia Regis Rolls*. (In progress.)
Dan	Danish.
Daniell	J. J. Daniell, *History of Warminster*, 1879.
DB	Domesday Book.
Deed	Unpublished deeds (in private hands).
Deeds Enrolled	Enrolments of Deeds at the PRO.

DEPN	E. Ekwall, *The Oxford Dictionary of English Place-names*, 1936.
Depositions	Exchequer Special Commissions and Depositions (PRO).
DeVaux	Cartulary of the College of St Nicholas de Vaux (*Add* 28870) (BM).
Devizes	Unprinted documents in the County Library, Devizes.
DKR	*Deputy Keeper's Reports*, vols. 35–43.
Do	Dorset.
Du	Dutch.
Dugd	Dugdale, *Monasticon Anglicanum*, 6 vols., 1817–30.
DuLa	Duchy of Lancaster documents in PRO (*Ct*, *Rentals* and *MinAcct*).
Earle	J. Earle, *A Handbook to the Land-Charters and other Saxonic Documents*, 1888.
EcclCom	Documents in the possession of the Ecclesiastical Commissioners (deposited at the PRO).
ECP	*Early Chancery Proceedings* (PRO Lists and Indexes, nos. 12, 16, 20, 29, 38, 47, 48, 50, 51, 54), 1901–33.
Edington	Cartulary of Edington Priory (Lansdowne MS 442) (BM).
EETS	Early English Text Society.
E.H.G.	*Ex inf.* Canon E. H. Goddard.
EHR	*English Historical Review.* (In progress.)
ElyM	Liber M (14th) in Ely Diocesan Registry.
EPNS	English Place-name Society.
ES	*Englische Studien.* (In progress.)
Ethelw	*Fabii Ethelwerdi Chronicorum...libri quattuor* (Mon. Hist. Brit., ed. Petrie), 1848.
Eton	Documents in the possession of Eton College.
Exch	The Exchequer Domesday Book.
Exon	*The Episcopal Registers of the Diocese of Exeter*, ed. T. L. Hingston-Randolph, 1886 ff.
ExonDB	The Exeter Domesday Book.
Extent	Extents of Manors at the PRO.
Eyns	*Cartulary of the Abbey of Eynsham* (Oxford Hist. Soc.), 1906–8.
FA	*Feudal Aids*, 6 vols., 1899–1920.
Fees	*Book of Fees*, 3 vols., 1922–31.
Feilitzen	Olof von Feilitzen, *The Pre-Conquest Personal Names of DB*, 1937.
FF	*A Calendar of the Feet of Fines for Wiltshire*, 1195–1272, ed. E. A. Fry, 1930. *Somerset Feet of Fines* (SRS 6, 12, 17, 22).
FF	Feet of Fines (unpublished), 1273–1760 (PRO).
Fine	*Calendar of Fine Rolls.* (In progress.)
FineR	*Excerpta e rotulis finium*, 2 vols., 1836.
For	Forest Proceedings (Chancery, Exchequer, King's Remembrancer) (PRO).
Förstemann	Förstemann, *Altdeutsches Namenbuch, Personennamen* (PN), *Ortsnamen* (ON), 2 vols. in 3, 1901–16.
France	*Calendar of Documents preserved in France*, 1899.
Fry	*Hannington, the Records of a Wiltshire Parish*, ed. C. B. Fry, 1935.
FW	Florence of Worcester, *Chronicon ex Chronicis*, 2 vols., 1848–9.

G	C. J. Greenwood, *Map of the County of Wiltshire*, 1826.
Gaim	Gaimar, *Lestorie des Engles*, 2 vols. (Rolls Series), 1889–90.
G.B.G.	*Ex inf.* Dr G. B. Grundy.
GDR	Gaol Delivery Rolls (PRO), Nos. 71, 72.
Ger	German.
Gl	Gloucestershire.
Glam	Glamorgan.
GlastFeod	*A Feodary of Glastonbury Abbey* (SRS 26), 1910.
GlastInq	*An Inquisition of the Manors of Glastonbury for* 1189, ed. J. E. Jackson (Roxburghe Club), 1882.
GlastRl	*Rentalia...Monasterii Glastoniae* (SRS 5), 1891.
G.M.Y.	*Ex inf.* Mr G. M. Young.
Goodrich	*Trowbridge and its Times*, ed. Rev. P. J. Goodrich, 1932.
Gough	Camden's *Britannia*, ed. Gough, 1789.
Grundy	G. B. Grundy, *The Saxon Land Charters of Wiltshire*, First and Second Series as printed in *Archaeological Journal*, vol. lxxvi, 143–301 (1919), and vol. lxxvii, 8–126 (1920).
GrundyGl	G. B. Grundy, *Saxon Charters and Field Names of Gloucestershire*, 2 parts, 1935–6.
GrundyH	G. B. Grundy, *The Ancient Highways and Tracks of Wiltshire*, etc. (*Arch. Journ.* lxxv, 69–194), 1918.
GrundySo	G. B. Grundy, *The Saxon Charters and Field Names of Somerset*, 1935.
Ha	Hampshire.
Harl	Harleian MS (BM).
H.C.B.	*Ex inf.* Mr H. C. Brentnall.
He	Herefordshire.
Heath	F. R. Heath, *Little Guide to Wiltshire*, 1931.
HH	*Henrici Huntendoniensis Historia Anglorum* (Rolls Series), 1895–9.
HMC	Historical Manuscripts Commission.
HMC Var	*HMC Reports on Manuscripts in Various Collections*, 8 vols., 1901–23.
Hoare	R. Colt Hoare, *History of Modern Wiltshire*, 6 vols., 1822–44.
Holthausen	F. Holthausen, *Altenglisches etymologisches Wörterbuch*, 1934.
Hutton	E. Hutton, *Highways and Byways of Wiltshire*, 1917.
Inq aqd	*Inquisitiones ad quod damnum*, 1803.
Ipm	*Calendar of Inquisitions post mortem.* (In progress.)
Ipm	Unpublished Ipm (PRO).
IpmR	*Inquisitiones post mortem*, 4 vols., 1806–28.
IPN	*Introduction to the Survey of English Place-names*, 1923.
JEGPh	*Journal of English and Germanic Philology.* (In progress.)
Jones	W. H. Jones, *Domesday for Wiltshire*, 1865.
Jones-Beddoe	W. H. Jones, *Bradford-on-Avon*, ed. J. Beddoe, 1907.
Karlström	S. Karlström, *OE Compound Place-names in -ing*, 1927.
KCD	Kemble, *Codex Diplomaticus*, 6 vols., 1839–48.
Kelly	Kelly's *Directory of Wiltshire*, 1935.
Kidston	G. J. Kidston, *A History of the Manor of Hazelbury*, 1936.
Kings	Documents in the possession of King's College, Cambridge.
L	Leland, *Itinerary*, ed. L. T. Smith, 5 vols., 1906–10.
L	Lincolnshire.

Lacock	Cartulary of Lacock Abbey (*penes* Miss Talbot of Lacock Abbey).
Lat	Latin.
Lay	Layamon's *Brut*, 3 vols., 1847.
Lewis	W. J. Lewis, *History of the Parish of North Wraxall*, 1913.
LGer	Low German.
Lib	*Calendar of Liberate Rolls.* (In progress.)
LibCust	*Liber Custumarum* (Munimenta Gildhallæ London), ed. H. T. Riley, 1859–62.
LibHyda	*Liber monasterii de Hyda* (Rolls Series), 1866.
LibLand	*Liber Landavensis*, Oxford, 1893.
LibWinton	Liber Wintoniensis in DB, vol. iv.
LL	Late Latin.
LN	*Liber Niger Scaccarii*, 1774.
Longford	Documents in the possession of the Earl of Radnor at Longford Castle.
Longleat	Documents in the possession of the Marquess of Bath at Longleat House.
Longnon	A. Longnon, *Les noms de lieu de la France*, 1920–9.
LP	*Letters and Papers, Foreign and Domestic, Henry VIII*, 21 vols., 1864–1932.
LRMB	Miscellaneous Books, Land Revenue, vols. 191, 203, 207 (PRO).
LVD	*Liber Vitae Ecclesiae Dunelmensis* (Surtees Society 136), 1923.
Maclean	Sir John Maclean, *History of the Deanery of Trigg Minor*, 1868.
Magd	Documents in the possession of Magdalen College, Oxford.
Malm	Cartulary of Malmesbury Abbey (Lansdowne MS 417) (BM).
Manydown	*Manor of Manydown* (Hants.Rec.Soc.), 1895.
Map	Unpublished maps.
Marsh	C. E. W. Marsh. *History of the Borough and Town of Calne*, 1903.
MCorn	Middle Cornish.
MDu	Middle Dutch.
ME	Middle English.
Merton	Documents in the possession of Merton College, Oxford.
Middendorff	H. Middendorff, *Altenglisches Flurnamenbuch*, Halle, 1902.
Migne	*Patrologia Latina*, ed. J. P. Migne.
MinAcct	Ministers' Accounts (PRO).
Misc	*Calendar of Inquisitions Miscellaneous.* (In progress.)
MLG	Middle Low German.
Mo	Monmouthshire.
ModEng	Modern English.
ModFr	Modern French.
ModGaelic	Modern Gaelic.
ModWelsh	Modern Welsh.
Morden	Morden, *Map of Wiltshire*, 1695.
Morris-Jones	Sir J. Morris-Jones, *A Welsh Grammar*, 1913.
Moulton	*Palaeography, Genealogy and Topography.* Selections from the collections of H. R. Moulton (1930).
Naish	*The City of Salisbury, surveyed by W. Naish*, 1751.

Naumann	Hans Naumann, *Altnordische Namenstudien*, 1912.
Nb	Northumberland.
NCPNW	B. G. Charles, *Non-Celtic Place-names in Wales*, 1938.
NCy	North-country.
NED	New English Dictionary.
NewColl	Documents in the possession of New College, Oxford.
Nf	Norfolk.
NI	*Nonarum Inquisitiones*, 1807.
NoB	*Namn och Bygd*. (In progress.)
Noyes	Ella Noyes, *Salisbury Plain, its Stones, Cathedral and City*, 1913.
NPN	E. Björkman, *Nordische Persönennamen in England*, 1910.
NQ	*Wiltshire Notes and Queries*, 8 vols., 1893 ff.
O	Oxfordshire.
OBreton	Old Breton.
OBrit	Old British.
OCeltic	Old Celtic.
OCorn	Old Cornish.
ODan	Old Danish.
OE	Old English.
OE Bede	*The Old English Version of Bede's Ecclesiastical History* (EETS 95–6, 110–11), 1890–8.
OET	Sweet, *Oldest English Texts* (EETS), 1885.
OFr	Old French.
OFris	Old Frisian.
OGer	Old German.
Ogilby	Ogilby, *Itinerarium Angliae*, 1675.
O.G.S.C.	*Ex inf.* Mr O. G. S. Crawford.
OHG	Old High German.
OIr	Old Irish.
ON	Old Norse.
Orig	*Originalia Rolls*, 2 vols., 1838–55.
O.S.	Ordnance Survey.
OSax	Old Saxon.
Oseney	*The English Register of Oseney Abbey* (EETS, 133, 144), 1907, 1912.
OSw	Old Swedish.
OW	Old Welsh.
p.	post.
(p)	Place-name form derived from personal name.
P	*Pipe Rolls* (Record Commission, 3 vols.), 1833–44. Pipe Roll Society. (In progress). *Great Roll of the Pipe* for 26 Henry 3, ed. Cannon, 1918.
Pap	*Calendar of Papal Registers*. (In progress.)
ParlSurv	Parliamentary Surveys (PRO).
ParReg	*Wiltshire Parish Registers, Marriages*, ed. W. P. Phillimore and John Sadler, 1905 ff. (In progress.) *The Registers of Bishops Cannings*, ed. J. H. Parry, 1906.
Pat	*Calendar of Patent Rolls*. (In progress.)
PCC	*Wills Proved in the Prerogative Court of Canterbury* (British Record Society). (In progress.)
Pemb	Pembrokeshire.
PembSurv	*Survey of the Lands of William, 1st Earl of Pembroke*, ed. C. R. Straton, 2 vols. (Roxburghe Club), 1909.
Peramb	Forest Perambulations (PRO).

Phillipps	MSS of Thomas Phillipps relating to Wiltshire (BM).
PN Bk	*The Place-names of Buckinghamshire* (EPNS), 1925.
PN D	*The Place-names of Devon* (EPNS), 1931–2.
PN Db	B. Walker, *The Place-names of Derbyshire*, 1914.
PN Do	Fägersten, *Place-names of Dorset*, 1933.
PN Ess	*The Place-names of Essex* (EPNS), 1935.
PN Gl	Baddeley, *Place-names of Gloucestershire*, 1913.
PN Herts	*The Place-names of Hertfordshire* (EPNS), 1938.
PN in *-ing*	Ekwall, *English Place-names in -ing*, 1923.
PN K	Wallenberg, *Place-names of Kent*, 1934.
PN NbDu	Mawer, *Place-names of Northumberland and Durham*, 1920.
PN Nth	*The Place-names of Northamptonshire* (EPNS), 1933.
PN O	Alexander, *Place-names of Oxfordshire*, 1912.
PN Sr	*The Place-names of Surrey* (EPNS), 1934.
PN Sx	*The Place-names of Sussex* (EPNS), 2 vols., 1929–30.
PN Wa	*The Place-names of Warwickshire* (EPNS), 1936.
PN Wo	*The Place-names of Worcestershire* (EPNS), 1927.
PN WRY	Moorman, *Place-names of the West Riding of Yorkshire*, 1910.
Pococke	*The Travels through England of Dr Richard Pococke*, Camden Soc., 1888.
PRO	Public Record Office.
PRWinton	Pipe Roll of the Bishopric of Winchester, ed. Hubert Hall, 1903.
QW	*Placita de Quo Warranto*, 1818.
RBE	*Red Book of the Exchequer*, 3 vols., 1896.
RCH	R. Colt Hoare, *The Ancient History of South Wiltshire*, 1812. *The Ancient History of North Wiltshire*, 1819.
ReadingA	Cartulary of Reading Abbey (Egerton 3031) (BM).
Recov	Recovery Rolls (PRO).
RegMalm	*Registrum Malmesburiense* (Rolls Series), 2 vols., 1879.
Rental	Rentals and Surveys at the PRO, BM and in private hands.
RG	*Chronicle of Robert of Gloucester*, 2 vols. (Rolls Series), 1887.
RH	*Rotuli Hundredorum*, 2 vols., 1812–18.
RN	Ekwall, *English River-names*, 1928.
S	Saxton, *Map of England and Wales*, 1576.
Sadler	MS Collections of John Sadler in Wilts Museum at Devizes.
Saints	*Die Heiligen Englands*, ed. Liebermann, 1889.
StJ	*Admissions to the College of St John the Evangelist*, 2 vols., 1882–1903.
StNeot	Cartulary of St Neot's Priory (Cott. MS, Faust. A. IV) (BM).
StNicholas	*The Fifteenth Century Cartulary of St Nicholas Hospital, Salisbury*, ed. C. Wordsworth, 1902.
StOsmund	*Vetus registrum Sarisberiense alias dictum Registrum S. Osmundi, Episcopi* (Rolls Series), 1883–4.
Sarum	*Registrum Simonis de Gandavo*, ed. C. T. Flower and M. C. B. Davies, 1934.
SarumCh	*Charters and Documents Illustrating the History of... Salisbury in the 12th and 13th Centuries*, ed. the Rev. W. D. Macray (Rolls Series), 1891.

Sarum DandC	Documents in the possession of the Dean and Chapter of Salisbury Cathedral.
Sav	Documents relating to Savernake in the possession of the Marquess of Ailesbury.
Schönfeld	M. Schönfeld, *Wörterbuch der altgermanischen Personen- und Völkernamen*, Heidelberg, 1911.
SD	*Symeon of Durham*, 2 vols. (Rolls Series), 1882–5.
Selborne	*Charters and Documents Relating to Selborne* (Hants. Rec. Soc.), 1891, 1894.
Seld	Selden Society. (In progress.)
Sess	*Records of the County of Wiltshire, Extracts from the Quarter Sessions Rolls*, ed. B. H. Cunnington, 1932.
Shaston	The Shaftesbury Register (Harl. MS 61) (BM).
So	Somerset.
SP	State Papers Domestic (unpublished) (PRO).
SR	*Lay Subsidy Roll for Somerset for 1327* (SRS 3), 1869.
SR	Lay Subsidy Rolls (unpublished) (PRO).
SRS	Somerset Record Society. (In progress.)
Stowe	Stowe MSS 798 and 925 (Forest perambulations) (BM).
Studies[1]	E. Ekwall, *Studies on English Place and Personal Names*, 1931.
Studies[2]	E. Ekwall, *Studies in English Place-names*, 1936.
StudNP	*Studia Neophilologica*. (In progress.)
Survey	Surveys of Wiltshire manors in private hands.
Swithin	S. Swithunus, *Miracula*, ed. Huber, 1905.
Sykes	Collection of local names made by the Rev. W. B. Sykes, late Vicar of Wilcot.
TA	Tithe Award.
Tax	*Taxatio Ecclesiastica*, 1802.
Templars	*Records of the Templars*, ed. Beatrice A. Lees (British Academy Records Series), 1935.
Tengvik	Gösta Tengvik, *OE Bynames*, 1938.
Thorney	Red Book of Thorney (Cambridge Univ. Library, Add. MS 3020).
Torp	A. Torp, *Nynorsk Etymologisk Ordbok*, 1919.
TRE	Tempore regis Edwardi.
Trinity	Documents in the possession of Trinity College, Cambridge.
Trop	*The Tropenell Cartulary*, ed. Rev. J. S. Davies, 2 vols., 1908.
TRW	Tempore regis Wilhelmi.
VE	*Valor Ecclesiasticus*, 6 vols., 1810–34.
W	Welsh.
Wells	*MSS. in the Possession of the Dean and Chapter of Wells*, 2 vols. (HMC), 1907, 1914.
Wills	*Wiltshire Wills* (NQ).
Wilton	Documents in the possession of the Earl of Pembroke at Wilton House.
WiltonReg	*Registrum Wiltunense*, ed. R. Colt Hoare, 1827.
WiltsGloss	Dartnell and Goddard, *Glossary of Words used in Wilts* (English Dialect Soc. 69), 1893.
WinchColl	Documents in the possession of Winchester College.
Winton	*Wykeham's Register* (Hants. Rec. Soc.), 2 vols., 1896–9.
Winton	Documents in the possession of the Dean and Chapter of Winchester Cathedral.

WintonCart   *Chartulary of Winchester Cathedral*, ed. A. W. Goodman, 1927.

WIpm   *Wiltshire Inquisitions post mortem*, 1242 to 1377 and t. Chas 1 (Brit. Rec. Soc. 1901, 1908, 1914).

WM   *Wiltshire Archaeological and Natural History Magazine.* (In progress.)

WMP   William of Malmesbury, *Gesta Pontificum Anglorum* (Rolls Series), 1870.

Wood   *Life and Times of Wood*, 5 vols. (Oxford Hist. Soc.), 1891–1900.

Works   *Public Works in Medieval Law* (Selden Soc. 32, 40), 1915, 1923.

Wt   Isle of Wight.

PHONETIC SYMBOLS USED IN TRAN-
SCRIPTION OF PRONUNCIATIONS OF
PLACE-NAMES

p	*p*ay	ʃ	*sh*one	tʃ	*ch*urch	ei	fl*ay*
b	*b*ay	ʒ	a*z*ure	dʒ	*j*udge	ɛ	Fr. jam*ai*s
t	*t*ea	θ	*th*in	ɑˑ	*f*ather	ɛˑ	*the*re
d	*d*ay	ð	*th*en	ɑu	*c*ow	i	p*i*t
k	*k*ey	j	*y*ou	a	Ger. m*a*nn	iˑ	*fee*l
g	*g*o	χ	lo*ch*	ai	*fl*y	ou	*l*ow
ʍ	*wh*en	h	*h*is	æ	*ca*b	u	*goo*d
w	*w*in	m	*m*an	ɔ	p*o*t	uˑ	r*u*le
f	*f*oe	n	*n*o	ɔˑ	s*aw*	ʌ	m*u*ch
v	*v*ote	ŋ	si*ng*	oi	*oi*l	ə	*e*ver
s	*s*ay	r	*r*un	e	r*e*d	əˑ	b*i*rd
z	*z*one	l	*l*and .				

Examples:

Hardenhuish [hɑrniʃ], Cherhill [tʃeril]

Donhead [dɔnet]

NOTES

(1) The names are arranged topographically according to the Hundreds. Within each Hundred the parishes are dealt with in alphabetical order, and within each parish the names of primary historical or etymological interest are arranged similarly, but in a large number of parishes these are followed by one, or two, or even three further groups of names. These groups, so far as they are represented, always appear in the following order: (i) minor names of topographical origin found largely in the second name of persons mentioned in the Subsidy Rolls and other similar local documents; (ii) names embodying some family name of Middle English or Early Modern English origin; (iii) minor names of obvious origin, or minor names for which we have only very late forms, about whose history it is unwise to speculate. All three types are represented under Melksham (*infra* 129–30).

(2) Where a place-name is found only on the 6-inch O.S. map, this is indicated by putting 6″ after it in brackets, e.g. Ladywell Copse (6″).

(3) Place-names now no longer current are marked as (lost). This does not necessarily mean that the site to which the name was once applied is unknown. We are dealing primarily with names and the names are lost. These names are printed in italics when referred to elsewhere in the volume.

(4) Place-names marked '(local)' are not recorded on modern maps but are still current locally.

(5) The local pronunciation of the place-name is given, wherever it is of interest, in phonetic script within square brackets, e.g. Hardenhuish [hɑrniʃ].

(6) In explaining the various place-names, summary reference is made to the detailed account of such elements as are found in the *Chief Elements in English Place-names* and by printing those elements in Clarendon type, e.g. Hinton, *v.* heah, tun.

(7) In the case of all forms for which reference has been made to unprinted authorities that fact is indicated by printing the reference to the authority in italic instead of ordinary type, e.g. 'c. 1570 *Wilton*' denotes a form derived from a MS authority in

contrast to '1620 Aubrey' which denotes one taken from a printed text.

(8) Where two dates are given, e.g. 1065 (14th), the first is the date at which the document purports to have been composed, the second is that of the copy which has come down to us.

(9) Where a letter in an early place-name form is placed within brackets, forms with and without that letter are found, e.g. *Sturton(e)* means that forms *Sturton* and *Sturtone* are alike found.

(10) All OE words are quoted in their West Saxon form unless otherwise stated.

ADDENDA ET CORRIGENDA

For addenda with appended initials we are indebted to

A.C.W.   Mr A. C. Wood.
E.J.   Mr E. Jervoise.
E.J.S.   Professor E. J. Salisbury.
J.B.J.   Rev. J. B. Johnston.
P.H.R.   Dr P. H. Reaney.
R.H.W.   Dr R. H. Woodforde.
S.J.M.   Dr S. J. Madge.

VOL. I, PART I

INTRODUCTION

p. 122, l. 4. *Mussegros* is not a nickname but derives from the place-name Mussegros (Eure). Cf. *Dict. Top. de l'Eure* 152 and Tengvik 102.

VOL. I, PART II

CHIEF ELEMENTS

p. 17, l. 15. For 'clæfer' read 'clæfre.'
p. 44, *s.v.* (ge)læte. Delete 'Longleat (W).'

VOL. II

THE PLACE-NAMES OF BUCKINGHAMSHIRE

p. 60, under BUCKINGHAM parish. Add 'DUDLEY BRIDGE is *Dudley Brydge* 1554 Pat' (A.C.W.).
p. 84, *s.n.* LISCOMBE. Add '*Lychescumbe* 1270 Cl.'
p. 241, last line. For '*stocc*' read '*stoc*.'

VOL. III

THE PLACE-NAMES OF BEDFORDSHIRE AND HUNTINGDONSHIRE

pp. 105–6, *s.n.* COCKAYNE HATLEY. Add 'John *Cokayn* of *Brayhatley* (1479 Pat).' This suggests another alternative name (P.H.R.).
p. 211, *s.n.* OLD HURST. Add '*Old Hurst* 1606 *Depositions*' (P.H.R.).
pp. 229–30, *s.n.* WOODSTONE. Woodson in Pembrokeshire is alternatively *Woodeston* and *Le Wood* in the 14th century (NCPNW 85) and this is in favour of the possibility of a genitival compound.
p. 274, *s.n.* WARESLEY DEAN BROOK. Add '*Weresledene* c. 1185 *StNeot*' (P.H.R.).

VOL. IV

THE PLACE-NAMES OF WORCESTERSHIRE

p. 159, *s.n.* Southley. Mr E. F. Gray calls our attention to constant references in the Ripple Church Registers to *Sudleye* or *Soudley*, giving us later traces of this name, and notices that it survives in *Sudeley Lane* in the Ripple *TA* of 1807. It was the south end of the parish in the neighbourhood of Bow Cottages and Bow Fm.

VOL. V

THE PLACE-NAMES OF THE NORTH RIDING OF YORKSHIRE

p. 95, *s.n.* BLAKEY MOOR. Add '*Blakehoumore* 1341 Misc.'

VOL. VI

THE PLACE-NAMES OF SUSSEX (PART I)

p. 223, *s.n.* BRAMBER. Professor Max Förster notes that *bremer* should be rendered 'bramble' rather than 'broom', as in BCS 591 where a man scratched his face on a *brem(b)er.*

Through the kindness of Mr H. J. R. Murray and his daughter, Miss K. M. E. Murray of Girton College, further names (with early forms derived from documents at Petworth House) can now be given under the following parishes:

FERNHURST

p. 21. BALDWINS (6″) is *Baldwyn* 1455 *Ct.*

    s.n. OEBORNE COPSE (6″) add 'cf. *woburnan* BCS 1114 and *infra* xxxvi.

HEYSHOTT

p. 22. HOYLE was the home of Adam *atte Hulle* (1327 SR), *atte Hulde* (1332 ib.). Later forms are *Hylde* (1617), *Hoylde al. Hile* (1655), *Hoyle* (1681), *Hyle* (1704), *Hyle or Hoyle* (1756), all from Petworth deeds, and *Hiall or Hoyle* (1815 Dallaway). This is from OE hielde, 'slope.' Cf. Hyle Fm (PN Sr 265).

The home of William *Nethehulde* 1372 *Ct*, called *Netehull* 1486 ib., *Nethehild* 1518 ib., *Netherhild* 1577 *Deed*, *Neither Hill* 1700 ib. was at the house (unnamed) below the road from Heyshott to Ambersham Common, just north-west of Hoyle.

    BERRYWOOD FM. Cf. *Burywood* 1518 *CtBk.*

    DUNSTEAD (local) is *Dunstede* 1377 *AcctRoll, Dunstan* c. 1840 *TA.*

    HAMPSHIRE COPSE. Cf. *Hemeshyre Corner* 1530 *CtBk.*

    HEYSHOTT GREEN is *Berygrene* 1377 *AcctRoll, Beregrene* 1489, 1490 *CtBk.*

    HOE COPSE. Cf. *At Howe* 1486 *CtBk, How(e)land* 1489, 1490, 1509 ib. *v.* hoh, 'hill-spur.'

    LARKINGS BARN is *Larkyns* 1509 *CtBk, Lorkens Mead* 1577 *Deed, Larkins* 1662 ib.

    PETTY CROFT (*TA*) is *Purycroft* 1377 *AcctRoll, Perrycroft* 1577, 1661, 1717 *Deed.* 'Pear-tree croft,' *v.* pirige.

    SUNWOOL FM is *Sonnewolle* 1530 *CtBk, Sunwool(d)* 1707 *Deed.* Just to the south is SUN COMBE. *wolle* is possibly from wielle, 'spring.'

    UPTONS ASH (local) is *Oppetouneshasch* 1316 *Ct, Uptons Ash* 1586, 1627, 1662 *Deed.*

    Patchescumbe 1231 *Charter, Pachcombe* 1438 *AcctRoll, Paschecomb(e)* 1353, 1509 *CtBk, Pascombe* 1529–31 ib., *Pescombe* 1531 ib. give us apparently a further example of the personal name *Pæcci* found in Patching (PN Sx 248).

AMBERSHAM, NORTH and SOUTH

pp. 97–9. FERNDEN is *fearndun* 963 (12th) BCS 1114, *Farnden* 1395 *Ct*, t. Eliz *Survey*. 'Bracken-hill,' *v.* dun.

    RIDGE HILL (6″) is *Rugg* 1514 *Ct. v.* hrycg.

    SURNEY HATCH is *Southney in Farnhurst* t. R. 2 *Ct*, i.e. 'south of the river,' with the same history as Sidney (PN Sx 265). It lies on the Fernhurst border.

    s.n. ELIDGE. Add '*Erlichlond* 1386 *Ct*.'

    s.n. GUNTERS. Add '*Gounters* t. Eliz *Survey*.'

    s.n. REETH COPSE and WOOD. Add '*Wrethland* and *Writhplace in Farnest* t. Eliz *Survey*.' They lie on the Fernhurst boundary.

    s.n. SHEETLAND. Add '*Shetplace, Shetland, Sheet, the Shutt, Shuttland* t. Eliz *Survey*.'

Under minor names at the end add: BALDRUDE (6″) is *Baldred* 1395, 1505 *Ct*. Perhaps 'bare clearing,' see under Inchreed (PN Sx 378). BULL REEDS WOOD (6″). Cf. *Bulreede* 1537 *Ct* and Inchreed *u.s.* CRADLEHURST COPSE (6″). Cf. *Cradlers* t. Eliz *Survey*.

With reference to the Ambersham Charter (BCS 1114) discussed on pp. 97–8, note 2, Mr Murray makes two new and almost certain identifications. He suggests that Fernden in North Ambersham which gives name to a House, Copse and Hill (6″) and a school (1″) is to be identified with *fearndun* and notes that Fernden is really a ridge of high land to the west of the Wey valley standing up prominently between Black Down and the Marley heights. The landmark immediately preceding is *woburnan* and this may well be identified with the *Oeborne* of Oeborne Copse immediately south of Verdley Place, by a winding stream (cf. the history of Oborne (Do) in RN 469). He also gives forms *Unmymede* from a Court Roll of 1514, *Umly Mead* and *Umbly Mead* 1719–20 *Deeds*, which bridge the gap between *ummanig* in the Saxon charter and *Hombly Mead* in the *TA*.

VOL. VIII

THE PLACE-NAMES OF DEVON (PART I)

p. 27, *s.n.* BARNSTAPLE BRIDGE. Add '(*juxta*) *pontem Barnastapolie* 1312 Exeter Episcopal Registers' (E.J.).

p. 88, *s.n.* BIDEFORD BRIDGE. Add '*ponti de Bydeforde* 1326 Exeter Episcopal Registers' (E.J.).

p. 231, *s.n.* PETERTAVY. Mr A. C. Wood points out for us that the form *Patryxtavy* is found in the phrase 'Hampton Sechefeld or Heyaunton Sechefeld in the parish of Patryxtavy.' This clearly refers to Heanton Satchville (ib. 93) which is partly in the parish of Huish and partly in that of Petrockstow, suggesting that *Patryxtavy* is a strange blunder for Petrockstow.

VOL. IX

THE PLACE-NAMES OF DEVON (PART II)

p. 345, *s.n.* BRINSWORTHY. Add '*Brumsey* 1675 Ogilby.'

p. 487, *s.n.* SPARA BRIDGE. Mr E. Jervoise calls our attention to the form *Sparrowe Bridge* in the Devon Sessions Records of 1647. This makes it clear that the speculation in the Devon volume was unwise.

p. 541, *s.n.* BOLHAM. Add '*Boldham* 1675 Ogilby.'

p. 635. Add 'Bow BRIDGE is *Bowbridge* 1540 *MinAcct*' and unidentified '*Coldeharbrougth ex parte occideñ de Slymelake*' (A.C.W.).

p. 636, *s.n.* WESTWATER. Add '*Westwater* 1540 *MinAcct*' (A.C.W.).

VOL. X

THE PLACE-NAMES OF NORTHAMPTONSHIRE

p. 109, *s.n.* ARTHINGWORTH. Add '*Hardenworth* 1675 Ogilby.'

p. 133, *s.n.* BOUGHTON. Add '*Bouton* 1675 Ogilby.'

p. 201, *s.n.* DUDDINGTON. Add '*Dodinton by Clive* 1293 Ipm,' i.e. by King's Cliffe.

p. 211, *s.n.* BENEFIELD. Add '*Benyfeild* 1675 Ogilby.'

VOL. XII

THE PLACE-NAMES OF ESSEX

p. 69, *s.n.* NAVESTOCK. Add '*Navistok* 1361 Ipm.'

p. 71, *s.n.* DUDBROOK. Add '*Doddebrok* 1265 Misc (p).'

pp. 82–3, *s.n.* THEYDON. The explanation of Theydon given here must be withdrawn. The confirmation of the reading *þecdene* (*v. infra* 353) and the parallel of Braydon (Wilts) make it clear that the later development of Theydon is natural though unusual. The whole name must be interpreted as 'valley where *thatch* (material) grows,' and the occasional forms in *Tain-*, *T(h)eyn-* must be regarded as eccentric.

p. 89, *s.n.* Axe St. Add '*Axestrett* 1540 *MinAcct*' (A.C.W.).

p. 90, *s.n.* Upney. Add '*Upney* 1456 Rental (Barking Arch. Soc. Trans. 1936–7).'

Add 'Choat's Manor Way (6″) is probably to be associated with the family of John *Chotte* (ib.).'

p. 92, *s.nn.* Eastbrooks Fm and Hook's Hall. Add '*Estbrookes, Hookes, Hokestrete* 1456 Rental (Barking Arch. Soc. Trans. 1936–7).'

p. 93, *s.nn.* Frizland Fm, Valence Ho, Church Elm Lane, Eastbrook Fm. Add 'These are *Frystelynghalle, Valans, Cherchehelm, Estbroke* 1456 Rental (Barking Arch. Soc. Trans. 1936–7).'

p. 94, *s.n.* Triptons. Add '*Trypton* 1456 Rental (Barking Arch. Soc. Trans. 1936–7).'

p. 100, *s.nn.* Fulwell Hatch Fm, Bunting Bridge, Hedgemans. Add '*Fulwellhacch, Buntons Broke, Hegmans* 1456 Rental (Barking Arch. Soc. Trans. 1936–7).'

p. 101, *s.nn.* Carswell, Highland Fm, Ley Street. Add '*Careswell, Highlond, le lee, Leestrete* 1456 Rental (Barking Arch. Soc. Trans. 1936–7).'

pp. 117–18, *s.n.* Gidea Park. Add '*Gedybernlond* 1348 Ipm' in Creeksea.

p. 122, *s.n.* Marshfoot Ho. Add '*Marshfoot* 1696 DKR xli.'

p. 146, *s.n.* Billericay. Add '*Billirica* 1274 *Ass.*'

p. 150. Under Kitcatts, Northwick and Westwick add earlier forms *Kytcotmershe, North-West-wycke* 1536 *MinAcct* (A.C.W.).

p. 151, *s.n.* Corringham. Add '*Culingham* 1201 Cur.'

p. 266, *s.n.* Brockhill Ho. Cf. *Brochol* (part of the possessions of Richard *Gyffard*, cf. Gifford's Fm ib.) c. 1325 *CartMisc.*

pp. 266–7, *s.n.* Bensted Green. Add '*Betlested* 1201 Cur.'

p. 284, *s.n.* Scrip's Fm. Add '*Scripps* 1691 DKR xli.'

p. 327, *s.n.* Bovill's Hall. Add '*Bovyles* 1360 Ipm.'

p. 338, *s.n.* Elmstead Market. Add '*Elmestedemarchat* 1333 *Deed.*'

p. 345, *s.n.* Dengewell. Add '*Daneswell* 1201 Cur (p).'

p. 357, *s.n.* Pond Hall. Add '*Freshmylls alias Pondhall* 1691 DKR xli.'

p. 378, *s.n.* Drury Fm. Add '*Drories-tenement* 1441, 1454 *Deed.*'

p. 386, *s.n.* Dedham. Add '*Diham* 1202 Cur.'

p. 410, n. 2. Add '*le Vaux* 1360 Ipm.'

p. 433, *s.n.* Abel Cottages. Add '*Abeles* 1349 Ipm.'

p. 435, *s.n.* Gladfen. Add '*Gladefen* 1203 Cur (p).'

p. 441, *s.n.* Prayor's Fm. Add '*Bourghalle* 1360 Ipm.'

p. 442, n. 8. Add '*Bloys* 1349 Ipm.'

p. 446, *s.n.* Hosden's Fm. Add '*Hosedenes* 1349 Ipm.'

p. 451, *s.n.* Bradfield's Fm. Add '*Bradefeld* 1354 Ipm.'

p. 503, *s.n.* Bowsers. Add '*Bowsers* 1536 *MinAcct.*'

p. 504, *s.n.* Nun Wood. Add '*Aisshedowne Wood alias Nunwood* 1536 *MinAcct.*' It was part of the possessions of the *nuns* of Ickleton (C).

p. 525, *s.n.* Elmdon. Add '*Halmedon* 1201 Cur (p).'

p. 530, *s.n.* Catmere End. Add '*Kattemere* c. 1170 *ElyM.*'

p. 531, *s.n.* Bordeaux Fms. Add '*Burdew(e)sfeld* 1483 *Rental, Burduez* t. Hy 8 Bentham, *Ely Cathedral* ii, 108, *Burdewyce* 1536 *Deed, Byrdhowsefeyld* 1612 *Terrier.*' These forms show that *Bird House* is a late etymologising of a local pronunciation.

Add 'Bradley Grove (6″). Cf. *Bradleyffeild* 1549 *Ct.*'

p. 537, *s.n.* SAFFRON WALDEN. Add '*Waleden by Strethale* 1322–41 Misc,' i.e. Strethall, and '*Saffron Walding* 1647 Cambs PR i, 44.'

p. 552. Add 'LEY WOOD (6″) was probably the home of William de *la Ly* (13th *Trinity*).'

VOL. XIII

THE PLACE-NAMES OF WARWICKSHIRE

p. 129, *s.n.* FRANKTON. Add '*Frangeton* 1202 Cur (p).'

p. 26, n. 1. So similarly *Bolumhall* (1342 Ipm) has reference to Bonehill and not to Bole Hall as indexed in that volume.

p. 94, *s.n.* NETHER WHITACRE. Add '*Neothere Whitacre* 1354 Ipm.'

p. 107, *s.n.* COSFORD. Add '*Goseford* 1352 Ipm.'

p. 156, *s.n.* BINLEY. Add '*Bingley* 1675 Ogilby.'

p. 158, *s.n.* BRETFORD. Add '*Bredford* 1675 Ogilby.'

p. 304, *s.n.* ILMINGTON. Add '*Edelmeton*' 1200 Cur.'

VOL. XIV

THE PLACE-NAMES OF THE EAST RIDING OF YORKSHIRE AND YORK

p. 41, *s.n.* POLLARD. Add '*le Poller* 1337 Ipm.'

s.n. NEAT MARSH. Add '*le Netmersk* 1343 Ipm,' showing OE neat.

p. 159, *s.n.* BESWICK. Add '*Besseck* 1675 Ogilby.'

p. 163, *s.n.* HOLME ON THE WOLDS. Add '*Howom by Lokynton* 1331–2 Misc.'

p. 193, n. 1., l. 2. For '*castrorum*' read '*castorum*.'

p. 260, under CLIFFE township. Add 'WHITE MOOR is *Whytemore* 1553 Pat' (A.C.W.).

p. 300, *s.n.* *Buthil*. Add 'St Mary the old on *Buthill* 1345 Ipm.'

VOL. XV

THE PLACE-NAMES OF HERTFORDSHIRE

p. xiii, l. 8. For 'Thames' read 'Thame.'

p. xiv, n. 2. For 'indexed *infra* 315' read 'noted *infra* xx.'

p. xxxvii. For 'Berry Fm' read 'Berry Fen.'

p. 14, *s.n.* WEYLEYE. Add '*Weileg*' 1203 Cur.'

p. 24, *s.n.* WANDON END. Add '*Wewendenn*' 1200 Cur.'

p. 32, *s.n.* FLAMSTEAD. For 'Place of refuge' read 'Place of flight,' hence 'refuge, sanctuary' (J.B.J.).

p. 44, *s.n.* ABBOTS LANGLEY. Earlier references to *Lees Langley* are found in 1549, 1556 Pat (A.C.W.).

p. 70, *s.n.* BARNET. Add '*Chepyng Barnet* 1321 Cl, *High Bernet* 1575 Saxton' (S.J.M.).

p. 78, *s.n.* BEAUMONT HALL. Add '*Bemond Hall* 1675 Ogilby.'

p. 86, l. 11. For 'Οὐρυλάνιον' read 'Οὐρολάνιον.'

p. 98, *s.n.* PARK STREET. Add '*villa de Parco Soca* 1359 Ipm.'

pp. 137–8, *s.n.* STEVENAGE. Add '*Stithenæce* 1066 (t. Hy 2) *CottCh*' (P.H.R.).

p. 139, *s.n.* SIX HILLS. Mr O. G. S. Crawford (*Antiquity* xii, 435) notes that the barrows are Roman.

p. 148, *s.n.* WYMONDLEY. Add '*Wymly* 1461 *StJohns*, *Little Wimbly* 1745 Cole ix' (P.H.R.).

p. 153, *s.n.* ARBURY BANKS. Mr O. G. S. Crawford (*Antiquity loc. cit.*) suggests that Arbury may here go back to OE *here-beorg*, 'army-shelter.' Cf. the common Coldharbour as discussed in PN Sr 406–10. This derivation is supported by the modern pronunciation *Harburra*.

p. 153, *s.n.* HIGHLEY HILL. Mr Crawford (ib.) notes that air photographs show evident traces of barrow circles in the immediate vicinity. The biggest remaining barrow is known as Pancake Hill.

p. 155. CALDECOTE is pronounced locally [kɑˑkət] (R.H.W.).

p. 156, *s.n.* KINGSWOOD BURY. Add '*Kingeswod*' 1203 Cur.'

p. 159. SALTMORE FM is also known locally as Cold Harbour Fm (R.H.W.). Cf. PN Herts 263.

pp. 161–2, *s.n.* ROYSTON. In the 12th-century charters of the Colchester Cartulary, the spellings of the name of Eudo Dapifer's wife are consistent with the suggestion that she gave name to the place (P.H.R.).

p. 167, *s.n.* PEN HILL. Mr O. G. S. Crawford (*Antiquity* xii, 435) notes that there are a number of valley entrenchments or pennings here, probably of medieval date. He rightly suggests that Pen Hill must be a secondary derivative from Pen Bottom.

p. 168, *s.n.* METLEY HILL. Mr O. G. S. Crawford (ib.) notes that the hill is called Tree Barrow on the 2-inch map of 1845 from which the 1-inch O.S. map was engraved.

p. 174, *s.n.* ABBOTSBURY. An earlier reference to the alternative name is *Rowlettesbury alias Abbottysbury* 1556 Pat (A.C.W.).

p. 260, *s.v.* weyour. Delete 'first' (J.B.J.).

p. 263. Mr O. G. S. Crawford (*Antiquity* xii, 436) is doubtless right in suggesting that 'Deadman' in a good many of the names containing that element has reference to the discovery of human bones there rather than to any fatality such as a murder.

p. 305, l. 10 from bottom. For 'PN Sx' read 'PN D' (J.B.J.).

VOL. XVI

THE PLACE-NAMES OF WILTSHIRE

p. 7, *s.n.* HUNGERBOURN. Professor Bruce Dickins calls attention to the passage from William of Newburgh quoted in PN ERY 5 in which intermittent streams when in flood are said to be significant of future famine. This may well explain such a name as Hungerbourn.

p. 18, *s.n.* SALISBURY. Professor Bruce Dickins calls attention to the modern Welsh names *Caergaradog* and *Caersallog* for Salisbury. The former goes back at least to the 12th century. Geoffrey of Monmouth in his *Historia Regum Britanniae* (ed. Griscom) 377 speaks of '*Caercaradduc que nunc Salesberia dicitur.*' Further he notes the attempt by John of Salisbury in his *Policraticus* (ed. Webb, ii, 371) to associate the emperor Severus with it when he writes '*illum* (*sc. Seuerum*) *adhuc solum adiciam, ne Seuericae uel Seresberiae nostrae parcere uidear.*' Webb quotes the 16th-century Humphrey Lhuyd (p. 15), '*Caerseuerus aliis Caer Caradoc dicitur nunc uero Sarysbury ab Anglis uocitatur.*' The attempt to associate Salisbury with the emperor Severus may conceivably be a piece of folk-etymology. The authority for the identity of *Caradoc* is completely obscure.

p. 36, *s.n.* LYDIARD TREGOZE. Professor Bruce Dickins notes (cf. Planché, *The Companions of the Conqueror* ii, 298) that *cel qui donc teneit Tresgoz* was one of the companions of the Conqueror as recorded in Wace, *Roman de Rou* (ed. Andresen), l. 8563, and that Tregoz is in the arrondissement of St Lô (dept. La Manche).

p. 53, *s.n.* CHEDGLOW HUNDRED. Aubrey (213) notes that *Lowe* in Old English is the same with Tumulus or Barrow. Jackson adds a note 'of the barrows one or two are left. That at Chedglow has been hauled away to fill up quarries. The field is still called Barrow field.'

p. 85, *s.n.* WORMWOOD. Mr G. M. Young calls attention to Aubrey's observation (NH 50) that wormwood is exceedingly plentiful in all the waste

grounds about Kington St Michael, Hullavington and so to Colerne. We
are in this very district, so that folk-etymology to *Wormwood* would be very
natural.

p. 90, *s.n.* FOGHAMSHIRE. Professor Ekwall suggests derivation of the
river-name from OE *fācn-ēa*, 'treacherous stream,' used perhaps of one that
rapidly changes its volume. He compares Wylye (*infra* 11), OSw *Mēnā* from
Meinā, 'hurtful stream' (NoB xxiv, 286) and Norwegian stream-names in
Svik- (cf. Rygh, *Norske Elvenavne s.v.*).

pp. 175–6, *s.n.* KNOYLE. East Knoyle was also known as Knoyle *Regis*
from the king's holding (DB) later purchased by the Bishop of Winchester.

pp. 182–3, *s.n.* ZEALS. The first form for this name is taken from a grant
by King Edwy to his huntsman Wulfric of one and a half hides at a place
called *At Seale* and one hide at a place called *At Dunnynghefd.* The grant, as
printed by Kemble (KCD 458) is said to be found in MS Cotton Tib. B v,
a 12th-century MS, but Birch (BCS 968) says that he could not find it there
and prints his text from Kemble. In the rubric to the charter he says that
Seal was probably Zeal Monachorum near Exeter, but in a foot-note adds
'But cf. Zeal and Donhead Co. Wilts.' The Devon suggestion was probably
due to the fact that the Cotton MS contains certain additional entries con-
cerning Battle Abbey and its offshoot St Nicholas Exeter, but is really
irrelevant as Zeal Monachorum belonged to Buckfastleigh and not to Battle
or to St Nicholas. Professor Ekwall accepts the Zeal Monachorum identification and would further identify *Dunnynghefd* with *Dunheved*, an early name
for part of Launceston, but it is a far cry from Zeal Monachorum to Launceston
and nothing is known of any other link between them. Birch's alternative
identification seems the more likely. Zeals (or *Seale*) is only six miles from
Donhead and lies by Selwood Forest (*infra* 15) whose earliest form is *Sealwudu*.
The earliest forms of Donhead are *Dunheued*, *Dunheafdan*, etc. (*infra* 187)
and *Dunnynghefd* will suit the forms of Donhead as well (or as ill) as those
of the Launceston place-name.

p. 210, *s.n.* RAMSHILL FM. Ramshill Fm is in Donhead St Mary (*supra*
188–9) and not in Semley as given in the text.

p. 257, *s.n.* CALSTONE WELLINGTON. In Ipm, Volume II, p. 21, the father
of George de Cantilupo (who held the manor of Calstone) is said to have died
at *Calveston*, the man who made this deposition having himself come from
the parts of *Calveston*. If this is an error of transcription for *Calneston*, we
have at least one early form with an *n*.

p. 266, *s.n.* BUPTON. In 1232 (Ch) William Quintin gave to Bradenstoke
Priory five acres in *Bubbeclive*. It would seem, therefore, that part at least
of Clyffe Pypard was named *Bubbeclive* after William Bubbe, for William
Quintin and William Bubbe are mentioned together in 1255 (RH) as holding
one knight's fee in *Clyve*.

p. 291, *s.n.* SELKLEY HUNDRED. *Selkelye* is also mentioned in 1300 (Ch)
between Overton and Fyfield.

pp. 310–11, *s.n.* HACKPEN HILL. There is a well-known hill of this name,
near Letcombe Bassett (Berks) and it certainly has a projecting hook. Unfortunately we have no early forms for the name of this hill and we cannot be
sure if the name is original or has been transferred from the hill in
Wiltshire.

pp. 328–9, *s.n.* FIFIELD. This is also called *Fihide* (sic) *Episcopi* (1275 RH),
from the holding of the Bishop of Winchester.

p. 330, *s.n.* LINDEN COPSE. The presence of ling on chalk downs seems,
at first sight, remarkable, since ling or heather is a calcifuge species.
Actually, however, its presence on the more level summits of chalk downs is
not infrequent where continual action of the weather has leached the surface

soil. In this lime-free surface the heather can become established and its roots penetrate into the chalk below (E.J.S.).

p. 341, *s.n.* CONHOLT. Professor Salisbury and Mr Young call attention to the Wiltshire *coven-tree*, a name for the guelder-rose which is 'common about Chalke and Cranborne Chase' (AubreyNH 56). This may possibly be the first element in *Covenholt*, but the history of *coven* is entirely obscure and it would be dangerous on the ground of the modern form alone to assume connection.

p. 346, *s.n.* GODSBURY. Godsbury is in Collingbourne Kingston (*supra* 344) and not in Easton as given in the text.

p. 346, *s.n.* HARROW FM. Mr G. M. Young (WM xlv, 346), noting that Harrow Fm is by Crossford and that both are by the *holenstypbum* or 'holly stumps' of BCS 225, suggests that here, as in other *Harrow*-names, we have a heathen *hearg* or grove, later replaced by some Christian sign. No certainty is possible in the absence of early evidence for *Harrow*.

p. 360, *s.n.* STONEHENGE. Professor Bruce Dickins notes the reference in the 12th-century *Roman de Brut* of Wace (ed. Arnold), ll. 8175 ff.:

> Bretun les suelent en bretanz
> Apeler carole as gaianz
> Stanhenges unt nun en engleis
> Pières pendues en franceis

and the lingering tradition of this interpretation in Thomas Middleton's 16th-century reference to 'the Hanging stones in Wilts' (*A Fair Quarrel* v. i, 181). Layamon renders Wace's *carole as gaianz* by *eotende ring*, that is 'giants' ring.'

pp. 381–2, *s.n.* LAVERSTOCK. BCS 879 is a grant of one hide of land at a place called Winterbourne in the land of the *Gewisse* and in the grant there is more than one mention of a river *læfer*. Since Laverstock lies by the river Bourne, formerly known as *Winterbourne* (*infra* 2), and the grant is found in the Wilton Register, it is natural that attempts have been made to associate it with Laverstock, but it is difficult to identify any of the boundary points and we must with Grundy (ii, 22) leave the matter in doubt. The early forms of Laverstock are not consistent with derivation from *læfer* and could only be associated with it if we take the *Laverke-* forms to be due to some early process of folk-etymology.

p. 418. Add '*Beocca* (Bagshot), *Beotta* (Bedborough).'

p. 489, under WILTON. Add 'Rollington (*Rollandun, Rollendun, Wrollendun* 944 (13th) BCS 795, *Rowllyngton* 1570 PembSurv) is recorded by Straton (PembSurv xlvi) as the name of the hill running south of *The Temple* in Wilton Park up to Warren Down.'

WILTSHIRE

Wilsætan 9th ASC (A) *s.a.* 800, 878, *Wilsæte* 12th ib. (E) ib., *Wiltunscir* 9th ib. (A) *s.a.* 898, 955 (14th) BCS 912, (*to*) *Wiltunescire* c. 1000 (c. 1225) KCD 716, *Wiltescire* 1086 DB, *Wiltescira* 1130 P *et passim* to 1367 AD v, with variant spellings *Wylte-* and *-s(c)hire, county called le Wiltshire* 1447 Pat, *Wilsher'* 1523 *SR*, 1606 Sess, *W(h)ileshire* c. 1540 L, *Wilshere* 1565 *DuLa*. On the significance of the name *v.* Introd. xvi, xvii. Locally the name of the county is still often heard as [wilʃər]. Cf. the surname *Wilsher*.

RIVER- AND STREAM-NAMES

ABBERD WATER (Bristol Avon) is so named from Abberd in Calne *infra* 256. In 1540 (L) the stream is called *Cale water, Cawne Water* from Calne itself.

AVON, R. (Bristol Avon)

> *Abon* 688 (14th) BCS 71, c. 1000 Asser
> *Auene* 850 (13th) BCS 458, 1065 (14th) KCD 817, 1228 Cl, 1289 Ass, *Avone* 1205 ClR, *Havene* 1268 Ass
> (*be*) *Afene* 940 (15th) BCS 752, (*on*) *Afonæ* 987 (c. 1150) KCD 658

For further forms and for the etymology, *v.* RN 23. The meaning is simply 'river' (OBrit **abonā*).

AVON, R. (Salisbury Avon)

> (*on*) *Afene* 892, 943 (13th) BCS 567, 782, *be æfene stæþe* 892 (13th) ib. 567, *Afenan* (gen.) 934 (c. 1150) ib. 705
> *Avene* 1214 FineR *et freq* to 1279 For

v. supra. stæþe is 'bank,' *v.* stæþ.

BEDWYN STREAM (Kennet) is (*in*) *bedewindan* 778 BCS 225, (*fram*) *bedeuuindan* 968 (c. 1225) ib. 1213. *v.* Bedwyn *infra* 332.

M W   I

BISS, R. (Bristol Avon)

> *on bis* 964 (late copy) BCS 1127, *Bys* ib., t. Ed 3 *For*
> *Byssi, Bissy* 1001 (15th) KCD 706
> *le Bisse* 1468 *MinAcct, water of Bysse* 1545, 1563 *FF, Biss Head, The Biss* 1575 *For, Bisse Mouth* 1632 WIpm
> *Beysbroke* 1536 BM

Ekwall (RN 34) takes this to be a British river-name, identical with Welsh *bys*, Cornish *bis, bes*, 'finger' (from **bissi-*), which perhaps had here some transferred sense, such as 'fork or arm of a river.' If so, the name may have reference to the fact that the stream consists of two arms which unite near North Bradley. The *i, y* in the second series of forms may represent OE dat. *ie* from **ea**, 'river.'

THE BOURNE (Bristol Avon) is *Dameteseye borne* 850 (14th) BCS 457, *Dauntesbourne* 940 (15th) ib. 752, from Dauntsey *infra* 68. v. **burna**, 'stream.'

BOURNE, R. (Salisbury Avon)

> (a) (*of*) *Collengaburnan* 921 (14th) BCS 635, *aque de Colebourne juxta Laverstoke* 1348 *Cor*
> (b) (*andlang*) *burnan* 949 (13th) BCS 879, *la Bourne* 1518 Hoare
> (c) (*fram*) *winter burnan* 972 (13th) BCS 1286, *Winterburne (aqua)* t. Hy 3 *Stowe* 798, *water called Winterbourn* 1279, *Wynterborne* 1356 *For*

Near its source this stream was once known as Collingbourne (*v. infra* 342). *Winterbourne* survives in the names of three villages on its banks (*infra* 383). The name refers to a stream which normally flows only during the winter months. Cf. Ekwall RN *s.n.*

BRINKWORTH BROOK (earlier IDOVER) (joins Bristol Avon at junction of Great and Little Somerford and Dauntsey parishes) is *riuulum qui dicitur ydouere* 850 (14th) BCS 458 in the bounds of Dauntsey. The old name is preserved in Idover in that parish (*infra* 69) and was preserved as late as the O.S. map of 1816 in the name of the bridge now called Somerford Bridge (*infra*

74). Brinkworth Brook further up its course becomes Gritten-ham Brook, and near Dovey's Fm in Brinkworth that stream is fed by a small stream coming up from Wootton Bassett. An islet in this stream just east of Hunt Mill is called *Idivers* (c. 1840 *TA*), and if we follow the stream up to its headwaters at a point just north of Cotmarsh Fm in Broad Town we have another field called *Idovers* (ib.).

This name is found in connection with several other streams in the north-west of the county:

(i) A mile further up the Avon, a little stream comes in on the south bank, near Great Somerford, the *reodburna* which gives its name to Rodbourne in Malmesbury (*infra* 51). If we follow that stream up we find its headwaters in Grittleton Park in a field called *Idover* in *TA* (c. 1840).

(ii) Some two miles still further up the Avon the Gauze Brook comes in from the west. If we follow that stream up to where it rises in the high ground on which Littleton Drew stands, we find, at the south end of the village, fields called *Idover* (ib.).

(iii) In Brinkworth, just by the south-west corner of Webb's Wood, are fields called Great and Little *Idovers* (ib.) on a small stream known as Woodbridge Brook (*infra* 11), which is also a tributary of the Bristol Avon.

(iv) Half a mile south-west of Chedglow in Crudwell there are fields called *Idover* and *Grass Idover* (ib.) which mark the headwaters of a stream which flows east and south-east to join Braydon Brook, which becomes Swill Brook (*infra* 10).

(v) In Hankerton, half a mile west of Hankerton Field Fm, is a field called *Idover* (ib.) which must be named from the stream which rises just to the west and flows south-east and east to join stream (iv) near its junction with Braydon Brook.

(vi) There is also a small stream which rises near the south-east end of Hankerton parish and flows north-west to join Braydon Brook. Along this lie two fields called *Idover* (ib.).

(vii) In Cricklade, at the head of a tiny feeder of the Thames, flowing past Bournelake Fm, is a field called *Idovers* (ib.).

(viii) Charlton School also notes a field called *Idovers* (just west of the north-west corner of Nineteen Acre Wood) at the headwaters of a feeder of Braydon Pond.

The uniform appearance in all these stream-names of *Idover* rather than *Tidover* makes it probable that any attempt to explain the river-name on the basis of forms with initial *t* found for Idover Fm *infra* 69 (cf. RN 208–9) should be abandoned. The second element is clearly the British word for water, corresponding to Welsh *dwfr*. The first element might, as suggested by Ekwall (ib.), be from a British word corresponding to Welsh *yw*, 'yew,' with loss of *w* before the following consonant, but yews are not common here.

BROADMEAD BROOK (By Brook) is *alor broke*, i.e. 'alder brook,' in 944 (BCS 800). The present name is a later formation. There was a field named *le Brodemede* near by in 1422 (*Add*).

BY BROOK (Bristol Avon)

(*andlang*) *þe fer* (sic) 944 (15th) BCS 800
innan, andlang wæfer 957 (c. 1200) ib. 1001
(*in ripar' de*) *Wevre* 1268, (*piscar' de*) *Wefre* 1279, *Wefre* 1281, 1289 *Ass*, *le Wevere* 1363 *NewColl*, *Wevermulle* 1370 *Cor*, (*fishery in*) *Weber* 1635 *FF*
Weaverne Brooke 1623 WIpm, *Wavering Brook* 1862 Aubrey

In the first form OE *p* (wen) has been misread as *þ* (thorn). The river-name is identical with Weaver (Ch, D), cf. PN D 16. The meaning is uncertain. It may derive from a root meaning 'winding' (RN 444), related to Latin *uibrare*. The By Brook winds greatly throughout the greater part of its course. The old name survives in Weavern Fm *infra* 82 and in Weavern Mw in Colerne *infra* 470. The new name is probably a back-formation from Bybrook Ho *infra* 78.

BYDEMILL BROOK (Thames) is *Bidebrok* 1357 AD iii, *Bidebrooke* 1591 WM vi. The stream gives name to Bydemill in Hannington *infra* 25 and repeats itself in Byde Mill in Corsham *infra* 96, Byde Fm (with Byde Mill) in Potterne *infra* 244, Byde Mill Lane in Poulshot *infra* 130, Byde Mill Fd in Kington Langley *infra* 470, and *Bydemilne* (1318 *Magd*) in Wanborough. It is clearly identical with the Gloucestershire stream-name Boyd (RN 46) from earlier *Byd* (BCS 887). These all probably derive from OE *byd*, 'hollow, depression,' discussed under Bidwell Fm (PN Nth 222), which is very commonly compounded with *wielle*, usually when used of a spring but also of a stream. Cf. further Beardwell in Atworth (*infra* 116), *Bydewellake* (1341 *Rental*) in Steeple Ashton and Bidwell (Fd) in Heddington.

CAT BROOK (Marden) in *Cadeburne* 937 (14th) BCS 717, *Cadebrok* 1259 FF. Probably '*Cada*'s stream,' *v.* **burna**. See Cadenham *infra* 87.

COCKLEMORE BROOK (Bristol Avon) is *aque de Pewe* 1279, 1281, 1289 *Ass*, *rivulum de Pewe* t. Ed 1, t. Ed 3 *For*, *stream of Pewe* 1304 Pat. See further Pewsham Forest *infra* 14.

COLE, R. (Thames). This river is mentioned in the bounds of (*a*) Little Hinton, (*b*) Wanborough. The first reference is in 854 (12th) BCS 477, in the phrase *of smitan*, the second in 1043–53 (11th) ib. 479, in the phrase *innan smitan stream*. The contexts make it clear that *smite* is here an old name for the Cole, at least in this part of its course.

Mention is also made of one of its tributary streams in the phrases *innan, of Lentan* 854 (12th) BCS 477, in the bounds of Wanborough, where it clearly has reference to the unnamed stream, rising in Bishopstone, which joins the Cole a mile west of Bourton (Berks). The same name is used in BCS 675 (*on Lentan*) in the bounds of Watchfield (Berks), with reference to the main stream of the Cole, so that it is clear that in earlier days the Cole was known, at least in part of its course, as (*a*) *Smite*, (*b*) *Lente*. This early name for the Cole survives in Lynt Bridge and Lynt Fm in Inglesham which are on and by the Cole. Further references to the Cole in its lower stretches are *Lenta*, *Lente* 1221 Pat, *river Lente* 1227 Ch, *Liente*, *Lyenthe* t. Hy 3 Stowe 798, *Leynt* 1482 AD i.

We have no early authority for the name *Cole* as applied to this stream and the natural assumption has hitherto been that it is a late back-formation from Coleshill (Berks), past which the Cole flows. That may be the case, but it is a little disturbing to find that there was in Wanborough a *messuage voc. Colne* (1336 *Magd*), which would suggest the existence of a stream called *Colne* in Wanborough already in the 14th century, and if so, it could not be anything other than the present river Cole or one of its feeders, so that *Colne* may be yet another genuine early name for this stream.

There are other examples of Smite, Lent and Colne as river-names in England (cf. RN 249–50, 373–4, 87–90). Ekwall (*loc. cit.*) associates the first with the common word 'smite' and takes the name to be used of a swiftly moving stream. The second he takes to be allied to Welsh *lliant*, 'flood, stream.' For Coln(e) more than one origin is possible.

DEANE WATER (Salisbury Avon) is *Nhodden* 13th *For*, of unknown origin (H. C. B.).

DERRY BROOK (Thames). This is *river called Sanburne* 1651 WM xlvi, i.e. 'sand stream,' *v.* **burna**, the name being preserved in Sambourn in Minety *infra* 62. An alternative earlier name was *Grenebourne* 1368 *For*, *Greene bourne* 1630 NQ vii. For Derry, *v.* Derry Hill *infra* 257.

DEVERILL, R. (old name for upper part of Wylye R.) is *Deferael, Defereal* 968 (13th) WiltonReg, *ripam de Deverel* c. 1300 Trop, *stream called Deverell water* 1736 *Longleat*. See further Brixton Deverill *infra* 165. As a place-name it occurs as *Devrel* 1086 DB, *Deverel* t. Hy 2 (1270) Ch, c. 1160 StOsmund, 1186 P, *Deurel* 1164 ib., *Deureals* 1166 ib., *Deverell* 1190 ib., 1213 ClR, referring to one or other of the villages on its banks.

The first element is a form of British *dubro-*, 'water,' found also in Andover, Candover, Micheldever (Ha), cf. RN *s.n.* The second element is the British word corresponding to Welsh *ial*, 'fertile or cultivated upland region,' found also in Fonthill *infra* 190. Cornish parallels are Deveral in Gwinear (*Deverel* 1324, *Defriel* 1356 *Ass*) and Deveral in Sancreed (*Deverel* 1326, *Dyfryl* 1340 *Ass*). These are now farm-names, but were originally no doubt the names of the small streams near by.

Hoare (*Hundred of Mere* 137) dallies with the idea that the name is really *Dive-rill* and that the river is so called "from a spring, which afterwards assumes the name of the river Wily, diving under the ground for a considerable distance, till it reaches Kingston Deverill where it becomes a permanent stream." In Drayton's *Polyolbion* the goddess 'Dyver' is drawn as half buried in the ground, her feet coming out at one hole and her head at another (cf. WM xvii, 283).

DONCOMBE BROOK (By Brook) is *Donecombesbroke* 1296 Aubrey, i.e. the brook by Doncombe *infra* 94.

EBBLE, R. (Salisbury Avon) is (*on*) *ebblesburnon, Ybbleş burnan* 672 (c. 1150) BCS 27, (*on*) *Eblesburnan* 826, 932, 947, 957 (c. 1150) ib. 391, 690, 832, 1004, (*innan*) *Ebbeles burnan* 955 (13th) ib. 917, (*on*) *Yblesburnan* 948 (c. 1150) ib. 863, *Ebelesburne* 1288 FF, *aqua de Ebbelesborne* 1289 *Ass*. See further Ebbesborne Wake *infra* 207. Leland (c. 1540) calls the stream *Chalkbourn* from Chalke *infra* 203. Ekwall (RN 141) interprets the name as '*Ebbel*'s stream,' noting the personal name *Ebbella* (BCS 154) and that this name seems also to be found in *Ebbleswell* (river) (1251 Ch) in Warwickshire. Ebble or *Ebele* itself is a late back-formation from the longer name, due to Bowles, the author of the *Hundred of Chalke* in Hoare's *History of Wiltshire* (161).

FISHER'S BROOK (Marden) is probably to be associated with the family of Thomas *le Fissere* (1289 *Ass*). It is called *Fishers Brook* c. 1840 TA.

FLAGHAM BROOK (joins the Thames above Ashton Keynes) is a late formation from a lost place recorded in *two meadows called Flaghams* (1633 WIpm).

FONTHILL BROOK (Nadder) is referred to in (*to*) *Funtgeal* 984 (15th) KCD 641, v. Fonthill *infra* 190.

GAUZE BROOK (joins the Bristol Avon below Malmesbury) is *Corsaburna* 701 (c. 1125) BCS 103, *Corsborne* 854 (14th) ib. 470, *Corsbrok* 956 (14th) ib. 922, *Coresbrok* 982 (14th) KCD 632, *Gosbrooke* 1599 Devizes, *Gaze Brook* 1753 Eton, *Gauze Brook* 1773 A and D. The first part of the name is related to Welsh, Cornish *cors*, 'reeds, bog,' Breton *kors*, 'reeds,' cf. RN 95. The stream gave name to Corston *infra* 50. See also Corsley *infra* 152. It is to be noted that its later English name was Rodbourne (*infra* 51–2), which itself means 'reed-stream.'

HUNGERBOURN STREAM (1773 A and D) is the name of an intermittent stream which comes down in wet years from Rockley to Bay Bridge *infra* 303 (H. C. B.). See Addenda *supra* xxxix.

Isis, R. The name for the upper part of the Thames. The earliest reference in a Wiltshire context is *The Isis* c. 1540 L. The name is an antiquarian one, due to artificial division of *Tamesis* and *Tamise*, as if from Thame(s) and Isis. *v.* RN 215.

Kennet, R. Forms found in Wiltshire documents are (*of*) *cynetan* 939 BCS 734, 972 (13th) ib. 1285, *Kenet* t. Hy 2 (1268) Ch, *aqua de Kenett* 1228 SarumCh, *Kenite* 1228 Cl, *Kenete* 1228 FF, 1289 *Ass*, 1331 *Stowe*, *Kenet* 1280 Pat, *Kynette* 1360 AD vi, *Kennet* 1540 *MinAcct*, *Kynnet* 1565 WM xxxviii, *Kinnet* 1670 Aubrey. The river-name goes back to OBrit *Cunētio*, *v.* RN *s.n.*, of doubtful meaning. The upper part of the Kennet from its source to Avebury was known at one time as *Winterburna*. The name is preserved in Winterbourne Bassett and Monkton *infra* 309. Crawford (WM xlii, 58) notes that there are fields called *Sambourne* by the Upper Kennet Horslip Bridge in Avebury and in West Overton by George Bridge on the Lower Kennet, which suggests yet another name for the Kennet. One of the feeders of the Kennet was *Gadbourne* (c. 1840 *TA*), and this survives in Gadbourne Bridge (*infra* 280).

Key, R. (Thames). This stream is named *Braden water* in 1540 (L) from Braydon Forest *infra* 11, and would seem to be identical with *Lortinges bourne* 796 (14th) BCS 279 A. It flows past Keycroft in Purton (*infra* 40), of unknown origin. The present name may be a back-formation from Keycroft.

Lid Brook (By Brook) is *Lydbroke* t. Eliz *LRMB*, *Lidbrooke* 1630 *Devizes*, while the valley through which the stream flows is *Ludecombe* 13th RegMalm. The name probably goes back to OE *hlȳde*, 'loud one.' "The stream falls down a steep stony bank near its source and is noticeably a noisy one in contrast with other streams in this countryside" (G. M. Y.). *v.* Liddington *infra* 283–4.

Lilly Brook (6″) (Brinkworth Brook) takes its name from a lost *Lynley*. See Lillybrook in Lyneham *infra* 271. A bridge by here was called *Lyllyesbrugge* 1512 *Ct*.

Marden, R. (Bristol Avon) is *aqua de Melkeden* 1228 Cl, *aquae de Merkedene* 1245 WM xvi, *aqua que voc' Merkeden* 1279,

t. Ed 3 *For, aqua de Melkeden, Merkeden* t. Hy 3 *Stowe* 798, *Water of Merkeden* 1300 *For, Markedeane* 1557 Pat. Marden (*merke(n)dene* 937 (14th) BCS 717) was originally a place-name, 'boundary valley,' *v.* mearc, denu. It was one of the boundaries of Chippenham Forest (G. B. G.).

NADDER, R. (Salisbury Avon)

Noodr 705 (c. 1125) BCS 114

(*be, on, to*) *Nodre* 860 (15th) ib. 500, 901 (13th) ib. 588, 956 (15th) ib. 970, *aqua de Nodere* t. Hy 3 *Stowe* 798

(*æt, of, andlang*) *Noddre* 937 (13th) BCS 714, 956 (14th) ib. 985, *Noddre* 1255 RH, t. Hy 3 *Shaston*, 1279, t. Ed 3 *For, Noddere* 1275 RH

Nadder 1540 *MinAcct*, 1544 LP, 1551 Pat

A British river-name, probably a derivative of the root found in Latin *natare*, 'to swim' (RN 298). Hoare indulges in a piece of folk-etymology, saying that "from its numerous windings (it) has obtained the vulgar name of Adder" (Hoare 109).

NINE MILE RIVER (Salisbury Avon) is so named in 1773 (A and D) and is *le Borne* t. Jas 1 *LRMB. v.* burna. The stream is only about four miles long but joins the Avon nine miles from Salisbury. Drovers perhaps named it from this fact (G. M. Y.).

OG, R. is a late back-formation from Ogbourne *infra* 303.

RAY, R. (Thames) is *Rea* 1630 WIpm, *the Rea* 1733 WM xl, from ME *atter ee*, 'at the water,' *v.* æt, ea. The old name was (*on*) *uuorf* 962 (c. 1225) BCS 1093, *Worfe* 796 (14th) ib. 279 A, (*on*) *Wurf* 943 (c. 1150) ib. 788, 956 (c. 1150) ib. 983, *Worfe stream* 1008 (c. 1225) KCD 1305, *Werfe, Werffe* 1228 Cl. *v.* Wroughton *infra* 278. The old river-name is identical with Wharfe (Y) and the root-idea is that of something which twists and turns (RN 470).

SEM, R. (Nadder) is (*on*) *Semene* 984 (15th) KCD 641, *Semene, Semenhaved* 1244 Hoare. Cf. also John de *Semene* (1327 *SR*) and William de *Semene* (1333 ib.) in Semley *infra* 209. A pre-English river-name, probably going back to a British *Sumina*, and identical with Somme (France), cf. RN 355–6.

SEMINGTON BROOK (Bristol Avon) is *aqua de Semelton* 1249 *Ass.* Semington (or *Semelton*) itself contains as a first element the old name of the stream, referred to as *semnit* 964 (late copy) BCS 1127, *aqua de Semnet, Semet'* 1228 Cl, *aqua de Semelet, Semnet* t. Hy 3 *Stowe* 798, t. Ed 3, *Semenet* 1279 *For.* Ekwall (RN 356) compares the French rivers *Sumenat* and a lost *Sumeneta*, which may be diminutives of the *Sumina* noted above.

SHEAR WATER (Wylye) is *Sherewater* 1675 Ogilby. Cf. *Shear Water Spring Head* c. 1840 *TA*. Probably Hoare (*Heytesbury* 81) is right in deriving it from scir, 'clear.' "The reason of the name I presume was the comparative purity or clearness of the water, though we now see no peculiar claim which it has to such distinction" (*loc. cit.*). The present lake is an artificial creation.

STOUR, R. Nearly all the course of this river is through Dorset, and the only reference noted in Wiltshire records is *ryver of Stowre* c. 1540 L. Cf. Ekwall (RN *s.n.*) and Stourton *infra* 181.

SWILL BROOK (Thames) is *aqua que voc' la Suelle* 1267 FF, cf. also *Swilbrigge* 1568 *DuLa, Swele bridge* 1591 WM vi. An old name for the stream was *Bradenebrok(e)* 956 (14th) BCS 922, 974, 1065 (14th) KCD 584, 817, 1289 *Ass*, t. Ed 3 *For, -broc* 1228 Cl. *v.* Braydon Forest *infra* 11. It is preserved in BRAYDON BROOK, a hamlet in Crudwell.

THAMES, R. References in Wiltshire documents are *Thamisia* t. Hy 3 *Stowe* 798, *Tameyse* 1282 Ipm, *Tamyse* t. Ed 3 *For, le Temes* 1603 *AOMB*. For a full list of spellings and etymology cf. RN 403, PN Ess 13.

TILL, R. (Salisbury Avon). This is a late back-formation from Tilshead *infra* 237. It was formerly *Winterbourne Water* c. 1540 L, a name preserved in Winterbourne Stoke *infra* 237.

WERE, R. (6") (Wylye). It is *Little River Were* 1695 Morden, *Were* 1822 Hoare. *v.* Warminster *infra* 157. Ekwall (RN 449–50) shows that there is good reason to believe in the genuineness of the river-name and not to take it, as has sometimes been done, as a back-formation from earlier forms of Warminster. He derives the stream-name from a lost *worig, allied to OE wōrian, 'to wander about,' and OE *wērig*, 'weary.' Celtic origin for the river-name is also possible. Roseworthy (Co) is *hryd worwig* (960 BCS 1056), later *Redwuri*, *Rydwory* (cf. Welsh *hryd*, 'ford').

WOODBRIDGE BROOK (Bristol Avon) was earlier *Geresbourne* 956 (14th) BCS 922, *Garseburn'* 1228 Cl, *Garisburne* t. Hy 3 *Stowe* 798, 1300 *For*, *Garesbourne* 1228, t. Ed 3 *For*. *v.* Garsdon *infra* 59. The modern name is a late formation from a lost *la Wodebrigge* 13th RegMalm, t. Ed 3 *For*.

WYLYE, R. [waili]

> *Wileo* 688 (c. 1125) BCS 70
> *Wilig* 860 (15th) ib. 500 *et freq* to 988 (13th) KCD 665
> *Guilou* c. 1000 Asser
> (*on*) *wili stream* 1045 (13th) KCD 778, *Wyly* 1268, 1279 *Ass*, 1330 Cl, *Wili*, *Wylie* 1279, *Wily* c. 1300 *For*
> *Wile* c. 1125 WMP, c. 1540 L
> *Wylyborne Water* 1541, *Wylborne Water* 1544 LP, *Williborne Water* 1551 Pat

A pre-English river-name of uncertain etymology. It may mean 'tricky stream' though it has no direct connection with the adj. *wily*. For a full discussion cf. RN 457–60.

FORESTS

BRAYDON FOREST

> (*silva*) *Bradon* 688 (c. 1125) BCS 70, 1243 FF, 1611 *DuLa*
> (*silva*) *Braden* 796 (14th) BCS 279, *Braden* 1240 Lib, 1328 Ch
> (*on*) *Bradene* c. 925 ASC (Ā) *s.a.* 905, 956 (14th) BCS 922 *et freq* to 1321 *Ass*
> *Brædene* c. 1100 ASC (D) *s.a.* 905, *Braedone* 1272 Ipm
> *Braddene* 1311 *AD*, *Braddon* 1424 Pat, *Breden*, *Bredon* 1316 Cl
> *Braydon* 1589 *FF*, 1634 *Recov*

Ekwall (DEPN) notes that this name is probably identical with Bradon (So) for which he quotes forms *Bredde*, *Brede*, *Bredene*, *Brade* 1086 DB, *Braden(e)* 1266 Episcopal Registers. The name is clearly pre-English, and the etymology is obscure.

The Wiltshire wood seems at one time to have had an alternative name, cf. *Ordwoldeswode nunc Bradene* 13th RegMalm, and must have been so called from its sometime owner *Ordweald*.

CHIPPENHAM FOREST is *foresta de Chepeham* 1215 ClR, *forest of Chippenham* 1252 Cl.

CHUTE FOREST[1]

silvae quae vocatur Cetum 1086 DB, *Cet* 1210 Cur, 1222 Pat, 1223 ClR, 1231 Cl, *Cett'* t. Hy 2 (1270) Ch, 1231 Cl, 1232 Pat, 1236 Lib, *Ceth* 1235, *Cette* 1244, 1253 Cl

Ceat 1100–1117 (1329) Ch

Ceit 1178 BM, *Ceite* 1274, *Chiet* 1282, 1289 Cl

Chet 1231, 1245 ib., 1236 FF, 1240 Lib, *Chett(e)* 1233 Lib, 1248 Ch, *Schet* 1245 Pat, *Chete* 1253, *Ched'* 1254 Cl, *Chette* 1272 Pat

Chut 1252 Misc, 1257 *For*, 1259 Ipm *et passim*, *Chute* 1283 Cl, 1284 Ch, *Chutte* 1284 Cl, *Shut(e)* 1291, 1463 Pat

Ceute 1278, *Cheut* 1281, 1324 Cl, *Chewte* 1553 WM xii

Choete 1285, 1291 Cl, *Cheote* 1297 Pat

Chuet(e) 1285, 1291 Cl, 1297 Pat

Chuyt 1289 ib., 1290 Cl, t. Ed 2 *For*, 1428 FA, *Chiute* 1356 Cl

This is OBrit *cēto-, 'wood' (from *kaito-, ModWelsh *coed*, 'wood'). See further Introd. xv.

CLARENDON FOREST

(*a*) *Pancet* t. Hy 1 SarumCh, 1222 ClR, 1225, 1231 Cl, t. Hy 3 Fees, *Pauncet* 1223 Pat, 1224 ClR, 1234 Cl, 1269 Pat, *Panchet* 1220 ib., 1221 ClR, 1238 Cl, 1370 FF, *Ponchet* 1251 Cl, *Panset* 1255 RH, 1356 *For*, *Paunsett al. Panshett* 1650 NQ viii

Penchet 1279, 1331, t. Ed 3 *For*, *Penchyt* 1298 Cl, *Penchiet* 1313 Inq aqd, *Penchut* 1356 FF, *Penchetes myll* 1428 Hoare

(*b*) *foreste de Clarendon* 1231, 1234 Cl, *Claryndon forest* 1298 Ipm, 1348 Cl

Claringdon 1320 Cl, *Claryngdon* 1356 *For*, *Claryngdon al. Paunchet* 1457 IpmR, (*al. Paunset*) 1466 Pat, (*al. dict. Paunsett*) 1488 DuLa

---

[1] Part of Chute Forest lies in Hampshire.

The old British name *Penchet* means 'end of the wood' (ModWelsh *pen coed*), being identical with Penquit (PN D 272). It no doubt referred originally to a definite place, i.e. where the wood ended, perhaps in the Avon valley above Salisbury, but at an early date the name was taken over by the English and applied to the whole of the medieval forest of Clarendon. Clarendon was properly the name of a manor and parish within the forest area. For that name *v. infra* 375–6.

GROVELY WOOD

(*on*) *grafan lea* 940 (13th) BCS 757
foresta de Gravelinges 1086 DB, 1196 P, 1223 ClR, 1281, -*ingges* 1283 Ipm
Graveling(*a*) 1190 P, t. Hy 2 (1270) Ch *et freq* to 1352 Ipm, with variant spellings -*ing*', -*inge*, *Gravelinch* 1255 RH
forest de Gravele 1154 RBE, 1159 P *et freq* to 1279 *Ass*, -*lea* 1167 P, -*lee* 1307, -*ley* 1320 Cl, 1603, 1829 Hoare
Graveninge 1155 RBE, 1254 Cl, *Gravenel* 1231 ib.
Grofle 1317 Cl, *Grovelegh* 1402 FA, 1412 *MinAcct*, *Grofeley* 1434, *Groveley* 1448 Pat, 1605 *Recov*

This is a difficult name. OE *grāfan lēa* looks as if it were a genitival compound of grafa[1], 'copse, grove,' and leah, 'clearing,' 'clearing of or in the grove.' This should have developed to *Grovele* but no such form is found before the 14th century. The explanation is perhaps to be found in the existence, side by side with grafa, of græfe, which in Wessex would give ME *grave*, as indeed in southern England generally. OE *grǣfan lēa* would explain all the *Gravele* forms, and perhaps *græfanlea* was really the more usual form in OE. Confusion between *grave* (from græfe) and *grove* (from graf(a)) is common even in stressed syllables (cf. PN Herts 244). Alternatively, as suggested by Professor Bruce Dickins, the *a* might be explained as due to trisyllabic shortening. *Gravelinges* is probably, as suggested by Ekwall (DEPN), an ingas-formation from *grafanlea* or *græfanlea*, denoting the people who lived in or near Grovely.

---

[1] Ekwall (DEPN) suggests that the first element may be OE *grafa*, 'ditch,' with reference to the old ditch or Roman road which runs through the wood, but no such word seems to be on independent record.

MELCHET FOREST

> *Milchet(e) silva* 1086 DB, *Milchet* 1231 Cl, 1281 Fine, 1289
> Cl, 1300 *For*, *Mylcet* 1252 Ch, *Milcet* 1255 RH, *Milchete*
> 1320 Cl
> *Melset* 1243 ib., *Melchetwode* 1255 *Ass*, *Melcet* 1255, *-chet*
> 1275 RH *et passim*, *Melkset* 1275 Fine, *Melchuyt* 1538 LP
> *Mulchet* 1287, 1324, 1327 Ipm, 1297 Cl, 1400 Pat

This is another old British forest-name, the second element
being the OBrit *cēto-*, 'wood,' discussed under Chute *supra* 12.
Ekwall (DEPN *s.n.*) takes the first element to be OBrit *mēl-*,
'bare, bald' (ModWelsh *moel*). This word is common in Welsh
and Cornish place-names in combination with the word *bre*,
'hill' (cf. Welsh *Moelfre*, Cornish *Mulfra*, *Mulvra*, *Mulberry*),
but its exact sense in connection with a wood is uncertain.

Melchet was an outlying part of Clarendon Forest. The name
is preserved in Melchet Court *infra* 383.

MELKSHAM FOREST is *foresta de Melkesham* 1236 Cl, taking its
name from the town *infra* 128.

PEWSHAM FOREST is *forest(a) de Peusham* 1238 Cl, 1263, 1319
Pat, *Peuseham* 1245 Cl, *Peuwesham* 1245 WM xvi, *bosco de
Pevesham*, *foresta de Pevenesham* 1249 *Ass*, *Beuisham* 1261 Cl,
Peuesham 1268 *Ass*, *Pewesham* 1279 *For et freq* to 1374 Pat,
Peuesham 1279, 1289 *Ass*, 1291 Cl, *Peausham* 1297 Pat, *Peawsham*
1486, 1508 ib., *Pewsham alias Pevesham* 1558 FF.

Pewsham and other names in *Pew* in Wiltshire present a very
difficult problem. Pewsham itself is on Cocklemore Brook, of
which the old name is *Pewe* (*supra* 5), common in the 13th and
14th centuries, and surviving in the field-names *Bennetts Pew*,
Panns Pew (*TA*), lying by Cocklemore Brook. We have further
(i) Pew Hill in Langley Burrell *infra* 106 which lies near the
headwaters of another feeder of the Avon, (ii) Pew's Hill in
Slaughterford *infra* 112 at the head of a valley down which a
tiny stream flows to join By Brook *supra* 4. All these names
suggest the possibility of an early stream-name *Pewe*. No
suggestion can be made as to its ultimate origin. If *Pewe* is a
river-name, Pewsham would then mean 'ham or hamm by the
Pew.'

SAVERNAKE FOREST [sævərnæk]

> *silva quae appellatur Safernoc* 934 (c. 1300) BCS 699
> *Savernak* 1155 RBE, 1222 Pat, -*ac* 1156, 1159 P *et passim*,
>   with variant spelling -*ak, Savernage* 1333 Ipm
> *Severnak* 1224 ClR, 1264 Cl, 1305 *Ass*, 1307, 1333, 1355 Cl
> *Savernack* 1675 Ogilby, *Savernake* 1684 ParReg (Marl-
>   borough)

Savernake is clearly a derivative with the OCeltic suffix -*āco*
of the word found in the river-name Severn. Ekwall (DEPN
s.n.) suggests that it was so named from an older name for one
of the streams near by, possibly the Bedwyn.

SELWOOD FOREST[1]

> *Sealwudu* 9th ASC (Ā) *s.a.* 878, 894, *Selewudu* c. 1000 ib. (B)
>   *s.a.* 878, *Sealuudscire* c. 1000 Ethelw
> *Selwudu* c. 1000 Asser

Later forms found in Wiltshire documents are *Selewod(e)*
1228 Cl, 1232 Pat, 1248 Ch. Asser calls it *Selwudu, Latine
autem sylva magna, Britannice Coit Maur.* The British name
corresponds to ModWelsh *coed mawr*, 'big wood.' Cf. Morchard
(PN D 380). The English name apparently has as first element
OE *sealh*, 'sallow, withy.' Cf. the neighbouring Zeals *infra* 182–3.

ROADS, ETC.

FOSSE WAY. In Wiltshire documents this road is referred to as
stratam publicam que ab antiquis stret, nunc fos nuncupatur (BCS
922), in the bounds of Brokenborough and as (*on*) *strete* in 940
(BCS 750) in the bounds of Grittleton, and later as *regia via
vocata Foos* c. 1300 *Malm, Fosse, Fos* 13th RegMalm, *le Fossewey*
1422 *Add, Force waie* 1591 WM vi. For a discussion of this
name, which is ultimately from the Latin *fossa*, with reference
to the 'ditch' on one or both sides of it, *v.* PN Wa 7.

GRIM'S DITCH. There have been at least three dykes of this
name in the county, of which two survive on the modern map.
The first is the ancient dyke which runs through Grovely Wood
to the Wylye and gave name to Ditchampton *infra* 219. This is

---

[1] Most of Selwood Forest lies in Somerset.

referred to as *grimes dic* 956 (13th) BCS 935, 968 (13th) Wilton-Reg, 1045 (13th) KCD 778, *Grymmesdich* 1352 Ipm, *Grymes-*1380 Pat, 1570 PembSurv, *Grymsdyke* 1603, *Grimes Dike* 1651 Hoare. The second is the old dyke along the present county boundary north of Martin. This is *Gryms ditche* 1618 *Map* and is referred to as *þer strete dich* in BCS 817, perhaps, as suggested by Grundy, because it crosses the old Sarum-Dorchester road. The third is the remains of an old dyke on Wick Down between Downton and Breamore (Ha). This gave name to *Grymesdiche-sende* 1297 *DuLa* and would seem to be referred to as *on tha dic* in BCS 27.

This is a common name for an ancient earthwork, cf. PN Ess 375 and PN Herts 7–8. Ekwall (*Studia Germanica tillägnade E. A. Kock* 41 ff.) has shown that *Grim* here is probably another name of Woden, to whose activities these ancient earthworks were ascribed. Cf. Wansdyke *infra* 17.

ICKNIELD WAY. This name is not now found in the county, but we have documentary evidence that two roads were so named in Saxon times and later. The first example is *icenhilde weg* 1045 (12th) BCS 479, *way called Ykenilde* 1270, *Ikenyldeweye* 1292 *Magd*, *Ickleton Way* 1649 Ct. These all refer to a road in Wanborough, and have reference to the well-known Icknield Way which, coming from the Chilterns, makes its way westwards below the Berkshire downs and so south-west to Wanborough. The second example is *Ykeneldestrete*, *Yknildestrete* 1279, *Ikenyldestret* t. Ed 3 *For*, (*super montem de Wynterborne*) *juxta Ikeneldestret* 1348 *Cor*, *Ykenylstrete* t. Hy 7 Hoare. The Forest references are to Clarendon Forest, and the *montem de Wynterborne* is probably Figsbury Ring (*infra* 384). It would seem, therefore, that the name refers to the ancient road which runs down from here to St Thomas' Bridge.

We may note also *Ikinildestreta fossata* in 1184 (P), but the context is insufficient to fix the locality of this 'street.'

PORT WAY as in OE *portweg* (KCD 778) is used in OE charters and later documents of a road leading to a **port** or town. The only one of which the name survives on the map is the ancient track which enters the county at Hampshire Gap near Newton Tony and runs through Idmiston to Old Sarum. It is referred to as *Portwey* 1364 *DuLa*, *Porteway* 1518 Hoare. Cf., however, Portway Ho in Great Hinton *infra* 142.

RIDGE WAY is the name of an ancient track entering the county near Bishopstone on the Berkshire border and running through the parishes of Bishopstone, Little Hinton, Liddington, Wanborough, Wroughton to East Kennett, where it crosses the Kennet, then across the downs to Alton Priors. It is referred to as (*andlang*) *hric weges* 939 BCS 734, *hric weg* 956 (c. 1150) ib. 948, *Rigweie* 1270 *Magd*, *la*, *le Rigweye* 1281, 1289 *Ass*. Another RIDGE WAY, still so named, on the downs above Lavington is referred to as *Rigwey in decenn' de Lavynton* 1348 *Cor*, *Ryggewey* 1422 *Ct*.

There are frequent references in OE charters and in other documents to other ridgeways besides these. There is a full discussion of those mentioned in OE charters in Grundy's *The Ancient Highways and Tracks of Wiltshire* (*ArchJourn* xxv, 69–194).

WANSDYKE [wɔnzdaik] is *wodnes dic* 903 (13th) BCS 600, 939 ib. 734, 961 (c. 1200) ib. 1073, *wondesdich* 936 (14th) ib. 710, t. Ed 3 *For*, *Wodenesdich* 1259 Ch, *-dik* 1260 *Survey*, *Wodnesdiche* 1279 Ch, *Wannysdiche* 1499 ib., *Wansdiche* 1563 *NewColl*, *Wannesdichesherde* 1567 PembSurv, *Wensditch* 1670 Aubrey, *Wansditch* 1819 RCH. 'Woden's dike.' In BCS 734 it is mentioned in close connection with a *wodnes dene*. The 'dyke,' which runs from the hills south of Bath to a point east of Bedwyn *infra* 332, was clearly associated with the god Woden. Cf. Grim's Ditch *supra* 15. The normal development was to *Wansditch*. The form in *dyke* must be a late antiquarian form, perhaps due to Stukeley. The *sherd* in the last form but two has reference to a gap in the dike. Cf. **sceard** *infra* 445.

MISCELLANEOUS

MARLBOROUGH DOWNS. Cf. *le Downe* 1540 *MinAcct*, *le Downe in Marleborough* 1553 Pat.

SALISBURY PLAIN is *planum Sar'* 1346 *Ipm* (Fisherton de la Mere context), *the Playne* c. 1540 L, *Salesburye Playne* 1610 S, *Salisbury-plaines* 1670 Aubrey. Westbury is called *West(e)bury under the Playne* 1551 NQ i, *subter le Playne* 1585 WM xxi, *v. infra* 149.

Salisbury[1]

SALISBURY [sɔ·lzbəri]

Sorvioduni, Sorbiodoni 4th (8th) AntonItin

(*æt*) *Searobyrg* 9th ASC (Ā) *s.a.* 552, (*to*) *Searbyrig* c. 1150 ib. (E) *s.a.* 1003, (*to*) *Searebyrig* ib. *s.a.* 1085, (*on*) *Searbyrig* ib. *s.a.* 1096, 1099, 1100, 1106, (*of*) *Særesbyri*(*g*) ib. *s.a.* 1123, 1125, 1126, 1130, (*of*) *Searesbyrig* ib. *s.a.* 1123, (*of*) *Seresberi* ib. *s.a.* 1132, (*of*) *Sereberi* ib. *s.a.* 1137

Salesberia a. 1086, (*apud*) *Salesburiam* 1096 France, *Salesberia* 1087–1100 (1306) Ch, 1131, *-berie* 1142 SarumCh, *-bir'* 1202 P, 1212 Cur, 1235 Fees, *-bury* 1227 FF, 1385 Trop, Cl, 1394 *Ass*, 1422 Pat, *Sallesbury* 1422 *Add*, *Neu Salesbery* 1450–3 ECP, *Newe Salysbury* 1457 Pat, *Salsbery* 1575 WM xxxvi

Sarisberie 1086 DB, *-beria* 1158, (*Vetus*) 1187 P, *-biria* c. 1200 RBE, *-beri* 1212 Cur, *-berie* 1237 Bracton, *Saresbury* 1294 Ch, 1385 Trop, *-birie* 1309 Sarum, *Saresbir'* t. Ed 3 *For*, *New Saresbury* 1427 Pat, *Nova Sarisburia* 1428 FA

Sarrisbiriæ 1154 RBE, *Sarrisburie* 1230 Cl, *-biri* 1232 Ch, *-biria* 1232 Pat, *-byr'* 1279, 1289 *Ass*, *-birie* 1315 Sarum

Cyty of Newe Sarum 1586 AD v

Forms from coins include *Searber, Ser(e)byri, Serebrig, Sereb, Serbri* 979–1016, *Searbir, Ser, Sereb, Sere, Serebyr, Serbirge, Serbie, Serbyr, Serb* 1016–66, *Sear(b), Særeb, Serbir, Serburi* 1066–1135.

The name *Salisbury*, like that of many other Romano-British settlements, is the result of a process of folk-etymology. The name of the original settlement at Old Sarum is preserved in the Antonine Itinerary in the forms *Sorvioduni, Sorbiodoni* (gen. sg.). The only suggestion of any value which has been put forward with regard to this name is the very tentative one made in 1901 by Henry Bradley in the *English Miscellany presented to Furnivall* (15). It was that the first element *Sorvios* or *Sorvia* might be a Celtic river-name applied to the Avon as it flows just to the west

---

[1] Until the closing years of the 12th century, when a new settlement was coming into being on the plain beneath Old Sarum (*infra* 372), all the forms must refer to the latter place, but they are included here in order to have a complete sequence of early spellings for the name.

of the site. It would be related to Irish *soirbh*, 'gentle.' He suggested that this might have become *Sarva* by the 8th century (cf. *Sarva*[1] as recorded by the Ravenna Geographer as the name of a British river) and could then by a process of folk-etymology be associated with OE *searu*, gen. *searwe*, *searwes*, 'trick,' so that we had in *searoburh*, 'trick-stronghold,' a name which had arisen from the old Celtic name in much the same way as OE *eoforwic*, 'boar-dwelling,' from *Eburācum*. The second element in the old name was British *dūnon*, 'fort,' which would appropriately be rendered by OE *burh*. A little later the first element in this name was given genitival form on the model of the numerous *burh*-names with a personal name in the genitive singular as their first element, and lastly in Anglo-Norman times the sequence *r-r* interchanged with *l-r* (cf. IPN 106 and see further *Collected Papers of Henry Bradley* 90, 106–7, 114 and WM xxxix, 28–9). See Addenda *supra* xxxix.

With regard to the form *Sarum* it is impossible to carry the matter further than the note, in the form of a query, contributed by the late Canon Wordsworth to NQ (iv, 418–19) in 1904. He notes that the earliest authoritative references for it are in a printed volume of 1460 and on tombs dated 1416 to 1418, with a form *Sarum* on episcopal seals from 1330 onwards. In earlier printed texts where editors now give *Sarum* this is only an editorial expansion of *Sar*' and the like. *Sarum* is a late Latinised form of the common early abbreviation *Sar*'.

SALISBURY STREET-NAMES

BARNARD ST led to *Barnard's Cross* 1751 Naish, earlier *Bernewellcros* 1428 HMC Var iv, *Bernwelcros, Barn(e)wellescros* 1455 WM xxxvii, from some lost 'spring by the barn,' *v.* wielle. BEDWIN ST is *Bedwin Row* 1429 Hoare, 1751 Naish, probably named from some man from Bedwyn *infra* 332. BLUE BOAR ROW is *Blew Bore Row* 1751 ib., so named from an inn, *le Blew Bore* (1549 Pat). BRIDGE ST leads to Fisherton Bridge (*Fysherton Brygge* 1438 HMC Var iv). *v.* Fisherton *infra* 22. BROWN ST is *Brounstrete* 1275, 1338 StNicholas, *Brounestrete* 1339 *DeVaux*, 1358 HMC Var iv, 1504 Ipm. The reason for the name is unknown. BUTCHER ROW is *le Bocherewe* 1339 *DeVaux*, *le Boucherrowe* 1406 Trop. An alternative early name was *le, la Potrew(e)* 1362 *Cor*, 1377 Ipm, 1455 WM xxxvii, i.e. where pots were made or sold. CASTLE ST is *Castelstrete* 1339 *DeVaux*, 1396 Trop, *Castrumstrete*

[1] It is, however, *Sarna* in two of the MSS (cf. Haverfield in WM xxxix, 29).

1455 WM xxxviii, leading towards the castle of Old Sarum *infra* 372. The lower end of this street, near Market Place, was once known as *le Cokerewe* 1339 *DeVaux*, 1504 Ipm, i.e. 'cooks' row.' CATHARINE ST is *Carterestrete* 1339 *DeVaux*, *Caterne strete* 1393 IpmR, 1554 *FF*, *Carternestret* 1393 Inq aqd, 1553 AD v, *Carternstret* 1421, *Carter(e)strete* 1424 Cl, 1540 WM xxxvii, *Katherine Street* 1623 WIpm. There can be little doubt that this was originally 'carters' street,' with the same weak genitive plural which we have in *Carterne strete* in Exeter (PN D 23). Later falsely associated with (St) Katherine. CHIPPER LANE is *Chipperystrete* 1331, *Chiperestret* 1343 Trop, *Chiperiestret*, *Shiperestrete* 1415 AD vi, *Cheppare strete*, *Chiperstret*, *Chipperlane* 1455 WM xxxvii, *Chipperyslane* 1457, (*alias dicta Chipperistrete*) 1459 Trop. The first element in this name is apparently ME *chepere*, *chipere*, 'market-man,' with an alternative first element *chiperie*, 'place of the market-men,' formed after the fashion of *draperie*, which sometimes denotes 'place where drapers assemble.' THE CLOSE is *clausū ecclie* 1327 Hoare, *the Close of Salisbury* 1469, *The Cathedral Close* 1549 Pat. COLD HARBOUR LANE is *Cold Harbour* 1751 Naish. Cf. *infra* 451. CRANE BRIDGE and STREET are *Crane Bridge* c. 1540 L, *Crane Streete* 1637 *SR*, so named from an inn called *le Crane* in 1455 (WM xxxviii). CULVER ST is *Colverstret* 1428 HMC Var iv, *Culvirstrete* 1455 WM xxxvii, probably from ME *culver*, 'dove, pigeon.' DE VAUX ROAD preserves the name of the college of the *Vallis Scholarum Beati Nicholai* from Champagne, established in 1261, *v.* Hoare 50, 601. DRAGON ST (now EXETER ST and ST JOHNS ST) is *Drakehallestret* 1339 *DeVaux*, *Drakehalestret* 1362 *Cor*, *Drakenhallestrete* 1400 StNicholas, *Drakehalstrete* 1413 Trop, *Drakhalstrete*, *Draghall strete* 1455 WM xxxvii, *Dragon Strete* 1554 *FF*, *Draghall or Exeter Street* 1822 Hoare. Hoare is probably right in suggesting that this street is named from '*Drake*'s hall or mansion,' from the family of John *le Drake*, found in the city in 1297–1315 (Hoare 92). ENDLESS ST is *le Endelsstrete* 1339 *DeVaux*, *Endelesestret* 1362 *Cor*, 1432 WM xxxvii, *Endelestrete* 1415 AD vi, 1455 WM xxxvii, *Endelistret* 1535 VE, *Endless strete* 1554 *FF*. Probably the name means just what it purports to, for originally it led out beyond the northern limits of the city. FISHERTON ST is so named in 1610 (S). It led to Fisherton *infra* 22. FISH ROW is *Fissherowe* 1554 *FF*. Cf. *Fysshamels* 1314 Pat, i.e. 'fish benches or stalls.' FRIARY LANE is *Frererenstrete* 1362 *Cor*, *Frerenstrete* 1413 Trop, *Frerynstrete* 1455 WM xxxvii. The Friars Minor were granted a messuage here in 1357 (WIpm). Cf. also Hoare 57. GIGANT ST [dʒigənt] is *Gygornestrete* 1451, *Gigorstrete*, *Gicorstrete* 1455 WM xxxvii, *Gigor strete* 1504 Ipm, *Gygornstrete* 1544–53 ECP, *Gigerstrete alias St Edmunds Street* 1485 AD v, *Giggon, Gigant or Gigger Street* 1808 Hoare. This is a difficult name but the probability is that the first element is ME *gigour*, 'fiddler,' and that there were alternative forms of the street-name, *gigo(u)rstrete* and *gigo(u)rnestret*, the latter showing a would-be weak gen. pl. form such as we find in Catharine St *supra*. Hence 'fiddler(s)' street,' cf. *infra* 164. GREEN CROFT ST is so named in 1751 (Naish), from a field called *Grenecrofte* (1455 WM xxxvii), still preserved as GREEN CROFT (6″), an open space or public gardens. The older name for the street was *Mel(e)monger Stret(e)* 1403 WM xxxv, 1413 Trop, 1455 WM xxxvii, *Millemongerstrete* ib., 'street of the meal-mongers or sellers.' GUILDER LANE is so named in 1751 (Naish), of unknown origin. It is possibly identical with *Gudelstret* 1530 FF. HIGH ST is *the Heystrete* 1429, *(in) alto vico* 1439 Trop, *Highstreete* 1672 *Rental*. 'Chief street,' *v.* 'high' (NED). IVY ST is *Ivye Street* 1629 WIpm. Near by was *Yvibrigge* 1455 WM xxxvii. LOVE LANE is *Lovelane* ib., a common street-name in old towns. MARKET PLACE is *Chepyngplace* 1357 GDR, *le Market place* 1528 Recov. *v.* cieping, 'market.' Old names for parts of this may have been *Shipstrete* 1455 WM xxxvii, 'sheep street,' *Wheler Rew* ib., *le Whele Rewe* 1509 FF, *Iremonger Rew, Cordewanerrew* 1455 WM xxxvii, where the cordwainers or bootmakers congregated, *Beddrewstrete* t. Hy 8 AOMB. MILFORD ST is *Milford strete* 1535 VE, leading to Milford *infra* 382. The earlier name was *Wynemannestret* 1362 Cor, *Wymanstrete* 1451 WM xxxvii, *Wynman Street* 1461 Hoare, *Waymonte strete* 1554 FF, probably named from some man *Winman* (OE *Wineman*). MINSTER ST is *Minstrestrete* 1265, *Munstrestrete* 1270 SarumCh, 1289 Ass, *Munsterstrete* 1330, 1336 Trop, *Ministrestrete* 1371 WIpm. 'Street leading to the minster.' Originally the name was applied to the whole stretch of the present Castle St, Minster St and High St, leading from Old Sarum to the present Cathedral and Close (Hoare 92). *v.* mynster. NEW CANAL (locally THE CANAL) is so named in 1751 (Naish). A main cut of the river formerly ran along here and was not closed over till the 19th century (Noyes 126). NEW ST is *Newstrete, novo vico* 1265 StNicholas, *le Newestrete* 1289 Ass. This street is one of the oldest in the City, and must have been named originally in distinction from some still earlier street, perhaps Minster St *supra*. OATMEAL ROW is *(in) novo aventato* 1455 WM xxxvii, *Oatmeale Rowe* 1625 WIpm, i.e. where oatmeal was sold. The earliest form is a late Latin derivative of *avena*, 'oats.' PAYNE'S HILL is *Paines Hill* 1813 Hoare, from the family of *Payn* found in early records quoted by Hoare, e.g. William *Payn* (1361), Richard *Payn* (1428). PENNYFARTHING ST is *Penny Farthing Street* 1751 Naish, perhaps a nickname of contempt. Cf. *infra* 455. POULTRY CROSS is *Poultrecrosse* 1547 Hoare. The old street or district of *Pultri strete* 1316 NomVill, 1535 VE, *la Poletrie* 1362 Cor, *Poletria* 1455 WM xxxvii, was near by. The street may have been on the line of the present Silver St *infra* 22, a modern name. For the name *Poultry*, i.e. 'place where poultry was sold,' cf. Poultry in the City of London, *Polettar'* 1275 RH, *Poletria* 1303 LibCust, *Puletrie* 1315 AD ii. RAMPART ST is named from the old city ramparts, part of which were still marked here in 1751 (Naish). ROLLESTON ST is *Rolveston* 1455 WM xxxvii, *Rollestonstrete* 1547 Hoare, *Rowlstonstrete* t. Hy 8 AOMB, *Rossen strete* 1610 S, *Rolson Street* 1751 Naish. According to Hoare (93) this was so named from one *Rolfe* who "built a collection or row of houses called a town." Similarly there is a lost *Nuggeston* 1455 WM xxxvii to be associated with the family of John

Nugge (1316 NomVill), *v.* tun. ST ANN ST is *St Annes Street* 1751 Naish, taking its name from the gate leading into the Close called *Seynt Anne Gate* 1455 WM xxxvii, *The Tann Gate* 1629 WIpm, now TAN GATE (local). Cf. Tan Hill *infra* 312. ST EDMUNDS CHURCH ST is *St Edmundis strete* 1540 WM xii, *Church Street* 1751 Naish, from the old *ecclesia Sci Edmundi Sar'* 1291 Tax. ST MARTINS CHURCH ST is *vico Sancti Martini* 1455 WM xxxvii, leading to the *ecclesia Sci Martini Sar'* 1291 Tax. ST NICHOLAS ROAD is by ST NICHOLAS'S HOSPITAL (6″), an ancient hospital founded in 1220 (cf. Hoare 80). Cf. *Hospit' Sancti Nich'i* 1291 Tax. ST THOMAS SQUARE is *Square* in 1822 Hoare. The church is *ecclesia Sci Thome Sar'* (1291 Tax). SALT LANE is so named in 1610 (S), presumably where salt was sold. SCOTS LANE is *Scotteslane* 1424 Trop, *Scottislane* 1455 WM xxxvii. It probably derives from the family of Antony and William *Scot,* found in a city record of 1297–1315 (Hoare 741). SILVER ST is so named in 1751 (Naish). There are some eight examples of this common street-name in the county. Five are in important towns (Calne, Corsham, Marlborough, Trowbridge, Wilton), two in villages (Chittoe and Compton Bassett). SWAYNE'S CLOSE is named from the family of Henry *Swayne* (1462 Hoare). TRINITY ST is *Trinity Street* 1751 Naish, from the Trinity Hospital (now alms-houses) mentioned in city records in 1397 (Hoare). WATER LANE is *Watir Lane* 1455 WM xxxvii. It leads to the Avon. WINCHESTER ST is *Winchestrestrete* 1339 DeVaux, leading to Winchester.

Lost street-names include *Leystrete* 1455 WM xxxvii, *Burye Strete* 1524 Recov, *Mylwarp strete* 1540 WM xii. Other lost names include *la Ryole* 1356 WIpm, possibly a name for the wine merchants' headquarters, so called either from the corresponding *la Ryole* or *Royal* in London or from the ultimate source of that name, viz. *La Reole* in Gascony (cf. PN Sr 60), *la Bolehalle* 1388 BM, *le Colecorner, Stapulhall, Cauntolescorner, Cage, Blackebrigge* 1455 WM xxxvii, *Pryors Garden, Covent Garden* 1538 ib. xviii, cf. Covent Garden (London), 'convent garden,' *Bountes Court al. Bownes Court* 1553 AD v, *Weepinge Crosse* 1617 Sess. *Bridewell* (1751 Naish) was the name of a former house of correction, no doubt copied from the London name (originally the name of a spring by St Bride's church).

FISHERTON ANGER[1] [eindʒə]

Fiscartone 1086 DB, *Fiskerton* 1194 Cur, 1232 Ch, *Fisserton* 1242 Fees, *Fissherton* 1262 StNicholas *et passim,* with variant spellings *Fisch-* and *Fys(c)h-, Visertone* 1275 RH

Fischereston 1274 Cl, *Fyshereston* 1279, *Fisshereston juxta Sar'* 1305 *Ass*

Fisshereton juxta Novam Sarr' 1281 ib., *Fissereton juxta Salisbury* 1286 Ipm

---

[1] A former manor and village, now absorbed into Salisbury.

Fissherton Aucher(e) 1324 Pat, 1356 *Ass*, 1376 *FF*, 1404 *Ass*,
    (*Aucer*) 1412 FA
Fyssherton Aunger 1432, (*Ancher*) 1439 Trop, (*Anger*) 1553
    Pat, 1596 *FF*

'Farm of the fishermen,' *v.* tun. Cf. Fisherton de la Mere
infra 161. Richard *filius Aucheri* held the manor in 1242 (Fees).
Later this was misread as *Ancher* (cf. Henry son of *Anger* 1295
Pat) and a new spelling pronunciation arose.

BUGMORE (local) is *Bugmore* 1563, 1623 Hoare, *Bugmore Street*
1591 AD v. *v.* mor, 'marsh.' See further Bugley *infra* 158.
BUTTS FM. Cf. *le Buttes, Letelbuttes* 1393 StNicholas, with reference to ancient archery butts. MIZMAZE HILL (local) is *Mismass*
Hill 1773 A and D, 1818 O.S. *Mizmaze* is the old term for a
labyrinth or maze. There must at some time have been such
a maze on this hill, probably a place of play. Cf. Mizmaze
Wood (Fd) in West Ashton (*infra* 478). MUTTONS BRIDGE (6″)
is so named from *The Shoulder of Mutton*, a field near by (WM
xliv, 200). *v. infra* 455.

I. HIGHWORTH HUNDRED

Wrde hundred 1086 Exon and ExchDB, *Wurðhundredo* 1177 P,
Hundred de Wurþe 1196 Cur, *Hundred de Hautewrth* 1249 *Ass*,
v. Highworth *infra* 25. The present hundred of Highworth
includes the former hundreds of Staple and Cricklade which
existed down to the 14th century (*v. infra* 34, 40) and also the
DB hundred of *Scipe*.

Castle Eaton

CASTLE EATON [*olim* jetən]
    Ettone 1086 DB, *Etton(a)* 1195 P, 1242 Fees, 1249 *Ass*
    Etune 1086 DB, *Eton(e)* 1228 Cl *et freq* to 1332 *SR*, (*Meysi*)
        1302 *AD*
    Eattona 1133 Dugd vi, *Eaton* 1200 P, (*Meysy*) 1428 FA
    Easte Yetton 1442 WM xii
    Castel(l) Eton 1469 IpmR, (*al. dicta Eaton Moisy*) 1470 Cl,
        Eiton Castelle c. 1540 L, *Castle Eaton al. Eton Meysye* 1601
        Recov

'Farm by the river,' *v.* ea, tun and cf. Eton (PN Bk 236). *East* to distinguish it from Water Eaton *infra* 45. Robert de *Meysy* had a holding here in 1242 (Fees). For *Yetton*, cf. *Water Yetton* (*infra* 45).

LUS HILL

    Rusteselle (sic) 1086 DB[1]
    Lusteshulla, -e 1166 LN, 1227 FF *et passim* to 1428 FA
    Lustreshulle t. Hy 3 *Edington*, 1281 *Ass*, 1415 AD iv, *-helle*
      1240 Ch (p), *Lustrushulle* 13th AD v, *Lostreshulle* 1278 *Ass*
    Losteshulle 1275 RH (p), 1279 *Ct*
    Lussell c. 1500 ECP, *Lusshull* 1528 *Recov*
    Lushill al. Lishill 1600 FF, *Lissell* 1637 *Phillipps*

The first element may be the OE *lūs-þorn*, 'spindle-tree,' as suggested by Ekwall (DEPN). In that case the name must be a genitival compound *lusþornes-hyll*. Cf. Lostiford (PN Sr 255). The spindle-tree is specially common in North Wiltshire (E. J. S.). The alternative would be a lost OE personal name *Lusthere*. Cf. *Lustwine*, which is on record.

BLACKFORD FM, DROVEWAY[2] and MARSH COTTAGES[3] (6″) were the homes of John de *Blakeford* (1321 *Ass*), Henry *atte Drove* (1332 *SR*) and Richard de *Marisco* (1279 *Ass*).

BOTANY BAY (6″) is in the south-east corner of the parish and bears a common nickname denoting remoteness, cf. *infra* 435. FORTY ACRE BARN (6″). Cf. *Great Forty Acres, Forty Acre Meadow* c. 1840 *TA*. FROGPIT BARN (6″). Cf. *Froggpit Laynes* 1627 WIpm and lain *infra* 439.

Hannington

HANNINGTON

    Hanindone 1086 DB, *Hanindon(e), -y-* 1289 *Ass et freq* to
      1398 Pat, *Hanydon* 1322 ib.
    Hanedon(e) 1211 RBE, 1218 ClR *et freq* to 1289 *Ass*, *-dun'*
      1235 Fees

---

[1] Jones (230) makes this identification, since this *Rusteselle*, as distinct from the one recorded *infra* 323, is in Highworth Hundred.
[2] *Drove Way* 1820 G, cf. *infra* 429.
[3] Cf. *close called Marshe* 1627 WIpm.

Hanendon 1226 Pat, 1242 Fees, 1279 *Ct*, 1289 *Ass*
Hanyngdone 1300 Pap, 1316 FA, 1535 VE, 1564 *FF*
Hannyngton 1576 *FF*, *Hannington al. Hanningdon* 1683
    Recov

Probably *Hanan dūn*, ' *Hana*'s hill,' *v.* dun, with connective
ing.

NOTE. BEDLAM LANE. Cf. *Bidlam* 1427 Fry.

HANNINGTON WICK is *Wyk* 1289 *Ass*, *Hanyndoneswyk* 1364 ib.,
Hanyngdon Weke 1547 *SR*, *v.* wic, 'dairy-farm.' *Wick* is often
thus added to the name of a manor and denotes the dairy-farm
of the manor.

STERT'S FM is *le Steurte* 1277 *Rental*, *Stert* 1646 *Recov*, *Stert-
grounds* 1692 *Longleat*, and was the home of William *atte Sterte*
(1327 *SR*) or *atte Steorte* (1332 ib.) and Robert de *Stert* (1362
Fry), *v.* steort, 'tail, point of land.' The farm is on a tongue of
land between the Thames and the Bydemill Brook. The *s* is
pseudo-manorial.

BRIDGE FM[1] (with HANNINGTON BRIDGE), BYDEMILL FM[2] and
GORE FM were the homes of Robert de *la Brigge* (1281 *Ct*), Rose
de *Byde* (1391 Fry) and Richard de *la Gore* (1279 *Ass*), *v.* gara,
'angle of land, gore,' and Bydemill Brook *supra* 4.

NELL FM. Cf. *The Nell hedge* 1680 *Devizes*. STAPLER'S BARN
(6"). Cf. *Stapling* 1427, *Stapling Hill* 1632 Fry.

Highworth

HIGHWORTH

Wrde 1086 DB, *Wortha* 1094 StOsmund, *Worde* 1155 RBE,
    Wurda 1158 P, *Wrdha* 1158 HMC Var i *et freq* to 1263 Ipm,
    with variant spellings *Worth(e)*, *Wurth(e)*
Hauteworth 1231, 1299, 1310, 1370 Pat, 1316 Ipm
Hegworth 1232 Cl, *Heworth* 1249 FF, *Heyewurth* 1272 ib.,
    -*worth* 1279 FF, *Heywrth* 1284 Pat, -*worth* 1289 *Ass*, 1316
    FA
Alta Whorth 1257 Ch, *Altaworth* 1305 Sarum

---

[1] Cf. *Bridgend* 1452 Fry, *Thomes bridge* (i.e. Thames bridge) 1591 WM vi.
[2] *Bide Mill* 1773 A and D.

Heyghewrthe 1281 *Ass, Hegheworth* 1312 ib., 1333 *SR, Heygh-* 1321 *Ass*

Hyghworth 1296 *FF, Highworthe* 1312 ib., *Hieworth* 1388 Pat, *Hiegh-* 1503 *MinAcct*

Originally known simply as *Worth,* 'farmstead,' *v.* worþ. In the 13th century the epithet *High* was added, the town being situated on a well-marked hill, the highest ground for many miles round. *Haute* is a partially gallicised form. Cf. Halt-whistle (PN NbDu 100) and further examples given there.

NOTE. CRICKLADE RD is *Cryckeladys way* 1463 *Ct.* MARKET PLACE. Cf. *in foro de Hieghworth* 1503 *MinAcct.* SHRIVENHAM RD is *Shriven-ham way* 1540 *Rental,* i.e. the road to Shrivenham (Berks). Lost names are *Langlane* 1503 *MinAcct, Pycards lane* 1540 *Rental.* A lost estate is *Beaumys* 1322 Pat, 1382, 1465 IpmR, 1409 Cl, *Belmyse* 1463 *Ct.* This goes back to OFr *belmeis,* LL *bellus mansus,* 'fine house.' Cf. Beamish (PN NbDu 14) which is found in the form *Bellus mansus* in 1251 (Cl).

BELLINGHAM FM (6″) is *Bullingesham* 13th AD vi, 1278 *Ct, Billinges-* 1263 Ipm, *-is-* 1493 *MinAcct, Byllinges-* 1277 *Rental, Billingtham* (sic) 1608 WM xxxvi. The first part of the name is clearly a personal name. It may be *Billing* (cf. Billingshurst, PN Sx 147) with occasional *bull*-forms under the influence of initial *b.*

CROUCH HILL and LITTLE CROUCH HILL (6″) are *Crouch Hills* 1773 A and D. We have no early forms for these hill-names though we may have reference to them in *Croucheslond* (1452 Fry) in Hannington, which borders on Highworth at this point. They probably go back to British *cruc,* 'hill, barrow.' They are well-marked rounded hills.

EASTROP and WESTROP appear as *Esthropp in Worthe* t. Hy 3 BM, *Estrop* 1268 *Ass, Est(t)horp* 1318 *FF,* 1336 Pat, *Estthrop* 1332 *SR, (by Heghworth)* 1335 Misc, *Westrop* 1249, 1268 *Ass, West Thorp juxta Heyworth* 1302 ib., *Westthorp* 1318 *FF,* 1327 Pat, *-throp* 1332 *SR, Westropp* 1468 AD i. 'East and west hamlets,' *v.* þorp. Eastrop is just east of Highworth, but Westrop is due north and must have been named because west of Eastrop.

FRESDEN FM [*olim* fristən]

Fersedon 1263 Ipm, 1277 *Rental,* 1278 *Ct, -den* 1307 *FF*
Fressinden 1267 Abbr

Fershesdon 1308 Ipm, 1310 *FF*, 1332 *SR*, (*juxta Heyworth*)
   1360 *FF*, *Fersheston* 1314 ib., *Fersshedon by Esthrop* 1360 Cl
Freshesden 1344 *FF*, *Fresshedoun* 1392 Cl, *Freshden* 1439
   IpmR, *Fressheden* 1535 VE, *Freshdeane* 1540 *MinAcct*,
   Fresshdeane al. Ferchesdeane 1541 LP
Versshedon 1365 Ipm, 1367 Pat
Fersthusdon 1369 BM
Frissheton 1392 Cl, *Frisheden* 1418 IpmR, *Frysdon* 1516
   Recov, *Freshdean al. Frisden* 1699 ib., *Frisston* 1773 A and D

The persistent *sh*-forms now available and the absence of any
u-forms make it impossible to take *fyrsen*, 'covered with furze,'
as the first element, as in DEPN. Rather it would seem to be
the adjective *fersc*, 'fresh,' perhaps applied to the pasturage of
the denu or dun. Cf. Surrendell *infra* 71.

HAMPTON is *Hantone* 1086 DB, *Hamton* 1227 FF, *Hampton* 1242
Fees *et freq*, (*Turevill juxta Heyewurth*) 1272 FF, (*Turvyle*) 1402
FA. This may be from OE hamtun or, as it lies on sharply
rising ground, from OE (*æt þæm*) *hēan tūne*, '(at the) high farm.'
Robert de *Turneville* held the manor in 1279 (*Ass*). If this is the
same man who held the not far distant Acton Turville (Gl) in
1236 (Fees), it is likely that the *n* in the family name is a clerical
mistake (cf. DEPN *s.n.* Acton Turville).

SEVENHAMPTON [seniŋtən] is *Sevamentone* 1086 DB, *Suvenham-
tone* 1211 RBE, *Sevenhamton* 1216 ClR, *-hampton* 1227 FF *et
passim*, *Sevehampton* 1216 ClR, 1276 BM, 1294 *Rental*, *Sevene-*
1281 *Ass*, *Senhampton* 1330 Pat, 1331 *FF*, *Sennington* 1608
WM xxxvi, *Sennington al. Sevenhampton* 1616 *Recov*, *Seving-
hampton* 1629 *SR*, *Senehampton al. Synnington* 1657 PCC. For
the etymology *v.* Sevington *infra* 107. Close by was *Seven-
hamehulle* (1332 AD i), *Sevenamhyll* (1487 ib.), the hill of the
Seofonhǣme or the dwellers at Sevenhampton, *v.* hǣme.

COOMBES COPSE (6"), HILL FM[1] and WICKSTED FM[2] (6") were
probably the homes of Richard de *Combe* (1294 *Rental*), John
atte Hulle (1332 *SR*) and Nicholas de *Wykestede* (1279 GDR)
v. wic, stede, 'dairy-farm site.'

---

[1] Cf. *Hilleacre* 1493 *MinAcct*.
[2] *Wexstede* 1422 *Ct*, *Wekestede* 1463 ib.

FRIARS HILL, HUNGERFORD BARN[1] (6″), PICKETT'S COPSE[2] (6″), RANDALL'S BUILDINGS (6″) and WARNEFORD PLACE[3] are to be associated with the families of William *le Frere* (1281 *Ass*), Sir Thomas *Hungerford* (1365 Aubrey), William *Picard* (1277 *Ct*), Jamys *Randal* (1524 *SR*) and Richard *Warneford* (1422 *Ct*).

FOLLY PLANTATION (6″). See *infra* 451. GROVE HILL HO (6″). Cf. *The Grove* c. 1840 *TA*. HIGHMOOR COPSE. Cf. *Highe Moore* 1641 WIpm. NORTH LEAZE FM. Cf. *North Leaze* c. 1840 *TA*, v. læs, 'pasture.' PENTYLAND FM is *Penty Land* 1841 *Devizes*. QUEEN LAINES FM is *Queen Lanes* 1773 A and D. See *infra* 439. RAG FM. Cf. *Sevyngtons Ragge* 1540 *Rental* and *infra* 453. RED DOWN is *Reddowne* 1463 *Ct*, *le Redde downe* 1540 *Rental*. REDLANDS COURT is *la Redelanda* 1171 P, *Redelonde* 1277 *Rental*, *Redlonde* t. Hy 4 *Ct*. Probably self-explanatory, *red*, as is often the case in place-names, denoting a golden-brown soil, cf. *infra* 318. ROUNDHILL FM. Cf. *Roundhill* 1659 WM xxxvi. ROUND ROBIN FM. Cf. *Round Robin Coppice* c. 1840 *TA*. ROVES FM. Cf. *le Roue* 1357 AD iii, *Rovyswell* 1442 *Ct*. STARVEALL BARN (6″), a common nickname of contempt, *v. infra* 455.

Inglesham

INGLESHAM [iŋgəlsəm]

    (*æt*) *Inggeneshamme* c. 950 (11th) ASWills, *Incgenæsham* c. 970 (c. 1150) ib.

    Inglesham 1160 SarumCh *et passim*, with variant spelling *Yng*-, *Hinglesham* 1198 Fees

    Englesham 1190 P, 1225 Pat, 1242 Fees, *Overenglesham* 1279 *Ass*
    Ingelesham 1211 RBE, 1249, 1268, 1279 *Ass*, *Yngeles-* 1279 *Ct*
    Ingelsham 1291 Tax, *Ingelsom* 1693 ParReg

The first element would seem to be a personal name *Ingen* or *Ingin*, an unrecorded *n*-derivative of *Inga*. The second element is hamm, 'enclosure,' or here perhaps 'land in the bend of a river.' The place is almost surrounded by the Thames and the Cole. *Overenglesham* is the present Upper Inglesham. For interchange of *n* and *l* cf. IPN 106–7.

---

[1] *Hungerford pece* 1463 *Ct*, *terra voc. Hungerford* 1540 *MinAcct*.
[2] Cf. *Pykardes lanysende* (i.e. 'lane's end') 1463 *Ct*, *Pycards lane* 1540 *Rental*.
[3] *Warneford Place* 1635 WIpm.

Lynt Bridge and Lynt Fm (6″)

> Lente 1279 Ct, 1289 Ass et freq to 1581 BM, Lent 1518–29 ECP
> Leente 1348 AD i (p), Leente Hulle 1513 FF
> Lyntys Courte 1416 AD i, Leyntes Courte 1483 ib., Lynte 1580 Recov

This was originally the name of the river Cole, v. supra 5, the farm and bridge taking their name from it. The hill may be that over which the main road goes, just south-west of the bridge.

Marston Meysey

Marston Meysey [vulgo maˑsən]

> Merston(e) 1199 FF, 1211 RBE, 1239 Cl, (Meysi) 1259 FF, Northmerston 1281 Ass
> Marshtone Meysi 1302 AD, Northe Mershton 1316 FA, Mers(s)hton Meysy 1316 FF, (Meyse) 1398 Pat, Mason 1738 Sadler, Marston Measey 1773 A and D

'Marsh farm,' v. tun. North to distinguish from South Marston infra. Roger de Meysi held the manor in 1211 (RBE).

Cox's Fm (6″) is to be associated with the family of Edmonde Coxe (1571 SR).

Hill Mead Bridge (6″). Cf. Hillemede 1493 MinAcct. Marsh Hill Fm (6″). Cf. marisco de Merston 1281 Ass, Marsh Hill 1773 A and D. Oxleaze Fm. Cf. Oxleaze c. 1840 TA and læs infra 438.

South Marston

South Marston[1]

> Merston 1204 FF, with a similar run of forms to Marston Meysey supra, Suthmershton 1331 FF, Meryshton 1392 Cl, Southemaston 1553 WM x, Southmarson 1568 PCC

South to distinguish from Marston Meysey supra.

Burton Grove Fm is Berton 1625 WIpm, Barton al. Berytoune al. Berton 1688 Recov, Bearton 1773 A and D and was the home of John de Burchtone (1327 SR), de Bourton (1332 ib.). v. burhtun, 'fortified farm.'

---

[1] A parish formed from Highworth in 1894.

HUNT'S COPSE FM is to be associated with the family of Thomas *le Hunt* (1279 *Ct*).

LONGLEAZE FM. Cf. *Long Leaze* 1773 A and D and læs *infra* 438. OXLEAZE FM (6″), *v. infra* 438. ROWBOROUGH FM is *Rowborowe* 1634 WIpm, 'rough barrow or hill,' *v.* beorg *infra* 423.

Stanton Fitzwarren

STANTON FITZWARREN

> *Stantone* 1086 DB, *-ton* 1196 Cur, 1228 Cl, *Staunton juxta Hegheworth* 1312 *FF*
>
> *Stontone* 1327 *SR*, *Staunton Fitz Waryn* 1394 IpmR, *Stanton al. Stanton Fitzwarren* 1553 *FF*

v. stan, tun. Possibly *stan* refers to the large standing stone here (WM xlii, 50) and the name is to be interpreted as 'farm by the stone' rather than as 'stone farm-enclosure' (E. H. G.). Fulco *filius Warini* held the manor in 1196 (Cur).

MILL FM (6″) was the home of Thomas *atte Mulle* (1327 *SR*).

BROADMOOR COPSE (6″). Cf. *Brademore* 1277 *Rental*, *Bradmore* 1442 *Ct*. 'Wide marsh,' *v.* brad, mor. GREAT WOOD. Cf. *boscus de Stanton*' 1187 P. SHEEPSLEIGHT PLANTATION (6″). Cf. *Sheep Slaights*, *Sheep Slaits Wood* c. 1840 *TA* and *infra* 454. SOUTH FIELD (6″) is *Southfeld* 1442 *Ct*. Cf. *infra* 41. STARVEALL BARN (6″) is *Starveall* 1773 A and D, *v. infra* 455.

II. SCIPE HUNDRED

This DB hundred (*Scipe*, *Scipa* 1086 ExonDB) is not mentioned in any later records. It is thought by Jones (163) to have contained the parishes of Blunsdon, Rodbourne Cheney and Stratton St Margaret, later placed in Highworth Hundred.

Blunsdon

BLUNSDON ST ANDREW, BROAD BLUNSDON [*olim* blʌnsən]

> *Bluntesdone*, *Blontesdone* 1086 DB, *Bluntesden*' 1177 P, *-dun(a)* 1204 FF, 1233 Bracton, 1242 Fees, *-don* 1235 Cl
>
> *Blundesdon* 1232 Cl

Bradebluntesdon(e) 1234 FF, *Brode-* 1263 Ipm, 1279 *Ct*,
    Brodeblountesdone 1455 Pat
Hangingebluntesdon 1242 Fees, 13th AD ii, *Hanginde-* 1277
    Rental
Churibluntesdon 1242 Fees, 1422 *Add*
Bluntesdon Seynt Andreu 1281 *Ass*, (*Sancti Andree*) 1299
    Sarum, *Andrewblountesdon* 1542 LP
Bluntesdone Gay t. Ed 2 Ipm, *Blountesdon Gay* 1348 Cl
Blondeston Sci Andree 1379 BM
Lytelblountesdon 1397 Cl
Blounesdon Andrewe 1429 Cl, *Androblunsdon* 1544 *SR*
Blunsen 1744 *Map*

'*Blunt*'s hill,' *v.* dun. Cf. Blundeston (Sf) in DEPN, *Bluntesig*
(KCD 666) and *Bluntesheth juxta Bromham* (1293 *FF*) in this
county. *St Andrew* from the dedication of the church. For
Broad, i.e. 'great' or 'chief,' cf. *infra* 204. *Churi-* is no doubt
for 'church,' i.e. Blunsdon St Andrew, cf. Cheriton (PN D 59).
Little also refers to this place. *Hanging* and *Blunsdon Gay* are
alternative names for Broad Blunsdon. Cf. Limpley Stoke *infra*
121. Walter *le Gay* held part of the manor in 1281 (*Ass*).

BURYTOWN FMS. Cf. *Buribluntesdon* 1279 *Ass*, *Bury-* 1297 Ipm,
Berytown alias Berybloundeston 1523 *FF*, *Beryblunesden* 1546
LP, *Bury Blunsden alias Burytowne* 1586 *Recov*, *Berritowne* 1633
FF. *Bury* refers to the ancient camp on Castle Hill, *v.* burh.

GROUNDWELL HO is (*a*) *Grundewylle* 962 (c. 1200) BCS 1093,
Grundewlle 1242 Fees, 1294 *Rental*, *-well(e)* 1249, 1268 *Ass*,
1257 *For*, 1277 *Rental*, 1428 FA, *-wull'* 1279 *Ct*, (*b*) *Grindewylle*
962 (c. 1250) BCS 1093, *Gryndewelle* 1281 *Ass*, (*c*) *Grendewelle*
1086 DB, (*d*) *Groundewelle* 1289 *Ass*, (*e*) *Grundwelle* 1332 *SR*,
(*f*) *Groundwell* 1339 Ipm *et passim*, (*g*) *Grondewelle* 1356 Pat.
This is a spring and not a stream (*v.* wielle). The first element
is uncertain. The series of forms (*a*), (*d*)–(*g*) suggest initial
grunde, others are in favour of *grynde*. *grund-wielle* might mean
'deep spring,' but even then we should have expected *grund*
rather than *grunde* in the early forms. There is an OE poetic
word *grynde* which means abyss; possibly the words have been
confused.

GROVE FM and HYDE were the homes of William de *Grova* (1279 *Ct*) and Thomas de *la Hyde* (1255 RH). *v.* **grafa, hid.**

FOWLER'S FM (6″) is to be associated with the family of Henry *le Fowelar* (1281 *Ct*) and William *le Foulere* (t. Ed 3 *For*).

ASHMEAD BRAKE (6″). Cf. *Ash Mead* c. 1840 *TA*. BRICKKILN COTTAGE. Cf. *Brick Kiln Fd* ib. CASTLE HILL is so named in 1773 (A and D). *v.* Burytown *supra* 31. COLDHARBOUR is *Cole Harbour* ib., *Coldharbour Field* 1778 NQ vii, *v. infra* 451. NEWLANDS FM is *la Niwelond* t. Hy 4 *Ct*. NEWMEADOW COPSE (6″). Cf. *New Meadow* c. 1840 *TA*. OXLEAZE FM (6″). Cf. *Ox Leaze* ib. ST LEONARD'S FM (6″) takes its name from the chapel of St Leonard in Broad Blunsdon which is called *Bluntesdon Sci Leonardi* (1291 Tax). STUBB'S HILL (6″) is so named c. 1840 (*TA*).

Rodbourne Cheney

RODBOURNE CHENEY[1]

> *Redborne* 1086 DB, *-burn(e)* 1185, 1199 P *et freq* to 1281 *Ass*
> *Rodeburn* 1291 Tax, 1329 *FF*, *-bourne* 1410 Cl, (*Chanu*) 1439 *FF*
> *Rodburne Chanu juxta Puriton* 1304 *Ass*, *Rodburne* 1316 FA, *Rodborn(e) Chanu* 1346 *FF*, (*Chaynewe*) 1541 ib., (*Chanew*) 1544 LP
> *Rudbourne* 1370 *Ass*

The stream here is referred to as (*on*) *hreodburnan* in 943 (12th) BCS 788, 962 (12th) ib. 1093, i.e. 'reed stream,' *v.* **burna.** Cf. Rodbourne in Malmesbury *infra* 51 and Redbourn (PN Herts 78). Ralph *le Chanu* held the manor in 1242 (Fees).

HAYDON, HAYDON WICK is *Haydon(e)* 1242 Fees, 1332 *SR*, 1428 FA, *Heydon(e)* 1249, 1279 *Ass*, 1255 FF, 1291 Tax, *Haydonwyk* 1249 *Ass*, *Wykeheydon* 1268 ib., *Haydoneswyk* 1321 ib., *Wyke* 1332 *SR*, (*juxta Bluntesdon*) 1419 *FF*, *Heydon Week* 1595 ib. The first element may be either OE (ge)hæg, 'enclosure, hedge,' or heg, 'hay.' The second element is **dun.** Haydon Wick means 'the dairy-farm attached to Haydon Manor,' *v.* **wic** and *supra* 25.

---

[1] Now included within the borough of Swindon, except the tithing of Haydon, which is now a separate ecclesiastical parish (Kelly).

MOREDON is *Mordun* 943 (12th) BCS 788, 962 (12th) ib. 1093, *Mordone* 1086 DB *et freq* to 1332 *SR* with variant spelling *-don*, *Moredowne alias Moreton* 1632 WIpm. 'Marsh hill,' *v.* mor, dun. Cf. Morden (PN Sr 53).

CHURCH HILL (6") is *Churchhill* 1626 WIpm. HURST FM is *Herste* 1235 Fees, *le Hurst* 1256 FF, *v.* hyrst, 'wooded hill.' MOULDON HILL (6"). Cf. *Far, Hither Moulden* c. 1840 *TA*. NORTH LEAZE, SOUTHBROOK FM and TADPOLE FM (all 6") are so named ib.

Stratton St Margaret

STRATTON ST MARGARET

> *Stratone* 1086 DB
> *Strettuna, -e* c. 1150 France, t. Hy 3 AD iii, *-ton* 1253, 1268 Ass, (*Seynt Margarete*) 1370 ib., *Margrete Stretton* 1446 Inq aqd
> *Stratton(e)* 1195 P, 1199 FF, (*Overe*) 1240 FF, *Nether-* 1268 Ass, *Michele-* 1279 ib., *Nuthere-, Muchele-* 1281 Ct, *Stratton Sce Margarete* 1294 FF (*juxta Altam Swyndon*) 1294 Ipm, (*superior, inferior*) 1316 FA, *Upper, Lower Stratton* 1509 Pat, *Stratton Sce Margarete al. Nether Stratton* 1578 *FF*, *St Margarett Stratton al. Nethetowne al. Throppe* 1630 Recov

'Farm on the Roman road,' *v.* stræt, tun. The place lies by Ermine Street. Upper Stratton lies on higher ground than Lower Stratton or Stratton St Margaret where the church is dedicated to that saint. For *Throppe* see þorp *infra* 417.

DOCKLE FM (6") was the home of Henry de *Dochull* (1278 *Ct*) and William de *Dokhulle* (t. Ed 2 *For*). 'Hill where dock grows,' *v.* hyll.

PEN HILL was probably the home of Adam de *la Penne* (1279 *Ct*) and John *atte Penne* (1327 Pat). The *pen(n)*-names in Wiltshire present some difficulty. They may go back to OE penn, 'pen, enclosure,' or they may go back to a British word corresponding to Welsh and Cornish *pen*, 'head, top, height,' which we undoubtedly find in Penselwood on the borders of Wiltshire and Somersetshire (*æt Peonnum* (dat. pl.) c. 900 ASC (Ā) *s.a.* 658).

Topographical conditions in relation to the chief *pen*-names in Wiltshire are as follows: (i) Pen Hill is a prominent isolated hill with a farm on it, (ii) Penn's Lodge (*infra* 67) is at the end of a well-marked hill, (iii) Penleigh (*infra* 48) lies low by a stream with no prominent hill near, (iv) Pen Hill (*infra* 174) is a prominent well-marked hill, (v) Penridge (*infra* 182) is by Penselwood, (vi) Penn Fms in Calne and Hilmarton (*infra* 269) lie on a long well-marked hill. The topographical possibilities, except in the case of Penleigh, are in favour therefore of the *hill*-interpretation. See further Hackpen *infra* 310. Pen Hill must be *ættan penn* (BCS 1093) in the bounds of Moredon. The hill may have been so called from a sheepfold there, the possession of one *Ætta*, or the British word for a hill may have been so far naturalised that it could be used in a compound with an OE personal name.

BREACH FM (6″) is *la Breche* 13th AD vi, *v.* bræc *infra* 423. CLAY FM (6″). Cf. *Cleye* 14th *Bradenstoke*. KINGSDOWN is *Kingesdon(e)* 1277 *Rental*, 1278 *Ct.* The King held the manor of Stratton in 1227 (*Ass*). MARSHGATE HO (6″). Cf. *The Marsh* 1773 A and D. THE MOORS is *Mora* 1277 *Rental*, *v.* mor, 'marshland.' PEAT MEADOW (6″) is so named c. 1840 (*TA*). SLADE KEYS (6″). Cf. *la Slade* 1277 *Rental* and slæd *infra* 446. THE STREET (i.e. Ermine Street). Cf. *Streteforlong* 1442 *Merton*.

III. STAPLE HUNDRED

Staple, *Stapla hundred* 1086 ExonDB, *Stapele* 1187 P, *Hundred de Stapele* 1196 Cur, 1198 Abbr, *Stapel* 1255 RH, 1259 *Ass*, 1297 Ipm, *-lee* 1275 RH, *Stapele* 1316 FA. From OE stapol, 'post, pillar.' The site of the Hundred meeting-place must have been in Purton, for we have reference to *Staple Cross Way* in Purton (1631 WIpm). Possibly the name is preserved in *Steeple Piece* (c. 1840 *TA*), a field just to the north of Purton Church. There was another *stapol* further west, on the parish boundary, called *le Westapele* (BCS 279).

Lydiard

Lydiard Millicent and Tregoze [lidjəd]

(*æt*) *Lidgerd, Lidgeard, Lidegæard* 901 (c. 1150) BCS 590,
Lidgeard 901–24 ib. 591, *Lidgard Milisent, Tregos'* 1257
For

Lediar (sic), *Lidiarde* 1086 DB

Lidiard 1166, 1169 P *et passim* to 1567 *FF*, with variant
spellings *Lyd-* and *-yard*, (*Milisent*) 1275 Abbr, (*Milicente*)
1289 *Ass*, (*South*) 1305 ib., (*Treigos*) 1323 Pat

Lydierd 1228 Ch, *Lydyerd Mylisent, Tregoz* 1268 *Ass*, *North-
lydyerd* 1279 ib., *Northlideyerd* 1283 Pat, *Lydeyerd* 1285 Ch,
Lydyherd 1308 Ipm, *Lydyerd* 1316 FA, (*Mulcent*) 1379
WM xxxvi, *Northlydyerd al. Lydyerd Milsent* 1412 Pat

Lidiart, Lidewarte 1228 Cl

Lydiert 1249 *Ass*, (*North*) 1252 FF, *Lidyert Milsent* 1357 Pat,
Lydeyert Tregoz, Mulsent t. Ed 3 *For*

Ledyerd 1316 FA, *Northledeyerd* 1346 Pat, *Ledeyerd Milcent*
1412 FA

Lyderd 1376 Ch, *Southlydeard* 1426 *Ass*

Luydeyard Mylcent 1473 WM xxxvi, *Ludyerd Milcent* 1502
ECP, *Luddyard* 1615 FF

The name is identical in origin with Lydeard (So), *Lidegeard*
854 (c. 1150) BCS 476, *Lidgeard* 904 (13th) ib. 610, *Lidegeard*
1065 (13th) Wells, *Lidigerd* 11th (c. 1150) KCD 897, and is also
found in *lidgeardes beorge* (BCS 834, 1125) in Washington
(PN Sx 240 n. 1). Ekwall (DEPN) takes the second element to
be the equivalent of Welsh *garth*, 'hill.' A Welsh parallel is
Litgart, Litgarth c. 1150 Liber Landavensis (possibly to be
identified with Lydard in Mitchell Troy (Mo)), while a possible
Cornish parallel is Liggars in St Pinnock, *Lodegard* 1280 Journ.
Royal Inst. of Cornwall iv, *Lutegard* 1327 *SR*, *Lugger* 1663 *FF*[1].
The first element in all these names is obscure.

---

[1] Mr Gover notes possible Welsh parallels (the references being to the
Pop. 1″ map): Cefn-llidiart (68 N 5), containing *cefn*, 'ridge'; Llidiart-y-rhos
(59 B 13), containing *rhos*, 'hill-spur'; Llidiart-fawr (51 B 1) from *mawr*,
'great,' with mutation, showing that the compound was feminine; Ty'n-y-
llidiart (42 K 11), 'house on the Lidiart'; Ty'n-llidiart (41 G 6), id.; Llidiardau
(49 J 3), with a common plural ending. One may also suspect that the

In 1199 (FF) Hugh gave Richard the vill of Lydiard to hold by the service of one knight after the death of *Millisent*, mother of Richard. Lydiard Tregoose was held by Robert *Traigoz* in 1242 (Fees) and by John *Tregos* in 1275 (RH). This family name, which appears in the Pipe Rolls as *Tresgoz*, *Trezgos*, etc. is no doubt of French, probably Breton, origin. It cannot, as suggested by Ekwall (DEPN *s.n.* Eaton Tregoze) be derived from the Cornish Tregoose. That is *Tregois*, earlier *Tregoyt*, *Tregoid*, meaning 'farm by the wood.' See Addenda *supra* xxxix.

Lydiard Millicent

BRICKKILN COPSE (6") is *Brick Hill Copse* c. 1840 *TA*. *kill* is a common dialect-form for *kiln* and *Brickkill* is often thus folk-etymologised to *Brick Hill*. Cf. Brickhill St Fm (PN Wa 43).

PARLEY COPSE is *le Purlye*, *les Purliewes*, *le Purlymere* 1611 *For*, *Purlieu* 1744 *Map*. v. purley, purlieu *infra* 453. It lies on the edge of the old Braydon Forest (*supra* 11).

SHAW is *Shaghe* 1332 *SR*, *Shawhyll* 1512 *Ct* and was the home of Peter de *la Shawe* (1289 *Ass*), v. sceaga, 'coppice.' SHAW BRIDGE is *Shaghebrigg'* 1228 *For*.

SPARCELL'S FM is *Speresholt* 1263 *For*, *boscum de Speresholt* 1281 *Ass*, *Speresholte* t. Ed 2 *For*, *Spersholte* t. Ed 3 ib., *Spressels* 1733 WM xl, *Sparswell* 1744 *Map*. The name is clearly identical in origin with Sparsholt (Berks, Ha), the former being (*æt*) *Speresholt* 963 (c. 1200) BCS 1121 with uniform *Speres*-forms, the latter (*æt*) *Sweoresholt* (sic) 901 (c. 1150) BCS 594, *Spæresholt* 1060–6 (c. 1150) KCD 820, *Speresholt* 1167 P *et passim*, *Sparesholt* 1257 *FF*, *Sparshall* 1591 *Recov*.

It is difficult not to connect the first element in this name of threefold occurrence with the common word *spere*, 'spear,' as does Ekwall (DEPN *s.n.* Sparsholt) and then to interpret the name as 'wood from which spear-shafts are taken.' The

following names are to be identified with Lydiard, folk-etymology having substituted *llwyd*, 'grey': Llwydiarth (51 F 4), Llwydarth (109 A 3), Llwydarth (101 G 7), Llwydiarth (59 D 13), Mynydd Llwydiarth (41 F 11) in Anglesey, written *Mynydd Lidiart* by Borrow in *Wild Wales*, as taken down orally from a small boy.

genitive singular in the first element of a compound with such a sense is strange, but cf. Haxmore *infra* 38.

CHURCH FM (6″) and THE GROVE[1] were the homes of John *atte Churche* (1327 *SR*) and Thomas *de la Grave* (1281 *Ass*). *v.* **græfe** and *infra* 432.

GODWIN'S FM, PIKE'S STALLS (both 6″) and WEBB'S WOOD are to be associated with the families of Charles *Godwin* (1701 ParReg), William *Pyk* (1289 *Ct*) and Henry *Webbe* (1618 ParReg). The last is *Webbs wood* 1733 WM xl.

BREACH BARN (6″). Cf. *la Breche* 13th *Bradenstoke*, *v.* **bræc** *infra* 423. THE BUTTS (6″). Cf. *infra* 425. COW LEAZE COPSE (6″). Cf. *Cow Leaze* c. 1840 *TA*. GREAT FIELD (6″) is so named ib. Cf. *Feldhous in Lidierd* 1391 Pat. GREENHILL FM. Cf. *Green Hill Pound* c. 1840 *TA*. LYDIARD PLAIN (6″) is *Liddiard Plain* c. 1825 O.S. NINE ELMS is so named in 1773 (A and D). PEATMORE COPSE (6″). Cf. *Patmore* c. 1840 *TA*. ROUGHMOOR is *Rowmore* 1820 G.

Purton

PURTON

> *Perytun* 796 (14th) BCS 279, *Peritun* 854 (14th) ib. 470, *Peryton(a)* 1156 RegMalm *et freq* to 1282 Ipm, *Pereton* 1195 P, *Pertune* 1211 RBE
>
> *Puriton(e)*, *-a* 796 (14th) BCS 279 A, 1242 Fees, 1332 *SR*, *Purtun* 1247 Cl, *Puryton* 1289 *Ass et freq* to 1428 FA, *Puryngton* 1327 Ipm
>
> *Piritune* 1065 (14th) KCD 817, *-tone* 1086 DB, 1275 RH, (*juxta Creckelade*) 1304 *Ass*, *Pyryton* 1281 QW, 1299 BM, t. Ed 3 *For*, *Pyri-* 1291 Ipm, *Piryton Keynes* 1375 Pat, *Pyryton al. Puryton* 1430 *FF*
>
> *Perinton* c. 1250 *Rental*, *-y-* 1349 FF, *Pyrinton* 1268 *Ass*, *Pyrynton* 1281 ib., *Piryn-* 1289 ib., *Puryn-* 1297 Ipm
>
> *Pyreton* 1298 Pat, 1304 *FF*, *Pyrton al. Puryton* 1580 ib.

'Pear-tree farm,' *v.* **pirige, tun**. An earlier form of the name is *æt Piergean, et Pirigean*, as recorded respectively in RegMalm (i, 291) and WMP (388), i.e. '(at the) pear tree.' This appears

---

[1] Cf. *Grofforlang* 14th *Bradenstoke*.

in a corrupt form in *æt Piertean* 796 (14th) BCS 279. Sub-
sequently *tun* was added, sometimes to the nom. form *pirige*,
sometimes to the oblique case-form *pirigean*. John *Keynys* held
the manor in 1428 (FA).

NOTE. HOG'S LANE is *Hog(g)eslane* 1257 *For*, 1281 *Ass*. MOPES
LANE. Cf. *Mopes Mead* c. 1840 *TA*. SMITHMEAD LANE was near
Smethemede t. Hy 3 RegMalm, *Smithmeade* 1625 WIpm, i.e. 'smooth
mead,' *v. smeþe*.

BENTHAM HO [bentəm] is *Benetham* 1249 *Ass* (p), 1257, 1270 *For*,
1325 Pat, 1406 IpmR, *Bentham al. Benthams haye* 1625 WIpm,
Bentem 1744 *Map*. A compound of OE beonet, 'bent-grass,' and
ham or (more likely) **hamm**.

BROCKHURST FM is *Brokouere* 796 (14th) BCS 279, *Brochuvere*
1257 *For*, *Brokevre* 1270 ib., *Brokhure, Brochure* t. Ed 3 ib.,
Brocufere 1362 ib., *Brokehurste* 1611 ib., *Brockhurst* 1744 *Map*,
cf. *Brockhowse Coppice* c. 1840 *TA*. The OE form is in a late
text. The name seems to be a compound of OE **broc**, 'brook,'
and **yfer**, 'edge, slope,' etc. There is a steep hillside here below
Ringsbury Camp.

HAXMORE FM (6″) is *Hassukes more* 796 (14th) BCS 279 A,
Haskemores-furlonge 13th RegMalm, *Haskemore* c. 1400 *Malm*,
Haxmore 1744 *Map*. 'Swampy land where coarse grass grew,'
v. **mor, hassuc**. In the first form the first element has been given
pseudo-genitival form.

HURSTED FM is *Hursteeds Close* 1630 WIpm and was the home
of John de *la Houstede* (1281 *Ct*), William de *Hustede* (1284
RegMalm) and Nicholas de *Hustede* (t. Ed 3 *For*). This must be
the OE *hūsstede*, 'site of a house.'

PAVEN HILL is *Pevenhull* 1257 *For*, 1284 RegMalm (p), 1370
Ipm, *-hill* 1628 WIpm, *Pewenhill* 1578 FF, *Peavenhill* 1632
Recov, *Pavenhill* 1744 *Map*. The forms are too late for any
certainty. It may be that the first element is a personal name,
the weak form of *Pefe, v.* Pewsey *infra* 350. A Roman pavement
has been discovered here (WAM xli, 393). This may have
affected the latest forms of the name but clearly has nothing to
do with its origin.

Purton Stoke is *Stoche* 1086 DB, *Stoke* 1257 *For* (p), (*juxta Puryton*) 1312 *Ass*, *Purytonstoke* 1422 AD vi, *Pirton Stoke* 1509 *Pat*. The stoc attached or belonging to Purton. For this use of stoc as a name for a secondary settlement cf. Ekwall, *Studies*[2] 23, and such doubles as Basing and Basingstoke (Ha), Chard and Chardstock (So, D). See also Bradenstoke *infra* 270.

Restrop is *Radestrope* c. 1250 *Rental* (p), 1284 RegMalm (p), 1323 Pat, Inq aqd, 1327 *SR* (p), c. 1400 *Malm*, *Radesthrop* 1332 *SR* (p), 1341 NI (p), 1353 Pat, *-thorp* 1356 Cl, *Restrop* 1544 *SR*. The second element is OE *þorp*, *þrop*, 'village,' the first would seem to be a personal name but the forms are too late to enable us to determine what it is.

Church Fm, Coombefield[1], The Hill, Marsh Fm[2], Mill Fm[3] and Well's Fm (all 6″) were probably the homes of John *Attechirche* (1281 *Ass*), Henry de *Coumbe* (t. Ed 3 *For*), Henry de *la Hulle* (1284 RegMalm), Geoffrey de *Marisco* (1289 *Ass*), William de *Molendino* (ib.), Adam de *Puteo* (1281 ib.) and John de *la Welle* (1288 *Ct*). In the last the *s* is pseudo-manorial.

Barstroppe Ford, Harding's Fm (6″), Plummer's Bridge (6″) and Rodger's Fm are to be associated with the families of John de *Barsthrop*[4] (1282 WIpm), Nicholas *Harding* (1279 *Ct*), John *Plumer* (1629 *SR*) and Evan *Rogers* (1562 ParReg).

Abbot's Bridge (6″) is *Abbotts bridge* 1553 *DuLa*. The Abbot of Malmesbury had a manor here. Bagbury Fm (6″) is *Beggebur'* 1289 *Ass*, *Begberie* 1615 PCC, *Begburies* 1630 WIpm, *Bagbury Green* 1733 WM xl. Battle Lake (6″). There was a *Battle Field* not far away in 1744 (*Map*). This is *Bettlefield al. Battlefield* in 1641 (WIpm). Blacklands Fm is *Blackeland* 1512 *Ct*. Blake-hill Fm. Cf. *Blake Hill* 1744 *Map*. Bremell Fm (6″) is *Brimhill* 1733 WM xl, *Brimmal* 1744 *Map*. Cf. *infra* 424. Brickkiln Coppice (6″). Cf. *Brickkiln Ground* ib. Bury Hill is *Berry Hill* 1611 *For*, *Buryhill* 1650 ParlSurv, *v.* burh. There is an old 'camp' here. Clardon Ho (6″) is *Claverdon* c. 1400 *Malm*, *Clardon* 1641 WIpm. 'Clover hill,' *v.* dun. Cf. Claverdon

---

[1] *Combefeeld Common* 1625 WIpm, *v.* cumb, 'valley.'
[2] *Pirton marshe* 1553 *DuLa*.   [3] Cf. *Millmore, Millclose* 1632 WIpm.
[4] No place of this name has been found elsewhere and it is difficult to be sure whether the whole name is manorial or local in origin.

(PN Wa 206). COLLEGE FM (6″). Cf. *College Hill* c. 1840 *TA*. The property of Worcester College (Aubrey 155). COMMON PLATT is *Common Platt Mead* 1744 *Map*, v. platt *infra* 443. DOGRIDGE is so named in 1839 (*Devizes*). DOWN FM. Cf. *Dunweye, le Westeredune* t. Hy 3 RegMalm, *The Downe* 1630 WIpm. DRILL FM is so named in 1820 (G). ELBOROUGH BRIDGE (6″) is *Elvers Bridge* 1630 WIpm. GREEN HILL is *Greenehills* ib. HAYES KNOLL. Cf. *Great, Little Hayes, Haynole* 1773 A and D. KEYCROFT COPSE (6″) is *Keycroft* 1744 *Map*. See Key, R. *supra* 8. MILK HO (6″). Cf. *Milk House Gd* c. 1840 *TA*. MOONS-LEAZE FM. Cf. *Momes leaze* 1662 *Depositions*, 1733 WM xl, *Mumsley* 1773 A and D, v. læs *infra* 438. OXLEAZE COPSE (6″) is *Oxe Leaes* (sic) 1650 *ParlSurv*, v. læs. POND FM (6″). Cf. *Pond Ground* 1744 *Map*. POST STREET (6″) is so named ib. PRY FM is *Prye* 1625 WIpm, *Prye close* 1632 ib., *The Prys* 1744 *Map*. There are several fields so named in 1744 (*Map*). PYTCHARDS STALLS (6″). Cf. *Pitchworth* and *Pitchworth Lane* ib., now NEWTHS LANE. QUARRY FM is on the site of *Pukpitt* ib. It is *Pokkeput* 1398 *Ct*, 'goblin pit,' from puca. QUEEN STREET. Cf. *Queen Ham* 1733 WM xl. RIDGEWAY FM (6″). Cf. *Ridgwaye grounde* 1635 WIpm, *Rudgeway* 1744 *Map* and *supra* 17. RINGS-BURY CAMP is *Ringesburye* 1630 WIpm. Probably 'circular camp,' v. burh. There is a 'camp' here. WEST MARSH FM (6″). Cf. *West Marrish* 1650 *ParlSurv*. WIDHAM is so named in 1773 (A and D). WOODWARD'S BRIDGE (6″) is *Woodwardes Bridge* 1630 WIpm.

IV. CRICKLADE HUNDRED

Crichalade, Crichelada, Crechelade 1086 ExonDB, *Crickelad* 1227 Fees, *Kerkelad, Crikkelad'* 1255 RH, *Crekklade* 1316 FA, v. Cricklade *infra* 42. The hundred is not mentioned after the 14th century and was merged in Highworth Hundred *supra* 23.

Ashton Keynes

ASHTON KEYNES [keinz]

Æsctun 880–5 (c. 1000) BCS 553

Essitone 1086 DB, *Eston* 1242 Fees, *Eshton* 1281 *Ass*

Aston 1256 FF, (*juxta Bradene*) 1281 *Ass*, (*Keynes*) 1589 NQ
vii, *Aystin* 1299 BM, *Asshton next Cryckelade* 1306 Ipm,
Ashtone 1316 FA, *Aysshtone* 1332 *SR*, *Asheton by Chele-
worth* 1386 Pat
Aysheton Keynes 1572 *Recov*, *Asheton Kynes* 1588 *FF*, *Aishen
Kaines* 1691 ParReg (Brinkworth)

'Farm by the ash-tree,' *v.* tun. William de *Keynes* held the
manor in 1256 (FF). Cf. Somerford Keynes *infra* 46.

NOTE. *Brodwaye* 1603 *AOMB*; *Portwayfurlong* t. Jas 1 *LRMB*.
See *supra* 16.

KENT END is to be associated with the family of Ralph *Kent*
(1327 *SR*). It is *Kent End* 1773 A and D.

ASHTON DOWN. Cf. *the Downe* t. Eliz *LRMB*. ASHTONFIELD.
Cf. *Eastfeld*, *Westfeld* 1603 *AOMB*, referring to the open fields
of the township. Cf. PN Nth 16. ASHTON MILL. Cf. *Milclose*,
le Mill hamme ib., *v.* hamm. BROOK HO (6″). Cf. *Brokemede*
t. Jas 1 *LRMB*. CLAYHILL COPSE. Cf. *Cleyhill* t. Eliz ib. THE
DERRY (6″). Cf. *Derry Road* 1841 *Devizes* and *infra* 257. HAPPY
LAND. Cf. *infra* 455. NORTH END is so named in 1773 (A and
D). RIXON FM (6″) is *Ryckeston* 1603 *AOMB*. Possibly we
should compare Richardson *infra* 309.

Braydon

BRAYDON is a small modern parish formed from Cricklade
in 1868. It includes the central part of the old forest (*v. supra*
11).

BRICKILN COPSE (6″) is so named in 1744 (*Map*). DUTCHY RAG.
Cf. *Dutchie Marsh, Wood, Ragg* 1651 WM xlvi and rag *infra* 453.
It is the property of the Duchy of Lancaster. MAPLE SALE FM
(6″) is *Mapell Zell* 1591 WM iv, *Maplesalls* 1650 *ParlSurv*, *The
Maplesalls* 1651 WM xlvi. RED LODGE and WHITE LODGE are
so named in 1773 (A and D).

Cricklade

Cricklade

Crecca gelad c. 925 ASC (Ā) *s.a.* 905, *Creocc gelad* c. 1050 ib.
(D) *s.a.* 905, *Creaccgelad* ib. (B), *Crecalad* c. 1200 ib. (F)
s.a. 1016, *Cricgelad* c. 1050 ib. (D) *s.a.* 1016

(*into*) *Cracgelade* c. 975 (14th) ASWills

Crocgelad 1008 (c. 1225) KCD 1305

(*æt*) *Cræcilade* c. 1120 ASC (E) *s.a.* 1016, *Crecalade* c. 1050
ib. (C), *Cricgelade* c. 1120 ib. (D)

Crecgelade c. 1050 (16th) BurghalHidage

Crichelade 1086 DB, 1177 P, *Cricce-* c. 1150 FW, *Crike-* 1190 P
et freq to 1290 Pat, *Cricke-* 1205 ClR *et freq* to 1397 Pat, with
variant spellings *Kricke-, Crikke-, Crikeford quod est Crike-
lade* c. 1400 Liber de Hyda

Criechelada 1164–79 France, *Crekelade* 1196 Cur *et freq* to
1290 Misc, with variant spelling *Kreke-, Creckelade* 1205
ClR *et freq* to 1319 *FF*, with variant spelling *Crekke-
Kirkelade* 1249 *Ass*, *Kyrke-* 1260, 1370 Pat

Creyeklade 1294 Pat, *Creyklade* 1311 Pap

Crekklade 1316 FA, *Creklade* 1446 Pat, 1675 Ogilby

Cricklett 1637 *Phillipps*

Forms from coins include *Croci, Croc, Croccel, Crocglad*
t. Canute, *Crecelā, Crec, Croc, Creccelad, Creeca, Crecel, Crecla*
t. Edw Conf, *Cric, Criic, Cri* t. Wm i

The second element is OE (*ge*)*lād*, 'passage,' probably with
reference to a crossing of the Thames here. The same second
element is found in Lechlade (Gl) about ten miles to the north-
east (cf. PN Gl *s.n.*). The early spellings of Cricklade show that
the first element cannot be the British *cruc*, 'hill.' It may be
the British word corresponding to Welsh *craig*, 'rock' (OW
creic), cf. Crick (PN Nth 68–9). The reference would then be
to the prominent isolated hill half a mile to the west of the town.

Note. Horse Fair Lane is *Horsfayre lane* 1633 WIpm. In other
old records we find *Westret*, probably the present Bath Road, *Estret*
t. Hy 4 *Ct, the east street* 1633 WIpm, probably the present Calcutt
Street, *Riggewey, Snoweslane* t. Hy 4 *Ct.*

Calcutt [kɔ·kət] is *Colecote* 1086 DB, 1257 For *et freq* to 1342
Pat, *Colcote* 1297 Cl, 1348 Ipm, *-kote* 1300 ib., (*juxta Cheles-*

worth) 1374 IpmR, *Calcotte* 1351 *FF*, *Calecote* 1493 Ipm, *Cold-cott* 1543 *FF*, *Callcott* 1623 BM, *Corkett* 1773 A and D. '*Cola*'s cot(e).'

CHELWORTH

> (*æt*) *Ceolæswyrðæ* c. 970 (c. 1150) ASWills
>
> *Celewrde* 1086 DB, *Celesworda* 1130 P, *Cheleswurda* 1155 RBE *et freq* to 1374 IpmR, with variant spelling *-worth,* *-wurth*, (*Magna*) 1289 *Ass*
>
> *Chelwurða* 1197 P, *Cheleworthe* 1211 RBE, (*juxta Creckelade*) 1314 *FF et freq* to 1482 ib. with variant spellings *-wurth,* *-wrth*, (*Litel*) ib.
>
> *Chedeleswurthe* 1229 Bracton
>
> *Chulewurth* 1263 *For*, *-worth*(*e*) 1268 *Ass*
>
> *Chulesworth* 1279 *Ass*, *-wrth* 1281 ib.
>
> *Chylewerth* 1300 Ipm, *Chelleworth* 1377 Pat

'*Cēol*'s farmstead,' *v.* worð. It is not always easy to separate the forms for this name from those for the not far distant Chelworth in Crudwell *infra* 57. The form *Chedeleswurthe* in Bracton is curious. Side by side with it *Chelewurthe* is found in the same document.

DUDGEMORE FM (6") is *Dodesmere, Duddesmere* t. Hy 4 *Ct, Dodesmere* 1406 IpmR. '*Dodd*'s or *Dudd*'s mere or pool.' For the sound development cf. Dadglow (PN Wa 171).

THE FORTY (6") is *Vorty* 1841 *Devizes* and was the home of Nicholas de *la Fortye* (1281 QW) and Richard de *la Fortheye* (1289 *Ass*). This *Forthey*, like others described under Forty Green (PN Wo 202–4), thrusts itself out into low-lying marshland. It is a compound of forð, 'forward' and eg. For the first form, *v.* Introd. xxi. Other examples in the county are to be found in Calcutt Forty *infra* 44, Forty in Bishopstone *infra* 286, (Adam) *atte Fortheie* (1333 *SR*) in Sherston, (William) *atte Fortheye* (ib.) in Bremhill, (John) *atte Fortheie* (ib.) in Pool Keynes, and in *pastura voc. Forty* 1463 *Ct* in Highworth.

HAILSTONE is *Halagheston* 1228 *For*, *Halweston* 1263 WIpm, *Haghelstan* 1268 *Ass*, *Halgestane* t. Hy 3 *Stowe* 798, 1300 *For*, *Halegheston, Haleweston* t. Ed 3 ib. It is clear that there has been confusion with regard to this name from early times, and it is difficult to say whether it is from OE *hālig-stān*, 'holy stone' or *hagolstān*, 'hailstone,' ME *hawelston*, *hailston*. If it is from the latter, then the farm was perhaps named from the small isolated Hailstone Hill, north-north-west of it, which may have been nicknamed 'hailstone' from its small rounded character.

WIDHILL [*olim* widəl] is *Widehille* 1086 DB, *Widehill(e)* 1205 *FF et freq* to 1428 FA, with variant spellings *Wyde-* and *-hull(e)*, *Westwydehulle* 13th AD ii, *Wydihulle* 13th AD vi, 1276 *FF*, 1277 *Rental*, *Withihull'* 1245 WM xvi, *Wythehull* 1249 *Ass*, *North-wythihull* 1305 ib., *Withihill* 1344 Cl, *Widdle* 1585 WM xxi, *Widhill al. Widdell* 1726 *Recov*. Probably 'withy hill.' There is low ground by the river Ray just near the farm.

BOURNE FM[1] and LITTLEWORTH[2] (both 6″) were the homes of Henry de *la Burne* (1289 *Ass*) and Milo *atte Bourne* (1327 *SR*) and William de *Litlewurth* (1279 *Ct*) and William de *Luttelworth* (1332 *SR*), *v.* burna, worþ.

ABINGDON COURT[3] (6″), COX HILL, GODFRAY'S HURNE[4] (6″), KING'S BARN[5], STONE'S FM[6] (6″) and WOODWARD'S FM are to be associated with the families of Robert de *Abendon* (1279 *Ct*) and John de *Abyngdone* (1327 *SR*) (which must have come from Abingdon (Berks)), William *le Cok* (1333 ib.), John *Godefrey* (1345 *Ass*), Thomas *le Kyng* (1333 *SR*), Thomas *Stone* (1503 *MinAcct*) and Hamo *le Wodeward* (1370 Pat).

ARMYN CROSS (6″) is *Armyn Crosse* 1591 WM iv. BALLICKACRE FM (6″) is *Balokacres* t. Hy 4 *Ct*. BOURNELAKE FM and STALLS. Cf. *Burne Lake* 1630 NQ viii, *Burnlake* t. Chas 1 *For*, *Bone Lick* 1773 A and D. There is a small stream here, *v.* burna, lacu. For the form *bone*, cf. Bohun Lodge (PN Herts 71). BROADLEAZE FM (6″) is *Broad Leaze* ib. BUSHEY LEAZE STALL (6″). Cf. *Bushey Leys* c. 1840 *TA* and læs *infra* 438. CALCUTT FORTY (6″), *v. supra* 43. DANCE COMMON. Cf. *The Dance* 1773 A and D. FARFIELD FM is *Furfeild* 1650 *ParlSurv*. Probably 'further

---

[1] Cf. *Borneclose* t. Hy 4 *Ct*.   [2] *Litilworth* 1493 *MinAcct*.
[3] *Abyndonescourt* t. Hy 4 *Ct*.
[4] *Godefrayeshurne* 1368 *For*, *v.* hyrne, 'corner, angle.'
[5] Cf. *Kinges Marsh* 1650 *ParlSurv*.   [6] *Stones* t. Jas 1 ECP.

field.' It is in a remote part of the parish. FIDDLE FM (6"). Cf.
Fiddle Close and *Field* c. 1840 *TA.* GOSPEL OAK FM. Cf.
Gospell oke 1553 *DuLa.* It is on the parish boundary and
probably takes its name from the reading of the Gospel here in
the beating of the parish-bounds. THE HATCHETTS (6"). Cf.
Hawchat, Hawchet t. Hy 4 *Ct.* HEADLANDS FM (6"). Cf. *Long
Headlands* c. 1840 *TA, v. infra* 439. HORSEY DOWN. Cf.
Horsseylane t. Hy 4 *Ct, Horsley Down* 1841 *Devizes.* LEIGH-
FIELD LODGE seems to be identical with *Slyefeild lodge* 1650
ParlSurv, Slyfield Lodge 1739 NQ vii. NORTH MEADOW (6") is
Northmede t. Hy 4 *Ct.* RAVENSBROOK FM may be identical with
la Ravenesik t. Ed 3 *For, v.* sic, 'ditch.' RAVENSHURST is *Ravens
hurste* 1611 *DuLa, v.* hyrst, 'wooded hill.' The two places are
close together. STANDING HO (6") is so named in 1826 (G).
TOWN BRIDGE (6") is so named in 1773 (A and D). WEST MILL
(6") is *la Westmulle* 1228 *For.* WHITEHALL FM is *White Hall*
1773 A and D.

Latton

LATTON

> *Latone* 1086 DB, *Latton(a)* 1133 Dugd vi, 1177 P *et passim*
> *Lacton* 1204 ClR, 1241 FF, 1281 QW
> *Latteton* 1249 *Ass*

The first element may be OE *lēac*, 'herb, vegetable,' *v.*
leactun. The OE lacu, 'small slow-moving stream,' is less likely,
since the place is by the Churn, a stream of some size.

EISEY [aizi] is *æt Esig* 775–8 (11th) BCS 226, (*æt*) *Esege* 855
(11th) ib. 487, *Aisi* 1086 DB, *Eisi* 1133 Dugd vi, *Esy* 1259 FF,
Eysy 1314 FF, 1370 *Ass*, 1428 FA, *Easy* 1544 *SR, Eisey or Isey*
1773 A and D. The second element in this name is OE eg, ieg,
'marsh land.' The first must remain an unsolved problem.

WATER EATON [*olim* jetən] is *Etone* 1086 DB, *Nunyeton* 1281
Ass, Eton Monial' 1332 *SR*, 1341 NI, *Waterheton* 1395 Pat,
Nunne Eiton c. 1540 L, *Water Yetton* 1553 WM xii, *Non Eaton
al. West Eaton al. Water Eaton* 1726 *Recov.* See Castle Eaton
supra 24. *Nun* from the holding of the Abbess of Godstow
(1275 RH).

SHEPHERDS HAM (6″) is to be associated with the family of Thomas *Shepherd* (1524 *SR*), *v.* hamm.

ALEX FM is *Harlicks Farm* 1773 A and D. COW LEAZE FM (6″). Cf. *pastura voc. Cow leaze* 1681 *Devizes*. THE FOLLY and THE GARSTON (both 6″). Cf. *infra* 451, 432. MILL HO. Cf. *le Millpole, Millham close* 1558 *Devizes*. SEVENBRIDGES FM is *Seven Bridges* 1773 A and D, so named from seven bridges over the Ray (School). SHEEPPEN BRIDGE (6″) is recorded by the School in the field-name *Sheeppen Berds*, just by, showing that the local pronunciation is *burge*, cf. Introd. xxi. WESTFIELD FM is *Westfeld* 1232 Ch, *the Westfeild* 1558 *Devizes*. Cf. *supra* 41.

Leigh

LEIGH [lai] is *Lia* 1242 Fees, *la Leye* 1249 *Ass*, *la Legh* 1279 ib., *Legh juxta Ashton* 1289 ib., (*juxta Crekelade*) 1368 *FF*, *Lighe* 1561 ib., *Lye al. Ligh al. Leigh* 1699 *Recov*, *v.* leah, 'clearing or wood.'

COVE HOUSE FM is *la Cove* t. Ed 3 *For*, *Covehouse* 1633 WIpm and was the home of Richard de *la Cove* (1270 *For*, 1289 *Ass*). This must be from OE *cofa*, cf. Cove (PN D 542). As the place is on low-lying land not far from the Thames, there can be no question of any meaning 'hollow, recess in hillside.' The word may here have the sense 'shed, building.'

ARCHER FM (6″) is perhaps to be associated with the family of Nicholas *le Archer* (t. Ed 3 *For*).

BROOK FM. Cf. *Brookmead* 1680 *Devizes*. COTE HO. Cf. *Cott mead* ib. KNAPP FM is *Knappes* 1585 *For*, *v.* cnæpp, 'hill.' WATERHAY, *v.* (ge)hæg *infra* 433. WHITE SPIRE (all 6″). Cf. *White Spire Coppice* 1650 *ParlSurv*.

Somerford Keynes

SOMERFORD KEYNES[1] [keinz]

    Sumerford 683 (c. 1125) BCS 65, 931 (14th) ib. 671, 1211 RBE, 1242 Fees, *Somerford Kaynes* 1289 *Ass*, (*Keynes*) 1291 Tax

---

[1] Transferred to Gloucestershire in 1897.

'Ford passable during the summer months,' cf. Somerford *infra* 73. William de *Kahaines* held the manor in 1211 (RBE), spelt *Kaaynes* in 1222 (FineR), *Kignes*, *Kaignes* (1242 Fees). The family name derives from Cahagnes in Normandy.

SHORNCOTE[1] [*vulgo* ʃɑˑnkət]

> *Schernecote* 1086 DB, *Scerncote* 1242 Fees, *Shernecot* 1249 FF
> *Cernecote* 1198 P, 1199 FF *et passim* to 1566 *FF*
> *Sernecote* 1235 Cl, 1289 *Ass*, 1535 VE, *-kote* 1269 Ipm,
>   *Serncot* 1242 Fees, *Sarnecote* t. Hy 3 Ipm
> *Sharncote* 1375 Ipm, *Sharcote* 1387 ib.
> *Sernecote al. Sharncote* 1418 IpmR, *Sharncote al. Cerncote*
>   1568 *FF*, *Sharnecott al. Cernecott* 1631 WIpm

Probably a compound of OE *scearn*, 'dung' and cot(e). The later numerous spellings with initial *c* and *s* must be due to the influence of the neighbouring river Cerne (*v.* RN *s.n.*) and South Cerney (Gl) on that stream. It is not likely that it is actually named from the river; the forms make it improbable, and it is more than a mile distant. It is really nearer to the upper Thames.

MILL FM. Cf. *Mulleham* 1327 WIpm, *v.* myln, hamm. NEIGH BRIDGE (6″) is *le Ebrigge* 1327 WIpm, *Ney bridge* 1591 WM vi. From ME *atten ee*, 'at the river,' *v.* æt, ea and cf. Reybridge *infra* 103.

V. MALMESBURY HUNDRED

This is first mentioned as *Hundredum de Malmesbury* in 1226–8 (Fees). The abbot of Malmesbury then held the three hundreds of Malmesbury, Chedglow and Startley (*infra* 53, 65).

Malmesbury

MALMESBURY

> *Mealdumesburg* 675 (14th) BCS 37
> *Meldunesburg* 681 (14th) ib. 58, 59, 844 (14th) ib. 447,
>   *Maeldunesburg* 892 (14th) ib. 568
> *Maeldubesburg* 683 (14th) ib. 65

[1] Originally a separate parish, it was amalgamated with Somerford in 1894.

Maldumesburuh 701 (10th) BCS 106, *Maldumesburg* 956
(14th) ib. 921, 974 (14th) ib. 1301, 982 (14th) KCD 632,
c. 1125 BCS 37, 65, 569

Maildufi urbs c. 730 Bede, *in Maldubiensi monasterio* 758
(14th) BCS 185, *Maldubia civitate* c. 770 (9th) Boniface,
Maildubiensis æcclesia c. 1125 BCS 569

(*ad*) *Maldunense monasterium* 745 (14th) ib. 170

Maelduburi, Malduberi 892 (14th) ib. 568, *Mailduberi*
c. 1125 ib. 584

Meldulfuensis Burgi 934 (15th) ib. 720, *Meldulfesbirg* c. 1125
ib. 58, *Maldulfes burgh* c. 1000 OE Bede

Maldelmesburuh 974 (14th) BCS 1301, *Maldmesbyrig* c. 1050
BurghalHidage

(*into*) *Mealdælmæsbyrig, -elmes-* 10th (c. 1150) ASWills,
c. 1120 ASC (E) *s.a.* 1015

Ealdelmesbyrig c. 1050 ib. (C, D) *s.a.* 1015

Malmesberie 1086 DB *et passim*, with variant spellings *-bury*,
-biry

Mamesberie 1086 DB, *Mamesbur'* 1198 Abbr

A shortened form *æt Meldum* is recorded in BCS 106 (10th).
Forms from coins include *Maldmes, Mald, Meald* 979–1016,
*Mealdmes, Mealmes, Meald, Mealm, Meal, Meale, Melmes,
Melme* 1016–66, *Malme, Malm* 1066–1100. Post-Conquest
forms of interest are *monasterium quod Meldum religiosæ
memoriæ condidit, quod etiam nunc Meldumesburg vocatur* c. 1125
WMP, *Maumesberi* 1200 Cur, *Maumesbir* 1201 FF, *Mawmesbiri*
1252 Ch, *Mamsbury* 1652, 1737 *FF*.

According to William of Malmesbury the monastery here was
founded by one *Mailduf* or *Maildulf*, an Irishman. This is the
OIr personal name *Maeldub* or *Maildub*, meaning 'black prince
or chief,' from *maglo-*, 'prince,' and *dubo-*, 'black' (cf. Mod
Gaelic *dubh*, Welsh *du*). St Aldhelm was once abbot of Malmesbury, and, as suggested by Plummer (Bede, *Historia Ecclesiastica*
ii, 311), the modern form of the name is due to confusion between
Ealdhelm and *Mailduf*. It should be noted that the forms from
Bede and St Boniface, coming from 8th-century documents
preserved in good texts are really much earlier and more
valuable than any of those which precede them.

NOTE. ABBEY ROW is so named in 1670 (Aubrey). BURNIVALE is *Burneval* 12th, *vico qui appellatur Burneval* t. Hy 3 RegMalm, *Burnevalle, Burnefal, Burnevale* c. 1300 *Malm, Burnevall* 1512 *Ct, Burneyvall* 1563 NQ viii. This street faces the river Avon which may be the *burna* in question. There is a small weir here and it may be that the whole name derives from earlier *burn(ge)feall*, 'river-fall.' For *v* for *f* cf. Introd. xxi. CROSS HAYES is *Croshayes* c. 1300 *Malm, Crosseheys* 1545 LP, with reference presumably to the market cross. *hayes* is from OE (ge)hæg, 'enclosure.' EAST GATE is *portam orientalem* 13th RegMalm. HIGH ST is *la Heystrete* t. Hy 3 ib., *magna strata* c. 1300 *Malm, alta strata* 1556 *Eton*. Cf. *supra* 21. THE HORSEFAIR is so named in 1670 (Aubrey). INGRAM ST is *Ingerameslane, Engerameslane* c. 1300 *Malm*, probably from some early owner or resident. KINGSWALL is *Kyngeswalle* 13th RegMalm. MARKET CROSS and OXFORD ST are so named in 1670 (Aubrey).

Lost names include *Unkerestret, Griffinslane, Phelipeslane, la Blyndelane, Lokeputtestrete, la Posterne, la Barre* 13th RegMalm, *Bynne-, Bynport* (cf. Bimport in Shaftesbury (Do), probably from *binnan port*, 'within the town'), *Dounstrete* c. 1300 *Malm, Hen lane* 1544–53 ECP, *Turne againe lane* 1603 Sess, probably a blind alley. *Estret* 13th RegMalm is possibly the present SILVER ST, on the east side of the town.

ANGROVE FM is *Angrave* c. 1300 *Malm, Anne Grove* 1547 Pat, *Angrove* 1563 NQ viii, *Aungrovesmede* t. Eliz *LRMB. v.* græfe and *infra* 432. The grove lies by the Avon and it is possible that *Auene* is the first element of the name. Cf. Avoncliff *infra* 122.

BACK BRIDGE is *Baggebrugge* t. Hy 3 RegMalm, c. 1300 *Malm*. '*Bacga*'s bridge,' cf. Bagshot (PN Sr 153).

BINCOMBE WOOD. Grundy (ii, 43) identifies this with *Beucumbe* (BCS 922) and suggests that *Beucumbe* is a mis-reading for *Bencumbe*. The identification may well be correct but examination of the MS gives no support for the idea of a mis-reading. If *Bencumbe* is the right reading, the corrupt reading must be of still earlier date.

BURTON HILL

　Boruhtone 13th RegMalm, 1285 Ipm, *Boruton* 1376 FF
　Burʒtone 1248 RegMalm, *Burghton juxta Malmesbury* 1315
　　FF, 1321 *Ass*
　Burton 1332 SR, *Bourton* 1535 VE, *Burton Felde* 1548 Pat,
　　Bourtonhill 1571 SR, 1601 FF, *Burtonhill* 1626 WIpm

v. **burhtun.** The meaning here is probably 'tun by the **burh,**' i.e. Malmesbury. The place lies south of the town on a hill above the Avon. Cf. Boreham *infra* 158 and Bourton (PN Bk 60).

Cole Park

Cusfalde (sic) 1065 (14th) KCD 817, *Cufaldam* 1191 Reg-
Malm, *Coufaud* 1275 RH, 1284 Misc, *Couefaude* 1289 *Ass*,
Coufauld 1376 FF, *Cowfold* 1535 VE
Cowfold parke t. Eliz *LRMB*, *Coleparke* 1637 *Phillipps*, *Cole
Park al. Cowfield Park* 1727 *Recov*

Originally OE cu-falod, 'cow fold or enclosure.' *Cole* may be
a colloquial reduction of the earlier name.

Corston [*vulgo* kɔˑɪsən]

Corstuna 1065 (14th) KCD 817, *Corstone* 1086 DB, -*ton* 1177
P *et passim*, *Coreston* 1242 Fees, *Corston juxta Malmesbury*
1302 *Ass*, *Corsen* 1673 *Sadler*

The place is on Gauze Brook *supra* 7 and the meaning is
'farm on the Cors (stream),' *v.* **tun.** Cf. Corston in Pembrokeshire (NCPNW 10) in which however *cors* probably denotes
'bog, swamp.'

Filands Fm is *Fulinge* 1194, 1195 P, 1263 *For*, c. 1270, 1284
RegMalm, *Fulinges* 1196 Cur, *Fulenge* t. Hy 3 RegMalm, *Fulyng*
1400 FF, t. Hy 6 ECP, 1483 FF, *Fulyngs* 1527 ib., *Fulings* 1535
VE, *Filence* 1711 ParReg (Minety), *Filents* 1773 A and D.
Professor Ekwall would interpret this as from OE *fielging, fælging*,
'newly cultivated land,' OE *ie* becoming *u* after *f* in the same
way as after *w* in *wulle* from *wielle*, occasionally found in Wilts
(*Contributions* 47 ff.). Dr Ritter takes it to be from OE **fȳling*,
'miry, muddy place' (cf. Deeping (L)), and notes a possible
parallel in OGer *Winter fulinga* (Förstemann ON i, 961, ii, 1382).
The difficulty in both interpretations is the consistent *u* in the
long run of early forms. No parallel for such consistent development of either *ie* or *y* is found elsewhere in the county.

Hyam Fm is *Heyham, Litleheiham* 13th RegMalm, *Hyham* c.
1300 *Malm*, *Higham juxta Malmesbury* 1526 Ct, *Greate Higham
Coppes* 1547 Pat, *High Ham* 1816 O.S. 'High ham or hamm.'

The latter element is perhaps the more probable here, since the farm lies on rising ground near a big bend in the Avon.

INGELBURNE MANOR. This was originally the name of the little stream which rises near Burntheath. It is referred to as (*ad*) *aquam que Ingelbourne appellatur* 956 (14th) BCS 922, *Yngelburne* 13th RegMalm, *Ingelborne* c. 1300 *Malm*, *aqua vocata Ingelborne* 1341 *Cor*. The material is insufficient for any satisfactory suggestion as to its interpretation. The earliest form is really a ME and not an OE one.

KINGWAY BARN. Cf. *Kingweye* 931 (14th) BCS 672, *Kingwei* 956 (14th) ib. 922, *Kyngesweye in villa de Redburne* (i.e. Rodbourne *infra*) 1289 *Ass*. This must have been the old name for the road between Malmesbury and Chippenham. Cf. *infra* 71 and GrundyH 73–4.

MILBOURNE is *Melburne* 1249 *Ass*, *Muleburne* 1270 *For*, *Mulburne juxta Malmsbury* 1314 Inq aqd, *Milburn juxta Malmesbury* 1316 Orig, *Muleborne* 1332 *SR*, *Nuthermulburne* 1394 *Ass*, *Mylburn* 1483 *FF*. 'Mill stream,' *v.* burna. This must originally have been the name of the small stream which rises near Quobwell Fm and joins the Avon below Charlton. Just south of the junction of the two streams there is still a mill. *Nuther* is OE *neoðera*, 'nether, lower,' *v.* Introd. xx.

QUOBWELL FM. Cf. *la Quabbe* t. Ed 1 RegMalm, *le Quabbe* c. 1300 *Malm*, *Quabwelle* 1349 Ipm, *Cobwell* 1816 O.S. The first element is the dialectal *quob*, 'boggy place,' fully discussed in PN Sx 368, *s.n.* Quabrook. Cf. Quobbs Fm *infra* 261 and quabbe *infra* 445. *well* is a later addition. A small stream rises here.

RODBOURNE and RODBOURNE RAIL FM (6″)

Reodburna 701, 758 (14th) BCS 103, 185, 982 (14th) KCD 632
Rodburne ib., *Rodeborne* 1526 *Ct*, *Rodborne* 1535 VE, -*brone* 1547 *SR*
Redburn(a) c. 1125 WMP, 1198 Abbr, 1232 Cl, -*borne* 1289 *Ass*, *Redborne al. Rodborne* 1548 Pat
Rudburne 1289 *Ass*
Rodborn Rayles 1650 *ParlSurv*, *Rodborn Rail* 1773 A and D

'Reed stream,' *v.* hreod, burna. Cf. Rodbourne Cheney *supra* 32. *Rail* perhaps with reference to some form of enclosure, cf. *s.v. rail(s)* (PN Sr 370).

ROWDEN WOOD (6″) is *Rolidone* (sic) 982 (14th) KCD 632, *Rowedone* t. Hy 3 RegMalm, *Rowedune* c. 1400 *Malm.* Probably from ruh and dun, 'rough-hill', with corrupt early form.

WESTPORT (6″) is *Westeporte* t. Hy 1, 13th RegMalm, 1232 Ch, 1289 *Ass, Westport* 1232 Ch. This was originally a separate settlement lying to the west of Malmesbury. Probably the OE form of the name was *bi westan porte*, 'west of the town,' i.e. Malmesbury, *v.* port and cf. *Bynport supra* 48.

HALCOMBE[1] was the home of Agnes de *Holecombe* (1321 *Ass*) and Henry de *Holecoumbe* (1332 *SR*). 'Hollow valley,' *v.* holh, cumb.

ARCHES FM and PARSLOE'S FM (both 6″) are probably to be associated with the families of Richard *le Archer* (1270 *For*) and William *Parslowe* (1571 *SR*). The former is *Archars Farm* 1773 A and D.

BURNTHEATH is *Barndeheþe* t. Hy 3 RegMalm, *-hethe* c. 1400 *Malm.* CAM'S HILL is *Camps Hill* 1650 *ParlSurv.* There are earthworks here. COLDHARBOUR FM is *Cold Harbour* 1773 A and D. Cf. *infra* 451. COW BRIDGE and MILL (6″) are *molendin' de Coubrigge* 1284 RegMalm, *Coubryge* 1410 FF, *Cowebridge Mill* 1540 *MinAcct.* Probably self-explanatory. DANIELS WELL (6″) is *Daniels Well* 1604 DKR xxxix, cf. *Danyelles* 1547 Pat. HOLLOWAY (Kelly) and HOLLOWAY BRIDGE (6″) are *Hollewey* 1540 *MinAcct, Holwey Bridge* ib. LAWN FM. Cf. *the Lawne* 1650 *ParlSurv* and launde, 'open country' *infra* 440. MALMESBURY COMMON is *Kings Heath or Malmesbury Common* c. 1840 *TA.* ORCHARD FM (6″). Cf. *Orchardbrigge* 1341 *Cor.* PORT-MEADOW COTTAGES (6″). Cf. *Port Meadow* c. 1840 *TA.* The town-meadow. Cf. Portmeadow in Oxford and Port Hill *infra* 299. ROUNDMEAD (6″) is so named in 1650 (*ParlSurv*). STA(I)NES BRIDGE (6″) is *Staynes bridge* 1553 NQ viii, 1603 Sess. THORNHILL FM is *Thornhulle juxta Malmesbiria* t. Ed 1 Reg-

---

[1] *Holcombes, Greate, Little Holcombes* 1628 WIpm.

Malm. WEST PARK FM. Cf. *Westpark* 1453 *Eton, Weste parke*
t. Eliz *LRMB*. WHITCHURCH FM with WHYCHURCH MARSH
BRIDGE (6″). Cf. *Whitechurch* 1252 Ch, *la Whytechurche* 1284
RegMalm. "Here hath been a church; it is now converted
into a dwelling house: but the steeple remaynes still" (Aubrey
267). WHITEHEATH FM is *Whiteheath* 1793 *Recov*. WINYARD
MILL (6″). Cf. *porta de Wyneierd, Wynyerd* 13th RegMalm,
Wynyardesbrigge 1526 Ct, *Wyneyerds Mill, Whynyards Mill* 1650
ParlSurv. From OE *wingeard*, 'vineyard.'

V*a*. CHEDGLOW HUNDRED

Hundred de Ceggeslau 1156, *Cheggeslawahdr* 1167, *Cheggeslauua*
1168, *Cheggelewa* 1176, *Chedeleslawehdr* 1184 P, *Chegelawe* 1196
Cur, 1198 Abbr, *Cheggelewe* 1316 FA. The hundred meeting-
place was evidently at Chedglow *infra* 57. In DB the hundred
was called *Hundred de Chechemetorn, Cicimethorn* (Exon),
Cicemertone (Exch). This must be a compound of *þorn* and
Chicheme, i.e. the thorn-tree of the dwellers at Chedglow,
a compound of the first element of Chedglow and *hæme*,
'dwellers.' The thorn-bush doubtless marked the hundred
meeting-place. See Addenda *supra* xxxix.

Ashley
ASHLEY

> *Esselie* 1086 DB, *-lega* 1196 Cur, 1198 Abbr, 1236 FF,
> *Eshleye* 13th RegMalm
> *Asseleg* 1222 SarumCh, *-leye* t. Hy 3 BM, *Assheleye* 1281 *Ass*
> *Ayssele* 1268 *Ass, Aysshele* 1289 ib.

'Ash clearing or wood,' *v*. leah.

ASHLEY MARSH. Cf. *Marsh Barn* c. 1840 *TA*.

Brokenborough
BROKENBOROUGH

> (*in*) *brokene beregge* 956 (14th) BCS 921, *Brokeneberge* ib.
> 921–2, *Brokeneberg* 1065 (14th) KCD 817
> *Brocheneberge* 1086 DB, *Brokeneberga* 1156 RegMalm *et freq*
> to 1268 *Ass*, with variant spellings *-berg(e), -berwe*

Brokenburgh 1232 Ch, *-bergh* 1340 ib., *Brokynborgh* 1394 *Ass*,
  Brokyngbergh 1410 *FF*, *Broken Bergh* t. Hy 6 ECP
  Brokeberge 1251 Pat, *Brockenborough* t. Eliz WM xxi

'The broken hill or barrow,' *v.* beorg. Cf. Brokenborough in
Almondsbury (Gl), *Brokeneberwe* 1307 *FF*, *(to) brocenan beorge*
(BCS 596) in Micheldean (Ha) and *Brokeneberge* (1232 Selborne) in Basingstoke. The reference in one or more of these
places may be to a barrow rather than a hill.

There would seem to have been an earlier Celtic name for
this place, cf. "non longe fuit a castello apud *Kairdurberg* quod
Saxonice dicitur *Brohamberg* nunc vero *Brokenberg*" (Migne
lxxxix, 309 A). We seem to have here the OE beorg added to a
British compound of *caer*, 'fort, camp,' and **duro-*, 'stronghold,'
etc., found in *Durobrivā*, the old name of Rochester (cf. DEPN
s.n.).

Twatley Fm is *Tothele* 956 (14th) BCS 922, *Totele* 13th, t. Hy 3
RegMalm, *Totley* 1547 Pat, 1563 NQ viii[1]. The medial *e* of the
early spellings perhaps points to the personal name *Tota*, rather
than *tote*, 'look-out place,' as the first element, though topographically the second interpretation is also possible. Cf. the
not very distant *Totleie* in the bounds of Charlton (BCS 59 A).

Bell Fm. Cf. *Bell End* c. 1840 *TA*. Boakley Fm is *Bokeley*
1456 IpmR, *-ly* 1773 A and D. Probably 'beech-wood,' *v.* leah.
Fosse Fm is *Foss Farm* ib. It is on the Fosse Way (*supra* 15).
Gilboa Fm. Cf. *Mount Gilboa Close* c. 1840 *TA*.

Charlton

Charlton [tʃɔ·ltən]

  Cherletune 680 (14th) BCS 59, *-ton* 1225 Pat *et freq* to 1332
    SR, *Cerletone* 1086 DB, *Cherelton* 1268 *Ass*, *Cherleton juxta
    Malmesbury* 1289 ib.
  (*æt*) *Ceorlatunæ* 10th (c. 1150) ASWills, *Cheorletun* 1065
    (14th) KCD 817, *Chorletone* t. Hy 3 RegMalm, *Cheorletone*
    t. Ed 3 *For*, *Chorelton juxta Malmesburye* 1523 *SR*

---

[1] The form may have been influenced by the name of the barn to the
north-west, not now recorded but named *Whatley* 1773 A and D.

'Farm of the churls or free peasants,' v. ceorl, tun. *juxta Malmesbury* to distinguish it from Charlton *infra* 319.

KINGS HAY[1] (*TA*) is *Kynegareshey(e)* 13th RegMalm, 1263 *For*, *Kyneger(e)shey* 1279 *Ass*, t. Ed 1 RegMalm, *Kenegrasheye in hundredo de Cheggelewe* 1305 *Ass*, *Kyngaresheys* 1479 *FF*, *Kings Hayes* 1527 ib. '*Cynegār*'s enclosure,' v. (ge)hæg.

LIPE FM is *Lupe* 1489 *FF*, *Lipe* 1773 A and D and was the home of Richard de *la Lupe* (1255 RH, 1258 *Ass*), William de *la Lupe* (1284 RegMalm) and Roger *atte Lupe* (1332 *SR*), v. hlype, 'steep place,' with reference to the descent to the river here. Cf. Lipe in Luxborough (So), *atte Lipe* 1327 SR (p).

PINK LANE FM (6″) is *Pinckeland* t. Hy 3 *Stowe* 798, *Pynkelond* 1327 *SR* (p), *Pyncklane* 1605 PCC. Possibly '*Pinca*'s land,' cf. Pinkworthy (PN D 164, 388). Förster (*Anglia* lxii, 66 n. 1) discusses very fully this personal name, first found as a second name or nickname in Devon in the 11th century. He links it with the dialectal *pink*, used very widely of the chaffinch. It may well be that in Pink Lane and in other *pink*-names we have the bird-name rather than any personal name deriving from it. See also Pincombe Fd *infra* 486 and Tengvik 328 *s.n.*

SWATNAGE WOOD is *Swetehegge* t. Hy 3 *Stowe* 798, *Swetenhegge* t. Hy 3 RegMalm, *Swetenehegge* c. 1400 *Malm*. Either '(at the) sweet hedge,' from the adj. swēte, or '*Swēta*'s hedge,' cf. Swettenham (Ch), *Swetenham* 1259, 1288 Ct, and Sweethay in Trull (So), *Swetehegh* 1327 SR (p).

PERRY GREEN and WORTHY HILL FM[2] were the homes of Walter de *la Purye* (t. Ed 3 *For*) and Robert de *la Worthy* (1270 ib.) and Thomas *atte Worthi* (1327 *SR*), v. pirige, 'pear tree,' and worþig, 'enclosure.'

GRIFFIN'S BARN and WOODCOCK FM (both 6″) are perhaps to be associated with the families of William *Griffen* (1763 ParReg) and William *Wodecok* (t. Ed 3 *For*). The former is *Griffin Barn* in 1773 (A and D).

---

[1] The field just north of the foot-bridge to the north of Pond Fm (School).
[2] *Worthy Hill* 1733 WM xl.

BAMBURY HILL FM is so named in 1773 (A and D). HEATH FM
is so named c. 1840 (*TA*). MOOR FM (6″) is *la More* 1245 Misc,
v. mor, 'marsh.' POND FM. Cf. *Pond Hill* c. 1840 *TA*. THE
ROUGHETT (6″). Cf. *infra* 430. STONEHILL FM is *Stonhull*' 1257
For, *Stonehill* 1483 *FF*. STREET FM is *Charlton Street Farm*
c. 1840 *TA*.

Crudwell

CRUDWELL[1]

Croddewell(e) 854 (14th) BCS 470, 1362 Pat, 1383 Cl, *Crode-
welle* 1353 Pat, 1362 BPR

Cruddewell(e) 901 (14th) BCS 586, 1270 FF, *Crudewill*' 1242
Fees, *Crudewelle* 1291 Tax, 1332 *SR*, (*Est*, *West*) 1340 Cl,
Estcruddewell 1345 *Ass*, *West-* 1367 Cl, *Chirche*, *West
Crudwell* 1624 *Recov*, *Crudgewell* 1637 *Phillipps*

Creddewilla 1065 (14th) KCD 817, *Credvelle* 1086 DB,
Credewella 1180 P, *-walle* 1196 Cur, 1198 Abbr, *-welle* 1211
Seld iii, 1222 SarumCh, *-wlle* 1242 Fees, *Westcred(d)ewelle*
c. 1250 *Rental*, 1284 RegMalm

Criddanuille c. 1125 BCS 470, *Est-*, *Westcridewell* 1268 *Ass*

Cradewella 1183 P

Croudewelle 1300 Sarum, *Crowdewell* 1543 *FF*

Curdwell 1599 ib.

Near by must have been *Cruddemores lake* 974 (14th) KCD
584, *Credemore*, *Credehemefeld* 1360 Arch xxxvii, *Crudmore*
t. Ed 6 *DuLa* and *Crudehamwlleslake* 956 (14th) BCS 922, *v.* mor,
lacu.

Crudwell is probably 'Crēoda's spring or stream,' *v.* wielle.
Cf. Credenhill (He), *Cradenhille*, *Credenelle* 1086 DB, *Creddehull*
1242 Fees, and Creddacott (Co), *Crodecote* 1298 *MinAcct*,
Croudecote 1302 *Ass*. We have reference to the boundaries of
Crudwell in the phrases *Cruddesetene imere* (956 (14th) BCS 921)
and *Crystetenmore* (901 (14th) ib. 586), where *Cruddesetene* is a
compound of the first element in Crudwell and sæte, 'inhabitants.' For such formations cf. the history of Broadwas
(PN Wo 103–4). The mor-compound survives in Great Crud-
moor (Fd), three furlongs east of Murcott. For *Credehemefeld*
cf. *Chechemetorn supra* 53.

[1] Including West Crudwell.

CHEDGLOW

> *Chegghemwllesbroke* 956 (14th) BCS 922
> *Chegeslei* 1086 DB, *Chegelawe* 1242 Fees, -*lewe* 1255 RH,
> *Cheggeslewe* 1258 *Ass*, *Cheggelowe* 1270 FF, -*lewe* 1305 *Ass*,
> 1332 *SR*, 1341 NI, -*lawe* 1428 *FF*, *Chedglo* 1587 ib.
> *Cheieslave, Cheseslave* 1086 DB
> *Cheggelawe* c. 1150 RegMalm, -*lewa* 1177 P, *Cheggeslawa*
> 1168 P
> *Chichelewe* 1203 FF, *Chigelawee* 1257 Ipm, *Chigelewe* 1399 *FF*
> *Chaggely* 1300 Ipm
> *Chedslowe* 1670 Aubrey

For further forms see Chedglow Hundred *supra* 53 and note *Chegge berwe, Chegge berge* (RegMalm) in the neighbourhood. The second element is clearly hlaw, 'barrow.' The first must remain uncertain in view of the absence of good and consistent early forms.

CHELWORTH [*olim* tʃeləθ]

> *Cellanwurd* c. 890 (c. 1125) BCS 569, *Cellewird, Cellanwirdan*
> 901 (c. 1125) ib. 584, 585, *Choellewrthe* 901 (14th) ib. 585,
> *Cheleworthe* 901 (14th) ib. 586, *Chelewrthe* 956 (14th) ib.
> 922, *Ceollanwurd* 1042–66 (13th) RegMalm, *Chellewrða*
> 1065 (14th) KCD 817, *Celeorde* 1086 DB, *Chellewrth* 1232
> FF, 1272 BM, -*worth* 1297 Ipm, *Chel(l)eswrth* 1275 RH
> *Cheleworth juxta Magna Credewelle* 1281 *Ass*
> *Challoth* 1773 A and D

'*Ceolla*'s farmstead,' *v.* worþ. The forms are not always easy to distinguish from those for Chelworth *supra* 43, but those with a double consonant certainly refer to this place.

EASTCOURT [eskət] is *Escote* 901 (14th) BCS 586, 1332 *SR*, 1638 *Recov*, *Eastcotun* 974 (14th) BCS 1301, *Estcote* 1222 SarumCh, 1268 FF, 1279 *Ass*, *Estcott otherwise Eastcourt* 1736 *FF*, *Eastcourt otherwise Escot* 1772 *Recov*, *Escott* 1773 A and D. 'East cottage(s),' *v.* cot(e). *cotun* is from the OE dative plural *cotum*. Cf. Coton (PN Nth 67). For the modern -*court* cf. Earl's Court *infra* 287.

FLISTERIDGE WOOD is *Flusrige* c. 1250 RegMalm, *boscus de Flusrugge* c. 1270 ib., c. 1400 *Malm*, *Flusrigge* 1284 RegMalm.

The first part of the name would seem to be OE *flīes*, 'fleece.' Possibly used of a hill where the sheep bore good fleeces.

MURCOTT is *Morcotun* 1065 (14th) KCD 817, *Morcote* 1202 FF, 1284 RegMalm, *Morecote* 1440 *FF*. 'Cottage(s) by the swampy land,' *v.* mor, cot(e). Cf. Eastcourt *supra* 57 for the earliest form.

QUELFURLONG FM is *Quelleforlong* t. Hy 3 RegMalm, *Quelverlands* t. Ed 6 *DuLa*, *Quelverland* 1773 A and D, 1816 O.S. There is a well here (6″) and the first element is probably OE *cwylle*, 'spring.' The second is the common word furlang. Cf. *infra* 431.

THE GROVE was probably the home of William *atte Grove* (1332 *SR*), *v.* graf.

MORGAN'S TININGS[1] and OATRIDGE FM (6″) are to be associated with the families of Mary *Morgan* (1662 ParReg) and Henry *Oatridge* (t. Ed 6 *DuLa*). For *Tinings, v. infra* 449.

BROAD LEAZE (6″) is so named c. 1840 (*TA*). *v.* læs. CHURCH GREEN is *Churchgreene* t. Ed 4 *DuLa*. HAYLEAZE (6″) is *Hay leaʒe* t. Ed 6 ib. MORLEY FM (6″) is *Morleia* 1196 Cur, *-le(e)* 1242 Fees, 1337 Ch, 1346 *Ass*. *v.* mor, leah. NOTGROVE (Fd) is *note grave* 974 (14th) KCD 584. Probably 'nut-thicket,' *v.* græfe *infra* 432. PILL BRIDGE (6″). Cf. pyll *infra* 444. POUND FM (6″). Cf. *Pound Mead* c. 1840 *TA*. ROMMELLS COTTAGES (6″). Cf. *Ramwell* t. Ed 6 *DuLa*. A spring is marked here. STADBOROUGH COPSE. Cf. *Stadborough* c. 1840 *TA*. WOODLANDS. Cf. *bosco de Chileworth* 1231 Cl, *Woodlands* 1535 VE.

Garsdon

GARSDON

> *Gersdune* 701 (14th) BCS 103, *-dunam* 1066–87 (13th) RegMalm, *-don* 1279, 1281 *Ass*
>
> *Garsduna* 1066–87 (13th) RegMalm, *-don* 1082 (1385) Pat, 1248 RegMalm, 1257 *For*, *-dune* 1156 RegMalm
>
> *Gardone* 1086 DB
>
> *Garesdon(e)* 1228, 1270 *For et passim* to 1551 Pat, *Garrys-* 1512 Ct

---

[1] *Morgan's Tyning* c. 1840 *TA*.

Garsedon 1228 Cl, *-done* 1268 *Ass*, *Garsindun* c. 1250 *Rental*
Gresdon 1279, 1289 *Ass*
Geresdon 1281 ib., 1288 RegMalm, *Geersden* 1675 Ogilby
Garston t. Eliz WM xxi

'Grass hill,' *v.* gærs, dun. We probably have the same first
element in the old name for Woodbridge Brook (*supra* 11) which
flows just south of Garsdon.

TANNER'S BRIDGE (6″) is to be associated with the family of John
le Tannere (1281 *Ass*).

CHURCH FM. Cf. *Over Churchleys* 1677 NQ vii. PARK FM. Cf.
the Parke ib.

Hankerton

HANKERTON

Hanekyntone 680 (14th) BCS 59A, 901 (14th) ib. 589,
    Hanekinton(e) c. 1150 RegMalm, 1222, 1284 SarumCh, *-yn-*
    1279 Ipm
Honekynton 1065 (14th) KCD 817
Haneketon 1249, 1258, 1268, 1279 *Ass*, *Hanketon* 1428 FA
Hanekyngton(e) 1341 NI, *Hankyngton* 1399 FF, 1412 FA
Hankerton 1535 VE, (*Hankenton al.*) 1541 LP

'*Haneca*'s farm,' *v.* ingtun. Cf. Hankham (PN Sx 447),
Hankford (PN D 92).

BISHOPER is *Bissupesberuwe* c. 1300 *Malm*, *Bushiper* 1773 A and
D. There is hardly any hill here, so it looks very much as if we
have to do with a lost barrow (*v.* beorg *infra* 423), though why
it should have become associated with a bishop it is impossible
to say.

CLOATLEY is *Clotleye* c. 1250 RegMalm, *-lee* 1257 *For*, *-lye* 1388
Cl, *Clotele* 1268 *Ass*, t. Ed 3 *For*, *-legh* ib. 'Clearing or wood
where the clote grows,' *v.* leah. The first element is OE *cláte*,
'burdock,' cf. Clothall (PN Herts 155–6). In western dialect
clote is used of the yellow water-lily and also of Great Mullein.

WOBURN is *Woubourne* 956 (14th) BCS 922, *-borne* 13th Reg-
Malm, *Woburne* 1257 *For*, *-borne* 1595 DKR xxxviii, *Woghe-*
bourne 1375 *For*, *Owborne* 1540 *MinAcct*. 'Crooked stream,'
v. woh, burna. Cf. Woburn (PN BedsHu 143).

DOLMAN'S FM is to be associated with the family of Edith *Dolmen* (1622 ParReg) and John *Doleman* (1667 ib.).

BROOK FM (6″). Cf. *camp. de Brok* c. 1300 *Malm.* BULLOCK'S HORN is so named in 1773 (A and D). NORLEY COPSE. Cf. *Great, Little Norley* c. 1840 *TA.* PERLIEU PLANTATION (6″). Cf. *Parlieu Head* ib. and purlieu *infra* 453.

Kemble

KEMBLE[1]

> *Kemele* 682 (14th) BCS 63, 854 (14th) ib. 470, 1065 (14th) KCD 817, 1180 P *et passim* to 1316 FA, *Chemele* 1086 DB, *Kemela* 1156 RegMalm
> *Cemele* 688 (c. 1125) BCS 70
> *Kemeleshage* 956 (14th) ib. 922
> *Kemelegh* 1242 Fees, 1341 NI
> *Kembyll* 1523 *SR*, 1535 VE

This is a pre-English place-name, but the etymology is uncertain. Ekwall (DEPN *s.n.*) tentatively suggests a derivative of the name *Camulos*, a Celtic war-god, denoting possibly a spot dedicated to his worship. Alternatively one might compare the place-name Penkevil (Co), *Penkevel* 1208–13 Fees (p), 1259 Exon, 1278 *Ass*, etc., *Penkefel* 1265 Maclean, with the regular later British change of medial *m* to *v*. *Kemeleshage* refers to some boundary *haga* of Kemble.

The second element of Penkevil may, as suggested by Professor Max Förster, be cognate with the Welsh *cyfyl*, 'border, brink, edge,' etc. According to Morris-Jones (159), this is from PrimCeltic **com-pel*, OBrit **komel*. One or two of the above early spellings of Kemble show that the last syllable was occasionally associated with the ME *leghe* from leah.

EWEN [juˑən]

> *at Awilme, Awelm* 931 (14th) BCS 671
> *Euulme* 931 (14th) BCS 673, *Ewulm* 937 (c. 1125) ib. 719, *Ewlma, -e* 1156 RegMalm, 1332 *SR*, *Ewelme* t. Hy 3 ib., 1289 *Ass*, 1428 FA, *Eywelm* 1227 FF, *Ewolme* 1284 RegMalm, *Yowelme* 1623 *FF*
> *Ewyn* 1571 *SR*, *Ewen* 1621 *FF*, *Yewelme alias Yewen* 1736 Recov, *Yeoing* 1773 A and D, 1820 G

---

[1] Transferred to Gloucestershire in 1897.

This is OE æwielm, 'spring, source,' cf. Ewelme (PN O 102). Ewen derives its name from one of the springs which rise in this neighbourhood and this must be the one known as 'Thames Head,' since the field in which it is situated is called 'Yeoing Field' (Akermann in *Archaeologia* xxxvii, 116).

KEMBLE WICK is *Weeke* 1591 *Map.* *v.* wic and *supra* 25. LYDWELL (local)[1] is *Lydewelle* 931 (14th) BCS 673. Cf. *s.n.* Liddington *infra* 282–3. PEASTON LANE (6″). Cf. *Perestone* ib.

Lea

LEA is *Lia* 1190 P, *la Le(e)* 1242 Fees, 1248 RegMalm, *Lya* 1249 *Ass*, *Legh* 1268 ib., *la Lee juxta Malmesbury* 1346 ib., 1370 Cl, *Lea al. Lee* 1581 FF, *la Lye al. Lea* 1600 Recov, *v.* leah, 'clearing or wood.'

NOTE. CRESSWELL LANE. Cf. *Cresswell* 1788 *Map*.

CLEVERTON is *Claverdon(e)* t. Hy 3 RegMalm, 1257 *For*, *Cleverdon(e)* 1284 RegMalm, 1327, 1332 *SR*, *Cleverton* 1627 *Recov*. 'Clover hill,' *v.* clæfre, dun.

WINKWORTH FM is *Winekeswurda* 1193 P (p), *Wynekewrth(e)* t. Hy 3 RegMalm, 1286 Pat, -*worth* 1332 *SR* (p), *Winkew(o)rthe*, -*y*- 1248 RegMalm, 1388 Cl, t. Hy 6 ECP. '*Wineca*'s farmstead,' *v.* worþ. Cf. Winkleigh (PN D 373) and Winkfield (Berks), *æt Winecan felda* 942 (c. 1225) BCS 778.

COMBE GREEN was the home of Ralph de *Combe* (1346 *Ass*), *v.* cumb.

BRILLSCOTE (6″) is *Brill's Court* c. 1885 O.S. CRABB MILL (6″) is *Crabb Mill Meade* 1632 WIpm. CROSS FM. Cf. *The Cross*, *The Cross Ground* c. 1840 *TA*.

Minety

MINETY[2] [minti]

Mintih, Mintig 844 (14th) BCS 444, *Minty* 844 (14th) ib. 447 *Minti* 1156 RegMalm, 1185, 1190 P *et passim* to 1314 Pat, with variant spellings *Myn-* and -*ty*, *Minthi*, -*y* t. John (14th) Dugd vi, 1232, 1321 Ch, 1249 Cl

[1] Near WELL HEAD (6″).
[2] The church and surrounding houses with two or three other areas (some 40 acres) were originally in Gloucestershire, but the whole was placed in Wiltshire c. 1890.

Menthi 1232 Ch, *Munte* 1247 *Ass*
Minitide t. Hy 3 *AD*, *Minety* 1282 Cl, *Mynetye* 1552 *FF*

Ekwall (DEPN) derives this name from an OE *mintīe*, dative of *mintēa*, 'mint stream,' *v.* **ea** and cf. Otter R. (PN D 11–12). If this is so the name must have referred to the small stream a little to the west of the present village. 'At Mintie is an abundance of wild mint' (Aubrey NH 49). There is no very marked hill just here, otherwise one might think of a compound of British *monijo-, 'hill' (Welsh *mynydd*, adopted into OE as *myned*), and *tig-, 'house' (Welsh *ty*). Cf. Minehead (DEPN).

Note. Rigsby's Lane is to be associated with the family of John *Rigsby* (1790 ParReg).

Brandier is *Brandyres al. Branyrons* 1633 WIpm, *terra voc. Brandiron* 1681 *Devizes*, *Brandeers* 1773 A and D, 1820 G. Cf. *le Brondyre* 1540 *Rental* in Highworth, *Brandiers* 1694 *Brazenose* in Broad Town and *Brandiers* c. 1840 *TA* in Purton. There can be little doubt that these names contain the word *brandier*, *brandiron*, used of a gridiron in Scotland and the North and North Midlands. Not hitherto recorded from the South, it may have reference to a well-ridged field (B.D.).

Gibb's Fm, Kemble's Fm, The Mansells, Pleydells Fm (all 6″), Sawyers Hill, Telling's Fm (6″), Waits Wood and Woodward's Fm are to be associated with the families of Francis *Gibbs* (1670 ParReg), Thomas *Kemble* (1692 ib.), John *Mansell* (1689 ib.), Edward *Pleydell* (1611 *DuLa*), Jacob *Sawyer* (1622 ParReg), Henry *Tellin* (1671 ib.), William *Waight* (1633 ib.) and Mary *Woodward* (1716 ib.).

Brownockhill Plantation. Cf. *Browning Oke* 1591 *Map*. Buckswell Fm (6″) is *Books Well* 1773 A and D. The Row (6″) is *Mynetye Row* ib. Sambourn (6″) is *Sand(e)burne* 1196 Cur (p), 1279 *For*. 'Sand stream,' *v.* **burna**. Stert Fm is *Sterteslade* 13th RegMalm, *la Stoerte* t. Hy 3 ib., *Sturt Fm* 1773 A and D. 'Tail or point of land,' *v.* **steort**, **slæd** *infra* 446 and cf. Stert *infra* 314. Wellfield (6″). Cf. *Well mede* 1540 WM xii.

Long Newnton

LONG NEWNTON

Niuentun 681 (c. 1125) BCS 58, *Newentone* 1086 DB,
   Newenton 1258 *Ass et freq* to 1387 Cl, with variant spellings
   Niwen-, Nywen-, (*juxta Malmesbury*) 1364 *Ass*
Long Newenton 1337 Cl, *Newnton alias Longe Newnton* 1571
   NQ vii

From OE (*æt þām*) *nīwan tūne*, 'at the new farm,' *v.* tun. The
epithet *Long* is hard to justify. The hamlet lies along a road but
is not a particularly long one.

CHURCH FM[1], NEWNTON MILL and SLADS FM were probably
the homes of John *atte Churche* (1327 *SR*), John *atte Mulle* (1332
ib.) and Robert de *la Slade* (1279 *Ass*), *v.* slæd *infra* 446. The *s*
is probably pseudo-manorial.

BOLDRIDGE FM (6″) is *Great, Little Boldridge* c. 1840 *TA*. THE
FOLLY. Cf. *The Folly House* ib., and *infra* 451. HAM BRAKE
COTTAGES (6″). Cf. *Ham Brake* ib. LARKHILL FM is *Lark Hill
Farm* 1773 A and D. WALLGUTTERS COVERT (6″). Cf. *Wall
Gutter* c. 1840 *TA*.

Oaksey

OAKSEY[2]

Wochesie 1086 DB, *Wokesai* 1196 Cur, *-eia, -eye, -ey* 1197 FF
   et freq to 1428 FA, *Wogasca* c. 1180 Berkeley Charters
Wockesheye 1279 *Ass*, *Wokkeseye* 1289 ib., *Wockesygh* 1299
   Ipm, *-ey(e)* 1300 Misc, 1324 FA, 1337 Ipm, *Woxey* 1452
   Pat
Okyssey 1535 VE, *Oxhay* 1547 *SR*, *Oxey* 1585 FF, *Ocksey*
   t. Jas 1 ECP, *Wokesey alias Oxhey* 1638 *Recov*, *Okesey alias
   Woxy* 1620 Aubrey

'*Wocc*'s well-watered land,' *v.* eg. Cf. Woking (PN Sr 156).
For the loss of the initial consonant cf. Ockendon (PN Ess
125–6) and Oaktrow in Cutcombe (So), *Wochetreu* DB, *Woke-
trowe* 1280 *Ass*, 1331 Ipm.

---

[1] Cf. *Church Leaze* 1773 A and D.
[2] The old pronunciation [wɔksi] is still occasionally heard (*ex inf.* Rev. W.
Sole).

CLATTINGAR is *Clothangare* 1332 *SR* (p), *Cladhangre* 1337 Ipm, *Clodhangere, Cladhangur', Clathangere* 1347 *Ct, Clathanger* 1420 *MinAcct, boscus voc. Clattanger* 1488 *DuLa, Clatangre* 1568 ib. The name would seem to be a compound of OE *clāte* and hangra, 'slope.' Cf. Cloatley *supra* 59. Close by is a field called *Clodd* (*TA*), which may account for the variant *d*-forms.

CHURCH FM (6″) and OAKSEY WOOD[1] were the homes of Robert *atte Churche* (1347 *DuLa*) and John *atte Wode* (1333 *SR*).

COURT FM. Cf. *Court Field* c. 1840 *TA*. DEAN FM. Cf. *Netherdene* 1347 *DuLa, Overdene* 1568 ib., *Dane Barn* 1773 A and D, *Oaksey Dean* 1816 O.S. 'Valley,' *v.* denu and Introd. xx. FLINTHAM HO is *Flinton* 1773 A and D. MOOR FM. Cf. *Wokhamesmore* 1568 *DuLa, The Moor* 1773 A and D, *v.* mor. NORWOOD CASTLE (6″) is *Northwode* 1337 Ipm. OAKSEY PARK. Cf. *le Park* 1337 Ipm, *Okesey Park* 1633 WIpm. SODOM FM (6″) is *Sarhams* 1816 O.S. WOODFOLDS FM (6″) is *Woodfeldes* 1568 *DuLa*. WOODLANDS is *Greate, Litle Woodlands* 1633 WIpm.

Poole Keynes

POOLE KEYNES[2] [keinz]

> *Pole* 931 (14th) BCS 673, 1086 DB, 1268 *Ass*, 1291 Tax, *La Pole* 1242 FF, 1305 FF, *Poole* 1539 LP, *Pole Canes* 1610 S, *Pool Keynes* 1793 Cary

'Pool,' *v.* pol. John Maltravers held the manor in 1327. He left two daughters, of whom the elder married Sir John *Keynes* (Aubrey 279). Cf. Somerford Keynes *supra* 46–7.

MILL FM was the home of John *atte Mulle* (1327 *SR*). Cf. *Milleplace* 1488 *DuLa*.

OAK WELL (6″). Cf. *Okewell hed* 1591 WM iv.

---

[1] *bosco de Wokkesey* 1321 *Ass*.
[2] Transferred to Gloucestershire in 1897.

V*b*. STARTLEY HUNDRED[1]

Hundred de Starcheleia, Sterchelee, Sterchelai 1086 ExonDB, *Sterchelai* 1156 P, *Sterchel' hdr* 1159 ib., *Starchelea* 1164 ib., *Sterkelaihdr* 1174 ib., *Sterkeleg' hdr* 1186 ib., *Sterkelewe* 1255 RH, *Stercheslegh* 1281 *Ass, Sterkele* 1316 FA. The meeting-place was at Startley in Gt Somerford *infra* 73.

Brinkworth

BRINKWORTH

Brinkewrða 1065 (14th) KCD 817, *Brinkeswurda* 1190 P, *Brinkeworþe* 1191 RegMalm *et passim* to 1479 PCC, with variant spellings *Brynke-* and *-worth, -wrth, -wurth*

Brenchewrde, Brecheorde 1086 DB, *Brenkewrtha* 1156 Reg-Malm, *-wrþe* t. Hy 3 ib., *-wurth* 1236 FF *et passim* to 1370 Cl, with variant spellings *-wrth, -worth*

Brankeswurda 1186 P, *Brankewurd* 1247 Pap

Brengewurth 1242 Fees, *Bringewurth* 13th AD vi

Brunkwurth 1242 Fees, *Brunkeworth* 1428 FA

Brenchesworth 1279 *Ass, -wrthe* 1281 ib.

'*Brynca's* farmstead,' *v.* worþ. Cf. Brinklow (PN Wa 98–9), where it is shown that the recorded personal name *Brynca* is much more likely to be the first element in this name than any unrecorded OE *brinc*, denoting a slope.

NOTE. SLOUGH LANE was probably near the home of William *atte Slowe* (1257 *For*) and John *atte Sclo* (1343 *Pat*), *v.* sloh, 'slough, mire.'

CALLOW HILL is *Calewehulle* 1300 WM iv, c. 1300 *Malm*, (*le*) t. Ed 3 *For, Callowe Hill* t. Eliz ChancP, *Calley Hill* 1815 O.S. 'Bare hill.' Cf. Callowhill (PN Sr 120).

---

[1] From the township of Christian Malford in this Hundred, together with Grittleton and Nettleton in the old Hundred of Thorngrove and Kington St Michael in the Hundred of Chippenham, all Glastonbury manors, was formed in 1321 a separate Hundred, later known as the Hundred of North Damerham, in contrast to the original Hundred of Damerham (now called South Damerham) in the south of the county, which from the first was purely Glastonbury property (see Aubrey 124 n. 1).

GRITTENHAM

> *Gruteham* 850 (14th) BCS 458, 1288 RegMalm, 1289 *Ass*,
> *Grutenham* 1065 (14th) KCD 817 *et freq* to 1349 WM xxxiii
> *Greteham* 1156 RegMalm, *Gretheham* 1268 *Ass*, *Gretenham*
> 1291 Tax, 1362 BPR, *Gretenham*, *Gretnam* t. Eliz WM xxi
> *Gryteham* 1268 *Ass*, *Gritnam* 1595 *FF*, *Grittingham* 1602 ib.
> *Grotenham* 1279 *Ass*

The soil here is gravelly and the place lies low by Brinkworth
Brook; the probabilities therefore are that we have a compound
of OE *grīeten*, an unrecorded OE adjectival derivative of *grēot*,
'gravel,' and *hamm*. Hence 'gravelly water-meadow or enclosure.' We may perhaps compare *Grotelinche*, *Grotenberwe*
1341 Trop (in Codford), *Grotenhill* 1448 *Kings* (in Brixton
Deverill), *le Groten* c. 1350 Trop (in Chicklade). Ekwall
(DEPN *s.n.*) suggests that *Greote* was an old name for Brinkworth Brook itself, but we know now that its usual earlier name
was Idover. Cf. *supra* 2–3.

SUNDEYS HILL is *Sondheye* 680 (14th) BCS 59 A, *Sundeys Hill*
1773 A and D. The 14th-century form points to a compound of
OE *sand*, 'sand,' and (ge)hæg, 'enclosure.'

WOODSIDE FM may have been the home of Cristina *Bythewode*
(1332 *SR*). Cf. *Brinkworth woode* 1585 *For*.

BARNES'S GREEN, BELLAMYS, GILES'S GREEN, GODDARD'S FM,
HULBERT'S GREEN, LATIMER'S FM, LUKER'S FM, PINNELL'S FM,
VINE'S FM, WALDRON'S FM (all 6"), WEEKS'S FM, WHITE'S FM
and YORK'S FM (6") are to be associated with the families of
Joyce *Barnes* (1605 ParReg), William *Belamy* (1289 *Ass*), Mary
Giles (1724 ParReg), Edward *Goddard* (1585 *For*), William
Hurlebalt (1669 ParReg), *Hulbart* (1762 ib.), William *Latnar*
(1572 *FF*), John *Looker* (1726 ParReg), Richard *Pinell* (1655 ib.),
Edward *Vines* (1734 ib.), Francis *Waldron* (1611 *DuLa*), Arthur
Wickes (1605 ParReg) and Margaret *Weekes* (ib.), Ralph *le Wyte*
(1270 *For*) and Hugh *le Whyte* (1281 *Ass*) and Charles *Yoarke*
(1668 ParReg).

BOXBUSH FM (6"). Cf. *Box Bush House* 1841 *Devizes*. BRAYDON
SIDE is so named c. 1840 (*TA*). Beside Braydon Forest *supra* 11.

CLITCHBURY (6″) is *Clinchboroughe al. Clitchboroughe* 1636 WIpm. Cf. Clench *infra* 349. DOLLAKER'S GREEN is *Gallykers Green* (sic) 1773 A and D, *Doleacres Green* c. 1840 *TA*. *doleacres* is doubtless used of lands which have been shared out, *v*. dal *infra* 429. FARM HILL (6″) is so named ib. FERNHILL is *Farnhull* 1347 Cl. Self-explanatory. FRITTERSWELL FM (6″). Cf. *Fritters Well* c. 1840 *TA*. GROVE FM (6″). Cf. *Grove close* 1585 *For*. LODGE FM. Cf. *Old Lodge plecke* 1611 *DuLa*. For *pleck*, 'plot of ground,' *v. infra* 444. LONGMAN'S STREET FM (6″). Cf. *Longmans Street* 1773 A and D. PENN'S LODGE. Cf. *la Penne* t. Ed 3 *For* and Pen Hill *supra* 34. PITTSLAND FM is *Pits Land* 1820 G. RAMP HILL. Cf. *Great, Little Ramp* c. 1840 *TA*. TROW LANE FM (6″) is *Troweye* t. Ed 3 *For*, *Trow Lane* 1773 A and D. 'Tree way,' *v*. treow, weg. WEST END FM (6″) is *Westend* 1600 *Recov*. WINDMILL HO (6″). Cf. *Windmill leaze* 1640 WIpm, *v*. læs.

Christian Malford

CHRISTIAN MALFORD

> *Cristemal(l)eford* 937 (14th) BCS 717 *et freq* to 1330 Ch, (*at*) *Cristemalford* 940 (15th) BCS 752, 1330 Ch, *Cristimalford* 1242 Fees, *Chrystemalforde* 1539 *Phillipps*
>
> *Cristemeleford* 1086 DB, 1189 GlastInq, 1232 Ch, 1275 Cl, *Cristesmeleford* 1166, 1168 P, -*meles*- 1167 ib., *Crestemeleford* 1197 ib., *Cristmel(l)(e)ford* 1227 Ch, 1241 FF, 1395 Pat
>
> *Cristemere(s)ford* 1181, 1186 P, -*mare*- 1195 ib.
>
> *Cristesmaelford* 1196 Cur, *Crystmoelford* 1428 FA
>
> *Cristine Malford* 1374 Pat, *Christine Maleford* c. 1540 L, *Christen Malford* t. Eliz ChancP, *Christon Malford al. Christian Malford* 1611 *Recov*
>
> *Curst Mavord* 1585 WM xxi

'Ford by a cross,' *v*. cristel-mæl.

DODFORD FM is *Dodeford* 1255 RH (p), *Doddeford* 1278, 1289 Ass, 14th Bradenstoke, *Duddeford* 1279 Ass (p), *Dodford* t. Eliz ChancP. '*Dodda*'s ford.'

MELSOME WOOD is *Milesham* 1232 Ch, c. 1350 *Bradenstoke*. The forms are too late for any interpretation to be possible. The second element is ham or hamm.

THE GREEN (6″) was the home of Rosemond *atte Grene* (1327 *SR*).

BRIGHT'S FM is to be associated with the family of Abraham *Bright* (1692 ParReg).

BEANHILL FM. Cf. *Great, Little Bean Hill* c. 1840 *TA*. BITTLE-SEA FM is *Bittelsheare al. Bittelser* t. Eliz ChancP, *Bittlesea* 1773 A and D. THE CITY (6″). Cf. *City Mead* c. 1840 *TA* and *infra* 455. FRIDAY STREET FM is *Friday Street* 1773 A and D. Cf. *infra* 452. MERMAID FM (6″) is so named c. 1840 (*TA*) and is so called from the *Mermaid Inn* ib. PARADISE FM, RIDGEWAY FM, SELSTEAD FM and SWALLETT FM are so named ib. THORNEND is so named in 1744 (WM xli). UPPER TOWN is so named in 1773 (A and D).

Dauntsey

DAUNTSEY [dɑ·nsi]
  Dometesig 850 (14th) BCS 457, 1065 (14th) KCD 817, (*at*) *Domeccesige* 854 (14th) BCS 470
  Daunteseye, Dameteseye 850 (14th) ib. 458
  Dantesie 1086 DB, 1160 RBE, *-ia* 1164, 1166 P, *-eia* 1166 RBE, *-i* 1178 BM, 1198 P, *-eye* 1257 FF, 1312 Cl
  Dauntesa t. Hy 2 (1270) Ch, *Dauntesi* 1220 AD iv, *-(h)eye* 1268 *Ass*, 1303 Sarum, 1316 FA
  Doundsee al. Daundesey 1407 Pat, *Daundeseye* 1416 Cl
  Daunsey 1516 *Recov*, *Dancy* 1655 ParReg (Brinkworth)

The second element in this name is OE **eg, ieg,** 'island, well-watered land.' Ekwall (DEPN *s.n.*) suggests that the first may be a lost OE personal name *Dōmgeat*. The development of *o* to *a* has its parallel in the forms of Damerham *infra* 400, with more persistent early *o*-forms. Professor Ekwall points out that the *a*-forms are due to early shortening of $\bar{o}$ to *o*, with substitution of [ǫ] for [o] as in Brampton (DEPN) from *brōm* and Frampton (ib.) from the river Frome. It should be noted that the same first element is found in *Dauntesbourne* (BCS 752) in the bounds of the adjacent parish of Christian Malford. The stream is now known simply as The Bourne (*supra* 2).

IDOVER DEMESNE FM

> *Ydouere* 850 (14th) BCS 458, *Idoure* 956 (14th) ib. 922, 13th
> RegMalm, *Idovers* 1670 Aubrey
>
> *Tidoure* 1214 FF, 1228 Cl, *Didoure* 1228 ib., *Tydovere* 1242
> Fees, 1257 FF, 1301 Ipm, *Tydo(u)re* 1288 RegMalm, 1293,
> 1313 Abbr, -*overe* 1312 Cl
>
> *Tideur* 1228 ib., *Tydeuere* 1293 Abbr

In the OE and in the 1228 Close Roll forms the reference is
to a stream, viz. Brinkworth Brook *supra* 2–3, just to the north
of the farm; in the other cases the reference is to the farm itself.
For the history of the name Idover, cf. under Brinkworth Brook
supra 2–3. The forms with initial *t* would seem to be due to fusion
of final *t* in *æt* and the initial vowel in Idover.

SMITHCOT FMS is *Smitecote* 1086 DB, *Smidecota* 1190 P,
Smithecot(e), -*y*- 1242 Fees, 1257 FF, 1321 *FF*, 1342 Cl, *Smeþe*-
1242 Fees, *Smethe*- 1327 *SR et freq* to 1428 FA, *Smiskett or
Smithcot* 1773 A and D. 'Cot(e) of the smiths,' cf. Smithacott
and Smynacott (PN D 93, 389).

WAITE HILL FM was the home of Cristina *atte Waitehull* (1327
SR) and Philip *atte Waytehulle* (1332 ib.). 'Watch or look-out
hill,' the first element being ME *waite*, 'watch,' cf. White
(PN D 108).

CREW'S FM (6″) is *Crow's Fm* 1816 O.S. DAUNTSEY GREEN is
Dantsey Green 1773 A and D. DAUNTSEY PARK is *Dauntasey
Parke* t. Ed 6 *DuLa*. SODOM (6″) is so named in 1841 (*Devizes*).

Draycot Cerne

DRAYCOT CERNE

> *Draicote* 1086 DB, *Draycota* 1198 Fees *et passim*, with variant
> spellings -*cot(e)* and *Drai-*, (*juxta Northlangeleye*) 1307 *FF*,
> (*Cerne*) 1345 Ipm
>
> *Dracote* 1086 DB
>
> *Dreycota*, -*e* 1221 Bracton, 1275 RH, *Dreighcote Serne* 1394
> Pat

v. dræg, cot(e) and Ekwall (*Studies*[1] 46 ff.). There can be no
question of any 'portage' or the like here, but there is a

steep hill just to the north of the place which may have been called a *dræg*. Henry de *Cerne* held the manor in 1225 (Pat). The family probably came from Cerne (Do).

CLANVILLE is *Clanvell* 1638 WIpm, *Clanvill* 1700 Longford, 1773 A and D, *Clanfield* c. 1840 *TA*. 'Clean open land,' i.e. without weeds. Cf. Clanville in Alford (So), *Clanefeld* 1219 Fees, *Clanvil* 1675 Ogilby, Clanville in Wey Hill (Ha), *Clanefeud* 1256 *Ass*, *Clanvell* 1654 ParReg, and *Clanvill(e)* (*TA*) in Biddestone and Sherston *infra* 467, 472.

BUSHES LEAZE (6″). Cf. *Bushy Leaze Wood* c. 1840 *TA*. *v*. læs. DRAYCOT PARK is *Draycott Park* 1637 WIpm. LAKE FM. Cf. *Upper*, *Lower Lake* (fields) c. 1840 *TA* and lacu *infra* 438.

Foxley

FOXLEY

> *Foxelege* 1086 DB, *Foxlegh* 1227 Ch *et passim*, with variant spellings -*le*(*e*), -*ley*(*e*), (*juxta Malmesbury*) 1314 *FF*, *Foxly* t. Eliz WM xxi, *Foxley*, *Faxley* 1675 Ogilby
> *Voxlee* t. Hy 8 *Rental*

'Clearing or wood frequented by foxes,' *v*. leah and Introd. xxi.

NOTE. HONEY LANE is probably so called as a muddy lane. Cf. *infra* 139.

BREMILHAM MILL (6″)

> *Brimelham* t. Hy 2 (1270) Ch, 1208 Cur
> *Brumilham* 1178 BM, *Brumel-* t. John Dugd ii, 13th RegMalm, 1279 *Ass*, 1332 *SR*
> *Bremleham* 13th AD ii, *Bremel-* 1249 FF *et freq* to 1327 *SR*, *Bremham* 1675 Ogilby, *Bremenham al. Bremilham* 1752 Recov

'Bramble ham' or more likely 'hamm.' The place is in a big bend of the Avon. *v*. bremel, hamm.

COWAGE FM is *Covage* (sic) 1773 A and D, *Colwich* 1820 G. See *infra* 269.

Hullavington

HULLAVINGTON [hʌliŋtən]

Hunlavintone 1086 DB *et freq* to 1343 Pat, with variant
  spelling -*yn*-, *Honlavynton* 1279 *Ass*
Hundlavinton, -y- 1203 FF *et freq* to 1310 FF, *Hundelavinton*
  1242 Fees
Hunlavyngton 1347, 1415 Pat, *Hund-* 1428 FA
Hundlaunton 1422 Pat
Hullavington al. Hullonton 1583 AD v, *Hullyngton al.
  Hullavyngton* 1583 FF, *Hull Lavington* 1645 WM xix

'*Hūnlāf's* farm' or '*Hundlāf's,*' *v.* ingtun. No personal
name *Hundlāf* is on actual record. Cf. Hullasey (PN Gl 88),
DB *Hunlafsed.*

BRADFIELD FM is *Bradefelde* 1086 DB *et freq* to 1258 *Ass*, with
variant spelling -*feld*, -*vyld* 1453 *Eton*, *Brodefyld al. Bradfyld*
1579 *FF*. 'Wide open space,' *v.* brad, feld.

SURRENDELL is *Sorendene* 1211 RBE, *Surinden*' 1242 Fees,
Surenden' 1278 *Ass*, *Suryndon* 1289 ib., -*den(e)* t. Ed 1 Ipm,
1316 FA, *Cyrendene, Sirenden* c. 1330 BM, *Surrenden* 1425
IpmR, 1576 *FF*, *Serenden* 1428 FA, *Sorenden* 1507 BM,
Surrendel 1695 Gough, (*or Surrenden*) 1773 A and D. This is
possibly from OE (*æt þǣre*) *sūran dene*, a compound of *sūr*,
'sour' and denu. The opposite of Fresden *supra* 26–7.

GARDENER'S FM, HEYWARD'S PATCH, MAY'S FM and NEWMAN'S
FM (all 6″) are to be associated with the families of Alexander
le Gardiner (t. Ed 3 *For*), Richard *Hayward* (1611 *DuLa*), John
Maye (1571 *SR*) and William *Neweman* (1257 *For*).

COURT FM (6″). Cf. *Courtfeild* 1599 *Devizes*. FURLEAZE FM is
Fur Leaze 1773 A and D. Probably 'further læs.' It is in a
remote part of the parish. HILLAYS is *Hillhayes* 1599 *Devizes*.
v. (ge)hæg. KINGWAY BARN (6″). Cf. *Kingway* ib. It is on the
same road as Kingway Barn *supra* 51. LITTLE WORTH WOOD
(6″). Cf. *infra* 455. PICCADILLY (6″). Cf. *infra* 455. It is at the
end of the village. STOCK WOOD is *Stokewod(e)* 1460 *Eton*, 1560

FF, *Stockwood Coppice* 1599 *Devizes*. The first element is probably stocc, 'stump.' TOWNLEAZE BARN (6″) is *le Toune leaze* 1566 *Eton*, v. læs and tun *infra* 449. Cf. *Tonforlang* 14th *Bradenstoke*. WINDMILL HILL is so named in 1599 (*Devizes*).

Norton

NORTON

> *Nort(h)un* 931 (14th) BCS 671, 937 (14th) ib. 719, *Nortone* 1086 DB *et passim*, with variant spellings *-ton*, *-tun(e)*, (*by Malmesbury*) 1408 Pat
>
> *Northton* 1281 *Ass*, 1291 Tax

'North farm,' v. tun. *North* perhaps with reference to Hullavington.

ELLSTUB[1] (1807 O.S.) is *ellernestubbe* 931 (14th) BCS 672, *Ellstubs* c. 1840 *TA*. 'Elder-tree stump,' v. ellern, stubb.

MAIDFORD is *maȝþe ford* 931 (14th) BCS 672, *Madeford* 1773 A and D. The first element is probably OE *mægþe*, 'mayweed.' Cf. Mayfield (PN Sx 381).

BUCKLANDS FM (6″) is to be associated with the family of Thomas *Buckland* (1727 ParReg).

GORSEY LEAZE is *Gossey Leaze* 1820 G, v. læs.

Seagry

SEAGRY [*olim* segəri]

> *Segrie* 1086 DB
>
> *Segrete* ib., *Segreth* 1399 IpmR, *Over Segreve* 1420 *FF*, *Over Segrith* 1465 ib.
>
> *Segrea* 1190, 1191 P, *Segreya* c. 1220 BM, *Segrey(e)* 1224, 1236 FF, 1232 Ch, *Secre* 1242 Fees, *Segre* ib., 1249 *Ass et freq* to 1363 *FF*, *Nethere-* 1218 ClR
>
> *Seggereye* 1225 Pat, *Segere* 1332 SR, *vulgo Segary* 1670 Aubrey
>
> *Segree* 13th Aubrey, 1258 *Ass*, 1344 Pat, *Seggree* 1301 Ipm, *Oversegree* 1318 FF
>
> *Seagrey* 1699 Recov, *Seagry, Over and Nether* 1773 A and D

---

[1] The field north-west of the Vine Tree.

This is probably OE *secg-rīð*, 'sedge stream,' as suggested by Ekwall (DEPN). *Over* and *Nether* have now been replaced by Upper and Lower.

NOTE. FIVE THORN LANE. Cf. *Five Thorns* c. 1840 *TA*.

HUNGERDOWN is *campo qui vocatur Hungerdowne super Shitarshulle* c. 1350 *Bradenstoke, Hungerdowne mead* 1658 *FF*. The name describes poor soil or pasture. Cf. *infra* 93. It has supplanted the earlier and cruder name of the hill.

SEALE'S FM (6") is probably to be associated with the family of John *Sealy* (1735–81 WM xxvi).

NEW LEAZE FM (6") is *New Leaze* c. 1840 *TA*, *v*. læs. SEAGRY HEATH is so named in 1671 (WM xxxi).

Somerford

GREAT and LITTLE SOMERFORD

> *Sumerford* 937 (c. 1125) BCS 719, *Somerford* 956 (14th) ib. 921 *et passim*, with variant spelling *Sum-*, *Sumerford Mauduyt, Mautravers* 1268 *Ass*, (*Mauduth, Mautravers*) 1275 RH, (*Matreface*) 1553 WM x
> *Somreford, Sumreford* 1086 DB
> *Brode Somerford* 1409 *FF*, 1428 Pat, *Somerford Magna alias Brode Somerford* 1588 *FF*, *Somerford Magna al. Somerford Matravers al. Broad Somerford* 1610 *Recov*, *Little Somerford al. Somerford Mauditt* 1681 ib.

'Ford usable during the summer months,' cf. Somerford Keynes *supra* 46–7. Great Somerford was held by Walter *Maltravers* in 1196 (Cur), Little Somerford by John *Mauduth* in 1275 (RH). For *Broad* in the sense 'great,' cf. *infra* 204.

Great Somerford

STARTLEY FM is *silvum q.v. Stercanlei* 688 (c. 1125) BCS 71, *Sterckle* 13th RegMalm, *Sterkele* 1249 *Ass*, *Sterkle* 1409 *FF*, *Startley* 1558–79 ECP, *Starkley grove* 1603 NQ iii. Possibly from OE (*æt þǣm*) *stearcan lēage*, a compound of OE *stearc*, 'stiff, unbending' and leah, probably with reference to the wood or forest.

Brook Fm (6″), Grove Fm[1] and Mills Fm (6″) were probably the homes of Nicholas de *Brok* (1289 *Ass*), Thomas *atte Grove* (1332 *SR*) and John *atte Mulle* (ib.).

Down Field Fm is *Downefields* 1608 NQ viii, *-fielde* 1672 ib. ii. Goosegreen Fm (6″) is *Goose Green* 1773 A and D. New Leaze Fm (6″) is *the New Leaze* 1608 NQ vii, *v.* læs.

Little Somerford

East End Fm (6″). Cf. *East End Piece* c. 1840 *TA*. Hill Ho. Cf. *Hillecroft* 1451 *MinAcct*. Kingsmead (6″) is *Kyng(e)mede* ib. Maunditts Park Fm preserves the name of the medieval holders of the manor, *v. supra* 73. Cf. *le Parkefeld* 1451 ib. Somerford Bridge is *Idoverbridge* 1610 S, 1816 O.S., *v. supra* 2.

Sutton Benger

Sutton Benger

> (*at*) *Suttune* 854 (14th) BCS 470, *Sutton(e)* 956 (14th) ib. 922, 1115 Osmund, (*Berengeres*) 1377 IpmR, (*juxta Braden-stoke*) 1415 Aubrey, (*Benger*) 1488 Ipm, (*Leonard juxta Christmalford*) 1497 Aubrey
> *Sudtone* 1086 DB

'South farm,' *v.* tun. *South* perhaps with reference to Hullavington. *Berenger* was under-tenant TRW. The reason for the *Leonard* addition is unknown.

Nabal's Fm (6″) [næbəlz]

> *Knabbewelle* 1196 Cur (p) *et freq* to 1492 Ipm, *Cnabbe-* 1242 Fees, t. Ed 1 *DuLa*, *Cnabe-* 1250 FF, *Cnabbewlle by Dray-cote* 1292 Ipm
> *Cnabwell(e)* 1275 RH (p), 1309 Ipm, *Knab-* 1279 *Ass* (p), *-wolle* 1411 Cl
> *Knavewell* 1318 Ch
> *Knabwell vulgarly called Knabbals* 1670 Aubrey, *Nabbols* 1773 A and D

---

[1] *The Grove* 1652 NQ iii.

The first element in this name must be a personal name *Cnabba*, allied to OE *cnafa*, 'boy,' and the recorded personal name *Cnebba*. '*Cnabba*'s spring,' *v.* **wielle**.

HARDING'S FM (6″) is to be associated with the family of Adam *Herdyng* (1281 *Ass*).

OAK HILL (6″) is *Oat Hill* c. 1840 *TA*. SCOTLAND HILL. Cf. *Scotland* 1773 A and D and *infra* 454. SUTTON DOWN. Cf. *montem de Sutton* 1249 *Ass*.

VI. DUNLOW HUNDRED

Duneslawi, Denelau (bis) 1086 ExonDB, *Duneslawahdr* 1167, 1168 P, *Dunilewe* 1196 Cur, 1198 Abbr, *Dunelawe, Dunelewe* 1268 *Ass*, *Dynlewe* 1317 Pat, *Donlowe* 1474 ib. The meeting-place was at Dunley in Littleton Drew *infra* 76. This hundred, with Thorngrove *infra* 78, is now merged in Chippenham Hundred.

Alderton

ALDERTON

    Aldri(n)tone 1086 DB, *Aldrinton, -y-* 1196 Cur *et freq* to 1316 FA, *Aldrenton* 1321 FF

    Aldrington, -y- 1249 FF *et freq* to 1428 FA, *Alderyngton* 1426 *Ass*, 1433 Pat

    Alderton al. Aldrington t. Jas 1 ECP, 1628 *Recov*

'*Ealdhere*'s farm,' *v.* **ingtun**.

CRANHILL WOOD (6″) is *Crawenhulle, Crawehulleputte* 1317 NQ viii. The ME forms suggest 'crows' hill,' from OE gen. pl. *crāwena*, *v.* **hyll**.

HUGH'S FM (6″) is to be associated with the family of Joseph *Hughes* (1758 ParReg).

ALDERTON GROVE FM. Cf. *Aldrington Grove* 1820 G. BROADMEAD COVERT (6″) is *Brodemede* 1460 Eton. TOWNFIELD FM (6″). Cf. *Town Field* c. 1840 *TA*. It is just at the end of the village, cf. *infra* 449.

Easton Grey

Easton Grey

> Estone 1086 DB, Estuna t. Hy 2 (1268) Ch, Eston 1243 Pat,
> 1258 Ipm, Eston Grey 1289 Ass
> Aston(e) Gray 1311 Sarum, (Grey) 1341 Ipm, 1460 Pat

'East farm,' v. tun. John de Grey held the manor in 1243 (Pat).

Normeads Covert is so named c. 1840 (TA).

Littleton Drew

Littleton Drew

> Litletun 1065 (14th) KCD 817, Liteltone 1086 DB, Litleton(a)
> 1191 RegMalm, 1220 Bracton, 1242 Fees, Littleton Dru
> 1311 Cl, Litleton Drewe 1316 FA, Littletone Dryeu 1332 SR
> Lutleton 1249 Ass, Lutlyngton Dru 1352 FF

'Little farm,' v. tun. Walter Driwe held the manor in 1220 (Bracton), spelt Dreu in 1242 (Fees). Cf. Drewsteignton (PN D 431). Dreu is a Norman-French personal name of Germanic origin (OHG Drogo).

West Dunley Fm is Dynelawe in villa de Lytleton 1289 Ass, Dunelewe 1308 Ipm, Donlewe 1348 Cor, Donelewe 1425 FF, Dunley Hill 1630 WM xliv. This was the hundred meeting-place, v. supra 75. The name is also found in East Dunley Fm and Cottages in Hullavington and Dunley Wood in Grittleton, so it is difficult to say just where the hlaw was. Probably it was at the top of the hill now marked Elm and Ash where Alderton, Littleton Drew and Hullavington parishes meet. The Elm and the Ash may have marked the actual meeting-place. The first element is uncertain as the forms are inconsistent with one another. For lewe, v. Introd. xx.

Gatcombe Hill is Gatecombe 1346 AddCh, Gatcombe cliff 1354 ib., Gatcombe mille 1422 Add. Probably OE gāta cumb, 'goats' valley,' cf. Gatcombe (Wt), Gatecome 1086 DB.

Brimsol Spring (6"). Cf. Brinshill, Brinsell Tyning c. 1840 TA and infra 449. The Gib is Gibraltar c. 1830 RCH. It is the

name for the extreme south projection of the parish. OLDLANDS
WOOD (6″). Cf. *Oldland* 1513 *Add*. STEP HILL (6″) is so named
c. 1840 (*TA*). TOWNSEND FM (6″). Cf. *Townsend Close* ib. and
infra 449. It is at the end of the village.

Luckington

LUCKINGTON

> *Lochintone* 1086 DB, *Lokinton(e), -y-* 1201 Cur *et freq* to 1341
> NI
> *Luchinton* 1198 Abbr, *Lukintona* 1242 Fees
> *Lokyngton* 1296 *FF*, 1298 Pat, 1349 *FF*, 1360 BPR, *Lookington*
> 1585 NQ vii
> *Luckington* 1598 *FF*, *Lockington alias Luckington* 1684 *Recov*

'*Luc(c)a*'s farm,' *v.* ingtun. The same man must have given
name to Luckley *infra*.

NOTE. CHERRY ORCHARD LANE. Cf. *Cherry Orchard House* 1820 G.

LUCKLEY is *Lokelee* 1332 WIpm, *Lokkele* 1335 Ipm, *Luckley*
1648 *Recov*. '*Luc(c)a*'s clearing or wood,' *v.* leah and *supra*.

LYPPIATT BARN[1] (6″) and WICK FM[2] were the homes of Roger
atte Lupзete (1332 *SR*) and William *atte Wyke* (1289 *Ass*). *v.* wic
and Lypiatt *infra* 96.

BRIDGES COURT and HANCOCK'S WELL are to be associated with
the families of John *Bridges* (1819 ParReg) and John *Hancock*
(1522 *SR*). The latter is *Hancocks-well* in 1670 (Aubrey).

ALLENGROVE FM is *Allen Grove* 1773 A and D. ASHBRIDGE
COTTAGES (6″). Cf. *Ashbridge Mead* c. 1840 *TA*. BROOK END.
Cf. *Brook House* ib. GIANTS CAVE (with tumulus). Cf. *Giants
Grave, Cave Tump* c. 1840 *TA*. It is a long barrow, with chamber.
HEBDEN FM is *Ebden* 1773 A and D. HUNDRED ACRES FM is
Hundred Acres House 1820 G. It takes its name from the
adjoining *Hundred Acres Fd* in Sopworth (*TA*), which is really
1 acre 2 roods and ironically so called, cf. *infra* 455. SHALLOW
BROOK (6″) is so named c. 1840 (*TA*).

---

[1] *Lypзate* 1438 *Eton*.   [2] *Weeke* t. Hy 8 *Rental*.

VII. THORNGROVE HUNDRED

Thornegraue, -a hundred 1086 ExonDB, *Torgravahdr* 1160 P, *Tornegravehdr* 1167, 1168 ib., *Thorngrave* 1227 Fees. The meeting-place must have been at Thorngrove in Castle Combe *infra*. The hundred is now merged in Chippenham Hundred *infra* 82. 'Thorn-thicket,' *v.* græfe *infra* 432.

Castle Combe

CASTLE COMBE

    Come 1086 DB, *Cumbe* 1186 RBE, 1242 Fees, 1249 *Ass*, 1270 Ipm

    Castelc(o)umbe 1270 (1383) Pat, 1322 Ch, 1330 Ipm

    Chastelcombe 1305 *Ass*, 1422 *Add*

    'Valley,' *v.* cumb. *Castle* from the Norman castle here.

COLHAM (6″) is *Colham* 1338 Ipm, 1346 *AddCh*, *Collamwode* 1416 *Add*, *Coleham* 1422 ib., *Colhamwood* 1513 ib. The first element is possibly col, 'charcoal,' the second may be ham or hamm, but the forms are too late for any certainty to be possible.

SHRUB HO is *la Schrubbe, la Scrobbe* 1354 *AddCh*, *la Shurbe* 1422 *Add*, *le Shrubbe, le Shrubbes* 1513, 1547 ib. This is ME *s(c)hrubbe*, 'shrub,' etc., descriptive of land overgrown with bushes or brushwood. Cf. The Shrubs (PN Sx 42).

PITLANDS[1] and WESTWAY (both 6″) may have been the homes of William *atte Putte* (1354 *AddCh*) and John *atte Weye* (1341 NI), *v.* pytt.

BYBROOK HO is *Bybrok* 1545 *Add*. 'By the brook,' *v.* By Brook *supra* 4. EAST COMBE FM (6″) is *Overcombe juxta Castelcombe* 1453 Trop. COMBE LEYS (6″) is *Comb Leaze* 1773 A and D, *v.* læs *infra* 438. CREWS CROFT (6″). Cf. *Crews Craught Wood* c. 1840 *TA*. THORNGROVE COTTAGES (6″). Cf. *Thorngrove crosse* 1422 *Add*. The hundred meeting-place, *v. supra*. WHITE GATE PLANTATION (6″). Cf. *White Gate* c. 1840 *TA*. WOODBURY HILL (6″) is so named *ib*.

---

[1] *Pitlands* c. 1840 *TA*.

Grittleton

GRITTLETON

Grutelington(e) 940 (15th) BCS 750, 1242 Fees, *-lin-* 1236 FF, *-lyng-* 1289 *Ass*, 1341 NI, *-ling-* 1354 *AddCh*, *Grutlyngton* 1327 Pat, 1360 *FF*, (*alias Gritleton*) 1601 *Recov*

Gretelintone 1086 DB, *-ton* 1186 P, 1216 ClR, 1268 *Ass*, 1291 Tax, *-ling-* 1186, 1197 P, 1268 *Ass*, 1269 FF, *-lintona* 1189 GlastInq, *-linc-* 1235–61 GlastRl, *Gretylinton* 1249 *Ass*, *Gretelingeton* 1267 Abbr

Gridelington 1241 FF

Gritelington 1279 *Ass*, *-lyng-* 1330 Ch, *-lin-* 1300 Pap

Grittelynton 1308 Cl, *-lyng-* 1321 Pat, 1327 *SR*, *Gritlington* 1641 *Sadler*

Gratelington 1316 FA

Gritilton 1337 Pat, *Grittleton al. Grittlington* 1687 *Recov*

Gretleton t. Eliz WM xxi

This is a difficult name. Ekwall (DEPN) suggests that the first element is either OE *grēot-hlinc*, 'gravel-hill,' or *Grēotlingas*, 'dwellers in a (lost) place called *Grēotlēah*.' A compound of *grēot* is possible in relation to the soil, but the assumption of a lost place-name is difficult and both suggestions are open to the objection that the great majority of the early forms point to a first element *Gruteling-*, *Greteling-*, rather than *Grutling-*, *Gretling-*. More probably we must look to an English personal name *Grytel*, cognate with the Germanic personal name *Grutilo*. Cf. Schönfeld 114 and Naumann 41. Hence 'Grytel's farm,' *v.* ingtun.

NOTE. *Blind lane, Possett lane* 1628 WM xliv.

CLAPCOTE is *Clopcote* 1196 Cur *et passim* to 1535 VE, *Cloppekote* 1263 *For*, c. 1350 GlastFeod, *Clappecote* ib., *Clapcott* 1589 *FF*. The place is on a hill and the first element must be OE **clop*, 'hillock, hill, lump,' as suggested by Ekwall (*Studies*[2] 136). The second element is cot(e).

FOSCOTE and EAST FOSCOTE are *bi este foxcotone* 940 (15th) BCS 750, *Foxcote* 1166 RBE (p), 1189 GlastInq (p), 1198 Abbr, 1268 *Ass*, *Voxcote* c. 1250 *Rental*, *Foscott* 1659 WM xliv. The meaning may be 'fox earths or burrows' rather than 'fox cottages.' Cf. PN Wo xxxix.

Grove Barn (6″) was the home of William de *Grava* (1189 GlastInq) and Richard de *la Grave* (1289 *Ass*). It is *le Grove* 1616 WM xliv. *v.* græfe *infra* 432.

Deadhill Wood (6″). Cf. *Dead Hill* c. 1840 *TA*. Limekiln Cottages (6″). The 'Limekiln' is mentioned c. 1840 (*TA*). Newlands Fm is *la Newelonde* 1279 *Ass*.

West Kington

West Kington [kaintən]

> *Weskinton* 1195 P, *Westkinton* 1196 ib., 1202 Seld i, 1227
> Fees, 1235 Ch, 1281 QW, *West Keynton* 1607 *FF*
> *Westkington(e)*, -*y*- 1211 RBE, 1236 Fees, 1244 Ipm, *West*
> *Cyngton* 1322 Cl, *Westkynkton* 1323 Ipm
> *Westkineton* 1242 Fees

Probably OE *cyne-tun*, 'royal farmstead or manor.' *West* to distinguish from Kington St Michael *infra* 100.

Church Fm (6″) and Mill Ho were the homes of Richard *atte Cherche* (1289 *Ass*) and Nicholas *atte Mulle* (1346 *AddCh*).

Ebbdown Fm (6″) is *Ebdowne* 1670 Aubrey. Hanger Wood (6″) is so named c. 1840 (*TA*). *v.* hangra. Harcombe Wood (6″) is *pastura de Harcombe* 1585 *AOMB*, *Harecombe* 1626 *FF*. 'Boundary valley,' *v.* har, cumb. It is on the parish boundary. Hazel Grove (6″) is *Hazle Grove* c. 1840 *TA*. Kingtondown Fm. Cf. *le Downe* 1585 *AOMB*. Latimer Ho (6″) is so named after Bishop *Latimer* who was Rector here (G. M. Y.). Maggs Grove Fm (6″). Cf. *Maggs Grave* (field) c. 1840 *TA*. Rownham Fm (6″). Cf. *Great, Little Roundham* ib. Shire Hill is on the county boundary. West Kington Wick. Cf. *la Wyke* 1270 Aubrey and *supra* 25.

Nettleton

Nettleton

> *Netelin(g)tone* 940 (15th) BCS 800, *Netelyntone* 1332 *SR*
> (*at*) *Netelingtone* 956 (15th) BCS 933, -*yng*- 1289 *Ass*, 1305
> Sarum, *Netelinctona* 1189 GlastInq, *Netelingtune* 1235–61
> GlastRl, *Netlington* 1256 FF
> *Niteletone* 1086 DB

Netlinton 1186 P, 1249, 1268 *Ass*, 1291 Tax, *Nett-* 1242 Fees
Netleton 1197 P, 1236 FF, 1279, 1281 *Ass*, 1331 Pat, *-tune*
  1250 *Rental*
Nettelintone, Nettelinctone 1235–61 GlastRl
Netelton 1242 Fees, 1330 Ch, 1341 NI, *-tone* 1316 FA

This is not an easy name. The forms from the charters come
from late ME transcripts. Persistent early *Net(e)lington, Netlinton* make Ekwall's suggestion (DEPN) of an adj. *netlen* as the
first element unlikely on the score of form. Perhaps we should
rather take the name as containing the OE personal name
*Nēðel found in Netteswell (PN Ess 46) and Nettlesworth
(PN Sx 465), with connective ing. Hence '*Nēðel*'s farm.'

NOTE. MARSH LANE. Cf. *le Mershe* 1562 *Add*. WOOD LANE is
Wodestrete ib.

WOODFORD BRAKE (6″). Cf. *to wodeford* 944 (15th) BCS 800.

MILL FM and NETTLETON GREEN were probably the homes of
William *Molendinar*' (i.e. 'miller') (1189 GlastInq) and William
atte Grene (1354 *AddCh*).

BROTTON HILL (6″) is *Brolton* (sic) *Hill* c. 1840 *TA*. BURTON is
Burton 1204 FF, *Borton* 1274 *Ass*. *v*. burhtun and cf. Burton
Grove *supra* 29. FOSSE FM. Cf. *Foss Hill* c. 1840 *TA*. On
Fosse Way (*supra* 15). HATCH (6″) is *Hache* 1289 *Ass, la Hachche*
(sic) 1354 *AddCh*, *v*. hæcc. HORSEDOWN is *Horse Down* c. 1840
TA. LITTLEWORTH PLANTATION (6″). Cf. *Littleworth* ib. and
infra 455. LONG DEAN is *Langdene* 1451 Trop. 'Long valley,'
v. denu. LUGBURY is *Lugburys* 1670 Aubrey. There is no camp
here, only the chamber of a long barrow. NETTLETON SHRUBB.
Cf. *the Shrubbe* 1604 PCC. Not far from Shrub Ho *supra* 78.
PRIORY FM. Part of the parish belonged to Malmesbury Abbey.
WALL LEAZE FM (6″). Cf. *Wall Leaze* c. 1840 *TA* and læs
infra 438. WESTFIELD FM. Cf. *le west fylde* 1585 *AOMB*. Cf.
supra 41.

VIII. CHIPPENHAM HUNDRED

Cepeham hundred 1086 ExonDB, *hundred de Cepeham* 1130 P, *Chepeham* 1176 ib., *Cippeham* 1196 Cur. *v.* Chippenham *infra* 89.

Biddestone

BIDDESTONE [bidstən]

Bedestone 1086 DB, 1181 P, 1337 Pat, *-ton* 1222 FF

Bedeneston' 1187 P

Buddeston 1215 ClR, 1464 BM, *-tun* 1221 ClR, *Butteston* 1428 FA

Budeston(e) 1236 Fees *et passim* to 1350 Ipm

Bydesden' 1274 Ass, *Byddeston* 1339 Ipm, 1523 *SR*, *Bydeston* 1339 Pat, (*al. Budston*) 1575 *FF*, *Biddeston* 1339 Cl, *Bidston, -y* 1487 Pat, 1552 *SR*

Biedestone 1297 Lewis, *Bittson* 1539 *Phillipps*, *Bydson, Bedson* 1585 WM xxi, *Biteston* 1675 Ogilby

If the 1187 form is to be trusted, the first element is probably a personal name *Bīedin*, a derivative with an *n*-suffix of *Bīeda*. The second element is tun. Cf. Ekwall DEPN *s.n.*

WEAVERN FM. Cf. *Weverysplace, Weversmylle* 1536 *MinAcct, Weaverne meade* 1640 WIpm. It was the home of William de *Wevere* (1332 *SR*). The name preserves the old name of the By Brook (*v. supra* 4).

THE BUTTS (6″) is so named in 1841 (*Devizes*). Cf. *infra* 425. CHAPSCROFT WOOD (6″). Cf. *Chapps Mill* 1712 *DuLa*. ERKWELL WOOD (6″) is *Harequill Brake* c. 1840 *TA*. The second element is probably OE *cwylle*, 'spring,' cf. *supra* 58. HONEYBROOK FM is *Honey Brook Farm* 1841 *Devizes*. SKIMPOT (6″) is probably a nickname of contempt. Cf. Skimpot Fm (PN Herts 31) and *infra* 455. TYNING BELT (6″). Cf. *New, Over, Lower Tyning* ib. and *infra* 449. WHITE CLIFF WOOD (6″) is *White Cliff Coppice* ib.

Box

Box

Boczam (acc.) 1144 AC

la Boxe, -a 1181 P, late 12th BM, 1242 Fees, 1259 Ipm, *la Bosse* 1216 ClR, *Boxe juxta Ferlege* 1226 SarumCh, *la Box* 1340, 1367 Cl, *Box* 1435 ib.

This is OE *box*, 'box-tree,' cf. Box in Awre (Gl), *la Boxe* 1221 *Ass*, and in Minchinhampton (ib.), *la Box* 1307 *Custumal*, and Box Hill (PN Sr 270). Box is not common here now, but "in all probability it took its name from the Box-trees which grew there naturally, but now worne-out" (Aubrey NH 55). *Ferlege* is Monkton Farleigh *infra* 120.

ALCOMBE is *Alecumbe* 1279 *GDR* (p), *-combe* 1307 WIpm, 1332 *SR* (p), *-coumbe* 1307 WIpm, *Alcombe* 1497 Ipm, *Awcon* 1650 *Map*, *Alcombe or Akeham* 1773 A and D, *Aucombe* c. 1840 *TA*. The forms are too late for any certainty. The name may be from OE *Ǣllan cumb*, 'Aella's valley,' *v*. **cumb**.

CHAPEL PLASTER [pleistər] is *Pleystede* 1268 *Ass*, *Chapell' de Pleystede* 1425 *GDR*, *Chappelfylde*, *Playster* 1558 *FF*, *The Chapell(e) of Playster* 1670 Aubrey, *of Plaistow* 1728 WM xlv, and was probably the home of John *atte Pleistede* (1333 *SR*). There was a chapel here, belonging to the monks of Glastonbury. The second part of the name is an OE *pleg-stede*, 'place of play,' identical in meaning with the more common **pleg-stow**, with which indeed it has been confused in later records. The latter often appears later as *Plestor, Playster*.

DITTERIDGE

    Digeric 1086 DB, *-riga* 1167 P (p)
    Dicherigga ib., *-rug'* 1236 FF, *-rigge* 1249 ib. *et freq* to 1428 FA, with variant spellings *-rugge*, *-rygge* and *Dyche-*, *Dichrigge* 1276 *Ass*, *Dychrugge* 1283 *FF*
    Dicheriche 1345 *Ass*, *Dichriche* 1412 FA, *Dichricke* 1553 WM x *Dykerigge* 1376 IpmR
    Dytchridge al. Ditridge 1581 *FF*, *Ditcheridge* 1628 WM xliii, 1728 ib. xlv

'Dike or ditch ridge,' *v*. **dic**, **hrycg**. Perhaps so named because the ridge is a spur of land running eastwards from the Fosse Way.

HATT Ho is *Hatt* 1575 *FF* and was the home of Reginald de *Hette* (1259 WIpm), Robert de *Hatte* (13th Trop) and John *atte Hatte* (1485 *Ct*). The name is identical in origin with Hett (PN NbDu 113) and Hatt (Co), *la Hatte* 1305 *Ass* and is from

OE *hætt*, 'hat.' The reason for the name is not obvious. Possibly it may have been a nickname for one of the tumuli in the grounds of Hatt Ho (cf. Old Hat Barrow *infra* 343), but the application is not obvious. It might also have application to some feature in the landscape itself but no site has been discovered which readily lends itself to such an interpretation[1].

HAZELBURY Ho is *Heselberi* 1001 (14th) KCD 706, *-bur* 1232 Ch, *-bere* 1235 Fees, *-biri* 1245 WM xvi, *Haseberie* 1086 DB, *Haselberga* 1189 WM xvi, *-bur'* 1239 *Ass*, *-berg* 1265 Pat, 1268 *Ass*, *-ber'* 1268, 1289 ib., *-berwe* 1300 Ipm, *-bury* 1325 *FF*, 1342 Cl, *Hasilberg(h)* 1249 *Ass*, 1261 Ipm. The forms are conflicting and it is difficult to decide whether the original second element was **burh** or **beorg**. Probably **burh** was the original one but there was early confusion. The first element is the common plant-name.

HENLEY is *Henlega* 13th Trop, *-leya*, *-e* t. Hy 3 *Lacock*, 1355 Pat, *-lege* 1399 *AddCh*, *Henele* ib., *Henly* 1629 WIpm. 'At the high clearing,' *v*. **leah**.

RUDLOE HO

> *Riglega* 1167 P (p), *Ryggelawe*, *-i-* 1249 FF, 1268, 1310 *Ass*, 1398 Trop, *Riglawe* 1268 *Ass*, *Ruggelewe* 1330 *FF*
> *Ridlawe* 1249 Ipm, *Rydlawe* 1338 Trop, *Redelawe* 1409 *FF*, *Ridelawe* 1476 ib., *Ridlowe* 1497 Ipm, *Rudlow* 1713 Recov
> *Rudlowe otherwise Ridgelow* 1767 ib.

There can be little doubt that this is a compound of OE **hrycg** and **hlaw**. Hence 'ridge hill or barrow.' It lies on a well-marked ridge. The sound group [dʒl] was simplified to [dl]. For the survival of the ME *u*-sound cf. Introd. xx.

SLADE'S FM is *Slade* t. Hy 2 BM, *la Slade* t. Ed 1 *Lacock*, 1333 AD iv (p), *le Slade* 1623 WIpm, *Slade livinge* 1628 WM xliii. OE **slæd**, 'valley,' etc., the modern *s* being pseudo-manorial. *livinge* is here used in the sense 'holding of land, tenement,' cf. Poundliving (PN D 585).

---

[1] We are much indebted to Mr H. A. Druett for all the trouble he has taken on our behalf in enabling us to arrive even at these somewhat negative conclusions.

WADSWICK is *Wadeswica* late 12th BM, *-wyk(e)* 1341 *Rental*, 1385 *FF*, 14th *Bradenstoke*, 1413 *Ct*, *Waddeswyk* 1310 *Ass*, 1314 *FF*, *-wik* 1512 *Ct*, *Wadsick al. Waddeswicke* 1623 WIpm, *Wodswick* 1758 *FF*. Ekwall (DEPN) notes the parallels of Wadsley and Wadsworth (PN WRY 197–8). We may add Wadgworthy (Co), *Wadesworthi* 1298 *MinAcct*. In all these names the first element is genitival in form and in Wadswick itself the only possible significant word, viz. wæd, 'ford,' which could be brought in in explanation, is inapplicable, so we are doubtless right in assuming with Ekwall (*loc. cit.*) a personal name *Wæddi* or the like in explanation of it. *v.* **wic**.

WORMCLIFF (6″) and WORMWOOD FM appear as (*a*) *la Wormeclyve* 1274 *Ass* (p), *Wornyclive* (sic) 1332 *SR* (p), *Wormecliffes mede* 1558 *FF*, *Wormecliffe* 1629 WIpm, and (*b*) *Wormhirde* 1259 WIpm, *atte Wormherd* 1312, 1345 *Ass*, 1322 *FF* (all p), *Wormyerd* 1391 *AddCh*, *Wormherde, Wormehurde* 1409, 1418 *FF*, *Wormerde* 1411 ib., *Wormewood* 1684 *Recov*. These places are far apart, but the first element in each is probably OE *wyrm*, 'worm, snake, dragon,' possibly in the genitive plural form *wyrma* in the first name. Wormcliff is at the foot of a steep slope and there may have been some legend of a dragon associated with it. *v.* **clif**. The second element in Wormwood is **geard**, 'enclosure,' as in Derriads *infra* 90, and the name may be descriptive of a snake-infested farm. See Addenda *supra* xxxix.

HILL HO FM was the home of Nicholas de *la Hulle* (14th *Bradenstoke*). It is *Hill House* 1628 WM xliii.

CHENEY COURT[1], COLE'S FM, DREWETT'S MILL[2] (6″), HULBERT'S FM[3] (6″), HUNT'S WOOD[4] and LENT'S GREEN (6″) are to be associated with the families of John *Chayne, Chenye* (1478, 1555 Kidston), Robert *Cole* (1362 *Cor*), John *Drewett* (1715 WM xlv), John *Hulbert* (1642 *SR*), Simon *Hunt* (1572 *FF*) and Thomas *Lent* (1727 WM xlv).

ASHLEY is *Aissheley* 13th Trop, *Ayslegh juxta la Boxe* 1281 *Ass*. 'Ash clearing or wood,' *v.* **leah**. BARN HO (6″). Cf. *Barne close*

---

[1] Cf. *Cheyneys Courte* 1530 *MinAcct, Cheynes Court* 1554 Pat, 1773 A and D.   [2] *Drewett's Mill* 1773 A and D.
[3] Cf. *Hulberts Hayes* c. 1840 *TA*.   [4] *Hunts Wood* c. 1840 *TA*.

1623 WIpm. BEN MEAD (6″) is *Ven Mead* 1630 *Map, Ben Mead* c. 1840 *TA*. Possibly 'fen mead.' Cf. Sutton Veny *infra* 154. BLUE VEIN. Cf. *Blue Vein Turnpike* 1773 A and D. BOTLEAZE WOOD (6″). Cf. *Bod lease* 1630 *Devizes*. BOX FIELD (6″) is so named in 1650 (*Map*). CHAPEL BARN. Cf. *Chapel Field* ib. CHARLWOOD (6″) is *Charle Wood* 1630 *Devizes*. 'Churls' wood.' Cf. Charlwood (PN Sr 287). ENNOX WOOD (6″) (locally *Hinnocks*) is *Innok* 1258 FF, *Innox* 1549 NQ iv, *close called Innockes* 1623 WIpm, *v. infra* 134. FOLLY FM (6″), *v. infra* 451. GROVE HO (6″) is *Grove* 1539 *FF*, (*le*) 1623 WIpm. HUNGERFORD BOTTOM (6″). Cf. *Hungerford Wood* c. 1840 *TA*. It takes its name from a small manor of the Hungerford family (Aubrey 56). INGHALLS COTTAGE (6″). Cf. *Ynyhalle* 1391 *AddCh*, *Engolls meadowe* 1623 WIpm, *Ingolles* 1630 *Devizes*, *Inglis* c. 1840 *TA*. KINGSDOWN is *Kyngesdon juxta la Boxe* 1334 *Ass*. KINGSMOOR (6″) is *Kingsmore Coppice* 1623 WIpm. LITTLEFIELD (6″) is *Little Field* c. 1840 *TA*. LONGLEASE COTTAGES (6″). Cf. *Long Lease* ib. *v.* læs *infra* 438. MIDDLEHILL is *Myddlehyll* 1558 *FF*. MILL HO. Cf. *Milsplat* 1721 *Recov*. *v.* splot *infra* 446. OLD PITS (6″) is *the Tile Pitte Feilde* 1630 *Map*. QUARRY HILL. Cf. *Haselbury Quarre, le Quarrefield* 1623 WIpm. See quarre *infra* 445. ROADHILL WOOD (6″). Cf. *Rode Hill* 1630 *Devizes*, leading to Rode (So). ROUND WOOD (6″) is so named c. 1840 (*TA*). STOWELL WOOD (6″) is *Stowerd* 1630 *Map*. TOTNEY FIRS (6″) is close to *Totenhill* ib. TYNING COTTAGES (6″). Cf. *The Tyning, Great, Little Tyning* c. 1840 *TA* and *infra* 449. WASHWELLS (6″) is *Wash Wells* 1630 *Devizes*. WEAVERN COTTAGES (6″). Not far from Weavern Fm and By Brook. *v. supra* 4, 82. WHITEWOOD is *Wytewode* t. Hy 3 RegMalm, *Whitewood Peece* 1623 WIpm. WOODLANDS is *Great, Little Woodlands* c. 1840 *TA*.

Bremhill

BREMHILL [*olim* brimbəl]

　　Brœmel 937 (14th) BCS 716, *Breomel* 937 (c. 1125) ib. 719
　　Bremel 937 (14th) ib. 716–7, 1190 P *et passim* to 1428 FA, *Brembel* 1268 *Ass*, *Bremul*(*l*) 1332 *SR*, 1416 Trop
　　Bremela 1065 (14th) KCD 817, *Bremele* 1233 Bracton *et freq* to 1342 Pat
　　Breme (sic) 1086 DB

Bromel 1196 Cur, *Bromell* 1316 FA, *Brumele* 1344 Pat
Bremhill 1430 ib., *Bremehill* 1516 Recov, *Bremehyll al. Bremble*
1561 ib., *Bremble* 1637 WIpm, *Bremell al. Bremhill* 1744
Recov

OE **bremel**, 'bramble, collection of brambles.' Cf. *infra* 424.

AVON is *Avene* 1065 (14th) KCD 817, 1242 Fees, 1249 *Ass*, 1428
FA, *Avon* 1642 *SR*, the hamlet taking its name from the river
supra 1.

BREMHILL WICK is *Brembelwyk, Bremleswyk* 1279 *Ass*, *Wyke*
1428 FA, *Bremell weke* 1564 *Add*. 'Dairy farm attached to
Bremhill manor,' *v.* **wic** and *supra* 25.

CADENHAM is *Cadehā* 1086 DB, *Cadenham* t. Hy 3 RegMalm,
t. Ed 1 Dugd iv, (*juxta Bradenstoke*) 1295, 1347 *FF*, *Kadenham*
1242 Fees, *Caddenham* 1546 LP, *Cadnam* 1595 *FF*, (*al. Caddenham*) 1665 *Recov*. '*Cada*'s ham.' Close at hand is Catcombe in
Hilmarton *infra* 268, while in the bounds of Bremhill itself we
have *Cadeburne* (BCS 717) now Cat Brook *supra* 5. All must
take their name from the same man. This personal name is
found also in *Cadinglæge* in Westwood (W) (KCD 658) and in
Cadley *infra* 245.

CHARLCOTE is *Cherlecote* c. 1300 *Malm*, *Charlcotte* 1564 *Add*.
'**Cot(e)** of the churls or free peasants,' *v.* **ceorl**.

FOXHAM is *Foxham* 1065 (14th) KCD 817, 1219 SarumCh *et
passim*, *Voxham* 1553 *Phillipps*. The meaning is 'ham or hamm
where foxes were common.' For *Voxham*, see Introd. xxi.

GODSELL FM (6″) is *Godeshulle* 1225 *Edington*. Possibly 'God's
hill,' cf. Godshill (Wt), *Godeshull* c. 1270 Winton, but the
personal name *God, Godus* is recorded from Wiltshire in DB
(TRE). Cf. Feilitzen 262 and Godswell *infra* 148.

HARE STREET FM. Cf. *Hare Street Mead* 1775 *Map*. It lies by
HARE STREET (6″), presumably from OE *herestræt*, 'army-road,'
cf. Hare Street (PN Ess 118). Usually the term is used of a more
important road.

HAZELAND is *Heselholt* 1227 FF, *Haselholt(e)* 1279 *Ass*, c. 1300 *Malm*, 1284 RegMalm, *Hasland* 1570 *Add*, *Hasill holte alias Haseland* 1576 ib. Originally 'hazel wood,' *v.* holt.

SPIRTHILL is *Speerful* (sic) 1065 (14th) KCD 817, *Spertella* 1153 RegMalm, *Spercella* 1156 ib., *Sperchulle* 1284 ib., *Sperthull* 1305 *Ass*, *Spirthille* 1535 VE, *Spirte-* 1546 LP, *Spert-* 1575 *FF*. The form from KCD is clearly corrupt. The first element would seem to be the word *spirt*, 'jet of liquid,' noticed in Spurt Street (PN Bk 158), Spurtham (PN D 642). Although the charter in KCD is a late copy, there is no reason to suppose that the place-name did not exist in the 11th century, and if so the history of the word is carried back to OE times. There is a spring close at hand.

STANLEY is *Stanlege* 1086 DB, *-legam* 1107 (1300) Ch, *-leia*, *-lea* 1187 AC *et passim*, with variant spellings *-legh*, *-ley(e)*, *-le*, *abbas de Stonleg'* 1206 Abbr, *Stonlegh* 1346 *Ass*, *Standley* 1558–79 ECP, 1773 A and D. 'Stony clearing or wood,' *v.* leah. STANLEY BRIDGE (6″) is *Stanley bryge* 1570 *Add*, replacing an earlier *Stanleyesforde* (1348 *Cor*).

STOCKHAM MARSH is *Stokham* 1289 *Ass*, *Stokeham marshe* 1553 *Devizes*, *Stockham*, *Stockham mershe* 1564 *Add*. Perhaps a compound of stocc, 'stump' and hamm.

NAISH HO is *Nasshehouse* 1570 *Add* and was probably the home of Nicholas *atten Assche* (1327 *SR*), i.e. 'at the ash,' with the usual ME development.

LEEKSHEDGE FM is to be associated with the family of William *Lyke* (1340 WIpm). It is *Lykeshedge* 1571 *FF*, *Lickshedge* 1820 G.

AVON GROVE WOOD (6″) is *Haven Grove* 1775 *Map*. BENCROFT FM is *Bencrafte* 1592 *Add*. BREMHILL FIELD (6″) is *Bremell field* 1570 ib., with reference to the common fields of the parish. BREMHILL GROVE is *Bremells grove coppes* 1564 *Devizes*. CHARWOOD COPSE (6″). Cf. *Charrwood greene* 1576 *Add*. ENNIX WOOD (6″) is *le Inhoke* 13th RegMalm, *le Innocke hedge* 1570 ib. *v. infra* 134. GATE FM. Cf. *The Forest yate* 1593 *Devizes*, with reference to one of the gates of Pewsham Forest. HAM VILLA (6″). Cf. *le Hame* 1564 *Add*, and fields called *Ham* and *Gt. Ham* 1775

(O.G.S.C.). *v.* **hamm.** HANGER PARK is *Hangre* 1284 RegMalm, *Hangerfeld* 1416 Trop, *v.* hangra, 'slope.' HONEYBED WOOD (6″) is *Honybett coppice* 1564 *Add.* *Honeybed Fd* 1773 *Map* is adjacent, with a stream flowing through it. Doubtless soft and marshy ground. KINGFIX BRIDGE. Cf. *Kingfix Mead* 1775 *Map.* It is possibly to be connected with *Kyngebrydge sharde* 1576 *Add*, *v.* sceard, 'gap.' LOW BRIDGE is *Low Bridge Close* 1775 *Map*, *Ley Bridge* 1816 O.S. MOUNT PLEASANT (6″). Cf. *infra* 455. PARK FM (6″). Cf. *le parke pale* 1592 *Add.* SIDEROW FM (6″) is *Syderowe* ib. UNDERDOWN COTTAGES (6″) is *pastura voc. Underdownes* 1570 ib., *Under Downs* 1820 G. WEST END is *Westende house* 1564 *Add.*

Chippenham

CHIPPENHAM

> (*to*), (*æt*) *Cippanhamme* 9th ASC (Ā) *s.a.* 878, 880–5 (c. 1000) BCS 553, c. 1000 (*s.a.* 853) Asser, (*æt*) *Cippan homme* 901–24 BCS 591, *Cyppan hamm* 930 ib. 1343
>
> *Chipehā* 1086 DB, -*ham* 1176 P, 1208 Cur
>
> *Chepehā* 1086 DB, -*ham* 1156, 1158 P, 1232 Ch
>
> *Cheppeham* 1155 RBE, 1161 P *et freq* to 1235 Fees
>
> *Cipeham* t. Hy 2 (1268) Ch, 1241 FF
>
> *Chyppeham, -i-* 1177 P, 1189 WM xvi, 1211 RBE, 1219 Abbr, *Chypham* 1313 Ch
>
> *Chippenham* 1227 Ch *et passim*, *Chypp-* 1307 Ipm
>
> *Chuppeham* 1250, 1259 Ipm
>
> *Cyppe-, Cippeham* 1255 RH, *Cyppenham, -i-* 1276 Cl, 1317, 1331, 1345 Pat, *Sippen-* c. 1300 Gaim, *Shippen-* 1319 Cl
>
> *Chep(p)enham* 1305 Ass, t. Ed 3 *For*, 1404 *Ass*, 1435 Cl
>
> *Chipnam, -y-* 1455 Pat, 1493–1500 ECP, 1503 *FF*, *Chippyngham* 1541 LP, *Chipping-* 1597 *FF*

'*Cippa*'s hamm.' See further *s.n.* Cippenham (PN Bk 217) and cf. Chipley (So), *Chippelegh* 1253 Ass, -*ley* 1280 Ipm.

NOTE. BATH RD. Cf. *Batheweye* c. 1300 *Malm.* THE CAUSEWAY is *The Causway* 1603 BorRec. CRICKET'S LANE is *Cricketts lane* 1674 ib. EMERY LANE. Cf. *Ymbyri* 1314 WM iv, *Emerygate* 1592 *Add.* FOGHAMSHIRE. *v. infra* 90. HIGH ST is *alta strata* 1326 Trop, *alto vico* 1378 BorRec. Cf. *supra* 21. KING'S ST is *vico regali* 1369 BorRec. MARKET PLACE is (*in*) *foro* 1412 MinAcct, *The Markett Place* 1580 BorRec. NEW ROAD may be identical with *le Newestrete* 1406 Trop. ST MARY ST is *Seynt Marystrete* 1514, *Seynt Maries strete* 1561 *Ct*, from the parish church of St Mary. THE SHAMBLES is so named in 1570 (BorRec) from OE *scamol*, 'stall'. WOOD LANE is so named in 1559 (ib.).

Lost names include *Langstret* 1245 WM xvi, *Luttesweye* 13th RegMalm (cf. Lutsey Fm *infra* 248), *Coltestret* 1347 Trop, *Cokestrete* 1487 *MinAcct*, 1514 *Ct*, *Chese Markett* 1570 BorRec, *the Buttercrosse* 1685 *Add* (all three, the last two probably parts of the Market Place), *le Backe lane* 1561 *Ct*, *Corsham waye* 1605 (i.e. the road to Corsham *infra* 95), *Rotten Reawe* 1608 (probably a term of contempt, 'rats' row'), *the Derry* 1671 BorRec. For the last *v. infra* 257.

ALLINGTON is *Alentone, Allentone* 1086 DB, *Alinton(e)* t. Hy 3 RegMalm, 1276 Abbr, 1278 Cl, *Alyn-* 1286 Pat, (*juxta Chippenham*) 1307 Ipm, *Alyngton(e)* 1289 Ass, (*juxta Chipenham*) 1397 BM, *Allington* 1590 *Add*. 'Ælla's or Ælle's farm,' *v.* ingtun.

CHEVERDEN FM [tʃivədən] is *Chiverden(e)* t. Ed 1 RegMalm, 1304 Pat, 1305 *Ass*, 1332 *SR* (p), *Chyverden* t. Ed 1 *For*. It is possible that the first element here is OE *cefer*, 'beetle,' a form which is found side by side with the more common *ceafor*. Cf. NED *s.v. chafer* sb.[1] *e* is often thus raised to *i* before following *v*, though the change is not often evidenced as early as the 14th century. *v.* denu.

DERRIADS FM [*olim* derits] is *Durhirda, Durhierd* 1167 P (p), *Derierd* 1227 Ch, *Durierd* 1232 (14th) *Lacock*, 1245 WM xvi, *Dereyerd* 1514 *Ct*, *Duryards* 1605 BorRec, *Duriard* 1647 *Recov*, *Derratt feild* 1685 *Add*, *Derrits* 1773 A and D. A compound of OE *deor*, 'animal,' and geard, 'enclosure, yard.' Cf. Duryard (PN D 436).

FOGHAMSHIRE[1] (street-name) is *Fokene juxta Chyppeham* 1289 *Ass*, *Fokene* 13th RegMalm, *Fokenestret* 1370 Cor, *Foggramshire, Foggamshyre* 1514 *Ct*, *Foggamshier* 1564 *Add*, *Foggamshere* 1587 *FF*. This district of Chippenham clearly takes its name from the tributary of the Avon which is called in 1232 in the Lacock Cartulary (14th) *aqua que vocatur Fokena, aqua que vocatur Focane*, and with regard to which we also have the phrase *ultra Fokene*. The stream is now known as Hardenhuish Brook. For the etymology *v.* Addenda *supra* xl.

---

[1] Canon Goddard notes for us that this name is given locally in Hilmarton to a group of cottages lying on the other side of the brook from the village. This would seem to be a case of transference of a name from one place to another. Cf. the history of Giggan St in Codford *infra* 164.

FOWLSWICK FM is *Fugeleswik* 1231 Pat, *Fuleswik* 1236 FF, *Foweleswyke* t. Hy 3 RegMalm, *Fouleswik* 1273 *AD*, 1284 RegMalm, *-wyk* 1300 Ipm, *Foleswick* 1773 A and D. 'Fugol's **wic** or dairy farm.' *Fugol* is the OE *fugol*, 'bird,' here no doubt used as a personal name. Cf. Fugglestone *infra* 226.

LOWDEN is *Lolledon* 1249 *Ass et freq* to 1464 BM, *Loldon* 1474 Pat, *Lowdon* 1642 *SR*. 'Lolla's hill,' *v.* **dun**.

MAUD HEATH'S CAUSEWAY takes its name from one *Maud Heath* who lived at Langley Burrell in 1474. She left money to maintain a footway from Wick Hill to Chippenham Clift. Tradition has it that she was a market woman but this has been denied in favour of some more substantial woman of the neighbourhood. For further details *v.* WM i, 256 ff. It is called *le Cawseye* 1592 *Add*.

ROWDEN is *Rueden'* 1208 Cur (p), *Rughedon(a)* 1224 Bracton (p), 1229 Cl (p), 1257 ib., *Ruge-* 1245 WM xvi, t. Ed 1 *Lacock*, *Rowen-* 1275 Cl, *Rugh-* 1280 Abbr, *Rowe-* 1300 Ipm, *Rou-* 1307 ib. 'Rough hill,' *v.* **ruh, dun**. The name referred originally to ROWDEN DOWN, called *Rowdensdowne* in 1561 (*FF*).

SHELDON

> *Shyldune* t. Hy 3 RegMalm, *Shildene* 1428 FA, *-done* 1432 BM
> *Shuldon(e)* 1287 Ipm, 1320 Ch, 1324 *FF*, 1337 Pat, *Schul-* 1338 Ipm, *Shulden* 1417 BM
> *Sholdon* 1308 Ipm

The name is probably identical in origin with Sheldon (PN Wa 48), a compound of OE **scylf** and **dun**. The place is on a hillside, though the slope here would seem to be a very gradual one.

TYTHERTON LUCAS and EAST TYTHERTON

> *Tedelintone, Tedrintone, Terintone* 1086 DB, *Tederington* 1249 *Ass*
> *Tiderinton* c. 1155 StOsmund, 1199 P, *Tidrinton(e)* 1196 Cur, 1198 Abbr, 1242 Fees, *Tidderinton* 1248 *AD*, *Tiderintun* 1272 AD vi, *Tyderyngton* 1428 FA

Tuderington 1202 FF, 1249, 1268 *Ass*, -*yng*- 1279 ib., 1291 Tax, (*Lucas*) 1289 *Ass*, *Tuddrintone* 1211 RBE, *Tudrintone* t. Hy 3 RegMalm, *Tuderinton* 1242 Fees, 1273 Ipm, (*Lucas*) 1303 *FF*, *Tuderyngton Lucas* 1428 FA

Tethryngton Lucas 1513 *Ct*, *Titherton Lucas* 1603 PCC, *Tytherton Lucas al. West Tytherton* 1721 *Recov*

In PN D (654) *s.n.* Tytherleigh it was noted that in that name and also in Tytherley (Ha) the first element was, as suggested by Professor Ekwall, the OE adj. *tīedre*, 'fragile, weak,' and it was suggested that the same adj., used as a personal name of the nickname type, might lie behind Tytherton in Wiltshire. Since then Ekwall (DEPN *s.n.* Tytherington in Cheshire) has suggested that we may have this personal name not only in the Cheshire place-name but also in Tytherington (Gl), Tytherington *infra* 168, and the present place. Cf. also Tytherington in Marston Bigot (So), *Tyderington* 1242 Ass, *Tudryngton* 1425 FF. The interpretation would in all these names alike be ' *Tīedre*'s farm,' *v.* ingtun. Adam *Lucas* had a holding here in 1249 (WIpm.)

FIELD'S FM (6″), GASTON'S FM[1], THE HAM[2] (6″) and WOODLANDS[3] (6″) were the homes of Roger *in ȝe Felde* (1327 SR), Richard *atte Gerston* (1299 WIpm), Roger *atte Hamme* (1384 AD) and Walter de *la Wudelande* (1289 *Ass*). *v.* feld, gærstun, hamm. In the first two the *s* is probably pseudo-manorial.

BAILEY'S FM, BATTEN'S FM, BAYNTON HO, BEARD'S FM (all 6″), HARDEN'S FM[4], LORD'S BARN[5], PITT'S COTTAGES (6″), SCOTT'S MILL and STOKES FM are to be associated with the families of Richard *Bayly* (1512 *Ct*), William *Baten* (1523 *SR*), John *Beynton* (1453 Trop), Thomas *Beard* (1763 ParReg), William *Harding* (1245 WM xvi), Thomas *Lord* (1642 *SR*), Thomas *Pytt* (1523 ib.), John *Scott* (1535 *Rental*) and Nicholas *Stokes* (1425 Pat).

BOSMERE FM (6″) is *Barsmore* 1773 A and D. BUMPER'S FM (6″) is *Bumper* ib. CAMP BARN (6″). Cf. *Camp Corner* c. 1840 *TA*.

---

[1] *le Garston* 1564 *Add*, *Gaston* 1592 ib.
[2] *The Ham* 1685 ib. Cf. *Great Ham* c. 1840 *TA*.
[3] *le Wodelonde* t. Hy 3 RegMalm.
[4] Cf. *Hardyngesbreche* 1414 Trop, *v.* bræc.
[5] Cf. *Lordshill* 1666 NQ vi.

CURRICOMB FM (6″) is *Currycombe* 1773 A and D. ENGLANDS (6″) is *Ende-*, *Indeland* 1514 *Ct*, *Eng-*, *Inglands* 1604, 1695 BorRec, *Inlands* 1659 ib. It may be identical with *Hinlond* 1275 WM vi, i.e. *inland*, close to the reputed site of the king's villa (WM vi, 82). Cf. *infra* 439. THE FOLLY (6″). *v. infra* 451. FOREST FM. Cf. *Forrest leaze* 1640 WIpm. *v.* læs. FROGWELL is so named c. 1840 (*TA*). Cf. *Froggehull* 1274 WIpm. HOLY WELL (6″). Cf. *Holywell Meadow* c. 1840 *TA*. HUNGERDOWN is *Hungerdowne* 1685 *Add*. *v.* Hungerdown *supra* 73. ISLE OF REA (6″). Cf. *Raymead* c. 1840 *TA*. From OE (*æt þære*) *īeg*, 'at the island.' LANDSEND is *Lands End* 1820 G. LAN HILL is *Lannell Hill* c. 1840 *TA*. Probably *Lannell* is for earlier *Langenhill*, 'long hill,' and the second *hill* is redundant, cf. Lannock (PN Herts 146). MIDDLEHILL FM. Cf. *Middle Hill* c. 1840 *TA*. MONKTON HO is *Monketon* t. Hy 8 *AOMB*, *Mounckton lands* 1605 BorRec, *Monckton juxta Chippenham* 1626 WIpm. Malmesbury Abbey held land in the parish. MOUNT PLEASANT (6″). *v. infra* 455. MOUNT SCYLLA (6″) is *Mount Sylla Farm* c. 1840 *TA*. So also in Colerne *infra* 95. NEW LEAZE FM. Cf. *Neweleaze* 1628 *FF*. PIPSMORE FM (6″) is *Pippesmore* 1270 *For* (p), *Popplesmore al. Pipsmore* 1605 BorRec. POUND FM (6″). Cf. *le Pounde* 1564 *Add*, i.e. 'cattle enclosure.' SHIPWAY'S FM (6″) is *Schepwashe* 1362 *Cor*, i.e. sheep-wash. STARVEALL FM is *Starveall* 1747 NQ ii, *v. infra* 455. WESTMEAD is *Westmed(e)* 1245 WM xvi, 1364 AD i.

Colerne

COLERNE [kʌlərn]

> *Colerne* 1086 DB *et passim*, *Colerme* (sic) 1186 RBE
>
> *Culerna, -e* 1156 RegMalm, 1177, 1180 P *et passim* to 1302
> Orig, *Cullerne* 1572 *Recov*, t. Jas 1 ECP, 1651 *FF*, 1728
> WM xlv
>
> *Cullerne al. Collern* 1270 Ipm, *Collerne* 1327 *Ass*, *-arne* 1585
> WM xxi

The early and persistent alternation between *Colerne* and *Culerne* makes the name difficult to interpret. The second element is clearly ærn, 'house.' *col-ærn* might well denote a house where charcoal was made, used, or stored. Ekwall (DEPN *s.n.*) suggests that there was an alternative OE form *cul*, corresponding to OSw, Dan *kul*. Cf. *Culputtehalve infra* 434. The modern pronunciation derives from the *Cul*-forms.

DONCOMBE [dʌnkəm] is *Donenecombe* 1363, 1382, 1406 *NewColl*, *Donencombe* 1363 ib., *Doncomb* 1471 WM xxxiv, *Duncombehill* 1522 *NewColl*. The forms are too late for any certainty to be possible. It may be for earlier *Dunnan cumb*. '*Dunna*'s valley,' *v*. cumb. The adj. *dunn*, 'gray,' is also possible. Cf. Middendorff *s.v.*

EASTRIP is *Asshetrop* 1327 Banco, *Asshethrop(e)* 1406, 1522 *NewColl*, *Eastrupp* 1665 ib., *Estropps* 1712 *DuLa*, *Eastrop* 1820 G. 'Ash-tree village or hamlet,' *v*. þorp. The later alteration may be in part due to folk-etymology, the place lying to the north-east of Colerne.

EURIDGE FM (6″) is *Ewerigga* 1156 RegMalm, *Ywerigge* 1248 ib., *Iwerugge* c. 1250 *Rental*, *-rigge* 1288 RegMalm. 'Yew-tree ridge,' *v*. iw, hrycg. "At Euridge they (i.e. yews) also grow indifferently plentiful" (Aubrey NH 55).

LUCKNAM is *Lukeham* 1199 FF, *Lokenham* 1274, 1327 *Ass*, 14th Bradenstoke, t. Ed 3 *For*, *Lockeham* 1284 RegMalm, *Lokkenham* 1332 *SR* (p), *Lukmans* (sic) t. Eliz *LRMB*, *Luckenham* 1638 FF, *Lucknam* c. 1830 RCH. '*Locca*'s or *Lucca*'s ham(m).'

THE RIPPLES (6″) is *Repelis* 1363, *Rypples* 1382, *Rypelles* 1406, *les Rupples* 1522 *NewColl*. This is probably the plural of OE *rippel*, 'strip of land.' See PN Wo 58 and PN K 219, 403, 574.

SEWELL BARN (6″). Cf. *Sywelegh* 1382 *NewColl*, *Sewell*, *Sewells Coppice* 1712 *DuLa*. A spring is marked here and there are a good many others in the neighbourhood, so this may be another example of 'seven springs' with the element *legh* from leah added in the first form. Cf. PN Nth 40, PN Sr xliv, PN Wa xlvi.

THICKWOOD is *Ticoode* 1086 DB, *Thikwude* 13th AD v, *þycwode* t. Hy 3 RegMalm, *þickewde* c. 1250 *Rental*, *Thikkewode* 1289 *Ass*, *Thikwode* 1339 Trop. The name probably referred to a dense wood. Cf. Thinwood (Co), *Thynnewode* 1289 *Ass*, 1317 Exon, *Thunnewode* 1342 NI (p).

WIDDENHAM FM (6″) is *Wydenham, Wedenham* 1363, *Wydenham* 1382 *NewColl, Widenham mead* 1583 WM xiii, *Widham* 1773 A and D. The first element is probably OE *wiðegn*, 'withy,' hence 'hamm where withies grew.'

HALL FM was the home of Thomas de *Aula* (1289 *Ass*) and Edward *atte Halle* (1332 *SR*). It is *Hall Farme* 1670 Aubrey.

DAUBENEY'S FM, TILLEY'S WOOD and TRIMNELL'S FM (all 6″) are to be associated with the families of William *Dabney* (1730 ParReg), John *Tyly* (1701 ib.) and William *Trimmell* (1642 *SR*).

ABBOTSCOMBE WOOD (6″). Cf. *mede called Abbotts* t. Eliz *LRMB*. Possibly from the Abbots of Stanley, who had a holding (Aubrey 122) at Euridge. BREACH WOOD (6″). Cf. *Breches* 1363 *NewColl*, *v.* bræc. BURY CAMP. Cf. *le Bury* 1397 *NewColl, In burywood is a Camp, double workes* 1670 Aubrey, *v.* burh. COLERNE DOWN is *Cullerne Down* t. Eliz ChancP. FIDDLE CLUMP (6″) is so named from its shape. GILLING GROVE (6″) is *Julyans grove* t. Eliz *LRMB,* 1570 *Add.* LICTUM SPRING (6″). Cf. *Lictums* c. 1840 *TA*. MARTIN'S CROFT (6″) is so named ib. Cf. *Martynesham* 1406 *NewColl.* MEDLEYS WOOD (6″). Cf. *Medd Leys* c. 1840 *TA*. MONKS WOOD (6″). Cf. *Munke close* t. Eliz *LRMB*. From the holding of the Abbot of Stanley at Euridge Fm *supra* 94. MOUNT SCYLLA (6″) is *Mount Scilla* 1841 *Devizes.* It stands on the edge of a deep valley. NORTHWOOD FM is *Northwode* 1268 *Ass, Norwood* 1712 *DuLa.* ROOKS' NEST FM (6″) is *Rook's Nest Farm* 1841 *Devizes.* STONEY BRIDGE (6″). Cf. *Stony Bridge Mead* c. 1840 *TA*. THE TYNING (6″). *v. infra* 449. VALE COURT (6″). Cf. *Vale Vue House* c. 1840 *TA*. VINEYARD FM (6″). Cf. *Vineyard Tyning* ib. *v. infra* 449. WATERGATES (6″) is *Wateryate* 1406 *NewColl, Watergate* 1773 A and D, *v.* geat. WATERSNAPS COTTAGE (6″). Cf. *Water Snap* c. 1840 *TA*. 'Marshy ground,' *v.* snæp *infra* 446. WESTWOOD FM is *Westwode* 1363 *NewColl*.

Corsham

CORSHAM [*olim* kɔsem]

    Coseham 1001 (14th) KCD 706, 1336 Pat
    Cossehā 1086 DB, *Cosseham* 1130 P, 1134 Cl, 1424 Pat
    Corsham 1160 P *et passim, Corsholm* 1201 Cur

Cosham 1185 P *et freq* to 1367 Pat, *Cossam* 1196 Cur, 1242 Fees, 1296 Pat, t. Eliz WM xxi

Cosham al. Coshamlond 1411 Pat, *Corsham al. Cosham* 1572 FF, (*oth. Cossum*) 1741 *Recov*

Probably '*Cosa*'s or *Cossa*'s ham.' Cf. Cosham (Ha) (*æt*) *Cosham* 1015 (12th) ASC (E), 1204 Cur, 1212 Fees, *Cos(s)eham* 1086 DB, 1174 P, 1236 *Ass*. The r is probably a later insertion, for the topography of the place makes any connection with the Celtic *cors*, noted under Corston *supra* 50 and Corsley *infra* 152, most unlikely.

NOTE. *via regia voc. London Roade* t. Ed 6 *Ct*.

BROCKLEES FM (6″) is *Brockele* 1279 *Ass*, *grava de Brockele* 1281 ib., *Brocklyes lane* t. Jas 1 *Ct*. OE *brocca lēah*, 'badgers' wood or clearing,' *v.* leah and græfe *infra* 432.

BYDE MILL (6″) is *Bidemille* 1273 Aubrey, -*mulle* t. Ed 1 *Lacock*, *Bydemel* 1300 *For*, *Bydemulle* t. Ed 3 ib., *Bydemylle* 1450 Trop. The mill lies on an unnamed tributary of the Avon which joins that river at Reybridge in Lacock. For the history of the name, *v.* Bydemill Brook *supra* 4.

GASTARD is *Gatesterta*, -*e* 1154 RBE, 1167, 1168, 1179 P *et freq* to 1279 *Ass*, -*sterd*' 1172 P, *Gastard* 1428 Trop, 1773 A and D, *Gadsteed* 1601 PCC. 'Goats' tail of land,' i.e. where they feed, *v.* gat, steort.

HARTHAM is *Heorthā* 1086 DB, *Herthā* ib., *Hertham* 1202 FF *et freq* to 1333 *SR*, *Hortham* 1196 Cur, 1464 Trop, *Hurtham* 1257 *For*, *Hoert*- 1281 *Ass*. The first element is *heorot*, 'hart, deer.' The second element is therefore most likely hamm, 'enclosure.'

LYPIATT FM [lipjət] (6″) is *la Lupeʒete* t. Hy 3 RegMalm, *Lepeyatis* 1414, *le Lepeyate, le Lupeyate* 1449, *Lypezatestrete* 1453 Trop and was the home of William *atte Lupʒate* (1332 *SR*). This name is found in an OE charter (BCS 1282) in the form *hlypgeat*. It is no doubt identical with the modern *leapgate*, a 'low gate in a fence that can be leaped by deer but not by other animals.' Cf. Lypiatt (PN Gl 104), Lipgate Fm in Brewham

(So), *la Lupeȝete* 1276 Ass (p), Lypeate in Holcombe (So), *atte Lipeȝate* 1327 SR (p). Further examples in Wiltshire are Lyppiatt *supra* 77, Henry *atte Lupeyete* (1327 *SR*) in Alderton, John *atte Lupghate* (1333 *SR*) in Nettleton, Walter *atte Lupeyate* (1333 *SR*) in Mere, *le Lypeȝete* (1430 *Ct*) in Bromham, *la Lepyate* (1488 *MinAcct*) in Trowbridge, *Lypyate* (1564 *Add*) in Bromham. Its frequency is doubtless due to the large amount of ancient forest land in Wiltshire.

NESTON is *Neston* 1282, 1288 *Ass*, 1332 *SR* (all p), 1337 Pat, 1373 Trop, 1503 Ipm. It stands on an isolated hill which may perhaps be here described as a *næss*, 'ness, headland.' *v.* tun and cf. Neeston (NCPNW 62).

PICKWICK is *Pykewyk(e)* 1268, 1289 *Ass*, 1327 *SR* (p), 1333 AD iv, 1375 Trop, *Pycwyk* 1279, 1281 *Ass*, *Pickweeke* 1686 *Rental*. The name seems to be a compound of OE *pic*, 'sharp point,' etc., and *wic*, 'dairy farm.' Upper Pickwick stands on a well-marked spur of land. Cf. Picton and Pickle Wood (NCPNW 42).

POCKEREDGE FM (6″) is *Polkerugge* 1346 *AddCh*, *-rygge* 1363 *NewColl* (p), *Pockeridge* t. Jas 1 *Ct*, and was the home of Henry de *Poltrigge* (1327 *SR*). The early forms vary too much for any suggestion to be made as to the first element, *v.* hrycg.

THINGLEY is *Thingele* 1275 WIpm, *Tyngle* 1289 *Ass*, *Thyngele* ib. (p), 1332 *SR* (p), 1349 Trop, 1356 *Ass*. The first element in this name looks like late OE *þing*, 'assembly,' possibly of native rather than Scandinavian origin, as has commonly been assumed (PN Bk xvii), but the persistent *Thinge*-forms are a little surprising; cf. Tinkfield Fm *infra* 313. The second element is leah, 'clearing.'

THRASHNELL BARN[1] (old 6″) is *Threshnels* 1625 *Ct*, *Thrashnells* 1641 *SR*, *Dresnols* 1773 A and D, *Dressnells* c. 1840 *TA*, and was the home of Henry de *Throstenhale* (1327 *SR*) and Henry de *Throstenhill* (1337 Pat). This is perhaps from OE *þrostlena healh*, 'nook or corner of land frequented by thrushes,' *v.* healh. The *s* is probably pseudo-manorial.

---

[1] South-south-east of Pond Close Fm, south-west of Boyd's Fm.

BROADSTONE COTTAGES[1] (6″), STOWELL FM[2], WESTROP[3] and WESTWELLS[4] were probably the homes of Thomas de *Bradestan* (1340 Pat), Richard de *Stawell* (1255 RH), Henry de *Westthrop* (1332 *SR*) and Walter de *Westwell* (1305 *Ass*). *v.* þorp, **wielle**.

HILLSGREEN, JAGGARDS HO[5], LOCK'S CROSS[6] (6″), MONK'S FM[7] and PITS FM (6″) are to be associated with the families of William *Hill* (1523 *SR*), Henry *Jagard* (1327 ib.), John *Lok* (1345 *MinAcct*), William *le Monek* (1333 ib.) and John *Pytte* (1523 *SR*).

AVILL'S FM (6″) is *Avell* t. Jas 1 *Ct*. BEAN CLOSE (6″). Cf. *Bean Ground* c. 1840 *TA* and *infra* 452. BECKHILL COTTAGES (6″). Cf. *Beckhill Wood* ib. CHAPEL KNAPP. Cf. *Chapell clos* 1453 Trop, *Chapel Nap* 1841 *Devizes*, *v.* cnæpp. THE CLEEVE (6″) is *The Cleve* c. 1840 *TA*, *v.* clif. COPENACRE (6″) is *Coppenacre* ib. COPPERSHELL (6″) is *Copper Shells* ib. CORSHAM SIDE is so named in 1773 (A and D). EASTON is *Eston* 1375 Trop, *Easton* t. Jas 1 *Ct*. 'East farm,' *v.* tun. It is just east of Westrop *supra*. ELLEY GREEN (6″). Cf. *Broad Elley* c. 1840 *TA*. FOLLY FM. Cf. *infra* 451. GREENHILL (6″) is *le green hill close* t. Jas 1 *Ct*. GUYER'S COTTAGES (6″) is *Guyers* 1773 A and D. HOLYWELL FM is *Hollywell* c. 1840 *TA*. HUDSWELL is so named in 1773 (A and D). KNOWL FM (6″) is *Knowl* c. 1840 *TA*, *v.* cnoll. THE LINLEYS is *Linleaze* t. Jas 1 *Ct*, perhaps a compound of *lin*, 'flax,' and *læs*, 'pasture land.' Cf. *infra* 438. MEADLANDS (6″) is so named c. 1840 (*TA*). MOOR BARTON (6″) and GREEN are *la More* 1268 *Ass*, *Moorgreen* t. Jas 1 *Ct*, *v.* mor, 'marsh,' and **barton** *infra* 451. MYNTE LODGE. Cf. *Myntemede* 1332 Trop, *Minte-* 1503 *MinAcct*. Presumably 'mead where mint grows.' OVERMOOR (6″) is *Overemore* t. Hy 3 RegMalm. PARK FM. Cf. *parcum suum de Corsham* 1242 Cl, *Est-*, *Westpark* 1300 Ipm. PATTERDOWN is so named c. 1840 (*TA*). POND CLOSE FM (6″) is *Pond Close* ib. POUND MEAD is *Poundemede* 1503 *MinAcct* from *pound*, 'cattle enclosure.' POUND PILL (6″). Cf. *infra* 444.

---

[1] *Broadstone* 1841 *Devizes*.
[2] *Stowell mead* t. Jas 1 *Ct*. Cf. Stowell *infra* 326.
[3] *Westhorpe* 1400 Inq aqd, *Westropp* t. Jas 1 *Ct*.
[4] *Westewell* 1382 Trop, *Westwells* t. Jas 1 *Ct*.
[5] *Jargetts* 1609 PCC, *Jaggard Ho* 1773 A and D.
[6] *Lockes* 1650 *ParlSurv*.   [7] *Monkes* 1429 Trop.

Prestley Wood (6″). Cf. *Prestley* c. 1840 *TA*. Presumably 'priests' clearing,' *v.* leah. Purleigh Barn (6″) is *le Purleys, Purley Rayles* t. Jas 1 *Ct*. Probably from *purley, purlieu infra* 453. It is in the old forest of Pewsham. Ridge is *le Rygge* 1503 Ipm, *Rudge* t. Jas 1 *Ct*. Sandpits Fm is *Sandpits* c. 1840 *TA*. Silver Street (6″) is so named ib. Smith's Mead (6″). Cf. *Smithes parke* t. Jas 1 *Ct*. Vauxhall Fm is *Vossells* ib., *Faxhall* 1773 A and D. Velley (6″) is *Velly quarr'* t. Ed 6 *Ct*.

Hardenhuish

Hardenhuish [hɑrniʃ]

> *Heregeardingc hiwisce* 854 (11th) BCS 469
> *Hardenehus* 1086 DB, *Hardehiwis* 1177 P
> *Herdenewiz* 1242 Fees, *Hardenewiche* ib., *Herdenehywys* 1258 Ipm, -*hewys* 1268 *Ass*, *Hardenehywish'* 1289 ib., *Hardene Hywich* 1291 Ipm, *Hardynghuwyssh* 1410 Pat
> *Hardnyshe* 1316 FA, *Hardnesshe* 1512 Ct, *Hardnash* 1535 VE, *Harden Hewysh al. Harnysh* 1568 FF, *Hardenish* 1746 ib.

'The hiwisc or family-holding of one *Heregeard,*' *v.* ing.

Yew Stock (6″) is *Yeo Stock* c. 1840 *TA*.

Kellaways

Kellaways

> *Tuderinton(e)* 13th RegMalm, (*Kaylewai*) 1257 *For*, *Tuderyngton Kaylewey* 1289 *Ass*, (*Caillewey*) 1412 FA, *Tutheryngton Cayleweys* 1453 FF, *Tytherton Keylewayes* t. Eliz WM xxi
> *Tiderington* 1227 FF, *Tyderinton Kaylewey* 1268 *Ass*
> chapel of *Caillewey* 1304 Sarum, *Keylewayes* 1585 FF, *Keilwaies* 1628 WIpm, *Kellawayes* 1637 ib., *Kelwayes* 1651 FF, *Kalloways or Kelways* 1773 A and D

Originally one of the manors of Tytherton in Chippenham (*supra* 91–2). It was held by William de *Caillewey* (13th Reg-Malm) and by Elias de *Kaillewey* (1227 FF). Later the place-name itself was dropped from the compound as in Chenies and Latimer (PN Bk 221, 225), Virley (PN Ess 323), Cottles and Pinkney (*infra* 110, 115), the manorial addition alone remaining.

KELLAWAYS BRIDGE is *Caisway* c. 1540 L, *Kelloways bridge* 1584
WM xxi. The first form may derive from the neighbouring
Maud Heath's Causeway (*supra* 91).

Kington St Michael

KINGTON ST MICHAEL [kaintən]

   (*at*) *Kingtone* 934 (15th) BCS 704, *Chinctuna* 1174–91 BM,
     Kincton(*a*) 1189 GlastInq, 1232 Cl, 1233 Pat, *Kink-* 1242
     Fees, *Kingtun* 1244 BM

   Chintone 1086 DB, *-tun'* 1156, 1158 P, *Kinton*(*e*) 1186 ib.,
     1211 RBE, 1221 ClR, *Kyn-* 1238 Cl

   Kyngton Michel 1279 Ass, *Kynton Mich'is* 1281 QW, *Kyngton*
     Michaelis 1428 FA, *Michells Kynton* 1503 Ipm, *Kynton Sci*
     Michaelis al. Miles Keynton 1672 Recov

   Minchinkinton 1284 Cl, *Munchenekyngton* 1321 ib., *Mynchene-*
     1356 Ass

   Estkington 1327 ib.

Either 'royal farm' (OE *cyne-tun*) or 'king farm' (OE *cyning*),
probably the former. *Minchin* from the Priory of Benedictine
nuns here (*infra* 101), *v.* myncen and cf. Minchinhampton (Gl).
The memory of the nuns is preserved in a field called *Minchin
Piece* (c. 1840 TA). *Michael* from the dedication of the parish
church.

   NOTE. NASH LANE. Cf. *le Nayshe* 1517 WM iv. 'At the ash,'
v. Naish *supra* 88.

BULIDGE Ho[1] is *Bolhides* 1606 PCC, *Bulhyde* 1636 Recov and
was the home of Thomas de *Bolehide* (1275 Aubrey) and John
de *Bulhyde* (1333 SR). 'Bull-hide (of land),' *v.* hid. The *s* is
no doubt pseudo-manorial.

CROMHALL FM [krɔmǝl] is *Crumhale* 1250 Aubrey, 1258 Ass (p),
1279 ib., *Cromhale* 1268 ib. (p), 1428 Aubrey, *Cromwells* 1670 ib.
A compound of OE *crumb*, 'crooked,' and healh, 'angle, corner.'

EASTON PIERCY is *Estone* 1086 DB, *Eston Pyeres, Peres, Pieres*
13th Aubrey, *Eston Peres juxta Kyngton Michũs* 1304 Ass, *Eston
Peers al. Eston Pyers* 1559 Recov, *Eston Pearce* 1578 FF, *Easton*

     [1] Now again officially *Bolehide* (E. H. G.).

Pearcey al. Easton Pearce 1702 *Recov*, *Easton Percy* 1773 A and D. 'East farm,' *v.* tun. It is west of Kington and must have been so named because east of Yatton Keynell *infra* 114. The manorial addition is the personal name *Pier(r)e*, 'Peter.' *Peter de Estune* was a tenant in the parish in 1189 (GlastInq) and in 13th-century deeds printed by Aubrey we have mention of William filius *Petri* de Eston and Johannes filius *Petri Fitz-Pieres*.

MOORSHALL FM is (*betweox*) *morsceagan* 1043 (c. 1225) KCD 767, *la Morshawe* 1279 *Ass* (p), 1360 *FF*, *Moreshall* 1517 WM iv, *Moreshawe Mead* 1582 NQ iii. 'Wood or copse in the marshy place,' *v.* mor, sceaga.

SWINLEY FM is *Swineleghe* 1243 Aubrey, -*le* 1249 *Ass*, *Swynlegh* c. 1350 GlastFeod, -*ley* 1450 IpmR. 'Swine wood or clearing,' *v.* leah.

DOWN FM. Cf. *The Down* 1773 A and D. FOLLY ROW (6″). *v. infra* 451. GRUBBINS WOOD (6″). Cf. *Hither, Further Grubbins* c. 1840 *TA*. HEYWOOD FM is *Haiwode* 1189 GlastInq, *Heiwode* t. Hy 3 RegMalm. 'Enclosed wood,' *v.* Heywood *infra* 149. LODGE FM is so named in 1820 (G). PRIORY FM. Cf. *Priory Downe* 1670 Aubrey. There was a Priory of Benedictine nuns here. TOR HILL is *Toor Hill* c. 1840 *TA*, *v. infra* 448. WHITE WOOD is *Wytewode* c. 1400 *Malm*.

Kington Langley

KINGTON LANGLEY

> *Langhelei* 1086 DB, *Langela* 1189 GlastInq, *Langeleghe* 1243 Aubrey, *Longley* 1547 *SR*
> *Northlangele* 1289 *Ass*, -*leye* 1305 ib., 1307 *FF*, *North Longley* 1544 LP
> *Langley Kington* 1636 *Recov*, *Kington Langley* 1699 ib.

'Long clearing or wood,' *v.* leah. *North* with reference to Langley Burrell *infra* 105. *Kington* from Kington St Michael near by.

FITZURSE FM is *Nether Langley, Langley Fitzurs* 1568 *FF*, *Langley Fitzhurst* 1746 ib. and represents the DB manor of *Langhelie* of which one *Urso* was under-tenant (TRW). In 1243

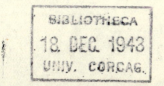

(Aubrey) Jordan *Fitzurse* held the manor, called in the same document Jordanus *Filius Ursi*.

CALIFORNIA COTTAGES (6″) are in a remote part of the parish, cf. *infra* 455. COLDHARBOUR (6″) is *Cold Harbour* c. 1840 *TA*. See *infra* 451. MORRELL COTTAGES (6″) is *Marhill (Lane)* 1746 *Sadler*, *Marhill* 1773 A and D, 1820 G. The cottages lie on the parish boundary close by a spring and it is probable that both forms alike are a corruption of an earlier compound *Marwell* or *Marrell* from (ge)mære and wielle. NEW HOUSE GREEN is so named c. 1840 (*TA*). SOUTH SEA FM (6″) is *South Sea Barn* 1773 A and D. Possibly so named because in a remote corner of the parish. STEINBROOK HO (6″). Cf. *Stein Brook* c. 1840 *TA*. SYDNEY'S WOOD (6″) is *Sydenham Wood* 1839 *Devizes*. WHITE-LANDS FM is *Whitelands* c. 1840 *TA*.

Lacock

LACOCK [leikɔk]

 Lacok 854 (14th) BCS 470, t. Hy 1 (1329) Ch, 1230 ib., Pat, 1232 Cl, *Lacoc(h)* 1086 DB, *Lachocha* 1166 P, *Lakoc* 1189 WM xvi, 1252 BM, 1267 SarumCh, 1306 Pap, *Lacoc* 1198 P, 1223 ClR, 1229, 1238 Cl, 1242 Fees, *Lacoq* c. 1210 BM, *Lakok* 1255 Cl

 Lacheoche 1185 Templars

 Lacoke 1193 P, *Lacocke* 1316 FA, *La Cocke* 1543 LP

 Laycock 1439 IpmR, *-cocke* 1584 *FF*, 1653 *Recov*

This is a difficult name. Lacock lies on a small tributary of the Avon and it may be that the stream was called *Lacuc*, a diminutive of the common word *lacu* for a small stream. If that is the case the history of the name is quite different from that of Laycock in Yorkshire with similar forms, for the topography of Laycock would not admit of this explanation. The matter is further complicated by the nearby Lackham *infra* 103. This looks as if it might be a compound of *lacu*, but there are diffi-culties in such an interpretation. There is the formal difficulty that if it were a compound of *lacu*, we should expect *Lakeham* rather than *Lakham* in the early and later forms alike. On the topographical side, Lackham lies in a bend of the Avon, which can hardly be described as a *lacu*, while the little stream on the south side of Lackham Park is even smaller than that on which Lacock lies, so that the latter could hardly be 'little *lacu*' if this one were '*lacu*.' Perhaps the explanation of Lackham should be sought elsewhere. The first element may be OE *lēac*, as in Latton *supra* 45. Leckhampstead (Berks), Leckhampton (Gl), and Lackham denote the 'ham(m) where leeks grew,' or more probably, where garden-plants generally grew.

NOTE. MONS LANE is *Manneslane* 1308 NQ viii.

BEWLEY HO is *Beuelee* 1257, t. Ed 3 *For*, *-leye* c. 1290 *Lacock*, 1392 *AD*, 1415 Cl, *-legh* 1330 AD iv, *Beuleye* 1332 *SR* (p), *Beauley*, *Bewley* 1540 *MinAcct*, *Beawley* 1542 LP. Perhaps a compound of OE *bēaw*, 'gadfly,' and leah, 'clearing.' Cf. Beaford and Bowcombe (PN D 86, 284).

BOWDEN PARK is *Bovedon(e)* c. 1240 *Lacock*, 1249 *Ass* (p), 1270 *For*, *-doune* 1332 *SR* (p), 1336 FF, *Bouedon* 1374 *FF*, 1411 IpmR, *Bovedon al. Bowdon* 1561 *FF*, *Bowden al. Bowdowne* 1539 *MinAcct*. '(Place) above the down,' from OE (*on*) *bufan dūne*.

LACKHAM is *Lacham* 1086 DB, 1242 Fees, 1252 BM, 1289 *Ass*, *Lakham* 1232 *Lacock*, 1249 *Ass*, 1300 Ch, 1307 Ipm, *Lackeham* 1513 *Ct. v.* Lacock *supra* 102.

NASH HILL is *le Hasshe* 1270 *For*, *le Asshe* 1304 Pat, *loc. voc. Atten Asche* 1331 *For*, *Naysshahull* 1375 Trop, *Naisshehulle* 1430 AD iv, and was the home of Richard *atte Nayssch* (1341 NI), i.e. 'At the(n) ash.' *Hill* is a later addition. The form ASH HILL, apparently for the same hill, is found in Pewsham *infra* 109.

NOTTON is *Natton* 1232 *Lacock*, 1257 *For*, 1286 FF, 1536 *Min-Acct (juxta Lacok)* 1304 *FF*, *Notton* 13th AD iv, *Netton* 1284 CtWards, *Naatone* 1309 AD iv. 'Cattle farm,' from OE neat, 'cattle,' and tun. Cf. Netton (PN D 258) and *infra* 364.

REYBRIDGE [reibəˑrdʒ][1] is *Ebrigge* t. Ed 1, t. Ed 3 *For*, 1330 Inq aqd, *Ebrigge juxta Lacok* 1394 *Ass*, *Raybrigge* 1513 *Ct*, *Rhe*

---

[1] There is a local rhyme

On Philip and Jacob
The bells rang at Lacock;
The great bell went with such a surge
That e' fell in at Reyburge. (G. M. Y.)

Bridge c. 1540 L, *Rye Brudge* 1539 *MinAcct, Rea bridge* 1670 Aubrey, *Ebridge* c. 1840 *TA*. It was the home of Robert *del Ebrige* (1232 *Lacock*) and John *atte Rebrigge* (1384 NQ viii). 'Bridge by the river,' from ME *atter ebrigge*, *v.* æt, ea. The **ea** is here the Avon.

Wick Fm is *Wyke* 1232 *Lacock, Lacokeswyk* 1289 *Ass, Cherlaweswyke* 1316 *CtWards*[1], 14th AD v, *Charloweswyke* 1371 *CtWards*[1], *Wyke* 1338 Pat, *Lacokwyke* 1415 AD iv, *Weke* 1576 *FF, Week al. Charles Week* 1742 *Sadler*. 'Dairy farm belonging to Lacock,' *v.* wic. *Cherlawe, Charlowe* must be the surname of its sometime owner or occupier. It can hardly go back to the Lacock tenant *Carlo* (TRE) as suggested in Kidston (67).

Lacock Bridge was the home of Galfridus *atte Brigge* (1333 *SR*). It is called (*de*) *ponte de Lacok* c. 1250 *Lacock, Lacockesbrigge* 1370 *Cor*.

Arnold's Fm (6″) is to be associated with the family of Richard *Arnold* (1642 *SR*). It is *Arnoldes* 1632 WIpm.

Abbey Fm (6″) recalls the abbey of Lacock. The Barn (6″). Cf. *Barn Fd* c. 1840 *TA*. Briary Wood (6″) is *Briery Wood* ib. Catridge Fm is so named in 1718 (*FF*). It is *Catrich Fm* in 1773 (A and D). Cuckoo Bush Fm (6″). Cf. *Cuckoo Bush* ib. Folly Cottages (6″). Cf. *The Folly* ib. and *infra* 451. The Griffin and Griffin's Wood (both 6″). Cf. *Griffins Wood* c. 1840 *TA*. Halfway Ho Fm is *Halfway House* 1773 A and D. Inwood (6″) is *bosco de Lacok' voc' Inwode* 1289 *Ass, Inwood* 1540 *MinAcct*. The meaning is no doubt 'wood in the demesne land.' Cf. PN Sr 138 and *infra* 450. Mill Fm. Cf. *le Melehamme* 1308 NQ viii, *v.* **myln, hamm.** Nethercote is *Nether(e)cote* ib., 1337 Pat. 'Lower cot(e).' Plucking Grove (6″) is *Plucky Grove* c. 1840 *TA*. Rey Mill (6″) is so named ib. *v.* Reybridge *supra* 103–4. Showell Fm is *Showell* 1773 A and D. Stroud Fm (6″). Cf. *Strowd lease* 1540 *MinAcct*, *v.* strod, 'marshy land,' and læs. Whitehall Fm (6″) is *Whitewell* 1490 *For*.

[1] References from Kidston (266, 274).

Langley Burrell

LANGLEY BURRELL

Langelegh 940 (14th) BCS 751, *Langhelei, Langefel* 1086 DB,
  Langelega 1181 P *et freq* to 1392 Pat, with variant spellings
  -leye, -lee, (Burel) 1289 *Ass*, 1333 *SR, (Borel)* 1327 Pat
Longley Burell 1535 VE, *Longlye Buryll* 1592 *Add*

'Long clearing or wood,' v. **leah**. Peter *Burel* held the manor
in 1242 (Fees), probably a descendant of *Borel* who was under-
tenant TRW.

BARROW FM is *Barwe* 1227 Fees, *Barewe* 1237 Cl, *(la)* 1255 RH,
1351 *Ass*, *la Baruwe* 14th *Bradenstoke* (p), *Little Barrowe* 1640
WIpm. Probably OE **bearu**, 'grove.'

COCKLEBURY (6″) is *Kokelesberga* 1181 P, *Cokelbergia* 1189
WM xvi, *-berge* 1232 Ch, *-bere* 1236 FF, *-berwe* t. Ed 1 RegMalm,
Ko(c)kelberwe, C- 1232 *Lacock*, t. Ed 1 RegMalm, 1249 FF,
Cockeleberewe 1289 *Ass*, *Kokkelbergh* 1301 Ipm, *Cokkeberwe*
1332 *SR*. Aubrey (NH 45) notes that the rough stone about
Chippenham, especially at Cockleborough, is full of petrified
cockles. Hence perhaps 'cockle-hill,' v. **beorg**. Otherwise,
'corn-cockle hill' (E.J.S.).

PECKINGELL ['pekindʒel]

Pegenhullis 940 (14th) BCS 751, *Peggehull* 1268, *Peginhulle*
  1289 *Ass*, *Pegyngill* 1332 *SR*, *Peggynghulle* t. Ed 3 *For* (all p)
Pechinhilla 1189 WM xvi
Pegingehulle 1273 Aubrey, *Pegangehull* 1289 *Ass* (p), *Pegingge-
  hull* 1305 ib.
Pichinghulle 1281 ib.
Pekynghulle 1298, 1304, 1312 ib., *Pekyngille* 1332 *SR* (p)
Peckingell, Peckinghull 1517 WM iv, *Peckyngell* 1581 *Recov*

This is not an easy name, partly because of the uncertainty as
to the medial consonant in the first element. There is some
evidence for an OE personal name *Pecg*, presumably allied to
the common word *peg*, though that word is first recorded in late
ME. It seems to be found in Pegswood (PN NbDu 156) and
pecges ford (BCS 1023) in Staffordshire. A weak form *Pecga* is
perhaps found in Pignes in Bridgwater (So), *Peghenes* 1086

ExonDB, *Pegenes* 1208 FF, *-nesse* 1240 Ass, 1250 Fees, *Peggenasse* 1219 ib., and possibly also in Paglinch in Foxcote (So), *Pegeling* 1296 Ipm, *Pekelinch* 1303 FA, *Peglinche* 1304 Ipm, *Peclynch* 1327 SR, *Pykelynch* 1346 FA, *Pekelynche* 1380 FF, *Pegelynche* 1431 FA, with the same interchange between *k(c)* and *g* as in Peckingell. Peckingell may be 'hill of the people of *Pecg(a)*' (*v.* ingas), but it should be noted that on the whole it would be easier to explain *g* from earlier *c* than *ck* from earlier *g*. The only alternative in the case of Paglinch and Peckingell would be to take the first element as *peac*, 'peak,' and take Peckingell as coming from OE *peacingahyll*, 'hill of the dwellers on the projecting hill,' but that does not seem a very likely name.

HILL CORNER was probably the home of Robert de *Hulle* (1333 *SR*).

RAWLINGS FM is to be associated with the family of John *Rawlinges* (1569 *For*).

BIRDS MARSH is *Birch Marsh* c. 1840 *TA*. GREENWAY LANE (hamlet) is *the greene waye* 1605 BorRec, *Greenway Lane* 1773 A and D. GROVE FM. Cf. *Grove Leaze* 1638 WIpm, *v.* læs. MARSH FM. Cf. *Outer, Inner Marsh* c. 1840 *TA*. PEW HILL would seem to be the same place as *Cawsehyll* 1592 *Add*. Close by was *Pewemeade al. cawseymeade* ib. *v.* Pewsham Forest *supra* 14. The *cawse(y)* is Maud Heath's Causeway *supra* 91. POOR LAINS COPPICE (6″) is *Poor Laines Coppice* c. 1840 *TA*. Cf. *Layne Hills* 1640 WIpm and *infra* 439. THORNHILL FM. Cf. *cottage called Hayward alias Thornehill* 1638 ib.

Leigh Delamere

LEIGH DELAMERE [lai dælimɔ·r]

> *Leye* 1236 FF, *la Legh, Lega* 1242 Fees, *Lye juxta Lokyngton* 1412 FA, *Legh juxta Castelcomb* 1534 *FF*, *Lye Dallamer* t. Eliz WM xxi, *Lydallimore* 1637 *Phillipps*, *Leigh de la More* 1641 *Sadler*, *Lye Dallemore* 1645 WM xix, *Ligh Dallimor* 1722 *Recov*

'Clearing or wood,' *v.* leah. Adam de *la Mare* held the manor in 1236 and 1242. Cf. Fisherton de la Mere *infra* 161.

SEVINGTON

> (æt) *Seofonhæmtune* 1043 (12th) KCD 767
>
> *Sevamentone* 1086 DB, *Sevenhamton* 1281, *Sevehampton*,
> *Sovenehampton* 1289 *Ass*, *Sevenhampton* 1522 *SR*, *Seving-*
> *hampton* 1662 Wood
>
> *Seyvyngton* 1512 *Ct*, *Sevington* 1607 WM xix, *Seventon* 1773
> A and D

In PN Wo (35), when dealing with a lost *Sevenhampton* in that county, that name was associated with Sevenhampton (Gl), Sevenhampton *supra* 27, the *seofonhæmtun* which gave rise to Sevington, and with Seavington (So), DB *Seovenamentone*, and it was suggested that all alike were compounds of OE *seofon*, 'seven,' hæme and tun, and that the term denoted a village or hamlet with seven ham(s) or homesteads, and reasons were given why, on the basis of early custom, a group of more than six homesteads (e.g. seven) might have significance as against six or less. That there may have been real significance in these numbers receives some slight measure of further support from the name Syrencot discussed *infra* 366.

Ekwall (DEPN *s.n.*) suggests that these names take their rise from compounds of tun with *seofonhæme*, denoting 'the dwellers at places called "seven wells"' and the like. Such hæme-compounds attached to the first element of a place-name are regular formations, as in *Neoðerehæma gemære* (KCD 764) from *Neoðeretun* (BCS 235), now Netherton (PN Wo 150). He supports this suggestion by noting that Sevington in Tichborne (Ha) is near *syfanwyllan* (BCS 731) in the bounds of that parish and that there is a *Seofenwyllas* (BCS 165) in the bounds of Aston Blank, three or four miles from Sevenhampton (Gl). Unluckily, it is impossible to build much on these foundations. *Seofenwyllas* is four to five miles from Sevenhampton, we have no evidence of any settlement at *Seofenwyllas*, and it is difficult to see how people from these springs can be thought of as settling at Sevenhampton and giving name to it. For Sevington (Ha) unluckily we have no early forms at all, and it is difficult to be at all sure that Sevington is really from *seofon hæmatun*, especially when it is by no means certain that *syfan wyllas* itself denotes 'seven springs,' for *syfan* is not a common OE form for *seofon*. In the case of the other places we have no trace of any 'seven springs,' and it may be noted further that none of the numerous other 'seven wells' known to us have ever given rise to names of this type. Cf. *s.n.* Seawell (PN Nth 40), where mention is made of Sinwell (Gl), Sowell (PN D 565), Seven Wells Fm in Stoke Doyle (Nth) and Sywell (PN Nth 139) where note is made of Sewell (PN BedsHu 129 and O), and other minor examples. Ekwall (*loc. cit.*) does not exclude the possibility of compounds of *seofon* with other elements. It should be noted however that such compounds are not very common and, so far as our knowledge goes, have never given rise to Sevenhampton-names. We have noted Seabeach (PN Sx 68), Sevenoaks (PN K 64–5), Seaborough (PN Ess 164, PN Do 303), Sevenash (PN D 50), Zeaston (ib. 287) and Soussons (ib. 482), but no corresponding Sevenhampton.

No certain conclusion is possible, but it should perhaps be noted that the limitation of these Sevenhampton names to the adjacent counties of Worcestershire, Gloucestershire, Wiltshire and Somerset is in favour of the 'homestead' solution. Other *seven*-names are widely scattered and if they are the source of the Sevenhamptons there seems no reason why we should not find examples of this name as widely distributed as the other *seven*-names[1].

GREEN BARROW FM (6″). Cf. *Green Barrow* c. 1840 *TA*. There is a tumulus here. RAT HILL (6″). Cf. *Rathill* ib. RYLEY's FM (6″) is *Rileys Farm* 1773 A and D, *Reylis Farm* 1841 *Devizes*.

Pewsham

PEWSHAM HO

The earliest forms found which refer to this place as distinct from the forest *supra* 14 are *Peuisham* 1448, *Peuesham* 1449 Pat, *Pewsham* 1610 *FF*. The parish is a modern one, formed from Calne, Bremhill, Chippenham and Corsham in 1840 (Kelly). For the etymology *v. supra* 14.

LOXWELL FM is *Lokeswelle* 1158 RBE, *Locheswella* 1158 P, *Lokeswelle* 1171, 1202 ib., 1242 Fees, *Lockeswelle* 1245 WM xvi,

---

[1] It is perhaps worthy of note that in the Pembroke Survey (1570) we have mention of a field called *Sevenhams* in South Newton.

Lokkeswelle t. Ed 1 *For.* '*Locc*'s spring,' *v.* **wielle**. Cf. Loxbeare, Loxhore (PN D 540, 63).

NETHERMORE FM is *Nithermor* 1227 FF, *Nethemore* 1245 WM xvi, *Nethmore* 1257 *For*, *Nuthermore* 1327 Ipm, *Nethermor* 1535 VE. 'Lower mor or marsh.'

NOCKETTS HILL is *Nocket Hill* 1598 *Depositions*. The name repeats itself in Nockatt Plantation *infra* 167, for which we have no early forms, and in an unidentified *Nokete* (1347 *DuLa*), *Nocketts* (1591 WM vi) in Oaksey. Probably it is unwise to speculate upon the name with so little early material, but if we do it may well be that Professor Ekwall is right in suggesting that *Nokete* is from *at then okette* and explaining *okette* as an *ett*-derivative from ac, 'oak,' denoting an oak plantation. Cf. ett *infra* 430 and *la okette* (PN Sr 359).

ASH HILL FM (6″). Cf. *Nash Hill* 1808 *Map* and Nash Hill *supra* 103. LODGE FM. Cf. *Great Lodge Homestead* c. 1840 *TA*. NICHILLS PLANTATION (6″) may possibly derive from OE **(i)ecels*, 'additional land taken in,' found in Etchilhampton *infra* 313, with affixed *n* as in Nechells (PN Wa 30). PITTER'S FM is *Pittars* t. Jas 1 *SP*. ROOKS NEST FM (6″). Cf. *Great, Little Rooks Nest* c. 1840 *TA*. SPITAL FM (6″) is on the site of an ancient hospital. TYNING PLANTATION (6″). *v. infra* 449.

Sherston

SHERSTON [*olim* ʃɑ·s(t)ən]

> *Scorranstan* 896 (11th) BCS 574, *Scorastan* 11th Encomium Emmae
> *Scorstan*[1] 11th ASC (D) *s.a.* 1016, *Sceorstan* c. 1150 ib. (E)
> *Sorstain* 1086 DB, *Sorestan* 1142–54 France, *Scorestan* 1167 P, 1206 ClR, *Sorestane* c. 1200 HMC Var i, 1204 ClR
> *Sorestone* 1086 DB, *Scoreston* 1236 Fees, *Shoreston* 1245 Ipm *Sarestan*' 1215 ClR

---

[1] Recorded in *Knútsdrápa*, a contemporary Norse poem, in the form *Skorsteini* (dat.).

Shorestan 1236 Cl, 1237 Ch, 1245 Misc, *Schorestan* 1237 Pat,
  Schorstane 1268 *Ass*
Scherstan 1258 *Ass*, *Scerstan* 1292 *Rental*, *Sherstan* 1305 Pat
Scherston 1291 Tax, *Scerston* 1293 *FF*, *Sherston* 1316 FA
Sharston 1335 Cl, *Shareston* 1337 ib., *Great Shaston* 1558–79
  ECP, *Sharson Magna* 1598 *FF*, *Shireston Magna* 1693 *Sadler*

The first element is probably the OE word **scora*, found in
Shoreham (PN Sx 246) meaning perhaps 'steep slope or de-
clivity.' The second element is **stan**, 'stone, rock.' It is not
certain that the first form refers to this place but the probabilities are that it does. If so, it is an irregular one. The form
sceorstan shows West Saxon *sceo* for *sco* as in *sceort* for *scort*
(Bülbring § 303). This form ultimately prevailed and yields later
Sherston, Sharston.

NOTE. BACK ST (6″) is *le Backstret* 1670 NQ vii. LEACH LANE (6″)
is *Leach Lane* ib. SHALLOWBROOKS LANE (6″). Cf. *Challowbrook* ib.

PINKNEY

Parva Scorstan' 1242 Fees, *Parva Sherestone* 13th RegMalm,
  Parva Sherstan 1268 *Ass*
Sherston Pinkeneye 1351 *FF*, *Pynkeney al. Sharston Pynkeney*
  1552 ib., *Sharston Parva al. Pinckney* 1602 *Recov*

This corresponds to the manor of Sherston held by Ralph de
Pinkenny in 1201 (Cur), spelt *Pinkenye, Pinkene* (1268 *Ass*). For
the family name cf. Moreton Pinkney (PN Nth 41). For the later
dropping of the first part of the compound, cf. Kellaways *supra* 99.

SILK WOOD is *Selkwode* 1292 *Rental*, 1334 *Ass*, 1342 *GDR*,
Silkwode 1332, *Silkewood* 1640 WIpm. The first element here
is probably the OE personal name *Seolca*, hence ' *Seolca*'s wood.'
Cf. *Silkden* (really Selden in Patching) in PN Sx 166.

WILLESLEY is *Wyvelesleye* c. 1207 BM, *-leg'* 1256 FF, *-le* 1306
FF, *Wylsleye* t. Hy 8 *Rental*, *Willesley* 1589 *FF*. ' *Wifel*'s
clearing or wood,' *v.* **leah**. Cf. Wilsford *infra* 326.

BYAM'S FM, GAGG'S MILL and THOMPSON'S HILL (all 6″) are to
be associated with the families of Samuel *Byam* (c. 1840 *TA*),
Richard *Gagg* (t. Ed 2 *DuLa*) and William *Tompson* (1682
ParReg).

COMMON WOOD FM (6″). Cf. *The Common Wood* 1640 WIpm.
EASTON TOWN is *Estentowne* t. Hy 8 *Rental, Eston Towne* 1639
FF. It lies just east of Sherston and probably comes from (*bi*)
ēastan tūne, 'east of the tun.' Cf. *infra* 138. FORLORN (6″) is a
nickname of reproach, cf. *infra* 455. GROVE HO. Cf. *The Grove*
c. 1840 *TA*. HALFWAYBUSH. Cf. *Holly Bush House* 1773 A and
D. HILL HOUSE FM (6″). Cf. *The Hill* c. 1840 *TA*. KNOCK-
DOWN is *Knock, Knockdown* 1773 A and D. LORDS WOOD is so
named c. 1840 (*TA*). NET BUSH (6″) is *Nettle Bush* 1820 G.
POOL LEAZE COVERT. Cf. *Pool Leaze* c. 1840 *TA*. ROUGHILL FM
is *Rokhulle* 13th *Malm, Rough Hill* c. 1840 *TA*. Apparently from
earlier 'rook-hill.' STANBRIDGE FM (6″) is *Stanbrugge* c. 1300
Malm, Stonebridge Mead 1673 NQ vii, *Standbridge* 1773 A and
D. VANCELETTES FM (6″). Cf. *Vancelot Furlong* c. 1840 *TA*.
WICK (lost) is *Sherstoneswyk* 1356 *Ass, Sherston Weeke* 1594 *FF*,
Wick House c. 1840 *TA*. *v*. wic and *supra* 25. WIDLEY'S FM
is *Wydeleye* 1322 Trop. Probably 'withy leah,' *v*. wiðig.

Slaughterford

SLAUGHTERFORD

Slachtoneford 1176 P, *Slatheneford* 1279 *Ass, Slaghteneford*
    1298 Cl, *Slaghtenford* 1300 Pat, *Slaughtenford* 1341 NI,
    Slaghtonford 1393 IpmR, *Slaghtynford* 1446 Pat, *Slaghtne-*
    ford 1467 ib., *Slaighteneford* 1472 ib., *Slawʒtenford* 1532
    SR, Slattenford 1549 Pat
Sclachtesford 1186 P, *Slahteford* 1291 Tax
Slaterford 1242 Fees, *Slauchterford* 1268 *Ass, Slatre-*,
    Slahter-, Slahtter- 1274 ib., *Sclater-* 1281 Trop, *Slauter-*
    1284 RegMalm, *Slahtere-* 1291 Tax, *Slaughter-* 1301 Abbr,
    Slag- 1303 Sarum, *Slaughtre-* 1343 Pat, *Slaghter-* 1356 ib.,
    1382 *NewColl*
Slauterneford 1289 *Ass, Slatrenford* 1321 ib.
Slawtenford(e) 1552, 1590 *FF*, 1553 WM x
Slawterford, Sletterford t. Eliz ib. xxi, *Slatterford* 1682 *Sadler*
Slaughterford al. Slaughtenford 1699 *Recov*

A compound of OE *slāh-þorn*, 'sloe-thorn or bush,' and ford.
This etymology, which was apparently first suggested by
Stevenson (Asser 276–7) is strongly supported by the Assize
Roll forms quoted above. *slāh-þyrne* is also possible (B.D.).

Mercombe Wood (6″) is *Merecumb'* 1245 WM xvi, *Marcombe-wode* 1536 *MinAcct.* 'Boundary valley,' *v.* (ge)mære, cumb. The place is on the parish boundary.

Mill Ho was the home of Matilda *atte Mulle* (1327 *SR*).

Cloud Quarry (6″) (locally *Cloud Quarr*). Cf. *Cloud Common, Hill, Lees* c. 1840 *TA.* See Clouds Ho *infra* 176 and *quarre infra* 445. Pew's Hill is *Pewshill, Pewsells* ib. *v. supra* 14.

Sopworth

Sopworth

> *Sopeworde* 1086 DB, *-wrth* 1201 Cur, *-worth* 1249 *Ass*, *Sopesworth* 1206 Cur
> *Soppewarda* 12th *AD*, *-worth* 1281 *Ass et freq* to 1351 Pat
> *Sopwarde* ib., *-wrth'* 1251 Cl, *-worth(e)* 1298 *Ass*, 1332 *SR*
> *Scopewurth* 1242 Fees, *Shopwurth* 1252 Ch
> *Sapworth* 1665 *FF*, 1773 A and D

'*Soppa*'s farmstead,' *v.* worþ. For the personal name cf. Sopwell (PN Herts 95).

Ashen Bottom (6″) is *Ashing Bottom* 1773 A and D, *Ash Down Bottom* c. 1840 *TA.* Bullpark Wood. Cf. *Bull Park Plantation* ib. Crow Down. Cf. *Crowdown Hill* ib. The Diddle (6″). Cf. *Diddle Wood* ib.

Stanton St Quintin

Stanton St Quintin

> *Stantone* 1086 DB, 1211 RBE, *-ton* 1236 FF, *Staunton Quyntyn* 1317 Cl, (*Seynt Quyntin*) 1339 Pat, (*Sancti Quintini*) 1428 FA

'Stone-enclosure' or 'farm in the stony spot,' *v.* stan, tun. Herbert de *Sancto Quintino* held the manor in 1211, John de *Sancto Quintino* in 1236 and 1242 (Fees).

Avil's Fm is *Avils* c. 1700 *Longford.* Greenhills Fm (6″). Cf. *Greene hill* 1604 ib. Stanton Park. Cf. *The Parke of Stanton Quinton* 1602 ib. Woodman Croft (6″) is *Woodmancraft* (sic) c. 1700 ib.

North Wraxall

NORTH WRAXALL

Werocheshalle 1086 DB, Wrocheshal juxta Netelton 1305 Ass
Wrockeshal(e) 1229 Cl, 1249, 1268, 1281 Ass, 1314 Cl
Wrokeshal(e) 1229 ib., 1268, 1279, 1289 Ass, 13th RegMalm,
  1281 Trop
Wraxhal' 1229 Cl
Wroxhale 1300 FF, 1316 FA, 1333 SR, 1341 NI, (by Mars-
  feld) 1363 Pat, Wroxhalle juxta Castel Combe 1357 FF
Northwroxhall 1468 IpmR, Northe Wraxhale 1506 Pat, North
  Wraxall 1582 FF, Upper Wraxall 1773 A and D
Racxell 1659 PCC, Raxall 1709 Recov

This place-name has been fully discussed in PN Wa 228 *s.n.*
Wroxall. The first element is a lost OE *wrocc, 'buzzard,' possibly
in some cases used as a personal name. The second element is
healh, 'angle, corner,' etc. *Marsfeld* is Marshfield (Gl).

CHURCH FM (6″) was the home of Margery *atte Churche* (1327
SR).

BOND'S WOOD, CULLIMER'S WOOD and HALL'S BARN (all 6″) are
to be associated with the families of William *Bonde* (1513 *Ct*),
Henry *Cullimore* (1642 Lewis) and Isaac *Hall* (c. 1840 *TA*).

CHANTRY WOOD (6″). Cf. *Chantry Ground* c. 1840 *TA* and *infra*
456. COLD HARBOUR (6″) is so named ib. *v. infra* 451. DRY
LEAZE (6″). Cf. *Dry Leaze Wood* ib. FORD is (*la*) *Forde* 1249 *Ass*,
1297 Lewis, *Foorde* 1422 *Add*. FOSSE BARN (6″). Cf. *Fosse
Tyning* c. 1840 *TA* and *infra* 449. On the Fosse Way. HORSE
GROVE (6″). Cf. *Horse Grove Wood* ib. LIPPET (1820 G) is
Lypyate 1588 WM xxxiv, *Lippeat Lease* ib. Cf. Lypiatt *supra*
96. MOUNTAIN BOWER is *Mnctons* (sic) *Bower* 1608 Lewis.
Cf. Monkton *infra* 119. NEWLEAZE WOOD (6″). Cf. *New Leaze*
c. 1840 *TA*. OUT WOODS (6″) is *Outwoods* ib. PRESTGROVE (6″)
is *Prest Grove Hill* 1608 Lewis. SHEEPSLEIGHT WOOD (6″). Cf.
Sleights 1704 WM xliv, *Sheep Slaits* c. 1840 *TA* and *infra* 454.
WHEATRIDGE BARN (6″) is *Wheat Ridge* 1608 Lewis.

Yatton Keynell

YATTON KEYNELL

> *Getone* 1086 DB, *Yeton* 1247 FF, 1289 *Ass*
>
> *Yatton(e)* 1242 Fees, (*Kaynel*) 1289 *Ass*, (*Kaignel*) 1306 ib.,
> (*Kynel*) 1346 *FF*, *Iatton* 1258 Ipm
>
> ȝitton 1242 Fees
>
> *Jettun'* 1245 WM xvi, *Yetton Caynel* 1334 *Ass*, *Yetton* 1348
> Pat, *Yettonkenell* 1553 *FF*
>
> *Yeatton Kaynell* 1522 ib.
>
> *Churcheyatton* 1530 *Recov*, *Yatton Keynell al. Eaton Keynell
> al. Churche Eaton* 1618 *FF*

A compound of geat, 'gate, gap,' and tun, the 'gap' being the
head of the well-marked valley to the west of the village. Henry
Caynel had a holding here in 1242 (Fees). *Church* in distinction
from West Yatton *infra*.

GIDDEAHALL is *Giddy Hall* 1773 A and D. Probably a nickname
of contempt. Cf. Gidea Park (PN Ess 117–8) where other
examples are cited, *la Gidielond* (1276 StNicholas) in Broad
Chalke and *Gediacre* (1224 FF) in Lavington.

KENT'S BOTTOM is to be associated with the family of Thomas
Kent (1752 ParReg).

BROOMFIELD is *Bromfield* 1773 A and D. BROOM'S FM is *Broomes*
1638 WIpm, *Bromseys* 1773 A and D. DEAN MILL (6") is *Dane
Mill* 1816 O.S. *v.* Introd. xx. THE FOLLY and FOLLY FM (both
6"). Cf. *infra* 451. THE GRANGE. Cf. *Graungemille* 1422 *Add*.
GROVE FM. Cf. *le Grove* 1513 ib. HAMMERDOWN (6") is
Great, Little Hammer Down c. 1840 *TA*. LONG DEAN is *le Longdene* 1422 *Add*. 'Long valley,' *v.* denu. PARK FM. Cf. *le Parkemede*
1354 *AddCh*. QUARR PLANTATION (6"). Cf. *Quarr Hill* c. 1840
TA and *infra* 445. WARR HILL PLANTATION (6"). Cf. *Warhill*
ib. WESTWELL COTTAGES (6"). Cf. *Westwells* ib. WEST YATTON
is *Westyatton* 1279 *Ass*.

IX. BRADFORD HUNDRED

Bradefort, Bradeford hundred 1086 ExonDB, *hundred de Bradeford* 1130, 1190 P. It takes its name from Bradford on Avon *infra* 116.

Atworth

ATWORTH [*vulgo* ætfərd]

Attenwrðe 1001 (14th) KCD 706
Hettewrthe t. Hy 1 *Shaston*
Atewurth 1242 Fees, *-worth* 1324 FA
Attewurth 1249 *Ass et passim* to 1369 Cl, with variant spelling *-worth*
At(t)ewarde 1354 Cl, (*near Bradeford*) 1358 ib., (*Magna*) 1421 ib., *Mechell Attewarde* 1451 ib., *Great Atte Ward* 1458 Pat, *Attewarde* 1475 ib.
Ateforde 1427 Trop, *Atford* 1480 *FF, Atford al. Atworth* 1615 *Recov, Afford al. Atworth* 1637 WIpm

'*Ætta*'s farmstead,' *v.* worþ. *Great* (*v.* micel) in contrast to Little Atworth, now Cottles *infra*.

GREAT and LITTLE CHALFIELD [*vulgo* tʃɑ·vil]

Chaldfeld 1001 (14th) KCD 706, *Chaldefeld(e)* 1191 Templars, 1216 ClR, 1242 Fees, 1428 FA, *Chaude-* 1196 Cur, 1198 Abbr, *Scaude-* 1201 FF, *Chade-* 1316 FA
Caldefelle 1086 DB, *-feld* 1176 P
Cheldefeld 1281 *Ass*
Chaldevile 1526 Ct, *Chawfeld* 1583 *FF, West Chawfield* t. Eliz WM xxi, *Chafeilde* 1646 Sess, *Little Chavill* 1659 PCC

'Cold or exposed open space,' *v.* ceald, feld. *West* is an alternative epithet for Little Chalfield.

COTTLES Ho is *Atteworth* 1278 *FF, Attelworth Parva* (sic) 1298 Sarum, *Atteworth Cotell* 1402 FA, *Cotelys* 1412 ib., *Cotelatteword* 1428 ib., *Cotelles* 1458 Trop, *Attewarde Parva alias dict' Cotels Atteward* 1460 ib., *Cuttels Atteward* 1503 Ipm, *Cottles al. Cottles Attford* 1718 Recov. This represents the old manor of Little

Atworth, held by the family of *Cotel*. Cf. Richard *Cotel* (1242 Fees), John de *Cotele*, Richard *Cotele* (1278 Trop), Richard *Cotel(e)* (1278 *FF*, 1298 Sarum).

LYNCH BOTTOM (6″) may have been near the home of Robert de *Lyncheford* (1281 *Ass*). It is *Linch Bottom* c. 1840 *TA*. *v*. hlinc *infra* 436.

MOXHAMS (lost) is *Mockesham* 1236 FF, 1278 Ipm, 1338 Trop, *Mokesham* 1255 RH (p), *Moxham* 1411 *FF*, 1460 Trop, *Moxhams* 1711 *FF*, *Bushes or Moxhams* c. 1840 *TA*. *v*. ham(m). The first element is probably a personal name *Mocc*, identical with that found in Moxhull Park (PN Wa 52).

THE HAYES is *le Heyes* (1573 WM xli) and was the home of Egidius de *la Haye* (1279 *Ass*) and William *del Haye* (1289 ib.). *v*. (ge)hæg, 'enclosure.'

BEARDWELL (6″) is *Bedewelle* 1353 Trop, *Bidwell* 1631 WIpm, *Beard Well* c. 1840 *TA*. Cf. Bydemill Brook *supra* 4–5. COCK-ROAD PLANTATION. Cf. *infra* 427. DENLEYS FM (6″) is *Denley* ib. GANBROOK FM is *Gangbroke* 1451, *Gangbrokes Crosse*, *Gangebroke* 1460 Trop. GROVE MEAD (6″). Cf. *Overgrove* 1634 *Longleat*. LENTON FM. Cf. *Lynton*, *Lyntonesford* 1338 Trop. Perhaps 'flax-farm,' *v*. lin, tun. MEDLEYS (6″) is *Medelee* 1353 ib. MOUNT PLEASANT (6″). *v*. *infra* 455. NEWHOUSE FM is *New House Farm* 1820 G. PURLPIT is *Purlepittes* 1634 WIpm. STUDLEY FM (6″) is *Stodleg'* 1257 *For*, *v*. Studley *infra* 135.

Bradford on Avon

BRADFORD ON AVON

(æt) *Bradanforda be Afne* c. 900 ASC (Ā) *s.a.* 652, *Bradanford* 705 (c. 1125) BCS 114, 955 (14th) ib. 912

(æt) *Bradeforda* 1001 (14th) KCD 706, *Bradeford* 1086 DB *et passim* to 1244 Cl, *Bradford* 1415 Inq aqd

Brodeford 1340 Ipm, 1412 FA, 1485 *Ct*

'Wide ford,' *v*. brad.

NOTE. HIGH ST is (*in*) *alto Streete*, *High Street* c. 1660 WM xli. Cf. *supra* 21. KINGSTON RD was earlier *Frogmerestret* 1329 ib. i, taking its name from some lost 'frog mere or pool.' MARKET ST is *le Markett streete* 1612 ib. xli. PIPPET ST (local) is *Pep(p)ut street* 1583 ib. xiii, *Pepitt Streete* 1660 ib. xli. ST MARGARET ST is so named from the hospital of St Margaret, still standing in Leland's time (ib. xx, 315). WOOLLEY ST was formerly *Seynt Olesstret* 1426 AD i, *St Toles streete* 1612, *Tuley streete* 1660 WM xli, from the chapel of St Olave which once stood here. Cf. Tooley St (PN Sr 33). The street leads to Woolley *infra* 118. Lost names include *Elbridge Lane*, probably from þelbrycg, 'plank-bridge', *Pando Street*, *Millstreete* 1660 WM xli, *Selestrete* 14th AD vi, *Seale Streete* 1660 WM xli.

BUDBURY HO is *Bodeberie* 1086 DB, *Budeberia* t. Hy 2 *Shaston*, *-bir'* 1204 FF, 1272 *Ass*, *Buddeber'* 1268 ib., *-bury* t. Ed 1 WM i, 1303 FF, *-bur'* 1288 *Ass*. '*Budda*'s burh.'

CUMBERWELL

> *Cūbrewelle* 1086 DB, *Cumbrewelle* 1245 WM xvi, 1255 RH (p), 1257 *For*, *Combrewell(e)* 1249 *Ass*, 1330 Ipm, 1331 Cl *Combereswell'* t. Hy 2 *Shaston*
> *Cumberwella, -e* t. Hy 2 *Shaston*, 1236 FF, *Comberwell* 1289 ib.
> *Comerwell(e)* 1232 *Lacock*, t. Ed 1 WM i *et freq* to 1364 *Ass*, *Comerell al. Comerwell* 1691 *Recov*
> *Comerewelle* 1288 *Ass*, *Cumerewelle* 1291 WIpm

'*Cumbra*'s well or spring,' *v.* wielle. Cf. Cumberlow (PN Herts 163) and Cumberworth (L), *Combreuorde* 1086 DB, (WRY), *Cumbreuurde* 1086 DB. *Cumbra* originally denoted a Welshman.

ELMS CROSS (6″) is *Elmes Cros* 1630 WIpm, *Elms Cross* c. 1840 *TA* and is possibly identical with *Elmescroft* 1204 FF. For possible confusion of the second elements cf. South Croft *infra* 248 by South Cross Lane.

TROWLE FM and COMMON and TROWLE BRIDGE [troul]

> *Trole* 1086 DB, *Trol* t. Hy 2 *Shaston*, 1263 *For*, 1333 *SR*, 1352, 1355 Pat
> *Trul* t. Hy 2 *Shaston*
> *Trulle* 1242 Fees, *Bradfordestrull* 1504 Ipm
> *Trolle* 1242 Fees, 1268, 1289 *Ass*, 1327 *SR*, 1384 Cl, *Troll* 1349 BM
> *Troulle* 1571 PCC, *Great Trowle* 1611 *SR*
> *le Trullebrugge* t. Ed 4 *DuLa*

This is a difficult name and the solution of it is not made easier by our not knowing just where the site called *Trowle* really lay. Trowle Bridge lies on a tributary of the Biss. At the headwaters of one of the feeders of that tributary lies Trowle Fm, with Trowle Ho and Trowle Wood in Wingfield close at hand. A mile north-east of Trowle Fm lies Trowle Common, with Trowle Manor Court Fm and Trowle Cottage close at hand, but well away from the stream. It is just possible that *Trul(l)* was originally the name of the stream. There is evidence for such a stream-name denoting something which turns; cf. Trill, Trull (RN 418), Trulley Brook (PN Sr 6). From this Trowle Fm and Trowle Bridge would appropriately be named. The name may have been extended to other places in the neighbourhood or possibly a compound of *Trul* and leah, denoting 'clearing by the Trull,' was formed and that may have had the same development as we find in some of the names noted under Keevil *infra* 142.

WIDBROOK is *Wyggebrok* 1279 *Ass* (p), 1281 ib., *Wyge-* 1327 *SR* (p), *Wygbrooke* 1439 *MinAcct*, *Widbrook* 1773 A and D. Probably '*Wicga*'s brook' (*v.* broc), with common variation between *g* and *d* at a later date.

WOOLLEY is *Wlfleg'* 1242 Fees, *Wulvele* 1255 RH (p), *Wolvelegh* t. Hy 2 *Shaston*, 1279 *Ass*, *Wlfleye* 1288 ib. (p), *Woolflege* 1324 WM i, *Wolleye* 1332 *SR* (p). 'Wolves' clearing or wood,' *v.* leah.

WOOD COTTAGES (6″) were perhaps the home of John de *Bosco* (t. Hy 3 WM i) and William *atte Wode* (1523 *SR*).

ARNOLD'S FM and POTTICK'S FM[1] are to be associated with the families of Thomas *Arnold* (1642 *SR*) and Ralph *Poteck* (1523 ib.).

BARTON FM (6″). Cf. *Barton Stile* 1655 WM xli and *infra* 451. BEARFIELD is *Berefeld* t. Ed 1 WM i, *Bearefeelde* 1639 WIpm, *Berfeld* 1773 A and D. BELCOMBE COURT is *Belcombe* 1640 WIpm. BRADFORD BRIDGE is *Avenebrygge* 1426 AD i. GREAT BRADFORD WOOD is *Bradefordewod* 1277 Cl. CONIGRE HILL (6″). Cf. *Coniger* 1631 WIpm and *infra* 427. THE FOLLY (6″). Cf.

---

[1] *Pothooks* c. 1840 *TA*.

Folly Piece c. 1840 *TA* and *infra* 451. FRANKLEIGH FM is *Franckly* 1637 *Phillipps*. GREENLAND MILL (6″) is so named c. 1840 (*TA*). GRIP WOOD (6″). Cf. *6 acres of wood in the Grippe* 1632 WIpm. See *infra* 452. KINGSFIELD HO is *Kyngesfeld* 1332 AD i, 1446 Trop. LADY DOWN FM. Cf. *Ladydowne* 1632 WIpm. LEIGH HO is *Lighe* 1412 FA, *Bradfordslye* 1571 *FF*, *Bradforde Leighe* 1637 *Phillipps*. *v.* leah. MAPLECROFT (6″) is so named c. 1840 (*TA*).

Broughton Gifford

BROUGHTON GIFFORD [brɔˑton dziʃərd]

    Broctun 1001 (14th) KCD 706, *-ton(e)* 1086 DB, 1196 Cur *et freq* to 1288 *Ass*, (*Parva*) 1228 Cl, (*juxta Melkesham*) 1268 *Ass*, (*Magna*) 1278 ib., *Brok-* 1242 Fees, 1375 Pat, *Brocton Giffard* 1288 *Ass*

    Brochetone 1267 Sarum, *Magna Broghton* 1269 FF, *Brochton* 1281 Ch

    Brouhton 1279, 1281 *Ass*, *Browhton* ib., *Broughton* 1333 *SR*, 1347 Pat, 1402 FA, *Browton* 1401 IpmR, *Broughton Gyffard* 1409 *Ass*, *Brughton* 1412 IpmR, *Broton Gifford* 1637 *Phillipps*

    Borghton 1410 Pat

'Farm on the brook,' *v.* broc, tun. John *Giffard* held the manor in 1281 (Ch). Hence GIFFORD HALL (6″) in the parish.

MONKTON HO is *Broctune* 1086 DB, *Monketon* 1325 Pat, *Munketon* 1428 FF, *Monketon juxta Broughton* t. Hy 8 *AOMB*, *Mounton* 1611 SR, *Mountain Farm* 1773 A and D. 'Farm of the monks,' *v.* tun. For the later forms cf. Mounton (NCPNW 250). A manor in Broughton was granted to the Priory of Monkton Farleigh in the 12th century (WM v, 330).

CHALLYMEAD HO (6″) is *Chaldmede* 1525 WM v, *Cherrymead* 1773 A and D. 'Cold meadow,' *v.* Introd. xxi. FRYINGPAN FM (6″) is *Frying Pan* 1773 A and D, *v. infra* 455. HOLLYBROOK HO. Cf. *aqua de Holebrok* 1397 Trop. 'Brook in the hollow,' *v.* holh. LEECHPOOL FM. Cf. *Leech Pool* c. 1840 *TA*. NORRINGTON COMMON. Cf. *Norrington Green* ib. and *infra* 200. It is in the north part of the parish.

Monkton Farleigh

MONKTON FARLEIGH

> *Farnleghe* 1001 (14th) KCD 706, *-lege* 1196 Cur, 1249 *Ass*,
> *-ligh* 1272 ib.
> *Farlege* 1086 DB, *-lega* 1155 RBE, *-le* 1241 Ch
> *Ferleia* 1131 AC, 1203 Cur, *-lega* 1156, 1158 P, t. Hy 2 BM
> *Ferneleia* 1198 Abbr, *-leg'* 1245 WM xvi, 1257 Cl
> *Franleye* 1267 Pat
> *Farley Monachorum* 1316 FA, *Monekenefarlegh* 1321 *FF*,
> *Munkesfarlegh* 1364 IpmR, *Farleye Monketon* 1370 *Ass*,
> *Monks Farlegh* 1384 Pat, *Monkenferlowe* 1462 ib., *Mounton
> Farley* 1773 A and D

'Fern or bracken clearing,' *v.* fearn, leah. A Cluniac priory
was founded here in 1125; cf. Monkton Deverill *infra* 174. For
Mounton cf. *supra* 119.

NOTE. LINK LANE. Cf. *Link Mead, Great Links* c. 1840 *TA*.
v. hlinc *infra* 436.

CHURCH FM (6″) was the home of William *atte Churche* (1346
Ass).

DUCKMEAD FM (6″). Cf. *Duck Mead* c. 1840 *TA*. FARLEIGH
WICK is *Farlegh Wyke* 1257 AD iii, *la Wyke* 1485 *Ct*, *v.* wic and
supra 25. HAYS WOOD (6″). Cf. *Great Hayes, Hayes Ground*
c. 1840 *TA*, and (ge)hæg *infra* 433. INWOOD FM. Cf. *Inwodestret*
1485 *Ct* and Inwood *supra* 104. THE MONKS' CONDUIT (6″).
Cf. *Conduit Close* c. 1840 *TA*. PARK WOOD. Cf. *le Estparke* 1513
Ct. RUSHMEAD FM. Cf. *Rush Mead* c. 1840 *TA*.

Holt

HOLT[1]

> *Holt(e)* t. Hy 2 Shaston, 1242 Fees *et passim*, *la Holte* 1257
> *For, Holte juxta Bradford* 1332 FF, *Hol, Holte, Houlte*
> t. Eliz WM ii, *Hoult* 1637 *Phillipps*

'Wood,' *v.* holt.

[1] A parish formed from Bradford in 1894.

G ASTON [gæsən] F M and W OODGATE (both 6″) were probably the homes of Eustace de *Garston* (1257 *For*) and William *atte Garstune* (1282 *Ass*) and John *atte Wode* (1327 *SR*). *v.* gærstun, 'grass paddock.'

B RADLEY'S F M, H ALL'S F M (6″) and H UNT'S H ALL are to be associated with the families of William de *Bradelegh* (1332 *SR*), Thomas *Hall* (1642 ib.) and Henry *Hunt* (c. 1840 *TA*). The first probably came from North Bradley *infra* 138, a few miles away.

B LACKACRE F M is *Blackacre* 1583 WM xv. F OREWOOD C OMMON is *Farrads Common* 1762 Act. Cf. *Forewoods Mead* c. 1840 *TA*. In front of Great Bradford Wood. G LAN-YR-AFON is a modern house by the river Avon. It is an artificial Welsh name, meaning 'bank or shore of the river (Avon).' O XEN L EAZE F M. Cf. *Oxen Leaze* 1773 A and D. S TANBRIDGE F M is *Stanbridge* c. 1840 *TA*. T HE S TAR (6″). Cf. *Star Fd* ib.

Limpley Stoke

L IMPLEY S TOKE[1]

Hangyndestok 1263 *For*
Hanging Stoke 1322 WM xxiii, 1585 ib. xxi, *Hangyngestoke* 1362 *Cor*
Stoke 1333 *SR* (p), 1522, 1611 ib., 1539 WM v, *Stokewere* 1348 *Cor*
Lymply Stoke 1585 WM xxi, *Limplystoke* 1613 PCC, *Limpley* 1670 *FF, Lympley Stoke in the parish of Bradford* 1784 *Recov*

v. stoc. Originally called *Hanging* from its position below a steep hillside; cf. Hanging Houghton (PN Nth 126). There is a weir here by Avon Mill. The addition of *Limpley* remains an unsolved mystery.

A SHLEIGH (6″) is *Ashley* 1642 *SR*. C HATLEIGH H O is *Chatteley* 1513 *Ct*. C LEEVEHILL H O (6″). Cf. *Upper, Lower Cleeves* c. 1840 *TA* and clif *infra* 426. D ODLEAZE W OOD (6″). Cf. *Dodleaze* ib. S HORT W OOD (6″) is *Shortwood* ib. W ATER H O is so named in 1773 (A and D). W INYATTS (6″) is *Winyatt* c. 1840 *TA*, i.e. wind-gate or gap, *v.* geat.

---

[1] Formerly a detached part of Bradford on Avon.

Westwood

WESTWOOD

> (to) *Westwuda* 987 (12th) KCD 658, *Westwode* 1086 DB
> *et passim*, with variant spelling *-wude, Overwestwode, Nether
> Westwode* 1363 Inq aqd

Self-explanatory. Upper and Lower Westwood still exist.

AVONCLIFF [*olim* ænklif] is *Aveneclife* t. Hy 2 *Shaston* (p),
Aveneclive 1249, 1289 *Ass, Avenclyve* 1357 *FF, Aveneclyfessmille*
1432 *MinAcct, Anclyff* 1554 Pat, *Ann Cliff* 1773 A and D. *v.*
clif. There is a steep hillside here above the Avon valley.

IFORD

> *Igford* 987 (12th) KCD 658, *Yford* 1289 *Ass, Iford* 1357 *FF,*
> *Yforde* 1435 WM xiv, *Yford juxta Farley Hungerford* 1487
> *FF*
> *Nyfordyshegge* 1458 *Ct*

v. ieg, ford. There is no island here, but the name may have
reference to the flat marshy land by the Frome just to the south
of the place. Distinguished as near Farleigh Hungerford (So).
The 1458 form must be due to wrong division of a ME *atten
iford*; cf. Nash Hill *supra* 103.

LYE GREEN[1] and WELL HO (6″) were the homes of John *atte
Legh* (1327 *SR*) and Alvric de *Wella* (t. Hy 2 *Shaston*). *v.* leah.

BECKY ADDY WOOD (6″) is *Addy Wood* c. 1840 *TA*. HAYGROVE
PLANTATION (6″) is *Hay grove* ib. THE QUARRY (6″). Cf. *Quarry
Piece* ib. SHRUB DOWN is so named ib.

Winkfield [2]

WINKFIELD[3]

> *Winefel* (sic) 1086 DB, *-feld* 1241 FF, *Wynefeld* 1268 ib. *et
> freq* to 1428 ib., *Wynyfeud* 1281 *Ass*
> *Winesfeld* 1242 Fees, *Wynes-* 1281 *Ass*

---

[1] *Leigh Green* c. 1840 *TA.*   [2] WINGFIELD (6″ O.S.).
[3] As Grundy notes (ii, 74) there is a form *Wuntfeld* in BCS 1127 which
must refer to this place, but the form seems to be entirely corrupt.

Wenfeld 1428 FA, *Wynfeld* ib., 1446 Pat, 1535 VE, 1541 *FF*,
  Winfeilde 1549 NQ iv
Wynkefeld(e) 1535 VE, 1556 *FF*, *Wyngfeld* 1542 LP, *Winge-*
  feld al. Wynfyeld 1576 *Recov, Wingfeild al. Wynefeild* 1645
  ib., *Winkfeild al. Wingfeild* 1707 ib.

'*Wina*'s open land,' *v.* **feld**. The *k* is a late and irregular
intruder in this name.

FRESHAW (lost)[1] is *(onbutan) færs scagan* 987 (12th) KCD 658,
Fershawe 1263 *For* (p), 1268 *Ass*, 1279 ib. (p), *Fresshaw* 1411 *FF*,
Frechehawe 1458 BM, *Freshawe* 1494 ib. The second element is
sceaga, 'copse.' The first element is uncertain.

POMEROY WOOD
  Pumberig 1001 (14th) KCD 706, *Pumbur'* 1257 *For*, -*buri*
    1306 *FF*, -*bury* 1311 ib., -*bery* 1312 *Ass*, -*berie* 1576 *FF*,
    Poumbery 1336 *FF*, *Pombury* 1412 FA, -*bury* 1428 ib.
  Ponberie 1086 DB, *Punbir'* 1242 Fees
  Plumbyr' 1282 *Ass*
  Pumbrye 1535 VE, -*brey* 1585 BM, *Pombre* 1723, 1762 *Recov*
  Pombre oth. Pomber oth. Pomroy oth. Pomrey 1826 ib.
  Pomeray Farm House, Pumbury Wood c. 1840 *TA*

It is possible that the original form of this name was *plumbyrig*
(dat.), with later loss of *l*, as is suggested by Ekwall (DEPN) for
Puncknowle (Do), *Pomacanole* 1086 DB. The name would then
mean 'burh marked by a plum-tree.'

ROWLEY COPSE[2] (6″) and WITTENHAM (lost)
  (*a*) (*at*) *Wutenham* 1001 (14th) KCD 706
    Withenhā 1086 DB, -*ham* 1376 IpmR, *Wythen*- 1316
      NomVil, *Wytham* 1268 *Ass*, *Wytteham* 1268 FF,
      Witham 1316, 1324 FA, *Wittenham* 1339 Pat, 1412,
      1428 FA, 1474 Pat, *Whittenham* 1401 IpmR, *Whiten-*
      ham 1428 *FF*
  (*b*) *Rueleia* 13th WM xiii, *Roweleye* 1306 *FF*, *Ruweleye* 1311
      ib., *Roghele* 1333 *SR*, *Rowelegh* 1412 FA, 1428 *FF*
  (*c*) *Rowelegh al. Witnam* 1430 Cl, 1487 Pat, *Rowley al.*
      Witnam 1558 Pat, 1585 *Recov*, (*al. Wittenham*) 1619 ib.

---

[1] Near Stowford.   [2] In Farleigh Hungerford (So).

Rowley is 'rough clearing or wood,' *v.* ruh, leah. Wittenham seems to be identical in origin with Witham (So), *Witeham* 1086 DB, 1156 P, *Wuttheham, Witheham* 1212 Fees, '*Wit(t)a*'s ham.'

SNARLTON FM is *Snarleton* 1820 G. This name repeats itself in Snarlton in Melksham and Snarlton in Steeple Ashton (*infra* 130, 137). For none of them have we early forms and the name must remain unsolved.

STOWFORD FM is *stanford* 987 (12th) KCD 658, *Stafford* 1199 FF, *Stovord* 1327 SR (p), *Stowford* 1458 BM, (*al. Stovord*) 1576 *Recov, Stoward* 1773 A and D. 'Stony ford,' cf. Stoford *infra* 228.

SWANSBROOK FM is (*inne*) *Swinbroch* 1001 (14th) KCD 706. If the 14th-century form is to be trusted this was originally 'swine brook.'

THE STREET was probably the home of William *atte Stretende* (1327 *SR*).

MIDWAY MANOR. Cf. *Midway Farm* 1820 G. Half-way between Winkfield and Bradford. OXSTALL FM is so named in 1773 (A and D). SLEIGHT HO. *v. infra* 454.

Winsley

WINSLEY[1]

> *Winesleg'* 1242 Fees, *-lege* 1249 *Ass et freq* to 1332 *SR*, with variant spellings *Wynes-* and *-leye, -legh, Weneslegh* 1341 *Rental, Winslegh* 1363 FF, *Wynnesley* 1523 SR

> '*Wine*'s clearing or wood,' *v.* leah.

CONKWELL is first so called in 1778 (*Recov*). It is close to the place called *cunuca leage* (BCS 1001) as noted by Grundy (*The Saxon Charters of Somerset*, 216) and it is clear that the first element in these two names must be the same. Grundy suggests that *cunuc* is "the name of the streamlet which runs from Conkwell to the Avon" but there is no such stream. More probably *cunuc* here has reference to the steep hill with its rounded top rising to over 500 feet. See Conock *infra* 312.

[1] A parish formed from Bradford in 1894.

TURLEIGH is *Turlinge* 1341 WM i, *Torlyng* 1362 *Cor*, *Turlin* 1699 *FF*, *-lyn* 1748 ib. This would seem to be from OE *þȳrelung*, 'piercing through,' with reference to the deep and curving valley here.

HAUGH FM (6″) was the home of John de *la Haghe* (1281 *Ass*). It is *Haugh* 1432 *MinAcct*, *Ashleyhaugh* 1705 *Recov*. *v*. haga, 'enclosure, hedge.' See Ashley *infra*.

DANES HILL (6″) and FRY'S WOOD are to be associated with the families of John *Danys* (1523 *SR*) and Robert *le Frye* (1289 *Ass*).

ASHLEY is *Ashelegh* 1279 *Ass*, (*juxta Bradeford*) 1357 *GDR*, *Aysshe-* 1332 *SR* (p), *Aishe-* 1485 *Ct*. 'Ash wood or clearing,' *v*. leah. CROCKFORD (6″) is so named in 1727 (*Map*). DANE BOTTOM (6″) is *Dean Bottom* c. 1840 *TA*. Cf. Introd. xx. HARTLEY is *Hortleye* 1289 Ipm (p), *Horteleye* 1299 WIpm, *Hortlie* 1634 ib., *Hartley* 1773 A and D. OE *heort(a) leah*, 'hart clearing,' *v*. leah. MURHILL. Cf. *Murrell mead* 1634 WIpm, *Marvill* 1773 A and D. ROWAS LODGE (6″). Cf. *Great*, *Little Rowas* c. 1840 *TA*.

South Wraxall

SOUTH WRAXALL

> *Wroxhal* 1227 FF, *Wrokeshal'* 1242 Fees with a similar run of spellings to those for North Wraxall *supra* 113, *Wroxhale juxta Bradeford* 1302 *Ass*, 1313 *FF*, (*by Broughton*) 1432 Pat. First distinguished as *Suthwroxhall* in 1468 (IpmR)

Identical in origin with North Wraxall *supra* 113. The two places are about ten miles apart and must have been named independently.

CHESLAND WOOD (6″) is *Cheslands* c. 1840 *TA*. We may perhaps compare *Chesthull*, *Chisthull* (1453 *MinAcct*) in the same parish. This has its parallel in Chessel (Wt), *Chesthull* 1228 Pat, *Chusthull* 1346 FA. The place lies on the border of the parish and it may be that the first element is ME *cheste*, 'strife.'

CHURCH FM was probably the home of Simon *Attechurche* (1292 *FF*).

MISON'S FM and WHATLEY'S BRAKE[1] (both 6″) are to be associated with the families of Allen *Myson* (1611 *SR*) and William *Mison* (1642 ib.) and John de *Watelegh* (1279 *Ass*).

NORBIN is *Narbing* 1773 A and D. Possibly for *norð-binnan* 'north within.' It is in the far north of the parish. NORBIN BARTON (6″). *v.* barton *infra* 451. WILD CROSS is so named c. 1840 (*TA*).

X. MELKSHAM HUNDRED

Melchesam hundred, *Melchessam* 1086 ExonDB, *Hundred de Melkesham* 1227 Fees. See Melksham *infra* 128.

Bulkington
BULKINGTON
> *Boltintone* 1086 DB
> *Bolkintone* 1211 RBE, *Bulkinton'* 1225 FineR *et freq* to 1395 *Ct*, with variant spelling *-yn-*, *Bolkenton* 1279, 1281 *Ass*, *Bulkyng-* ib. *et freq*, with variant spelling *-ing-*, *Bolkyng-* 1332 Pat, 1345 *Ass*, *Bulkyngdoun* 1437 Cl
> *Buckington* 1544 FF, *Bulkyngton al. Buckyngton* 1560 Recov

'*Bulca's* farm,' *v.* ingtun. Cf. Bulkworthy (PN D 91) and Bulkington (PN Wa 100).

NOTE. SHORTMARSH LANE. Cf. *Short Marsh* c. 1840 *TA*.

BLACK CROSS. Cf. *Blackcross Ground* c. 1840 *TA*. BRASSPAN BRIDGE (6″) is *Brass Pan Bridge* 1820 G. MILL FM (6″). Cf. *Mill Mead* c. 1840 *TA*.

Erlestoke
ERLESTOKE
> *Stokes* c. 1200 BM
> *Erlestok(e)* 1227 FF, 1239 Ch, 1249 *Ass*, *Erlys-* 1325 Cl, *Eorlestoke* 1340 WIpm, 1392 Pat, 1393 IpmR, *Erelstoke* 1518–29 ECP, *Earlestoke* 1611 *SR*
> *Littlestok(e)* 1310 *Ass*, 1344 FF
> *Herrylstoke* 1517 NQ i

[1] *Whatleys* c. 1840 *TA*.

v. stoc. Jones (224) says that this parish was in DB included under Melksham. Melksham was held by Earl Harold (TRE); it is just possible that he is the earl to whom reference is here made.

PUDNELL FM is *Podenhulle* 1309 WM xxxiv, 1341 Ipm, *Pudenhulle* 1309 ib. '*Puda*'s hill,' cf. Pudmore Pond (PN Sr 168).

BROUNCKER'S FM is *Brounkers Farm* 1773 A and D and takes its name from the family of William *Brunker* (1572 *FF*).

BITHAM WOOD (6″). Cf. **bytme** *infra* 425. The wood is in a hollow. STOKEHILL FM. Cf. *The Hull* 1309 WM xxxiv.

Hilperton

HILPERTON

> *Help(e)rinton, Helperitune* 1086 DB, *Helpringeton* 1205 FineR, *Helprington* 1282 FF
> *Hulprincton(a)* 1232 Lacock, *-ing-* 1279 *Ass*, *-yng-* 1416 Pat, *Hulprinton(e)* 1242 Fees, 1260 Misc, *-ryn-* 1289 *Ass*, 1316 FA, 1325 Pat
> *Hilprington* 1263 Pap, 1305 Cl, *-yng-* 1402 BM
> *Hylperton* 1268 *Ass*, *-pre-* 1351 Cl, *-pir-* 1359 ib., *-ber-* 1361 ib., *Hulper-* 1283 *FF*, *-ir-* 1359 Cl
> *Hylperton al. Hylprynton* 1571 NQ vii, *Hilprington al. Hilperton* 1598 Recov, *Helperton* 1675 Ogilby

The same first element occurs in *hulpryngmor* 964 (late) BCS 1127 in the bounds of Steeple Ashton just near. Ekwall (DEPN) is probably right in taking this as from a personal name *Hylpric*, a side-form of *Helpric* which is on record. Hence '*Hylpric*'s farm,' *v.* ingtun.

PAXCROFT FMS

> *Packelescroft(e)* 1249 *Ass*, 1254 Ipm, *Pakelescrofte* 1279, 1281, 1289 *Ass*, *Pachelescrofte* 1281, 1289 ib.
> *Paxcroft* 1574 *FF*, *Plaxcroft* 1667 Recov

'*Pæccel*'s croft or small field.' For the personal name cf. Patchway (PN Sx 309).

HILPERTON MARSH was probably the home of William *atte Mersshe* (1332 *SR*).

POUND FM (6″). Cf. *Pounde close* 1635 WIpm. SOUTHFIELD
COTTAGES (6″). Cf. *South Field* c. 1840 *TA*. WYKE HO is *Wyke*
1252 Ch, *Hylperton Wyke* 1491 *Ct. v.* wic and *supra* 25.

Melksham

MELKSHAM [melksəm, melsəm]

> Melcheshā 1086 DB, -*ham* 1144, 1156 P, 1204 ClR
> Melkesham 1155 RBE, 1172 P *et passim* to 1254 Ipm, *Melc-*
>   *sham* 1240 Pap
> Milkesham 1229 Cl, 1249 *Ass et passim* to 1553 WM x
> Mulkesham 1281 Cl
> Mylsham 1558–79 ECP, *Melsham* 1661, 1724 *FF*, *Milsham*,
>   *Melsam* 1675 Ogilby

There can be little doubt that at some stage in its history this
name has been associated with OE *meoloc*, 'milk,' but what its
ultimate history may be it is impossible to say.

NOTE. CHURCH ST is *Cherchestret* 1370 *Cor*. PRATER'S LANE is to be
associated with the family of William *Prater* (1642 *SR*).

BEANACRE [*vulgo* binəgər] is *Benacre* 1276 *FF*, 1286 Ch, 1351
Ipm, *Beneacre* 1296 Abbr, 1412 FA, *Beneger al. Benacre* 1573
FF, *Bineger* 1670 Aubrey, *Bennecar* 1773 A and D. 'Bean field,'
v. æcer.

BLACKMORE FOREST is *Blakemor(e)* 1230, 1260 Cl, 1268 *Ass*, (*la*)
t. Ed 3 *For*, *Black-* 1613 DKR xxxix. 'Black marshy land,'
v. mor. *Forest* because within the old Melksham Forest *supra*
14.

COWFOLD (lost) is *la Cufaude in foresta de Melkesham* 1224 ClR,
Cufaude 1251 Cl, *la Coufaud(e)* 1289 *Ass*, t. Ed 1 *For*, 1305
AD iii, (*la*) *Coufolde* 1321 *Ass*, 1341 Ipm. Identical in origin
with Cole Park *supra* 50.

RHOTTERIDGE FM is *Raderygge* 1331 *For*, -*rigge* 1334 Aubrey,
-*rigg* 1419 IpmR, *Ratarigge* 1490 *DuLa*, *Rotteridge* 1618 *FF*.
The early forms suggest the possibility of an interpretation 'red
ridge' from read and hrycg, but local enquiry does not much

favour such an interpretation even if we bear in mind the use of OE *rēad* in the sense 'golden-brown' (cf. Red Shore *infra* 318). There is sand here, mixed with a certain amount of gravel[1].

SHAW and SHAW HILL are *Schawe* 1256 FF, *Shaghe* 1286 Ch, *Shawe juxta Melksham* 1379 FF, *Shaa* 1641 *Recov*, 1652 *FF*, *Shawhill* 1671 *Recov*. 'Wood or copse,' *v*. sceaga.

WHITLEY is *Witlege* 1001 (14th) KCD 706, *Witelie* 1086 DB, *Whitlee* 1286 Ch, *Wytelegh* 1296 *Rental*, *Whitele* 1381 IpmR. 'White clearing or wood,' *v*. leah.

WOODROW HO (6") is *la Woderewe* 1248 *Ass*, 1252 FF, *la Wuderewe* 1257 *For*, *Woderewe juxta Melkesham* 1321 *Ass*, *alias le Quenecourt* 1408 *FF*, *Quenescourt* 1411 Cl, *la Grove al. Woderewe al. Quenecourte* 1464 Pat. 'Row of trees.'

WOOLMORE FM (6") is *Wolvemere, Wlve-* 1249 *Ass*, *Wulve-* 1257 *For*, 1296 *Rental*, *Wulmeresmershe* t. Ed 3 *For*, *Wolmere* 1412 FA, *Woolmer* 1629 *FF*. 'Wolves' pool or mere.' Identical in origin with Woolmer Forest (Ha).

CHURCH FM (6"), CROFT HO (6"), SLADE'S FM and TOWNSEND FM were the homes of Margery *atte Churcheheye* (1346 *Ass*), Hugh de *Crofte* (1272 ib.), William de *la Slade* (1263 *For*) and William *atte Tounesende* (1333 *SR*). *v*. croft, slæd and (ge)hæg, 'enclosure.' In Slade's the *s* is no doubt pseudo-manorial.

DANIEL'S WOOD (6"), LOVES FM (6") and SELVES FM are to be associated with the families of Stephen *Daniel* (1296 *Rental*), William *Love* or *Loove* (1597 NQ viii) and William *Self* (t. Ed 3 *For*). The last is *Silves Farm* (1773 A and D).

BERRYFIELD (6") is *Bereghfeld* 1286 Ch, *Berry feild* 1682 NQ iv, *v*. beorg, 'hill,' 'barrow.' BOWERHILL is *Bowrehill* 1741 *Recov*. Cf. *Bowermede* 1540 *MinAcct*, *Bowerhill Mead* 1597 *Sadler* and *infra* 424. BUSHEY MARSH FM is *Bushy Marsh* 1773 A and D. CHAPEL PLANTATION. Cf. *Chapel Mead* c. 1840 *TA*. CLACKERS BRIDGE (6") is so named in 1773 (A and D). Cf. *Clackers* c. 1840 *TA* (Seend). CONIGRE FM (6") is *Coniger* 1632 WIpm. See *infra* 427. CRAYSMARSH FM (6") is *Craies marshe* t. Jas 1 *SP*.

---

[1] *Ex inf*. Mr W. B. Tonkin.

Cf. *Cray Croft* c. 1840 *TA*. HACK FM (6″) is *Hack House* 1773 A and D. HANGING WOOD (6″). Cf. *Hanging Ground* c. 1840 *TA*. HOLBROOK FM is *Holebroke* 13th Trop, *Holbrooks feild* 1682 NQ iv. Cf. Hollybrook *supra* 119. KITE'S STILE (6″). Cf. *Kyte close* t. Jas 1 *SP*. LONG LEAZE (6″) is so named c. 1840 (*TA*). MELKSHAM BRIDGE is *the Great Bridge* 1637 Sess. MOONGROUND PLANTATION (6″). Cf. *Moon Ground* c. 1840 *TA*. NEWTON FM is *Neuton* 1289 *Ass*, *la Niwetoune* 1341 *Cor*, *Newtowne* 1640 WIpm. OUTMARSH FM is *Out Marsh* 1682 NQ iv. POPLAR FM (6″). Cf. *Poplar Ground* c. 1840 *TA*. QUEENFIELD is *Queenefeild* 1637 *Phillipps*. Cf. *Quenemore* 1469 *FF* and *s.n.* Woodrow *supra* 129. REDSTOCKS is *Red Stocks or Stoke* 1773 A and D. SANDRIDGE is *Sandrug'* 1268 *Ass*, *-regge* 1281 ib., *-rigge* 1419 IpmR, *Saunderighill* 1484 Pat. Self-explanatory. SHURNHOLD is *Shurnell* 1778 WM xliii, 1820 G. SNARLTON is *Snarlton Row* 1773 A and D. Cf. Snarlton in Winkfield *supra* 124. SOHO FM (6″) is *Soho* ib., probably a nickname from the London place of that name. It is on the border of the parish. SOUTHBROOK FM (6″). Cf. *South Brook* c. 1840 *TA*. STUB COPPICE (6″). Cf. *Stub Ground* ib. TANHOUSE FM (6″) is *Tan House* 1773 A and D. WEST HILL is so named in 1801 (*Recov*). WESTLAND'S FM is *Westlond* 1362 *Cor*.

Poulshot

POULSHOT [poulʃət]

    Paveshou (sic) 1086 DB

    Paulesholt 1187 P, 1216 ClR, 1255 RH, 1272 FF, 1274 *Ass*, 1395 *Ct*, *Palesholte* 1331 Ch

    Pawelesholt(e) 1242 Fees, *Pauelesholt(e)* 1249, 1268 *Ass*, 1332 SR

    Powelesholt 1268 *Ass*, *Poulesholt* 1335 Cl, 1428 FA, *Powlesholde* 1553 WM x

    Pollesholde 1585 NQ vii, *-holt* 1613 *FF*, *Polshed* t. Eliz WM xxi, *Pousall al. Polshead* 1675 Ogilby

    Polshott al. Powlsholt 1632 *Recov*, *Polsholde* 1666 *SR*

Poulshot is at first sight a difficult name. The probabilities are however that we should associate it with one or two other similar West Country names. There is a Poleshill in Milverton (So), (*æt*) *Pauleshele* c. 1070 (c. 1150) KCD 897, *Pouselle* 1086 DB,

Pauleshulle, Pawleshele 1278–84 Ipm, *Pouleshele* 1327 SR, 1391 FF, and a Polsham in the same county, *Paulesham* 1065 (13th) Wells, *Poulesham* 13th ib., 1284 FF. All three names alike suggest that the Christian name *Paul* was early current in the West Country. The normal development of *Paul* is to *Poul(e)* in ME. Hence '*Paul*'s wood,' v. **holt**.

NOTE. BYDE MILL LANE (6″). Cf. *Byde Mill* c. 1840 *TA* and *Byde Mill Mead* ib. in the neighbouring parish of Seend and *supra* 4. HOOKS LANE (6″). Cf. *Hooks* ib. LEIGHBALL LANE. Cf. *Layball breach* 1634 WIpm, v. **bræc** and *balle infra* 422–3.

SUMMERHAM BRIDGE is *Sumerham* 13th AD vi, *Somerham* 1332 *SR* (p), t. Ed 3 *For.* Perhaps 'summer **ham** or **hamm**' because used at that time. Cf. the place-name Somerton found in L, Nf, O and So.

BARLEYHILL FM (6″). Cf. *Barley Hill* 1773 A and D. GREEN FM. Cf. *Poulshot Green* ib. THE MARSH (6″). Cf. *Marsh Furlong* c. 1840 *TA*. TOWNSEND FM. Cf. *Townsend Piece* ib.

Seend

SEEND [*olim* si·n]

Sinda 1190, 1195 P

Seinde 1194, 1200 ib., 1235 Fees, *Seynde* 1249 *Ass*, 1553 WM x, *Scheynde* 1283 Ipm

Sende 1211 RBE, 1227 FF *et passim* to 1322 Pat, (*juxta Divyses*) 1289 *FF*

Senede 1279 *Ass* (p)

Seende 1330 Pat, *Syend* 1541 LP

Seene al. Seend 1602 *Recov*, 1635 *FF*, *Sceene* 1650 *ParlSurv*, *Send vulgo Seene* 1670 Aubrey, *Sean* 1675 Ogilby

This is a difficult name. Topographically the site is a distinctive one. Seend is on the top of an isolated hill (an outcrop of iron-sand) which rises steeply up from the valley 150 ft. below[1]. This makes it difficult to accept Ekwall's suggestion that it is named from Semington Brook *supra* 10. That stream is a mile and a half away and its old name is persistently *Sem(e)net*. Ekwall suggests that it had an alternative form *Semned*, but there

[1] Aubrey (302–3) has some interesting comment on the soil.

is no evidence for such a form in this name and it would hardly explain the forms for Seend with their persistent final *e*. It should be noted further that *semnet* shows no such tendency to develop to *seint* in Semington *infra* 143.

It would seem therefore that the suggestion made in PN Sr 146, *s.n.* Send, that the name goes back to OE **sænde*, 'sandy place,' is still the most likely explanation. The spellings in the Pipe Roll forms are difficult but the *ei*-forms are probably due to attempts to represent the *e*-vowel as lengthened before the consonant-group.

NOTE. COLBOURNE LANE. Cf. *Caburn* c. 1840 *TA*.

INMARSH is *Hennemershe* 1225 *Edington*, 1341 *Cor*, 1345 *Ass*, *Henmersshe* 1432–43 ECP, *-marsh(e)* 1553, 1659 *FF*, *In Marsh* 1654 *Sadler*. Originally 'hen marsh' with reference probably to some kind of waterfowl. The later corruption is identical with that found in Moreton in the Marsh (Gl), cf. PN Wa 299–300.

SEEND HEAD, PARK and ROW are *Sendheved* 1227 FF, *Shende-heved* 1249 ib., *Sendenheved* 1281 *Ass*, *Synd(e)hede* 1443, 1444 Pat, *Sendhede* 1503 Ipm, *Seenehead* 1597 *FF*, *park of Sende* 1421 Pat, *Sendenerewe, Senderowe* 1268 *Ass*, 1279, 1289 ib., *Shende Rew* 1546 *SR*. The heafod or 'head' clearly has reference to the well-marked projection at the south-west end of the hill on which Seend lies, the ræw or 'row' is the name of the straggling hamlet which lies along the western end of the ridge.

PILE FM was the home of William de *la Pyle* (1257 *For*) and *atte Pyle* (1332 *SR*). This must be OE *pīl*, 'stake, pile.' Cf. Pilemoor (PN D 420).

MARTINSLADE[1], MITCHELL'S FM (6″) and TURNER'S FM are to be associated with the families of Roger *Martyn* (1327 *SR*), Edward *Mitchell* (1642 ib.) and Roger *le Turnur* (1270 *For*).

BERHILLS FM is *Berehille* 1305 AD vi. SEEND CLEEVE. Cf. *Clyve* 1255 RH, *les Cleves* 1341 Pat, *Seend Cleeve* 1773 A and D and clif *infra* 426. EGYPT FM (6″) is so named c. 1840 (*TA*). REW FM (6″). Cf. *Rewham* 1681 NQ iv and Introd. xx. By SEEND

---

[1] *Martin Slade* 1773 A and D, *v.* slæd.

Row *supra* 132. ROWCROFT FM is *Row(e)croft* 1377 *MinAcct*, 1582 *FF*, 'rough croft.' SELLS GREEN (6"). Cf. *Selfestreet* 1639 *Sess*, probably taking its name from the family noted under Selves Fm *supra* 129. THE STOCKS. Cf. *Stocks Ground* c. 1840 *TA*. THORNHAM FM is *Thorneham* 1609 NQ iii, *Thornam* 1681 ib. iv.

Staverton

STAVERTON[1] [stævətən]

Stavretone 1086 DB

Stanerton (sic) 1206 Abbr, *Staverton* 1212 Cur *et passim*, -*tona* 1230 Bracton

Stafferton 1509 *DuLa*, 1642 *SR*, 1733 *Recov*

This name, as explained *s.n.* Staverton (PN Nth 28–9), is probably a compound of OE *stæfer*, 'pole, stake,' dialectal *staver*, and tun, hence 'stake-enclosure.'

SMALLBROOK is *Smalebroc* 1086 DB, 1242 Fees, -*broke* 1231 Bracton, -*broch* 1232 FF. 'Narrow stream,' *v.* smæl, broc.

Trowbridge

TROWBRIDGE [troubridʒ]

Straburg (sic) 1086 DB

Trobrigge 1184 P, -*breg* 1222 FF, -*brige* 1235, 1242 Fees

Troubrigg(e) 1211 ClR, 1227, 1322 Ch, 1332 *SR*, -*brig* 1236 Ch, 1249 *Ass*, 1265 Pat, -*brygge* 1316 FA

Treubrige 13th AD iv, -*brigge* 1232 Lacock, -*bregg*' 1268 *Ass*, *Trewbrigge* 1250 SarumCh, -*bregge* 1279 *Ass*, *Trewebrugge* 1281 ib.

Trowbrugg(e) 1230 Bracton, -*brigge* 1316 *FF*, *Trowebregge* 1289 *Ass*

Trebrugg' 1257 Cl, -*brigge* 1311 Ipm

Trubrigge 1275 RH, t. Ed 4 *DuLa*, *Trubridge* 1553 WM x

Troughbrigge 1358 BPR, 1395 IpmR, *Throughbrygge* 1489 *MinAcct*, *Trowghbrygge* 1509 *DuLa*

'Tree bridge,' i.e. 'bridge made by a tree trunk or of wood generally,' *v.* treow, brycg. Some of the late spellings may have been influenced by the word 'trough.' Cf. Trobridge (PN D 406).

[1] A tithing of Trowbridge, made into a separate parish in 1895.

NOTE. ADCROFT LANE is so named in 1671 (WM xv), leading to Adcroft *infra* 135. BACK ST is *Bakstrete* t. Ed 4 *DuLa*. CASTLE ST is *Castelstrete* ib. CONIGRE. Cf. *Ye Conygere paddock* 1671 WM xv. 'Rabbit warren,' *v. infra* 427. FORE ST is probably *alte strate* 1468 *MinAcct*, *le Highstrete* t. Ed 4 *DuLa*. Cf. *supra* 21. MARKET ST. Cf. *in foro* 1509 ib., *the Market Place* c. 1600 WM x. POLEBARN RD. Cf. *Powle barne* 1594 NQ i, *Polebarne ground* 1671 WM xv. ROUND-STONE ST was earlier *Lovemead St* (Goodrich). Cf. *Luvemede* 1262 Seld ii, *Lovemede* 1348 *Cor*. It takes its present name from a round stone which once stood here at the end of Polebarn Road. SILVER ST is so named in 1773 (A and D). TIMBRELL ST. The manor of Trow-bridge passed to Thomas *Timbrell* in 1807 (Goodrich). WEST ST is *Westrete* 1488 *DuLa*.

Lost names include *lez Barres* 1468 *MinAcct*, *Crooked Lane* 1516 WM xli, *Newladyslane alias Newlandyslane* 1509 *DuLa*.

COCK HILL (6″) and COCKHILL FM are *Cochulle* 1303 *GDR*, *Cockhill* 1632 WIpm, *Cockell House* 1773 A and D. Ekwall (DEPN *s.n.* Cock Beck) connects this and other examples of *cock hill* with a lost OE **cocc*, 'hillock,' found in *haycock* and various place-names. The *cock hills* are too numerous for us to explain them from the bird name, which is only very rarely found in place-names.

INNOX MILL (6″). Cf. *la Inhoke* 1232 Lacock, *Inhok* 1332 AD i, *Estenneke, Northynnok, Southennok* 1468 *MinAcct*, *le Inhoke, Northinoke, Southinoke, Estinoke* 1488 *DuLa*, *Inhokmede* 1500 Pat, *Upper Innox, Nether Innox* 1553 *DuLa*. This is the word *inhoc, inhoke* sb. (obs.) discussed in NED. Its sense is clear; it is used in the 13th and 14th centuries of land temporarily enclosed from the fallow and put under cultivation. The quota-tions illustrating its use and meaning given in NED are from the Sarum Statutes, from the Oseney Register and from the Malmesbury Cartulary, and it is in the counties of Wiltshire, Oxfordshire, Gloucestershire and Somersetshire that this word, generally in the plural form *Innocks, Innox* and the like, is most common (see *infra* 438). Its history is obscure. It has been associated with OE *hōc*, 'hook,' used possibly in the sense 'corner, angle,' but in those circumstances the *in* does not seem to have much meaning. More probably *inhok* is what results from a process of 'in-hooking,' i.e. hooking or bringing into cultivation, the vb. *inhokare* being on record from medieval documents.

STUDLEY is *Stodlega* 1167 P, *-leg(h)* 1232 Ch, 1279 *For*, 1332 *SR*, *Stodelegh* 1490 *DuLa*. 'Clearing for horses,' *v.* stod, leah.

ADCROFT HO (6″) is *Addecrofte* t. Ed 4 *DuLa*, *v.* croft. GALLEY FM (6″). Cf. *pasture called the gallie* 1594 NQ i, *the Gallye* 1635 WIpm. *gallie* probably stands for *gallow*. HOLBROOK FM (6″) is *Holebrok* 1341 *Cor*, *Holbrooke* t. Jas 1 ECP. Cf. Hollybrook *supra* 119. LONDON BRIDGE (6″) is so named c. 1840 (*TA*). LONGFIELD is *Long Field* ib. SILVER STREET FM (6″). Cf. *Silver Street* 1773 A and D. WESTFIELD (6″) is *West Field* c. 1840 *TA*. WYKE HO is *Wyk* 1289 *Ass*, 1332 *SR*, *Weeke* 1666 ib., *v.* wic and *supra* 25.

XI. WHORWELLSDOWN HUNDRED

(*and lang*) *wereforesdone* 964 (late) BCS 1127
woresotes doune 968 (15th) ib. 1215
Weruedesdona 1086 ExonDB, *Wervedeston* 1274 *Ass*
Hweruelesdena 1234 Bracton, *Wherewelesdone* 1279 *Ass*,
    Wheruelesdon 1289 ib., *Whereweldoune* 1402 FA
Weruelesdon 1249 *Ass*, *-vel-* 1255 RH, 1268 *Ass*, 1288 *FF*,
    Wervollesdone 1275 RH
Wherflesdone 1279, 1281 *Ass*, *Whorlesdown* 1565 WM i

All these forms refer to the hundred. The following refer to an actual place: *villa de Werflesdon* 1281 *Ass*, *Wherflesdon* 1289 ib., *Woreweldown* 1531 *FF*, *Horwells Down* 1575 Hoare.

The first element in this name is OE *hwyrfel* recorded independently and in various compounds in OE charters. The clearest application of this word is found in the Culmstock charter (BCS 724) where it is used of a well-marked circular hill (cf. PN D 612 n.). The same word or its Scandinavian cognate is found in Whorl Hill (PN NRY 177), a high round hill in Cleveland. The primary idea is of something circular. We have it compounded with dun in the unidentified *wirfuldoune* in the Idmiston charter (BCS 867) and here we have a similar compound but in a genitival form. Here, as is often the case, the original name of the hill is put into the genitival form with the common word for hill added, hence *hwirfles-dun*, later

Whorwellsdown. The pseudo-OE forms are found in late ME transcripts, setting forth the boundaries of Steeple Ashton and Edington respectively, and Whorwellsdown must be identified with the low rounded hill on which the boundaries of Steeple Ashton, Edington, Bratton and West Ashton meet, near Crosswelldown Fm *infra* 138. The local pronunciation is [wərlidən].

Ashton

ASHTON, STEEPLE and WEST

(*to*) *Æystone*, (*at*) *Aystone* 964 (late) BCS 1127

Aistone 1086 DB, *Aystone al. Aysstone* 1299 Ipm, *Aysshtone* 1333 *SR*

Westaston 1248 *Ass*, 1257 *For*, *West Asshton juxta Stupel Asshton* 1305 *FF*

Stepelaston 1268 *Ass*, 1289 *FF*, *Stupel A(y)shton* 1289 *Ass*, 1341 *Rental*, *Stapelashton* 1363 Pat, *Stipelasshtoun* 1391 ib.

Chirchaston 1268 *Ass*

Gyldeneaston 1279 ib., *Guldene Ashton* 1281 ib., *Gildenasheton* 1289 ib., *Gyldon Ashton* 1533–8 ECP

'Ash farm,' *v.* tun. *Steeple*, as may be seen from its early forms, clearly goes back to OE *stīepel*, 'steeple,' and not to OE *stapol*, 'staple, market.' The reference must be to the church steeple. In WM (xxxii, 182) it is stated that in deeds of Ed 1 and 2 it is called Ashton *Forum* and that there is a charter of 1349 at the PRO granting a market here to the Abbess of Romsey. If so, the place may have also been known as *Staple* Ashton (cf. the 1363 form) but that cannot be the source of the *stepel*, *stupel* forms. *Gyldene*, etc., apparently an alternative name for Steeple Ashton, cf. *s.n.* Moreton Pinkney (PN Nth 41). It is probably descriptive of a wealthy manor.

Steeple Ashton

NOTE. DROVE LANE. Cf. *le Drove* 1341 *Rental*, *le Drovelane* 1526 *Ct*, i.e. a cattle road. MUDMEAD LANE. Cf. *Mudmede furlong* 1491 ib. In old records we find also *le Suthestrete*, *Ballard lane* ib., *Sweltenham lane*, *le Morelane*, *Mershelane* 1526 ib.

AMOURACRE (6″) is *Ammer acre* c. 1625 WM xxiii, *Amour Acre Farm* 1841 *Devizes*. *ammer* is probably from OE *amore*, the name of a bird, cognate with Ger *ammer* and identical with the element *hammer* found in yellow-*hammer*. Cf. *ammer* (NED).

SMITH'S WELL WOOD (6″) is *le Smytheswelle* 15th WM xxxvi, *Snytwell oth. Smitwell oth. Snytefield* 1630 WIpm. There was also a *Snyteforlong* (1341 *Rental*) in this neighbourhood. It looks as if compounds of OE *snite*, 'snipe,' and OE *smiþ*, 'smith,' found in names of neighbouring places had in the course of their history been completely confused.

ASHTON MILL[1] and BROOK FM[2] (6″) were the homes of Nicholas *atte Mulle* (1370 *Ass*) and John *atte Brok* (1327 *SR*).

SPIERS PIECE and WATTS FM (6″) are to be associated with the families of Thomas *Spire* (t. Jas 1 *Rental*) and Roger *Watts* (c. 1840 *TA*).

ABURY (old 6″) is *Aldebury in Stepulashton* 1262 *Cor*, *Albery* t. Hy 8 *Rental*. 'Old burh.' There are no remains here now. BULLENHILL. Cf. *Bolenham* 14th WM xxxvii, *High, Low Bullen Coppice* 1606 Hoare. ELMSGATE HO. Cf. *Elms Gate* c. 1840 *TA*. LOPPINGER FM (6″) is *Lobbingeh'* 1273 *Ct*, *Lopyngell* t. Hy 8 *Rental, Loppinger, Loppyneger* t. Eliz *LRMB, Loppingers* 1633 WIpm. RAY DOWNS (6″). Cf. *Revedoune lane* 1431, *Redowne* 1494 *Ct*, *Reydowne* 1550 Pat, *Raydowne* 1604 DKR xxxix. SNARLTON (6″). Cf. *supra* 124. WHITE LAWN LANE (6″). Cf. *launde infra* 440.

West Ashton

ROOD ASHTON

> *Chapel As(s)hton* 1307 Cl, 1339 Pat, *Chapelasshtoun* 1391 ib., *Chappelaston* 1476 IpmR
>
> *Rode A(y)ssheton* 1474 ib., 1500 Ipm, *Road Ashton* 1575 Hoare, *Rowde Asheton* 1596 BM, *Chapple Ashton al. Roode Ashton* 1631 *Recov*

This Ashton must have been distinguished by the presence of a *rood* or cross. It is almost certainly the same which is mentioned in *rodestan* (BCS 1127) in the bounds of Ashton.

---

[1] Cf. *le Wyndemyll* 1491 *Ct*.
[2] *Broke* ib., *Broke place* t. Eliz *LRMB*.

KETTLE LANE COTTAGES (6″). The lane is *Kytelleslane* 1526 *Ct*, *Kittles Lane* 1830 Hoare and the first element probably goes back to the first element in *Kydewelgarston* (15th WM xxxvi), i.e. 'kid-spring or stream.' There is still a field close by called *Kittles* (c. 1840 *TA*).

YARNBROOK is *Yondebrok* 1367 *FF*, *Yondbroke* 1599 ib., *Yanbrook* 1802 *Map*. '(Place) beyond the brook,' from OE *begeondan brōce*. Cf. Yonderlake (PN D 383). Names of this type are very common in Devon (PN D Pt. 1, xxxvii). Some other examples are found in Wiltshire in early documents but they seldom survive on the modern map. We may note *Binorthe the cumbe* (1276 StNicholas) in Broad Chalke, *Bovetheclyve* (1360 *Winch-Coll*) in Durrington, *Nethenebrugge* (1279 *Ass*) in Wilton, *Bovethethornes* (1310 Ipm) in Yatesbury. We have possible survivals in Easton Town *supra* 111 and Norney *infra* 244.

FLOWERS WOOD is to be associated with the family of John *Flowre* (1491 *Ct*).

BLACKBALL BRIDGE. Cf. *Blackballe* 1491 *Ct*, *Black Ball* 1793 Carey, and *infra* 422. CROSSWELLDOWN FM is *Crowswell Down(s)* 1663 NQ iv, *Crowswell Downs* 1804 *Recov*. THE DROVE (6″) is probably *Motweye* t. Hy 3 *Edington*, leading to the *moot* on Whorwellsdown (*supra* 135–6). EAST TOWN FM is *Estaston* 1257 *For*, 1268 *Ass*, *East Towne* 1628 *Recov*. Also known as *Sulden* or *Silden's Ashton* (Aubrey 355) from a former owner. STOURTON PLANTATION (6″). Cf. *Sturton Farm* 1773 A and D. The Lords Stourton, former owners of Stourhead, had property here.

North Bradley

NORTH BRADLEY

Bradlega 1174 P
Bradelege c. 1210 SarumCh, 1225 FF, -*legh* 1232 Cl, (*juxta Trowebregge*) 1281 *Ass*
North Bradlegh 1352 *FF*, *Northbradeleye* 1394 *Ass*, *North Broadly* 1632 Sess

'Wide clearing,' *v.* leah. *North* to distinguish from Maiden Bradley *infra* 172.

BROKERSWOOD [*olim* brɔkəˑzwud]

> Brochuuere 1257 For, Brokeure 1327 SR (p), 1375 Ct, Brok-
> evere 1334 Ass, Brokeuereswode 1426 Ct
> Brokerswode c. 1460 Rental, le Brockerswode 1491 Ct, Brockers
> Wood 1803 Act

The name is apparently identical in origin with Brockhurst *supra* 38, a compound of OE brocc, 'badger,' or broc, 'brook,' and yfer, 'slope, bank.'

CUTTERIDGE

> Cuderug(g)e 1241 FF, 1279, 1289 Ass
> Coterugge c. 1250 Edington, 1356 FF, -rigge 1289 Ass, 1332
> SR (p), 1353 Cl, -rygge 1396 IpmR, Cl, 1412 MinAcct
> Coderugge 1289 Ass (p), -rigge 1304 FF
> Cudderygge 1305 Ass

Probably '*Cūda*'s ridge,' *v.* hrycg.

HONEYBRIDGE FM (6″) is *Hunybrigge* t. Ed 1 *DuLa, Honnebrigge* 1278 *Ass, Honybrigge* 1327 *SR* (p), 1341 *Rental*, 1388 IpmR, 1399 Pat, *Honyngbrugge* 1365 *MinAcct, Honybrugge* 1412 ib., *-burge* t. Eliz *LRMB*. No certainty is possible with regard to this name. Were it not for the forms *Honnebrigge* and *Honyngbrugge* it would seem fairly certain that this was a compound of *hunig*, 'honey,' and brycg, denoting either a bridge where bees swarmed or one which had a sticky, muddy surface. Cf. the common Honey Lane. In that case it probably has a parallel in Honey-burge (PN Bk 116). The other forms suggest the possibility of the personal name *Hun(n)a* with connective ing and later folk-etymologising. Hence '*Huna*'s bridge.'

CARTER'S BRIDGE (6″) and DRUCE'S FM are to be associated with the families of William *le Cartere* (1327 *SR*) and Phineas *Druce* (1626 WIpm).

AXE AND CLEAVER FM (6″) is *Axe and Cleaver* 1802 *Map*. DRYNHAM is *Drynam* 1625 WM xxiii, *Drienham* 1671 ib. xv. Doubtless a compound of OE *drȳgean*, dat. of dryge, 'dry,' and hamm. HAZEL WOOD (6″) is *Hazle Wood* c. 1840 *TA*. HIGH WOOD is so named ib. IRELAND is so named in 1802 (O.G.S.C.)

and in 1841 (*Devizes*). The neighbouring farm is SCOTLAND in Southwick. Possibly so nicknamed because on the extreme edges of these parishes, cf. *infra* 454. ORGAN POOL FM (6") is *Organ Pool* 1802 *Map*. PICKET WOOD is *Picked Copse* 1617 *Map*, *Picked Wood* 1802 ib. *v. infra* 443. It is triangular in shape. POUND FM. Cf. *Pound close* 1631 WIpm, *Pound Ground* c. 1840 *TA*. THE RANK is *The Rank* 1841 *Devizes*. ROUND WOOD is *Rondwode* 1341 Pat, *Rounde woode* t. Eliz *LRMB*. WOODMARSH is *Wodemershe* 1432 Cl, *Woodmarsh* 1625 WM xxiii.

Coulston, East and West

COULSTON, EAST and WEST [koulstən, *vulgo* koulsən]

> *Covelestone* 1086 DB, *Coueleston* 1206 Abbr *et freq* to 1332 *SR*, with variant spelling *Cov*-
>
> *Cuuleston(e)* 1086 DB, 1242 Fees, *Cuveleston(e)* 1222, 1255 FF, (*juxta Devises*) 1304 *Ass*, *Couveleston* 1267 Ipm, 1363 *FF*
>
> *Couleston* 1316 FA, *Coweleston* 1484 Pat, *Cowlyston* 1512 *Rental*, *West Cowlston* 1632 *Recov*
>
> *Culston* 1501 ECP, (*West*) 1525 *SR*
>
> *Cowston* 1613 *FF*, *Cowlson* 1637 *Phillipps*, *Colson* 1675 Ogilby

'*Cūfel*'s farm,' *v.* tun.

Edington

EDINGTON [ediŋtən]

> (*æt*) *Eðandune* 880–5 (c. 1000) BCS 553, *Eþandun* c. 890 ASC (Ā) *s.a.* 878, -ð- 957 BCS 1347, *Ethandun* c. 1000 Asser
>
> *Edendone* 1086 DB, -*don(a)* t. Hy 3 *Edington*, 1257 *For*
>
> *Edindun* 1236 FF, *Edyndon* 1272 Misc, *Edindon(e)* 1275 RH, 1289 *FF*, 1297 Pat, *Edynton* 1361 *FF*
>
> *Edyngdon(e)* 1291 Tax, 1327 *SR*, 1392 Pat, 1398 BM, 1512 *Rental*, -*doun* 1386 Cl, -*ton* 1428 FA, *Eddington* 1546 LP

Ekwall (DEPN *s.n.*) takes the first element of this name to be the OE word *ēþe*, found once and cognate with ON *auðr*, OHG *odi* (German *öde*). The sense would then be 'waste, bare or uncultivated hill or downland,' *v.* dun. The place lies just below the chalk downs of the Plain. The name may equally well be derived from the pers. name *Ēða* recorded in the 8th century.

NOTE. *Kyngweye, Rugweye* t. Hy 3 *Edington*.

Baynton is *Beinton* 1203 Cur (p), *Bainton* 1204 ib., *Beynton* 1208 Abbr, c. 1250 *Edington et freq* to 1428 FA, *Beyntonesfeld* 1348 *Cor*. Possibly '*Bǣga*'s farm,' *v.* tun. *Bǣda* is also possible. For loss of *d* cf. Bainton (PN O 45).

Housecroft Fm is *Houscroft* t. Hy 3 *Edington*, 1354 Cl, *Hus-croftes*, *Houscroftes* 1397 *Ct*, *Housecroftes*, *Howe croftes* 1550 Pat. 'Croft or paddock near a house,' *v.* croft.

Tinhead

 Tunheda 1190 P, *-hyde* t. Hy 3 *Edington*, *-hid(e)* 1275 RH, 1373 *Ct*

 Tynhide 1242 SarumCh, 1249, 1253 *Ass*, *Tinhide* 1275 RH, *Tynhyde* 1332 *SR*, 1402 FA

 Tenhyde t. Hy 3 *Edington*, 1256 FF, 1270 *For*, *-hid*, *-y-* 1327 Banco, *SR*

 Teynhed 1255 RH (p), *-hid* 1258 *Ass*, *Teenhide* 1280 Ch

 Tyenhyde 1289 *Ass*, *Thienhide* 1305 ib. (p)

 Tynnehide 1397 *Ct*, *Tynehead* 1563 *FF*, *Tynhedd* t. Eliz WM xxi, *Tenehedd* 1571 *SR*, *Tinnet* 1657 *Devizes*

'Ten hides,' *v.* hid. See Mawer, *PN and History* 22. Cf. Teignhead (PN D 459) for another corruption of such a name. Unfortunately it is impossible to identify in DB the holding which gave rise to Tinhead.

Ballard's Fm, Butler's Fm, Hudd's Mill and Slade's Fm (all 6″) are to be associated with the families of Henry *Ballard* (1257 *For*), Laurence *le Boteler* (1289 *Ass*), Robert *Hudde* (1281 ib.) and Richard *Slade* (1587 NQ viii).

Barn Bottom (6″). Cf. *Barn Mead* c. 1840 *TA*. The City (6″). Cf. *City Piece* ib., *pasture called great Citties* 1642 WIpm in Broughton and *infra* 455. Court Fm (6″). Cf. *Courte Close* 1550 Pat. Ivymill Fm. Cf. *Ivey Mill* 1773 A and D. Lady Well (6″) is so named ib. Long Hollow is so named in 1839 (*Devizes*). South Down is *Southdoune* 1283 *MinAcct*. South Down Sleight is *South Down Sheep Sleight* c. 1840 *TA*. *v. infra* 454. Tenantry Down is so named ib. *v. infra* 431. West Down Fm. Cf. *la Westhulle* 1426 *Ct*, *Westerne downe* 1540 *MinAcct*. The Wilderness (6″) is so named c. 1840 (*TA*). Wood Bridge (6″) is *Wodebrigge* 1341 *Cor*.

Great Hinton

GREAT HINTON

Henton' 1216 ClR *et passim*, (*Greate*) 1547 *SR*, (*juxta Stepel Ashton*) 1349 *FF*

'High farm,' from OE (*æt þām*) *hēan tūne*, *v.* heah, tun.

CASTLE LEAZE (6″) is so named c. 1840 (*TA*). *v.* læs. COLD HARBOUR is so named in 1820 (G). *v. infra* 451. HAG HILL is *Hagg Hill* 1625 *For.* PORTWAY HO (6″). Cf. *Portway* 1494 *Ct*, *messuage voc. Portway* 1667 *FF*. It lies on the road to Keevil, cf. *supra* 16.

Keevil

KEEVIL

(*on*) *Kefle wirtrim* 964 (late) BCS 1127

Chivele 1086 DB, c. 1210 HMC Var i, *Chivelai* 1130, 1165 P, *Kivele*, *-y-* 1211 RBE, 1215, 1217 ClR *et passim* to 1425 Pat, *Keyvele* 1318 ib.

Kiuelea t. Hy 2 *Shaston*, *Kiveley* 1217 ClR, *Kyvelegh* 1240 Cl, 1284 Ipm, *-lee* 1268 *Ass*, *-leye* 1289 ib. *-leie* 1330 Inq aqd, *Kywelegh* 1412 FA

Keuele 1222 Bracton, *Keveleye* 1289 *Ass*, *Keveleigh* 1535 VE

Kivel 1231 Cl, *Kyvel* 1249 *Ass*

Cuvel 1242 Fees, *Kuvele* 1293 Pat, *Cuvele* 1327, 1397 Ipm

Kevell 1546 LP, *Keveleigh al. Kevell* 1560 *Recov*, 1561 *FF*

It may be that this is one of those names like Crowle (PN Wo 315) and such names as Acle, Bale, Eagle, etc. mentioned by Ekwall (DEPN *s.v.* leah) in which final *le* (from the dat. sg. of leah) has developed to ModEng [əl]. Ekwall suggests that the first element is either an OE personal name *Cyfa*, a mutated variant of the recorded *Cufa* or OE *cȳf*, 'tub, vessel,' and that the name *cȳfa-leah* denoted a wood where such tubs were made. Alternatively we may suggest that the first element was the OE diminutive *cȳfel* from *cȳf*, used here perhaps of the depression in which Keevil lies. The *wirtrim* of the first form is from OE *wyrtruma* and has reference to some part of the Keevil-Steeple Ashton boundary (cf. Grundy ii, 71).

NOTE. BUTTS LANE probably led to the archery butts. Cf. *infra* 425.

Baldham Bridge is *Baldeham* 1270 *For* (p), *Baldenham* 1289, 1305 *Ass* (both p), c. 1460 *Rental*, 1744 *Recov*, *Baldenham* 1341 *Rental*, *Baldenhamesbregge* t. Ed 3 *For*, *Baldnam Bridge* 1583 WM xxi. '*Bealda*'s ham(m).'

Pantry Bridge is so named in 1773 (A and D). It is earlier *Pyntrowebrygge* 1362 *Cor*, and would seem to denote a bridge made of pine-wood or (less probably) near a pine-tree (OE *pīn-trēow*).

Mere Fm[1] and Woodhouse Fm[2] (both 6″) were probably the homes of Walter *atte Mere* (1332 *SR*) and William *atte Wode de Kyvele* (1279 *Ass*). v. mere, 'pool.'

Martin's Fm (6″) is to be associated with the family of Anthonie *Martin* (1597 NQ viii).

Keevil Wick is *Kyvele Wyk* 1279 *Ass*, *Kevylweke* 1494 *Ct*, *Keevell Weeke* 1631 *Recov*. v. wic and *supra* 25. Longleaze Fm (6″). Cf. *Long Leaze* c. 1840 *TA*. Oxen Leaze Fm (6″). Cf. *Oxenlese* 1327 Ipm, *Oxenleaze* 1573 *FF*, v. læs.

Semington

Semington [semiŋtən]

> *Semelton* 1249, 1268 *Ass*, 1257 *For*, 1322 WM xxiii, 1344 *FF*, -*tun* 1270 *For*
> *Semeleton* 1249 *Ass*, t. Ed 2 *AD*, *Semleton* 1306 *FF*, 1491 *Ct*
> *Semneton* t. Hy 3 *Edington*, 1289 *Ass*, *Sempneton*' 1258 ib.
> *Sembleton* 1257 *For*, 1289 *Ass et freq* to 1555 *FF*, -*bel*- 1375 *Ct*
> *Semelynton* 1300 *For*
> *Sempleton* 1327 *SR*, Banco, 1341 *Rental*, t. Ed 3 *For*
> *Semington* 1470 BM, -*yng*- 1547 *FF*, *Simenton* 1675 Ogilby

The first element is the old name *Semnet* for Semington Brook *supra* 10. Hence, 'tun on the *Semnet*.' For interchange of *n* and *l*, cf. PN 106.

Note. (Robert) *atte Stanstret* 1333 *SR*, *Garlecke strete* t. Jas 1 *LRMB*.

Littleton is *Lytelton* 1268 *Ass*, 1332 *SR*, *la Litelton* t. Ed 1 IpmR, *Lyttleton* 1306 *FF*. 'Little farm,' v. tun.

[1] Cf. *Merelond* 1491 *Ct*.
[2] *Woodhouse* 1427 IpmR, cf. *Kyvelewode* 1331 Ipm.

WHADDON is *Wadone* 1086 DB, *Waddune* 1234 *Longleat*, *Waddon* 1249, 1268, 1289, 1394 *Ass*, 1254 Ipm, *Whadone* 1363 *FF*, 1428 FA, *Whadon* 1523 *SR*. 'Woad hill,' *v.* **dun**. The name would have reference to a hill where this plant grew. Later the name has been influenced, perhaps by association with *Whaddon* from OE *hwǣte-dūn*, 'wheat-hill.'

BARTLETT'S FM (6″) is to be associated with the family of William *Bartlet* (1624 *SR*).

LITTLE MARSH is *Lytell Mershe* t. Eliz *LRMB*. PENNY PLATT (6″) is so named in 1773 (A and D). See **plott** *infra* 444 SEMINGTON BRIDGE is *pontem de Semeleton* t. Hy 3 *Stowe* 798 *Sembletonesbrigge* t. Ed 3 *For*. STRANGER'S CORNER FM (6″) Cf. *Strangers Corner* 1773 A and D.

Southwick

SOUTHWICK [sauðik]

> *Sudwich'* 1196 Cur, 1198 Abbr, *Suwich'* 1204 Cur, *Suthwik* 1249 *Ass*, *Suthewyk* c. 1250 *Edington*, -*wike* 1275 RH *Sutwyk* 1302 Sarum, *Sothewyke* 1322 Ch, *Southewyk* 1342 *Rental*
> *Sowthick* 1539 *Phillipps*, *Southicke* 1637 ib.
> *Southweeke* t. Eliz WM xxi, 1683 *FF*

'South **wic** or dairy farm,' probably so named because south of Trowbridge.

> NOTE. BREACH LANE. Cf. *le Breche* 1341 *Rental*, *v.* **bræc**. In *LRMB* (t. Jas 1) we have *Blynd lane*.

LANGHAM FM (6″) is *Langeham* 1247 FF, *Longeham* t. Hy 3 BM, *Langenham* 1351 Ipm, 1401 IpmR, c. 1460 *Rental*, *Langham* 1552 *FF*. 'Long ham(m).' In some of the ME forms the *n* of the OE inflection has been preserved from (*æt þām*) *langan ham(me)*.

NORRIS HILL FM, VAGG'S HILL FM[1] and WHITAKER'S FM (all 6″) are to be associated with the families of William *Norris* (1641 WM xxxvii), Richard *le Vag* (1286 ib. xxiii) and Thomas *Whittacre* (1648 ib. xxxvii).

[1] *Vaggs Hill* 1625 WM xxiii.

CHANCEFIELD FM (6″). Cf. *Chance Field* c. 1840 *TA*. DILLYBROOK
FM is *Dilley Brook House* 1820 G. DUNKIRT (sic) FM (6″) is
Dunkirk ib. Cf. Dunkirk *infra* 455. GREENHILL FM is *Grene-
hulle* 1341 *Rental*, *Grenehyll* 1428 *FF*. GROVE'S HO (6″). Cf.
Upper, Lower Grove c. 1840 *TA*. HOGGINGTON is *Hockington*
1773 A and D. LAMBER'S MARSH is *Lamberts Marsh* c. 1840 *TA*.
MUTTON MARSH FM is so named in 1841 (*Devizes*). NEW POOL
COTTAGES (6″). Cf. *New Pool* ib. OVERCOURT FM is *Overcourt*
1617 *FF*. POLE'S HOLE is *Pauls Hall* 1773 A and D. POUND FM
(6″). The *Pound* stood here in 1802 (O.G.S.C.). RODE HILL.
Cf. *Rodehethe* 1491 *Ct*, *Road Hill* 1841 *Devizes*. So named from
the neighbouring Road (So). ROMSEY OAK FM (6″). Cf. *Rumsey
oak* 1625 WM xxiii. The oak stood on the parish boundary just
to the north of the farm. The Abbess of Romsey had a holding
in Southwick (Aubrey 346 n. 5). SCOTLAND. See *infra* 454.
WHITE ROW BRIDGE is *White rowe* 1553 *DuLa*, *White Trowe*
1625 WM xxiii, *Whiterewe* 1653 *FF*. WOODENTUN FM (6″) is
Wooden Tun 1841 *Devizes*.

XII. WESTBURY HUNDRED

Westberia hundred 1086 ExonDB, *Westberihdr* 1167 P. *v.* Westbury *infra* 149.

Bratton

BRATTON

    Bratton 1177 P, 1201 Cur, 1202 Abbr, 1212 ClR *et passim*
    Bracton(e) 1196 Cur *et passim* to 1333 Ipm, (*next Westbury*)
      1335 ib.
    Bractun 1221 FineR
    Brotton 1227 FF
    Bretton 1241 ib., 1256, 1267 Pat, 1281 *Ass*, t. Hy 8 NQ iii

This is a compound of OE **bræc**, 'newly cultivated land,' etc.,
and tun. Cf. Bratton Fleming (PN D 29–30).

DANES LYE (6″) is *Denelyghe, Deanelighe* t. Eliz *LRMB*. 'Valley
clearing,' *v.* denu, leah. In spite of the proximity of Edington,
this can have nothing to do with the Danes. The name has been
altered to support a legend (Hoare 45).

DUNGE is *Dengestret* 1395, 1397 NQ v, *Dunge* 1773 A and D. Probably OE *dyncge*, 'manure, manured land.' Cf. Denges Barn (PN Sx 145).

MELBOURNE HO (6″) is *Milebourne, on Mulbourne ewelmen* 968 (15th) BCS 1215, *Muleburne* t. Hy 3 *Edington*, 1304 *FF*, 1310 *Ass*, 1332 *SR*, *Mulleburne* 1289 *Ass*, *Melbourn* 1361 Pat. 'Mill stream,' *v.* myln, burna. *ewelmen* is OE *æwielm*, 'source,' cf. Ewen *supra* 60–1. Hoare (57) notes that the meeting of two springs here was anciently called *Ewelm*.

PATCOMBE HILL is *Papekehulle, Patekynhull* 1330 *Edington* and must have been near *padecan stan* 968 BCS 1215, *Pattens stone* 1575 Hoare. The stone is still marked on Patcombe Hill. The first element is clearly a personal name *Padeca*, a diminutive of *Pad(d)a*.

REDLANDS FM (6″) is *la Ridelonde* 1330 *Edington*, *Rodelondes mershe* 1375 Ipm, *Rodlandes* t. Hy 8 NQ iii, *Redland(s)* 1592 *Add*, 1685 NQ iv. 'Reed land(s),' *v.* hreod. The land is low and marshy.

CAP'S LANE FM[1], FLOWER'S BARN (6″), GRANT'S FM, REEVE'S FM and SCOTT'S FM are to be associated with the families of Edith *Cape* (1609 ParReg), John *Flower* (1642 *SR*), Thomas *Graunt* (1588 ParReg), Thomas *Reeves* (c. 1840 *TA*) and John *Scot* (1257 *For*).

BIRCHANGER is *Burchhangere* 1330 *Edington*, *v.* hangra, 'slope.' THE BUTTS. Cf. *Butts Furlong* c. 1840 *TA* and *infra* 425. COMBE FM. Cf. *Combe Tyning* c. 1840 *TA* and *infra* 449. HIGH DOWN is *Hidon* 1249 *Edington*. HILL FM. Cf. *la Hulle* 1330 ib. HORSE CROFT FM (6″). Cf. *Horse Croft* c. 1840 *TA*. KNAPP DOWN is *Knapp Downe* 1609 *FF*, *v.* cnæpp, 'hill.' LUCCOMBE (6″) is *Lovecombe* 1283 *MinAcct*, 1426 *Ct*, *Lovecum* 1550 Pat. Perhaps '*Lēofa*'s valley,' *v.* cumb. SUMMER DOWN is *St Maur's Down* 1830 Hoare, part of the 13th-century manor of St Maur. TISWELL SPRING (6″) is *Tysewelle* 1330 *Edington*. We may possibly compare Tisbury *infra* 194. THORNCOMBE FM is *Thorncombe* ib., *v.* cumb. TYNINGS (6″) is *Tyning* c. 1840 *TA*, *v. infra* 449. WHITE CLIFF is so named in 1773 (A and D).

---

[1] *Cops Lane Farm* 1773 A and D.

Dilton

DILTON[1]

Dulinton 1190 P

Dultun' 1221 FineR, 1265 Ipm, *-ton* 1236, 1242 Fees, 1249
  Ass et passim to 1553 WM x

Dolton 1250 Fees, 1281, 1289 *Ass*

Dilton 1516 *Recov, Dylton* 1535 VE, *Dulton al. Dylton* 1566
  FF, Dylton al. Dulton 1587 ib.

Delton 1666 *SR*

The complete absence of any spellings with *i* before the 16th
century, as well as the fact that no forms, except the first, show
any sign of an inflectional syllable (*e* or *ing*), make Ekwall's
derivation (DEPN *s.n.*) from OE *Dylla* improbable. It is more
likely that the later *i* has developed from OE and ME *u* (*v.*
Introd. xx) but no suggestion as to the etymology can be
offered.

BREMERIDGE FM [bremridʒ] is *Brembelrugge* 1268 *Ass, Bremel-*
rigge t. Ed 1 *Edington,* 1275 RH, 1332 *SR, -rugge* 1277 Cl, *-rygge*
1350 *FF,* 1367 Pat, *Brembrig* 1412 FA, *Brembridge* 1571 BM.
'Bramble ridge,' *v.* bremel.

CHALCOT HO is *Caldecote* 1249, 1268, 1279, 1281, 1289 *Ass,* 1257
For, Chaldecote 1268 *Ass,* 1318 Ch, t. Ed 3 *For, -cott* 1593 *FF.*
'Cold or exposed cottages,' *v.* cot(e) and Introd. xxi.

CHAPMANSLADE

Chipmannesled 1245 WM xvi, *-slade* 1332 *SR, Chypmaneslad*
  1268 *Ass, Chipmanslade* 1430 *FF,* 1456 IpmR, *Chippenslad*
  1575 Hoare

Chapman(n)(e)slade 1245 WM xvi, 1278, 1289 *Ass,* 1413 *FF*

Chepmanesled' 1245 WM xvi, *Chepmanneslad'* 1253 *Ass,*
  Chepmanslad(e) 1257 *For,* t. Ed 2 *AD,* 1397 IpmR, *Chep-*
  pynslade t. Eliz WM xxi

'The slæd or flat valley of the chapmen or merchants' (OE
cēapman, cȳpman). Cf. *cypmannadell* (BCS 179), *chypmanna*
ford (ib. 879) and Chapmans Combe in Bicknoller (So), *Chap-*
mannescumb 1327 SR.

---

[1] A parish formed from Westbury in 1894.

GODSWELL GROVE FM (6″) is *Godeswell'* 1189 WM xvi, *Godewul'* 1242 Fees, *Godewell'* 1245 WM xvi, *Godwell* t. Hy 8 *AOMB*, 1461 Inq aqd, 1537 LP, 1666 *FF*, *Goswell* 1751 ib. Cf. *Godeshulle* 1241 FF in Bratton and Godsell Fm *supra* 87. The probabilities are in favour of a personal name as the first element.

PENLEIGH[1]

> *Penleia* 1198 Abbr, *-legh* 1236 Fees, 1255 RH, *-lee* 1268 *Ass*, *-leiȝe* 1275 RH, *-ley* 1304 *Ass*, *-ligh* 1332 *SR*
> *la Penne* 1279, 1281 *Ass*
>
> *v.* Pen Hill *supra* 33–4.

SHORT STREET is *Sheterestret* 1257 *For*, *Schoterstret* 1315 WIpm, *Schotestre* 1327 *SR* (p), *Shortestret* 1367 *FF*, *Shotestret* 1394 *Ass*, *Shoarestreete* 1629 WIpm, *Shortstreet* 1637 ib. Probably 'the street of the shooters or archers' (OE *scȳtere*). Cf. Shooters Hill (PN Nth 177) and Hawk Street *infra* 254.

WANSEY'S COTTAGES (6″) are to be associated with the family of Henry *Wansey* (c. 1840 *TA*).

BLACK DOG WOOD is *Black Dog Woods* 1809 Hoare, from an inn so named. CLAY CLOSE FM (6″). Cf. *le Cleye* 1341 *Cor*, *Clay Close* c. 1840 *TA*. CLIVEY FM is *le Clyvey* 1430 *MinAcct*, *Clift Hays* c. 1840 *TA*. 'Slope-enclosure,' *v.* clif, (ge)hæg and *infra* 426, 433. DEAD MAIDS is *Dead Maid* 1820 G. DILTON MARSH is *Mersshe* 1332 *SR*, *Dilton le Marsh* 1638 NQ iii. FAIRWOOD FM. Cf. *Fairewood Coppice* 1636 WIpm. FIVE LORDS FM. Cf. *The waste of the five borderers or five lords of Leigh* 1575 *For*. The five manors of Stourton, St Maur, Leigh Priors, Arundell and Brembridge centred here (Hoare 43). GOLDEN GROVE (6″) is so named in 1575 (*For*). HISSOMLEY is *High Somley* 1812 RCH, *Isomley* 1820 G. THE LAWN (6″) is so named c. 1840 (*TA*). Cf. *infra* 440. OX LEAZE (6″) is *Oxen Leaze* ib. STORMORE is *Stormore Coppice* 1606 Hoare, *Starmore* 1767 *Recov*, *Stormore or Stourton's Moor* 1797 Hoare. STOURTON BUSHES (6″) is *Stourton's Bushes* 1830 Hoare, so named from the family of Lord *Stourton* (16 Hy 8) (Hoare 85).

---

[1] The earliest mention of PENKNAP, a mile south of Penleigh, is from 1812 (RCH) so that it is difficult to know if it is a genuine early name. This does lie by a prominent hill.

Heywood

HEYWOOD[1]

Heiwode 1225 FF, -wude 1245 WM xvi, Heywode 1289 Ass
Haywud 1241 FF, -wode 1249 Ass, Haiwude 1242 Fees, -wode
1245 WM xvi
Hewode 1268 FF, 1327 Banco, 1327, 1332 SR

'Enclosed or preserved wood,' v. (ge)hæg. Cf. Heywood
(PN Sr 89).

BROADMEAD COTTAGES (6″). Cf. Brodemede 14th (O.G.S.C.).
BROOK HO is Brooke 1666 SR. CLANGER WOOD is Clayhanger
Wood c. 1840 TA. v. hangra, 'slope,' and cf. Clinger (PN Gl
44). CONIGREE WOOD (6″). Cf. Conynghay 1277 For. 'Rabbit
enclosure,' v. (ge)hæg. FULLING BRIDGE is Felling Bridge 1773
A and D. HAWKERIDGE is Hauekerigge 1249 Ass, Hauecrugge
1279 ib., Hauekerygge 1327 Banco. 'Hawks' ridge.' LODGE
WOOD is Lodgewoode 1626 WIpm. LONGMEAD WOOD (6″). Cf.
Longmeade 1669 FF. NORLEAZE (6″) is Norleaze Common c. 1840
TA. v. læs. ROUND WOOD (6″) is so named ib. YOAD LANE.
Cf. Yoed 1773 A and D.

Westbury

WESTBURY

Westberie, Wesberie 1086 DB, Westbiri 1115 StOsmund,
-beria 1139 SarumCh et passim, with variant spellings -bury,
-buri, -bery, -biri, -biry
Westbury(e) under the playne 1518–29 ECP, (subtus le Playne)
1573 Recov

'West burh.' West perhaps because near the western border
of the county. The exact meaning of burh here is uncertain.
There is no ancient fort nearer than Bratton Castle. Under the
Plain, the town lying at the extreme north-west corner of
Salisbury Plain, v. supra 17.

NOTE. CHANTRY LANE. Cf. Gt, Little Chantry c. 1840 TA. Probably
so named from the Church or Chantry manor, the endowment of the
chanter of the Cathedral Church of Salisbury (Hoare 2). MARISTOW ST
may be part of the four bovates given by Henry 1 to the church of
St Mary Sarum (Hoare 2). v. stow. WEST END. Cf. Weststrete 1375
WIpm.

[1] Formerly a part of Westbury parish.

BROOK is *Broc'* 1216 ClR, *Broc* 1227 FF, *Brok* 1242 Fees, *Brouk* 1356 *Ass*, *Brooke* 1402 Pat. A lost place near by was *Brocweie* 1210 Cur, FF, *Brocweye* 1290 Ipm, *Brockway* 1740 *FF*. *v.* broc, weg.

WESTBURY LEIGH is *Lia* 1242 Fees, *Lye* 1249 *Ass*, 1257 *For*, 1275 RH, (*juxta Westbir'*) 1302 *Ass*, *Westbury Leyghe* 1581 *FF*. *v.* leah. The meaning here was no doubt that of 'wood.' LEIGHTON would seem to be a modern derivative of it.

POUND FM (6″) was the home of John *atte Pounde* (1332 *SR*). Cf. *Pownde Barton* 1626 WIpm and *infra* 444, 451.

BOURNE'S BARN (6″) is to be associated with the family of Richard and James *Bourne* (c. 1840 *TA*).

BEGGAR'S KNOLL is a term of contempt. Cf. *infra* 455. BERE'S MERE is *Beers Meer Hill* 1773 A and D. BRIDEWELL SPRINGS [bridəl] (6″) is *Brudewelle* 1341 *Cor*, *Breddell Spring* 1773 A and D, *Briddle Spring* 1830 Hoare. Probably 'brides' spring,' perhaps a fertility spring. CHALFORD. Cf. *Chalford Sands* c. 1840 *TA*. EDEN VALE is so named in 1820 (G). FOUR HUNDRED DOWN (6″) is *4 Hundred Down* c. 1840 *TA*. Cf. Thirteen Hundred Down *infra*. Probably both so called from their acreage. FROGMORE is *Frogmere* 1260 *Harl*, *v.* mere. HAM (6″). Cf. *le Hamme* 1332 NQ ii and hamm *infra* 433. MADBROOK FM is *Madebrook* 1820 G. NEW TOWN is so named in 1773 (A and D). RANSCOMBE BOTTOM (6″) is *Ranscombe* 1575 *For*, *Rambscombe* c. 1840 *TA* (Upton Scudamore). REDLAND HO (6″) is *Rodelond* 1375 WIpm. It is low-lying and may be for hreod-land, 'reed-land.' STORRIDGE FM (6″) is *Storegge* 1517 *Recov*, *Storige Mead* 1575 *For*. Probably 'stone-ridge.' Cf. Storridge (PN D 271, 310, 436). THIRTEEN HUNDRED DOWN is *13 Hundred Down* c. 1840 *TA*. Cf. Four Hundred Down *supra*. WHITE HORSE is *The White Horse* 1773 A and D. WINKLAND'S DOWN (6″). Cf. *Wincklands* 1575 *For*. As this is in a remote corner of the parish the first element may be wincel, 'corner.'

XIII. WARMINSTER HUNDRED

Hundred de Warminister, Warministro, -e 1086 ExonDB, *Were-menistrehðr* 1159, *Wermenistra hðr* 1170, *Werreministre hðr* 1174 P. See Warminster *infra* 157. The site of the meeting-place is unknown. There is a field called Moothill in Warminster *TA*, just south of Dirtley Wood on Warminster Down, and another Moothill in Bishopstrow *TA*, immediately south-east of Bigbury Wood. Both are high up on the Downs, about two miles from each other. Either or both may at some time have been the Hundred meeting-place.

Bishopstrow

BISHOPSTROW

> *Biscopestreu* 1086 DB, *Bissopestreu* 1121 AC, *-tre* 1195 P,
> 1201 Cur, 1206 Abbr, *Bissupestru* 1196 Cur, 1198 Abbr,
> *Bisshopestre* 1236 Ch, *-trewe* 1257 For, *Byscoppestrewe* 1270
> Ch, *Biss(c)hoppestrowe* 1300 Ipm, 1316 FA, *-true* 1331 Pat

'The bishop's tree,' *v.* treow. This is probably the place which William of Malmesbury (WMP 384–5) calls *Biscepes truue*, associating with it a legend that St Aldhelm once preached there and that when he placed his ashen pastoral staff in the ground it miraculously multiplied into numerous ash-trees so that the vill was henceforward known as *ad Episcopi arbores,* i.e. at Bishop's trees. The church is dedicated to St Aldhelm.

RAESTERS FM (6″) is possibly identical with *Radenhurste* c. 1189 GlastInq, 1271 *Longleat,* c. 1300 GlastFeod, *Radenherste* 1312 *FF, Radnester alias Radenhurst* 1576 *Longleat.* '(At the) red wood,' *v.* read, hyrst.

BARROW HO (6″) is *Baruwe* 1211 RBE, *Barwe* 1273 *FF.* 'Wood,' *v.* bearu. BISHOPSTROW DOWN is so named in 1575 (*For*). HORSEPOOLS COPPICE (6″). Cf. *Horspol* 1232 *Lacock,* 1331 Pat. MIDDLE HILL is *Middelhull* 1241 FF. SOUTHEY (6″) is *Sowthehay* 1609 *Corpus. v.* (ge)hæg. SWEETLAND COTTAGES (6″) is *Sweed-lands* (sic) c. 1840 *TA.* WOOD BURY (6″) is *Woodberry* ib.

Corsley

CORSLEY

> *Corselie* 1086 DB, *-lea* 1166 P, *-lega* 1179 ib. 1242 Fees, *-legh*
> 1275 RH, 1280 Cl, *-le* 1289 *Ass*, *-leghe* 1316 FA, *Parva*
> *Corsele* 1268 *Ass*, *Magna Corseleye* 1285 *FF*, *Estcorseley*
> 1574 ib.
>
> *Cosselega* 1190 RBE, P, *-ley* 1250 Cl, *Cosley* 1593 *Sadler*
> *Corslee* 1206 Cur, (*Magna*) 1268 *Ass*, *-leye* 1211 RBE, *-leg*'
> 1214 FF, 1232 Ch, Cl, (*Parva*) 1242 Fees, *-le* 1249 *Ass*,
> *-leyghe* 1286 Ipm

This is a hybrid place-name, the OE *leah* having been added
to OBrit *cors*, 'reeds, swamp,' cf. Gauze Brook *supra* 7. It
is possible, of course, that *Cors* was here also a stream-name, the
old name for Rodden Brook.

CLEY HILL is *Cly* 1316 *Longleat*, 1321 *AD*, *Cley hill* 1540 WM
xii, *Cley* 1560 *FF*, *Clye*, *Clyhill* c. 1560 *Longleat*, *Clee or Clay*
Hill 1812 RCH. Cf. *Clycombe* 1581 *Corpus*. The etymology of
this name is obscure. The hill is a prominent one, the soil is
chalk and it is impossible from the point of view of either topography or form, at least in the case of the two really early
forms, to associate the name with *clæg*, 'clay.'

HUNTENHULL

> *Heuedlingell'* 1165, *Hauellingehulle* 1168, *Hauelingehulla* 1169,
> 1170, *-hull'* 1172, *Heuedlingehilla* 1183, 1186 P, *Henedling-*
> *hill* (sic) 1298 Ch
> *Hauelingehull'* 1172 P
> *Hauedinghehull* 1257 *For*, *Havedynghulle* 1421 Cl
> *Hefdynghull* t. Hy 3 *Edington*, 1361, 1368 Cl, *Hefodynghull*
> 1361 WIpm
> *Hevedynghull(e)* t. Hy 3 *Edington*, 1324 Ipm, 1368 Cl, 1375,
> 1407 IpmR
> *Heneddingehull* (sic) t. Hy 3 Ipm
> *Heveninghull* 1376 IpmR
> *Hedynghull* 1402 FA, *-hill* t. Hy 8 NQ iii
> *Huntenhull* 1412 FA, *Huntell hill*, *hull* 1648 WM xxxvii

This is probably a compound of ME *heuedling(e)*, 'headlong,'
and **hyll**, the hill being so called from its steepness (B.D.).

STURFORD is *Stereford* t. Ed 1 *For*[1], *Sturforde* 1558 *Longleat*. The place lies near the headwaters of the stream which gives name to Whitbourne *infra*. If reliance may be placed on the first form the name is a compound of OE *stēor*, 'steer' (or *stēora*, gen. pl. of the same word), and **ford**. Hence 'steer's ford' or 'steers' ford,' because frequented by such. *ēo* might well appear later as *u*. Cf. Introd. xx.

TRUSSENHAYES is *Trowsonhey* 1376 *Longleat*, *Trusen haies* 1615 ib. The first element in this name is probably an adjectival derivative of OE *trūs*, 'brushwood,' hence 'enclosure covered with brushwood,' *v.* (ge)**hæg**.

WHITBOURNE is *Wyte-*, *Wytteburne* 1249 *Ass*, *Wyteburne* 1263 Cl, *Hwytburn* t. Hy 3 *AD*, *Whytebourne* 1327 *SR*, *Whiteborn* 1412 FA. 'White stream,' *v.* **burna**.

LYE'S GREEN was probably the home of William de *Lye* (1277 *Longleat*) and John de *Lye* (1332 *SR*). *v.* **leah**. The *s* may be pseudo-manorial. It is *Lyes Greene* 1607 *Longleat*.

BISSFORD (6″) is *Bisford* 1500 Pat. 'Ford over the river Biss' (*supra* 2). CORSLEY HEATH is *Corseley heath* 1558 *Longleat*. CORSLEY MILL FM. Cf. *Mill wood, Milham* 1615 ib. DERTFORD'S WOOD is *Dartfords wood* 1650 *ParlSurv*. The Prioress of Dartford (K) held lands here (Hoare 78). LADY'S COPPICE (6″) is *Lady Copise* 1615 *Longleat*. LANDHAYES is *Landheyes* 1620 ib., *Landhurst* 1820 G. MAD DOCTOR'S FM is *Mad Doctors* 1773 A and D. The reason for the name is not known. PARK BARN. Cf. *The Parke* 1648 WM xxxvii. RAGLAND COPPICE (6″) is *Ragland* 1615 *Longleat*. Cf. *Ragland Coppice* (Fd) c. 1840 *TA* in Norton Bavant and **rag** *infra* 453. RUSHPOOL (6″) is so named in 1726 (*Longleat*). SANDHAYES (6″). Cf. *le Sonde* t. Hy 4 *Longleat*. SOUTHCROFT. Cf. *Southcroft Ditch* 1575 *For*. TEMPLE COPPICE and FM (6″). Cf. *Whitbournetemple* 1574 *FF*, *Temple feilds* 1575 *For*. The reason for the name is unknown. THE VENN (6″). Cf. *Venn Way* ib. 'Marsh,' *v.* **fenn** and Introd. xxi. WHITBOURNE GATE (6″) is *Whitbourne Turnpike Gate* c. 1840 *TA*.

[1] *Ex inf.* Dr G. B. Grundy.

Norton Bavant

Nortone 1086 DB, *Northton* 1242 Fees, *(Scidemor)* 1305 *Ass*,
Nortonbavent 1381 Pat, *Norton Bavan* 1675 Ogilby

'North farm,' *v.* tun. *North* with reference to Sutton Veny
infra. Geoffrey de *Escudemor'* held the manor in 1242, but
it had passed to the family of Alesia de *Bavent* in 1301 (Pat).
Adam de *Bavent* married Alice, only daughter and heiress of
Peter de *Scudamore* (Hoare 77).

MIDDLETON (6″) is *Mideltone* 1086 DB, *Middeldon* 1275 RH,
1332 *SR*, -*ton* 1281 *Ass*, *Middleton* 1648 WM xxxvii. 'Middle
farm,' *v.* tun.

COTLEY HILL is *Cottley Hill* 1773 A and D. SCRATCHBURY HILL
is *Scratchburie* 1609 Hoare, *v.* burh. There is an old camp here.
Scratch is a West Country name for the Devil and may be
the first element here. TYNING COTTAGE (6″). Cf. *infra* 449.

Sutton Veny

Sudtone, Sutone 1086 DB, *Suttone juxta Bysshopestrowe* 1412
FA
Magna Suttuna 12th *AD*, *(Michel)* 1365 Cl
Fennisutton 1268 *Ass*, *Fenny Sutton* 1291 FF, *Fennyesottone*
1294 Ipm, *Fenne Sutton* 1297 Pat, *Fennisoutton* 1304 Sarum,
Fenneysutton 1325 *FF*
Litel Sutton 1365 Cl
Veny Sutton 1535 VE, *Vennye Sutton* 1632 *FF*

'South farm,' *v.* tun. *South* in relation to Norton Bavant
supra. Fenny from its marshy situation. For *Ven(n)y, v.*
Introd. xxi.

ILEY OAK (lost), also called the Hundred Oak, was the meeting-
place of the Hundreds of Warminster and Heytesbury (cf.
Hoare, *Warminster* 11, *Heytesbury* 2). Early forms for Iley are
Ilegh 1394 GDR, 1461 WM xiii, *Iligh, Ilegh* 1470 ib., *Elye* 1546
LP, and there can be little doubt that Stevenson (Asser

271–2) is right in identifying it with *Iglea* ASC (Ā, B, C) *s.a.*
878, *Aecglea* c. 1000 Asser, *Aeglea* ASC (D, E), *Ecglea* c. 1118
FW. It was presumably on the boundary common to Sutton
Veny and Longbridge Deverill. Traditionally it was by Lord
Heytesbury's Lodge at Southleigh Wood, of which Iley forms
the eastern part (WM xiii, 108), i.e. presumably near Southleigh
Cottage, just on the border, where five roads and footpaths
met. There is documentary evidence for their proximity in
the phrase *woodland called Sowley and Eleigh*, used of land
in Sutton (1640 WIpm). All this makes it very probable
that Iley is to be identified in site, if not in name, with the
present Eastleigh Wood, adjacent to Southleigh Wood *infra*.
The interpretation of the first element in the name is difficult. It would seem to be OE ieg (eg) in spite of the *Aeg*-
form and the *cg*-forms in Asser and FW, but if so, ieg must
be used in the sense 'island of high ground,' which is aptly
descriptive of this whole woodland patch, rather than of low-
lying marsh land, for that can only be found to the west and not
to the east of Southleigh. We may have a parallel for such usage
in Ram Alley *infra* 353.

NEWNHAM (Kelly and old 6″) is *Newenham* 1242 FF, 1268 *Ass*,
1323 BM, 1412 FA, *Neweham* 1279 *Ass*, *Nywenham* 1323 BM,
Niwenhamme 1413 *FF*, *Newname* 1571 *SR*, *Newnham* 1820 G.
The name goes back to OE (*æt þām*) *nīwan ham(me)*, v. ham(m).
The site is immediately north-west of Sutton.

SOUTHLEIGH WOOD is *bosc. de Suthle* 1257 *For*, *Southle* 1348
Pat, *bosc. de Southlegh* 1470 Cl, *Sowley* 1625, 1640 WIpm.
v. leah. The meaning is here no doubt 'wood.'

CHURCH FM was perhaps the home of Agnes *atte Churcheye*
(1327 *SR*), i.e. probably 'church enclosure,' v. (ge)hæg.

BAKE BARN (6″) is *messuage called Beak* 1631 WIpm. See bake
infra 450. BOTANY FM is probably for *Botany Bay* (cf. *infra* 455).
It is in the remote western extension of the parish. HAYCOMBE
BARN. Cf. *Haycombe* 1421, 1488 *MinAcct*, *Heycome* t. Jas 1
LRMB. LITTLECOMBE HILL is *Littlecombe Hill* 1820 G. It is
by *Litelcombe* 1328 WIpm. PIT MEADS (6″) is *Putmede* 1400
WM vii, v. pytt. WHITEN HILL is so named in 1773 (A and D).

Upton Scudamore

UPTON SCUDAMORE

> (æt) *Uptune* c. 990 ASWills, *Uptone* 1086 DB, *Upton* 1216
> ClR, *Uppton* 1242 Fees, *Upton Squydemor* 1275 Abbr,
> *Uptone Escudemor'* 1281 *Ass*, *Upton Skydemour* 1301 Ipm,
> (*Escudmor*) 1312 *FF*, (*Skidmore*) 1359 ib., t. Eliz WM xxi
> *Opetone* 1086 DB, *Upeton* 1203 Cur
> *Skydemorysupton* 1439 *MinAcct*, *Skydmores Upton* 1488 ib.,
> *Skedmers Upton* 1623 WM i

'Higher farm,' *v*. uppe, tun. Peter de *Skydemore* held the
manor in 1216 (ClR), Geoffrey de *Escudamor* in 1242 (Fees) and
Peter *Scuydemor* in 1275 (Abbr).

CLEAR WOOD (6″) is *Clerwode* 1348, *Clerewod* 1516 *Longleat*,
Clerewood 1568 BM. The first element is probably OFr *clere*,
'glade,' as noted in Clearfields (PN Bk 119). Cf. Clears Fm *infra*
247, *le Est*, *West Clere* (1448 *Kings*) in Brixton Deverill, and
Bridge Cleere (1651 WM xlvi) in Braydon Forest.

NORRIDGE is *Northrigge* 1203 Cur, 1270 *For*, -*rugge* 1276 *Ass*,
Norrigge 1203 Cur, 1242 Fees, *North Rugge* 1289 *FF*, *Northrigge
by Werministre* 1322 Ch. 'North ridge.'

THOULSTONE

> *Tholveston(e)* 1257 *For*, 1268, 1279, 1289 *Ass*, 1316 FA, 1332
> SR, 1397 IpmR
> *Tholfueston* 1263 *For*, *Tholfeston* 1428 FA
> *Tolleueston*, *Tolveston* 1278 *Ass*
> *Tholston* 1439 *MinAcct*, 1626 *FF*

The name is probably of post-Conquest origin, the first
element containing the Anglo-Scandinavian name *Tholf* from
ON *Þólfr*, ODan, OSw *Tholf*. Feilitzen (389) notes examples
of the name in Do and Ha.

MILLARDS FM and TEMPLE'S FM (both 6″) are to be associated
with the families of John *Milward* (1445 *Ct*) and Thomas *Temple*
(1594 NQ viii).

BEARCLOSE COTTAGES (6″). Cf. *Bereclos* 1439 *MinAcct*. KEYFORD
COTTAGES (6″). Cf. *Keyfords Tyning* c. 1840 *TA*, *v. infra* 449.
NORRIDGE WOOD is *Norigeswod* 1428 *MinAcct*, *Norregewod* 1513
Ct, from Norridge *supra* 156. UPTON COW DOWN is *Cow Down*
1575 *For*, *v. infra* 430.

Warminster

WARMINSTER

> *Worgemynster* 899–925 BCS 591, *Worem'* 1253 Ipm
> *Gverminstre* 1086 DB
> *Werminister* 1115 StOsmund, *-menistra*, *-e* 1157, 1158 P,
> 1198, 1206 Cur, 1207 FF, *-munstre* 1186 RBE, *Wermester*
> 1294 Pat, *-tre* 1420 Trop
> *Warmenistre* 1155 RBE, *-ministre* 1158 HMC Var i, *-tra*
> 1169 P, *-mynystre* 1289 Cl, *Warmestre* 1448 *FF*, 1458 Trop,
> *-ter* 1471 BM, 1578 *Recov*, *Warmister* t. Eliz WM xxi
> *Wyrmenistre* 1249 *Ass*
> *Wereministre* 1253 Cl, 1269 FF, *-mynstre* 1316 FA, 1343 Pat,
> *-mystre* 1324 FA, *-mestre* 1357 *GDR*, 1409 *MinAcct*,
> *-moustre* 1374 Pat, *Werreministre* 1257 Pat
> *Wormenestre* 1350 Cl

Forms on coins include *Worimen*, *Wori* 979–1016, *Worim*,
Wori, *Wor* 1016–40.

'The church or **mynster** on the river Were' (*v. supra* 10).
The coin-forms make it clear that the *o* in the OE form
Worgemynster is correct, as was to be expected in an original
document of the 10th century. The normal development would
have been to *Wor(i)minster* and not *Werminster*, but Ekwall (RN
450) compares the similar irregular development of *Wodnesdæg*,
Wodnesbyrig, *Wodnesfeld*, and, we may add, *Wodnesleage*, to
Wednesday, Wednesbury and Wednesfield (St) and Wensley
(Db). *Werm-* developed normally to *Warm-*. Curious are the
persistent trisyllabic forms *ministre*, etc., from OE **mynster**.

NOTE. CHAPEL ST is *Chapel style* 1363 Hoare. CHURCH ST. Cf.
Churchewey 1581 *Corpus*. HIGH ST is *Heghestrete* 1279 *Ass*. Cf. *supra*
21. MARKET PLACE is *The Market place* 1633 Sess. PORTWAY was
formerly *Newport* 1360, *Nyweport* 1382 Hoare. POUND ST is so named
in 1727 (Daniell). WEST ST is *le Weststrete* 1344 Longleat, *Westerstreet*
1581 *Corpus*.

Arn Hill Down is so named in 1773 (A and D). It is earlier *Arnyngge-, Ernynggedown* 1308 *Longleat*, i.e. 'down of the people of *Earna*.'

Battlesbury Hill is *Pattelsbury, Patelsberye* 1589 *Corpus, Battlebury* 1754 Pocock, *Battlesbury Castle* 1773 A and D. The second element is burh, with reference to the ancient camp here. The forms are too late for any certainty, but the first element might be a personal name *Pættel*, an *l*-derivative of OE *Patta*. In any case it is likely that the later modern spellings are due to folk-etymology.

Boreham and Boreham Down

> *Buriton* 1241 FF, 1242 Fees, *Burython'* 1258 *Ass*, *Borton juxta Wermenistre* 1281 ib., *Bouriton* 1327, *Buryton* 1332 *SR*, *Boryton juxta Bisshopestrowe* 1440 FF
>
> *Burton Delamare al. Booreham* 1573, *Burton Delamore al. Boreham* 1574 ib., *Boorham Down* 1575 *For*, *Boreham al. Burton in Warmester* 1582 PCC, *Boram al. Burton* 1585 WM xxi, *Bourton al. Boreham* 1592 Daniell, *Bowram* t. Eliz ChancP
>
> *Borams downe* 1589 *Corpus*

The original name represents an OE (*æt*) *byrigtun*, 'farm belonging to a burh' (cf. Burton *supra* 49–50, *infra* 178), the burh in this case being Warminster. For the earlier forms cf. Buriton (Ha) which is *Buriton* from 1227 (Ch) onwards. The reason for the later corruption is not clear.

Bugley

> *Buggele(g')* 1236 FF, *-le(y)* 1279, 1289 *Ass*, *Boggeleye* 1350 Cl *Bugele* 1249 *Ass*, *-leg'* 1257 *For*, *-ley* 1290 FF, *Bogeleye* 1254 Cl, *-legh* 1332 *SR*, 1412 FA, 1430 FF, *Boggele* 1369 WM xxxvii *Bogley* 1351 FF, *Buglie* 1593 Sadler

'*Bucge*'s clearing or wood,' *v.* leah. *Bucge* is a woman's name in OE. It is possible, however, that this name and Bugmore (*supra* 23) contain ME *bugge*, 'hobgoblin,' of obscure origin.

Chadlanger[1] is *Chedelhangere* t. Hy 3, *Chedelhanger* 1284 *Longleat, Chadelangre, Chedelangre* 1363 Hoare, *Chaddelhangre*

---

[1] No longer on map but the School shows this to be the slope south-east of Norridge Wood.

1562, *Chedlanger in Warminster* 1585, *Chadlenger* 1677 *Longleat*, *Chidlanger* 1690 *Recov.* Apparently '*Ceadela*'s slope,' *v.* hangra. Identical in origin with Chaddlehanger (PN D 185).

EMWELL ST (6″). Cf. *Emewell* 1249, 1394 *Ass*, *Emewelle* 1332 *SR* (p), *Emwell* 1344 Misc, Cl, 1348 Pat, *Emwell al. Emble Coppice* 1650 *ParlSurv.* The forms are too late and indecisive for any etymology to be suggested.

SAMBOURNE is *Sandeborne, Samborne* 1249 *Ass, Est Samborne* 1307 Hoare, *Sandburne* t. Ed 3 *For.* 'Sand-stream,' *v.* burna.

MILL HO was the home of Emma *atte Mulle* (1327 *SR*), *v.* myln.

BUCKLER'S WOOD, BUTLER'S COOMBE and LUDLOW'S FM are to be associated with the families of John *Buckler* (1665 Daniell), John *Botiller* (1393 Pat) and Jane *Ludlow* (1622 WM xlv).

BEGGAR'S BUSH (6″) is *Beggers bushe* 1581 *Corpus.* BRICK HILL is *Brickhill* 1615 *Longleat.* Cf. Brickkiln Copse *supra* 36. COLD HARBOUR is so named in 1820 (G). It is *la Goslonde* 1292 *Longleat, Gooseland al. Coleharborow* 1609 *Corpus.* See *infra* 451. COLLOWAY CLUMP (6″). Cf. *Coleway* 1650 *ParlSurv*, 1727 Daniell. Perhaps 'charcoal-road,' cf. *Colrode* (1300 *For*) in Savernake. COP HEAP (tumulus) is *Cop Head Hill* 1773 A and D. "It is called in old deeds *Rite Heap* and now they call it *Cop Heap*" 1754 Pocock. CRADLE HILL is so named in 1727 (Daniell). ELM HILL is so named ib. FOLLY FM (6″) is *Folly* 1773 A and D. *v. infra* 451. GALLERY BRIDGE (6″) is so named in 1649 (*Sarum D and C*). HENFORDS MARSH with HENFORD HO (6″) may be identical with *Helmesford juxta Wermenester* 1398 IpmR. HERONSLADE (6″) is *Heronsladd* t. Hy 8 *Corpus, Heringslade* 1589 ib., 1658 PCC. HILL BARN (6″). Cf. *Hulle* 1307 Hoare. KING BARROW is so called in 1812 (RCH). LONGCOMBE is *Longecombe* 1352 *Longleat.* MANCOMBE (6″) is *Mancombe* 1363 Hoare, *Mancum* 1812 RCH. It is near the parish boundary and the first element may be OE (*ge*)*mǣne*, 'common.' NUNS PATH is *Nunpathe* 1577 *Longleat.* Tradition has it that this led up from a spot which was still called the Nunnery in Hoare's day (Hoare 12). OXENDEAN FM is *Oxendeane* 1589 *Corpus, v.* denu. OXSTALLS FM. Cf. *Oxstall* 1773 A and D. PARSONAGE FM is so named in 1820 (G). SACK HILL is so named in 1727 (Daniell). SMALLBROOK FM

is *Smalebroke* 1275 RH, *Smalbrok* 1337 Cl. 'Narrow stream,'
v. smæl, broc. It is another name for the Were *supra* 10.
WARMINSTER DOWN is so named in 1575 (*For*). WIND HILL is
Wyndehill 1565 *Longleat*, *Wine hill* 1625 WM xxiii, *Windhill Lodge*
1820 G. WOODCOCK FM is *Woodcock Farm House* c. 1840 *TA*.

DETACHED PARISHES OF WARMINSTER HUNDRED

Dinton

DINTON
> *Domnitone* 1086 DB
> *Dunyngtun*, -*ing*- t. Hy 2 *Shaston*, 1225 *SR*, 1227, 1236 FF,
> 1268 *Ass*
> *Duninton* 1184 P, 1203 FF, 1208 Cur, 1242 Fees, -*yn*- 1249
> *Ass*, *Donynton* 1324 FA
> *Duniton*, -*y*- 1198 P, 1205 Cur, 1210 FF, 1249 *Ass*, *Donyton*
> 1458 Trop
> *Donington* 1268 Pat, 1316 FA, -*yng*- 1305 *Ass*, 1327 *SR*, 1354
> Pat, 1428 FA
> *Dynton* 1505 Ipm, *Dynton*, *Denyngton* 1535 VE, (*al. Donyng-
> ton*) 1571, 1591 *Recov*

'*Dunna*'s farm,' *v.* ingtun. For the vowel *v.* Introd. xx.

NOTE. BROAD WAY is *Brodwey* c. 1570 *Wilton*.

DALWOOD FM (6″) is (*swa þurh*) *dellwuda* 901 (14th) BCS 588,
Dalwode c. 1240 *Wilton* (p), 1279, t. Ed 3, 1362 *For*, 1289 Ipm,
1418 *MinAcct*, *Dallewode* 1281 *Ass*. The present form of the
name is no doubt identical in origin with Dalwood (PN D 638)
from dæl and wudu, 'valley wood,' though the OE form suggests
that the original first element may have been dell, 'dell.'

COTTRELLS[1], FITZ'S FM, HYDE'S COPSE[2] and JESSE FM (all 6″)
are to be associated with the families of William *Cottrell* (1632
Wilton), Richard *Fitze* (1642 *SR*), Robert *Hyde* (1674 NQ vii)
and John *Jesse* (1648 WM xxxvii).

THE HANGING (6″). Cf. *Hanging Croft* 1844 *Wilton*. MARSH-
WOOD FM is *Merswode* 1276 *Ass*, *Mershwod* 1362 *For*, *Mashwood*

---

[1] Cf. *Cotterills Close* c. 1840 *TA*.   [2] *Hyde's Coppice* ib.

1589 *Map*. OAKLEY (6″) is *Hacleia* 1224 *Wilton*, *Ocle* 1236 FF, *Okle* 1279, 1289 *Ass*, *Wockley* 1820 G. 'Oak clearing or wood,' *v*. leah. PITT COPPICE (6″) is *Pytt copice* 1570 PembSurv, *copice called Pyttes* c. 1570 *Wilton*. Cf. *Pittmeade* 1570 PembSurv. SNAPES (6″). Cf. *Snapes copice* ib. and snæp *infra* 446. SWINDLEY COPSE (6″) is *Swyneslee* ib., *Swinley Cops* 1589 *Map*, *Swinely Ground* 1800 ib. WICK BALL. Cf. *Wyke* 1428 *MinAcct*, *Weekball Coppice* 1844 *Wilton*. *v*. balle and wic *infra* 422, 450.

Fisherton de la Mere

FISHERTON DE LA MERE

> *Fisertone* 1086 DB, *Fisserton* 1173, 1194 P, *Fiskerton* 1275 RH, *Fisshereton juxta Wili* 1289 *Ass*, *Fisherton juxta Code-forde* 1318 WIpm, *Fyssherton Dalamare* 1412 FA, *Fisherton Dalamore* t. Jas 1 ECP
>
> *Fissentona* 1158 France, *Fisselton*' 1200 Cur

'Fishermen's farm,' *v*. tun. Cf. Fisherton Anger in Salisbury *supra* 22–3. *Next Wylye* and *Codford* to distinguish it from that place. John *de la Mare* held the manor in 1377 (*FF*).

BAPTON

> *Babinton* 1221 FF, 1242 Fees, *-yn-* 1249, 1289 *Ass*, *Babington* 1249 ib., 1316 FA, *-yng-* 1312 Ipm
>
> *Babeton* 1276 *Ass*, 1332 *SR*, *Babbeton* 1413 BM
>
> *Babton* 1455 *MinAcct*, 1502 Ipm, *Bapton* 1526 *Ct*, 1600 *FF*

'*Babba*'s farm,' *v*. ingtun. This may well be the same man who gave name to Baverstock *infra* 212, about six miles away across the down.

THE BAKE is *The Beake* c. 1840 *TA*. *v*. *infra* 450.

Teffont Magna[1]

BRACHE COPSE (6″). Cf. *Est-*, *Westbreach* 1570 PembSurv. *v*. bræc. SPRING HEAD (6″) is *The Spring of Teffont* 1589 *Map*, *Spring Head* c. 1840 *TA*. TEFFONT DOWN. Cf. *Overteffont Hill* 1560 *FF*, *le Downe* 1690 *Wilton*. THICKTHORN COPSE (6″). Cf. *Thickthornesdoune* 1570 PembSurv.

---

[1] For the parish name, *v*. *infra* 193.

XIV. HEYTESBURY HUNDRED

Hestredeberia hundred, *Extredeberie* 1086 ExonDB, *Hichtredeberi*
hđr 1167, *Hechtredeberi hđr* 1168 P, *Hegtretesbur'* 1198 Abbr.
See further Heytesbury *infra* 167.

Boyton

BOYTON

> *Boientone* 1086 DB, *Boynton* 1366 Ipm
> *Boiton'* 1166 P, *Boiton* 1242 Fees *et passim*, with variant
>   spelling *Boy-*

'*Boia*'s farm,' *v.* tun. Cf. Boyton (PN Ess 426), Boyton (Co),
Boietone 1086 DB. The personal name *Boia* occurs in Cornwall
in the 10th-century Bodmin Manumissions. See further
Feilitzen 204, *s.n.*

CORTON

> *Cortitone* 1086 DB, *-ton* 1227 FF
> *Corton(e)* 1242 Fees, 1316 FA, *Estcorton* 1356 *Ass*
> *Cortinton*, *-y-* 1259 FF, *Est-* 1279, *Westcortynton* 1281 *Ass*
> *Cortyngton* 1291 Tax, 1304 Sarum, 1325 Pat, 1332 *SR*, 1348
>   Cl, *Corton al. Cortington* 1570 *FF*

'Farm of *Cort* or *Corta*,' *v.* ingtun. For the personal name
cf. *Corteshamme* BCS 917 (a Wiltshire charter) and Courteen-
hall (PN Nth 145). *East* Corton was probably the present
Manor Fm in contrast to *West* Corton, now West Fm in the
village itself.

BARROW HILL (6″) is so named c. 1840 (*TA*). BOYTON BRIDGE
(6″) is *Boyton brygge* 1514 *Ct*. BOYTON FIELD FM (6″). Cf.
Boyton Field c. 1840 *TA*, i.e. the township open field. CHATTLE
HOLE (6″). Cf. *Chattle Hill Coppice* ib. There is a deep
cauldron-shaped hole here with water at the bottom. CRATT
BARN (6″) is by Cratt Hill *infra* 185. PICKET GROVE (6″). Cf.
infra 443. STARVEALL (6″). *v. infra* 455. WEST WOOD (6″) is
The West Wood c. 1840 *TA*. WHATCOMB BOTTOM is *Whatcomb*
ib., i.e. (probably) 'wheat valley.'

Chitterne

CHITTERNE (ALL SAINTS and ST MARY)

Chetre, Cheltre (sic) 1086 DB

Cettra 1166 P, 13th BM, 1232 Ch, *Cettre* 13th BM, 1227,
1249 FF, 1242 Fees, 1248 Ch, 1268 *Ass*, *Cetra* 1206 ChR,
Cetre 1279 *Ass*

Chittra 1232 Lacock

Chytterne 1268, 1289, *Chyttyrne* 1281, *Chitterne* 1321 *Ass*,
1325 Pat, *Chittern* 1381 ib., *Chyttern Mary*, *Chittern
Allalwes* 1542, 1556 PCC, *tithyng of bothe Chittornes* 1571
SR, *Chitterne Mary* 1646 Sess

Chetherne 1279, 1289, *Chetterne* 1281, 1305 *Ass*, 1304 BM,
1341 NI, *Chetteren* 1289 *Ass*, *Chetaron* 1533–8 ECP vi

Chuterne 1289 *Ass*, 1316 FA, *Chuttre* 1305 *Ass*

This is a very difficult name. Ekwall (DEPN *s.n.*) takes it to
be a compound of British *cēto-*, 'wood' (*v.* Chute *supra* 12),
and OE ærn, 'house.' A hybrid compound with ærn, however,
seems unlikely, and if the first element is British, the second
element may be the well-known Celtic suffix *-erno* found in
Savernake *supra* 15. Cf. also Iwerne (RN 220). There is now no
large wood here though the area immediately around the village
is well wooded, but there may once have been more woodland,
since, though the soil is now shallow, the slope of the valley
would result in a rapid erosion of surface soil after felling of
the forest by the early settlers (E.J.S.).

Another possibility (suggested by Mr G. M. Young) is to take
the first element to be the word *cȳte, cīete* discussed under
Preshute *infra* 307 and to interpret the name as a compound of
cyte and ærn, hence 'cottage house(s).' This is perhaps the
more likely solution. For such a compound cf. Hulcott (PN Bk
151–2), 'hovel-cottages.'

BREACH HILL is *Brechehulle* 1269 *De Vaux*. *v.* bræc and *infra*
423. BREAKHEART HILL. Cf. *infra* 455. CHITTERNE DOWN. Cf.
Comyndown 1437 *MinAcct.* PENNING BARN (6″). *v. infra* 453.

Codford St Mary and St Peter

CODFORD ST MARY and ST PETER

> *Codan ford* 901 (12th) BCS 595
> *Coteford* 1086 DB, 1203 Cur, 1316 FA, 1327 *SR*, *Cutiford*
>   c. 1167 BM, *Cotesford* c. 1180 ib.
> *Coddeford* 1211 RBE
> *Codeford* 1212 FF *et freq* to 1428 FA, (*Est*) 1282 Ipm, *Est-*,
>   *Westcodeford* 1310 *FF*, *Codeford Sce Marie, Sci Petri* 1291
>   Tax, *Codford Marys* 1552 WM xxxviii, *West Codford al.*
>   *Codford St Peter* 1619 Recov, *Codvert* 1675 Ogilby

'*Cod(d)a*'s ford.' For this personal name cf. Coddimoor
(PN Bk 74), Coyton (PN D 272), Codham (PN Ess 466). The
places are distinguished by the dedications of the churches.

Codford St Mary

NOTE. GIGGAN ST would seem to be an imitation of the Salisbury
Gigant St *supra* 20.

CLAY PIT HILL. Cf. *Cleyputtes* 14th AD ii. FOXHOLE BOTTOM
(6″) is so named ib. LAMB DOWN is so named in 1773 (A and D).
MALMPIT HILL (6″) is *Manpet Hill* ib. STARVEALL. *v. infra* 455.
STONY HILL is so named in 1773 (A and D).

Codford St Peter

NOTE. CROUCH'S LANE (6″). Cf. *Croucheland* 1317 Pat, *Crouch's
Mead* c. 1840 *TA*. *v.* crouche, 'cross.'

ASHTON GIFFARD (6″)

> *Aston* 1242 Fees, *Ashton* 1289 Ass, *Assh(e)ton juxta Hegh-*
>   *tredebury* 1305 *Ass*, (*near Boyton*) 1327 Cl, (*Giffard*) 1412 FA
> *Eston Giffard* 1279 Ass
> *Aihston* 1281 Ch, *Aisshton by Codeford* 1362 Ipm

'Ash-tree farm,' *v.* tun. Elias *Giffard* held the manor in 1242
(Fees).

WRAXWORTHY BARN (6″). This name is probably manorial in
origin, deriving from the family of Anne *Raxworthy* mentioned
in 1829 (WM xii).

Brixton Deverill

BRIXTON DEVERILL

Devrel 1086 DB (held by *Brictric* TRE), *Deverell quod fuit Bristicii* 1087 (15th) EHR xl

Britricheston 1229 FF, *Bri(g)htricheston* 1242 Fees, 1291 Tax

Brighteston(e), -y- 1316 FA, 1332 *SR*, (*Deverell*) 1462 Pat

Brighston Deverell 1410 ib., *Burston Deverell* 1551 *FF*, *Birgheston Deverell* 1553 WM x, *Brixston Deverell* 1555 PCC

'Farm of *Beorhtric* (*Brihtric*),' so named after the holder TRE, *v.* tun. For Deverill, *v. supra* 6.

BRIMS DOWN is *Brunnesdon* 1282, *Brymysdown* 1505, *Brimes Downe* 1592 *Kings*, *Brimsdon* 1812 RCH. Possibly '*Bryni*'s down,' but the forms are too late for certainty.

WHITECLIFF FM [witli] is *Witeclive* 1086 DB, *Whiteclive* 1242 Fees, *-clyve* 1282 *Kings*, *Gretwhitclyf, Litle Whitclyff* 1516 WM xxxvii. 'White clif or steep place.' "This place is by the common people very generally called *Whitley* rather than Whitecliff" (Hoare, *Heytesbury* 7).

BUSHCOMBE was possibly the home of Robert de *Butlescomb* (1289 *Ass*). The single form makes any attempt at explanation unwise.

BOTLEY OAK. Cf. *Potley Oak Field* c. 1840 *TA*. COLD KITCHEN HILL is so named in 1820 (RCH). It is named after a Midden Mound here. LANGLEY FM (6") is *Langeleghe* 1270 *For*. 'Long clearing or wood,' *v.* leah. WOODCOMBE is *Wodecumbe* 1248 Ch, *-combe* 1300 Ipm. *v.* cumb.

Hill Deverill

HILL DEVERILL

Devrel 1086 DB

Hull 1130–35 SarumCh, *Hulla* 1202 FF, *Hulle* 1211 RBE

Hulle Deverel 1227 FF, 1242 Fees, *Hulledeverel* 1324 FA

For Deverill, *v. supra* 6.

BIDCOMBE HILL is *Bytecombe, Britecombe* 1257 *For, Bidecumbe* 1262 Ipm, *Bidcomb(e)* 1263 *For,* 1812 RCH, *Bytcoumbe* 1319 *AD, Bitcum Wode* 1521 WM xxxvii. The forms are too late and uncertain for any suggestion to be worth while.

MILL FM was the home of John *atte Mulle* (1327 *SR*).

BURNBAKE (6″) is so named in 1788 (*Kings*). See *infra* 451. CHARLOCK HILL (6″) is *Charlockhill* 1540 *Add, Charloke hyll* 1548 *Longleat, Charlekhill* 1773 A and D, probably from the plant. LITTLE DOWN is so named in 1820 (G). Cf. John *atte Dounende* 1341 NI. RYE HILL FM is *Rye hill* 1540 *Add, Ray Hill Farm* 1773 A and D. WHITLEY COPSE (6″) is *Whitleys Copse* c. 1840 *TA*.

Longbridge Deverill

LONGBRIDGE DEVERILL

> *Devrel* 1086 DB
> *Peverel* (sic) *Lungpont* 1239 Bracton, *Deverelungpunt* 1241 FF, 1242 Fees, *-pund* 1249 *Ass, Longepont* 1275 RH, *Longpund* 1291 Tax, *Longepond* 1428 FA
> *Dever(ill) Langebrigge* 1316 FA, *Deverellangebrigg* 1324 Pat, *Deverel Langebrugge* 1339 ib., *Deverellangbrige* 1538 NQ i, *Deverall Longe Bridge* 1546 LP

For Deverill, *v. supra* 6. The distinguishing epithet is from the long bridge over the Wylye here. The earliest forms give it in French form.

NOTE. *Blyndestrete* 1341 *Cor.*

CROCKERTON is *Crokerton* 1249, 1305 *Ass,* 1257 *For,* 1351 *FF, Crock-* 1369 WM xxxvii, *Crokk-* 1430 *FF, Crokeriston* 1289 *Ass.* This is probably a late tun-name. There was a John *le Crocker* in the parish in 1268 (*Ass*) and a Stephen *le Crokker* in 1289 (ib.). The place takes its name from an earlier member of their family or from potters generally, cf. Potterton (PN WRY 150). Close by is Potter's Hill *infra* 167 and there are still Brick and Tile works.

SHUTE FM is *Shete juxta Deverel* 1278 *Ass, Shute* t. Eliz WM xxi. This is from OE **sciete,* 'nook, corner of land,' discussed in PN D 184, 417, *s.n.* Shute. It lies in a corner of the parish.

SWANCOMBE BOTTOM (6″) is *Swenecumbe* 1300 Ipm, *-combe* 1381, *Swynecombe* 1391 Pat, 1566 *Ct*. Probably 'swine valley' (*v.* cumb), cf. some of the forms for Swindon *infra* 276.

HILL FM (6″) and MILL FM were the homes of William *super la Hulle* (1235–61 GlastRl) and Roger *atte Mulle* (1327 *SR*).

COLLIERS[1], KINGS CORNER, POTTER'S HILL and STAR'S FM (all 6″) are to be associated with the families of Nycholas *Colyar* (1525 *SR*), Thomas *Kyng* (1524 ib.), Richard *le Poter* (1252 WIpm) and Richard *Starr* (1629 *SR*).

AUCOMBE BOTTOM (6″). Cf. *Aucombe Warren* 1655 *Longleat*. BROOM CLOSE (6″) is *Broome Closes* 1695 ib. BULL MILL (6″) is so named c. 1840 (*TA*). COW DOWN is *Cow Downe* 1655 *Longleat, v. infra* 430. DRY HILL is *Dryhill* c. 1840 *TA*. FOX HOLES is so named in 1820 (G). LONG IVER. Cf. *Long Ivey* (sic) *Barn* ib., *Ivercumhole* 1566, *Ivercombehole* 1632 *Longleat* and yfer, 'escarpment.' LYNCHETTS (6″). *v. infra* 453. MANS WOOD is *Manswood* 1660 *Longleat*. NOCKATT PLANTATION (6″). *v. supra* 109. SAND HILL FM (6″). Cf. *Sandhullesclade* 1236 FF, *Sand Hill* 1690 *Longleat, v.* slæd. WESTCOMBE (6″) is *Werescumbe* 1235 WM xxxiii, *Wustcombe* 1571, *Wuscombe* 1616 *Ct*, *Wescombe* 1640 WM xxix.

Heytesbury

HEYTESBURY [heitsbəri]

Hestrebe (sic) 1086 DB

Hectredebur 1107 (1300) Ch, *-beria* 1158 HMC Var i, *-bir* 1201 FF, *-byre* c. 1230 SarumCh

Hehtredeberi(a) 1109–17 ib., t. Hy 1 (1496) Pat, 1158, 1160 P, *-bir* 1202 FF, 1242 Fees, *Hehtredesberi* 1156 P

Hegtredebiri 1115 StOsmund, *-beri* 1187 P, *-byr* 1212 FF, *-buri* 1270 Ipm, *Hegtredesbir'* 1216 ClR

Heitredbiria 1155 RBE, *Heytredebur'* 1249 *Ass*

Hictredeberia 1174, *-beri* 1190, *Hictredesberia* 1194 P

Heichtredeberi 1183 P, *Hechtredebiri* c. 1200 RBE, 1215 ClR, *Heithtredebiri* 1211 RBE, *Hecghtridebiri* 1227 Ch, *Heʒtredebir'* 1242 Fees, *Hegthridebiry* 1282 Cl, *Hightredebir* 1283

---

[1] *Collyers* 1653 *FF*.

Ch, *Heghtredebury* 1291 Tax, 1307 Ipm, 1316 FA, *Heghteredebury* 1319 *FF*, *Hextrede-* 1334 Pat, *Istheghtredebury*, *Westheghtrebury* 1328 Ipm
Heghdresbury 1299 Ipm, *Heghtresbury* 1320 *FF*, 1428 FA
Haitesbury, -y- 1445, 1487 Pat, *Hatchbury al. Haitsbury* 1570 *FF*, *Haytreddysburye al. Haytesberye* 1574 ib., *Heytredebury al. Heytesbury* 1618 ib., *Hetsburie* 1632 Sess, *Haresbury*, *Hatchberry* 1675 Ogilby

'burh of a woman named *Hēahþrȳþ*.' This etymology was first suggested by Stevenson (*Dukery Records* 397) who pointed out that *Heahðryð* occurs again in *Hegtredebrug* (1232), the name of a bridge on the boundary of Sherwood Forest. The name is not on independent record.

BOWL'S BARROW is so named in 1773 (A and D) and is the *bodelusburgȝe* of 968 (15th) BCS 1215, *Bothelesbergh* 1348 *Cor*, *Boulsborough* 1675 Ogilby. '*Bodel*'s barrow,' *v.* beorg. The personal name *Boda* is on record. This would be a diminutive form of it. Cf. OGer *Bodilo, Bodila* (Förstemann, PN 322).

TYTHERINGTON

Tuderinton 1242 Fees, 1282 Cl, *-yng-* 1281 *Ass*, *-yn-* 1332 *SR*, *Tudryngton* 1347 *FF*, 1422 *Ct*, (*juxta Heyghtesbury*) 1465 Trop
Toderington 1279 *Ass*
Tederyngton 1459 *FF*, *Tedryngton* 1489 *MinAcct*
Tydryngton ib.

Identical in origin with Tytherton *supra* 91–2.

DUNSCOMBE (6″) is *Dunscomb Bottom* 1820 G. LITTLE LONDON (6″) is so named in 1773 (A and D). Cf. *infra* 455. Here used of the western end of the village. POUND COPSE (6″). Cf. *Southpounde* 1489 *MinAcct*, 1554 Pat.

Horningsham

HORNINGSHAM [*olim* hɔ·rnisəm]
Horningeshā 1086 DB, *-ham* c. 1155 StOsmund, 1202 FF *et freq* to 1332 *SR*, with variant spelling *-yng-*
Horningham 1086 DB, *Hornigeham* late 12th BM

Ornigesham 1242 Fees
Magna Hornynggesham 1289 *Ass, Little Hornyngesham* 1390
    Pat
Hornesham 1405 ib., *Hornyssame* 1535 VE, *Hornisham,*
    Hornisom 1585 WM xxi, *Hornson* 1675 Ogilby

The most likely suggestion for this name, as for Horningsea
(C) and Horningsheath (or Horringer) (Sf) is that the first
element is a personal name *Horning*, perhaps a weakened form
of OE *hornung*, 'bastard,' used as a surname. *Horning* is a
common OGer name (cf. Förstemann PN 867). *v.* ham(m).

NOTE. *Taddelane* 1415 Cl.

BAYCLIFF FM

Ballochelie 1086 DB
Bayleclive, -y- c. 1230 BM, 1257 AD vi, 1343 *AD, Baileclive*
    1242 Fees
Bailleclive ib., 1332 *SR, -clyve* 1325 *FF, -clyf* 1325 Pat
Bayllesclive 1316 FA, *Baylesclyfe* 1387 AD i
Baleclyff 1439 WM xiii
Baicliffe 1513 *Ct, Baycliffe* 1608 *FF, Bay Cleeve* 1773 A and D
Bakley 1648 WM xxxvii

Possibly '*Bægloc*'s clif or steep hillside.' For the personal
name cf. Bealy Court (PN D 377).

LONGLEAT HO

Langelete 1235 SarumCh, 1315 Ipm, (*le*) 1257 AD vi, *la*
    Langhelete late 13th BM, *le Langlete herne* 1366 WM xxiii
Longalete 1245 SarumCh, *Longa Leta* 1281 *Ass*, 1297 Pat,
    La Longe Lete 1297 Chanc, *Longleyte* 1546 LP

The second element is OE *gelæt* found in the compound
wæter-gelæt, 'water conduit, channel or *leat*.' The place is said
to take its name from the long *leat* or water-course which
brought water from Horningsham to the mill by the convent
on the site of which the house stands. *herne* is OE hyrne,
'corner, angle.'

EVERETTS WOOD and ROWE'S HILL are to be associated with the
families of Mary *Everett* and William *Rowe* (c. 1840 *TA*).

BARN FM (6″). Cf. *Barne Close* 1682 *Longleat*. COCK ROAD is *Cockroad* 1635 ib. See *infra* 427. COWERN COPSE (6″). Cf. *Cowern Rag* c. 1840 *TA*, from OE cu-ærn, 'cow-house.' For *rag*, *v. infra* 453. DOD POOL is so named ib. FAIRBROAD COPPICE (6″) [vərbərt]. Cf. *Fairbowd oake* 1625 *Longleat*. THE GROVE is so named in 1651 (ib.). GULLY COPSE (6″) is so named c. 1840 (*TA*). HAZEL COPSE (6″) is *Hasel Copise* 1615 *Longleat*. HIGH WOOD is so named ib. HITCOMBE BOTTOM (6″). Cf. *Hitcomes meade* 1540 *Add*. NEWBURY is so named in 1773 (A and D). PARK HILL. Cf. *parco de Hornyngesham* 1422 *Ct*. POTTLE STREET is so named in 1773 (A and D). SCOTLAND is so named ib. Cf. *infra* 454 TOMKINS POOL (6″). Cf. *Tomkins lane* 1540 *Add*. WHITE MARSHES (6″) is *Whitemarshes* 1625 WM xxiii. WOOD-HOUSE FM is so named c. 1840 (*TA*).

Imber

IMBER

Imemerie (sic) 1086 DB, *Immemera* 1146 SarumCh, 1164, 1167 P, *Immemer* 1198 Fees, *-mere* 1211 RBE, 1221 ClR, *Imimere* 1236 Fees, *Ymmemere*, *Ymemer* 1242 ib.

Imere 1291 Tax, *Immere* 1304 Sarum, 1316 FA, 1347 Pat

Himmemere 1200 SarumCh, *Immer al. Hymbemer* 1435 Cl, *Immer al. Imber* 1540 *FF*, *Ember* 1681 ParReg

This name must be taken with *Ymmanedene* found in the land boundaries of BCS 1215, and a lost name in the parish, *Imendone* 1161 RBE, *Himmedon* 1170 ff. P, *Hummendon* 1177, *Himmendon* 1178, 1182, 1186, *Hunmendon* 1187 P, *Immeden'* 1198 Fees, *Himendun'* 1202 P, *Imedone* 1212–16 RBE, *Humedon* 13th Fees, *Immedon* 1281 *Ass*. The first element of these names is almost certainly the OE personal name *Imma*. The *y*-spelling in BCS 1215 comes from a 15th-century copy. Hence '*Imma*'s pool and hill,' *v*. dun, mere.

BROWN'S FM (6″) is to be associated with the family of Thomas *Broun* (1332 *SR*).

CHAPPERTON DOWN. Cf. *Chaperton feld(es)* 1540 *MinAcct*, 1550 Pat. FORE DOWN is *Fore Downe* 1632 *Wilton*. WADMAN'S COPPICE (6″) is so called in 1812 (RCH).

Knook

KNOOK [nuk]

Cunuche 1086 DB, *Chenuka* t. Hy 1 (1496) Pat
Cnuca 1107 (1300) Ch, *Cnuke* 1211 RBE, 1236 Cl, *Knuke*
1227 FF
Cnuk 1220 StOsmund, 1242 Fees, *Knuch* 1249 BM, *Knuk*
1262 Ipm, 1268 *Ass*, *Knuc* 1296 Ipm
Cnoke c. 1300 SarumCh, *Knoke* 1310 *Ass*, 1327 Banco
Cnouk 1314 Ipm, *Knouk* 1316 FA, *Knouke* 1332 *SR*, *Knowke*
1403 IpmR, *Knooke* 1581 *FF*

This is probably a Celtic name, identical with ModWelsh *cnwc*, 'lump, hillock.' It may have reference to a tumulus, such as that marked half a mile south of the church. Cf. Introd. xv.

FLOWER'S FIELD BARN (6″) is to be associated with the family of Isaac *Flower* (1809 ParReg).

ANSTY HILL (6″) is *Anstrow Hill* 1773 A and D. The School gives *Ansty Trees* as the name of a row of trees along the road here. Possibly *Anstrow* is for *Ansty Trow* or *Tree*. KNOOK CASTLE. Cf. *Castle Barrow* ib.

Upton Lovell

UPTON LOVELL [lʌvəl]

Ubbantun, Ubbantuninga gemære 957 (13th) BCS 992
Ubeton 1199 Abbr, 1200 Cur, 1291 Tax, 1316, 1428 FA
Ubbeton 1200 FF, 1297 Pat, 1386 *FF*, 1430 Cl
Obeton 1242 Fees, 1387 Pat, *Obbetone* 1327 *SR*
Lovells Upton 1526 *Ct*, *Upton Lovell* 1597 *FF*, *Ubton* 1624 ib.

'*Ubba*'s farm,' *v.* tun. William *Lovell* held the manor in 1428 (FA). The second form means 'the boundary of the people of Upton.' Cf. ingas, (ge)mære.

HORSE HILL is so named in 1773 (A and D). QUEBEC BARN (6″) is at the extreme north end of the parish. Cf. *infra* 455. UPTON FOLLY is so named in 1773 (A and D). *v. infra* 451.

XV. MERE HUNDRED

Mere hundred 1086 ExonDB, *Merahðr* 1160 P, *Hundredum de Meyre* 1316 FA. See Mere *infra* 178. For the possible site of the meeting-place, *v.* Moot Fd *infra* 484.

Maiden Bradley

MAIDEN BRADLEY

Bradelie 1086 DB, *-lega* t. Hy 2 (1313) Ch, *-leia* t. Hy 2 Dugd vi, 1196 Cur, *-legh* 1232 BM
Maydene Bradelega t. John Dugd vi, *Maydenbradley* 1547 *SR*
Suht Bradeleigh t. Hy 3 WM xxx
Braddeley 1316 FA

'Wide clearing or wood,' cf. North Bradley *supra* 138. *Suht* (sic) in contrast to that place. There was a small cell here, belonging to Amesbury. In 1178 (BM) the place is referred to as *Deverell Puellarum* from these same nuns. It lies on the old Deverill stream, *v.* Deverill *supra* 6.

NOTE. CHURCH ST is *Chyrche strete* 1509 *Ct.* HONEYPOT LANE, a nickname for a muddy lane.

KATE'S BENCH CLUMP. Cf. *Cattenbenche* 1385, 1531, *Gatebenche* 14th Hoare, *Gadebenche* 1402 HMC, App. vii, *Cattebenche* 1535 VE, 1536 *MinAcct*, *Cattesbenche* t. Hy 8 ib. For *bench*, denoting 'a slope,' cf. benc *infra* 423. The whole name probably means '(Wild) cats' slope.'

YARNFIELD[1]

Gernefelle (sic) 1086 DB, *-feld* 1225 *Ass*, 1229, 1230 FF, t. Hy 3 BM, t. Ed 1 *For*, *-feud* 1260 BM
Jernefeld 1232 Cl, 1341 NI, *Yarnefeld* late 14th BM, 1509 *Ct*, *Yerne-* 1402 *AD*

It has been suggested (DEPN) that this is from OE *earnafeld*, 'eagles' feld,' but there is the serious difficulty that no parallel is known for the persistent appearance of an initial *g* or *j* before *ern* (earlier *earn*) from the earliest times onward. Possibly we

---

[1] Formerly in Somerset. Transferred to Wiltshire in 1895.

may have a stream-name *Gerne* identical with the Norfolk Yare found in Yarmouth (DB *Gernemutha*). A stream runs down from Yarnfield to join the Frome.

PENNY'S WOOD (6") is to be associated with the family of William *Penny* (1629 *SR*).

BARCROFT FM (6"). Cf. *Barcroft* c. 1840 *TA*. BRICEFIELD (6") is *Brysefeld* 1536 *MinAcct*. The first element is possibly the word *breeze*, 'gadfly,' which in the 10th and 11th centuries sometimes appears in the form *brise*. BRIMBLE HILL (6") is *Bremelhil brech* 1407 Trop. 'Bramble hill,' *v*. bremel, bræc. DEERWOOD COMMON (6") is so named c. 1840 (*TA*). LITTLE and LONG (6") KNOLL. Cf. *Knoll Wood, Knoll Hill, Long Knoll* ib. *v*. cnoll. MILL TYNING WOOD (6"). Cf. *Mill Tyning* c. 1840 *TA* and *infra* 449. NEWMEAD FM is *New Mead Farm* 1773 A and D. PENSTONES WOOD. Cf. *Penystonys* 1536 *MinAcct*. PROUTLY WOOD (6"). Cf. *Prowtleaze* c. 1840 *TA*. RAG WOOD (6"). Cf. *Ragg* ib. and *infra* 453. RODMEAD FM is *Redemede* 1422 WM xxx, *Rodmede* t. Eliz *LRMB*, i.e. 'reed-meadow,' *v*. hreod. TOM HOLE (6") is so named c. 1840 (*TA*). TYNING WOOD. Cf. *Tyning* ib. and *infra* 449.

Kingston Deverill

KINGSTON DEVERILL
> *Devrel* 1086 DB, *Kingesdeverell* 1206 ClR
> *Dewrelquinston* (sic) 1236 Pap, *Deverel Kyngeston* 1249 FF,
>   *Kingiston Deverel* 1260 Cl, *Kyngestone Deverel* 1282 *Ass*
> *Kyngeston(e)* 1291 Tax, 1428 FA, *Kingson* 1675 Ogilby

For *Deverill, v. supra* 6. "Shortly after the Conquest it was in the Crown and was among the early grants to the Earl of Cornwall.... It followed the fate of the Earldom, which frequently reverted to the Crown and was finally entailed on the King's eldest son. This circumstance, perhaps, gave origin to the appellation of *Kingston*, by way of distinction from the other Deverills, none of which, since the Conquest, have been royal property" (Hoare 137–8).

MARVINS (6") is to be associated with the family of George *Mervyn* (1629 *SR*).

Court Hill. Cf. *Courtende* 1609 *Ct.* Holcombe (6″) is *Holcombe* 1571 ib. Marcombe (6″) is so named t. Eliz (*LRMB*). It is on the parish boundary. *v.* (ge)mære, 'boundary.' Middle Hill is *Myddlehill* 1616 *Ct.*

Monkton Deverill

Monkton Deverill

> *Devrel* 1086 DB
> ·*Munketon* 1189 GlastInq, 1249 *Ass*, *Muneketon* 1242 Fees, 1249 *Ass*
> *Moneketon Deverel* 1270 FF, *Deverel Monketon* 1275 RH, *Est Monketon* 1525 *SR*, *Mounton Deverall* 1558 FF

For *Deverill*, *v. supra* 6. *Monkton* means 'monks' farm,' *v.* tun. The manor belonged to Glastonbury as early as DB. It was also known as *Over Deverill*, perhaps in the sense of 'upper.' to distinguish it from Longbridge Deverill which is lower down the stream (Hoare 176), and *Est Monkton* to distinguish it from another Monkton belonging to the same Abbey (ib. 177).

Boar's Bottom (6″) takes its name from the family of Robert *le Bor* (1327 Pat), *le Boor* (1334 *Ass*). Cf. *Boresmaner* 1439 *FF*, *Borres* 1516, *Bores* 1552 WM xxxvii, *Boars* or *Bores* 1740 *Sadler*.

Keysley Fm is *Keasley* 1648 WM xxxvii, *Keasley Sheep Sleight* 1702 *Longleat*, *Keesley* 1812 RCH. *v.* leah and *infra* 454. Pen Hill is so named in 1820 (G). Cf. Pen Hill *supra* 33–4.

Kilmington

Kilmington[1]

> *Chelmetone* 1086 DB
> *Cilemetone* ib., *Chilmatona* 1086 ExonDB
> *Culminton* 1251 Cl, 1284 FA, -*yng*- 1291 Tax, 1327 *SR*, 1396 Pat, 1544 LP, -*yn*- 1308 *FF*, 1310 Pat, *Kulmeton* t. Hy 3 Stowe 798, *Colemeton* t. Ed 1 *For*
> *Kylmyngton al. Culmyngton* 1403 Pat

Probably 'Cynehelm's farm,' *v.* ingtun. Cf. Kilmington (PN D 640).

[1] Formerly in Somerset. Transferred to Wiltshire in 1896.

NORTON FERRIS is *Nortone* 1086 DB, *Northon* 1227 Ch, *Norton* 1253 Ipm, (*Mussegros*) 1368 Pat. 'North farm,' *v.* tun. *North* with reference to Stourton *infra* 181. Joh de *Ferrers* held the manor in 1368 (Pat). Robert de *Muscegros* had a holding in 1253 (Ipm).

WHITE SHEET DOWN is *White Sheet* 1773 A and D and is called *The Beacon Hill* in 1610 (S) and 1695 (Morden). Here and in White Sheet Hill *infra* 184 and in White Sheet (Fd) in Boyton it is formally possible that *sheet* is from a lost OE *scēot*, corresponding to OHG *sciez*, 'slope, steep place,' as postulated by Ekwall (DEPN) for Shottle (Db). All the Wiltshire examples, however, are late and there can be little doubt that they are only late nicknames descriptive of the appearance of the hill-side.

HOMESTALLS. *v. infra* 434. THE KNOLL (6″) is *Knoll Hill* 1548 WM viii.

Knoyle

KNOYLE, EAST and WEST [nɔil]

(*æt*) *Cnugel* 948 (13th) BCS 870, *Cnugel* 956 (14th) ib. 956, (*on*) *Cnugellege* 984 (14th) KCD 641
Chenvel 1086 DB
Cnoel 1187, 1195 P *et freq* to 1332 SR, with variant spellings *Knoel, Cnoell'* 1200 Cur
Childecnoel 1202 P, 1205 Pap, 1236 FF
Cnohell' 1204 FineR, *Cnohill* 1236 FF, *Knoyhull* 1451 Trop
Childecnowell 1204 WintonCart, *Knowel* 1275 RH, (*Magna*) 1285 FF, *Cnowel* 1300 Ipm, 1327 SR, *Knouwell Magna* 1331 Pat, *Knowell Episcopi* 1346 FF, (*Odierne*) 1347 ib., *Knoel Hodyerne al. Knoel Parva* 1428 FA
Stepelknoel 1228 Cl, *Little Knoyell* 1408 Pat
Este-, Westeknoyle 1467 MinAcct, *Westknoyle al. Cnoyle Oderne* 1540 ib., *Estknoyle al. Bisshopes Knoyle* 1570 FF
Noyle 1693 ParReg

The ground here is very much broken and Ekwall (DEPN) is probably right in postulating a lost OE *cnugel*, 'knuckle,' which might be used of a rounded hill. East Knoyle was known also as *Great* Knoyle and *Bishop's* Knoyle from the holding of the *Bishop* of Winchester here (1204 WintonCart, 1236 FF). It was also known as *Childecnoel* (ib.), but the reason for this name is unknown. West Knoyle was also known as *Little* Knoyle or Knoyle *Odierne* from the holding of *Hodierna*, the mother of Alexander of Neckham and foster-mother of Richard Cœur de Lion (cf. *terra Hodierne nutricis* (1236 *P*) mentioned next to Mere in a document given in Madox, *History of the Exchequer* 488). For *Stepelknoel*, see Milton *infra*. See Addenda *supra* xl.

East Knoyle

CLOUDS HO (6″). Cf. *Clowdes* 1822 Hoare, *Clouds Park* c. 1840 *TA*, from OE *clūd*, 'rock, hill.' The ground is much broken here. Cf. *Shortcloude* (1412 *WinchColl*) in Compton Bassett, *Clowd hyll* (1545 *Deeds Enrolled*) in Easton Grey.

MILTON is *Middelton* 1281 *Ass*, *Midel-* c. 1300 Trop, *Milton juxta Knoell* 1445 ib. 'Middle farm,' *v.* tun. So named in relation to East and West Knoyle. Close at hand is STEEPLE COPSE (6″) (cf. *Stepple Close* c. 1840 *TA*), suggesting that *Stepelknoel* (1228 Cl) was another name for Milton. *Steeple* is from a lost OE *stīepel*, 'steep place,' discussed in PN Ess 226–7.

PERTWOOD FMS

> *Perteworde* 1086 DB, *-wurda Edwardi* 1166 P, *-wurth'* 1242 Fees *et freq* to 1431 Trop, with variant spellings *-worth*, *-wrth*
> *Purtewerthe* 1270 *For*
> *Perteworthy* 1411 *FF*
> *Pertewodde* 1535 VE, *Peertwode al. Peertworth* 1542 *FF*, *Partewoode al. Parteworthe* 1554 ib., *Peartworth* 1651 Hoare

This name must remain an unsolved problem. It may be that it is to be associated with the place-name Peart in Laverton (So), *le Perte* c. 1250 Wells, but that name is obscure. Professor Ekwall and Dr Ritter suggest the possibility of associating this last name with Welsh *perth*, 'bush, brake,' British *pertā*, 'wood, copse,' the source of Perth (Scotland).

HOLLOWAY[1] and UPTON[2] were the homes of John de *Holeweye* (1279 *Ass*) and Stephen de *Upton* (1289 ib.). *v.* holh, tun.

---

[1] *la Holeweye* 1289 *Ass*.   [2] *Upton'* ib.

COLEMAN'S FM (6″), FRIAR'S HAYES FM, KING'S BUSHES (6″) and SLADE'S FM (6″) are to be associated with the families of John Colman (1529 *Rental*), Richard *Fryer* (1624 ParReg), Thomas *le Kyng* (1332 *SR*) and James *Slade* (c. 1840 *TA*). *v.* (ge)hæg *infra* 433.

BARN'S HILL (6″). Cf. *le Barne* 1616 *Ct*, *Barnesfurlang* 1632 *EcclCom*. BLACK HOUSE FM (6″) is *Blackhouse* 1598 ib. THE GROVE (6″). Cf. *Grove meade* 1563 *Rental*. HIGH CROFT (6″) is *Highcroft* c. 1840 *TA*. KINGHAY is *Kinghayes* 1668, *Kingshayes* 1692 Moulton. *v.* (ge)hæg. LEIGH FM is *Lie in parochia de Estknoyle* 1541 *FF*, *Lyghe* 1632 WIpm. *v.* leah. MOOR'S FM. Cf. *Moore meade* 1563 *Rental*, *le Moore* 1598 *EcclCom*. *v.* mor. NEW LEAZE FM. Cf. *New Leaze* 1773 A and D. PARK FM. Cf. *parcum suum de Knoel* 1253 Cl. PEAKED FD (6″). Cf. *infra* 443. RED HOUSE FM (6″) is *Red House* 1773 A and D. SHEEPHOUSE FM. Cf. *lez Shepehowse* 1570 PembSurv. SKIDMARSH WOOD (6″). Cf. *Skydmarshe* 1563 *FF*. SUMMERLEAZE FM is *Symerlees* (sic) 1549 Pat, *Somerleaze* 1563 *Rental*, (*al. Easthaies*) 1616 *Ct*. 'Summer pasture,' *v.* læs, (ge)hæg. THRODMILL COTTAGE (6″). Cf. *Trodmill Coppice* c. 1840 *TA*. UNDER HILL (6″) is so named ib. VERNHILL (6″) is *Fern Hill* ib. Cf. Introd. xxi. WINDMILL HILL is so named in 1632 (*EcclCom*). WITHYBED PLANTATION (6″). Cf. *Withy Bed* c. 1840 *TA*.

West Knoyle

CLEEVE HILL was probably by the home of Samson de *Cliva* (1225 *SR*). *v.* clif, 'hillside.'

MITCHELL'S COPPICE and PINNOCK'S COPPICE (both 6″) are to be associated with the families of Anthony *Michel* (1673 ParReg) and Walterus *Pinnok* (1273 RH). Cf. *Pinnock* c. 1840 *TA*. The last form probably stands for *Pinnocks*.

BROADMEAD FM is *le Brodemed* 13th AD i, *Broade meade* 1616 *Ct*. HANG WOOD (6″) is *Hangwood* c. 1840 *TA*. LONGMEAD COPPICE (6″). Cf. *Long Mead* ib. OXLEAZE FM (6″). Cf. *Ox Leaze* ib. PUCK WELL (6″) is *Puckwell* ib. 'Goblin well.' WEST HILL FM. Cf. *Westhill* 1609 *Ct*. WOOD FM. Cf. *bosco de Knoel* 1279 Ass, *Woodfurlonge* 1570 PembSurv.

Mere

Mera 1086 DB, 1091, 1098 StOsmund, 1139 SarumCh, 1155 RBE, 1156 ff. P, *Mere* 1086 DB, 1166 RBE, 1196 Cur *et passim*, *Meyre* 1281 *Ass*, *Meere* 1308 Pat, *Mayre* 1316 FA, *Miere* 1337 Pat, *Meere* 1359 Cl, 1416 Pat, *Myre* 1502 ib., *Meare* 1616 *FF*, *Mere oth*. *Mare oth*. *Meere* 1753 ib.

As Mere is near the point where Dorset, Somerset and Wiltshire meet, it is probable that the name is derived from OE (ge)mære, 'boundary.'

NOTE. BOAR ST is *Bore streat* 1574 *Rental*. CASTLE ST is *Castell streate* 1567 *Ct*. CHURCH ST is *Churchelane* 1495 ib., *Churche streat* 1574 *Rental*. CLEMENTS LANE is to be associated with the family of John *Clement* (1552 WM xxix). SALISBURY ST is *Salesburye streate* 1567 *Ct*, leading to Salisbury. WATER ST is *Water streat* 1574 *Rental*. WET LANE is *Wetlane* 1502 Ipm, *Weatelane* 1567 *Ct*.

Lost names include *Lanshare lane* (i.e. 'boundary lane,' from OE *land scearu*), *Shobbe lane*, *Woodelane*, *le Narrowe lane* 1568, *Darcklane* 1609 *Ct*, *Grean lane*, *Mylle lane*, *Hollow lane* 1595, *the Markett place* 1606 WM xxix, *Fryes lane*, *Shaftesbury streate* (i.e. leading to Shaftesbury (Do)) 1616 *Ct*, *London rode* 1650 *ParlSurv*.

BARROW STREET (hamlet). Cf. *la Baruwe* 1285 *MinAcct*, *Barowstreate* 1566 *Ct*, the home of Thomas *atte Barwe* (1327 *SR*). 'Barrow,' *v*. beorg. A large barrow once stood at the end of Barrow Street Lane (WM xxix, 257). Cf. Hawk Street *infra* 254.

BURTON

Burinton' 1204 Cur
Burtona 1236 Bracton, *-ton* 1237 Cl, *Burtone juxta Mere* 1281, 1289 *Ass*
Burghton 1268 ib., *Burgton* 1284 WIpm (p)
Bourton 1327 *SR* (p), 1398 Ipm (p), 1428 FA, 1566 *Ct*

As in the case of Burton and Boreham *supra* 49, 158 the compound is **burhtun** used in the sense 'farm by a borough.'

CHADDENWICK *alias* CHARNAGE

Chedelwich 1086 DB, *Chadelewic* 1196 FF
Chadenwik 1224 Bracton, *-wych* 1279 *Ass*, *-wich* 1300 Ipm, *-wyche* 1332 *SR*, *Chadewich* 1242 Fees, *-wiz* 1284 Ipm

Chadenewiche 1263 *For*, *-wyk* 1270 ib.
Cheddenwych 1289 *Ass*
Chadneswych 1397 IpmR, *-che* 1397 Cl
Chadenwych...sometimes called Charnage 1822 Hoare

Probably '*Ceadela*'s dwelling,' with the same personal name as in *Chadlanger supra* 158–9. *v.* wic. For confusion of *l* and *r*, *v.* IPN 106–7.

CHETCOMBE BARN (6"). Cf. *Chatecombe* 1300 Ipm, *Chetcombe* 1569 ChwAcct, 1650 *ParlSurv*. This is probably '*Ceatta*'s combe,' *v.* cumb.

CONRISH FM (6") is *parco de Kunewyk* 1268, *Couewych*, *Couewiz* 1281 *Ass*, *la Couewyche* 1285 *MinAcct*, *la Conewich*, *atte Conwich* 1300 Ipm (Hoare), *Couewyche* 1391 Pat, *park of Meere al. le Couewich* 1453 Pat, *Couwych comon* 1616 *Ct*. This, with CUNNAGE LANE (leading to it), is from OE *cūna* (gen. pl.) *wīc*, 'cows' farm.' Some of the *n*'s have been wrongly transcribed as *u*'s.

DEVERELLS WOOD (6") is *Devereleswode* 1281 *Ass*, *Deverlingewode* 1300 Ipm, *Deverelwode* 1391 Pat, *Deverlongwood* 1566 *Ct*, *Deverlonge woode* 1606 *LRMB*. This name must go back to an OE *Deferelinga wudu*, 'wood of the people by the river Deverill' (*supra* 6), *v.* ingas. The Deverill valley is only a few miles away on the other side of the chalk ridge.

HORSINGTON LANE (6") is *Horsington* 1502 Ipm and was near the home of Henry de *Horsington*, member for Mere in 1305. The place is mentioned in the metes of Gillingham Forest ib. 1567 and survives to this day in *Horsingtons Fds* in Mere. Cf. WM xix, 235 ff. The place-name is probably of manorial origin, from Horsington (So), not far distant.

KNOWL is *cnol* 956 (14th) BCS 956, *Cuffes cnoll* 948 (14th) ib. 70, in the bounds of West Knoyle. As Grundy notes (ii, 20–1), the knoll is the hill three-quarters of a mile to the north-east, marked by the 400 ft. contour line. *v.* cnoll.

MAPPLEDORE HILL (6") is *Mapeldreshille*, *Mapelderhil* 1281 *Ass*, *Mapeldorehulle* 1285 *MinAcct*, 1300 Ipm, *Maperdorehill* 1563

Rental, Mapedere hill 1606 *LRMB*. 'Maple-tree hill,' c▮
Mappowder (PN Do 206). The name repeated itself a few mile▮
to the east in *mapeldere hille* (KCD 641) in the bounds of Tisbury▮

PIMPERLEAZE RD (6″)

> *Pimperlega* 1193 P, *Pymperlegh* 1321 *Ass* (p), 1332 *SR* (p▮
> *Pymperleys* 1502 Ipm, *Pymperleighes lane, Pymperleyg*
> *hedge* 1568 WM xxix
> *Pinperlege* 1196 Cur, 1198 Abbr, 1208 Cur (p), *Pynperley*
> 1284 WIpm

There can be little doubt that we have here, in the first pa▮
of the name, a repetition of the name Pimperne found in Dors▮
as the name of a village (PN Do 56–7) and probably going bac▮
to an old river-name (cf. Ekwall RN 326, DEPN *s.n.*). There ▮
a small stream here.

LYEMARSH FM[1], MERE MILL, WELL HEAD[2] were the homes ▮
Robert de *la Lye* (1288 *Ass*), de *la Legh* (1289 ib.), Arnulph▮
Attemulle (1300 Hoare) and John *atte Mulle* (1332 *SR*), Cristi▮
atte welle (1300 Hoare) and Walter *atte Welle* (1332 *SR*). *v.* lea▮

ASHWELL (6″) is *Ayshwell* 1616 *Ct*. BLACK HOUSE FM (6″)
Blackhouse 1609 ib. BREACHES FM (6″). Cf. *la Brech* 1300 Ip▮
The Breaches 1650 *ParlSurv. v.* bræc. BUSHAYES (6″) is *Bussh*
hayes 1566 *Ct, v.* (ge)hæg. CASTLE HILL (6″) is *Castell Hill* 157▮
Rental. CHANTRY HO (6″). Cf. *Chantry Mead* c. 1840 *TA* an▮
infra 456. EAST HILL is *Easthill* 1616 *Ct*. EDGE BRIDGE (6″)
Edbrydge 1566, 1568, *Edbridge sherde* 1571 *Ct*. For *sherde* s▮
infra 445. HINCKE'S MILL (6″) is *Hympkes myll* 1566 ib., *Hincke*
mill 1578 ChwAcct. HOLWELL (6″) is *Holewelle* 1227 StOsmun▮
Holwell 1495 *Ct*. 'Spring in the hollow.' THE ISLAND (6″)
le Ilande 1616 *Ct*. IVY MEAD (6″) is *Ivye meade* 1563 *Renta*
LIMPERS HILL is *Lympereishill* 1574 *Rental, Lympershill* 15▮
ChwAcct, *Lympardshill* 1609 *Ct*. LORD'S MEAD HO (6″) is
Lordismede 1495 *Ct*. LYNCH (6″). Cf. *Linche close* 1563,
Lynche 1574 *Rental. v.* hlinc. MERE DOWN. Cf. *Downesi*▮
1606 *LRMB, le Downe* 1616 *Ct, Meere downes* 1650 *ParlSur*▮
MERE PARK is so named in 1568 (WM xxix). POND BOTTOM (6″

---

[1] *Leigh Marsh* 1568 WM xxix, *Lye Marsh* 1574 *Rental*.
[2] *Welle head* 1568 *Ct*.

Cf. *Ponde meade* 1563 *Rental*. ROOK STREET (hamlet) is *Rooke-treete* 1563, *Rokestreate* 1574 ib. SHEEPHOUSE (6"). Cf. *Shepe-house meade* 1563 ib., *Shepehouse* 1616 *Ct*. SOUTHBROOK is *Sowth brok* 1563 *Rental*. SWAINSFORD FM is *Swaynes foorde* 1563 *Rental*, *Sway(e)ng fourde* 1566, 1568 *Ct*. TOWN'S END (6") is *le Townes ende* 1616 ib. WHITE HILL is *Whitehill* 1563 *Rental*. WOODLANDS is *la Wodelonde* 1300 Ipm, *Merewoodlond* 1502 ib., *Eastewoodland* 1566 *Ct*.

Stourton

STOURTON [stɔːrtən]

> *Stortone* 1086 DB, -*ton* 1279, 1310 *Ass*, 1285 *MinAcct*, 1657
> Sadler
> *Sturton(e)* 1182 P *et freq* to 1327 *SR*, (*juxta Mere*) 1310 *FF*,
> *Sture*- 1290 WIpm
> *Steortone* 1302 *Ass*
> *Stourton* 1332 *SR*, 1386 *FF*, *Stoure*- 1383 Pat, 1513 *Ct*
> *Stowerton* 1606 Sess, *Stowrton* 1640 *FF*

'Farm on the river Stour,' *v*. tun and *supra* 10.

NOTE. COXFIELD LANE is to be associated with the family of Thomas Cox (1639 ParReg).

BONHAM (6") is *Bonham* 1356 BM, 1435 Cl and was the home of John de *Bonham* (1323 Hoare) and Nicholas de *Bonham* (1371 Pat). The house is mentioned in Leland who writes "There is on an hille, a little withoute Stourton, a grove, and yn it is a very praty place caullyd *Bonhomes*...*Bonhome* (proprius *Bonham*) of Wileshire, of the auncientie house of the *Bonhomes* there, is lords of it" (Hoare 89). The forms are too late for any etymology to be satisfactory.

GASPER[1] is *Gayespore* 1280 Ass (So), *Gayspore* 1376 FF, 1411 BM, 1435 Cl, 1566 *Ct*, *Gasper* 1812 RCH. The final element in this name is probably OE *spora*, 'spur,' used of a projecting hill. The first element must remain uncertain.

SHAVE COTTAGES (6") was the home of Goscelin de *la Shaghe* (1289 *Ass*) and Robert *atte Schawe* (1327 *SR*). It is *Shave* 1625

[1] Formerly in Somerset (Kelly).

FF, 1820 G, *v.* sceaga, 'wood, copse.' For the change of *w* to *v*, cf. Shave (PN Do 290) and PN D Pt. I, xxxv.

Brook Ho (6"), Coldcot Fm and Combe Wood were the homes of Gilbert *Bithebroke*, i.e. 'by the brook' (1285 *MinAcct*), Nicholas de *Caldecote* (1321 *FF*) and Nicholas de *la Cumbe* (1302 *Ass*), *v.* cumb, and Chalcot *supra* 147.

Bottle's Hill, Dyer's Well and Perfect's Copse (all 6") are to be associated with the families of Anne *Botwell* (1570 ParReg), Thomas *Dyer* (1566 *Ct*) and Henry *Perfect* (1728 ParReg).

Church Hill (6") is *Churchyll* 1566 *Ct.* Friezeland is so named c. 1840 *TA.* Hart Hill is *Hort Hill* ib. Penridge Fm, Pen Pits (6"). Cf. *Penne ende* 1616 *Ct.* This is the *penn* or hill which gives name to Penselwood (So). Cf. Pen Hill *supra* 34. St Peter's Pump (6") is so named in 1825 (Hoare). It was erected about 1768, being brought from Bristol. Search Fm is so named in 1820 (G). Shootershill Copse (6") is *Shooters Hill Coppice* c. 1840 *TA.* Six Wells Bottom. Cf. *The Six Wells* 1822 Hoare. The sources of the river Stour. Stourhead is a house built in 1720 (ib.). Tucking Mill. Cf. *Tucking Mill Mead* c. 1840 *TA*, i.e. 'fulling mill.' Writh Copse (6"). Cf. *Writh Coppice* ib., from OE wriŏ, 'thicket.'

Zeals

Zeals

> *at Seale* 956 (12th) BCS 968, *Netherseales* 1495 *Ct*, both *Sealles* 1571 *SR*
> *Sele, -a* 1086 DB
> *Seles* 1176 P, 1203 FF *et passim* to 1377 *FF*, *Celes* 1264 Ipm, *Ovre Seles juxta Mere* 1289 *Ass*, *Seeles* 1302 Ipm, *Sceles* 1302 Pat, 1303 Ipm, 1332 *SR*, *Netherseles* c. 1415 ECP, *Selesaylesbury* 1428 FA, *Selyscleverdon* 1502 Ipm
> *Sayles* 1629 *SR*, *Zailes* 1637 Sess, *Zeales* 1665 *FF*, 1719 Recov

This is OE *sealh* (dat. *sēale*), 'willow, sally.' Most of the forms point to the plural *sēalas*. "It contains two manors, which are distinguished by the titles of Seals Ailesbury or Over Zeals and Seals Clevedon, or Nether Zeals. The former of these manors derives its name from a grant in 1292 to Walter de *Ailesbury....* Zeal Clevedon I imagine is so called from a family of that name, whose arms are depicted in the parish church of Mere" (Hoare 31). See Addenda *supra* xl.

WOLVERTON is *Wolfertun* 1219 AD iii, *Wolverton* 1327 *SR* (p), 1377 *FF*, 1394 *Ass*, 1412 IpmR, *Wolfreton* 1357 Cl. Probably '*Wulfhere*'s farm,' *v.* tun, with omission of the genitival *s*.

CASTLE GROUNDS FM and THE GREEN (6″) were the homes of Jocelin de *Castello* (1257 *For*) and Walter *atte Castel* (1327 *SR*) and John *atte Grene* (ib.). Cf. *Sealisgrene* 1495 *Ct*.

ARK WATER (6″). Cf. *Ark Common* c. 1840 *TA*. NOR WOOD is *Nortwud* 1257 *For*, *Northe woodes corner* 1566 *Ct*. ROW FM (6″). Cf. *Rewend* 1566 *Ct* and Introd. xx. WESTFIELD COTTAGES (6″). Cf. *Westfelde* 1548 Pat. WHITE CROSS is so named in 1773 (A and D). ZEALS ST MARTIN FM (6″) is so named from the dedication of the parish church.

XVI. DUNWORTH HUNDRED

Donouuorde hundred 1086 ExonDB, *Duneward hdr* 1158, *Duneswurðe* 1167, *Duneswurde hdr* 1168, *Dunewurd hdr* 1193 P, *Hundred de Dunewrth(e)* 1196 Cur, 1255 RH, *Donewurth* ib., 1289 *Ass*. The meeting-place must have been at or near Dunworth in Wardour *infra* 197.

Ansty

ANSTY

   Anestige 1086 DB, *Anesty* 1220 Bracton, 1225 FF, *Anestie* 1227 ib., *Anestig* 1242 Fees, *-stye* 1249 *Ass*, *-steye* 1251 Ch, *-stygh* 1281 *Ass*

   Anstighe t. Hy 1 *Shaston*, *Ansteia* 1245 StNicholas

'Narrow path (generally up a steep place),' *v.* anstig. In the Ham Charter (BCS 677) we have reference to *bares anstigan*, a path of this kind used by a boar. Another example of this name is found in Ansty Fd in Horningsham *infra* 482.

COOMBE is *Cumbe* 1281 *Ass*, 1311 *FF*, *v.* **cumb**. COOMBE CRATE (6″). Cf. *infra* 427–8. DENMEAD COPSE (6″) is *Denemede* 1331 *MinAcct*. 'Valley meadow,' *v.* **denu**. HORWOOD FM is (*la*) *Horewod*(*e*) 1303 *GDR*, 1305 *Ass*, 1571 Hoare. Perhaps 'boundary wood,' *v.* **har**. It lies on the borders of Wardour parish. WATERLOO BARN (6″) was earlier *Cholen Barn* (1773 A and D). It is adjacent to Choulden Lane *infra* 193. WHITE SHEET HILL is *Whiteshete Hille* c. 1540 Leland, *White Sheet* 1608 Hoare. Cf. *supra* 175.

Berwick St Leonard

BERWICK ST LEONARD

   Berewica t. Hy 1 *Shaston*, *Berewyk* 1249 *Ass*, (*Sci Leonardi*) 1291 Tax, *Berwyk Seynt Leonarde* 1534 *FF*, *Barwyke Sci Leonard*' 1544 *SR*

   Barwyke alias Cold Barwyke 1545 Hoare, *Cole Barwike* 1553 WM x, *Barwick oth. Cold Barwick oth. Barwick Saint Leonard* 1805 *Recov*

   v. **berewic**, 'grange, outlying part of estate.' St Leonard from the dedication of the church. COLD BERWICK HILL preserves the earlier distinctive epithet.

BAKE BARN (6″). Cf. **bake** *infra* 450. CHILFINCH HANGING (6″). Cf. Chilfinch *infra* 217. PENNING WOOD (6″). *v. infra* 453.

Chicklade

CHICKLADE

   Cytlid c. 912 *BCS* 591, *Chitlad* (*boscus de*) 1300 *Stowe* 798
   Ciclet 1211 *RBE*, (*in*) *bosco de Siclat* 1232 *Lacock*, *Ciklet* 1242 Fees
   Chicled 1232 *Lacock*, *boscum de Chikled* 1279, *Chykled* 1281, 1289 *Ass*, *Chiklede* 1297 Pat, 1369 Ipm
   Chyclet 1275 *RH*, 1289 *Ass*, *Chikelet* 1330 Trop, 1347 Pat
   Chikkelade 1279 *Ass*, 1325 Pat, 1442 Trop, *Chikelade* 1281 QW, 1308 Sarum, 1365 *FF*, 1390 IpmR
   Chicklad(*e*) 1289 *Ass*, *Chiklade* c. 1350 Trop, *Cheekelead al. Chicklade* 1657 Hoare, *Chicklade al. Chicklett* 1686 *Recov*, 1746 *FF*
   Chikelet 1330 Trop, 1347 Pat, *Chicklat* t. Eliz WM xxi
   Chekelade 1409 Cl

Ekwall (DEPN *s.n.*) takes the first element to be the British *cēt-*, 'wood,' as in Chute *supra* 12. For the interchange of *cl* and *tl* we may compare Watling Street (cf. PN Herts 7). As for the second element, it is doubtful if the full list of forms given *supra* will allow us to accept Ekwall's tentative suggestion of OE *hlid*, 'gate.' Hybrid compounds of this type are not very common in English place-names. It may be that we have to do with the obscure British word found in Lydiard *supra* 35. At an early date the second element may have been associated with the OE (*ge*)*lād*, cf. Cricklade *supra* 42.

GREAT RIDGE is *Chicladrygh'* 1348 *Cor*, *Chikeladerugge* 1362 *For*, *Chikladerigge* 1367 Pat, *Chikladrugge* 1547 Pat, *Chicklade Ridge Woods or Chicklade Ridge Coppices* 1635 WIpm, *Chicklad Ridge or Great Ridge* 1773 A and D.

BOCKERLY HILL. Cf. *Bookerley Coppice* 1773 A and D. CRATT HILL (6″) is *Croft Hill* 1812 RCH. *v. infra* 427–8. SOUTH-RIDGE HO. Cf. *Southrigge* 1446 Trop, *Sutherage* c. 1840 *TA*.

Chilmark

CHILMARK

æt Chieldmearc 929–40 (14th) BCS 745, *Childmerk(e)* 1195 Wilton, 1242 Fees
cigel marc, to cigelmerc broce 984 (14th) KCD 641
Chilmerc 1086 DB, 1166, 1194 P, 1195 *Wilton*, 1206 FF, -*merk* c. 1190 *Wilton*, 1289 *Ass*, *Chylmerk* 1302 Sarum, *Chilmark* 1306 *Ass*
Chelmerk 1279, 1289 *Ass*, -*mark* 1326 Pat, *Chelesmerke* 1289 *Ass*
Chilemark 1297 Pat, -*merk* 1351 *Ass*

Ekwall (*Studies*[2], 165) is doubtless right in taking the form *Chieldmearc* to be a piece of folk-etymology for the more correct *cigelmearc* and in explaining the name on the basis of the latter form. For this name he suggests a first element *cigel*, a West Saxon form of Anglian *cegel* (cognate with OHG *kegil*, 'peg, pole,' Swedish dial. *kage*, 'stumps') found in Cheal (L), *Cegle* (dat.) 852 (c. 1200) BCS 464. Chilmark must have been so named from some mark or sign formed by a pole on the site of the present village[1].

NOTE. FRICKER'S LANE is to be associated with the family of Richard *Fryker* (1570 PembSurv). MILL LANE. Cf. *Milway copice* c. 1570 *Wilton.*

CLEEVE COPSE (6″) is *Cleves* 1570 PembSurv, *pasture called Cleeve* 1632 *Wilton* and is probably identical with *hoddes clif* 860 (14th) BCS 500. *v. infra* 426. '*Hodd*'s clif or sloping place.' Curiously enough there are two other places of this name in Wiltshire, viz. *Hoddesclyf juxta Wycheford* (i.e. Wishford) 1381 *Cor*, and yet another *hoddisclive* 940 (15th) BCS 752 in the bounds of Christian Malford.

MOORAY is *Morwyeve* 1428 *MinAcct*. This is clearly another example of OE *morgen-giefu*, 'morning-gift,' i.e. the gift given the morning after marriage by the husband to the wife. Cf. Moor Fm (PN Ess 276), Marraway (PN Wa 224), *le Moregheue-place* c. 1350 Trop in the neighbouring Chicklade, and *Morwyeve-croft* 1363 Ipm in Grimstead. It is interesting to note that we have in BCS 591 a document dealing with land in the neighbouring parish of Fonthill (five hides in extent) which was the *morgengifu* of one *Aeðeldryð* (c. 915).

CHILMARK DOWN is *North Downe* 1693 *Wilton*. HART COPPICE (6″) is *Heart Coppice* 1820 G. HENLEY COPSE (6″) is *Henley Coppice* c. 1840 *TA*. KNAP FM (6″) is *Nap Farm* 1820 G, *v.*

---

[1] Ekwall (*loc. cit.*) takes the *cigel marc* to be the actual boundary of the land in question and interprets it as 'boundary made of poles,' but it is difficult to accept this. *æt Chieldmearc* is the name of a large estate (20 cassatae) doubtless the present parish of Chilmark. The other forms are found in the bounds of Tisbury which begin *Arest ðe cigel marc scheð on nodre andlang stremes*... and end *ðanen to cigelmerc broce anlang stremes eft on nodre.* The eastern point of Tisbury, where Tisbury, Teffont and Sutton Mandeville meet, is at a point on the Nadder where the little stream which further up its course forms the eastern boundary of Chilmark joins the Nadder. Grundy is doubtless right therefore, since the Chilmark boundary does not itself touch the Nadder, in suggesting (ii, 91) that *cigel marc* at the beginning should really be *cigel marc broc*, and the defective opening of the boundary should doubtless be amended to *ærest ðær cigel mearc broc sciett*, i.e. where Chilmark brook 'shoots' to the Nadder, rather than amended as by Ekwall who takes *ðe* to be an otherwise unparalleled use of the later form of the definite article, and *scheð* as for *scīett* from *scīedeð*, 'separates,' and interprets the phrase as "First the *cigelmearc* forms the boundary to the Nadder." In either case *ðær* must be supplied.

cnæpp. LADY DOWN is so named in 1773 (A and D). PICKETT
FURLONG (6″) is *Pyked furlong* 1570 PembSurv, (*Piked*) 1632
Wilton, v. *infra* 443. PITS WOOD (6″) is *Pyttes woodde, wood
called The Pyttes* c. 1570 *Wilton*. PORTASH. Cf. *claus voc.
Portaishe* 1570 PembSurv, *Portash* 1693 *Wilton*. It is close to
the village itself. Perhaps from **port**, 'town,' v. *infra* 444.
RIDGE is *Rigge* 1195 *Wilton*, *Rygge* 1249 *Ass*, *Rydge* 1540
MinAcct, *Ruygge* 1547 *SR*, *Rudge* 1570 PembSurv. STOCKLEY
WOOD (6″). Cf. *Stockley* ib., *Stockly, Stocklies* 1632 *Wilton*.
UNDERHILL COPSE (6″). Cf. *Underhill* 1676 ib. WOLLARD COPSE
(6″) is *Wallwood coppice* 1632 ib.

Donhead St Andrew and St Mary

DONHEAD ST ANDREW and ST MARY [*vulgo* dɔnət]

Dunheved, Dunehefda 871 (c. 1400) BCS 531, *Dunheued* 956
   (14th) ib. 970, *Dunheved* 1242 Fees, 1249 *Ass*
(*to*) *Dun heafdan* 955 (14th) BCS 917, *Dunhefde* 1275 RH
Dunnynghefd 956 (12th) BCS 968, *Dunneheved* 1199 FF
Duneheve 1086 DB, *-heved(e)* t. Hy 2 *Shaston*, 1279 *Ass*
*Donheved Sancte Marie, eccl. Sancti Andree de Dunheved,
   Dounheved Mar'* 1298 Sarum, *Sancti Andree* 1302 ib.,
   Seynt Andreu 1324 *FF*, *Do(u)nhefde Sci Andree* 1346 *Ass*,
   (*Marie*) 1362 Pat, *Donhefd* 1498 ib.
Donhed Andreu 1373 ib., *Dounhede* 1406 ib., *Donyet Andrewe*
   1537 *FF*, *Dunhed(d) Mary* t. Eliz WM xxi, (*Androwe*) 1573
   FF, *Over, Nether Donet* 1618 WM xxii, *Dunhead* 1673
   Recov, Donet, Donett 1675 Ogilby, *Donnett St Andrewe* 1690
   Recov, Over, Nether Donhead 1693 ib.

'Top of the down, down-head,' v. **dun**. Cf. *Dunheved*, the old
name for Launceston (Co), Downhead (So), *Dunehefde* DB, and
Dunnett in Compton Bishop (So), *Duneheved* 1242 Ass. The
application of this name is not without difficulty. It is clear that
it cannot refer to the site of the tiny hamlets which cluster round
the churches of Donhead St Andrew and St Mary respectively,
for the former at least is in a hollow. Rather it must apply to
the whole extent of the parishes stretching south right up to
the ridge of the downs. The dative plural form *Dunheafdan*

possibly suggests that already at an early date the area was divided into two townships. *St Mary* and *St Andrew* from the dedication of the churches, known respectively as *Over* and *Nether* from their relative positions[1].

Donhead St Andrew

FERNE HO is *Ferne* 1256 FF, 1275 RH, 1297 *FF*, *Ferne al. Verne* 1561 ib., *Verne House* 1675 Ogilby, and was the home of Philip de *Ferne* (1225 *SR*, 1255 RH). OE fearn, 'bracken,' is unlikely, for we should have expected *la ferne* if that was its history. An alternative possibility is the OE *fiergen*, 'wooded hill,' which lies behind Ferryhill (PN NbDu *s.v.*). Cf. also Fern Down (Do) in DEPN.

WHITESAND CROSS is *Whitson Cross* 1608, *Whitsun Cross* 1677 Hoare. Probably *Whitson* here represents the local pronunciation of *Whitsand*, descriptive of the soil.

BROOK WATERS was the home of Walter *atte Broch'* (1225 *SR*) and William *atte Broke* (1338 *GDR*).

ARUNDELL FM takes its name from the *Arundells* of Wardour, the owners. DENGROVE FM (6″) is *Dengrove* 1608 Hoare. THE HANGING (6″) is so named c. 1840 (*TA*). LEIGH COURT FM is *manor of Donhead Legh now called Lyes Court* t. Hy 8 Hoare. MILKWELL. Cf. *Milkwell Close* c. 1840 *TA*. NOWER'S COPSE. Cf. *Nowers* 1608 Hoare. Probably from OE ora, 'bank,' with affixed *n* from *atten ore*, *v.* æt. PILE OAK COPSE (6″) is *Pile Oak Coppice* c. 1840 *TA*. ROWBERRY FM. Cf. *Rowbury Cross* 1820 G. SANDS' FM. Cf. *Zons Barn* 1773 A and D, *Sands Farm* c. 1840 *TA*. WEST END is so named in 1773 (A and D). WHITESHEET COTTAGES (6″). Cf. *White Sheet* 1608 Hoare and *supra* 175.

Donhead St Mary

CHARLTON is *Cherlton* 1249 *Ass*, *Cherleton* 1256 FF, 1279 *Ass*, (*juxta Lodewell*) 1382 *FF*, *Charlton* 1412 FA. 'Farm of the *churls* or free peasants,' *v.* ceorl, tun. CHARLTON DOWN is *Charleton Downe* 1618 *Map*.

[1] The early forms show that any suggestion of interpreting the name as 'head of a river *Don*' is out of the question.

LUDWELL is *Luddewell'* t. Hy 1 *Shaston*, *Ludewell* 1195 FF, *-wll'* 1225 SR (p), *-welle* 1281, 1298, 1321 *Ass*, 1450 *FF*, *Lodewulle* 1341 *Cor*, *-well* 1365 *FF*, *Ludwell* 1498 Pat, 1576 *FF*. 'Loud spring or stream,' *v.* wielle. Cf. Ludwell in Hutton (So), *Ludewell* 1276 RH (p), 1277 Ass, *Lydewelle* 1280 ib., *Lode-welle* 1327 SR (p).

TITTLEPATH HILL is *Tittlepath Hill* 1773 A and D, *Ticklepath Hill* 1830 Hoare. Possibly the correct form is *sticklepath*, 'steep path.' Cf. that name as found twice in Devon (PN D 27, 166) and in the unidentified *sticelan paδ* (BCS 588) in the bounds of Fovant, a few miles to the east. *v.* sticol. Dropping and adding of an initial *s* before a consonant is fairly common. Cf. *Speckledean* for Pickledean *infra* 306 and *tittlebat* for *stickle-back*. Interchange of *k* and *t* is even more common.

COOMBE FM[1], DONHEAD MILL, THE GROVE (6″), HILLSIDE FM, SHUTE FM (6″) and WELL HO were the homes of Nicholas *in Cumba* (1225 SR), John *atte Mulle* (1332 ib.), William *atte Grove* (ib.), John *atte Hulle* (1281 Ass), John *atte Shute* (1332 SR) and William *atte Welle* (ib.). *v.* cumb, grafa, OE *scīete* ('nook, corner') and wielle.

BURLTONS, GUILDINGS FM, KNIGHT'S FM, MULLINS' BRIDGE (all 6″) are to be associated with the families of William *Burlton* (1629 SR), John *le Gylden* (1332 ib.), William *Knyght* (1426 Ass) and John *Mullens* (1714 WM xlv).

BERRY COURT (6″) is so named in 1628 (WIpm). BIRDBUSH (6″). Cf. *Bird Bush Close* c. 1840 *TA*. DOCKHAM is *Dokham* 1351 Ipm. DONHEAD CLIFT is so named in 1830 (Hoare). For *clift*, *v. infra* 426. FIVE WAYS (6″) is *Five-ways* 1704 ib. HAWCOMBE (6″) is so named c. 1840 (*TA*). HEATH FM. Cf. *Northheathe* 1673 *Recov*. HORSE HILL (6″) is *Horse Hills* c. 1840 *TA*. LANDSLEY FM is so named in 1773 (A and D). NORTH DOWN (6″). Cf. *Northdown Close* c. 1840 *TA*. PICKET CLOSE (6″) is *Peaked Close* ib. Cf. *infra* 443. WHITECLOSE FM (6″). Cf. *Whit Close* c. 1840 *TA*. WINCOMBE is *Winecumba* 1225 SR (p), *Wincombe* 1637 *Phillipps*, *Windcombe* 1773 A and D. The forms are too uncertain for any satisfactory etymology to be possible.

---

[1] *Cumbe* 1279 *Ass*.

Fonthill Bishops and Giffard

FONTHILL BISHOPS and GIFFARD [fʌnt(h)il]

Funtial 901 BCS 591, *Funtgeall* 901 (12th) BCS 590, *Funteal* 977 (12th) KCD 610

Fontel 1086 DB, 1288 Ipm, (*Epi*), (*Giffard*) 1291 Tax, *Fontell* 1316 FA, *Fontelgyffard* 1345 AD ii, *Fontel Episcopi* 1367 WM iii, *Overfonthill* t. Eliz WM xxi

Funtel' 1166, *Funtel* 1187 P, 1224 Bracton, 1257 Ch, *Funtell* 1243 Pat, *Funtele* 1284 Ch, *Funtel Giffard* 1297 Pat, *Funtill al. Fountell* 1651 Hoare

Fountell Gifford 1316 FA, *Fowntell* 1547 SR, *Founthill* 1587, *Fountell* 1635 FF, *Bishop Funthill* 1695 Morden

The second element of Fonthill is the British word noted under Deverill *supra* 6. The first is difficult. The Late Latin *fontana* is found as a loan word in the British languages (W *ffynnon*, Corn *fonten, fenten*, Breton *feunteun*) but the ordinary word *fons* (*font-*) is not found. It may be that it did once exist, cf. Font (PN NbDu 88). Ekwall (ES liv, 103–8) derives the second element of names like Bedfont, Teffont, etc. from Latin through Celtic. See further his note on funta in DEPN. *Bishops* and *Giffard* from the DB holdings of the *Bishop* of Winchester and *Berenger Gifard* respectively. Fonthill Giffard was also known as *Over* or Upper Fonthill.

Fonthill Bishops

BAKE BARN. *v. infra* 450. BITHAM LAKE (6″). Cf. *Bittum Wood* c. 1840 *TA*. From OE *bytme*, 'bottom,' *v. infra* 425. HIGH PARK. Cf. *The Parke* 1648 WM xxxvii. PITCHPENNY CLUMP (6″). Cf. *Pitch Penny Castle* 1820 G.

Fonthill Giffard

STOP BEACON and FM (6″) is *Stoppe* 1249 *Ass*, 1373 AD ii, 1459 IpmR, *Stopp* 1467 *MinAcct*, c. 1500 ECP, 1630 WIpm. It is impossible as between the beacon and the farm to know just where the *stoppe* was from which the places take their name.

There is an OE *stoppa*, 'pail,' with which the name may ultimately be associated.

JERRARD'S FM is to be associated with the family of Nicholas *Jerrard* (1547 *SR*).

GREENWICH is *Greenwhich* 1773 A and D. Probably 'green farm,' *v.* wic. HODWAYS HANGING (6″) is *Hodways Coppice* c. 1840 *TA*. NEWCLOSE HANGING (6″) is *New Close* ib. ROUGH LAWN (6″). *v. infra* 440.

Hindon

HINDON

> *Hendon* 1249 *Ass*, 1675 Ogilby
> *Hynedon(e)* 1268 ib., 1275 RH, 1279, 1281 *Ass et freq* to 1356 ib.
> *Hyndon, Esthindon* 1281 *Ass*, *Hyndon* c. 1300 Trop, (*Markett*) 1553 *FF*, *Hyndoun* 1411 Cl, *Hindon streete* 1632 *EcclCom*

This is probably from OE *higna dun*, 'down or hill belonging to a religious or secular household,' *v.* higna. It is worthy of note that we have mention in the neighbouring parish of Fonthill (BCS 591) of one *Aeþelm Higa* who clearly belonged to such a household, possibly to the household of King Alfred himself at Wardour.

HAWKING DOWN FM is *Hocken Down* c. 1840 *TA*.

Sedgehill

SEDGEHILL

> *Seghull(e)* t. Hy 1 Shaston, 1241 FF, 1289 *Ass*, 1320 FF, 1332 SR, 1529 Rental, *Segghull* 1241 FF
> *Segilla* t. Hy 1 Shaston, *Segill* 1439 WM xiii
> *Segeshull* 1249 *Ass*, *Seggeshull* 1354 *AD*
> *Segehull* 1279, 1281, *Seggehull* 1289 *Ass*, 1399 IpmR, 1514 DeedsEnrolled, *-hill* 1495 Ipm
> *Sedghyll* 1547 SR, *Sedgehull* 1556 *Ct*, *Sedghull* 1611 *FF*, *Sedgell* 1716 ib.

Inappropriate though such a compound may seem at first sight, it is probable that this name means what it says and is descriptive of a hill where sedge grows. Sedgehill, it should be noted, is the name of a district and not of any precise village or hamlet, and the whole of the parish is remarkable for its many pools and small streams, even in the higher ground in the south of the parish. Whitemarsh Fm *infra* is on some of the highest ground in the parish.

NOTE. BUTTERSTAKES LANE. Cf. *Butterstakes* 1558 *FF*, c. 1840 *TA*. WELLGROVE LANE. Cf. *Well Grove* ib. *Blynd laine* 1586 NQ iii.

WHITEMARSH FM (6″) is (*on ðere*) *hwiten mercs* 984 (14th) KCD 641, *Witemers* 1225 *SR*, *Whytemers*(*h*) 1241 FF, 1279 *Ass. Whitmarsh* 1582 ChwAcct. Self-explanatory.

HAYS[1] and WOOD HO[2] (both 6″) were the homes of Thomas *en la Hay* (1288 *Ass*) and Thomas *atte Wodehouse* (1332 *SR*).

BERRYBROOK HO (6″). Cf. *water called Beriebroke* 1620 Sess. DEWDOWN COPSE (6″). Cf. *Dew Downs* c. 1840 *TA*. GUTCH POOL HO (6″) is *Gowge Pole* 1567 WM xxix. HULL COPSE (6″) is *Hole Coppice* c. 1840 *TA*. It lies in a hollow. MOUNT PLEASANT (6″) is so named in 1773 (A and D). Cf. *infra* 455 SWEETWELL FM is *Swetwell* 1648 WM xxxvii. WESTMARSH FM (6″) is *Westmarshe* 1586 NQ iii.

Swallowcliffe

SWALLOWCLIFFE [*olim* sweikli]

> *rupis irundinis, id est Swealewanclif* 940 (13th) BCS 756
> *Svaloclive* 1086 DB
> *Swaleweclive* c. 1155 StOsmund, 1236, 1242 Fees, *-klive*
>   c. 1240 *Wilton*, *-clyve* 1294 Pat, *Svaleweclive* 1202 FF
>   *Swaluweclive* 1277 Ipm
> *Swaleclive* 1241 FF, *-clyve* 1277 Ipm, 1289 *Ass*, 1316 FA
> *Swalfklyfe* 1276 Ipm, *Swalowcliffe al. Swaclyff* 1546 LP
>   *Swacliff* 1594 *Recov*, *Swakley* 1618 Sess, *-lie* 1648 WM
>   xxxvii

Probably 'swallow clif or slope,' but *swealwa*, 'swallow,' as the name of a stream is also possible. Cf. the history of Swalecliffe on the Swale (KPN 281), earlier *swalewanclif* (BCS 1345).

---

[1] *Estheyes* 1548 Pat, *Hayes* 1630 NQ vii, *Haise* 1648 WM xxxvii. *v* (ge)hæg.
[2] *Woodhouse* 1608 NQ vii.

Swalcliffe (PN O 201) is well away from any stream and must contain the bird-name. It shows the same development to *Swakley* as the Wiltshire name.

CHOULDEN LANE (6″) is in the neighbourhood of (*andlang*) *chealfa dune* 940 (14th) BCS 756. It is *Chaldon* in 1737 (*Wilton*). 'Calves' down,' cf. Chaldon (PN Sr 42). The name appears also in *Cholen Barn* (1773 A and D), the present Waterloo Barn *supra* 184.

MILL HO and POLE'S FM (6″) were probably the homes of John *atte Mulle* (1327 *SR*) and Matilda *atte Poule* (ib.). The *s* is probably pseudo-manorial.

BUXBURY HILL is *Bucksbury* 1737 *Wilton*, *Boxbury Hill* 1773 A and D. CRIBBAGE HUT (6″) is *Cripperidge* 1737 *Wilton*, *Cribidge Hutt* 1773 A and D. MIDDLEDEAN (6″). Cf. *Dean Mead* c. 1840 *TA*. STONEHILL is *Stone Hill* 1737 *Wilton*. SWALLOW-CLIFFE DOWN. Cf. *The Down* ib.

Teffont Evias and Magna

TEFFONT EVIAS and MAGNA[1] [*olim* tefənt juˑəs, *nunc vero* iˑvaiəs]

be Tefunte 860 (c. 1400) BCS 500, *Tefonte* 1086 DB, *Tefunte* 1241 FF

Teofuntinga gemære 940 BCS 757, (*at*) *Teofunten* c. 965 (13th) BCS 1138, *Theofunta*, *Teophonte* t. Hy 2 *Shaston*

Tifhunt 1236 FF, *Tyfunte* 1268 *Ass*, *Tefhunte* 1293 Pat

Hewyas Tefunte 1242 Fees, *Teffunt Ewyas* 1275 RH, *Teffonte-eweyas* 1284 *FF*, *Teffunte Euwyas* 1302 *Ass*, *Teffont Evyas* 1304 Pat, *Teffunte Eweas* 1378 Cl, *Tevaunte Evyas* 1553 Hoare

Over Tefunte 1268 *Ass*, *Overtevente* 1553 WM x, *Upperteffont* 1584 *Recov*

Teffount Hungerford 1418 *MinAcct*

Tevent(e) 1428 FA, 1547 *SR*, *Teffen* 1671 *Recov*

'Boundary spring or stream,' *v.* funta. The first element is identical with that of Tyburn (Mx), derived by Ekwall (RN) from an OE *tēo*, corresponding to OFris *tiā*, 'boundary, boundary line.' Teffont is on the borders of two hundreds, but

---

[1] For Teffont Magna parish, *v. supra* 161.

the name must go back to an earlier date than the formation of
the OE hundreds. Teffont Evias belonged to the barons of
Ewyas Harold (He). Cf. "Robert tenet de honore de *Hewyas*"
(1242 Fees). *Over* or *Upper* Teffont (now Magna) lies above
Teffont Evias. In 1428 (FA) Walter *Hungerford* held immediately
of the castle of *Ewyas*. The form *Evias* is a late corruption.
Teofuntinga gemære, i.e. 'boundary of the people of Teffont,' is
found in a Wylye charter and has reference to the boundary
between Teffont and Wylye.

Teffont Evias

MILL FM was the home of Richard *atte Mulle* (1332 *SR*). Cf.
Mill tayle 1690 *Wilton*.

LEY FM is *Ley* 1571 *SR*. v. leah. UPPER HOLT (6″) is *wood called
Holte copice* 1554 Pat. v. holt.

Tisbury, East and West

TISBURY, EAST and WEST [tizbəri]

> *Tyssesburg, Dyssesburg* c. 800 Willibald, *Life of St Boniface*
> (*to*) *Tyssebyrig* c. 915 BCS 591, (*æt*) *Tissebiri* 984 (14th) KCD
> 641, *Tisseberie* 1086 DB, *-biri* 1218 Pap *et passim* to 1316
> FA, with variant spellings *Tysse-* and *-bury, -bir*'
> *Tussebur*' 1289 *Ass*, *-bury* 1295, 1309 *FF*, 1305 *Ass*

Probably '*Tysse*'s burh,' though the name is not on record.
Tisse from *Tidsige* would be a natural formation but cannot
be reconciled with the 8th-century *Tysse*, supported as it is by
later forms in *Tuss-*.

East Tisbury

APSHILL FM is *Epsehilla* t. Hy 1 *Shaston*, *Abshulle* 1242 Fees,
Apshull juxta Tyssebury 1376 *FF*, *Apsehull* 1412, *Apshull* 1428
FA, *Apsell* 1773 A and D. 'Aspen-tree hill.'

CHICKSGROVE

> *Chichesgrave, -a* t. Hy 2 *Shaston*, 1225 *SR* (p), *Chikesgrava, -e*
> ib., 1268, 1312 *Ass*
> *Chykesgrove* 1279, 1281, 1289 *Ass*, *Chikes Grove* 1546 LP

Chekesgrave 1452 *FF*, *Chekisgrove* 1526 *Ct*, *Cheysgrove* 1552
   FF, *Checkgrove* 1557 Pat, *Chekesgrove al. Chickesgrove* 1571
   NQ vii, *Cheekesgrove al. Cheesgrove* 1636 WIpm
Chisgrove 1648 WM xxxvii

This may be for earlier *chiknesgrava* or it may be direct from
chicke which already appears independently in the 14th century
(NED *s.v.*) as a reduced form of *chicken*. In Chicksgrove, *chick*
may be used of the bird or it may be a nickname used as a
surname. *v.* græfe and *infra* 432–3.

Farnell Copse (6″). Cf. *Ferhilla Alurici* t. Hy 1 *Shaston*,
Fernhall, *Fernhull'* 1242 Fees, *Farnhull* 1258 FF, *Fernhull juxta
Tissebury* 1307 *FF*, *Fernhill* 1393 *AD*, *Firnhull* 1428 FA. 'Fern
or bracken hill,' *v.* fearn. It must at one time have been held
by a certain *Alfric*.

Haredene Wood is *Haredena* t. Hy 2 *Shaston*. Probably 'hare
valley.'

Lawn Fm, *olim* Rowcombe, is *Roughcombe* 1344 Ipm, *Rocombe*
1377 Inq aqd, *Roghcombe* 1382 *FF*, 1386 Pat, *Roucombe* 1495
Ipm, *Rowcomb(e)* 1553 *FF*, 1634 *Recov*, *Lawn Farm* 1773 A
and D, *the Lawns* 1809 Hoare. 'Rough valley,' *v.* ruh, cumb.
For the identification, cf. Hoare 435. For lawn, cf. *infra* 440.

Nippard[1] (*TA*)

   Nipret t. Hy 1 *Shaston*
   Nypred 1240 *AD*, 1289 *Ass*, 1337 *FF*, *Nipred* 1242 Fees, 1375
      AD, 1633 Hoare, *Nippred* 1255 RH, 1265 FF, *-rede* 1317
      AD ii, *Nypprede* 1344 Ipm
   Nippered 1241 FF, 1249, 1268 *Ass*, *Nypperede* 1382 *FF*
   Nuppered 1249 *Ass*, *Nuprude* 1327 WIpm
   Nyprad 1279, 1281 *Ass*
   Nepred 1289 ib.
   Nippride 1428 FA, 1533–8 ECP
   Nappen Mill 1773 A and D

This name must remain an unsolved problem.

[1] Part of Fonthill old park. The name survives in Nipper Meadow (School)
on Oddford Water immediately south-west of Lawn Lodge.

ASHLEYWOOD FM is *Asshellewood* 1552 *FF*. Cf. *Asseleya* t. Hy 2 *Shaston* (p). Self-explanatory. GASTON HO (6″) is *Gassen farm house* 1829 Hoare. See gærstun *infra* 432. HILLSTREET FM (6″) is *Hill Street Farm* 1820 G. LADY DOWN is so named c. 1840 (*TA*). QUARRY WOOD. Cf. *Quarr close* ib. and *infra* 445. SWELL HILL (6″) is *Swelled Hill* ib. THORNY BOTTOM (6″). Cf. *Thorny Hayes* ib. WEST WOOD is *Westwod* 1382 *Harl*.

West Tisbury

BILLHAY FM is (*to*) *Bilanleage* 955 (14th) BCS 917, *billan leah* 956 ib. 970, *Billeia* 1196 Cur (p), *Billeg'* 1225 *SR* (p), 1236 FF, 1242 Fees, -*leye* 1289 *Ass*, *Byllegh* 1344 Misc, 1409 *FF*, *Billey oth. Billhayes* 1744 *Recov*, *Binley al. Billhay* 1829 Hoare. '*Billa*'s clearing or wood,' *v.* leah. For the interchange of *l* and *n* found in the last form, cf. Binley (PN Wa 156).

EAST and WEST HATCH are *Hascia* t. Hy 1 *Shaston*, *Hache* 1200 Cur, 1202 Abbr, *Heche* 1201 Cur, 1202 Abbr, *Westhacha* 1225 *SR*, *Esthache* 1242 Fees, *Hecche* t. Hy 3 *Shaston*. *v.* hæcc. The meaning here may have been 'gate leading to a wood or forest' since this area has always been well wooded.

LINLEY FM is *Linlegia* t. Hy 1 *Shaston*, *Lindleg'* 1242 Fees, -*legh* 1249 *Ass*, *Lyndlegh* 1275 RH, *Linlegh* 1303 Chanc, *Lynlegh* 1428 FA, *Lynle* 1502 Ipm. 'Lime-tree wood,' *v.* lind, leah.

PYTHOUSE[1] and WICK FM[2] (6″) were the homes of William de *la Putte* (1225 *SR*) and Alfred de *Wicha* (ib.).

ABBOTT'S POND, DIBBEN'S COTTAGES and TURNER'S COTTAGES (all 6″) are to be associated with the families of Alexander *Abbot* (1546 *SR*), Thomas *Dibbyn* (1571 ib.) and Robert *Turner* (1544 ib.).

BRATCH POND (6″). Cf. *Bratch* c. 1840 *TA* and *infra* 423. CHERRYFIELD (6″) is *Cherry Field* ib. GREAT MEAD COPSE (6″). Cf. *Great Mead* ib. HAM WOOD (6″) is *Ham Coppice* ib. NEWTOWN is so named in 1820 (G). OLD STREET FM (6″). Cf.

---

[1] *Pythouse* c. 1500 ECP.
[2] *Wic* t. Hy 1 *Shaston*, *Wyke* 1345 AD i, (*juxta Tissebury*) 1428 FA, *Week* 1633 Hoare. *v.* wic *supra* 25.

Oldstreete Lane 1635 WIpm. PRIOR'S FM was held by lease under
the Hospital at Wilton (Hoare 133). RUDDLEMOOR FM is *Rodell-
more* 1553 *FF*, *Ruddlemore* 1634 *Recov*. TUCKINGMILL (6″). Cf.
Tuckingmill Mead c. 1840 *TA*, i.e. 'fulling mill.' WHITE MEAD
WOOD (6″). Cf. *White Mead* ib.

Wardour

WARDOUR [wɔrˑdər]

(*æt*) *weard oran* 899–925 BCS 591
Werdore 1086 DB, 1199 Abbr, 1200 FF, Cur, 1322 *FF*, 1350
    Ipm
Waredovre 1201 Abbr
Weredore 1242 Fees, 1318, 1324 Ipm
Werdure 1316 FA, 1319 *FF*, *-dour* 1393 Pat, 1430 Cl
Wardere 1461 Pat, *Warder* 1504 PCC, (*alias Wardoure*) 1569
    FF

The name is a compound of OE *weard*, 'watch,' and **ora**,
'slope,' etc. Cf. Wardle (PN La 57).

BRIDZOR FM [bridzər]

Bredesherd 1207 Cur (p), 1332 *SR* (p), *Bredesert* c. 1220
    Wilton (p)
Brudesherd 1208 Abbr (p), *Brudeserd* 1275 RH, *Brudesyerd*
    1279, 1281 *Ass*, *Brudeserde* 1341 NI (p), *Brudeserthe* 1428
    FA
Brideserd 1268 *Ass*, t. Hy 3 *Shaston*, 1289 *Ass*, *Brydesyerd*
    1385 *FF*, *Bridesherd* 1408 IpmR, *Brydeshurst* 1430 Cl
Briddeshird 1305 *FF*, *Bryddesherd* 1305 *Ass*, *Briddesherd* 1309
    FF, *Briddesyerde* 1331 *Phillipps*, *Briddeserd* 1423 IpmR
Byrdsour 1553 Pat, *Bridsor* 1634 *Recov*

This is a difficult name. The second element is probably OE
geard, 'enclosure,' as in Derriads *supra* 90. The first element
would seem to be a strong form *Brydi* of the personal name
Bryda, tentatively suggested as the first element in Bridmore
and Burcombe *infra* 201, 213.

DUNWORTH COPSE and COTTAGE (6″) is *Dunwrth* 1249, *Done-
worth* 1279 *Ass*, 1293 Ipm, *-wurth* 1289 *Ass*. 'Dunna's farm,'
v. **worþ**. For further forms *v.* Dunworth Hundred *supra* 183.

Hard by is SPELSBURY FM (local), recorded as *Spelsbury* in 1773 (A and D). The name must commemorate the meeting-place of the Hundred, for it is clearly a compound containing the element *spell*, 'speech.' For a parallel to such a name cf. the history of Spelhoe Hundred (PN Nth 131–2) and possibly also *Spelles-berwe*, a lost place in Worcestershire (PN Wo 61 n.). Spelsbury may well be for earlier *spelles-beorg*, for confusion between **beorg** and **burh** is common. For a further example of this name see *Spilsbury infra* 249, the meeting-place of Cannings Hundred.

HAYGROVE FM (6″) is *bosco de Heygrave* 1279, 1281 *Ass*, *Eigroves mead* 1635 WIpm. A compound of (ge)hæg, 'enclosure,' and græfe, 'thicket.' See *infra* 432–3.

HAZELDON FM is *Heselden* t. Hy 1 *Shaston*, 1207 Cur, 1208 Abbr (p), *Haselden(e)* 1199 P, 1242 Fees, 1249 *Ass*, *Haseldenefeld* 1382 *Harl*, -*don* 1200 P. 'Hazel valley,' *v.* **denu**.

TOTTERDALE FM

> *Totederehilla* t. Hy 1 *Shaston*, *Totedereshull* 1249 *Ass* (p),
> 　　*Toteredehulle* 1332 *SR* (p)
> *Tuturdesh'* t. Hy 2 *Shaston*
> *Toderdeulla* 1225 *SR* (p), *Todredehella* t. Hy 3 *Shaston*,
> 　　*Todrydhull* 1390 AD ii
> *Toterdehulle* 1383 AD vi
> *Toderhull* 1529 *FF*, *Totterdill* 1590 ib.

It is difficult to be certain with regard to this name, but perhaps the most likely explanation is to take the first element to be the word *tote*, 'look-out,' compounded with OE *dēor-hyll*, hence 'look-out deer-hill,' the hill standing high, with good views except to the south. Later the first part of the name seems to have been confused with the word *tottered*, a variant of *tattered* (cf. NED *s.v.*), a suitable description of the broken ground here.

TWELVE ACRE COPSE (6″). Cf. *be twelf Aceron* 984 (14th) KCD 641, a strange survival of an ancient area of land.

WALLMEAD FM is to be associated with the family of Theodric de *Walemade* (t. Hy 1 *Shaston*) and John de *Walemede* (1341 *Cor*). Perhaps '**mæd** of the serfs or Britons,' *v.* **wealh**.

Squalls Fm is *Upper, Lower Squall* 1773 A and D. It is possibly
to be associated with the family of Henry *Skylle* (1382 *Harl*).

Castle Ditches is so named in 1820 (G). High Wood (6″) is
so named in 1648 (WM xxxvii). Rowety Plantation (6″). Cf.
Rootey Croft c. 1840 *TA*. Wardour Park is *Warder parke*
t. Hy 8 Hoare. Westfield Fm. Cf. *West Field* c. 1840 *TA*.
Withyslade Fm is *Witheyslade* ib., *v.* slæd.

XVII. CHALKE HUNDRED

This was earlier *Stanforde hundred* 1086 ExonDB, *Stafford
hundred* 1174 P, *Hundred de Stafford* 1198 Abbr, 1224 ClR. It
appears first as *Hundred de Chelke* in 1249 (*Ass*), *Hundred de
Chalk* 1255 RH. The early name is preserved in Stowford in
Ebbesborne *infra* 207.

Alvediston

Alvediston [ɔ·lstən]

> *Alfwieteston abbatisse* 1165 P
> *Alvideston* c. 1190 *Wilton*, 1359 Cl, *Alvitheston* 1214 Cur,
>   Abbr, 1222 FF, *Alvit(t)eston(e)* c. 1220 *Wilton*, 1242 Fees,
>   *Alfitheston* 1250 FF
> *Alvetestun'* 1195 *Wilton*
> *Alvediston* 1209 FF, *Alvedeston* 1272 Ipm, 1279 *Ass*, 1353 Pat
> *Alvedston* 1331 Pat, *Alfedeston al. Alvedeston* 1337 Ipm
> *Alveston* 1428 FA, 1444 Pat, 1535 VE
> *Ilveston al. Ilvedeston* 1568 *FF*
> *Alstone* 1571 SR, *Alston, Awston* 1585 WM xxi, *Alston al.
>   Alvedeston* 1640 WIpm, *Alvediston or Aston* 1773 A and D

This is probably '*Ælfgeat's* farm' (*v.* tun), as suggested by
Ekwall, but the early forms are not entirely satisfactory. Jones
identifies it with the manor of *Chelche*, assessed at 2 hides,
which was held by the Abbess of Wilton (TRW).

Norrington

> *Norkington* (sic) 1198 Fees, *Northamtona* (sic) 1211 RBE
> *Northinton(e), -y-* 1227 SarumCh, 1270 FF, 1275 RH, 1307
>   Ch, *Norþinton* 1242 Fees

Northyngton, -i- 1289 *Ass*, 1304 Cl, 1327 *SR*, (*Chamberleyn*)
1409 *Ass*
Norrington al. Northington 1568 *FF*

This is from OE (*be*) *norðan-tūn*, 'to the north of the
tun,' i.e. of the main settlement. Cf. Southington in Selborne
(Ha), *Suthinton* c. 1245 Selborne, *Sudinton* 1240 Cl, *Suthington*
1256 *Ass*.

TROW FM and DOWN [trou]

(to) trogan 955 (13th) BCS 917
Troi 1086 DB
Triwa 1167 P (p), *Trewe, -a* c. 1190 *Wilton* (p), 1202 FF,
1203 Cur (p), 1225 *SR* (p), 1288 *Ass*
Trowe 1222 Pat (p), 1230 ib., 1242 Fees, 1293 Ipm, 1332 *SR*
(p), (*juxta magnam Chalke*) 1282 *Ass*, (*juxta Alvedeston*)
1409 ib., *Troe* 1799 *Recov*

This is a difficult name. It seems beyond question that *trogan*
which is twice mentioned in BCS 917 refers to the great hollow
which gives name to Trow Fm, Trow Bottom, Trow Clump
and Trow Down above that hollow (see Grundy ii, 28–9, 38–9).
The form should be *troge* (dat. sg. of the strong noun *trog*,
'trough') rather than *trogan*, as if from weak *troga*, but it is
possible that *trogan* is for *trogum*, 'at the hollows.' As the charter
is only found in a 13th-century cartulary we need not perhaps
press this point. OE *trogan* or *troge* would explain all the early
forms, except the series *Triwe*, *Trewe*, and would lead to the
modern form *Trow*.

With regard to the series of forms *Triwe*, *Trewe*, examination
of the contexts in which they occur makes it clear that some of
them must quite definitely be taken as referring to this place and
the probability is that all do. They must be explained as due to
confusion with ME *trow(e)*, deriving from OE *trēow*, 'tree,' as
illustrated in the history of Trowbridge *supra* 133 and to some
extent in Bishopstrow *supra* 151, where we have common and
legitimate alternation between ME *trowe* and *trewe*. When the
significance of *Trow* as coming from *troge* was forgotten,
alternation between *trow* and *trew* seems to have been established
for this name also as though it really came from OE *trēow*.

MANWOOD (6″) is *Manwood cops* 1618 *Map* and was the home
of Richard de *Manwode* (1332 *SR*). 'Common wood,' from
(ge)mæne *infra* 441. The place is by the parish boundary.

SAMWAYS FM is to be associated with the family of John *Samwaye*
(t. Hy 8 Hoare) and John *Samwise* (1570 PembSurv).

BIGLEY (6″) is *Bygley Corner* 1570 PembSurv. CHURCH FM (6″)
is *The Church Farm* 1813 *Kings*. COOMBE is *Combes* 1570
PembSurv. CROOK HILL (6″) is *Crookhills* 1788 *Kings*. It may
be that this was the earlier name of the neighbouring Windmill
Hill, a prominent, rounded hill. If so, we probably have Brit
cruc, 'hill,' as in Crooksbury (PN Sr 170). ELCOMBE (6″) is
Elcombe 1570 PembSurv. GALLOWS HILL. Cf. *Gallowes barrowe*
1590 *Wilton*. GOSCOMBE (6″) is so named in 1820 (G). MIDDLE
DOWN. Cf. *Myddelhill* 1570 PembSurv. WERMERE (6″) is so
named in 1618 (*Map*). WINDMILL HILL is so named in 1820 (G).

Berwick St John

BERWICK ST JOHN

> *Berwicha* 1167 P, *Berewic* 1196 P, 1209 FF, -*wich'* 1225 *SR*,
> -*wike* 1255 Pap
> *Berewyke S. Johannis* 1265 SarumCh, *Barwyke Seynt John*
> 1536 Recov, *Barrike St John* 1606 Sess, *Barwick* 1675
> Ogilby

> *v.* berewic, 'outlying grange,' etc. *St John* from the dedication
of the church.

BRIDMORE[1]

> *Brudemere* 1184 P, c. 1190 *Wilton*, 1225 *SR*, 1242 Fees, 1319
> Ipm, 1332 *SR*, *Brudmer* 1535 VE, 1544 LP
> *Bridemere* 1203 Cur, 1225 *SR*, 1301 Ch, *Bridmere* 1451 IpmR
> *Brudimere* 1241 FF
> *Bridmore* 1601 *FF*, (*al.* Bridmere) 1731 *Recov*

Near by must have been *Brydinga dic* 955 (13th) BCS 917,
Bridinghedic 970 (15th) ib. 956. For this name cf. Burcombe
infra 213. There is a pool here and the name probably denotes the
'pool of one *Bryda*.' The dic took name from him and his family.

---

[1] Near by is BRIMERGATE (6″), probably showing the sometime local
pronunciation.

EASTON FM (6") is *Estun* 956 (14th) BCS 970, *Eston* 1249 *Ass.* (*juxta Berewyk*) 1289 ib., 1382 *FF*, (*juxta Berewyk Sci Johannis*) 1307 ib. 'East farm,' *v.* tun.

RUSHMORE is *Rossemere* 1263 WIpm, 1289 *Ass*, 1292 *AddCh*, 1310 Pat, *Rosmere* 1279, *Rysshemere* 1321 *Ass* (all p), *Rushemere* 1570 PembSurv, *Rushmore* 1618 WM xxii. There can be little doubt that this is 'rush-mere.' The early forms are doubtless from *rosshe*, a variant ME form not hitherto noted before the 15th century.

TINKLEY DOWN (6"). Cf. (*to*) *tilluces leage* 955 (14th) BCS 917, *Tynckley copp'* 1567 *AddCh*, *Tynkeley copice* 1570 PembSurv. 'Woodland or clearing of *Tilluc*,' a diminutive of the personal name *Tilli*.

WINKELBURY CAMP. Cf. *Winterburge geat* 955 (13th) BCS 917, *Winkelbury Hill* 1773 A and D. 'Camp or stronghold used in winter,' *v.* burh. In the first quotation we have reference to a gate of the camp (*v.* geat).

PITT PLACE was the home of John *atte Putte* (1292 *AddCh*). *v.* pytt and cf. *Pytlandfeld* 1570 PembSurv.

MONK'S DOWN is to be associated with the family of William *Monke* (1641 NQ vii). There was a holding called *Monks* in 1830 (Hoare).

ARUNDELL COPPICE (6") is *Arundall Coppice* c. 1840 *TA*. So named after the *Arundell* family, Lords of the Manor. ASH-COMBE FM is *Asshecombe* 1537 *FF*. BARROW HILL is so named in 1618 (*Map*). BERWICK DOWN is *Barwick Downe* ib. BLIND WELL (6") is *Blundwell* (sic) *Bottom* c. 1840 *TA*. CARTWAY COPSE (6") is *Greate, Lytyl Carteway* c. 1570 *Wilton*. CHETTLES CLIFT (6") is *Chettells Clif* 1570 PembSurv. Cf. *boscus de Chetel* 1275 RH. Perhaps from OE *cietel*, 'kettle, cauldron.' There is a deep valley here. GREAT and LITTLE COKERS (6"). Cf. *Cockers Coppice* c. 1840 *TA*. COOMBE is *Barwikescomb* 1536 *Recov*, *Combe Bottom* 1570 PembSurv. COSTARD'S BUSHES and PLECK (6"). Cf. *boscus voc. Oldhewett al. Costerd* ib. For *Oldhewett*, *v. infra* 203. CUTTICE DOWN (6"). Cf. *Cuthayes* t. Hy 8 Hoare, *Cottehays* 1553 *MinAcct*, *Cotties or Cothayes* 1809 Hoare.

Probably 'cottage-enclosures,' *v.* (ge)hæg. FRYING PAN (6″) is *Frying Pan Coppice* c. 1840 *TA.* GLOVER'S COPPICE (6″) is *Glovers copice* 1570 *Wilton.* GRAVELLY WAY (6″) is *Gravell Way* 1618 *Map* and cf. *Gravelly Way Coppice* c. 1840 *TA.* HANGING RIDGE (6″). Cf. *Hanging Ridge Coppice* 1809 Hoare. HEWETTS COPPICE (6″). Cf. *Copic' voc' old hewett* 1567 *AddCh, boscus vocat' Oldhewett alias Costerd* 1570 PembSurv. From OE *hīewet,* 'hewing, cutting.' HORSE HILL. Cf. *Horsehillfeld* 1570 Pemb-Surv. INGRAM'S COPPICE (6″) is *Ingrames* 1618 *Map, Ingram Coppice* c. 1840 *TA.* IVERS WOOD (6″) is *greate, littell Ivers* 1570 PembSurv, *v.* yfer *infra* 450. LODGE COPSE (6″) is *Lodge Cops* 1618 *Map.* LONG CROFT is *Longcroftes* ib. MILES CHAIR (6″) is *Mighells cheare* 1570 PembSurv, i.e. Michael's. PARSON'S COPPICE (6″) is *Parsons copice* ib. POUND COPPICE (6″) is so named ib. ROTHERLEY DOWN is *Rotherley* ib. Cf. also *lez Rotherdowne* ib. The first element is OE hryðer, 'cattle.' SHIFT-WAY COPSE (6″) is *Shesteway Copice* (sic) ib., *Shyftwey copise* ib. STAPLE FOOT (6″) is *Staplefoote* 1567 WM xxxii, *-fote* c. 1570 *Wilton, Staplefoot Walks* 1809 Hoare. UDDENS COPPICE (6″) is so named in 1840 (*TA*). It is *Iwedene* 1227 FF, *Ewe Deans Copice* 1570 PembSurv. 'Yew-tree valley,' *v.* denu. UPTON FM (6″) is *Uppeton* 1242 Fees, *Upton in Berwyke* 1570 PembSurv. 'Up-farm.' WIN GREEN. Cf. *Wingreen Hill* 1812 RCH. WOOD-LANDS is so named in 1840 (*TA*).

Bower and Broad Chalke

BOWER and BROAD CHALKE

(*to*) *cealcan gemere* 826 (c. 1250) BCS 391

(*æt*) *Ceolcum* 955 (13th) BCS 917

Cheolca, (*to*) *Cheolcan* 974 (13th) BCS 1304

Chelche 1086 DB, *Chelk(e)* 1175 P, t. Ric 1 Cur, 1242 Fees, 1263 StNicholas, 1291 Tax, 1305 *Ass, Shalke* 1237 Cl, *Chalke* 1242 FF, 1316 FA, *Chawke* 1547 *FF, Est Chawke, Westchawke* 1553 *AddCh*

Burchelke 1225 *SR,* 1249, 1268 *Ass, -chalke* 1268, 1273 FF, 1316 FA

Boure Chalke 1276 StNicholas, *Bourchalk(e)* 1312 Sarum, 1332 *SR,* 1356 *Ass,* 1380 *FF, Bowerchalke* 1547 *SR*

Burghchalke 1279 *Ass*, 1456 IpmR, *Burgchalke* 1289, *Bourgh-chalk* 1305 *Ass*, *Burichalk* 1306 ib.

Magna Chelk 1289, *Grete Chalke* 1312 *Ass*, *Brode Chalk* 1380 FF, *Brodchalke* 1482 IpmR, *Brodechake* 1581 *Recov*

Bery Chalke 1482 IpmR, *Burr Chalke* 1607 WM xx

'Place of chalk, chalk down,' cf. Chalk (KPN 306). The forms are a little surprising. The form *ceolc* is not known elsewhere in OE and the ME form is regularly *chalke* rather than *chelke*. The dative plural forms may be explained perhaps from the early existence of the two settlements. *Broad* is used in the sense of 'great' or 'chief.' Cf. Broad Clyst (PN D 573) and Greatweek (ib. 426). Also called *East*. As the *g(h)* is not found in the earlier forms it may be that the first element is (*ge*)*būr*, 'peasant,' or (*ge*)*būra* (gen. pl.) rather than burh, with later folk-etymologising to *burgh*. Cf. (ge)bur *infra* 424. Straton (WM xxxii, 304–5) notes that in Chalke in the great Pembroke Survey the tenants paid certain grain rents called 'bower corn' which varied according to 'bower custom.'

Bower Chalke

NOTE. *North Strete* 1570 PembSurv.

KITT'S GRAVE (6″), where Wiltshire, Hampshire and Dorset meet, is on the site of *chetolesbeorge* 955 (13th) BCS 917. The reference is to the barrow here. Close at hand on the other side of the county boundary is CHETTLE HEAD COPSE (6″), deriving from *cheotoles heafde* in the same charter, later *Chytelheved* 1281, 1289 *Ass*, *Chettelhead* 1618 WM xxiii. We probably have to do with a personal name *Ceotol*.

MISTLEBERRY WOOD (6″). Cf. (*to*) *michelan byrg* 955 (13th) BCS 917. 'Big camp or stronghold,' *v*. micel, burh. It is really in Handley (Do) on the border of the two parishes.

WOODMINTON is *Wodmanton* 1254, *Wodemaneton* 1276 St-Nicholas, *Wudemanton* 1255 RH (p), *Wodemanton* 1289, 1305 *Ass*, 1310 Pat, 1456 IpmR, *Woodmington* 1773 A and D. 'Woodman farm,' *v*. tun.

BINGHAM'S FM, CUTLER'S CORNER, LAW'S FM (all 6″) are to be associated with the families of Richard de *Byngeham* (1288 *Ass*), John *Cuttler* (1570 PembSurv) and William *Lawes* (ib.).

BAKE BARN (6"), *v. infra* 450. COW DOWN HILL is *The Cowdown* 1690 *Wilton*, *v. infra* 430. GREAT DITCH. Cf. *Greatediche coppice* 1595 ib. MARLEYCOMBE is *Marlycombe* 1820 G. MESSCOMBE HEAD (6") is *Mescombe hedd* 1570 PembSurv, 1590 *Wilton*. MISSELFORE (6") is *Misleford* 1807–8 O.S. ROOKHAY FM is *Rokehay* 1570 PembSurv, *v.* (ge)hæg. SHIRE RACK is *Shire oke* 1618 *Map*. Probably 'shire oak,' the modern form being corrupt. It is on the county (shire) boundary. STANCHILL COTTAGES (6") is *Stanchill* ib., *Staunch Hill* 1788 *Kings*. STONEDOWN WOOD. Cf. *Standeane copice* 1590 *Wilton*, *Stonedene* 1618 *Map*, *Stone Dean* 1788 *Kings*, *v.* denu.

Broad Chalke

GURSTON

> *Gerardeston* 1237 Pat, 1254 StNicholas, 1312 Sarum, *-tona* 1242 Fees, *Estgerardestone* 1289 *FF*, *Westgererdiston* 1419 AD i, *Geradyston* 1533–8 ECP, *Geredston* 1547 StNicholas, *Geradston* 1602 *FF*, *Garrardston* 1637 *Phillipps*
>
> *Gerardstone al. Gerston* t. Eliz ChancP, *Gerardston al. Gurston* 1647 *Recov*

This is a post-Conquest tun-name. It represents the 3-hide estate in *Chelche* which *Girardus* held in DB. In 1166 (RBE) *Gerard* de Chelca held a knight's fee of the abbess of Wilton, to whose predecessor Chalke had belonged in 1086.

KNIGHTON

> *cnihta land* 955 (13th) BCS 917
> *Cnicteton* 1200 Cur, *Knichteton* 1200 FF, *Knictona, Cnihteton* 1242 Fees, *Knygteton* 1279 *Ass*, *Knyghteton* 1332 *SR*

'Farmstead of the household servants,' *v.* cniht.

MOUNT SORRELL *olim* MOUSEHILL. This name has been changed as shown by the succession of forms *Moleshulle al. Mountsorrell* 1568 *FF*, *Molleshillfeld* 1570 PembSurv, *Mousehill vel Mountsorell* 1590 *Wilton*, *Montshill* 1642 *SR*, *Mousehole* 1773 A and D, *Mousehill or Mussell* 1804 Hoare. It was originally the home of Robert de *Moles-, Molushulle* (1327, 1332 *SR*) and Roger de *Molleshulle* (1356 *Ass*), i.e. probably '*Moll*'s hill.' It came into the possession of the family of Henry de *Muntsorel* (1279, 1281 *Ass*), de *Montesorelli* (c. 1280 *Wilton*), from Mountsorrell (Lei), and was then given a new manorial name.

STOKE FARTHING

> (*be eastan*) *stoke, to stoc hæmalande* 955 (14th) BCS 917
> *Stokes* 1258 Ch, *Stokesverdun* 1268, *Stoke Verdon* 1289 *Ass*,
> 1312 Sarum, 1332 *SR*, (*Verdoun*) 1332 *MinAcct*, (*Vardon*)
> 1474 IpmR, (*Verthing*) 1570 PembSurv, (*Verdyn*) 1571 *SR*

Probably 'dependent settlement,' *v.* stoc and *Studies*[2] 23. *stochæma* (gen. pl.) denotes the dwellers at Stoke, *v.* hæme. John de *Verdun* held the manor in 1258 (Ch) and the present spelling is a piece of folk-etymology. The family came from Verdun in France.

VERNDITCH is *Ferndich'* 1275 RH, *Ferendich* t. Hy 3 *Stowe* 798, *Vernediche* 1570 PembSurv, *-dyche* 1590 *Wilton*. 'Bracken ditch,' *v.* fearn, dic and Introd. xxi.

BARNETT'S DOWN, REDDISH HO and RUMBALD'S BARN (all 6″) are to be associated with the families of Robert *Barnett* (c. 1840 *TA*), William *Rediche* (1570 PembSurv) and William *Rumbold* (c. 1840 *TA*).

BURY ORCHARD is *Beryorchard* 1570 PembSurv. There is an old camp here. CHICKENGROVE BOTTOM. Cf. *Chickengrove* c. 1840 *TA*. HATCHFIELD COTTAGES (6″). Cf. *Hatch Field* 1813 *Kings*. HYDON HILL is *Highdowne* 1590 *Wilton*. KNAPP DOWN is *Napp* 1660 ib. *v.* cnæpp. KNIGHTON WOOD is *Knighton cops* 1618 *Map*. KNOWLE FM is so named c. 1840 (*TA*), *v.* cnoll. LITTLE LONDON (6″). Cf. *infra* 455. It is in a far corner of the parish where three parishes meet. LONG BRIDGE (6″) is *Langebrigge* 1416 AD i. Cf. *Long Bridge Furlong* 1788 *Kings*. THE MARSH (6″). Cf. *Marshmeade* 1570 PembSurv. MIDDLETON HILL is *Middelton* ib. VITRELL GATE (6″) may be identical with *Vyrells Crosse* ib.

Ebbesborne Wake

EBBESBORNE WAKE

Eblesburna 826 (12th) BCS 391, (*æt*) *Eblesburnan* 902, 947,
956, 986 (12th) ib. 599, 832, 962 KCD 655
Eblesborne 1086 DB, -*burne* 1166 RBE, 1222 Pat, 1167 P,
Ebelesburn(e) 1202 Cur, *Ebulesburne* 1241 FF, *Ebbeles-
burne* 1242 Fees, 1244 StNicholas
Ebleburn' Simonis Wach 1167 P
Hebelesburn 1248 Ipm
Ebelesbornewak 1271 AD v, *Eblesburne Wake* 1285 Pat
Ebsborne 1571 *SR*, 1641 NQ vii, *Esbourn, Ellesburn* 1675
Ogilby

'*Ebbel*'s stream,' *v.* burna. See further Ebble river *supra* 7.

FIFIELD BAVANT

Fifhide 1086 DB, 1249 *Ass*, 1316 FA, *Fifide* 1275 RH,
Fyfhide 1301 Pat, *Fifhyde juxta Eblesbourne* 1345 *Ass*
Fiffehyde Beaufaunt 1436 FF
Fyfhed Bavent 1510 Sadler, *Fifehede* 1526 Ct, *Fifield al.
Fyfhed* 1567 FF

'Five hides,' *v.* hid. It was assessed at five hides TRE. Alesia
de *Bavent* held the manor in 1301 (Pat), Roger de *Bavent* in 1316
(FA).

STOWFORD BRIDGE (6″) is *Stoforde brigge* 1348 *Cor, Stovord* 1590
Wilton and was no doubt the Hundred meeting-place, *v. supra*
199. The earlier forms show the name to be 'stone-ford.'

CLEEVE COTTAGES (6″) must be near the home of Roger de *Clyve*
(1292 *AddCh*). *v.* clif, 'slope.' It is *Cleeve* 1788 *Kings*.

BARROW HILL is *Bury Hill* 1710 *Wilton*. GREAT BINGHAM (6″).
Bingham was the name of a rector of Berwick St John who died
in 1826 (Hoare 71). CHALKWAY HEAD (6″) is so named in 1740
(*Wilton*). Cf. *Chalkway furlong* ib. CHASE FMS. Cf. *The Chase*
1710 ib. This part of the parish was within the old Cranborne
Chase. EAST COMBE WOOD. Cf. *Estcombe* 1570 PembSurv,
Iscombe wood 1618 *Map, Escombe copice* 1740 *Wilton*. GREAT

and LITTLE FORLORN (6″) is *Foure lords* 1618 *Map*. Here Ebbes borne, Alvediston, Berwick St John and Handley (Do) meet *forlorn* from its remoteness, cf. *infra* 455. PITCOMBE (6″) i *Bit(t)combe* 1710, 1740 *Wilton*. PRESCOMBE is *Prestcoumbe* 144 *WinchColl*, *Prescombe bottom* 1710 *Wilton*. 'Priests' valley *v.* cumb. SOUTH DOWN is *Southdown* ib. SOUTHFIELD (6″) i *The Southfeeld* ib. WEST END. Cf. *West End Piece* c. 1840 *TA*

Tollard Royal

TOLLARD ROYAL

> *Tollard* 1086 DB, 1166 P, 1196 Cur, 1198 Abbr *et passim*
> *Toulard* 1227 FF, 1249, 1281 *Ass*, 1282 *FF*
> *Tollard Ryall* 1535 VE, *Toller Riall* 1547 AD, *Tollerd Ryal* 1601 NQ viii, *Tollard Royall* 1620 *Recov*, *Tollerd Ryall alia Toller Royall* 1671 ib., *Toller oth. Tollar Ryall oth. Tollar Ryall* 1763 ib.

This is no doubt a British hill-name, a compound of a word corresponding to ModWelsh *twll*, Cornish *tol*, Breton *toull* 'hole, cavity, pit,' and **ard*, 'height,' cf. Arden (PN Wa 11–12) *Royal* because John, Earl of Gloucester (afterwards King John) held a knight's fee here in right of Isabella his wife (Hoare 171)

ASHGROVE FMS

> (*to*) *erse grafan* 955 (14th) BCS 917
> *Ersegrave* 1241 FF, *Ersgrave* 1321 *Ass*, 1332 *SR* (p)
> *Eresgrove* 1255 RH (p), 1498 Pat, *-grave* 1289 *Ass* (p)
> *Asgrove* 1558–79 ECP, *Arsgrove* 1570 *AD*, *Arsegrove al Ersegrove* 1578 *FF*, *Arsgrove* 1606 ib.
> *Ashgrove* 1620 *Recov*, *Ashgrove olim Ersegrove* 1829 Hoare

The ground here is broken downland and the first element may be OE *ears*, 'arse,' with reference to the shape of the ground The second is OE **græfe**, 'thicket.' Cf. *Lands Arse Acre* (*TA* in Orcheston St Mary and Landcross (PN D 94). Later the name was probably altered deliberately.

LARMER GROUND (6″) is *lafres mere* 955 (14th) BCS 917, *Laver mere* 1227 FF, *Lauermere Gate* 1618 WM xlvi. 'Pool where rushes or irises grew,' *v.* mere. The first element is *læfer*, 'rush iris,' etc.

MALACOMBE BOTTOM is *mapuldor cumb, mapeldere cumb* 955 (14th) BCS 917, 970. 'Maple-tree valley,' *v.* cumb and cf. Mappledore Hill *supra* 179.

BENCHE'S FM and MUNDAY'S POND (6″) are to be associated with the families of Samuel *Bench* (c. 1840 *TA*) and John and William *Mondaye* (1641 NQ vii).

CORNER FM is *The Corner Farm* 1809 Hoare. GORE HANGING (6″). Cf. *Gore Coppice* c. 1840 *TA*. LANGDEN (6″) is *Langeden* 1535 VE, *Langdeane* 1590 *Wilton*. 'Long valley,' *v.* denu. LITTLE WOOD (6″) is so named c. 1840 (*TA*). TOLLARD GREEN is *Tollard greene* 1618 *Map*. TOLLARD PARK is *Tollard parke* ib. WOODLEY DOWN is *Wolly Down* (sic) 1807 O.S., 1820 G.

DETACHED PARISH OF CHALKE HUNDRED

Semley

SEMLEY

(*on*) *Semeleage* 955 (14th) BCS 917
Semele c. 1190 SarumCh, 1291 Tax, -*leg*(*h*) 1225 *SR*, 1242
  Fees *et passim* to 1344 *FF*, with variant spellings -*ligh*, -*lee*
Semlegh 1329 ib., *Semble* 1571 *SR*, *Sembly al. Sembleighe*
  1572 *FF*, *Semblie* 1650 *ParlSurv*

'Clearing or wood by the river Sem,' *v.* leah and Sem *supra* 9.

AMBER LEAZE FM (6″) is *Amberleyes* 1544 *Rental, Amberleaze* 1773 A and D, and is to be associated with the family of William de *Amberleg*' (1225 *SR*), Matilda de *Amberlegh* (1292 *AddCh*) and John de *Amberlegh* (1341 NI). Probably the place-name is manorial in origin, the family having come from Amberley (Sx or Gl).

BARKER'S HILL (local) is *beorcora* 956 (14th) BCS 917, *Berkore* 1241 FF. 'Birch bank,' *v.* beorc, ora. The hill is now called ST BARTHOLOMEW'S HILL from the neighbouring Catholic chapel (*Bertholemews Hill* 1773 A and D). The hill is now planted with conifers, but there are still a few stray birch-trees about.

CHALDICOTT'S FM (6″) is *Chaldecotis* 1448 *FF*, *Caldecots* 1541
Hoare, *Chalder Cutts* 1773 A and D, and is to be associated with
the family of William de *Cheldecot'* (1225 *SR*), John de *Caldecote*
(1292 *AddCh*), Walter de *Chaldecote* (1305 *Ass*). This may be
a genuine place-name 'cold cote,' or it may be manorial in origin,
taking its name from a family which came from Chalcot *supra*
147.

COPPIT DENNIS (6″) is *Coppit Dennis* c. 1840 *TA*. Hoare (44)
says *Copped Dinas vulgo Copped Dennis*, but this is no doubt an
archaic reconstruction influenced by Welsh *dinas*, 'fortress.'

RAMSHILL FM (6″) was the home of William de *Rameshulle* (1314
WM xxxvi), de *Rammeshull* (1321 *Ass*). '*Hræfn*'s hill' or
'raven's hill,' cf. Ramsbury *infra* 287. See Addenda *supra* xl.

CHURCH FM[1] (6″), HOLLOWAY'S COTTAGES (6″) and WHITE-
BRIDGE FM were the homes of John *atte Churche* (1346 *Ass*),
Thomas de *Holeweye* (1249 ib.) and Richard *atte Whytebrigge*
(1332 *SR*), *v.* holh, weg.

AMBROSE COPSE (6″), CALAIS COTTAGES[2] (6″), HATTS HILL[3] and
HATTS FM[3] (6″) are to be associated with the families of William
Ambrose (1641 NQ vii), John *le Calewe* (i.e. 'the bald') (1327
SR) and Richard *Hatt'* (ib.).

ALDERMOOR COPSE (6″) is *le Aldermore coppice* t. Jas 1 *SP*, *v.* mor.
BRACH COPSE (6″) is *Breach coppice* c. 1840 *TA*, *v.* bræc *infra*
423. BROCK'S PLANTATION (6″). Cf. *Brocks* c. 1840 *TA*. CRATES
FM (6″). Cf. *Cratt*, *West Cratt* ib. and *infra* 427–8. EAST END FM
is so named in 1541 (Hoare). GROVE HO (6″). Cf. *Grove Close*
c. 1840 *TA*. GUTCH COMMON is *Goch Common* 1773 A and D.
Cf. *messuage called Gutches* 1635 WIpm. HILLDOWN COPSE
(6″). Cf. *Hilden* c. 1840 *TA*. HOOK FM is *Hook* 1541 Hoare,
v. hoc. There is a projection of land here. LYEFIELDS COPSE

---

[1] *Church House Farm* 1541 Hoare.
[2] Hoare (27) says that the estate was called *Callis* from time immemorial
and represents the holding of Walter de *Caleston* in the Hundred of Chalke.
It is impossible without further evidence to be sure which suggestion is the
more likely.
[3] *Hatts* 1613 Hoare.

(6″). Cf. *Lyefields* ib. THE MARSHES. Cf. *Marsh Mead* c. 1840
TA. MUSTER'S FM (6″) is *Mousters* 1541 Hoare, 1820 G.
OYSTERS FM (6″) is *Ashton vulgo Oysters* 1541 Hoare. ROUND
HILL (6″) is so named c. 1840 (*TA*). SENIOR'S FM (6″). Cf.
Seniors Close ib. SHELOES COPSE (6″). Cf. *Shelves Close* (sic) ib.
SOUTH WOOD is *Sudwode* 1257 *For*. STIB ACRE WOOD (6″).
Cf. *Stib Acre* c. 1840 *TA*. *v.* stybb, 'stump.' TOKES COTTAGES
and LANE (both 6″). Cf. *Tolkeshayes* 1411 *FF*, *Tolkes al. Toakes
al. Tox* 1642 WIpm, *v.* (ge)hæg. WESTHAYS COTTAGE (6″) is
Westhays, Westey Croft c. 1840 *TA*. WESTWOOD FM is *Westwood*
1642 WIpm.

XVIII. CAWDON AND CADWORTH
HUNDRED

This Hundred is mentioned as the *Hundred de Cawdon et
Cadworthe* in 1547 (*SR*). It was formed by the union of the two
former hundreds of Cawdon and Cadworth.

XVIIIa. CADWORTH HUNDRED

Cadeuuorde, Cadeuurda, Cadeworda hundred 1086 ExonDB,
Cadewudehdr 1167 P, *Cadewurdehdr* 1168 P, *Hundred de Cade-
wurþe* 1196 Cur, *Cadewrth* 1198 Abbr, *Cadeswurðe* 1198 P,
Caddewurth 1227 Fees, 1255 RH, *Cadeworthe* 1316 FA. 'Cada's
farm,' *v.* worþ. The only references to the name as a place-name
in distinction from a Hundred name that have been found are
(*campus de*) *Cadeworth* 1293 Longleat, *Cad(d)ford* 1551, 1632
Wilton, *East Cadford, West Cadworth* 1705 ib. The documents
in question relate to the parish of Barford St Martin. The OE
survey of Baverstock in the Wilton Register includes an *eald
gemotwyll* in the boundary marks. Grundy (i, 269) identifies
this with a spring on the western boundary of Baverstock where
the Ox Drove cuts it.

Barford St Martin

BARFORD ST MARTIN

> *Bereford* 1086 DB, 1167 P *et freq* to 1598 *Recov*, (*juxta Bridecombe*) 1289 *Ass*, *Berevord St Martin* 1304 Ch, 1380 Pat, *Berford Seint Martyn* 1400 Inq aqd, *Bereforth* 1461 Pat, *Bereford al. Barford* 1598 *Recov*

'Barley ford' (i.e. one that could carry a load of corn), cf. PN BedsHu 50. *St Martin* from the dedication of the church. See Burcombe *infra* 213.

CROUCH'S DOWN is to be associated with the family of Thomas *atte Crouche* (1332 *SR*) and Stephen *Crouche* (1371 *For*). There are memorials to the Crouch family in the church (Hoare 93). They must originally have lived near the village cross (*v.* crouche) which is still standing.

HURDCOTT

> *Hardicote* 1086 DB
> *Hurdecot(e)* 1242 Fees, 1249, 1279, 1289 *Ass*, 1256 FF, 1332 *SR*, (*juxta Wilton*) 1305 *FF*, *Hurcott* 1659 PCC
> *Herdecote* 1249, 1268, 1281 *Ass*, 1283 Ch, *Hyrdecot'* 1268 *Ass*.

'Cot(e) of the herdsmen,' *v.* hierde. Cf. Hurdcott *infra* 384 and Hurcott (So), *Hurdecote* 1245 Ipm, *Herde-* 1327 SR (p).

MORRIS'S FM (6″) is to be associated with the family of Thomas *Moris* (1524 *SR*).

BARFORD HEATH is *Barford Heathe* 1557 *Wilton*.

Baverstock

BAVERSTOCK [bǽvərstɔk]

> *Babbanstoc* 968 (13th) WiltonReg
> *Babestoche* 1086 DB, *-stok* 1225 *SR*, 1231, 1323 Cl, 1242 Fees
> *Babbestoch'* 1225 *SR*, *-stok* 1249, 1268, 1279, 1289 *Ass*, 1291 Tax
> *Babstoke* 1375 Cl, 1394 Pat
> *Baberstoke* 1535 VE, *-stock* 1558–79 ECP, *Baverstocke* t. Eliz WM xxi, *Baverstoke* 1568 FF, *Baberstocke al. Baverstocke* 1716 *Recov*

'*Babba*'s stoc or settlement.' This may well have been the same man who gave name to Bapton *supra* 161, about five miles distant.

CROWDELL'S COPSE (6"). Cf. *Crowdell Bottom*, *Crowdells Coppice* c. 1840 *TA*. TARE COAT is *Terre Cotte* 1535 Hoare, *Terr Coty*' 1535 VE.

Burcombe

BURCOMBE

> *Brydancumb* 937 (13th) BCS 714
> *Bredecumbe* 1086 DB, -*coumbe* 1325 Pat
> *Brudecumba* 1225 *SR et passim* to 1428 FA, with variant spellings -*combe*, -*cumbe*, *Northbrudekumbe juxta Bereford* 1282 *Ass*, *Northbrudycombe* 1319 *FF*, *Southbrudecombe* 1345 *Ass*
> *Bridecumbe Salvage* 1268, *Northbridecombe* 1289 ib., *Bridecumbe* 1302 Sarum, *Bridcombe* 1316 FA
> *Bruddecombe* 1443–50 ECP
> *Northbritcombe* 1481 BM
> *Birdecombe* 1526 Ct, *Burcombe* 1535 VE, *Boorecombe* 1572, *South Burcombe* 1614, (*North*) 1640 *FF*
> *Brudcombe alias Burcom* 1539 Moulton

It would seem that in this name, in Bridmore *supra* 201 and the associated *Brydingadic* there noted, we must have a common element *brȳda* and it is difficult to see how this can be anything other than a personal name as suggested by Ekwall (DEPN). If *brȳd*, 'bride,' were the first element, then the Saxon form should be *brydecumb* and not *brydancumb*, and we should hardly expect a compound *brydingadic*, 'ditch of the bride's people.' Just how such a personal name arose it is difficult to say. The most probable rendering therefore is '*Bryda*'s valley,' *v.* cumb.

NOTE. *Bullocke streate* c. 1570 *Wilton*.

BURCOMBE IVERS [aivərz] is *boscus voc. Ivers* 1540 *MinAcct*, *Burcombe Ivers* ib., 1570 PembSurv and is referred to in (*forð be*) *yfre* in 937 (BCS 714) in the bounds of Burcombe. This is OE yfer, 'slope, escarpment' (*infra* 450), with reference to the steep slope of the chalk downs here. Cf. Rivar *infra* 355.

UGFORD

> *Ucganford* 956 (13th) BCS 1030, *Uggafordinga landscore* 1045
> (13th) KCD 778
> *Ogeford, Ocheforde* 1086 DB, *Ogeford(e)* 1332 *SR*, 1345 *Ass*
> *Huggeford* 1175 P, *Uggeford* c. 1190 SarumCh, 1195 FF,
> 1227 Ch, (*St Jacques*) 1382 FF, (*Sci Jacobi juxta Wilton*)
> 1409 *Ass, Northugford, Southugforde, Ugforde Abbesse* 1544
> LP

'*Ucga*'s ford.' Cf. Ugborough (PN D 284) and Ugley (PN
Ess 553). *St James* from the dedication of the former church,
Abbesse from the holding of the Abbess of Wilton. The 1045
citation refers to the boundary (OE *landscearu*) of the people of
Ugford, *v.* ingas.

FOLLY CLUMP (6″). Cf. *infra* 451. PRIORY FM (6″). The manor
of Burcombe belonged to Wilton Priory.

Fovant

FOVANT [fɔvənt]

> *Fobbefunte, Fobbanfuntan boc* 901 (13th) BCS 588, (*æt*) *Fobba-*
> *funtan* 994 (13th) KCD 687, *Fobbefunta* t. Hy 2, *Fobefonte*
> 1166, *Fobbefunte* 1224 *Wilton*
> *Febefonte* (sic) 1086 DB
> *Fobhunte* c. 1230 *Wilton*
> *Fofunte* 1242 Fees, 1267 SarumCh, *Fofonte* 1289 *Ass, Foffunte*
> 1291 Tax, 1332 *SR*, 1338 *FF*, 1371 Pat
> *Fovehunte* 1279, 1281, 1289 *Ass, Ovre Fofhunte, Nethere-*
> *fofhunte* 1306 *FF*
> *Upfovent* 1302 *Ass, Fovunte* 1305 Sarum, *Foffount al. Fovent*
> 1574 *FF, Feffen al. Fovent* 1592 *Recov*

'*Fobba*'s spring,' *v.* funta. Cf. Fobbing (PN Ess 156), Vobster
in Mells (So), *Fobbestor(re)* 1233 FF, 1327 SR (p), and Fob
Down in Alresford (Ha), *Fobedon(e)* 1327 *SR* (p), 1332 Winton.
Not far off in the bounds of Downton we have (*to*) *fobban wylle*
(948 BCS 863). See *Fobwell* in Downton *infra* 394. Some of the
later forms show the same tendency to develop final *hunt* which
was noted under Tolleshunt (PN Ess 306) and Chadshunt
(PN Wa 249–50).

CHISLEBURY CAMP is *Chiselbury* 1721 WM xi and is referred to as *cester slæd byrg* 901 (13th) BCS 588, *ceaster blæd byrig* 994 (13th) KCD 687. The two early forms (checked from the MS) are of equal authority. If the second is the more correct then we have a parallel in Chesterblade (So), *Cesterbled* 1065, *Chestreblad* 1259 Wells, a name which is very difficult of explanation (cf. DEPN *s.n.*). From the point of view of form and sense alike it is slightly easier to derive the name from *cesterslædbyrg*, the *slæd* being perhaps the shallow depression running east and west immediately south of the burh or camp.

TOUCHING HEAD COPSE (6″) is *Touching Head Coppice* c. 1840 *TA*. Possibly as in Touchen End (Berks), *la Twychene* 1351 Ipm, we have reference to cross-roads (OE *twicen(e)*). Cf. also Titching in Jacobstow (Co), *Twychene* c. 1150 *Launceston Cartulary*. There are cross-roads close at hand and not very far away was *ðere twichene* in the bounds of Tisbury (KCD 641).

DEAN COPSE (6″) and FOVANT WOOD were probably the homes of Richard *atte Dene* (1324 *FF*) and John de *Bosco* (1225 *SR*). The latter is *Foventeswode* 1362 *For*.

GUNVILLES WEIR[1] and JAY'S FOLLY (both 6″) are to be associated with the families of Henry *Goundeville* (1356 *Ass*) and Thomas *Jay* (1630 WM xlv).

CATHARINE FORD (6″) is *Cattarneford coppice* 1609, *Katherine ford close* 1700 *Wilton*. We may perhaps compare Catharine St *supra* 20. GALLOWS BARROW is so named in 1704 (ib.). HEATHY DOWN COPSE (6″). Cf. *Heathy Down* c. 1840 *TA*.

Grovely Wood

GROVELY WOOD

A former extra-parochial forest district. For the name *v. supra* 13.

EBSBURY (old camp) is *Ippesbury* t. Ed 2, 1331 *For*, *Ipesbury* 1570 PembSurv, *Ipsburie cops* 1589 WM xxxv. This name, like Ipsley (PN Wa 213) and Ipsden (PN O 135), points to an OE personal

---

[1] Cf. *meade called Gunvills* 1689 *Wilton*.

name *Ippi*. See the full discussion in PN Wa *loc. cit*. For Ipsley and Ipsden Ekwall (DEPN) has suggested a first element OE *yppe*, denoting in one case the Chilterns and in the other a small round hill. On the phonological side there is the serious difficulty that for all these names we have only one ME form in *u*, whereas all of them are found in areas where we should expect frequent *u*-forms. On the semantic side 'valley of the hill' is unsatisfactory as a place-name and there is the further difficulty that it would be very surprising if this unrecorded noun were found thrice over in a genitival compound, admittedly a rare type of formation.

HAMSHILL DITCHES (HIMSEL 6″) is *Henepeshulle* t. Ed 2 *For*, *Hemneshill* 1570 PembSurv, *Hempeshil cops* 1589 WM xxxv, *Hempell Copse* 1651 Hoare. The first element may be OE *henep*, 'hemp,' but if so the genitival compound is strange. Wild hemp is frequent in coppiced woods and clearings (E.J.S.). Cf. Hampage in Avington (Ha), *Hanepinge* 1256 *Ass*, *Hemepynge* 1305 Ipm, *Hanepynge* 1369 Winton.

POWTENSTONE (6″) is *(to) puntes stane* 956 (13th) BCS 934, *Poltin(g)stan* t. Hy 3 *Stowe* 798, *Pultingston* 1300 WM iv, *Poltyngston* t. Ed 3 *For*, *Pultingstone Copice* 1570 PembSurv, *Powtingstones Cops* 1589 *Map*, *Poltenstone* 1603 *For*, *Poultingstone* 1651 Hoare. If the OE form is to be relied on, the first element must be the recorded personal name *Punt*, cf. Pointers (PN Sr 89), Pounsley (PN Sx 393) and Poyntington (PN Do 301). The second element is stan, 'stone,' no doubt an old boundary stone. ing is used as a connective.

SHORTENGROVE is *Scortingrave* 1331 *Stowe* 925, *Shortingrove* 1331 *For*, *Shortyngrovt* (sic) 1475 Pat, *Shortingegrove* 1570 PembSurv. This name has a parallel in unidentified *Scortingrave* (13th *Bradenstoke*) in Burbage. Both alike must go back to OE *sceortan grǣfan*, 'short thicket,' *v*. grǣfe and *infra* 432–3.

APPLEDOE (6″) is *Apledoore Copice* 1570 PembSurv, *Appledore cops* 1589 WM xxxv. 'Apple-tree copse,' *v*. apulder. ASHGOE (6″) is *Ashgore* 1331 *For*, *Aishe Goore Copice* 1570 PembSurv, *Ashgore* 1603 Hoare. 'Ash gara or point of land.' BEMERHILLS (6″) is *Bemerhill Copice* 1570 PembSurv, *Bemerell* 1603 *For*,

Beamer Hill copps 1651 Hoare. Probably containing the same first element as Bemerton *infra* 225. CHILFINCH (6″) is *Chilfinch cops* 1589 WM xxxv, *-fench* 1603 Hoare. It is an old name for the chaffinch (WM xlvi, 486). FOUR SISTERS (6″) is *Rodnell alias the foure sisters cops* 1589 WM xxxv, *Rodnell cops* 1651 Hoare. GROVELY LODGE is *Grovele logge* 1362 *For.* HADDEN HILL. Cf. *Haddon cop(p)s* 1589 *Map,* 1651 Hoare, *Hadden* 1603 *For.* A compound of hæð and denu or dun. HAZEL PLANTATION (6″) is *Hasells copps* ib. SANDGATES (6″) is *Sandegates Copice* 1570 PembSurv, *Sangate* 1603 Hoare. STOTFIELD (6″) is *Stokfold* 1570 PembSurv, 1589 WM xxxv, *Stotefold* 1603 Hoare. THORN-HILLS (6″) is *Thornhulles* 1331, *Estthornhulle* (*copic' voc'*) t. Ed 3, *Thornell* 1603 *For.*

Netherhampton

NETHERHAMPTON [*olim* ˈneðəriŋtən]

> *Otherhampton* 1209 Cur, *Notherhampton* 1242 Fees
> *Netherhampton* 1249 *Ass et passim*, (*juxta Wilton*) 1324 *FF*, *Neþerehampton* 1279 *GDR*, *Nytherhampton* 1333 Ipm
> *Netheryng(e)ton* c. 1570 *Wilton*, 1571 *SR*, *Netherington al. Netherhampton* 1675 DKR xlii, *Nethington* 1675 Ogilby, *Netherington* 1777 *Sadler*

'Lower hamtun,' *v.* neoðere. *Lower* perhaps because south of the river with reference to Wilton. For the first two forms *v.* Introd. xx.

DAYE HOUSE (6″). *v. infra* 437. GROVE'S FOLLY and UPPER FOLLY. Cf. *infra* 451. NETHERHAMPTON DOWNS. Cf. *the Downs* 1682 *Wilton*.

Sutton Mandeville

SUTTON MANDEVILLE

> *Sudtone* 1086 DB, *Sutton(a)* 1224 Bracton, (*Maundeville*) 1278 *FF*, (*Maundvild*) 1535 VE, (*Mandfield*) 1561 *FF*, (*Manfylde*) 1571 *SR*, (*Manfille*) 1657 *Sadler*, (*Mandeville alias Manfeild*) 1675 Recov

'South farm,' *v.* tun. Robert de *Mandevilla* held the manor in 1224 (Bracton). For *Mandfield* etc. cf. Spinfield (PN Bk 189) from (*E*)*spineville*.

Row DITCH is referred to as (*on*) *rugan dic* 901 (13th) BCS 588 in the bounds of Fovant. 'Rough ditch,' *v*. ruh, dic.

FRICKER'S BARN (6″), LONG'S FM (6″), PANTERS and UMBER'S COPSE (6″) are to be associated with the families of Thomas *Fricker* (c. 1840 *TA*), Robert *Longe* (1641 NQ vii), William *Panter* (1524 *SR*) and Philip *Homber* or *Homeber* (1570 Pemb-Surv).

COMMON HILL (6″). Cf. *Common Down* c. 1840 *TA*. DASLETT FM (6″) is *Darslett* ib., probably from OE *dēor-slæd*, 'animal valley,' cf. Russlett Fd *infra* 502, Haslett (Wt), *Haresclad* 1294 *Ass*, *-slade* 1327 *SR* (p) and slæd. SUTTON IVERS (6″). Cf. *Ivers Coppice* ib. *v*. yfer and *infra* 450.

Wilton

WILTON[1]

> *Uuiltún* 838 BCS 421, *Wiltun* 854 ib. 469, c. 1000 Asser, (*æt*) *Wiltune* 9th ASC (Ā) *s.a.* 871, *Wiltun*(*e*) 933, 937 (13th) BCS 699, 714, c. 950 ASWills, (*to*) *Wiltune* 955 (14th) BCS 912, (*in*) *Wiltune* 968 (13th) ib. 1216, c. 975 (14th) ASWills, *Wiltune*, *-tone* 1086 DB *et passim*, with variant spellings *Wyl-* and *-ton*(*e*)

Coin-forms are *Wiltu*(*n*) t. Edgar, *Wilt*(*u*) t. Ethelred 2, *Wiltu* t. Canute, *Wiltun*, *Wiltu*, *Wilt Wiltune* t. Edw Conf.

'Farmstead on the river Wylye,' *v*. tun and Wylye *supra* 11.

NOTE. BREDE ST is *Bredstrete* 1268 *Ass*, 1428 FA, *Brydestrete* 1341 NI, *Bride-* 1540 *MinAcct*. CROW LANE is *Crawellane* 1494, *Crowelane*, *Crawell lane* c. 1570 *Wilton*, *Crowe Lane* 1570 PembSurv. Apparently 'crow-spring lane.' KINGSBURY SQUARE is *Kinggesbyri* 1296 Hoare, *Kyngesbury* 1348 *Cor*. See *infra* 256. MARKET PLACE. Cf. (*in*) *Atrio* 1428 FA, *Market mede* 1535 VE. MINSTER ST is *Munstre-* 1348 *Cor*, *Minsterstrete* 1540 *MinAcct*, *Munsterstret* c. 1570 *Wilton*, 'minster street,' i.e. monastery or nunnery. SILVER ST may be the earlier *Estret*(*e*) 1348 *Cor*, 1370 Ipm, *Estestrete* 1540 *MinAcct*. It leads eastwards from the Market Place. SOUTH ST is *Sudstrete* 1268, *Suth-* 1279 *Ass*, *Soth-* 1405 *MinAcct*. An alternative name may have been *Bolebriggestret* 1321 *Ass*, because leading to Bulbridge *infra* 219. WEST ST is *Westret*(*e*) 1348 *Cor*, 1370 Ipm, *Westestrete* 1540 *MinAcct*.

---

[1] Wilton was extra-hundredal, but may for topographical purposes be included in this hundred.

Unidentified names include *widan stræt* 988 KCD 665, *Nedlerstret* 246 WM xvi, i.e. 'needle makers' street,' *Gloverestrete* 1279 *Ass*, where he glove makers lived, *Shortestrete* 1540 *MinAcct*, *Froglane*, *Millne ane*, *Water lane* c. 1570 *Wilton*, *le Holowey* 1570 PembSurv, *Wassherne- tret* c. 1570 *Wilton*, leading to Washern *infra*.

BULBRIDGE is *Bulebrige* c. 1200 SarumCh, 1268 *Ass*, *-brigge* 1275 RH, *Bolebrigge* c. 1200 SarumCh, *-brig* 1236 FF, *-brugge* 1279 *Ass*, *Bollebrugge* 1275 Pat, *Bulbrygg* 1428 FA. 'Bull bridge.'

BURDENS BALL (6") is *Bordonesballe juxta Fogheleston* 1348 *Cor*, *Burdonesball* 1395 IpmR, *-balle* 1402 Pat, 1412 FA, *Burdensball bridge* 1599 WM xxi and is to be associated with the family of Robert *Burdun* (1263 WIpm). *Ball* is ME *ball(e)*, here used probably of a boundary-mark. See *infra* 422.

DITCHAMPTON [ditʃ'æmtən, *olim* ditʃiŋtən]

(*æt*) *Dichæmatune* 1045 (13th) KCD 778
Dicehantone 1086 DB, *Dichamton* 1202 Cur, 1203 FF, *-hampton* 1242 Fees, *Dychehampton* 1268 *Ass*
Dechementone 1086 DB
Dechington al. Dechehampton 1549 *FF*, *Dichington* 1674 ParReg

'tun of the dwellers by the dic,' *v.* hæme. So named from Grim's Ditch (*supra* 15) which runs north through Grovely Wood.

WASHERN GRANGE (6") is *Waisel* (sic) 1086 DB, *Wasserne* 1196, 1208 Cur, 1236 FF, 1275 RH, *la Wascherne* t. Ed 1 StNicholas, *Wa(ys)shehurne* 1279, 1289 *Ass*, *Washerne* 1307 *FF*, *la Wasshern'* 1318 Pat, *Washehorne* 1535 VE, *Wes(s)herne* 1540 *MinAcct*, c. 1570 *Wilton*. 'Wash-house,' *v.* ærn, or (possibly) '(sheep)- wash corner,' *v.* hyrne, 'corner.' It lies by the Nadder.

BURNBAKE is *Burnbacke* 1710 *Wilton*. See *infra* 451. HARE WARREN is so named c. 1840 (*TA*). NEALE'S BARROW (6") is *Neales Barowe* 1570 PembSurv. THE VENNEL (local) is the old name for the road to Netherhampton across Wilton Park. It is the word *vennel* (OFr *venelle*) in common use in Northern England for a narrow lane, but not hitherto noted in Southern England.

XVIII*b*. CAWDON HUNDRED

Cauuadone hundred, Cauduna 1086 ExonDB, *Caudona hundred*
1130, *Chaudune* 1158 P, *Caudon* 1196 Cur, *Chaudon* 1198 P
Caudona t. John BM, *Kaudon'* 1227 Fees, *Cawedon, Cauldon*
1255 RH, *Caudon* 1316 FA. The site of the Hundred meeting
place must have been in the parish of Coombe Bissett, since in
1473 (*WinchColl*) we have mention of a place in that parish
(*apud*) *Cawedon*. We also have the phrases *subtus Caudone*
t. John BM and *ad caput Caudone de Cawberg, hida terre subter*
Caudona t. Ric 2 Hoare in relation to this parish. In *TA* (c. 1840
there are six fields called *Cawdon* [kɑ·dən] *Dean* in Coombe
Bissett half a mile north of the village, on the east side of Drove
Lane. These adjoin a field in Homington called *Cawdean* (ib.)
situated in the northerly projection there of Homington parish
The *dean* is the hollow marked by the eastward projection of
the 250 ft. contour line, the *dun* is the down running northwards
up to the racecourse.

The first element is difficult. If we can lay any stress on the
1255 form the first element may be OE *cawel*, 'basket,' perhaps
used of one or more of the hollows in the southward slope of the
downs here, hence 'hollowed down.' Whatever its meaning the
same element is found in *caweldene* (BCS 762) in White Waltham
(Berks).

Britford

BRITFORD [bə·fəd]

Brytfordingea landscære c. 670 (12th) BCS 27, -*ingealana*
sceare 948 ib. 862, *Brytford* c. 1100 ASC (C) *s.a.* 1065
Brutford 826 (12th) BCS 391, 1243 FF *et freq* to 1428 FA,
Bruford 1167 P, *Brutteford* 1289 *Ass*, *Brute*- 1361 BM
Bredford 1086 DB, 1274 Ipm, *Bretheuorde* c. 1100 Life of
Edward the Confessor
Bretford 1086 DB, 1186 P *et freq* to 1325 Cl, *Breteford* 1186 P
Britford 1115 StOsmund, 1252 Cl, 1279 *Ass*, *Britfordstok*
1279, 1281 ib., *Brytford* 1399 *WinchColl*, *Brittford* 1474
Pat, *Brightford* 1708 *Sadler*
Brudefort 1175 France, *Brudford* 1211 RBE
Brideford 1203 Cur (p)

Bratford 1227 *Fees*
Birtford 1488 Ipm, *Byrteford* 1526 *Ct*, *Burtford* 1553 WM x,
    t. Eliz ib. xxi, 1609 *Longford*, *Britford al. Birtford* 1754 *Recov*

The first element here must be the word *Bryt* denoting British
or a Briton, which we find in *Brytland*, used in the Chronicle of
Wales and Brittany, and in the compound *Brytwealas*, 'Britons,'
and the whole name must denote a ford used by Britons,
possibly on some famous historical occasion. Cf. *brytta pol*
(KCD 778) in Ditchampton. We can hardly accept Ekwall's
explanation of the name as deriving from OE *brydford*. The OE
forms are too good for us thus to reject them in favour of an
interpretation which lays most stress on certain later forms. The
first two forms are found in the bounds of Bishopstone and
have reference to the bounds of the people of Britford so far as
they were at one time co-terminous with those of Bishopstone.

LONGFORD CASTLE is *Langeford* 1086 DB, 1202 FF, 1242 *Fees*,
1249 *Ass*, 1273 Ipm, *pontem de Langeford* 1279 *For*, *Longeford*
1281 Orig, *Langeford juxta Novam Sar'* 1370 *Ass*, *Langeford
Plokenet* 1372 Pat, *Langford* 1586 *Sadler*. Self-explanatory. The
Avon is wide at this point. Adam *Plukenet* held the manor in
1316 (FA).

BRIDGE FM and WELLHOUSE FM[1] were the homes of John *atte
Brugge* (1332 *SR*) and Nicholas *atte Welle de Bretford* (1305 *Ass*).

BAKE FM. Cf. *Lower*, *Middle*, *Peaked Bake* c. 1840 *TA*. See
infra 450. DOGDEAN FM is *Dogdean* 1773 A and D. THE
HEYMARSH (6″) is *Haymershe* 1535 *Rental*. KITT'S ISLAND (6″) is
St Kitts Island 1773 A and D. Probably a jest from the West
Indian island of that name. UPEND is *The Upende* 1650 *ParlSurv*.

Coombe Bissett

COOMBE BISSETT

Come 1086 DB, *Cumbe* ib., 1158 HMC Var i, *Cumba Maness'
    Biset* 1167 P, *Coumbe Byset super Ebelesburne* 1288 FF,
    Comb by Salisbury 1301 Ipm, *Combissett* 1639 FF

v. cumb, 'valley.' The form of 1167 records the tenure of
the village by Manasser Biset, *dapifer* of Henry II.

[1] *Well House* c. 1840 *TA*.

CHURCH FM (6″) was the home of John *atte Chyrch* (1307 WIpm)

COOPER'S FM, FELTHAMS, PALMER'S FM (all 6″) and TOTTEN
are to be associated with the families of William *Cooper* (152
SR), William *Feltham* (1598 NQ vii), Roger *le Palmer* (1332 *SR*
and John *Totyn* (1327 ib.).

COOMBE BISSETT BRIDGE. Cf. *ponte de Cumbe* 1249 *Ass.* COOMB
BISSETT DOWN. Cf. *montem de Cumbe* 1279 ib., *the downe c
Combe* 1594 *Longford.* NORTHDOWN is *North Down* c. 1840 TA
SHUTES FM (6″). Cf. *Shute Croft* ib.

Harnham

EAST[1] and WEST HARNHAM

> *Harnham* 1115 StOsmund, 1242 Fees, 1246 Cl, *Estharnhan
> t.* Hy 3 BM, *Hest-, Westharnham* 1275 RH, *Estharnham att
> Bryggeesend juxta Sarum* 1293 Trop, *West Harneham* 131
> FA
>
> *Hareham* 1130, 1168, 1171 P, 1158 HMC Var i, 1211 RBE
> 1234 Cl, *Haraham* 1244 StNicholas, *Harre-* 1249 *Ass*
>
> *Harinham* 1206 PatR, *Harenham* 1279, 1281 *Ass*, (*West*) 128
> *FF*
>
> *Haresham* 1224 Bracton
>
> *Harham* 1230 Ch, 1230, 1231, 1246, 1259 Cl, 1249, 1279 *Ass
> 1273 Ipm, *Harram* 1233 Ch, *Estharam* 1242 Fees, 124
> StNicholas, *Haram* 1268 *Ass*

The etymology of this name is uncertain. Ekwall's suggestior
of a lost OE adj. **hæren*, 'stony, rocky,' is ruled out by th
topography. More probably the first element is *hara*, 'hare.
Possibly the place was known alternatively as 'hare-hamm' and
'hares' hamm' with first element *hara* or *harena* (gen. pl.).

HARNHAM BRIDGE (6″) was formerly *pontem de Ayleswad*
Eleswade 1255 RH, *Ayleswade* 1279 *Ass*, 1300 Ipm, *Aileswade
brigge* 1348 Cor, *Ayleswaterbrigg* 1413 StNicholas, *Aylyswad.
brigge nowe called Harnham brigge by newe Salisbury 1471 Trop
Aylesford Bridge 1618 WM xxii. '*Ægel*'s ford,' v. **wæd**. Cf
Aylesbury (PN Bk 145).

---

[1] East Harnham is now included within the City of Salisbury.

DOWN BARN (6″). Cf. *Downe, Downforlonge* 1393 StNicholas.
FOXMORE DROVE (6″). Cf. *Foxmore* 1268 WM xxxviii, *v.* mor.
HARNHAM FOLLY (6″). *v. infra* 451. WALROND'S MANOR FM
(6″). Cf. *Crosse callid Walronds* c. 1500 StNicholas.

Homington

HOMINGTON [hʌmiŋtən]

> *Humming tun* 956 (12th) BCS 962
> *Humitone* 1086 DB, *Humintona, -e* 1130, 1190 P *et freq* to
>   1310 AD, with variant spelling *-yn-,* Hominton 1244
>   StNicholas, *-yn-* 1289, 1310 *Ass,* 1316 FA
> *Humminton* t. John *AD, Hommynton* 1244 StNicholas
> *Humington* 1236 FF, *-yng-* 1273 *FF,* 1299 AD vi

'*Humma*'s farm,' *v.* ingtun. *Humma* might be a pet form of
an OE personal name such as *Hūnbeald.*

HOMINGTON BRIDGE was by the home of John *atte Brigge* (1348
Cor). It is *Hummington Bridge* 1675 Ogilby.

BARBER'S FM (6″) is to be associated with the family of Edmund
Barber (1600 WM xlv).

HOMINGTON DOWN. Cf. *Homington Downe* 1594 *Longford, The
Downes* 1638 *Kings.* PENINGS FM is *The Pennyngs ib.* See *infra*
453. WESTEND FM (6″). Cf. *le Westende* 1393 StNicholas.

Odstock

ODSTOCK

> *Odestoche*[1] 1086 DB, *Odestokka* 1173 P, *-stok* 1199 FF, 1249,
>   1279 *Ass,* 1255 RH, 1316 Pat, *Est Odestoke* 1372 *FF*
> *Oddestok(e)* 1242 Fees, 1268 *Ass,* 1291 Tax, 1316 FA, 1319
>   Pat, *-stock* 1281 Ch
> *Odstocke al. Adstocke* 1732 *Recov*
> '*Od(d)a*'s stoc or stocc.'

ODSTOCK DOWN is *Odestocke Downe* 1594 *Longford.* SNAKES-
FIELD PLANTATION (6″). Cf. *Snakesfield* 1674 ib. GREAT YEWS
(wood) is *The Yew Trees, the west corner of the Yew Trees* 1693,
(*The*) *Yew Bushes* 1720 ib., 1773 A and D.

---

[1] In the MS *Odestote* was first written but was corrected to *Odestoche.*

Stratford Tony

STRATFORD TONY

(on) *stretford* 672 (12th) BCS 27, *on stret ford, on streat ford*
948 (12th) ib. 863
Stradford 1086 DB
Stratford 1242 Fees, 1249 *Ass*, *Strate-* 1275 RH, *Stratford*
To(u)ny 1332 *SR*, 1363 Cl
Stretford 1279, 1281 *Ass*, (*Tony*) 1338 Pat

'Ford where the (Roman) road crosses,' *v.* stræt. Ralph de
Touny held the manor in 1242 (Fees). Cf. Newton Tony *infra*
370. The *street* is the ancient Port Way, the same road which
gave name to Stratford-sub-Castle *infra* 371–2.

MAWERDEN COURT (6″) is *Mawerdens Court* 1538–44 ECP, 1686
FF and is to be associated with the family of Richard *Mawardyn*
(1394 *GDR*) which probably came from Marden (He), DB
Maurdine.

Whitsbury

WHITSBURY[1]

Wiccheberia 1132–5 (c. 1195) *Reading A*, *Wicheberi(a)* 1157 BM,
1171 P, *-biria* 1164 *AOMB*, *-buria* t. John (1227) Ch,
Wiccheburi 1207 Pap *et passim* to 1428 FA, with variant
spellings *Wyc(c)he-, Wic(c)he-, -bury, -beri, -biri*
Wuchebury 1327 *SR*
Whicchebury 1332 ib., *Whichbury* 1812 RCH
Whittisbury 1536, *Whitesbury* 1540, *Whyttesbury* 1545 LP,
1557 *FF*, *Whitsbury* 1611 S

Possibly 'wych-elm burh,' *v.* wice, though none have been
noted in the neighbourhood. The burh is the ancient camp called
Castle Ditches just to the north of the village.

CASTLE FM is near the ancient camp. Cf. *Castell Coppice*
1545 LP. SCOTLAND FM (6″). Cf. *infra* 454. It is in a remote
part of the parish. WHITSBURY COMMON is *Whyttesbury Comen*
1545 LP. WHITSBURY DOWN is *Whitsburie Downe* 1594 *Long-*
ford.

[1] Transferred to Hampshire in 1895.

XIX. BRANCH AND DOLE HUNDRED

This first appears as *Hundred de Brench et Dollefeld* 1428 FA, *hundred of Branchandole* 1646 Sess. It was formed from the two old hundreds of *Brencesberg* and *Dolefelt*.

XIX*a*. BRANCH HUNDRED

Brencesberge hundred 1086 ExonDB, *Brenchebergh* 1227 Fees, 1249 *Ass*, *Brenchesberg* 1255 RH, *Brencesbergh* 1268, *Brenchesberewe* 1279, *-burewe* 1281 *Ass*, *-burg'* 1285 Ipm, *Brencheberwe* 1289 *Ass*, *Brenchebrowe* 1316 FA

Branchesberga 1130, 1167, 1168, *Brancheberga* 1174, *Brankelesberg* 1198 P, *Branchesborwe* 1305 *Ass*

Hundred de Brench 1402 FA

The first element would seem to be a personal name *Brænci* of obscure origin but apparently found in Brenchley (PN K 189). The second element is **beorg**, 'hill, barrow.'

Bemerton

BEMERTON [bemərtən]

Bimertone 1086 DB, *-ton(e)* 1241 FF, 1242 Fees, 1258 Misc, 1281, 1289 *Ass*, *Bymerton* 1249 ib., 1262 StNicholas, 1271 FF, 1288 Ipm, 1306 Pat, 1325 Ipm, *Bimberton* 1259 Cl, *Bymirtone* 1306 *FF*

Beomertona 1107 (1300) Ch

Bumerton(e) 1281, 1289 *Ass*, 1316 FA, 1339 Ipm, 1346 Cl, 1368 Pat, 1386 IpmR

Bymerton al. Bemerton 1399 IpmR, *Bemerton* 1426 *Ass*, t. Eliz WM xxi, *Bymerton* ib.

Bymmerton 1460 IpmR, *Bimmerton* 1553 WM x

In BCS 27 we have mention of a boundary-mark *to bymera cumbe* which must be some five miles away. The names seem to mean 'farm and combe of the trumpeters' (*v.* tun), from OE *bӯmera*, gen. pl. of *bӯmere*, 'trumpeter.' Cf. Hornblotton (So and DEPN *s.n.*) which is probably 'hornblowers' farm,' Bemerhills *supra* 216 and *Bemerehill* (1574 WM xxxiv) in Winterbourne Stoke.

NOTE. *Cowlane* c. 1570 *Wilton*.

FUGGLESTONE [*olim* faulstən]

> *Fughelistone* 1236 FF, *Fugheleston juxta Wilton* 1304 *Ass*,
> *Fughleston* 1306, *Fougheleston(e)* 1346 Pat, 1377 IpmR
> *Fugeleston* 1242 Fees, *-tun'* 1245 WM xvi
> *Fuelestone* 1256 FF, *Fouleston* 1279, *Foweleston* 1305 *Ass*,
> *Fulston by Wylton* 1504 Ipm, *Foulston* 1627 WIpm
> *Fogheleston(e)* 1288 *Ass*, 1291 Tax, 1292, 1309 *FF*, 1294
> AD ii, 1341 NI, 1428 FA
> *Foggleston al. Foulston* 1570 *FF*, *Fugleston al. Fulston* 1598,
> *Fuggleston* 1639, *Fuggleston al. Fowleston* 1654 *Recov*,
> *Fugglestone or Foulston* 1773 A and D

'*Fugol*'s farm,' *v.* tun. *Fugol* is the OE *fugol*, 'bird,' here no
doubt used as a personal name. The normal development would
be to *Fowlstone*, but contracted forms such as *Fughleston* seem
to have led to a stopping of [g] before following [l], leading to
a pronunciation [fʌgəl].

QUIDHAMPTON [kwid'hæmtən, *olim* kwidiŋtən]

> *Quedhampton* 1249, 1268, 1279, 1281 *Ass*, 1306 *FF*, 1327 *SR*
> 1333 Pat, *-hamton* 1294 *Ass*
> *Quidhampton* 1289 ib., *Quyd-* t. Hy 8 *Rental*, *Quyddamton*
> t. Eliz WM xxi
> *Quidington* 1675 ParReg

This name is probably a compound of OE *cwēad*, 'dirt, dung,'
and hamtun, perhaps denoting a farm with good manure. Cf
Quidhampton *infra* 279, Quidhampton in Overton (Ha), *Quede-
mentune* DB, *Quedhampton* 1280 *FF*, *Quidhampton* 1316 FA and
Quither (PN D 216), denoting, like Mixerne (Gl), 'dung house.'
The persistent *e* in the early forms for these names suggests that
the first element is OE *cwēad*, 'dung,' rather than *cwidu*, 'cud,'
as suggested by Ekwall (DEPN). Cf. Sherrington *infra* 229.

BEMERTON HEATH (6″) is so named c. 1840 (*TA*). BOYS MEADOW
(6″). Cf. *Boysemed* 1314 Inq aqd. THE HERMITAGE (6″). Cf
Hermitage Hill 1773 A and D. HILL FM. Cf. *Hillemeade* c. 1570
Wilton. PEMBROKE PARK is named from the Earls of *Pembroke*
PIT FOLLY Ho (6″). Cf. *Gravel Pit Folly* c. 1840 *TA*. See
infra 451.

Langford

STEEPLE, LITTLE and HANGING LANGFORD

(*æt*) *langanforda* 943 (13th) BCS 783
Langeford 1086 DB, 1224 FF
Hangindelangeford 1242 Fees, *Hanginge* 1257, *Hangende-*
1270 *For*, *Hangynde* 1305 *Ass*, *Hengyng* 1365 *GDR*
Parva Langeford 1211 RBE, 1249 *Ass*, *Lutlelanggeford* t. Ed 2
For, *Litelangeford* 1332 *SR*
Stupellangeford 1294 *MinAcct*, 1310 Ipm, *Stepel-* 1294
MinAcct, *Steple Langford* 1305 Abbr, *Steppul Langford*
1316 FA, *Stapel Langford* 1331 Pat, *Steple Langford* t. Eliz
WM xxi, *Langford al. Steple Langford* 1605 *Recov*

'Long ford' (over the Wylye). *Steeple* from the church
steeple, cf. Steeple Ashton *supra* 136, also known as *Great*
Langford. *Hanging* from its position below a steep hill-side.
Cf. Limpley Stoke *supra* 121.

BATHAMPTON [baθ'æmtən, *olim* bætiŋtən]

Bachentune 1086 DB
Bethampton 1222 FF
Bachamwyly 1242 Fees, 1304 FF, *Bathamwyly* 1258 *Ass*,
1339 Cl, 1422 *Add*, *Bathampton al. Batham Wyly* c. 1440
BM
Batham 1279, 1289, *Bathampton* 1279 *Ass*, 1332 *SR*, *Bathe-*
1316 FA, *Badampton* 1428 FA
Batamtounewyly 1382 Cl, *Bathamtone Wyly* 1390 IpmR
Bathampton Wyly al. Batyngton Wily 1422 *Add*, *Battington*
t. Eliz WM xxi, 1648 ib. xxxvii
Bathampton sometimes called Battington 1825 Hoare

The place is probably so called from some bathing-place in
the Wylye, hence 'farm by the bathing-place.' There would seem
to have been alternative forms Batham and Bathampton, *v.* **ham**,
hamtun. *Bathamwyly* probably from its proximity to Wylye.

FARM DOWN is so named in 1709 (*Wilton*) and is identical in site
with (*on*) *mere dune* 963 (13th) BCS 783. This is an ancient
boundary-mark, so the first element is probably (ge)mære.

YARNBURY CASTLE is *Yarneberrie castell* 1591 WM vi. Possibly from OE *earna burh*, 'eagles' camp,' *v.* earn, burh.

THE MILL was the home of William *atte Mulle* (1327 *SR*).

CLIFFORD [klifit] BOTTOM (6″) is so named c. 1840 (*TA*). COW DOWN is *Cowe Downe* 1570 PembSurv, *v. infra* 430. HOLLOWAY HEDGE (6″). Cf. *Holloway* c. 1840 *TA*. LITTLE DOWN, PENNING BOTTOM and WEST HILL are so named (ib.). THE SPECTACLES (6″) is a plantation so named from its shape. STURTON HATCH (6″) is *Sturtons Hatte* 1589 *Map*.

South Newton

SOUTH NEWTON

> (*in*), (*æt*) *niwantune* 943, 946 (13th) BCS 782, 819
> *Nyweton* c. 1190 SarumCh, *Niweton* 1208 FF, *Sutneuton* 1242
> Fees, 1268 *Ass*, *Sutnewenton* 1281 ib., *Suth Newenton juxta*
> *Wilton* 1305 *FF*, *Niweton juxta Wilton* 1312 *Ass*

'New farm,' *v.*tun. *South* to distinguish from North Newnton *infra* 322.

> NOTE. *Bullokstrete* 1570 PembSurv.

CHILHAMPTON [tʃil′hæmtən, *olim* tʃiliŋtən]

> *Childamptun'* 1195 *Wilton*, *-hamton* 1203 Cur, *-hampton* 1242
> Fees, *Chyldhampton* 1262 StNicholas, 1317 *FF*, *Childe-*
> *hampton* 1324 Inq aqd
> *Chilhamton* 1202 FF, 1203 Cur
> *Chellyngton* 1500 Ipm

'The hamtun of the *cilds*,' *v.* cild, 'young man.'

STOFORD is *Stanford* 943 (13th) BCS 782, *Staneford* 1196 SarumCh, *Stafford* 1242 Fees, *Stoford* 1285 Ipm, 1303 *FF*, (*juxta Magnam Wychford*) 1321 *FF*, *Stouford* 1352 Cl, 1357 *FF*, *Stowe-* 1466 ib., *Stovorde* 1559 BM. 'Stony ford,' cf. Stowford *supra* 124.

LITTLE WISHFORD is *Wicheford* 1086 DB, *Litel Wycford* 1324 FA, *Lytelwychford* 1332 *SR*, *Parva Whicheford* 1316 FA, *Lytlewisheford* c. 1570 *Wilton*, *v.* Wishford *infra* 231. *Little* to distinguish it from that place.

MILL FM was the home of Richard *atte Mulle* (1332 *SR*).

CHAIN HILL is so named c. 1840 (*TA*). DOWN BARN. Cf. *Ye Downe, Newtons Downe* 1570 PembSurv. FOLLY FM. *v. infra* 451. MOUNT PLEASANT (6″). *v. infra* 455. SWANTON'S COVERT (6″). Cf. *Swantons* c. 1840 *TA*.

Sherrington

SHERRINGTON

Scearntune 968 (13th) WiltonReg

Scarentone 1086 DB, *Scharneton* 1268 Ass, *Scarenton* 1299 Ipm, *Scharnton* 1300 Pat, 1342 NI, *Sharne-* 1331 Misc, 1339 Cl, *Sharrenton* 1348 Ipm, 1428 FA

Sherinton' 1166 P, *Sherneton* 1248 FF, *Sernton* 1248, *S(c)hernton* 1282 Ipm, 1309 *FF*, 1327 WIpm, 1330 Cl, 1332 *SR*, *Sherenton* 1412 FA

Shernton al. Sheryngton 1560 *Recov*, *al. Sheryndon* 1561 *FF*

'Mud or dung farm,' from OE *scearn*, 'dung,' and tun. Cf. Shernick (Co), *Schernewyk* 1284 FF and Quidhampton *supra* 226.

SHERRINGTON MILL was the home of Adam *atte Mulle* (1327 *SR*).

ALSETTING COPSE (6″) is *Allsetting Coppice* c. 1840 *TA*. LONGDEAN BOTTOM (6″) is so named (ib.). MOUNT PLEASANT (6″). *v. infra* 455. STONY HILL is *Stoney Hill* 1773 A and D.

Stapleford

STAPLEFORD

Stapleford 1086 DB, t. Hy 2 (1252) Ch, *Stapel-* 1115 StOsmund *et freq* to 1219 FineR

'Ford marked by a post or staple,' cf. Stapleford (PN Herts 231). The actual post may be referred to in (*to þam*) *stænenan stapole* BCS 782.

SERRINGTON is probably *Suthampton Stapelford* 1314 Pat, *Wynterborn Suthynton* 14th *Bradenstoke*, *Southampton* 1314 Inq aqd, *Suthyngton* 1341 *Cor*, *Sothyngton* 1394 *Ass*, *Southyngton*

1432 AD ii, *Siddington* 1529–32 ECP. 'South hamtun,' cf. *Sunton infra* 344. For interchange of *d* and *r* cf. *Carrington* for Caddington (PN Herts 30–1), Darracott (PN D 43), *Dorrington* for Doddington (PN NbDu 65) and Derrington (St) and Derrythorpe (L) with earlier medial *d*.

UPPINGTON is *Uphampton juxta Stapulford* 1407 *FF*, *Uppington* 1411 BM, 1477 IpmR, *Uphampton* 1599 *FF*. 'Upper hamtun.'

CHURCH FM (6″) was the home of Adam *atte Churche* (1348 *Cor*).

COWDOWN FM. Cf. *Cow Down* c. 1840 *TA*, *v. infra* 430. DRUIDS HEAD FM (6″). Cf. *Druids Head* 1820 G. HORSE DOWN is so named (ib.). OVER STREET is so named in 1773 (A and D).

Stockton

STOCKTON

> *Stottune* 1086 DB, *Stoctun'* 1166 P, *-ton* 1189 BM *et passim* to 1350 *AddCh* with variant spelling *Stok-*, *Stocktun* c. 1250 *Rental*, *Stokton juxta Codeford* 1355 *FF*, *Stoketon* 1594 *Recov*

Probably 'tun made of stocks' (OE stocc).

ROAKHAM BOTTOM[1] (6″) was the home of William de *Roucombe* (1341 NI). It is probably referred to in the bounds of Stockton in 901 (BCS 595) in the phrase *ofer radune sweoran ofer nacum* (sic). Probably 'roe valley,' *v.* cumb.

CONYGAR BARN. Cf. *Conynger* 1570 PembSurv. 'Rabbit warren.' STOCKTON DOWN. Cf. *les Downes*, *lez Downe* ib.

Great Wishford

GREAT WISHFORD

> *Wicheford* 1086 DB, 1204 ClR, 1208 Abbr, 1227 Ch, 1242 Fees, (*Majori*) 1208 FF, *Wich-* 1211 RBE, 1242 Fees, *Wyche-* 1249 *Ass*, 1281 Ipm, *Wych-* 1291 Tax, *Muchelewychford* 1332 SR, *Michel Wychford* 1339 FF, *Magna Wyccheford* 1428 FA

---

[1] *Rokecombe* c. 1570 *Wilton*, *Rochum Bottom* 1808 O.S.

Wykford Majori c. 1190 SarumCh, *Wicford* 1212–17 RBE,
   1278 Ipm
Magna Whicheford 1316 FA
Wyssheford Magna 1513 BM, *Wycheford al. Wyssheford* 1574
   FF

'Ford by a wych-elm,' *v.* **wice**. *Great* in distinction from
Little Wishford *supra* 228.

DUTMAN'S CORNER (c. 1790 *Map*)[1] is to be associated with
Dudnams meade 1567 *Add*, *Wyllie mead alias Duttenham Mead*
1651 Hoare. It is the last relic of *duttan hamm* (BCS 757) in the
bounds of Wylye.

COBB'S MILL (6"). Cf. *Cobbes Milham* c. 1830 Hoare. The
hamm is by the Wylye. CUSTOM BOTTOM (6"). Cf. *Custom way*
1709 *Wilton*. Probably so named from one of the old Grovely
Forest customs. LOTMOOR (6") is *Lotmore* ib. Cf. *infra* 436.
PENNING BOTTOM (6"). Cf. *Lower Penning* ib., *v. infra* 453.
TOWN END (6"). Cf. *Townsend close* ib.

Wylye

WYLYE [waili]
   Biwilig 901 (12th) BCS 595, (*æt*) *Wilig* ib., 977 (12th) KCD
      611
   Wilgi, Wili 1086 DB, *Wili* t. Hy 2 BM, 1180 P, *Wyly* c. 1190
      SarumCh, *Wily* 1199 ClR *et passim* to 1418 *FF*, with variant
      spellings *Wyly, Wily, Wyli, Wili, Wyle* 1249, *Wyly
      Abbatisse* 1268, *Wyley* 1316 FA
   Wylgy 1378 IpmR
   Wely Abbatissa 1502 Ipm, *Weyleye* 1553 WM x, *Weilie* 1630
      FF

The village takes its name from the river (*supra* 11). *Abbatisse* from the holding of the Abbess of Wilton.

   NOTE. NETTLEMEAD LANE. Cf. *Nettelmeade* 1570 PembSurv.

DEPTFORD is *Depeford* 1086 DB, 1202 FF, 1242 Fees, 1316 FA,
Dupeford 1242 Fees, 1249, 1279, *Duppeford* 1281 Ass, *Doepeford*

---

[1] It was in the north-west corner of the parish, the hamm being by the
Wylye.

1341 *Cor, Deopeford* 1387 *FF*, 1422 *Add, Depford* 1432–43 ECP, *Detford* t. Eliz WM xxi, *Debtford* 1630 *FF*. 'Deep ford,' cf. Deptford (PN K 2).

THE BAKE is *Beake* 1808 O.S. See *infra* 450. BILBURY FM and RINGS. Cf. *Bylbury Downe* 1570 PembSurv, *Badbury or Belbury Ring* 1773 A and D. *v.* burh. COW DOWN is *Cowe Downe* 1570 PembSurv, *v. infra* 430. LITTLE DOWN is so named in 1773 (A and D).

XIX*b*. DOLE HUNDRED

Dolefelt, Dolesfelt hundred 1086 ExonDB, *Dolefeld* 1158 P, 1299 Ipm, *Dolesfeld* 1196 Cur, 1197 P, 1198 Abbr, 1275 RH, 1279, *Dollefeud* 1249 *Ass, Dollesfold* (sic) 1255 RH, *-feld* 1268 *Ass*, 1275 RH, *Dolle(f)feld* 1305 *Ass*, 1316 FA, *Dollenefeld* 1357 GDR. The modern name of the Hundred is misleading. The early forms show that it can have nothing to do with OE dal, 'share, portion' (cf. *infra* 429), for that would still be *dal(e)* in DB. If we may judge by the recurrent genitival form, the probabilities are in favour of an OE personal name. *Dol*, 'foolish,' is found as a nickname in Lewingus *Dol* (1066 LibWinton) and the weak form *Dola* is found c. 970 in a Devon manumission (BCS 1247). Hence '*Dol*'s open land,' *v.* feld.

Berwick St James

BERWICK ST JAMES

Wintreburne 1086 DB
Berewyk Sancti Jacobi c. 1190 SarumCh, 1268 *Ass*, 1291 Tax,
    Berwike 1275 RH, *Berewike* 1316 FA
Barwike St James 1595 FF, *Barwick* 1651 Hoare

'Outlying grange or farm,' *v.* berewic. *St James* from the dedication of the church. The place is pretty certainly one of the unidentified Winterbourne manors, *v.* Till R. *supra* 10.

NOTE. *Langforde waie, Mill waie, London waie, Maddington waie* 1591 WM vi.

ASSERTON is *Asshereston* 1279 *Ass*, *Asherton* 1289 *Ass*, *Winterbourne Ascertone* 1301 Ipm, *Asscherston* 1327 *SR*, *Asserton* 1327 Banco, 1340 *FF*, 1397 IpmR. '*Æschere*'s farm,' v. tun.

BERWICK DOWN is probably the *Cowe Downe* of 1591 WM vi, *v. infra* 430. HORSE DOWN is so named c. 1840 (*TA*).

Maddington

MADDINGTON

   Wintreburne 1086 DB

   Maydenwinterburne t. Hy 2 (1270) Ch, *Maydenewynterburna* 1178 BM, *Mayden Winterburn* 1241 FF, *Meidene Winterburn*' 1245 WM xvi, *Maydenes Winterburn* 1249 FF, *Maydene Wynterbourne* 1341 Ipm

   Medinton 1198 Fees, *Madinton(e)* 1211 RBE, 1281 *Ass*, 1292 Ipm, *Madyn-* 1309 Cl, 1316 FA, 1325 Pat

   Maidingtuna 1230 Bracton

   Maydenton 1268, 1289 *Ass*, *Maidenton* 1430 IpmR

   Madyngtone 1291 Tax, 1327 *SR*, 1428 FA

   Maydenton otherwise Winterbourne Maddington 1626 WIpm

   Madenton al. Marriton 1675 Ogilby

Originally Winterbourne from the stream (*v.* Till R. *supra* 10). Later 'maidens' tun' from the holding of the nuns of Amesbury. Cf. Maiden Bradley *supra* 172. For *Marriton* cf. *supra* 229–30.

ADDESTON (6″)[1]

   Wintreburne 1086 DB

   Abboteston 1279, 1289, *Abbodeston* 1289 *Ass*, 1316 FA, *Abbedeston* 1327 *SR*, *Abbateston* 1584 *Recov*

   Abdeston 1346 *Ass*, *Abbystone* 1660 PCC

This place-name represents the manor of *Wintreburne* held in DB by the Abbey of St Peter, Winchester. *v.* tun.

BOURTON FM is *Bourton(e)* 1327 *SR*, 1351 *Ass*, 1466, 1488 MinAcct, *Burton* 1332 *SR*, 1376 *FF*, 1455 MinAcct, 1626 WIpm. *v.* burhtun, 'fortified farm.'

[1] ABBASTON (old 6″).

HOMANTON FM

> *Hughemanton* t. Hy 3 BM, t. Ed 1 *Edington, Hughmanton* 1289 *Ass*
>
> *Hugmanton* 1268 *Ass*, 1332 *SR*, *Hugemanton* 1275 RH, 1277 Ipm
>
> *Hukmanton* 1278 *Ass*
>
> *Hoggmanton* 1289 ib., *Hoghemanton* 1319 *FF*, *Hogh-* 1330 WIpm
>
> *Wynterborn(e) Homanton* 1375 Cl, (*Homyngton*) 1471 Pat

This is clearly a place-name of post-Conquest origin, but the first element is obscure. Possibly on the model of such trade-names as *chapman*, *packman*, there was formed a trade-name *huk-man* for one who engaged in small trading (cf. *huckere, huckstere*), giving rise perhaps to a personal name *Hukman*. Hence '*Hukman*-farm,' *v.* tun.

ORAM'S GRAVE is so named from a suicide buried at the cross-roads here in 1849 (NQ iii, 275).

Orcheston St George and St Mary

ORCHESTON ST GEORGE and ST MARY

> *Orc(h)estone* 1086 DB, *Orcheston(e)* 1167 P, 1202 FF *et passim*, *Orchis-* 1236 FF, *Orcheston Seynt Jorge* 1279 *Ass*, (*Boyvile, Georgii*) 1291 Tax, (*Sci Georgii*) 1291 *FF*, (*Bovyle*) 1327 *Ass*, (*Marie*) 1404 Pat
>
> *Orkeston* 1227 Ch, 1316 Cl
>
> *Ordeston* 1296 WIpm, *Ordrycheston* 1315 Ipm
>
> *Orston Mary* 1524 *SR*, (*George*) 1535 VE, *Urston Mary* 1607 WM xix, *Orston al. Orcheston* 1688 *Recov*

Probably '*Ordric*'s farm,' *v.* tun, as suggested by the 1296 and 1315 spellings. The additions are from the dedication of the respective churches. Henry de *Bovile* held a manor in 1242 (Fees).

Orcheston St George

ELSTON

Wintreburne 1086 DB

Winterburn' Elye Giffard 1168 P, *Winterborne Helias Giffard*
1211 RBE

Elyston 1249, 1289, *Eles-* 1268 *Ass*, 1332 *SR*, *Elis-* 1310 *Ass*,
1316 FA, 1383 BM

Wynterbo(u)rne Eliston 1299 Cl, (*Elystone*) 1308 Sarum

This is a late tun-name. It represents the manor held in the
12th century by *Elias Giffard* (cf. Till R. *supra* 10).

COZEN'S FM (6″) and DRAX HO are to be associated with the
families of Ralph *Cosyn* (1327 *SR*) and I. S. *Drax* (c. 1840 *TA*).

THE CLEEVE (6″) is *The Cleeves* c. 1840 *TA*. v. clif *infra* 426.
HONEYDOWN RIDGE is *Honydowne* 14th *Bradenstoke*, *Honnie
downe balle* 1591 WM vi. For *balle*, v. *infra* 422. *honey* perhaps
from the bees that swarmed there. SILVER BARROW (6″) is so
named in 1812 (RCH).

Orcheston St Mary

OLD and LITTLE PENNING (6″) and WEST DOWN are so named
c. 1840 (*TA*). See *infra* 453.

Rolleston

ROLLESTON

Wintreburne 1086 DB

Rolveston(e) 1242 Fees, c. 1250 *Lacock et freq* to 1428 FA,
Wynterburne Rolveston 1325 *FF*

Rowston 1560 *FF*, *Rolleston al. Rolveston* 1566 ib., *Ralston*
1636 *Recov*

As the place is pretty certainly represented by one of the
unidentified *Wintreburne* manors, it is likely that the present
name is of post-Conquest origin, deriving from some 12th-
century holder *Rolf*, v. tun. *Rolf* is a Norman personal name of
Scandinavian origin (ON *Hrólfr*).

ROLLESTON BAKE FM. v. *infra* 450.

Shrewton

SHREWTON

Wintreburne 1086 DB

Winterbourne Syreveton 1232 Lacock, Winterburn Shyreveton 1236 Ch

Schyrreveton 1255 RH, Sherreveton 1279, Sherreveston 1281, Shyreveton 1282 Ass, Sherritone 1310 Ipm, Sherreveton al. Wynterborn Sherrevetone 1311 Ipm, Shirrefton 1348 Ipm

Shryfton 1529–32 ECP, Shreveton 1536 MinAcct, Shrewton alias Shreveton 1682 DKR xlii

This is another of the Winterbourne manors. Cf. Till R. supra 10. The later name means 'sheriff's farm,' v. tun. Edward of Salisbury, Sheriff of Wiltshire, held Wintreburne (TRW). Cf. Shurton in Stogursey (So), Sherrweton 1227 SRS xxxvii, Shurreveton 1279 ib.

NET DOWN

Netteton 1323 Ipm

Netton 1332 SR, 1566 FF, 1638 Recov, Necton 1432 AD ii

Nettefeld 1536 MinAcct, Netfeld 1566 FF

Nett, Net, downes of Net, Net feeld 1599 WM xxiii

Nett Downe 1682 DKR xli, Nett al. Netton 1754 FF

Nett, Nett Bush, Nett Drove, Nett Mead c. 1840 TA

This name is probably identical with Netton infra 364, from OE neat-tun, 'cattle farm.' At some stage in its history Netton would seem to have been interpreted as Net Down and then a series of names created from an imagined simplex Net(t).

LITTLE FOLLY (6"). Cf. infra 451.

Tilshead

TILSHEAD [tilzhəd, olim tilzed]

Theodulveside 1086 DB, Teolvesia 1180–7 France, Teovelsia 1246 Ch

Tidulfhide ib., Tidolfeshida 1167 P, Tidolveshyde c. 1190 SarumCh, Tidulveshida 1198 Fees, -hid' 1205 Fine, Thidulveshide 1225 Pat, Tydulfeshid 1242 Fees et freq to 1332 SR, with variant spellings Tid- and -olv-

Tydolside 1390 *FF*, *Tydelsyde* 1394 *Ass*, 1428 FA
Tyleshide 1403, *Tileshide* 1471 Pat
Tyleshed 1502 Ipm, *Titleside* 1535 VE, *Tylsehed* 1578 *FF*,
    Tidulsed al. Tilsett 1639, *Tilsheade* 1648, *Tilsett al. Tilshead*
    1695 *Recov, Tilsed* 1675 Ogilby, *Tilshead oth. Tulshead oth.*
    Tydelshead 1811 Act

'*Þēodwulf*'s hide of land' with later confusion with the name *Tidwulf, v.* hid. For the river Till, *v. supra* 10.

COPEHILL FM was the home of William de *Copehulle* (1289 *Ass*). In spite of the present form the first element would seem to be ME *coppe*, 'rounded hill.' The farm stands at the highest point in the neighbourhood.

EAST and WEST DOWN. Cf. *le Downes* t. Hy 8 *Rental*. THE ISLAND (6″) is probably so named from the moat here. KILL BARROW. Cf. *Gyllebarowys downe* 1461 *Ct*. WHITE BARROW is *Whitebergh* 1348 *Cor*. There are ancient barrows at both these places.

Winterbourne Stoke

WINTERBOURNE STOKE
    Wintreburnestoch 1086 DB, *Wintrebornestoca* 1086 ExonDB,
    Winterburnestoke 1169 P, 1211 RBE, -*stoch* 1176 P, *Winter-*
    burn' Stok 1242 Fees
    Wynterbourne juxta Chitterne 1325 *FF*

v. stoc. For Winterbourne *v.* Till R. *supra* 10.

GRANT'S BARN and GREENLAND FM (both 6″) are perhaps to be associated with the families of John *Grant* (c. 1840 *TA*) and Richard and Nicholas *Greene* (17th Hoare).

THE CONIGER. Cf. *Conyngarclose* 1466 *MinAcct, Conygeer* 1574 WM xxxiv. 'Rabbit warren.' HIGH DOWN is so named ib. KING BARROW (6″). "The rich contents of this *tumulus* has induced us to crown it with royal honours and to give it the title of King Barrow" (RCH 123). PARSONAGE DOWN is so named c. 1840 (*TA*). SCOTLAND FM is *Scotland* 1773 A and D. Cf. *infra* 454.

XX. POTTERNE AND CANNINGS HUNDRED

This appears first as *Hundred de Poterne et Canynges Epī* 1409 *Ass*, *Hundred de Canynges et Poterne* 1428 FA. It was formed by the union of the two hundreds of Cannings and Rowborough. In medieval times the latter was further sub-divided into Rowborough and Rowborough Regis Hundreds.

XX*a*. ROWBOROUGH REGIS HUNDRED

Hundred de Roubergh Regis 1327, 1332 *SR*, *Rowbergh Regis* 1428 FA, *Roborowe Regis* 1547 *SR*. *v.* Rowborough Hundred *infra* 242. The hundred of *Rubergh* was held by the king in 1316 (FA).

Great and Little Cheverell

GREAT and LITTLE CHEVERELL

Chevrel 1086 DB, *Cheverel(le)* 1166 RBE (p), *Cheverel* 1179 P, 1211 RBE, 1218 FineR, 1235, 1242 Fees, (*Magna*) 1227 FF, (*Parva*) 1236 Cl, *Cheverelles* 1198 Abbr, *Grete*, *Lytill Cheverell* 1522 *SR*

Capreolum 1103 France

Chiverell 1175, *Chiverel* 1178 P, 1204 Cur, 1242 Fees, 1287 Ipm, 1291 Tax, (*Parva*), (*Magna*) 1242 Fees, *Chyverel* 1250, 1275 Ipm, (*Litel*) 1362 Cor, *Magna*, *Parva Chyverell* 1316 FA, *Gretchyverell* 1554 FF

Little Cheveroill 1301 Ch

This name is pretty certainly identical with Keveral in St Martins by Looe (Co), *Kewerel* (sic) 1226 ClR, *Keverel* 1299, 1302 FF, *Keveral* 1302, *Over-*, *Nytherakeverel(l)* 1400, 1414 *Ass*, *Westkeverell* 1445 Pat. Professor Max Förster suggests for these names a possible compound of a word related to Middle Welsh *kyfair*, *kyfar*, *kyuar*, meaning (i) co-tillage, co-aration, (ii) a piece of land that is to be ploughed in common, and the word *ial*, discussed *supra* 6, *s.n.* Deverill. On the other hand it is difficult not to associate these names with Buckerell, Chackerell

(PN D 548, 610), Chickerell (PN Do 153) and Petteril (Cu, cf. DEPN *s.n.*), all of which would seem to contain a second element *-erel*. Note also Tregatherall (Co), *Tregaderel* 1308 Exon, 1327 *SR*, 1371 *Ct*, *-rell* 1577 *FF*. In all these names the last syllable may be the British diminutive suffix *-el(l)*. *Tre-* is Cornish *tre(v)*, 'farm.' The second element in this name and the first element in the Devon, Dorset and Cumberland names is obscure. It is clear from some of the forms for Cheverell that the name was at one time associated with French *chevreuil*, 'goat, roe-buck' (Lat *capreolus*).

Great Cheverell

Note. *Morganeslane, le Portewey, Ryggewey* 1422 *Ct*.

CHEVERELL WOOD was near the home of Peter *atte Wode* (1332 *SR*).

FOLLY WOOD (6"). Cf. *ground called Folly* 1797 *EnclA*. Cf. *infra* 451. GANG BRIDGE is *Gangbrugge* 1513 *Ct*, *Gangebrydge* 1542 *WinchColl*. The stream is of the tiniest and the phrase probably denoted a plank-bridge. Cf. *le Gangstighe* c. 1220 *Wilton*, probably used of a narrow path. THE GREEN is so named in 1797 (*EnclA*). GREENLANDS WOOD is *Greenlands* 1820 G. HENNING WOOD (6") is *Hanging Wood* 1797 *EnclA*. HIGHFIELD Ho (6") is *Heghefelde* 1289 *Ass*. HILL FM. Cf. *The Hill, Hill Field* 1797 *EnclA*. WITCHCOMBE (6") is *Whitcomb* ib.

Little Cheverell

FORE HILL. Cf. *Forehill Cliff* 1797 *EnclA*. NEW ZEALAND FM. This farm lies high up on the Plain in a remote corner of the parish, *v. infra* 455.

Easterton

EASTERTON[1]

> *Esterton juxta Stepellavynton* 1348 *Cor, Esterton* 1412 *FA et freq* to 1481 *FF*
> *Easterton Garnham* 1591 *WM* vi

'More easterly farm,' *v.* tun.

[1] A parish formed from Market Lavington in 1894 (Kelly).

BLACK HEATH is *Blacke Heath* 1610 S, 1695 Gough. EASTERTON
SANDS is *Easterton Sande* 1591 WM iv. TWENTYLAND (6″). Cf.
Twentie acres ib.

Market and West Lavington

MARKET and WEST LAVINGTON [læviŋtən]

> *Laventone* 1086 DB, *-ton(a)* 1175 HMC Var i, 1255 RH
> *Lavinton(e)*, *-(a)* 1091 StOsmund *et freq* to 1225 Bracton,
> (*Episcopi*) 1233 Cl, *Stupellavintona* 1242 Fees, *Stepel
> Lavynton* 1255 RH, *Stippellavyntone* 1309 Ipm, *Stapul
> Lavynton* 1316 FA, *Chepynglavynton* 1397 Pat
> *Stepel Lavington* 1274 Cl, *Lavyngton* 1291 Tax, 1402 FA,
> *Chepyng Lavyngton* 1402 Pat, *Lavyngton Gernon* 1412 FA,
> *Stapullavyngton* 1457 NQ i, *Lavington al. West Lavington*
> 1628, *Steeple Lavington al. Markett Lavington* 1681 *Recov*

'*Lāfa*'s farm,' *v.* ingtun. *Bishops* or *West* Lavington was held
in DB by the Bishop of Salisbury. Roger *Gernon* held Market
Lavington manor in 1242 (Fees). *Chepyng* is another name for
Market Lavington. It was also known as *Steeple* Lavington,
probably from the church steeple, but some of the forms show
confusion with *staple*, denoting 'a market.' Cf. Steeple Ashton
supra 136.

Market Lavington

FIDDINGTON

> *Fifede Lavynton* 1270 Pat, *Fyfhyde* 1281, *Fifhyde* 1289 *Ass*,
> *Fyfhyde Verdoyn* 1309 Ipm, *Fyfhide juxta Lavynton* 1319
> FF, *Fifhide Verdon juxta Steple Lavington* 1378 ib.
> *Fydynton juxta Stepellavyntone* 1306 FF, *Fydyngton juxta
> Steple Lavyngton* 1395 ib., *Fedyngton* 1450 IpmR, *Fytyngton*
> 1497 Ipm, *Fiddington* t. Eliz ChancP
> *Fiffehed Verdon alias Fidington* 1577 *Recov*

The older name means 'five hides,' *v.* Fifield *supra* 207 and
Introd. xviii. Later the element ingtun seems to have been added
to it so as to make it conform to a more usual type. The *Verdon*
family have not been noted in medieval documents nearer than
at Stoke Farthing (*supra* 206).

FRIETH FM[1], GROVE FM (6″), NORTHBROOK and WICK FM[2] (6″) were the homes of John de *la Frythe* (1268 *Ass*), John *atte Grove* (1327 *SR*), Roger de *Northebrok* (1282 *Ass*) and Richard de *Wike* (1332 *SR*). *v.* fyrhðe, 'wooded country,' grafa, wic. Northbrook means 'north of the brook,' cf. PN D Part I, xxxvii, for such formations.

DEWEY'S WATER and PARHAM WOOD are to be associated with the families of William *Dewy* (1717 ParReg) and William de *Perham* (1279, 1289 *Ass*, 1301 *Extent*).

BALL DOWN. Cf. *The Balles* 1591 WM vi. See *infra* 422. BLACK DOG FM (6″). Cf. *The Black Dog Public House* c. 1840 *TA*. BROADWAY HO (6″). Cf. *Broadway Close* ib. GIBBET KNOLL is *Gibbet Knowl* 1773 A and D. KNAPP FM (6″). Cf. *Nap House* c. 1840 *TA*. LADY WOOD is so named (ib.). LAVINGTON SANDS. Cf. *Great, Little Sands* ib. RIDGE WAY is *Rigweye* t. Hy 3 *Edington*. Cf. *supra* 17. SPIN HILL (6″) is *Spyneshull* 1225 ib., *Spynehill* 1540 *MinAcct*. SUMMER DOWN is so named c. 1840 (*TA*). TOWNSEND (6″). Cf. *Townsend Close* ib. WEST PARK FM is *West Park* ib. WHITE HILL is so named in 1773 (A and D).

West Lavington

ST JOAN À GORE FM

> *Gare* 1086 DB, 1232 Ch, 1242 Fees
> *Gores* 1232 Ch, *Gore* 1279 *Ass*, 1316 FA, *la Gorre juxta Lavinton* 1340, *la Gore by Lavyngton* 1370 Cl
> *Maner of St John of Goore* 1591 Recov, *St John Agore* 1614 FF

'Gore, wedge-shaped piece of land,' *v.* gara. The manor occupied the south-east angle of the parish. There was a small chapel here going back to the 14th century (NQ ii, 87–8).

LITTLETON PANNELL is *Liteltone* 1086 DB, *Litleton* 1249 *Ass*, *Lutleton(e)* 1255 RH, (*Paynel*) 1317 Imp, *Lytleton in the king's hundred of Roghebergh* 1319 ib., *Litelton juxta Lavington* 1335 FF. 'Little farm,' *v.* tun. William *Paynel* held the manor in 1249 (*Ass*). Cf. Newport Pagnell (PN Bk 21).

---

[1] *la Freth* 1355 FF.   [2] *Wyk* 1289 Ass.

ROUGH DOWN is *Ruwedunehulle, Ruggedunecumbe* 1224 FF, *Ruwedunehill* 1225 *Edington, Roghedone* 1301 Ipm, *Extent*. 'Rough down,' *v.* **ruh**.

MILL Ho and PITT Ho (both 6″) were the homes of John *atte Mulle* (1327 *SR*) and Thomas *atte Putte* (ib.). *v.* **pytt**.

A'BECKETTS, BUTLER'S CROSS and HUNT'S Ho (6″) are to be associated with the families of William *Beckett* (1523 *SR*), Rychard *Buttelar* (ib.) and William *Hunt* (1737 *Devizes*).

BOTTOM FM is so named in 1820 (G). CLYFFE HALL. Cf. *le Clyf* 1224 FF, *le Cliff* 1225 *Edington, Clyffe Hall* 1820 G, *v.* **clif**, 'slope,' etc. CONIGRE LODGE (6″). Cf. *Conygre* c. 1840 *TA* and *infra* 427. CORNBURY FM is *Cornbury Farm* ib. HIGHLAND FM is so named ib. NEW COPSE DOWN (6″). Cf. *New Copse Farm* 1839 *Devizes*. NEWGATE FM (6″) is so named in 1631 (WIpm). PENNING BARN (6″). Cf. *Great Penning* 1773 A and D and *infra* 453. RAMS CLIFF is *Remesclive* 1227 *FF*. Probably OE *hremnes*, clif, 'raven's slope.' RIDGE WAY is *Rigweie* 1224 FF. Cf. *supra* 17. WOODBRIDGE MILL (6″). Cf. *Wodebrigge* t. Hy 3 *Edington*.

XX*b*. ROWBOROUGH HUNDRED

Rugeberga hundred, hund *Rueberge* 1086 ExonDB, *Ruggeberga* 1167 P, *Rueberwe* 1249 *Ass, Ruberewe, Rugheberg* 1255 RH, *Roweberewe* 1279 *Ass, Rouberghe Episcopi* 1316 FA. 'Rough barrow,' *v.* **ruh, beorg**. Held by the Bishop of Salisbury in 1316 (FA).

Devizes

DEVIZES[1] [divaiziz]

    (*apud*) *Divisas* 1135–53 (1316) Ch, 1141 BM *et freq* to 1233 Cl, *Divise* 1282 Winton

    Divises 1152, 1157, 1227 SarumCh, 1280 Ipm, *Dyvises* 1279 *Ass*, 1318 Cl

    (*de*) *Divisis* 1176, 1187, 1196, 1199, 1202 P, 1205, 1212 ClR, 1234 Bracton, (*in*) 1249 *Ass*

[1] Devizes was extra-hundredal, but may for topographical purposes be included here.

Devises, -y- 1195 FF *et freq* to 1316 FA, *Devisis* 1260 Cl,
 Devysis 1327 Banco, *-sus* 1338, *les Divyses* 1381 Pat, *le
 Devisez* 1485 Ipm, *the Devizes* 1675 Ogilby
(*Castrum*) *Divisarum* 1223, 1229 Pat, 1242 Fees, (*Burgus*)
 1249, 1268, (*villa*) 1279 *Ass*
(*Castrum de*) *Vises* 1330, *la Vyses* 1335, *Vyse* 1376 Cl, 1397,
 1417, *Vise* 1442, *Visez, Vises* 1462, 1464 Pat, *The Vyse*
 1480–3 ECP, 1492, *the Vies* 1502 NQ i, c. 1540 L, *the toune
 of Vyes, The Vyes* 1529–32 ECP, *Veighes* 1620 NQ vii
Devys 1423 Cl, *Device* 1443–50 ECP, 1497 PCC
Devizes al. le Devize 1618 *FF, Devizes al. Vize* 1630 *Recov*

Devizes is a post-Conquest place-name. The name goes back
to the OFr *devise* (pl. *devises*), 'boundary,' from Latin *divisæ*,
cf. Viza (PN D 128) and Pipewell (PN Nth 176). The boundary
was that between the hundreds of Potterne and Cannings
which passed through the castle, the former being chiefly in the
king's hands, the latter belonging to the Bishop of Salisbury.
The town of Devizes grew up around the Norman Castle built
by Bishop Roger in the 12th century. The use of the definite
article alike with the full Devizes and the shortened *Vyse*
should be noted.

NOTE. THE BRITTOX is *la Britasche* c. 1300, *la Brutax* 1420 WM i,
the Brytax 1547 *Devizes*. This is the name also of two houses in old
London, for which Harben (*Dictionary of London, s.n.* Bretask) gives
14th-century forms *le Bretasse* and *la Bretask*. The word denoted a
place fortified with stockades, here perhaps the old battled way to the
Castle Gates (Heath 127). See further Longnon § 2286. Cf. NED
s.v. brattice. MARKET PLACE is *Ye Markett Place* 1603 Sess. NORTHGATE
STREET is *North Yate Street* 1547 *Devizes, v.* geat.
 Other unidentified minor names are *le Wolstrate* 1289 *Ass, la Rewe*
1302 WM i, *v.* ræw *infra* 445, *Cowas(h)lane* 1547 *Devizes,* 1553 Pat,
Shortstret 1589 ib.

SOUTHBROOM HO (6") is *Suthbrome* 1227 SarumCh, *Suthbrun*
(sic) 1227 Ch, *Suthbro* 1229 Cl, *Suthbrum prope villam Divisarum*
1231 Pat, *Suthbrom* 1289 *Ass*, 1308 BM, (*juxta Kanyngges Epi*)
1302 *Ass.* '(Place of) broom,' cf. Broom Manor *infra* 277.
Probably the southern part of some broom-grown tract.

DEVIZES GREEN (6") is *Devises Grene* 1555 Pat. DUNKIRK is so
named in 1820 (G). It is a late name from the Flemish town.
Cf. Dunkirk (PN K 495), also a name of late origin. ESTCOURT

HILL (6″) is *East Croft Hill* c. 1840 *TA*. NEWLANDS (6″) is *la Nywelond* 1281 *Ass*. OLD PARK. Cf. *in parco regis de Divisis* 1256 Cl, *Parkland juxta Devyses* 1379 IpmR, *The Devyse parke, Newe parke* 1568 *For, Devizes old parke* 1654 WM xli. SUNNYSIDE FM (6″) is *Sunny Side Farm* c. 1840 *TA*.

Marston[1]

MARSTON

> *Merston* 1198 FF, 1242 Fees, *Mers(c)hton(e)* 1289 *Ass*, 1291 Tax, *Merston juxta Poterne* 1306 FF, (*juxta Worton*) 1370 *Ass, Marston* 1559 *Recov*

'Marsh farm,' *v.* tun.

LONG STREET (6″) is so named in 1820 (G). NORNEY. Cf. *Norney Field* c. 1840 *TA*. Probably for (*bi*) *norðan ēg*, 'to the north of the marshy land,' cf. Norney (PN Sr 199). POUND FM (6″). Cf. *le Pounde* 1422 *Ct*. 'Cattle enclosure or pound.'

Potterne

POTTERNE

> *Poterne* 1086 DB, 1148 HMC Var i, 1195 FF *et passim* to 1291 Tax, with variant spellings *-ern* and *-erna*
> *Pottern* 1281 *Ass, Pottren* 1585 WM xxi, *Potterin* 1589 AD iv

'Building for pots or where pots were made,' *v.* ærn.

NOTE. COXHILL LANE. Cf. *Coxall* c. 1840 *TA*. WALLEN LANE. Cf. *Walelond* 1422 *Ct, Upper, Lower Wallen* c. 1840 *TA*. This would seem to be OE *wēala land*, 'land of the serfs or Britons.' It lies by fields still called Wallands (*TA*).

BYDE FM (6″) is *Bidesknappe* 1341 *Cor, Byde* 1346 *Ass* (p), *Bide* 1633 PCC. Byde Fm stands on a small isolated hill, doubtless here described as a cnæpp. Near by is BYDE MILL (6″) (disused). For this stream-name cf. Bydemill Brook *supra* 4.

CADLEY FM is to be associated with Thomas de *Cadele* (1332 SR, 1346 *Ass*). It is difficult to be sure whether this and the other Cadley names noted below (*v.* Index) are all of local origin or whether one or more of them are of local origin and the rest

---

[1] A tithing of Potterne. Made a civil parish in 1852 (Kelly).

of the manorial type, taking their name from a settler from one of the other Cadleys. The personal name *Cada* is on independent record and is well attested in place-names (cf. Cadenham and Cadworth *supra* 87, 211), so that the existence of more than one Cadley in the same county is quite possible.

FURZEHILL FM (6″) is *Forsthull* 1225 Edington, *Furze Hill* 1841 *Devizes*. This name is repeated in Forest Hill (O), for which Alexander (PN O 108) gives forms *Fostel* 1086 DB, *Fforsthull* 1158 Oseney, *Foresthulle* 1219 Eynsham, *Forsthull* 1274 RH, and in Fossil Fm (PN Do 139), *Foresteshull* 1227, *Forsteshull* 1254 FF, *Forstehull* 1280 Ch[1] and in a lost *Fosteshulle* (1292 *Magd*) in Wanborough. There can be little doubt that the first element repeats itself in the two examples of Fosbury *infra* 306, on high ground, in Foxbury in Crofton (Ha), *Forstebyr'* 1280 *Ass*[2], and in Forsham (PN K 351), *Fforsthamm, ffrosteshamm, Fortesham* 1261 *Ass* (p), also on high ground. All these names taken together are, as suggested by Tengstrand (StudNP vi, 100–1), in favour of a lost OE **forst*, used specially perhaps of a ridge-like hill such as we have at Furzehill, Forest Hill and Fosbury, deriving from a stem found also in MDu *vorst*, 'ridge of a roof.' See the full discussion of this suggestion by Tengstrand (*op. cit.*). It is related to OE *fyrst*, 'top, ridge.'

RANGEBOURNE MILL (6″)

> *Ryngesburne* 1252 FF, 1281, 1305 *Ass* (both p), -*borne* 1304, *Ringes*- 14th *Bradenstoke*
> *Ryngburne* 1279, *Rynge*- 1289 *Ass*
> *Rangesbourne* 1305 *Ass* (p), *Rangborne* 1657, *Range*- 1670 FF
> *Reyngeborn* 1450 IpmR, *Rengeborn by le Devisez* 1485 Ipm, *Rengeborne* 1504 NQ vii

Professor Ekwall compares Rangeworthy (Gl) for which (DEPN) he gives forms *Rengeswurda* 1167 P, *Ryngeworth* 1303 FA, *Rungeworthe* 1349 SR. We may add *Rungewurthy* 1248 *Ass*, -*worth* 1346 FA, *Ryngeworth* 1479 FF, *Rangeworth* 1492 Ipm. In both names he would find an OE **hrynge*, 'structure of rungs.'

---

[1] Another unidentified example is *Forsthull(e)* 1332 NQ ii, on the borders of Edington and Bratton.

[2] Here the sense cannot be topographical as the place is low-lying.

WHISTLEY FM is *Wyslegh, Whisle, Wyschele* 1289 *Ass, Whischele, Whistele* 1341 *Cor, Whystley* 1547 *SR, Whysheley* 1579 *Recov.* A compound of OE wisce, 'damp meadow,' and leah. Cf. Wisley (PN Sr 155). It is probable that this same compound repeats itself in fields called Whistley Leaze, Whistly Mead, Whistly Bottom and Whistle Mead, but we have no really early forms for these names.

BLOUNT'S COURT[1] and GRUBBE'S WOOD (6″) are to be associated with the families of Geoffrey *le Blunt* (1270 *Pat*), *le Blund* (1281 *Ass*), Richard *le Blount* (1332 *SR*) and Thomas *Grubbe* (1841 *Devizes*).

THE BUTTS (6″). Cf. *Potern Butts* 1773 A and D. See *infra* 425. COURTHILL FM (6″). Cf. *Court Hill House* 1841 *Devizes*. EASTWELL is *Estwell(e)* 1249, 1279 *Ass*. FIVE LANES. Cf. *Five Lanes Farm* 1773 A and D. HARTMOOR (6″) is so named in 1841 (*Devizes*). LARBOROUGH FM (6″) is *Laverkbergh* 1225 *Edington*. 'Lark hill or barrow,' *v.* beorg. MARSH FM. Cf. *Marshe Crofte* 1545 AD v. MONTECELLO FM (6″) is *Montecello* 1841 *Devizes*. MOUNT PLEASANT (6″) is so named in 1820 (G). POTTERNE FIELD is so named c. 1840 (*TA*). Cf. *infra* 247. POTTERNE PARK is *Potterne parke* 1591 WM vi. POTTERNE WICK is *Poternewike* 1203 FF, *Poterne Wyke* 1484 Pat, *Pottren Weeke* 1585 WM xxi. *v.* wic and *supra* 25. SLEIGHT FM is so named in 1820 (G). See *infra* 454. STROUD HILL FM (6″). Cf. strod, 'marsh,' *infra* 447. WOODBRIDGE HO (6″) is *Wodebrig'* 1249, *Wudebrigge* 1282 *Ass*, *Wood Breach* 1545 AD v.

Rowde

ROWDE [roud]

 Rode 1086 DB, (*la*) *Rode* 1230 Cl, 1254 Pat, 1283 Ch
 Rudes 1186, 1196 P, 1198 Abbr *et freq* to 1268 *Ass*
 Rodes 1196 P, 1217 ClR, 1228 Cl
 Rude 1212 Fees
 Roud' 1263 Cl, *Roudes* 1287 Misc, 1289 *Ass*, 1291 Tax, 1316
  FA
 Rowd(e) t. Eliz WM xxi

---

[1] *Blounts Courte* 1568 *FF.*

OE **hreod** is used both of the reed itself and of a place where reeds grow and Ekwall (DEPN) suggests that Rowde derives from this word. It would suit its low-lying situation. hreod commonly develops to ME *rod(e)*, *rud(e)* in Wiltshire (cf. Rodbourne *supra* 32, 51).

DURLETT FM

> *Durlete* 1255 RH (p), *Dorlegate* 1300 WM iv, *Durlezete* 1341 Cor, *Durlegate* t. Ed 3 *For*, *Durlett* t. Eliz *LRMB*, *Durleyate* 1630 BM, *Durlyatt's Close* and *Lane* c. 1840 *TA*
> *Thurlegate*, *Thurlegatesmethe* t. Ed 1, *Thurlegate*, *Thurlegatesmethet* t. Ed 3 *For*

A compound of **þyrel**, 'pierced,' and **geat**, 'gate.' It lies on the parish boundary. There is nothing in the topography which favours the interpretation of **geat** as 'gap.' The word *smethe*, *smethet* is found in the next name Smithwick. These places are a mile apart with somewhat broken country in between and this particular piece of 'smooth ground' must be different from that which gave name to Smithwick.

SMITHWICK FM is *Smethet*, *Smethet dyche* 1430 *Ct*. This name would seem to be an *ett*-derivative of OE *smēðe*, 'smooth,' referring to a smooth or level space. Cf. *infra* 430.

ROWDE FIELD FM may have been the home of William *atte Feld* (1327 *SR*), probably with reference to the open common lands of the parish.

CAEN HILL (6″) is *Canehill* 1612 Sess. CLEARS FM. Cf. *The Clears* 1610 Speed, *Rowd Clears* 1752 *FF* and Clear Wood *supra* 156. COCKROAD COTTAGES (6″). Cf. *Cockerode* 1592 *Add* and *infra* 427. CONSCIENCES BRIDGE and LANE (6″). Cf. *Consciences Lane* 1820 G. FOXHANGER'S FMS (6″) is *Foxangre* 1246 Cl, *-hangre* 1255 RH (p), *Voxhangre* t. Hy 3 Stowe 798, *Foxhangres mede* t. Ed 3 *For*, *Foxarnders al. Foxhangers* 1541 *FF*. 'Fox-frequented slope,' *v.* hangra. NINE HILLS is *Lyme hills* 1544 NQ vii. Ox Ho (6″) is *Ox House* 1820 G. ROWDECROFT (6″) is *Rowde Croft Farm* 1841 *Devizes*. ROWDE FORD is *Rowdford* 1773 A and D. ROWDE HILL is so named t. Eliz (*LRMB*).

SAND'S LANE (6"). Cf. *the Sands* c. 1840 *TA*. STROUD FM (6")
is *Strode* 1412 FA, *le Strowde* 1430 *Ct.* 'Marsh,' *v.* strod *infra*
447. WICK FM is *Wika* 1211 FF, *Wyke* 1249 *Ass*, *Roudewyk*
t. Ed 3 *For.* *v.* wic and *supra* 25.

Worton

WORTON[1] [wəˑrtən]

> *Wrton(a)* 1173 SarumCh, 1177 BM, *Wurton* 1195 P (p), 1254
> StNicholas, 1305 *Ass*, *Worton(e)* 1220 SarumCh, 1249 *Ass*
> *et passim*, (*by Poterne*) 1419 Pat, *Wourton* t. Eliz WM xxi,
> *Woorton* ib., 1622 *FF*

This is OE *wyrt-tūn*, 'herb enclosure, kitchen garden.' Cf.
Worton (Mx, O).

LITTLECOURT (6") is *Lytlecote* 1279 *Ass* (p), 1281, *Litle-* 1289 ib.
'Little cot(e).' For the modern form cf. Westcourt *infra* 338.

LUTSEY FM (6") is *Luteseye* 1279, 1281 *Ass*. There is an OE
personal name *Lutting* of which we have the simplex in *Luttes
crundel* (BCS 327), a Somerset charter, *Luttesweye* (13th
RegMalm) in Chippenham and *Lutteswell* (1227 SarumCh) in
Pitton, now Litchwells Fd *infra* 509, and the name is probably
from *Luttes-īeg*, '*Lutt*'s marshy land,' though the forms are too
late for any certainty.

WATTS FM (6") is to be associated with the family of Robert
Watts (c. 1840 *TA*).

CUCKOLDS GREEN is so named in 1773 (A and D). HURST FM is
le Herst 1196 SarumCh, *Hurst(e)* 1273 Ipm, (*boscus de*) 1279 *Ass*.
'Wood' or 'wooded hill,' *v.* hyrst. MARSH FM. Cf. *Marsh Mead*
c. 1840 *TA*. RAY BRIDGE (6") must be identical in origin with
Reybridge *supra* 103. SOUTH CROFT (6") is so named c. 1840
(*TA*). It is by SOUTH CROSS LANE. Cf. Elms Cross *supra* 117.

[1] A tithing of Potterne. Made a civil parish in 1852 (Kelly).

XX*c*. CANNINGS HUNDRED

hunđ de caninga, Canenge hundred, Chalenga hundred 1086
ExonDB, *Chaninge hđr* 1158, *Kanenges hđr* 1185 P, *Hundred de
Canynge Episcopi* 1255 RH. *v. infra* 230. Bishop's Cannings and
All Cannings are now in different hundreds, the one in Cannings Hundred and the other in Swanborough Hundred *infra*
312. There can be little doubt that they were at one time in the
same hundred. The meeting-place of Swanborough Hundred
was at Swanborough Tump *infra* 320, but in 1268 (*Ass*) we have
mention of a certain Walter de *Hundredesclyve* in All Cannings,
while in Etchilhampton, which at one time seems to have formed
part of All Cannings, there is a group of eight fields called
Spilsbury (c. 1840 *TA*) which if we may judge by the analogy
of Spelsbury *supra* 198 must have been a hundred meeting-place.
These fields lie on Etchilhampton Hill, a well-marked rounded
hill rising to 626 ft., where Etchilhampton and Bishop's Cannings
march with one another. Just west of Etchilhampton Hill lies
Tinkfield Fm (*infra* 313). This can best be interpreted as
'assembly-field' and further strengthens the suggestion that this
was a hundred meeting-place.

All and Bishop's Cannings

ALL and BISHOP'S CANNINGS[1]

Caneganmersc c. 1100 ASC (C, D) *s.a.* 1010, *Caningan mærsc*
c. 1120 ib. (E), *Caningmershe* 1289 FF, (*Stokes in*) *Kanynge-
mersh* 13th *Shaston*, (*Alyngton in*) *Canyngmershe* 1394 *GDR*
Caninge, Caininghā 1086 DB
Caninges 1091 StOsmund, 1148 HMC Var i, 1217 ClR, 1249
Ass, Canenghis 1139, *Caningas* 1148 SarumCh, 1175
HMC Var i, *Kaningis* c. 1150 ib., *Canengis* 1161 BM,
Kaninges 1186 P, 1242 Fees, *-yng-* 1249 *Ass*
Canninges 1146 SarumCh, 1177 BM, 1185 P
Keninges 1201 Cur, *Kening'* 1212 ClR
Aldekanning' 1205 FineR, *Aldechannigg'* 1205 ClR, *Elde-
kaninges* 1256, *Alle Kanyngs* 1258 FF, *antiqua Caninges*

---

[1] All Cannings is in Studfold Hundred *infra* 312.

1268, *Elde Canynges* 1279 *Ass*, *Alecaninges* 1283 Ipm *Allescannyng* 1306 Cl, *Alcanninges* 1316 FA

Canyng Episcopi 1294 Ch, *Bisshopescanyngges* 1314 FF *Bysshoppys Cannyngys* 1530 *Recov*

In relation to this name a word must first be said as to the identification of OE *caneganmersc*, *caninganmærsc*. In 1010 the Danes burned Northampton, gathered as large an army as they could, crossed the Thames into Wessex and made their way as far as *Caningan mærsc*, burning and ravaging, and then turned home. This marshland has commonly been identified with the well-watered land through which the Kennet and Avon Canal now runs, in which All Cannings and Bishop's Cannings lie, some three miles apart, with Allington between them and with Beechingstoke (cf. *infra* 318) still further to the south-east. Karlström (166) having noted a 16th-century field-name *Caningmersshe* in Damerham (VCH Ha iv, 586), suggested it was there that one must seek the site of *caninga mærsc*. In PN Sx Pt. I, xliii, the present writers accepted this identification but were certainly wrong in doing so. We have now three further references to *Caningmershe* and they certainly belong to the Cannings area and not to Damerham[1].

Caningas would seem to denote 'the people of *Cana*' (*v.* ingas and PN in *-ing* 69). The name is on record in DB in the forms *Cana*, *Cane*, *Cano*, *Canus* (Feilitzen 213), but the history of the name is obscure. Persistent single *n* prevents association with OE *canne*, 'can, cup.' All Cannings is *Old* Cannings, *v.* eald. Bishop's Cannings belonged to the Bishops of Salisbury already in DB.

Bishop's Cannings

BEDBOROUGH[2] (1773 A and D, 1820 G)

Betteberwe 1249, *-bergh* 1279, 1281, 1289 *Ass*, 1420 BM *Butteberewe* 1279, *-bergh* 1281 *Ass*

---

[1] The field-name in Damerham, taken by the VCH from Hoare, must for the present remain unexplained. It may well be a transferred name, a marshy field in Damerham being named after a famous marsh in another part of the county.

[2] In A and D Bedborough or Bedbury Lane is in Roundway Fields north-east of Devizes.

Betberwe 1315, *Betburgh* 1556 *FF*

Bedburgh 1493 Ipm, *-borough* 1522 *SR*, *-borowe* 1603 *FF*,
1632 *Recov*, *-borough* 1716 ib.

Professor Ekwall suggests the pers. name *Beotta* (cf. OE
Beotting) as the first element. The second element is beorg,
here used of a barrow as there is no hill.

BOURTON is *Burton* 1279, 1289 *Ass*, (*juxta Canynge Episcopi*)
1372 *FF*, (*by Canyngges*) 1385 Pat, *Bourtone* 1332 *SR*, *Boreton*
1649 *Sarum* D and C. *v.* burhtun and Burton Grove *supra* 29.

CALCOTE FM [kɔˑkət] is *Coldecote* 1442 AD i, *Coldecote(s)* 1493
Ipm, *Corcutt* 1773 A and D. 'Cold cot(e),' cf. Chalcot *supra* 147
and Introd. xxi.

HORTON is *Horton(a)* 1158 HMC Var i, 1195 P *et passim*, (*juxta
Canynges*) 1379 *FF*. 'Dirty farmstead,' *v.* horh, tun.

LYNES HO[1] (6″), MILL FM[2] and TOWNSEND FM were the homes
of Hugh de *la Lynde* (1394, 1409 *Ass*), Roger *atte Mulle* (1327
SR) and Richard *atte Tounesende* (ib.). *v.* lind, 'lime tree.'

MORGAN'S HILL is *Morgans Hill* 1773 A and D. The family of
Morgan is found in the ParReg first in 1804.

BISHOP'S CANNINGS DOWN. Cf. *The Downde* (sic) 1612, (*uppon
our*) *downes* 1634 ParReg. BLACKWELL FM (6″) is *Blackwell* 1568
Sav. BROADWAY FM is *Bradeweye* 1258 De Vaux, 1289 *Ass*.
COATE is *Cotes* 1255 RH, 1279, (*juxta Divises*) 1281, *la Cote* 1289
Ass, *Cotes juxta Canynges* 1324 *FF*, *Coate Grove* 1686 AddCh,
v. cot(e). EASTON FM is *Eston(e)* 1332 *SR*, 1385 Pat, 1428 FA.
'East farm,' *v.* tun. It is east of Bourton. HAREPATH FM. Cf.
Hare Path, Harepath Way c. 1840 *TA* and herepæð *infra* 435.
KITCHEN BARROW is *Kitchen Barrow Hill* ib. LAY WOOD is *Lay-
woods Copice* 1661 *Devizes*. NORTH DOWN is *North Downe* 1649
SarumD and C. ROUGHRIDGE HILL is *Roughbridge Hill* (sic) 1773
A and D, *Roughridge Hill* c. 1840 *TA*. SHEPHERDS' SHORE is
Shepherds Shard 1690 Aubrey, *Sheppards Shord* 1707 Act, *Shep-
herd Shore* 1773 A and D. *v.* sceard *infra* 445. The roadway here
makes its way through Wansdyke. STONE PIT HILL (6″) is so
named c. 1840 (*TA*). WEST END FM. Cf. *Westend* 1598 ParReg.

[1] Cf. *Lynes Close* c. 1840 *TA*.   [2] Cf. *Milham* 1641 WIpm, *v.* hamm.

Chittoe

CHITTOE [tʃituˑ]

Chetewe 1167 P (p), 1257 For, 1259 Ch, Cl, 1289, 1305 Ass,
  Cheteweie 1226 FF, Chetwe 1232 Lacock, Chetowe 1260 For,
  t. Hy 3 Dugd vi
Cuttewe 1196 Cur (p)
Chitewe 1202 P, 1257 For, Chytewe 1249, 1356 Ass, Chitwe
  t. Ed 3 For, Chitue 1409 Ass, Chitway 1773 A and D
Chetuwe 1263 For, Cheteye 1297 Pat
Chutewe 1310 FF, t. Ed 3, 1375 For, 1409 Ct, 1419 IpmR,
  Chutuwe 1354 Ct, 1390 AD iv, Chuteweheye 1375 For
Chittewe 1332 SR, Chidewe 1374 FF, Chittowe t. Eliz WM xxi

Chittoe was within the old Pewsham Forest and is probably
a British wood-name, the first element being the word for 'wood,
forest,' discussed under Chute *supra* 12. Ekwall suggests for
the second element either the British word for 'yew' corresponding to Welsh *yw*, or else an old derivative with the suffix
-oviā. The persistent final *e* in the ME spellings of the name
rather favour the latter alternative, as do also the occasional
spellings with *o* or *u*. But the second element may have been
early associated with the cognate English word 'yew.' Professor
Salisbury notes that yews are most naturally found on the
sides of a steep valley such as that in which Chittoe stands.

BROGBROOK (6″) is probably the *Froggebrooke* of 1592 (*Add*), i.e.
'frog brook,' with the same change of *f* to *b* which is found in
Broxwater (Co), *Frox(e)wade* 1263 FF, 1289 *Ass*.

SPYE PARK. Cf. *Spyestret* 1409, *apud le Spye* 1426, *Spyegate*
1430 *Ct*, *le Speehouse* 1553 *Devizes*, *Spye Bovedon al. Bowdon*
1562 *FF*, *Spie Park* 1605 WM xxii. The place lies high.

REYNOLDS HILL FM and SCUTTS COPSE (both 6″) are to be
associated with the families of John *Reynald* (1332 *SR*) and
Robert *Skotte* (1587 PCC).

GROVE FM (6″). Cf. *Grove pece* 1593 *Devizes*. SILVERSTREET is
Silver Street 1773 A and D.

Roundway

ROUNDWAY

(*apud*) *Rindweiam* 1149 SarumCh, *Rindway* 1262 FF, -*weye*
1289 *Ass*, *Ryndwey(e)* 1332 *SR*, 1535 VE, -*way* 1340 *FF*
Ryngweye 1289 *Ass*, *Ryng(e)wey(e)* 1428 FA
Ryndeweye 1305, 1394 *Ass*, 1315 *FF*, 1316 FA, 1327 *SR*,
1457 *AddCh*, 1484 Pat
Rundewey 1493 Ipm, *Rundwey* 1547 *SR*, -*way* 1618, 1632
Recov
Roundwaye 1619 *FF*, *Roundeway* 1637 *Phillipps*

Ekwall (DEPN) is doubtless right in explaining this name as
from OE *rȳmed weg*, 'cleared road,' with assimilation of *md* to *nd*.

NURSTEED is *Nutstede* 1249, 1279, 1289 *Ass*, 1484 Pat, *Notestede*
1289 *Ass*, *Notstede* 1315 *FF*, *Noutstede* 1332 *SR*, *Nustede* 1493
Ipm, *Nursted* 1730 *Recov*, *Nursteed* 1815 Act. 'Place where
nuts grow,' *v.* stede. Cf. Nurstead (Ha), *Nutstede* 1236 *Ass*,
1316 FA.

DREW'S POND (6″) is to be associated with the family of Robert
Drewe (1619 *SR*).

BROADLEAS is *Broadleaze* 1820 G. *v.* læs. THE FOLLY (6″). Cf.
infra 451. OLIVER'S CASTLE is an ancient camp, first so named
in 1820 (G). ROUNDWAY HILL is so named in 1652 (Sess) and
is *montem de Rindweye* 1327 *AddCh*. WICK GREEN. Cf. *Wyk*
1249 *Ass*, *Weeke* 1629 *SR*, *Weeke greene* 1631 *Recov*, *Week* 1815
Act. *v.* wic and *supra* 25.

XXI. CALNE HUNDRED

(*in*) *hundreto de Calna*, *Calne hundred* 1086 ExonDB, *Caune
hundred* 1193 P, *v.* Calne *infra* 256.

The meeting-place is unknown. Possibly it was at *The Motley*
(*TA*) in Compton Bassett, just east of Cherhill Low, where the
parishes of Calne, Cherhill and Compton meet. Motley probably
goes back to OE (*ge*)*mōt-lēah*, 'moot-clearing.'

Berwick Bassett

BERWICK BASSETT [barik]

> *Berwicha* 1168 P, *Berewic* 1185 Templars, *Berewica* 1196 Cur
> *Berewykbasset* 1321, (*juxta Ricardeston*) 1409 *Ass*, *Berwyk
>   Basset* 1325 Ch
> *Barwyk Basset* 1449 Pat, *Barwyck* 1523 *SR*

v. berewic, 'outlying grange or farm.' Alan *Basset* held the manor in 1211 (RBE). Cf. Wootton Bassett *infra* 272. Near Richardson in Winterbourne Bassett *infra* 309.

FIELD BARN (6″) was possibly the home of Henry *in the Velde* (1333 *SR*), *feld* referring to the open fields of the township. For the initial *v*, *v.* Introd. xxi.

Bromham

BROMHAM

> *Bromham* 1086 DB, t. early Wm 2 BM Facs *et passim*
> *Brumham* 1086 ExonDB, *Bromham al. Brumham* 1760 Recov
> *Bramham* 1168 P
> *Bromeham* 1433 Cl, 1458, 1494 Pat, 1576 *FF*

'Broom **ham** or **hamm** (enclosure).'

CLINGHILL (6″) is *Klynghulle, le Clynche* 1409 *Ct*, *Clynghill* 1569 *FF*, 1570 *Add*, *Clynche, Clyngehyll* 1592 *Add*, *Clinche* t. Eliz WM xxi, *Clingehill* 1652 ib. xlii. The name is repetitive, the first and second element alike denoting a hill, cf. more fully under Clench *infra* 349.

HAWK STREET FM and HAWK STREET (6″) are *Hauekestret* 1288 *Haukestret* 1399 *Ct*, *Hawkstreat* 1568 *Add*. In the 1288 reference there is mention of one Thomas *Hauek*, i.e. 'hawk,' and the hamlet probably took its name from his family rather than from the bird. *Street* is used of a 'straggling hamlet,' *v.* EDD *s.v.* and cf. Barrow Street *supra* 178.

NETHER STREET is *Netherstret* 1288, 1354, *Nethestrete, Binethestrete* 1288, *Nethestret* 1399, 1409 *Ct*, *Netherstrete* 1545 AD v

'Lower street,' the place lying lower than Bromham village.
For the meaning of *street*, *v.* Hawk Street *supra* 254.

ST EDITH'S MARSH. Cf. *Edithelegh* 1374 *FF*, *Ydethelee* 1398
AD iv, *Seyntydemershe* 1569 *FF*, *Tiddie Marsh*, *Tydworths
Marsh* 1640 Sess, *Idith Marsh* 1773 A and D, *Titty Marsh* 1862
Aubrey. *Edith* may be Queen Edith, cf. "*inde Rex de terra
Reginæ Edithæ in Brumham* 10 *hid. in domino*" (ExonDB). If so,
the *Saint* is a late incorrect addition.

MAPLES FM[1] and MOORHOUSE FM[2] (both 6″) were the homes of
Walter *atte Mapele* (1332 *SR*) and William *atte More* (1288 *Ct*).
v. mor, 'marsh.'

GABY'S CLAY BARN, HOBBS' FM and WYATTS (all 6″) are to be
associated with the families of Stephen *Gaby* (c. 1840 *TA*),
Robert *Hobbes* (1409 *Ct*) and John *Wyot* (1430 ib.).

ABBOTT'S WOOD FM. Cf. *Abbotts woode* 1570 *Add*. BATTLE HO
(6″). Cf. *Bromham Battell* 1558–79 ECP, *Battle crofte grove*
1570 *Add*, *Battle Bromham* 1820 *Recov*. Battle Abbey held the
manor by the gift of William ii. BERRYMOOR WOOD (6″). Cf.
Berrymore 1596 *Add*. BURBROOK'S WOOD (6″) is possibly to be
connected with *le Brodebrooke* 1570 ib. CLAY BARN (6″). Cf.
Upper, *Lower Clay* c. 1840 *TA*, *Cleystret* 1354 *Ct*, *Cleyfeld* 1377
MinAcct, *le South Cley*, *North Cley* 1564 *Add*. COLWELL COPSE
(6″). Cf. *Collwell* 1590 ib. HORSEPOOL is *Horsepol* 1261 FF.
LOOPHILL (6″) is *Lowpwellsforlong* 1377 *MinAcct*, *Lophull* 1426
Ct, *Loopehill* 1592 *Add*. NONSUCH is *None Such* 1773 A and D.
Cf. Nonsuch Park (PN Sr 73). Probably of nickname origin.
THE POUND. Cf. *Poundfald* 1377 *MinAcct*, *le Pounde* 1426 *Ct*.
PRICKMOOR WOOD. Cf. *Pyrtemore* 1409 ib. ROUGHMOOR
COTTAGES (6″). Cf. *le Rowmore* 1426 ib. *v.* mor. SLOPERTON
is *Slaperton* 1409, 1436 ib. STILL'S FM (6″). Cf. *Stills Hook*
1771 WM xlv. WESTBROOK is *Westebroch* t. Hy 2 BM, *-brok*
1288 *Ct*, probably from OE (*bi*) *westan brōce*, '(place) west
of the brook.'

---

[1] *la Mapele* t. Ed 3 *For*.
[2] *Morehous* 1402 *FF*, *Moorehowse al. Mooreplace* 1570 *Add*.

Calne

CALNE [kɑ·n, *vulgo* kan]

 et Calnæ 997 (c. 1150) KCD 698, *Calne* 955 (14th) BCS 912
 æt Cálne c. 1120 ASC (E) *s.a.* 978, *Calna* 1091 StOsmund
 1130, 1156 ff. P, 1144 AC, *Kalne* 1158 HMC Var i, *Caln*
 1198 Abbr *et passim*, *Caln* 1588 NQ viii
 Cauna, -e 1086 DB, 1167 P, 1199 FF, 1228, *Kaune* 123(
 Cl
 Calle al. Calne 1460 Pat, *Cane* 1672 StJ
 Cawne 1556 *FF, Cawen* t. Eliz ChancP, *Cawlne* 1588 *Sadle*

Ekwall (DEPN *s.n.*, RN 90) takes Calne to be a river-name
the old name of Abberd Brook and identical in origin with
Colne (La). If, however, Calstone *infra* 257 also contains thi
name as a first element, Calne must be an old name for th
Marden rather than for Abberd Brook.

NOTE. CASTLE ST is so named in 1695 (WM xliii). CHURCH ST i
le Cheretstret (sic) 1245 ib. xvi, *Chirchestrete* t. Ed 1 *Lacock, Churchestre*
14th *Bradenstoke*. CURZON ST is *Cusinstret* 1245 WM xvi, *Cosenstret*
1536 *MinAcct, Cowsyn strete* 1548 Pat, *Cozen Strett* 1695 WM xliii
THE GREEN is so named in 1695 (ib.). KEW LANE is *Kewe Lane* 164
SarumD and C. KINGSBURY STREET. Cf. *Kyngesbiri* 14th *Bradenstoke*
Kingsbery Greene 1649 *SarumD and C.* 'The king's burh or strong
hold.' Cf. the same name in Wilton *supra* 218 and Marlborough *infr*
299. Calne, Marlborough and Wilton were all royal manors. MARKE
HILL. Cf. *Market Place* 1695 WM xlvii. MILL ST. Cf. *Milleweye* 127
Ass. NORLEY LANE leads to Norley *infra* 260. PATFORD ST. Cf. *in vic*
voc. Patteford 1245 WM xvi, *Patford Street* 1695 ib. xlvii, from som
lost place-name '*Peatta*'s ford.' RAG LANE is so named in 1820 (G)
SANDY LANE is so named in 1812 (*Recov*). SILVER ST is *Silverstreet* 164
SarumD and C. WOOD ST is *Wodestret* 1232 *Lacock, Woodstrete* 155
Pat, presumably where wood was sold. Cf. Wood St in London, o
Cheapside.

 Among lost names we may note *Battestret* 1245 WM xvi, *Hernweie*
strete, Portstrete t. Ed 1 *Lacock*, the latter possibly the present Londo
Road, cf. *supra* 16.

ABBERD WOOD. Cf. *Abbreya* 1227 Ch, *Abrie* 1227 FF, *Aubre*
1245 WM xvi, 1264 Ipm, *Abbride* 1273 Ipm, *Abbard* 153
MinAcct, Abberde 1548 Pat, *Great Abberd* 1555 ib. This wa
originally a stream-name, *v. supra* 1. Probably from O
Abban rīð '*Abba*'s stream,' *v.* rīð.

BOWOOD HO [bouwud]. Cf. *Bunewode* (sic) t. Hy 3 Jones-Beddoe (p), *Bouewode* 1304, 1319 Pat, *-wod* t. Ed 2, *Bovewod* t. Ed 3 *For*. Probably from OE (*on*) *būfan wuda*, '(place) above the wood.'

CALSTONE WELLINGTON [*vulgo* kɑ·sən]

> *Calestone* 1086 DB, *-a* 1130 P, *Caleston(e)* 1164 P *et passim* to 1316 FA, *Calleston* 1281 *Ass*
> *Calston* 1242 Fees, 1255 RH, 1311 Ch, 1324 FA, 1326 Ipm
> *Calston Wely* 1500 Ipm, *Caulston Wellington* 1568 *FF*, *Cawston, Cawlston* 1585 WM xxi, *Calston al. Cawston Willington* 1607 *FF*

The first element in this name may be *Calne*, the name of the stream on which it stands (cf. *supra* 256). See Addenda *supra* xl. The manorial addition is from the family of Ralph de *Wilinton* (1228 Cl).

CHILVESTER

> *Chelfurstre* 1245 WM xvi
> *Chelfhurst* 1263 t. Ed 3 *For*, 1289 *Ass*
> *Chalfhurst* 1279, 1281, *-herst* 1281 ib.
> *Chelfestre* 1471 WM xxxiv, *Chelfester beside Calne* 1490 Ipm, *Chylfester* 1493–1500 ECP, *Chelvester* 1550 Pat

The first form is possibly corrupt. The other 13th-century spellings point to a compound of OE *cealf*, 'calf,' and **hyrst**, 'wooded hill.' For final *-ster* cf. Raesters *supra* 151.

DERRY HILL. Cf. *Derrie Gate* 1653 *Survey*, *Derry Hill* 1695 BorRec. Note also The Derry in Ashton Keynes (*supra* 40), *The Derry* (1653) in Chippenham, *Deryestreate* (1568) in Marlborough. The word would seem to be a variant of the usual *dairy*. The form is found in Fuller in the 17th century (cf. NED). Derry Brook in Ashton Keynes (*supra* 6) is not by The Derry. It lies south of it on the other side of Swill Brook.

HORSLEY UPRIGHT GATE (1725 Act) is *Horsliperith* 1279, *Horslaperythe* t. Ed 1 *For*, *-rithe* t. Ed 1 *Lacock*, t. Ed 3 *For*, 1331 Ipm, *Horslepride Gate* 1653 *Survey*. 'Stream (*v.* riþ) by the horse slæp or slippery place.' Restored on the 6″ map as HORSLEPRIDE GATE.

QUEMERFORD

> *Quemerford* 1199, 1232 FF *et passim,* (*juxta Calne*) 1346 *Ass,*
> *Quemmerforde* 1642 *SR*
> *Kemerford* 1227 Fees, 1279 *Ass*
> *Quembreforde* t. Hy 3, c. 1400 RegMalm, *Quember-* 1623
> WM i, *Quimberford* 1649 *Sarum D and C*
> *Comerford* 1476 IpmR, 1500 Ipm, *Commer-* 1539 *Phillipps,*
> *Comerforde al. Quemerford* 1560 *FF, Camberford* 1670
> Aubrey, *Gamarvon Bridge* 1675 Ogilby, *Cummerford* 1695 M

Quemerford is not far from the meeting of two streams. It is possible, therefore, that the first element is a Celtic place-name corresponding to Welsh *cymmer,* 'confluence,' etc. (from **cymber*). Cf. OBreton *comper, kemper* (Chrest 116) found in Breton place-names such as Quimper, and in Reskymmer (Co), *Reskemer* t. John AD i, *-kemmer* 1332 AD v, *Ryskymmer* 1342 NI (p), the first element of which is OCorn *rit,* MCorn *ris, res,* 'ford.' For confusion of initial *c* and *q,* cf. Queenhill (PN Wo 155, xliv).

STOCKLEY

> *Stokele* 1281, 1289, *Stokeleye juxta Calne* 1306 *Ass, Stokelegh*
> 1332 *SR*
> *Stoclygh* 1319 *FF, Stockeleye* 1327 *SR, Stokkeleye* t. Ed 3
> *For, Stockle* 1336 Pat, *Stokkele* 1351 *Ass,* 1372 *FF*

Probably from OE *stocca-lēah,* 'stump-clearing,' *v.* stocc, leah.

STOCK STREET (6″)

> *Stock*(*e*) 1232 *Lacock,* 1275 RH, 1295 Ipm, *Stok juxta Calne*
> 1289 *Ass, Stokke juxta Calne* 1313 Orig, *Stoke juxta Calne*
> 1324 Inq aqd
> *Stockstreete* 1637 *Phillipps, Stock al. Stock Streete* 1652 *FF*

From stocc, 'stump.' For *street* cf. *supra* 254.

STUDLEY is *Stodleia* 12th AD vi, 1196 Cur, 1198 Abbr, *-lega* 1175 P, *-legh* 1249, *-le* 1268 *Ass, Stodleye juxta Calne* 1296 *FF, Stodelegh juxta Bremel* 1370 *Ass, Studley Gate* 1653 Survey. 'Horse clearing,' *v.* stod, leah. *Bremel* is Bremhill *supra* 86.

TASWORTH (lost)

> *Tesewurth'* 1245 WM xvi, *Tesworth al. Tosworthes* t. Eliz
>   ChancP
> *Tasewarde* 1255 RH (p), *Thase-* 1265, *Tasseward* 1274 Ipm,
>   *Thasewarde* 1289 *Ass*, *Tasseworth* 1327 *SR* (p)
> *Taseworth* 1305 *FF*, 1332 *SR* (p), 1336 Pat, 1536 *MinAcct*

This name clearly contains the same first element as Tawsmead *infra* 318, found also perhaps in *Teasleye* (1509 *DuLa*) in
Aldbourne. It is probable that in all these names alike we have
the OE adj. *tǽse*, 'convenient, for general use.' *v.* worþ and
cf. Atworth *supra* 115.

WHETHAM is *Wetham* 1257, *Whet-* t. Ed 1 *For*, 1273, 1374 *FF*,
1503 Ipm, *Whetehamme* 1327 *SR*. 'Wheat ham(m).'

WHITLEY FM is *Wittelega* 1167 P, *Witele* 1242 Fees, *Whytele*
1279, 1321 *Ass*, *Whitelegh* 1332 *SR*. 'White clearing or wood,'
v. leah.

COOMBE GROVE[1] (6″), DEEPET'S WOOD[2] (6″) and HAYLE FM[3]
were probably the homes of Aylfrith de *Cumbe* (1268 *Ass*),
William de *Depegate* (1275 RH, 1279 *Ass*) and Alditha de *la Hele*
(t. Ed 1 *Lacock*). *v.* cumb, geat, healh, 'corner,' and *infra* 373.

BROAD'S GREEN[4], COLEMAN'S FM, CUFF'S CORNER[5] (6″), KNIGHT'S
MARSH[6] (6″), PINHILLS FM[7], SCOTT'S FM and THEOBALD'S
GREEN[8] are to be associated with the families of John *Brode*
(1369 *MinAcct*), William *Colman* (1547 *SR*), Edmond *Cuffe*
(ib.), Nicholas *le Knyght* (1368 *For*), Richard *Pinel* (1274 WIpm),
John *Scott* (1695 WM xlvii) and William *Teobald* (1369 *MinAcct*).

---

[1] *Coome Grove* 1562 Marsh.
[2] *Dippits* c. 1840 *TA*. 'Deep gate,' or 'gap,' the *s* being pseudo-
manorial.
[3] Cf. *Hayll Lanne* 1603 Sess, *Hayle Lane, Hayles Common* 1630 WIpm.
[4] *Brode juxta Calne* 1547 *FF*, *Broads pece* 1650 *ParlSurv*.
[5] *Cuffs Gate* 1653 *Survey*, *Cuffs Corner* 1773 A and D.
[6] *Knights Marsh* ib.
[7] *Pynelesplace* 1409 AD i, *Pynne Hills* 1557 PCC, *Pinnells Lane* 1763 *Map*.
Aubrey's grove of pines (NH 57) clearly had nothing to do with the name.
[8] *Thebalds* 1503 *MinAcct*, *Tibbals Green* 1694 Devizes, *Tebolds Green* 1773
A and D. The last two forms show a popular pronunciation, cf. Theobald
Street (PN Herts 61–2).

ABBOTT'S WASTE (6″) is so named in 1650 (*ParlSurv*). BASSETT'S MOOR (6″) is *Bassetts moore* ib. Cf. Compton Bassett *infra* 262 near by. BERHILLS FM (6″) is *Berehille* 1305 Pat, *Berihill* 1471 WM xxxiv, *Bury-* 1518 ECP, *Berrils* 1773 A and D. BLACKLAND is *Blakeland* 1195 P *et freq* to 1332 *SR*, with variant spelling -*lond*, *Blaklond* 1232 Ch, *Blacklonde* 1316 FA. BODNAGE COPSE (6″). Cf. *Bottenodge* (sic) t. Jas 1 BorRec. BRICKKILN WOOD (6″). Cf. *Brickhill* 1754 *Map* and Brickkiln Copse *supra* 36. BROKEN CROSS (6″) is *Brokencross* c. 1840 *TA*. BUCK HILL is *Buckhill* 1650 *ParlSurv*. CALNE LOW is *Ye Lowe* 1649 *SarumD* and *C*, *Calston Low* 1773 A and D, i.e. 'the hill.' CALNE MARSH is *la Mershe de Calne* 1305 *Ass*. CASTLEFIELDS (6″) is *Castylfelde* 1493–1500 ECP. CLARK'S HILL. Cf. *Clerkesmede* 1500 Ipm. CLOSE WOOD is *Closewood* 1592 *Add*. CONIGRE FM is *Conygre Farm* 1773 A and D. *v. infra* 427. COWAGE FM (6″) is *Cowich*, *Cowidge* 1642 WIpm, *Cowadge al. Cowidge* 1731 *Recov*. Cf. Cowage *supra* 70, *infra* 269. EASTMANSTREET (lost) is *Estman-stre(e)t* 1332 *SR*, t. Jas 1 ECP, *Eastman Street* 1695 WM xlvii. It is another name for the Hilmarton road. HIGHLANDS is so named in 1820 (G). HOLLY DITCH FM (6″). Cf. *Holly Ditch* 1773 A and D. HONEYBALL PLANTATION (6″). Cf. *Honeyball* c. 1840 *TA*. HOPYARD COPSE (6″). Cf. *le Hoppe yard* 1590 *Add*, *Hopgarden* 1642 WIpm, *v. infra* 452. THE KNOWLE (6″) is so named c. 1840 (*TA*). *v.* cnoll. LABOUR IN VAIN HILL. Cf. *Labour in vain* 1773 A and D and *infra* 455. LAGGUS FM is *Lagges* 1576 *Add*, *Lagas* 1763, *Laggus* 1829 *Map*. The land is low-lying and we possibly have the plural of dial. *lag* (So), 'long marshy meadow.' LICKHILL FM is so named in 1649 (*Sarum-D and C*). LODGE FM. Cf. *Upper, Lower Lodge* 1650 *ParlSurv*. MILE ELM is so named in 1773 (A and D). MONKS HILL WOOD (6″). Cf. *Monks Hill* 1653 *Survey*. NEWCROFT FM (6″) is *Niwe-crofte* 1245 WM xvi. NORLEY (6″) is *Northeley* 1377 *MinAcct*, *Norley* 1549 Pat. *v.* leah. NUTHILLS (6″) is *Nutthills* 1773 A and D. HIGH PENN FM and PENN HILL FM (6″). See Lower Penn Fm in Hilmarton *infra* 269. PILPOT WOOD (6″) is *Filpott Coppice* 1650 *ParlSurv*, *Pilpot Division* 1653, *Pilpot* 1725 *Map*. 'Fill-pot' is fairly common as a complimentary nickname. The later forms may be corrupt. POOLE'S FM (6″). Cf. *Pools Leaze* c. 1840 *TA*. QUEENWOOD is *The Quenes wood* 1568 *For*, *Queen*

Wood 1754 *Map*. QUOBBS FM (6″). Cf. *Quabbs* 1694 *Devizes* and *infra* 445. RANSCOMBE BOTTOM is so named c. 1840 (*TA*). RATFORD COTTAGES (6″). Cf. *pontem de Redford* 1289 *Ass*, *Ratford Bridge* 1773 A and D, *Radford Bridge* 1829 *Map*, now RATTLE BRIDGE. Probably 'reed ford,' *v.* hreod. RED HILL (6″) is *Redhill* 1650 *ParlSurv*. 'They digge plenty of ruddle' (Aubrey NH 39). ROUGH LEAZE (6″) is *Rowghlyes* t. Jas 1 *SP*, *v.* læs. RUMSEY HO. Cf. *Rumseys Pleck* 1653 *Survey*, probably named from a former owner. Romsey Abbey had no land here. SANDS FM. Cf. *Little Sandes* 1549 *Pat*, *The Sands* c. 1840 *TA*. SEARCHERS WOOD (6″) is *Searchers* ib. SPRAYS FM (6″). Cf. *Spray* 1242 SarumCh, *Sprays Mill* 1694 *Devizes* and Hamspray *infra* 348. TYNING BARN (6″). Cf. *The Tyning* c. 1840 *TA* and *infra* 449. WASHWAY is *The Washway* 1653 *Survey*. WESSINGTON (6″) is *Westyngton* 1527 Marsh, *Wessington* c. 1840 *TA*. It is not 'west' in relation to any part of Calne parish.

Cherhill

CHERHILL [tʃeril]

Ciriel 1155, 1194 RBE, 1275 Cl, *Cyriel* 1235 Fees, 1265 Ipm
Ceriel 1156, 1157, 1177, 1195, 1202 P, *Ceriol* 1166 RBE
Cheriel 1166 P, 1324 FA, *Cheryell* 1523 *SR*, 1546 LP
Chirieli (sic) 1198 Abbr, *Chiriel* 1221 ClR, 1235, 1242 Fees,
    1265 Ipm, 1275 RH, 1280 Ch, 1284 AD iv, 1299, 1315 Cl,
    Chiriell 1281 *Ass*, *Chiryell* 1402 FA, *Chiryel* 1446 Pat
Chyriel 1207 ClR, 1242 Fees, 1249, 1268 *Ass*, 1267 SarumCh,
    1277 FF, 1297 Ipm, *Chyryell* 1447 Pat
Churiel 1275 Ipm, t. Ed 2, 1345 *Ass*, 1332 *SR*, -*yel* 1397 Pat
Churhull 1294 Pat
Chyrrele 1316 FA
Cheryell al. Chirrell 1581 DKR xxxviii, *Chirrell* t. Eliz WM
    xxi, *Cherrell* 1637 *Phillipps*, *Cherle* 1656 *Devizes*, *Cherell*
    1668 FF

This is a difficult name. The second element is doubtless the British word *ial*, 'fertile upland,' etc. found in Deverill and Fonthill (*supra* 6, 190). For the first element Ekwall DEPN (*s.n.*) tentatively suggests the British *caer*, 'fort, camp,' common in the place-names of Wales, Cornwall and Cumberland, with reference to the camp at Oldbury Castle *infra* 262, but the full list of early spellings given above hardly allows this. It may be that we should, as suggested by Professor Max Förster, compare Polkerth (Co), *pollicerr* 977, *pollcerr* 1059 Earle, *Polkere* 1291 Exon. This may well be a stream-name, related to Ceri and Ceiriog (Wales), Carey (D), cf. Ekwall RN *s.n.* Carey. In Cherhill the reference might be to the small stream which joins the Marden at Quemerford. Professor Max Förster notes also OWelsh *ryt y cerr* (LibLand 247), *ryt* answering to ModWelsh *rhyd*, 'ford.'

MILL FM was the home of Stephen *atte Mulle* (1327 *SR*).

CHERHILL FIELD is *Cherrell feild* t. Eliz *LRMB*, with reference to the open common fields of the village. CHERHILL LOW (6″) is *The Low, The Low Common* c. 1840 *TA*, *v.* hlaw, 'hill.' GORES PLANTATION (6″). Cf. *la Gore* 1265 Ipm, *the Gore* t. Eliz *LRMB*, *v.* gara. THE LYNCHETTS (6″) is *Linchetts* c. 1840 *TA*, *v. infra* 453. OARE FM [*olim* hwə·r] (6″). Cf. *Oar Furlong* c. 1840 *TA* and ora *infra* 442. OLDBURY CASTLE is *Oldebyry* 1265 Ipm, *v.* burh. There is an old earthwork here.

Compton Bassett

COMPTON BASSETT

> *Contone* 1086 DB, *Comtona* 1182 BM, *Cumptone Basset* 1228 SarumCh, 1272 Ipm, (*juxta Calne*) 1282 *Ass*, *Compton juxta Calne* 1334 *Ass*, 1403 *FF*

'Farm in the combe or valley,' *v.* cumb, tun. Fulke *Basset* held the manor in 1242 (Fees).

NOTE. JUGGLER'S LANE. Cf. *Jugglers* c. 1840 *TA*. SILVER LANE is *Silver Street* 1818 O.S. Note also *le Drafwey* 13th AD iii, *v. infra* 429.

NOLANDS FM is *Aldelande, -lond* t. Hy 3 AD vi, *Oldelonde* 14th AD ii, *Nollens* 1773 A and D. 'Old land,' i.e. probably 'land out of cultivation,' cf. Yolland (PN D 465). The later and modern forms go back to ME *atten olde land*, *v.* æt.

BREACH FM was the home of Adam *atte Breche* (1327, 1332 *SR*). *v.* bræc *infra* 423.

DUGDALES HO (6″) is to be associated with the family of Richard *Dugdale* (c. 1840 *TA*).

Asн Bed (6″) is so named in 1818 (O.S.). Berry Mead (6″) is *Burymede* 1493 *MinAcct*, t. Hy 8, *Berry Mead* c. 1840 *TA*. Blackwell Wood (6″). Cf. *Great, Picked Blackwells* ib. *v. infra* 443. Freeth Fm is *Frith alias Freeth* 1671 *Recov*, *Freeth Fm* 1773 A and D. *v.* fyrhðe, 'wooded country.' Horn Wood (6″) is *Hornwode* 1270 *For*. Long Oatlands (6″). Cf. *Oatland Croft* c. 1840 *TA*. Oak Bed (6″) is so named c. 1840 (*TA*). Starve Knoll is no doubt an uncomplimentary nickname, *v. infra* 455. Withy Bed (6″) is so named c. 1840 *TA*.

Heddington

Heddington

> *Edintone* 1086 DB, *Hedinton(a)*, -*y*- 1203, 1229 FF *et freq* to
>   1332 *SR*
> *Heddendon* 1212 Cur, 1216 Abbr, *Hedyndon* 1289 *Ass*
> *Hedington* 1222, 1238 FF, 1229 Cl, 1316 FA, -*yngton(e)* 1307
>   Sarum, 1330 *FF*, (*Cantelo*) 1403 IpmR
> *Heddenton al. Heddington* 1618 *FF*

'*Hedde*'s farm,' *v.* ingtun. Robert de *Cantilupo* held the manor in 1316 (FA).

The Splatts is *le Splotte* 1526 *Ct*, *The Splatt* 1696 NQ ii, *Splats* 1773 A and D. This is OE *splot*, 'small patch of land,' discussed in PN D 137 and *infra* 446. Cf. Splot (Glam), *the Splott* 1393 NCPNW 161, *la Splotte* 1249 *FF* (in Long Sutton, Ha) and *Splotlond* 1351 Manydown (in Hannington, Ha).

Heddington Wick was the home of Alice *atte Wike* (1288 *Ct*) and is *Wike* 1540 *MinAcct*. *v.* wic and *supra* 25.

Eyres Fm is to be associated with the family of James *Eyre* (c. 1840 *TA*).

Beacon Hill is *Beacon Down Hill* 1773 A and D. Harley Cottages (6″) is *Harley* c. 1840 *TA*. As they are on the parish boundary the first element is probably har, denoting something on the boundary, hence 'boundary wood or clearing.' Kings Play Hill is *Kings Play Down* 1773 A and D and is said to be so called from the complete Royalist victory at Roundway Down in 1643 (WM vi, 137).

Yatesbury

YATESBURY

Etesberie 1086 DB

Hyatebir' 1199 FF, Yatebur' 1279 Ass, -bury 1297 Cl

Yttebir' 1207 FineR

Jetebur 1222 FF, Yetebir' 1249 Ass, -biry 1252 Pat, -bur' 1259 Cl

Getesbir 1226 SarumCh, Yetesbur 1239 Ch, -bury 1306 Ass, Jetesbir' c. 1250 Rental, Yetesbir 1247–51 Ch

Gytesbyre c. 1230 SarumCh, Yites-, Ʒitesbir' 1242 Fees, Ytesbyr' 1249 Ass

Yatesbur' 1242 Fees, 1249 Ipm, 1255 RH, -biry 1258 FF, -buri 1283 FF, Iatesbur' 1332 SR, Yhatesbyr' 1268 Ass

Yettesbiry 1263 Pat, -bur' t. Ed 1 DuLa

Yattebur' 1289 Ass, Yattesbur' 1291 Tax, -bury 1316 FA

Yeatesbury 1602 NQ vii, Yatsbury 1632 Recov, Yeatsbury 1700 FF

Examination of the site makes it very difficult to accept Ekwall's suggestion (DEPN *s.n.*) that the first element here is OE *geat* in the sense 'pass, gap,' for it is impossible to find such. A further difficulty in the name is to know whether the first element should really be taken as *geat* or *geates*. If the latter is correct, it is more likely that the first element is a personal name. As a personal name *Gēat* is only on very early record in OE but it is found as the first element in the woman's name *Gēatflǣd*. Cf. Eaton (PN Sr 88). Hence, possibly, '*Geat*'s burh.'

LITTLE LONDON. Cf. *infra* 455. It is on the outskirts of the village. STERT POND (6″). Cf. *Stert Leaze, Stert Penning* c. 1840 *TA* and steort *infra* 447. TOWN'S END. Cf. *Townsend Furlong* ib. VULPIT (6″) may be for earlier *Wulpit* or *Wolfpit* as suggested by Smith (93). If so, we have *v* for *w* as occasionally found in Devon, cf. PN D Pt. I, xxxv. YATESBURY FIELD. Cf. *North-, Suthfeld* 1570 PembSurv, with reference to the open common fields of the township.

XXII. KINGSBRIDGE HUNDRED

Chinbrige, Chingbrigge hundred 1086 ExonDB, *Chinbrigehðr* 1159, *Kingesbrigge hðr* 1174, *Kinbrigehðr* 1184 P, *Hundred de Kingbrig'* 1196 Cur, 1198 Abbr, 1255 RH, *Kinbrig* ib., *Kingbrygge* 1297 Ipm, *Kingbrigge* 1316 FA. The Hundred has absorbed the old Hundreds of Blackgrove and Thornhill *infra* 274, 281. The traditional meeting-place is in Clyffe Pypard parish, half a mile north-west of Woodhill Park (cf. NQ i, 413–5).

Broad Town

BROAD TOWN[1]

> *Bradetun* 12th AD v, *Labradeton* 1205 Cur, *La Bradetune*
> 1220 AD iv, *Bradeton* 1231, 1241 Cl, 1242 Fees
> *Brodetone* 1206 FF, 1272 Ipm, *la Brodetoun* 1280 AD iv
> *la Brode towne al. Brodeouer* 1295 StNicholas
> *Brodtoune* 1439, *-towne* 1503 Pat

'Great farmstead,' *v.* brad, tun. *Broad* or 'great' in contrast to Little Town *infra*, cf. Broad Chalke *supra* 203–4. *Brodeouer* presumably has reference to Broadtown Hill (*v.* ofer) on the lower slopes of which Broad Town lies.

NOTE. HORN'S LANE is to be associated with the family of Richard *Horne* (1669 ParReg). VIZE WAY (local), *la Visweia* 13th AD vi, is an ancient track running from Broad Hinton by Whyr Fm towards Devizes (E. H. G.).

COTMARSH FM is *Cotemershe* 1356 *Ass*, *-merssh* 1424 AD vi, *Cottemersh* 1454 IpmR, *Cotemarshe* t. Eliz WM xxi, *Cotmarshe* 1602 *FF*. Probably 'marsh marked by cottages.'

LITTLE TOWN is *Lytelton* 1247 FF, *Litel-* 1348 *FF*, *la Lyteletoune* 1349 WM xxxix, 1350 Ipm, *Liteltowne* 1497 Ipm. So named in contrast to Broad Town *supra*.

THORNHILL is *Tornelle, Tornvele* 1086 DB, *Thornehille* 13th AD vi, *Thornhull(e)* 1289 *Ass*, 13th *Bradenstoke*, 14th AD vi. Self-explanatory.

---

[1] A modern parish formed chiefly from Clyffe Pypard, partly from Broad Hinton in Selkley Hundred.

SEAGAR'S FM (6″) is to be associated with the family of Joseph *Seager* (1706 *Brasenose*).

BARNHILL FM (6″). Cf. *Barn Hill* 1773 A and D. BROAD TOWN HILL. Cf. *The Hill Furlong or Smock Acre* 1725 WM xlvi. See *infra* 446. GOLDBOROUGH (6″) is *Gold Borough* 1773 A and D, *Cole Borough Fm* 1818 O.S. HAM FM is *le Hamme* 1294 *Rental*, 14th *Bradenstoke, Ham* 1570 *FF, v.* hamm. MARSTON FM (6″). Cf. *Mersh juxta Brodetoune* 1320 *FF*. SNOW HILL (6″) is so named in 1773 (A and D). SPRINGFIELD HO. Cf. *Spring Field* c. 1840 *TA*. WHITE WAY (6″) is *Witeweya* 13th AD vi.

Clyffe Pypard

CLYFFE PYPARD[1] [*olim* kli·v pipər, *vel* pepər, *nunc vero* paipəd]

> *æt Clife* 983 (c. 1150) KCD 636
> *Clive* 1086 DB, 1191 P, 1231 Cl, 1242 Fees
> *Cliva in Wiltescira* t. Hy 2 (1290) Ch, (*Pipard*) 1242 Fees, *Pippardesclyve* 1282 Cl, *Clive Pip(p)ard* 1291 Tax, 1332 *SR, Piperesclyve* c. 1340 BM, *Cleve Pepper* 1570 *FF, Clevepeper, Clivepiper* t. Eliz WM xxi, *Cleeve alias Clieff Pypard* 1603 *Recov, Cleave Pepper* 1689 *Sadler, Cleve Pipper* 1714 WM xliv

> *v.* clif, 'slope,' etc. Richard *Pipart* held the manor in 1231 (Cl), spelt *Pipard* in 1242 (Fees).

NOTE. BREACH LANE is so named in 1773 A and D. Cf. *Breach* 1549 WM xliv and bræc *infra* 423.

THE BARTON (locally *Barken*) is the name of a group of cottages, *Barken Ham* 1818 O.S. Cf. *infra* 451.

BUPTON is *Bubbeton* 1283, 1529 *FF*, 1332 *SR* (p), *Bobeton* 1319, 1336, *Bobbeton* 1336, 1386, 1387, *Bubeton* 1532 WM xxxv, *Bubton* 1535 VE. This is a late tun-formation. William *Bubbe* owed service in *Clyve* in 1255 (RH). See Addenda *supra* xl.

BUSHTON is *Bissopeston, -y-* 1242 Fees, 1268 *Ass, Bushepeston* 14th *Bradenstoke, Bisshopeston* 1316 FA, *Bushton* t. Eliz ChancP,

---

[1] In WM xliv, 143 the local rhyme is quoted:
White Cleeve, Pepper Cleeve, Cleeve and Cleveancy,
Lyneham and lousy Clack, Cris Mavord (Christian Malford) and Dauntsey.

Busheton 1626 WIpm, *Bushen* 1753 *Map*. 'Bishop's farm,' *v.* tun. The name represents the manor of *Clive* held in DB by the Bishop of Winchester. It is therefore a late tun-formation. For the modern form cf. Bishton (Gl, Sa, St).

THE MERMAID (6″)[1] is locally called *Meremaid* but there is no tradition or likelihood of an inn here (E. H. G.). Perhaps the second element is mæd, 'meadow.' We are on the parish boundary here so the first element may be (ge)mære, 'boundary' (*infra* 441), but mere, 'mere,' is also possible as there are pools here.

STANMORE COPSE lies on the borders of Clyffe Pypard and Winterbourne parishes, while *Stanmore Meadow* (c. 1840 *TA*), just to the east, lies wholly in the parish of Winterbourne Bassett. Jones (232) shows good reason for identifying *Stanmore* with the DB manor of *Stamere* in Selkley Hundred, *Stanmere* 1242 Fees, 1275 RH. The only other reference that has been noted is *two closes called Stamner* (sic) 1626 Ipm. 'Stone pool,' *v.* stan, mere.

WOODHILL PARK [*olim* oudəl] is *Wadhulle* 1086 DB, *-hella* t. Hy 2 (1270), *-hull* 1269 Ch, *Wahulle* 1198 Abbr, 1233 Cl, 1242 Fees, 1248 Ch, *Wodhulle* 1242 Fees, *Wodehull* 1251 FF, *Woodhull* 1418 WM xxxv, *Odehill* 1497 Ipm, *Upper Woodhill* 1652 *FF*, *Oad Hill Park* 1773 A and D, *Oadle Park* 1820 G. 'Hill where woad grew,' from OE wad and hyll. Cf. Odell (PN Beds 34).

MILL MEAD is *Mill Meade* 1626 WIpm and was probably the home of John *atte Mulle* (1342 NI).

QUENTIN'S COPSE[2] and SMITH'S FM (both 6″) are to be associated with the families of Wm *Quintin* (1255 RH) and William *Smith* (1591 ParReg).

CLYFFE PYPARD WOOD is *Cleveswode* 1531 *FF*. Locally still always *Cleeves Wood* (E. H. G.). HYDE BARN (6″). Cf. *Hyde* c. 1840 *TA*. *v.* hid. NEBO FM is so named in 1818 (O.S.). It is on the top of the escarpment and is presumably so nicknamed from Mt. Nebo in Palestine. Near by is Jericho Field *infra* 494. NONESUCH is *None Such* 1773 A and D. Cf. *supra* 255. PARSONAGE

---

[1] *Mermaid Ground* c. 1840 *TA*.   [2] *Quentins* ib.

Fm (6″). Cf. *Parsonage Fd* c. 1840 *TA* and *infra* 456. Rebel Cottages (6″). Cf. *Rebbell* 1773 A and D, *Rebhill* c. 1840 *TA*. South Fm (6″) is so named in 1777 (*Brasenose*). Windmill Hill. Cf. *Windmylfeld* 1540 *MinAcct*, *Windmill Meade* 1626 WIpm. Wood Street is *Woods Street* 1773 A and D.

Hilmarton

Hilmarton [hil′maˑrtən]

>*Helmerdingtun* 962 (13th) BCS 1081
>
>*Helmerintone* 1086 DB
>
>*Helmertune, Adhelmertone* ib., *Helmerton* 1198 Fees *et passim* to 1428 FA
>
>*Hilmerton* 1349 Cl, 1574 BM, *Helmarton, Hilmarton* t. Eliz WM xxi
>
>*Hill Martyn* 1699 ParReg
>
>'*Helmheard*'s farm,' *v.* ingtun.

Beacon Hill is *Bignall Hill* 1773 A and D and is held by Jones (198) to be the *Bichenehilde, Bechenehilde* of 1086 (DB). If this identification is correct it may be that this name is a compound of OE *bēacen*, 'sign,' and hielde, helde, 'slope.'

Beversbrook is *Bevresbroc, Brevresbroc* 1086 DB, *Beveresbrok* 1242 Fees, 1249 *Ass*, 1298 Sarum *et freq* to 1381 *FF, Beversbrok* 1273 Cl, *Besbrooke al. Beversbrooke* 1622 *Recov*. 'Beaver's brook,' *v.* broc.

Catcomb is *Cadecoma* 1114 France, *-cumb'* 1241 Cl, *-combe* 1334, *Catecumbe* 1249 *Ass, Catcombe* 1570 *Add*. '*Cada*'s cumb.' Cf. the close-by Cadenham and Cat Brook *supra* 87, 5.

Clevancy[1] [kli′vænsi]

>*Clive* 1086 DB, c. 1220 *Magd*
>
>*Clif Wauncy* 1231 FF, *Clive Wancy* 1232 Ch, 1242 Fees, *Clyvewancy* 1249 *Ass, Clifwancy* 1255 RH, *Clyve Wauncy* 1316 FA
>
>*Clyve Auncy* 1428 FA, *Cleveansey* 1580, *Clevauncey* 1592 *FF, Cleeve Ansty al. Cleeve Ancey* 1726 *Recov*

[1] In Cliffansty Ho (6″) in Clevancy we have a name which has no authority except the fancy of a late owner (WM xliv, 143).

v. clif. Robert de *Wancy* held the manor c. 1220 (*Magd*), Ralph de *Wauncy* in 1249 (*Ass*). For the agglutination of the two words cf. Stogumber, Stogursey (So).

CORTON MANOR is *Corfton(e)* 1195 P, Cur *et freq* to 1332 *SR*, *Corfeton* 1195 Cur, *Corton* 1544 *SR*. The name is identical in origin with Corton Denham (So), *Corfetone* 1086 DB, *Corftona* 1167 P. Behind Corton there is a small gap in the escarpment up which you make your way to the ground on the top. This is doubtless the word *corf*, 'cutting' or 'gap.' Hence 'farm by the gap.' Cf. Corfe (PN Do 116–7) and *dich corf* (BCS 867) in Idmiston.

COWAGE FM is *Cowic* 1086 DB, *Cuwike* 1256 FF, *Kuwich* 1265 Ipm, *Couwych* 14th *Bradenstoke*, *Koweche* 1510 PCC, *Cowych* 1546 LP, *Cowage* 1704 WM xxiv, *Cowitch* c. 1840 *TA*. 'Cow dairy farm,' cf. Cowick (PN D 438), Cowage Copse in Steventon (Ha), *bosc. de Cowyk* 1269 *For* and Cowage Fm *supra* 70, 260.

GOATACRE is *Godacre* 1242 Fees, *Got-* 1268 FF, 1289, 1345 *Ass*, 1307 Ipm, 1332 *SR*, *Gateacre al. Goteacre* 1618 *FF*. Self-explanatory. *v.* gat, æcer.

HIGHWAY

> *Hiw(e)i* 1086 DB, *Hywey* 1219 SarumCh *et passim* to 1347 Pat, with variant spellings *Hi-* and *-wei(e)*
> *Heiewei* 1153, *Heywey* 1156 RegMalm, *Heyweye* 1321, 1346 *Ass*
> *Hieweye* c. 1250 *Rental*, 1364 Pat, *Hyeweye* 1287 *FF*
> *Hegheweye* 1289 *Ass*, *Heghweye* 1327 *FF*, 1345 *Ass*
> *Hygheweye* 1332 *SR*, *Hyghwey* 1512 *Ct*
> *Hewey* 1522 *SR*
>
> 'High' or (perhaps) 'hay' road. *v.* weg and cf. DEPN *s.n.*

LITTLECOTT is (*æt*) *lytla coton* 962 (13th) BCS 1081, *Litlecote* 1086 DB, *Littlecot'* 1232 Ch, *Litelecot* 1265 *Magd*, *Lettelecote* t. Ed 1 *DuLa*, *Luttlecote* 1332 *SR*, *Lytelcote by Lynham* 1412 Pat, (*juxta Helmerton*) 1447 *FF*. Self-explanatory. *v.* cot(e).

LOWER PENN FM[1]. Cf. *Penne* c. 1250 *Rental*, *la Penne* 1256 FF, 1279 *Ass* (p), 1369 *MinAcct*, (*juxta Calne*) 1438 *FF*, *Beveres-*

---

[1] With High Penn Fm and Penn Hill Fm (6″) in Calne. The latter is *Woodhills* 1829 *TA*.

brokes penne 1357 *GDR*, *Pennemersh* 1386 Cl, *Pen* 1704 WM xxiv. See Pen Hill *supra* 34.

WITCOMB FM is *Widecome* 1086 DB, *Widecumba* 1242 Fees, *Wydecumbe* 1249, 1279, *Widekumbe juxta Helmerton* 1282 *Ass*, *Wydecombe* 1505 FF, *Whytcoumbezate* 1512 *Ct*. 'Wide valley,' *v*. cumb. Cf. Widcombe (PN D 626).

SPILLMAN'S FM (6") is to be associated with the family of John *Spileman* (1332 *SR*).

CORTON HILL. Cf. *Hulleforlong* 1333 *Magd*, *v*. Corton *supra* 269. FOGHAMSHIRE (local). *v. supra* 90. HILMARTON PENNING (6"). *v. infra* 453. MARSH FM is *le Mersshe* 14th *Bradenstoke*, *Lytlecote Marshe* 1557 Pat. NEW ZEALAND is in a remote part of the parish, *v. infra* 455. RODWELL FM is *Rodwell* 1773 A and D. SANDY FURLONG (6") is so named c. 1840 (*TA*). SWILL PLANTATION (6"). Cf. *Swill Field* ib. It lies by a feeder of Cowage Brook and *swill* is doubtless the name of the small stream, cf. Swill Brook *supra* 10. UNDER SHERIFF'S CLUMP (6"), planted in memory of W. H. Poynder, sheriff.

Lyneham

LYNEHAM

> *Linham* 1224 SarumCh, *Lynham* 1268 *Ass et freq* to 1349 FF, with variant spelling *Lin-*
> *Lyneham* 1571 *SR*, *Linum* 1694 ParReg

'ham(m) where flax was grown,' *v*. lin.

BRADENSTOKE-CUM-CLACK [breidənstouk *vulgo* brædstɔk]

> *Stoche* 1086 DB
> *Bradenestoche* ib., -*stoch* t. Hy 2 (1355) Pat, -*stoca*, -*e* 1189 GlastInq, 1196 Cur, -*stok(e)* 1198 Abbr, 1205 ClR *et freq* to 1255 RH
> *Bradenstok* 1224 FF, 1349 *Ass*
> *Bradstock(e)* 1636 *Recov*, 1747 *Sadler*, *Broadstock* 1773 *Map*

'**stoc** or settlement attached to or belonging in some way to Braydon Forest' (*supra* 11). For **stoc** see Purton Stoke *supra* 39.

CLACK MOUNT is *Clak'* 1310 *Ass*, *Clacke* 1342 *GDR*, 1345, 1349 *Ass*, 1359 *AddCh*, *Clakke* 1427 *Pat*, 1535 *VE*, *Clack* 1639 *WIpm*. There is an earthwork here on a hill, the earthwork being of the castle-mound and bailey type. The name would seem to be identical with the Swedish *klack*, 'hill,' and other Scandinavian cognates discussed by Ekwall in NoB (viii, 89 ff.). It is difficult to believe that a Scandinavian loan-word could thus have come to be used in Wiltshire and we must probably look for some OE cognate. There is some evidence for an OE personal name *Clacc* (cf. PN Ess 334 *s.n.* Clacton) and it may be that side by side with this there was a common word *clacc*, its ultimate source. Cf. Clack Mead in Nettleton *infra* 467 and unidentified *Clack Linch* (1740 *Wilton*) in Ebbesborne Wake. Another example, just outside the county, is probably to be found in Clack Barn in Rockbourne (Ha), *molendin. de Clak* c. 1200 *Beaulieu Cartulary*, the home of Richard *atte Clakke* (1327 *SR*), *terra voc le Clacke* 1540 *MinAcct*, on a well-marked hill[1].

FREEGROVE FM is *le Frythe* 1249 *Ass*, *la Frith* 1343 *Phillipps*, *Frith grove* 1636 *WIpm*, *Freegrove* 1754 *Sadler*. *v.* fyrhðe, 'wooded area.'

LILLYBROOK (6″) may be connected with *Lynleye* 1289 *Ass* (p), *Lynleg'* 14th *Bradenstoke*, *Lynley* t. Hy 8 *AOMB*, the first element being the same as that in the parish name, *v.* leah.

POUND FM (6″) was the home of John de *la Punde* 1268 *Ass*. 'Cattle enclosure.' This example is some 150 years older than the earliest example of uncompounded *pund* as given in NED *s.v.* pound.

THE BANKS (6″) is so named c. 1840 (*TA*). COWLEAZE COPSE. Cf. *Cowleaze* 1636 *WIpm* and *læs infra* 438. CRANLEY FM is *Cranle* 1345 *Ass* (p), *Crandley* 1359 *AddCh*, *Cranleys* 1540 *MinAcct*. 'Crane (or heron) clearing,' *v.* leah. THE FOLLY. See *infra* 451. HILLOCKS WOOD. Cf. *Hillocks* 1773 *A and D*. LYNEHAM COURT is *Lineham Court* 1800 *Recov*. MIDDLEHILL FM is *Middlehill* 1635 *WIpm*. PRESTON is *Preston* 1289 *Ass*. 'Priests' farm,' *v.* tun. ROWLEY COPSE (6″). Cf. *Est-*, *West-*

---

[1] In the light of the evidence now collected, the conjecture with regard to this name made in PN Ess liv should probably be withdrawn.

rouleye 14th *Bradenstoke.* 'Rough clearing or wood,' *v.* ruh, leah. SHAW FM. Cf. *Shawe Croft* 1331 *MinAcct* and sceaga, 'wood.' THE STRINGS is the name of a narrow plantation in a long curving valley. Cf. *infra* 455. THICKTHORN FM. Cf. *Tikethorn* 1239 AD v, *prat. voc. Thyckethorne* 1540 *MinAcct.* Self-explanatory. Cf. Thickthorn in Marston Bigot (So), *Thikkethorn* 1238 Ass.

Tockenham

TOCKENHAM

> *Tockenham* 854 (15th) BCS 481, 1322 Cl, 1327 Pat, *Thokenham* 1202 FF, *Est Tokkenham* 1297 *FF*, *Tokkenham* 1316 FA, *Est-*, *Westockenham* 1332 *SR*, *Tokkenham by Lyneham* 1344 Pat
>
> *Tochehā* 1086 DB, *Tokeham* 1194 P, 1255 RH, *Thokeham* 1196 Cur, *Tocham* 1198 Fees, *West Tokeham* 1272 FF, *Tocke-* 1294 *FF*
>
> *Tokenham* 1289 *Ass*, *Tokynham* 1348 Pat

' *Toc(c)a*'s ham(m).' In the bounds of Clyffe Pypard adjoining (KCD 636) we have *tocan stan*, the same man giving name to the stone and the ham(m).

GREENWAY FM. Cf. *Green Way* 1773 A and D. TOCKENHAM WICK is *Tockenhamweke* 1559–79 ECP, *Tokenham Wike* 1561 *FF*, *Tottenham Weeke* t. Eliz WM xxi, *v.* wic and *supra* 25.

Wootton Bassett

WOOTTON BASSETT

> *Wdetun* 680 (c. 1125) BCS 54, 745 (14th) ib. 170, 937 (c. 1125) ib. 719
>
> *Wudetunnincga gemære* 983 (c. 1150) KCD 636, *Wutton* 1229 Cl, 1230 Ch
>
> *Wodetone* 1086 DB
>
> *Wotton(e)* 1211 RBE, *(Basset)* 1272 Ipm, *(juxta Bradestoke)* 1281 *Ass*, *Bassetteswotton* 1315 *FF*
>
> *Witun'* 1245 WM xvi
>
> *Olde Wotton* 1502 ECP, *(al. Wotton Bassett)* 1547 Pat

'Farm by the wood,' *v.* wudu, tun. Alan *Basset* acquired the manor before 1212 in right of his wife (Boarstall 312). The 983 form refers to the boundary of the people of Wootton, *v.* ingas, (ge)mære.

Note. Stoneover Lane. Cf. *Stoneover Mead* c. 1840 *TA. le Brode-weie* (1546 *Ct*) is later Broadway, part of the present Whitehill Lane (local). Cf. WM xxix, 195.

Vastern Manor

Fetstern 1229 Cl, 1230 Ch, BM

Fosterne 1235 AD ii, *la Fasterne* 1267 Pat, 1268 AD vi, 1281 Ipm, *Ass*

la Vasterne ib., 1300 AD iv, 1322 Cl, *Vasterne* c. 1300 Boarstall, *Vasterne al. Fasterne* 1547, *Vaston al. Fasterne* 1555 Pat

This is probably the OE *fæstærn*, 'stronghold,' the earliest spellings being corrupt. Cf. Vasterne Road outside the defensible area of medieval Reading. See also Holdfast PN Wo 140 and Buckfastleigh (PN D 293).

Woodshaw (6″) is *Wodeshawe* 1279 *Ass* (p), 1281 ib., *Wodeshaghe* ib., *Wydeschawe* 1327 *SR* (p), *Wodshawe* 1512 *Ct*. *v.* wudu, sceaga.

Greenhill Fm[1] and Grovehill Bridge[2] were the homes of John Simond de *Grenhulle* (1332 *SR*) and Henry *atte Grove* (1382 *MinAcct*).

Ballard's Ash[3], Hunt Mill[4] and Spratt's Barn (6″) are to be associated with the families of John *Baylard* (1332 *SR*), William *Hunt* (ib.) and Jacob *Sprot* (1279 *Ct*).

Brynards Hill is *Bryning Hill* 1676 WM xliv, *Brinders Hill* 1773 A and D. Coped Hall is *Coppid Hall* ib., i.e. a hall rising to a peak or *cop*, *v.* coppede and cf. Copped Hall (PN Ess 24). Coxstalls is *Coxtalls* 1783 *Devizes*. Dunnington Fm is *Downington* 1773 A and D. Folly Wood. Cf. *The Folly* c. 1840 *TA* and *infra* 451. Fowley (6″) is *Foulehille, Fowlehille* 1493 *MinAcct*. Bishop Fowley is *Bushey Fowlhill* (WM xxix, 195). 'Bird' or 'foul hill,' from OE *fugol* or ful. Harry's Croft is *Hariescrofte* 1493 *MinAcct*, *Harris Croft* 1659 Moulton. Hart Fm is so named c. 1840 (*TA*). Lawn Fm. Cf. *Wotton Launde*

[1] *Grenehull juxta Wotton Bassett* 1409 IpmR.
[2] Cf. *The Grove* 1676 WM xliv.
[3] *Baillardesasshe* t. Ed 3 *For*, *Baynards Ashe* 1602 WM xxxviii, *Banners Ash* 1773 A and D. [4] *Huntismylle* 1493 *MinAcct*.

t. Hy 8 *MinAcct* and **launde** *infra* 440. NORE MARSH is *Ore Marsh* 1815 O.S. It lies by a stream and the history of *Nore* is probably the same as that of *Nower* in Nower's Copse *supra* 188. OLD COURT (6″) is so named in 1281 (Ipm). OLD PARK FM. Cf. *parco de Wutton* 1230 Cl. PARADISE FM (6″). Cf. *Paradise* (field) c. 1840 *TA* and *infra* 453. WHITEHILL FM is *Whitehill* 1455 IpmR. THE WILDERNESS (6″) is so named c. 1840 (*TA*).

XXIII. BLACKGROVE HUNDRED

Blachegra(*ve*) *hundred* 1086 ExonDB, *Blakegrave* 1275 RH, 1280 Ipm, *Blacgrove* 1275 RH
Blachingravehðr 1159, *Blachingrave* hðr 1167, 1168 P, *Blachingegrave* hðr 1169 P, *Blakingrave* 1196 Cur, 1198 Abbr, 1211 RBE, 1255 RH, *Blakynggrave* 1249, 1305 *Ass*
Blakengrave 1255 RH, 1279 *Ass*

The meeting-place must have been at Blagrove Fm in Wroughton *infra* 279. The Hundred is now merged in Kingsbridge *supra* 265.

Lydiard Tregoze[1]

CHADDINGTON FMS

Chetindon 1242 Fees, *Chedington* 1324 Cl
Chatindon' 1245 WM xvi, *Estchatyndon* 1275 RH, *Chatyngton* 1301 Ipm, *Chatyndon*(*e*) 1303 Pat, 1330 Ipm, 1331 Cl
Estchatendon 1268 *Ass*
Chadinden', *Chadindone Bordevile* 1275 RH, *Est Chadynton* 1279, 1281, *Chadinton* 1289 *Ass*
Chadington 1281 QW
Chaddynton 1318 Pat, *Chaddenton* 1562 *FF*

'*Ceatta*'s hill or down,' *v.* ing, dun. William de *Burdeville* held the manor in 1242 (Fees).

HAGBOURNE COPSE is *Hagbourne Coppice* c. 1840 *TA*. The form *Hackburn* quoted *infra* 276 suggests that the stream here was so called from the numerous little turns in its course, deriving its name from OE *haca*, 'hook' and **burna**.

---

[1] For the parish-name, *v. supra* 35–6.

Hook and Hook Street are *la Hok(e)* 1238 Cl, 1257 *For*, 1268 *Ass*, 1275 RH, *Houke juxta Lydeyerd* 1327, *Hoke juxta Lydeyerd Treygos* 1345 *Ass*, v. **hoc**. Hook is on a well-marked spur of land. *hook* in Wiltshire dialect also denotes 'corner taken into cultivation,' cf. *supra* 134. Hook Street is a hamlet on a road leading to Hook, cf. *supra* 254.

Mannington

mehandun, mehhandun 900 (c. 1125, 14th) BCS 584, 585
Mekindon 1242 Fees
Meghedone 1275 RH, *Meghyndon* 1289 *Ass*, 1297 Inq aqd, 1304 Ch, *Meghynden(e), -i-* 1304, 1342, 1349 *FF*
Mehyndon 1289 *Ass*, *Meihyndon* 1332 *SR*
Mighenden 1353 *FF*, 1408 IpmR, *Myghendon* 1428 FA, *-den* 1529 *Rental*
Myhenden 1535 *FF*, *Myhinden* 1603 *Recov*
Mahington 1585 WM xxi, *Manington al. Mehington* t. Jas 1 ECP, *Marington* 1773 A and D
Meighendon 1805 O.S.

Professor Ekwall and Dr Ritter suggest a personal name *Mehha* as the first element in this name, but it is difficult to associate this with any known base and the history of the name must remain uncertain. The second element is **dun**.

Midgehall

(to) micghæma gemære 983 (c. 1150) KCD 636
Mighal' 1165 P, *Migghale* 1228 *For*, *Migehale* 1245 WM xvi, *Miggehale* 1257 *For*, 1320 Pat, *Michehale* 1268 *Ass*, *Myggehale* 1332, *Mygiall* 1524 *SR*, *Midgehall* 1558–79 ECP
Mudgehall 1571, *Mudghall* 1629 *SR*, *Mudghill al. Midghill al. Mygehale* 1686 *Recov*

'Corner of land frequented by midges' (OE *mycg*), v. **healh**. Cf. Midge Hall (PN La 133, 148). In the earliest form we have the OE *hæme* added as usual to the first element of the place-name to denote the inhabitants of the place, hence 'boundary of the people of Midgehall,' v. **(ge)mære**.

Frith Copse, Hern Barn (6″) and Lydiard Park[1] were the homes of Gilbert *del Frithe* (1257 *For*), John *atte Hurne* (ib.)

---

[1] Cf. *Parkwode* 1349 Ipm.

and Thomas *atte Hurne* (1281 *Ass*) and John *atte Park* (1332 *SR*). *v.* fyrhðe, 'wooded country,' and hyrne, 'angle, corner.'

BASSETT DOWN HO. Cf. *Bassettsdowne* 1637 *Phillipps*, from the family which held the nearby Wootton Bassett, *v. supra* 272. BROOK COTTAGES (6″). Cf. *Brook Mead* c. 1840 *TA*. CAN COURT is *Cancourt* 1560 *FF*, 1629 WIpm. CROW BRAKE (6″) is *Crow Breach* c. 1840 *TA*, *v.* bræc *infra* 423. FLAXLANDS is *Flexlands* 1722 *Sadler*, *Flackslands* 1773 A and D. GREENDOWN PLANTATION (6″). Cf. *Green Down Mead* c. 1840 *TA*. HIGHGATE FM. Cf. *Hie Gate* 1602 WM xxviii. HURST COPSE (6″) is *Hurst* 14th *Bradenstoke*, *v.* hyrst. THE MARSH is *Hackburn Marsh Farm* 1816 O.S. Cf. Hagbourne Copse *supra* 274 and *Lydyard merssh* 1512 *Ct*. PADBROOK FM is *Padbrooks* c. 1840 *TA*. PURLEY FM. Cf. *Great, Little Purlieu* ib. It lies on the bounds of Braydon Forest. Cf. purley *infra* 453. RED HOUSE (6″) is so named in 1820 (G). SPITTLEBOROUGH FM is *Spittelborough* 1554 NQ v. STUDLEY FM is *Stodlegh* 1275 RH, 1279 *Ass*. Cf. Studley *supra* 258. TOOT HILL is *Tothulle* 13th RegMalm, *Tutthill* t. Jas 1 ECP, *Marington Tootil* 1773 A and D. 'Look-out hill.' Cf. Mannington *supra* 275. *The Toot* is the name given to the isolated mound and ditch just to the east (School). WICK FM is *la Wik* 1235 Cl, *v.* wic and *supra* 25. WICKFIELD is *Wekefeld* 1554 NQ v, *Weekfield* 1590 *Sadler*, *Wakefield* 1815, *Wheatfield* 1818 O.S. WITHY BED (6″) is so named c. 1840 (*TA*).

Swindon

SWINDON

> *Suindone, -dune* 1086 DB, *Swindona, -e* 1156 RegMalm *et passim*, *Swinedon* 1205 ClR, *Nether, Alta Swindon'* 1275 RH, *West-, Heyswyndon, Chepyng Swyndon* 1289 *Ass*, *Hegheswyndon* 1311 Cl, 1324 FA, *Swyndon Valence* 1324 Ipm, *Higheswindon* 1409 IpmR, *Swyndon super montem* 1524, *East, West, Over, Nether Swindon* 1641 *Recov*, *East-swindon al. Netherswindon* 1642 WIpm
> *Swendone* 13th RegMalm, *Haute Swendon* 1255 RH, *West-sweyndon* 1279 *Ass*, *Sweyndon* 1473 Pat
> *Alta Swundone* 1275 RH

'Swine down or open land,' *v.* **dun**. *High* Swindon was no doubt the district round the old church, which stands high. *East, West* and *Nether* Swindon doubtless correspond to *Eastcott, Westcott* and *Nethercott infra. Chepyng* from the market here, *v.* **cieping**. Adomarus de *Valence* held the manor in 1316 (FA).

EASTCOTT, NETHERCOTT, WESTCOTT (lost)

> *Neyerkote* 1252 AD vi, *Nethercot(e)* 1255 RH, (*in the hundred of Blakegrove*) 1278 Ipm, (*juxta Hegheswyndon*) 1346 *Ass, Nethere-* 1276 FF, *Nuther-* 1337 Ipm
>
> *Estcote* 1276 FF, 1332 SR, (*juxta Hegheswyndon*) 1346 *Ass, Escote* 1340 FF, *Iskott* 1558–79 ECP, *Eastcott* 1820 G
>
> *Westcot(e)* 1289 *Ass*, 1332 *SR, Wescott* 1566 *Recov, Westcott* 1820 G
>
> *Nethercott oth. Eastcott oth. Westcott oth. Overcott* 1799 *Recov*

Former hamlets of Swindon, *v.* **cot(e)**, neoðera, 'lower.' Eastcott and Westcott are marked in Greenwood's map (1820), but the sites are now covered by the Railway works.

EVEN SWINDON[1] is *Theveneswyndon* 1247 FF, 1370 *Ass, Theuenesswendon* 1291 Cl, *Theveneswundon* 1313 FF, *Thevyng Swyndon* 1386 FF, *Swyndon al. Evon Swyndon* 1475, *Even-swendon* 1551 Pat, *Evanswindon* 1601 *Recov, Even Swindon* 1820 G. Probably the *even* or level Swindon in contrast to High Swindon. It is the site of New Swindon.

WALCOT is *Walecote* 1086 DB, *-cot(e)* 1198 FF, 1211 RBE, 1219 Abbr, 1242 Fees, (*juxta Swyndon*) 1281, (*juxta Heyswyndon*) 1289 *Ass, Wallecote* 1324 FA, *Walcote* 1477 FF. 'Cottages of the serfs or Britons,' *v.* **weala**, **cot(e)**.

KING'S HILL[2] and PIPER'S CORNER[3] (6″) are to be associated with the families of Robert *le Kyng* (1332 SR) and William *Pipard* (ib.).

BROOM MANOR is *Brome* 1242 Fees, 1249 *Ass*, 1305 Cl, 1332 SR, from OE *brōm*, 'broom' (the plant). BRUDDEL WOOD (6″) is

---

[1] Now covered by the Railway works. The name is still used officially of schools, etc. in this area (E. H. G.).

[2] *Kings Hill* 1773 A and D.

[3] *Pipers Corner* c. 1840 *TA*.

Brudenell c. 1840 *TA*. CHURCH FM is *Church Farm* ib. COATE is *la Kote* 1249 *Ass*, *la Cote* 1279 *Ct* (p), *v.* cot(e). MARSH FM (6"). Cf. *The Marshes* 1642 WIpm. OKUS is *Ocus* 1773 A and D, *Oak House* 1818 O.S., *Oacus* 1820 G. PARK FM. Cf. *the Parke* 1642 WIpm. RUSHEY PLATT (6") is *Rusia Platt* 1773 A and D, *v. infra* 443. WEST LEAZE is *Westleas* c. 1570 *Wilton*.

Wroughton

WROUGHTON [rɔ·tən]

(1) *Ellendun* c. 890 (*s.a.* 823 Ã) ASC, c. 1000 (ib. B), c. 1100 (ib. C), c. 1000 Ethelwerd, 956 (c. 1150) BCS 948, *Eallandun* c. 1100 (*s.a.* 823 D), *Ællandun* c. 1100 (ib. F), (*in*) *Ellandune, id est in monte Ealle* c. 1120 FW, *Ellandun* c. 1150 (*s.a.* 823 E) ASC, *Elendune* 1086 DB, *El(l)endon(e)* a. 1127 WintonCart, 1205 Pap, *Elendune* 1242 Fees, *Elindone* 1291 Tax, *Elyndon* 1324 WM xxxvi, *Elyngdon* 1330 FF, 1444 Pat, 1535 VE

(2) *Wertune, Wervetone* 1086 DB
Worfton 1196 Cur *et freq* to 1385 Pat, *Wourfton* 1285 Ch *Nether Werfton* 1236 FF, 1281, 1289 *Ass*, *Werfton* 1249 FF, *Ass*, *Overe-* 1279 ib., *Werfeton* 1399 Cl
Warfton 1236 FF, *Nether-* 1289 *Ass*, *Warghton* 1365 Cl *Worefton* 1242 Fees, *Nuther-* 1275 FF, *Uvere Werefton* 1242 Fees, *Wrfton(a)* 1242 Fees, 1300 Ch
Nether Wrofton 1418 Pat, *Nethyr Wroghton* 1428 FA
Over, Nether Wroughton 1466 IpmR, *Roahtun* 1655 ParReg

(3) *Elendone quod est Worftone* c. 1270 Winton, *Ellyngdon al. Wroughton* 1554 *FF*, 1555 Pat
Elington al. Wroughton t. Eliz ChancP, *Wroughton al. Elingdon* 1620 WM xxxvi

The present name means 'farm on the river *Worf*,' the old name for the Ray, *v.* tun and *supra* 9. The older alternative lost name is probably 'elder-tree down,' *v.* ellen, with early folk-etymologising in Florence of Worcester and elsewhere as if the name derived from a pers. name. Cf. *to þæm ællen stybbe* in the bounds of *Ellendun* (BCS 948).

BARBURY CASTLE and DOWN is (*æt*) *Beran byrg* c. 890 (*s.a.* 566 Ã) ASC, *Bereberia* 1180 France, *Berebyrie* 1252 BM, *-bury* 1332

SR, Berbyr' 1289 *Ass, -bury* 1391 Pat, *Barbery Downe* 1653, *Barbara(h) Down* 1673, 1759 *Recov.* '*Bera*'s burh.'

BLAGROVE FM is *boscus de Blakegrave, bosc. de Blakingrave, Blakengrove* 1268 *Ass, Blaggrave* 1287 Ipm, *Blakegrove* 1399 Pat, *Blakgrove* 1512 *Ct.* 'Black thicket,' see græfe *infra* 432–3. The Hundred meeting-place, *v. supra* 274. For the curious forms in *-ing-* found here and still more in the hundred-name, cf. the early forms of Shortengrove *supra* 216.

CHILTON (6″) is *Chilton* 1245 WM xvi, 1289, (*juxta Elecombe*) 1356, *Chylton* 1281, 1289 *Ass.* The forms are too late for us to decide whether this is OE *Cillan* tun, '*Cilla*'s farm,' or *cilda* tun, 'farm of the young men,' *v.* cild.

COSTOW FM is *Cotstowe* 1227 Ch, 1245 WM xvi, c. 1250 BM, *Cotestowe* 1231 Pat, *Costowe* 1242 Fees, *Cotestouwe* 1330 Ipm, *Castors Fm* 1815 O.S. 'Place or site of cot(e)' or cottage(s), *v.* stow. Cf. Costow (PN Nth 55) and *Costowesende* (1300 *For*) in Bedwyn Braile (H. C. B.).

ELCOMBE is *Elecome* 1086 DB, *-cumbe* 1242 Fees, 1253 FF, 1261 Cl, 1275 RH, *Ellecumba* 1168 P, *-cumb(e)* 1250 Ch, 1279, 1281 *Ass.* Probably 'elder-tree valley,' *v. Elyngdon supra* 278.

QUIDHAMPTON is *Quedanton* 1196 P, *Quidhampton* 1242 Fees, 1325 Ipm, *Quedhampton* 1242 Fees, 1268, 1324 WM xxxvi, 1279, 1289 *Ass*, 1332 *SR, Quidhampton al. Quiddington* 1832 *Recov.* Identical in origin with Quidhampton *supra* 226.

SALTHROP HO [sɔ·ltrəp]

  Salteharpe 1086 DB, 1279 *Ass, Sauteharp* 1198 FF
  Saltharp(e) 1241 Cl, 1245 WM xvi, 1268, 1303 *Ass*, 1330
    Ipm, *-harepe* 1242 Fees, *Saltharpesway* 1351 Pat
  Salthorp 1455 IpmR, *Salthroppe* 1524 *SR, Saltrop* t. Eliz
    WM xxi, 1603 *Recov, Saltrupp* 1629 *SR*

The same name apparently as *saltherpe* 956 (BCS 922) in the bounds of Brokenborough. Ekwall (*Studies* 82) takes both names as deriving from an OE **sealt-hearpe* used of a riddle for sifting salt, but has no suggestion to offer as to its local application. Note also South Harp in South Petherton (So), *Sutharpe* 1327 SR.

WESTLECOTT (6″)

> *Wichelestote* (sic) 1086 DB, *Wikelescote, -y-* 1175 P, 1225 FineR, 1286 *FF*, (*juxta Elyndon*) 1298 *Ass, Wicles-, -y-* 1228 FF, 1314 Ch
>
> *Wec(c)kelescote* 13th AD iv, 1242 Fees, *Wekeles-* 1274 *Ass*, 1337 Ipm, *Wec(k)les-* 1289 *Ass*, 1312 *FF*
>
> *Wykenescote* 1428 FA
>
> *Wiglescote* 1455 IpmR, *Wegillescote* 1497 Ipm, *Weglestok* 1541 WM xliv
>
> *Westlecot* 1629 *SR, Westcot al. Wigglescot* 1642 WIpm, *Weselcourt* 1677 *Sadler*

The first element here would seem to be a personal name *Wicel*, otherwise unrecorded, deriving perhaps from the element *Wic* found in the OE personal name *Uicbercht* (LVD). Hence 'Wicel's cottages,' v. cot(e).

COOMBE BOTTOM[1] (6″) and MILL Ho were the homes of Ralph *atte Combe* (1327 *SR*) and Nicholas de *Molendino* (13th AD iv) and Richard *atte Mulle* (1412 *WinchColl*).

BERRY COPSE (6″). Cf. *Berry close* 1608 WM xxxvi, *The Bury* 1805 O.S. BRIMBLE HILL (6″). Cf. bremel *infra* 424. GADBOURNE BRIDGE. Cf. *Gadbourne* c. 1840 *TA* and *supra* 8. HACKPEN FM and OVERTOWN HACKPEN. The latter is *Hackpen* 1550 *Sadler*. They take their name from Hackpen (Hill) *infra* 310. HAYLANE COTTAGES (6″). Cf. *Hay Lane* c. 1840 *TA*. THE IVERY (6″) is on the escarpment of a hill, cf. yfer *infra* 450. LADDER HILL (6″) is locally *Ladder Lane* or *Egg Lane* from rolling of coloured eggs down it on Good Friday (School). LORD'S COPSE (6″). Cf. *Lords Fd* c. 1840 *TA*. MARKHAM (6″) is *Merecombe* 1325 Orig, *Marcum Bottom* 1773 A and D, *Marcombe Bottom* 1815 O.S. Probably a compound of (ge)mære, 'boundary,' and cumb, though it is not on the parish boundary. MILLBROOK (6″) is *Millbroke* 1640 WIpm. OVERTOWN is *Overtowne* 1629 *SR*, 1661 *Recov, Novertowne* 1696 *Sadler, Overtown al. Overwroughton* 1779 *Recov*. v. Wroughton *supra* 278. SOUTH LEAZE is so named in 1773 (A and D). WEST LEAZE FM (6″) is *West Leaze* 1681 DKR xlii.

---

[1] *le Combe* 1503 *MinAcct*.

XXIV. THORNHILL HUNDRED

Thornehelle hundred 1086 ExonDB, *Tornhille hđr* 1174, *Thornhille hđr* 1175 P, *Hundred de Thornhull'* 1196 Cur, 1198 Abbr, 1249 *Ass*, 1255, 1275 RH, *Thorenhille* 1279 *Ass*, *Thornehull* 1316 FA. Self-explanatory. The meeting-place is unknown. The Hundred is now merged in that of Kingsbridge *supra* 265.

Chisledon

CHISLEDON

(*æt*) *Cyseldene* c. 880 (c. 1000) BCS 553, 925–41 ib. 648, *Ciseldenu* 891 (12th) ib. 565
(*æt*) *Ceolseldene* (sic) 901 (c. 1150) ib. 594, *Ceoseldene* 901 (14th) ib. 598
Chiseldene 1086 DB, -*den* 1202 FF
Cheselden(e) 1242 Fees, 1249, 1278 *Ass*, 1306 Ch, -*don* 1346 Pat, *Cheasledeane* 1353 WM i, *Chesulden* 1438 *FF*
Chuselden(e) 1281 *Ass*, 1318 Pat, 1332 *SR*, 1341 NI, 1393 IpmR, -*done* 1316 FA

'Gravel valley,' *v.* ceosel, denu.

NOTE. BERRYCOT LANE. Cf. *Berycott Bridge* 1773 A and D. BUTTS ROAD possibly led to the archery butts, cf. *infra* 425. HIGH ST is *High Street* 1608 NQ viii.

BADBURY is *Baddeburi* 955 (14th) BCS 904, -*beri* 1197 P, -*biri* 1235 GlastInq, -*bur'* 1241 FF, -*byr'* 1249 *Ass*, 1255 RH, -*bury* 1332 *SR*, *Badeberie* 1086 DB, -*beria* 1186 P, -*beri* 1189 GlastInq, -*bir'* 1242 Fees. '*Badda*'s burh.'

BADBURY WICK is *Baddehamwyke* 1425 AD i, *Badhamwyke* 1428 FF, 1440 AD i, *Badberrie Wyke* 1581 PCC, *Badbury Wicke* 1603 *Sadler* and may have been the home of Edward de *Wicha* (1189 GlastInq). *Baddehamwyke* probably stands for earlier *Baddanhæmewic*, having the same relation to Badbury as Liddington Wick (*infra* 283) to Liddington.

BURDEROP is *Burithorp* 1249 *Ass*, 1313 Inq aqd, Orig, *Burythrop(e)* 1279, 1281 *Ass*, 1445 Pat, -*thorp* 1281 *Ass*, 1327 Pat, 1401 AD vi, *Burythorpe al. Burderoppe* 1561 FF, *Burderopp al. Burythorpe al. Burythropp* 1619 WM xxxi, *Burdropp oth. Bury-*

thropp 1773 *Recov.* 'Village or hamlet near the **burh** or stronghold,' *v.* þorp. There is a rectangular camp here (WM xliv, 243).

DRAYCOT FOLIAT is *Draicote* 1197 FF, *Draycot* 1219 Abbr, *Dreycot'* 1235 Fees, 1241 FF, *Dreicote Foliot* 13th *Bradenstoke*, *Dreykote Folyoht* 1308 Ipm. *v.* Draycot *supra* 69–70. There can be no question of any portage here, but the place is below a hill near the top of the long valley running up from Ogbourne and this may have been called a **dræg**. Samson *Foliot* held the manor in 1219 (Abbr).

HODSON is *Hodeston* 1223 FF, 1249, 1258, (*juxta Chuselden*) 1312 *Ass*, 1497 Ipm, *Hoddeston* 1249, 1268 FF, 1482 IpmR, 1495 Ipm, *Hodson alias Hoddesdon* 1619 WM xxxi. '*Hodd*'s farm,' *v.* tun. Cf. Hoddesdon (PN Herts 228–9).

SNODSHILL is (*on*) *Snodeshelle* 940 (14th) BCS 754, *Snodshill* 1636 WIpm. '*Snodd*'s hill.' For the personal name *v.* Snodsbury (PN Wo 230 and PN Ess liv).

BALDWIN'S BARN, CROOK'S COPSE and TAYLOR'S COPSE (all 6″) are to be associated with the families of John *Baldwin* (1705 WM xxx), Thomas *Crooke* (1649 NQ viii) and Robert *Tayler* (1571 *SR*).

BURDEROP HACKPEN must take its distinctive addition from Hackpen Hill *infra* 310. COWLEAZE COPSE (6″). Cf. *Cow Leaze* c. 1840 *TA.* DAY HO. Cf. *infra* 437. FOLLY BARN (6″) is so named in 1820 (G). Cf. *infra* 451. GREEN HILL (6″) is *Greenhill* 1631 WIpm and is probably to be identified with *grenan byorh* (BCS 598). NIGHTINGALE FM is *Nightengall* 1773 A and D. STOCKBRIDGE (6″) is *Stokebrigge* 1300 *For.* 'Log bridge,' *v.* stocc.

Liddington

LIDDINGTON

> *at Lidentune* 940 (13th) BCS 754, *Lidetona, -e* 1156 RegMalm, 1166 RBE, *Lidinton* 1205 FineR, *Lydington* 1279 *Ass*, *Lyddenton* 1592 *FF*
>
> *Ledentone* 1086 DB, 1377 Pat
>
> *Ludinton* 1242 Fees *et freq* to 1394 *Ass* with variant spelling *-yn-,* (*juxta Wambergh*) 1334 *Ass*, *Ludyngton* 1321 *Ass*, 1341 NI, 1366 Cl, 1367 *FF*, *Luddington* 1636 *Sadler*

In BCS 754 the stream here is referred to in the phrases (*on*),
(*anlang*) *lyden* and in BCS 479 in (*andlang*) *Hlydan*, (*innan*)
hlydan æwylmas. This is from OE *hlȳde*, 'loud one,' found
elsewhere in England as a stream-name. Cf. RN 272–3 and Lid
Brook *supra* 8. Hence 'farm on the *Hlȳde*,' *v.* **tun.**

LIDDINGTON WICK is *Ludeemewyke* 1232 *Lacock, Wyk* 1249 *Ass,
Wika* t. Hy 3 *Shaston, Ludhamwyk* 1321 *Ass, Lidham Weeke*
1659 *Recov, Lydham Weeke* 1695 NQ viii, *Liddam Wick oth.
Liddington Wick* 1780 *Recov*. The earlier form would seem to
go back to OE *hlȳde hǣme* wic, 'dairy-farm of the men of
Liddington,' *v.* **hæme,** 'dwellers,' **wic.**

MEDBOURNE is *medeburne* 940 (14th) BCS 754, *medebourne* 955
(15th) ib. 904, *Medeburne* 1249 *Ass*, 1251 Cl, 1254 FF, *Medborne*
1268 *Ass, Medebourne juxta Ludynton* 1345 *Ass, Medebourne
Doynel* 1393 Cl. 'Meadow stream,' *v.* **burna.** Cf. Medbourne
(Lei). No association with a *Doynel* family is known; one Peter
Doynel held the manor of Huish (*infra* 319) in 1428 (FA).

LIDDINGTON CASTLE is called *Battle-bury* in 1670 (Aubrey).

LIDDINGTON HILL. Cf. *Lyddington Downes* 1639 Sess. LITTLE
MOOR (6″) is *Littlemoore* 1611 *DuLa*.

Wanborough

WANBOROUGH

(*æt*) *Wenbeorgan*, (*æt*) *Wænbeorgon* 854 (12th) BCS 477, 478
   Wemberge 1086 DB
Wamberg(*a*), -(*e*) 1091 StOsmund, 1160 SarumCh, 1177 P,
   1198 Cur, 1229 Cl, 1242 Fees, *Westwamberge* 1334 *Ass,
   Estwambergh* 1365 Pat
Wanberga, -*e* 1146 SarumCh, 1194 P *et freq*, with variant
   spellings -*berghe*, -*borghe, Wanbrow* 1553 *Phillipps, Wanbro
   al. Wanborough* 1805 *Recov*
Wenberge 1196, 1204 Cur, 1198 Abbr, -*burgh* 1354 Cl,
   Wanborowe al. Wenborowe 1542 LP
Waneberge 1268 *Ass*, -*bergh* 1374 Cl, *Wauneborough* 1500 Pat
Whanburgh 1325 ib., *Wonborough* 1685 ParReg

There can be little doubt that here, as in Wanbarrow (PN Sx
275), Wanborough (PN Sr 151) and Wambarrow (So), *Wan-*

burgh 1324 BM, we have a compound of OE *wenn, wænn,* 'wen,' the term being used of a barrow which suggested such an excrescence. It should be noted that in the OE reference we have the plural form (dat.). Mr Young points out that the reference is probably to a conspicuous group of four barrows close together on Sugar Hill (WM xxxviii, 156).

HARPIT is *Horput* 1249 *Ass, Horeputte* 1270 *Magd* (p), 1275 RH (p), *Horputte* 1282 AD vi, *Horepette* 1287 *FF, Horpitt* 1649 Ct. 'Dirty pit or hollow,' *v.* horh, pytt. It may be the *blacan pytt* of BCS 477.

NYTHE FM is (*in*) *niweam* (sic) 1232 *Lacock, le Nithe* 1283 *Magd,* (*juxta Wamburgh*) 1509 *DuLa, le Neiche* (sic) 1317 BM, *le Nythe* 1347 *Merton, East, West Nithe* 1553 AD vi, *le Nithe Brooke* 1649 *Ct, the Nighs* 1670 Aubrey[1]. Parallel names are Nythe in Greinton (So), *atte Nithe* 1327 SR (p) and The Nythe in Alresford (Ha), *Ye Nythen* c. 1550 *EcclCom.* Cf. also Nythefield in Alderbury *infra* 375. All these places are in low-lying marshy ground and they probably go back to OE *īggoþ,* 'islet, ait,' with affixed *n* from the definite article, ME *at then eithe, ithe* becoming *at the n(e)ithe.* Cf. the lost manor of *Neate* in Westminster (Mx), *la Neyte* 1320 Fine, on the marshes of the Thames, and un-identified *la Nyethe* (1323 Longleat) in Mere, *Nith ditch* (1654 Fry) in Hannington, *The Inner Nithie* (1608 WM xxxi) in Somerford, all in Wiltshire.

The *w* in the first form must be due to some earlier document in which the OE *thorn* and *wen* symbols were confused.

It may be noted that the site of Nythe must be just by *tha Ealdanig Dic* of the Wanborough Charter (BCS 479) where the simplex ig seems to be used of this land.

BREACH FM[2] (6″) and MOOR LEAZE[3] were the homes of John *atte Breche* (1332 *SR*) and William de *la More* (1233 *Magd*). *v.* bræc *infra* 423 and mor.

---

[1] This is just by a Roman station marked on the O.S. map as *Nidum.* Mr O. G. S. Crawford, however, informs us that although the Roman station or settlement is genuine, the name is a pure antiquarian invention for which there is no authority.
[2] Cf. *Northbreche* 1374 Cl.
[3] *Moreleaze* 1606 *DuLa, v.* læs.

BURYSCROFT ROW (6″) is *Berrycroft* 1649 Ct. CALLAS HILL is *Callice Hill* ib. COLLEGE FM (6″) is the property of Magdalen College. FOXBRIDGE is so named in 1649 (Ct). INLANDS FM (6″). Cf. *terra del Inlonde* 1270 *Magd* and *infra* 439. KITEHILL FM (6″) is *Kitehill* 1649 Ct. LOTMEAD FM is *Lottmeade* ib., *v. infra* 436. LYNCH FM (6″). Cf. *Langelinch* 1374 Cl and hlinc *infra* 436. ROTTEN ROW (6″). Cf. *supra* 90. SLATE FM (6″). Cf. *Slatthowse* 1649 Ct. SWANHILL (6″) is so named ib.

XXV. RAMSBURY HUNDRED

Ramesberie hundred 1086 ExonDB, *Hundred de Rammesbyr' Episcopi* 1255 RH. *v.* Ramsbury *infra* 287. Ramsbury was a manor of the Bishop of Salisbury.

Baydon

BAYDON

> *Beidona* 1146 SarumCh, *-dun* 1195 FF, c. 1200 HMC Var i,
>   *-don* 1226 StOsmund, 1227 FF *et passim* to 1412 FA, with
>   variant spelling *Bey-, Beydoun* 1399 Cl
> *Bedon* 1241 FF, 1316 FA, 1510 PCC, *Beadon* 1591 WM vi
> *Beyndon* 1249 *Ass*
> *Baydon* 1263 Cl

Ekwall (DEPN *s.n.*) suggests 'berry-down' as the meaning of this name, from OE *bēg-dūn. bēg* is found as the first element in OE *bēg-bēam,* 'blackberry bush.'

BAYFIELDS is *Bayfield* 1773 A and D and was the home of John de *Bayfeld* (1281 *Ass*). The first element may be the same as in Baydon, so also perhaps in Bailey Hill *infra*.

FINCHE'S FM, PAINE'S FM, PEAKS DOWNS[1] and WALROND'S FM (6″) are to be associated with the families of John *Finch* (1841 *Devizes*), Henry *Paine* (1637 WM xlv), Thomas *Peke* (1535 *SR*) and Robert *Walrond* (1594 NQ viii).

BAILEY HILL FM. Cf. *Bayleyhill, Bayley ground* 1570 Pemb-Surv. CONEYGRE COPSE (6″), i.e. 'rabbit warren,' *v. infra* 427.

---

[1] Cf. *Pecks Hill* 1773 A and D.

FORD FM is (*le*) *Ford* 1331 *Sarum D and C*, 1553 *AddCh*. GOORLANE FM is *Gorelaynes* 1570 PembSurv. *v. infra* 439. GREEN HILL is *Grenehill* c. 1570 *Wilton, the Greene Hill* 1587 *Rental*. THORN-SLAIT RIDGE (6″). Cf. sleight *infra* 454.

Bishopstone

BISHOPSTONE [*olim* buʃtən]

> *Bissopeston* 1186 P, 1223 SarumCh, *Bisshopeston* 1247 Misc,
> *Byssupeston'* 1249 *Ass*, *Busshopeston* 1332 SR
> *Bussheton* 1534 BM

'Bishop's farm or estate,' *v.* tun. Bishopstone was originally part of Ramsbury parish which was a manor of the Bishop of Salisbury.

CUE'S FM (6″) is to be associated with the family of Mary *Cue* (1751 ParReg).

BISHOPSTONE DOWNS. Cf. *ye Downe* 1649 *Sarum D and C*. BISHOP-STONE FOLLY (6″). *v. infra* 451. FORTY FM (6″). Cf. *Bishopston Forty* 1841 *Devizes*. It is on marshy ground, cf. The Forty *supra* 43. HILL BARN is so named in 1773 (A and D). LAMMY DOWN is *Lameng Down* ib., *Lameny Down* 1820 G. PREBENDAL FM (6″). Bishopstone is a prebend in the diocese of Sarum. RIDGEWAY FM is so named in 1820 (G) and is on the great Ridge Way, cf. *supra* 17. RUSSLEY is *Rushley* 1570 PembSurv, *Rusley* 1819 RCH. *v.* leah. STARVEALL FM is a nickname of reproach, cf. *infra* 455. TOWNSEND FM (6″) is at the end of the village, cf. *infra* 449.

Little Hinton

LITTLE HINTON

> *Hynyton* 12th BCS 477, *Hineton(e)*, -*y*- 1242 Fees, 1243
> WintonCart *et passim* to 1332 *SR*
> *Hinneton* 1205 Pap, *Hyniton* 1244 Pat
> *Hynynton* 1279, 1281 *Ass*, 1300 Misc, *Hynn-* 1285 Ch, *Little Hynyngton* 1311 Pat
> *Hynton* 1280 Pat
> *Lettell Hentune* 1663 ParReg (Bedwyn)

Probably OE *hīgna-tūn*, 'farm of the (monastic) community,' i.e. of Winchester, in spite of the curious forms in *Hynin(g)*-. Cf. Hindon *supra* 191.

Earl's Court Fm

Ardescote 1086 DB, 1204 FF
Erdescote 1196 Cur, 1198 Abbr, 1201–12 LN, 1242 Fees, 1268, (*juxta Wanbergh*) 1356 *Ass*, *Herdescote* 1428 FA
Erlescote al. Erdescote 1542 LP, *Erlescotte* 1558–79 ECP, *Earlescott* 1639 FF, 1650 *ParlSurv*

The DB form may be from earlier *Eardulfescote*, 'the cottage(s) of *Eard(w)ulf*,' or may contain a shortened form of that name, hence '*Eard*'s cottages.' Cf. Ardsley (PN WRY 10) and Ardley (PN O 40).

CHARLBURY HILL (6″) is *Shelbarrow Hill* 1773 A and D, 1820 G, *Shalborough Hill* c. 1840 *TA*. FOX HILL is *Foxhulle* 1276 StOsmund, *Fox Hill* 1773 A and D. GREEN CORNER (6″) is so named c. 1840 (*TA*). HASSOCK'S COPSE is *Hassock Coppice* ib. *v. infra* 452. HINTON MARSH. Cf. *terra in marisco* 1334 *Winton*, *Upper, Lower Marsh* 1791 *Devizes*. MOUNT PLEASANT. Cf. *infra* 455. THORN (6″) may be *thone Thorn* (BCS 477) in the bounds of Little Hinton, the thorn having been more than once replanted (Grundy 174). WEST HINTON is *Westhyneton* 1334 *Winton*, *West Town* 1773 A and D.

Ramsbury

RAMSBURY

Rammesburi 947 (14th) BCS 828, *Rammesbiri* 1091 StOsmund, *-beriam* 1146, *-byre* 1160 SarumCh, *-beria* 1175 P, *-bir'* 1227 ClR, *-bur'* 1228 FF, *-bury* 1240 Ch
Hremnesbyrig (dat.) c. 990 Crawford, *Remmisbiri(a)* 1227 Ch, 1239 Bracton, *Remmesbir'* 1275 RH, *-bury* 1291 Tax, 1294 Ch, 1310 BM, *-buri* 1335 AD ii, *Remsburye* 1577 *AD*
Reamnesbyrig c. 1050 SD, *Reamesbyrig* c. 1150 FW, *Remnesbery* 1281 QW
Ramesberie 1086 DB, c. 1125 ANG, *-biria* c. 1150 HMC Var i, *-beri* 1164 P, *-biri* c. 1220 HMC Var i, *-bur'* 1249 *Ass*, *-bir'* 1275 RH

Remesbir' 1232 HMC Var i, *-byr'* 1268 *Ass*, *-byri* 1275 RH, *-bur'* 1332 *SR*
Rammesbury al. Remesbury 1543 *FF*, *Remsbury* t. Eliz WM xxi

'Raven's burh' or '*Hræfn*'s burh.' *Hræfn* is the OE *hræfn*, 'raven,' possibly used here as a personal name. In late Latin documents of the OE period the church and diocese of Ramsbury occasionally appear as *ecclesia* and *parochia Coruinensis*. Just ten miles north-north-east of Ramsbury there was another *hremnesbyrig* (BCS 687, 899, 1121) identified by Grundy (*Berkshire Charters* 26) with Rams Hill in Uffington (Berks).

NOTE. HIGH ST is *High Streete* 1570 PembSurv. OXFORD ST is *Oxenfordstrete* 1331 *SarumD and C*, *Oxefordstret* 1384 AD vi, *Oxenfordstret* 1419 AD i. In 1570 (PembSurv) we have *Remesburye Streete, venella voc' Castell Wall*.

AXFORD is *Axeford* 1184, 1195 P, 1279 *Ass et freq* to 1428 FA, *Axford* 1255 RH, *Assheford* 1289 *Ass*. Probably 'ashes ford,' going back to OE *æsca ford*, 'ford of the ash trees,' with metathesis of *sc* to *cs* as in Axford in Nutley (Ha), *Ashore* 1272 *Ass*, *Axore* 1280 ib., 1330 Pat.

BOWER WOOD (6″) is *Bourwode* t. Ed 1, *haya voc' Boure* t. Ed 2 *For*. The forms are too late for any certain suggestion to be possible. The first element may be bur, 'dwelling,' or (ge)bur, 'peasant,' cf. *infra* 424.

HILLDROP is *Hullethorp* 1310, *Hyllethroppe, Hullethroupe, Hellethroup* 1329 BM, *Hullethorp juxta Remesbury* 1382 *FF*, *Hillethorp* 1412 FA, *Hildrop* 1510 BM, *Helthorpe* 1556 *AD*, *Helthrope* 1570 PembSurv. 'Hill village,' *v.* þorp. For the present-day form cf. Burderop *supra* 281.

KNIGHTON is *Knytteton* 1275 *FF*, *Knyghton by Remesbury* 1478 AD i, *Knyghton Marshe* 1570 PembSurv. 'Farm of the *cnihtas* or serving men,' *v.* cniht, tun.

LITTLECOTE is *Litlecota* 1187 P, *-cot'* 1279 *Ass*, *Littlecote juxta Remmesburi* 1329 AD v. 'Little cot(e).'

MARRIDGE HILL is *Masserugge* 1279, 1281 *Ass* (p), 1395 *SarumD and C*, *-rigge* 1281, *Maserugge* 1281, 1289 *Ass*, *Meserig'* 1331

SarumD and C, Marrygge 1456 *FF*, *Maredge* 1570 PembSurv.
Probably '*Mæssa*'s ridge,' *v.* hrycg. Cf. Massingham (PN in
-ing 138).

MEMBURY

Minbiry c. 1090 (14th) Footman, *History of Lambourne Church*,
   -berie c. 1150, 1175 HMC Var i, *-bir'* 1233 Cl, *Mynburi
   juxta Remmesburi* 1300 *FF*

Mimbyre 1196 SarumCh, *-bir'* 1233 Cl, *-byry* 1268 Pat, *-bur'*
   1275 RH, *Mymbur'* 1249 Cl, 1255 RH, *-bere* 1296 *FF*, *-bury*
   1323, 1340 ib., 1406 Pat, 1428 FA, *Mymbery walles* c. 1570
   Wilton

Mimmebir' 1263 Cl

Membir' 1289 *Ass*, *-bury* 1323 Inq aqd

The second element is burh, with reference to the large
'camp' here. The first element is difficult. If, as seems likely,
the spellings with *n* are the original ones, with later assimilation
of *nb* to *mb*, the first element might be the British word corresponding to Welsh, Cornish *min*, 'edge, brink, border,' etc., found in
a few Cornish place-names. The *camp* is on the western edge of
a high plateau with a fairly deep valley just below. A further
trace of the first element may be found in *Myndeane* (1553
AddCh) in Ramsbury.

PAXLET PLANTATION (6″) is *Pac(c)heslade* c. 1210 HMC Var i,
1403 *SarumD and C*, *Peccheslade* 1331 ib., *copice called Pasheslade*
t. Hy 8 *Rental*. Probably '*Pæcci*'s slæd,' cf. Patching (PN Sx
248). The personal name may also be found in *Paxdoune* (1570
PembSurv) in this parish.

THRUP FM is *Thrope* 1478, (*by Ramesbury*) 1498 AD i; and was
the home of Reginald de *Latrope* (1166 RBE). 'Village,' *v.* þorp.
Latrope contains the French definite article. *Esthorpe juxta
Remmesbury* (1420 *FF*) perhaps refers to this place, since it lies
to the east of Ramsbury.

WHITTONDITCH is *Whitedic* 1249 Cl, *Wytendyche* 1268, *Whyten-
dich* 1289 *Ass*, *Whitindich* 1298 *FF*, *Whydindych*, *Wydindiche*
1332 *SR* (p), *Whityngdiche* 1456, *Whittyndyche* 1562 *FF*. The
name would seem to go back to OE (*æt þām*) *hwītan dīce*, 'at the
white ditch,' *v.* dic.

WITCHA FM is *la Wychheye* 1331, *Wychehey* 1395 *SarumD and C*, *Wycheheydowne* t. Hy 8 *Rental*, *Wichehowe*, *Wychehey downe* 1570 PembSurv, *High Witchay* 1587 *Rental*, and was the home of Richard *atte Wycheheye* (1332 *SR*). The second element is (ge)hæg, 'hedge, enclosure,' etc. The first element may be OE *wice*, 'wych-elm.'

BRIDGE FM[1] and COMBE FM were the homes of Walter *atte Brigge* (1302 *FF*) and Robert *atte Combe* (1332 *SR*). v. cumb.

BALLARD'S COPSE (6″), BLAKE'S COPSE, HUNT'S COPSE[2] (6″), LARGE'S BARN (6″), LOVE'S FM[3] and MOON'S BARN (6″) are to be associated with the families of John *Balard* (t. Hy 8 *Rental*), William *Blake* (1570 PembSurv), John *Hunt* (1590 NQ vii), John *Large* (1841 *Devizes*), Walter *Lof* (1289 *Ass*) and Robert *Louf* (1305 ib.) and John *Mone* (1525 *SR*).

BARRIDGE BRAKE (6″) is *Berugge* 1336, *Berygge*, *Baryge* 1425 *MinAcct*. BOLTSRIDGE COPSE (6″) is *Bolstridge* 1777 *EnclA*, *Bowstridge Coppice* c. 1840 *TA*. BURNEY FM (6″) is *Burney* 1820 G. BURNT WOOD is *Burned Wood* 1570 PembSurv. CAKEWOOD[4] is *Cakewode* 1362 *For*. COAL BRAKE (6″) is *Coal Brake Coppice* c. 1840 *TA*. COCKED HAT COPPICE (6″). So named from its shape. In the 1900 edition of the O.S. map it is called *Three Corner Clump*. CROWOOD HO is *Crowewood* c. 1570 *Wilton*, *Crow Wood or Crowood* 1773 A and D. DWARF BRAKE (6″) is *Dwarfs Brake* c. 1840 *TA*. EASTRIDGE HO is *Estrigg* 1221 Pat, *Esterygge* 1255 RH (p), *Estrugge* 1279, 1289 *Ass*, *Astrudge* 1553 *AddCh*. Self-explanatory, v. hrycg. ELMDOWN FM is *Helme Downe* 1570 PembSurv, *Elm Down* 1773 A and D. FOXLEY WOOD (6″) is so named c. 1840 (*TA*). HAIL'S GROVE. Cf. *Hale copyce* t. Eliz *Rental*, *Haylescourt* 1584 PCC, *Hayles Court Farm* 1677 DKR xli. HENS WOOD is *copice called Hensedd* c. 1570 *Wilton*, *Hens Wood* 1773 A and D. HILL CLOSE (6″). Cf. *Hylfeld* 1570 PembSurv. HODD'S HILL is *Hoddhill copice* ib. HOWE MILL (6″) is *Hughmulle* 1331, *Howmulle* 1406 *SarumD and C*, *Howmyll* t. Hy 8 *Rental*, *Howe milne* c. 1570 *Wilton*. KEARSDOWN FM (6″) is *Karesden'* 1327 *SR* (p), *Caresdown*, *Carsedons* 1570

---

[1] Cf. *Burge end mede* 1570 PembSurv and Introd. xxi.
[2] Cf. *Hunts mead* 1682 *Recov*.   [3] *Lovys* 1538–44 ECP.
[4] Partly in Hungerford (Berks).

PembSurv. THE KNAPP (6″), v. cnæpp infra 427. LAMPLANDS (6″) is Lampe lands 1540 WM xii. It may be so called because providing light for the church. LEG OF MUTTON COPSE (6″), v. infra 455. LEIGH FM (6″). Cf. Lee copyce t. Hy 8 Rental. v. leah. LITTLE WOOD is Lyttlewoode 1553 DuLa. OAKEN COPSE is Oaken Coppice c. 1840 TA. OLDFIELD COTTAGES (6″). Cf. Tholde (i.e. 'the old') feldes t. Hy 8 Rental, Olde feild c. 1570 Wilton. PARK TOWN is Parkton 1395 SarumD and C, Parketowne t. Hy 8 Rental. PENTICO FM is so named in 1773 (A and D). PIT BARN. Cf. Pit Corner c. 1840 TA. PRESTON is Preston 1268, 1279 Ass, 1298 FF. 'Priests' farm,' v. tun. WESTFIELD (6″) is Westfeld 1570 PembSurv. WEST MARSH FM (6″). Cf. le Mersshe 1478 AD i. WHITEHILL COPPICE (6″) is so called c. 1840 (TA).

XXVI. SELKLEY HUNDRED

Selchelai, -laia, -laio (sic) hundred 1086 ExonDB, 1167, 1168, Selkelea 1191 P, Selkele 1196 Cur et freq to 1316 FA, Selkleye 1309 Ch
Selkeslea hundred 1187 P
Sulkele 1281 Ass, Sylkele 1305 ib.

The site of the meeting-place is not known[1]. In 1279 and 1281 (Ass) we have mention of a wood (in) bosco de Selkele, but there is no indication where it may be. We have on record in OE personal names Seolca and Seoloce (fem.) which may be found in the first part of this name. Hence possibly 'Seolca's wood,' v. leah. See Addenda supra xl.

Aldbourne

ALDBOURNE [olim ɔ·bərn]
(æt) Ealdincburnan c. 970 ASWills, Audingeburn' 1226 ClR
Aldeborne 1086 DB, -burna 1165 P et passim to 1454 IpmR, with variant spellings -borne, -bourne, -burne
Aldiburna 1181 P, 1230 Cl, Aldy- 1289 Ass, Audiburne 1217 ClR, 1229 Ch, 1229, 1250 Cl, 1242 Fees, 1248 Pat, -born(e) 1232 Lacock, 1456 PCC

---

[1] On the Marlborough-Broad Hinton road a mile short of the top of Hackpen is a knoll called MAN'S HEAD. It is just possible that this name marks the meeting-place (cf. Manshead Hundred, PN BedsHu 112–13).

Audeburne 1198 Abbr, 1214 ClR *et freq* to 1275 RH
Oldeborne 1347 WIpm
Aldbourne 1418 *FF*, *Alburne* 1476 Pat, -*bourne* 1535 VE,
    Alborne al. Aldiborne 1535 *FF*, *Auldeborne* 1573 ib., *Alborne*
    al. Aldeborne al. Awborne 1682 *Recov*, *Auburn* 1685 Aubrey
    NH

'*Ealda*'s stream,' *v.* ing, burna.

NOTE. SOUTH ST is *Southstrete* 1553 *DuLa*. WEST ST is *Westrete*
ib., *le West streate* 1614 ib.
    Lost names include *Portestrete* 1467 *MinAcct*, *Baydonwaye* (leading
to Baydon *supra* 285), *Portwaye* 1509, *Calfstrett* 1553, *Mylwaye* 1580
DuLa, *Forde lane*, *Ducke lane*, *Louers lane*, *High strate waie* 1591 WM vi.

LOTTAGE is *Luttewyk* 1249 *Ass*, *Lodewich'* 1270 *For*, *Lotwyk*
1281, *Lotewych'* 1289 *Ass*, *Lotwych* 1509, *Lotewiche* 1553 *DuLa*.
It is tempting, in spite of a good deal of uncertainty in the early
forms, to take this name as identical with Lutwyche (Sa) for
which Ekwall (DEPN) gives early forms *Loteis* 1086 DB,
Lotwych 1292 *Ass*, quoting the parallel of unidentified *Lootwic*
717 BCS 137 (Wo). The first element is quite uncertain.

PEAKS WOOD (6″) is probably identical with *Pikedewode* 1289
Ass (p), 1336 *FF*, (*la*) 1322 *AD*, *Pykedwood* 1427 IpmR,
Pykydwod 1450–3 ECP, *Pikewode* 1468 *MinAcct*, *Pykewood* 1509
DuLa, *Pickwood* 1677 DKR xli. The name must originally have
been used of a piece of woodland with many corners. Cf. *infra*
453. Probably influenced in form by the neighbouring Peaks
Downs *supra* 285.

SNAP is *Snape* 1268 *Ass* (p), *Snappe* 1332 *SR*, 1423 *FF*, (*by
Aldebourn*) 1361 Ipm. This is from OE *snæp*, 'boggy land,'
discussed in PN Sx 28 *s.n. Snapelands*. Cf. also Snapper and
Snape (PN D 44, 359). Snap lies in a bottom on the chalk downs,
and the ground is full of water so that the sense 'boggy ground'
would suit it well.

SUGAR HILL is *Suger Hill* (1773 A and D) and must have been
near (*innan*) *sceocera wege* 854 (12th) BCS 477, *Shuger waie* 1591
WM vi, *Sugerne Way* 1779 Grundy ii. 'The robbers' way or
path,' from OE *sceacere*, 'robber.' See more fully PN Wa 285,
s.n. Sugarswell. The *weg* is the old road which runs from east to
west here along the boundary of Wanborough and Aldbourne.

UPHAM is (*to*) *Uphammere* 955 (14th) BCS 904, *Upham* 1201 Cur, 1249 FF, 1332 *SR*, (*juxta Aldeburne*) 1281 *Ass*, *Hupham* 1314 Ch, *Uppham* 1327 *SR*. 'High ham.' *mere* is OE (ge)mære, 'boundary.' "It is on the top of everything" (E. H. G.).

HILLWOOD FM was probably the home of Thomas *atte Hulle* (1327 *SR*). It is *Hillewode* 1488, *Hillwood Coppice* 1608 *DuLa*.

BLAKE'S FM is to be associated with the family of Adam *le Blake* (1289 *Ass*).

ALDBOURNE CHASE. Cf. *in chas' de Aldeborne* 1381 *MinAcct*, *Aldborne Chace* 1561 *DuLa*. ALDBOURNE WARREN. Cf. *warren de Aldeburn* 1307 Pat. THE BUTTS is *Butts* 1841 *Devizes*, *v. infra* 425. THE DEAN may be the *Sheephouse dean* of 1650 (*ParlSurv*), *v.* denu, 'valley.' DUDMORE LODGE is *Dodmere* 1488 *MinAcct*, *-more* 1553 *DuLa*, *Dudmore Walk* 1689 WM xlii. EAST LEAZE is *Estlees* 1553 *DuLa*. EWIN'S HILL is *Ewens Hill* 1805 WM xlii, *Evans Hill* 1818 O.S. GIANTS GRAVE is a large barrow in a group of three (WM xxxiii, 157). LEIGH FM (6″). Cf. *Ley courte* 1553 *DuLa*, *Leigh Farm* 1773 A and D. *v.* leah. LOVE'S COPSE is *Loves coppice* 1606 *LRMB*. Cf. the adjacent Love's Fm in Ramsbury (*supra* 290). NORTH FIELD BARN. Cf. *le Northfeild* 1614 *DuLa*. SHIPLEY BOTTOM (6″). Cf. *Schepele* t. Jas 1 *LRMB*. SOUTHWARD DOWN may be by *Southwode* 1509 AD i, *Aldborne South Wood* 1820 G. STOCK CLOSE and LANE. Cf. *Stock Lane* 1600 *DuLa*, *Stockeclose* 1677 DKR xxxix. *v.* stocc, 'stump.' WILDING'S COPSE (6″) is *coppice called Lytle Wheleding*, *Greate Whelden* 1561 *DuLa*, *Welldon coppice* 1751 *Kings*. WOODSEND is *Wood End* 1773 A and D.

Avebury

AVEBURY [eivbəri, eibəri, *olim* ɔ·bəri]

Aureberie 1086 DB

Avesbiria 1114 France, *-beria* t. Hy 1 (1253) Ch, *-byry* 1256 Pat, *-bir'* 1289 *Ass*

Aveberia c. 1180 France, 1196 Cur, *-biri* 1232 Ch *et passim* to 1332 *SR*, with variant spellings *-bury*, *-biry*, *-bery*, *Avebere Priur* 1279 *Ass*

Avenesbur' 1255 RH, *Avenebyr'* 1268 *Ass*
Abury 1386 Pat, *Abery* 1535 VE, 1539 *Phillipps, Aibyri* c. 1540 L
Aubury 1494 Pat, 1670 Aubrey, *Awbery al. Avebury* 1689 *Recov, Aubury (Bridge)* 1773 A and D

No certainty can be attained with regard to this name. If we take the *Avenesbur', Avenebyr* forms seriously, the DB form *Aureberie* might be explained as due to common interchange of *ne* and *re* in Anglo-Norman spellings (cf. IPN 107) and the name be taken as 'burh by the Avon' on the supposition that this feeder of the Kennet, now called Winterbourne, was at an earlier stage known as Avon. Avebury *Priur* from the Prior of Avebury (1235 Fees).

BECKHAMPTON [bek'hæmtən *olim* bekiŋtən]

> *Bachentune* 1086 DB, *Bakhamtun* 13th AD v, *Bachamton* 1216 ClR, *Bachampton* 1242 Fees *et passim* to 1594 *FF*, with variant spellings *Bak-, Back-* and *-hamton*
> *Bechampton* 1249 *Ass*, 1267 Abbr, *Beckhampton* 1655 *FF*
> *Bakanton* 1268 *Ass*, *Bakenton* 1535 VE, *Bakington* t. Eliz *LRMB*
> *Beckhampton al. Backhampton al. Beckington* 1730 *Recov*

This is a difficult name. OE *bæc*, 'back,' which might be palatalised in the dative form *bæce*, will not suit the topography, for there is no ridge here. There is a small stream, a feeder of the Kennet, which might possibly be spoken of as a **bæce**. This should in later English have given [bætʃ], [betʃ]. Cf. *le Bache* 1460 *WinchColl, The Batch* 1790 WM xxxi in Durrington and Burbage *infra* 336. Some of the ME spellings point to this, but the majority suggest a pronunciation [bæk] or [bek], as in modern times. There was perhaps early confusion with the word **bæc**. If that could give ME *bak* and *beche*, the word *bæce*, which ought only to become *bache* or *beche*, may have been given an alternative form *bak*.

WEST KENNETT is *Chenete* 1086 DB, *Westkenete* 1288 *FF*, 1327 Banco, *Westkynet* 1332 *SR*, taking its name from the river (*supra* 8). *West* to distinguish from East Kennett *infra* 297.

SILBURY HILL is (*in regia via juxta*) *Seleburgh* 1281 *Ass*[1], *Selbyri, Selburi hille* c. 1540 L, *Selbarrowe hill* t. Eliz *LRMB*, *Selbury or Silbury Hill* 1663 Aubrey, *Selbury* 1754 Pococke. Unluckily we have very little to go upon in the interpretation of this name, and its meaning must remain as uncertain as the history of Silbury itself. From the form it is probable that the second element goes back to OE beorg, 'barrow,' rather than to burh, for names in burh nearly always appear in the dative form *bury* (from OE *byrig*) in ME forms. On the other hand *bury* is a common corruption of *burgh* from beorg in the 16th century and earlier. Formally, the first part of the name may be derived from OE *sele*, 'hall,' but no certain conclusions can be drawn from a solitary thirteenth-century form.

WADEN HILL is *Weadon* 1639 *Recov*, *Weeden* 1695 NQ iii, 1730 *Recov*, *Wadon Hill* 1818 O.S. In this area it is almost certainly from OE *wēo(h)-dun*, denoting a hill marked by some heathen site. It lies just above the Stone Avenue, looking down on the circle. Cf. Weedon (PN Bk 85, PN Nth 30–1) and *Wedone* in Damerham (1518 Hoare). There is a clear example of this first element in *Weolond* (13th *Bradenstoke*) in Tockenham. See also Introduction *supra* xiv.

AVEBURY TRUSLOE is *Truslows Abury* 1730 *Recov* and is to be associated with the family of Thomas *Truslowe* (1524 *SR*).

HORSLIP BRIDGE (6″) [hɔslip], probably from earlier 'horse-leap.' KNOLL DOWN is *Knoll downe* t. Eliz *LRMB*, v. cnoll. PENNING BARN is *Pennens Barn* 1820 G. v. *infra* 453. SWALLOWHEAD SPRINGS is *Swallow Head Spring* 1773 A and D. WESTBROOK FM (6″) is *Westbrok(e)* 1370 *Cor*, 1640 WIpm. WEST DOWN is *le Westerdownes* 1639 *Recov*.

Fyfield

FYFIELD

 Fifhide 1086 DB, 1205 Pap, 1242 Fees, *-hida* 1165 P, *Fiffhide* 1242 Fees, *Fifhude* 1257 *For*, *Fyfhide* 1300 Ch

 Fyfilde al. Fyfitt 1505 Pat, *Phiphild* 1553 *AddCh*, *Fyfelde* 1558 PCC, *Phipheld* 1570 PembSurv

'Five hides,' v. hid. It paid geld for 5 hides in DB.

[1] Assize Roll No. 1005 m. 117.

KEEPENCE COPSE and STONE'S WOOD (6″) are to be associated with the families of Christopher *Keepen* (1657 ParReg) and Margaret *Stone* (1667 ib.).

DELLING (6″) is *Dyllinge* 1570 PembSurv. TOTTERDOWN is so named in 1773 (A and D).

Broad Hinton

BROAD HINTON

> *Hentone* 1086 DB, *-ton(e)* 12th *AD*, 1204 Cur *et freq* to 1316 FA, *-tune* 1220 AD iv
> *Hantone* 1086 DB
> *Brod(e)henton* 1319 *FF*, 1327 Banco, 1348 *FF*, *Brodehanton al. Brodehenton* 1469 Pat
> *Brodhinton* 1339 Ipm, *Hynton* 1397 Pat
> *Henton Columbers, Henton Waas* 1428 FA

'(At the) high farm,' *v.* heah, tun. *Broad* (cf. *supra* 204), to distinguish from Little Hinton *supra* 286, though the *Hinton* in the two names is of different origin. Mathew de *Columbariis* had a holding here in 1242 (Fees) and John *Waas* in 1428 (FA).

BINCKNOLL CASTLE [bainəl]

> *Bienknoll(e)* c. 1220 *AD*, 1282 Cl, 1362 BM, 1428 FA, *-cnolle* 1242 Fees, *Bienknole* 1396 Cl
> *Benknolle* 1247 FF, 1279 BM, 1332 *SR*, *Bencnoll* 1268 *Ass*
> *Byngknoll* 1429 BM, *Byncknoll al. Bynoll* 1575 *FF*, *Bincknold* 1629 *SR*

Probably from OE *bēona cnoll*, 'bees' hill,' *v.* cnoll. "The earthwork is probably a Norman motte and bailey" (E. H. G.).

UFFCOTT

> *Ufecote, Ulfecote* 1086 DB
> *Uffecot(e)* 1115 StOsmund, 1207 FF, 1224 SarumCh, c. 1250 Rental, *-kote* 1282 *Ass*, *Huffecote* 1158 HMC Var i, *Uphcot* 1687 ParReg
> *Offecote* 1297 Cl

'*Uffa*'s cot(e).'

NORBORNE FM (6″) is to be associated with the family of Thomas *Norborne* (1708 WM xxxix).

CONEGAR COPSE (6″). Cf. *infra* 427. CRATCHCROFT (6″) is *Catche crofte* t. Eliz *LRMB*, *v.* croft. ELM CROSS is so named in 1773 (A and D). HIGHDEN is *Highdown* 1725 WM xlvi. SAND FURLONG FM is *Sandfurlong* 1820 G. THE WEIR [wair] is *The Wire* 1818 O.S., *Weir Close* c. 1840 *TA*.

East Kennett

EAST KENNETT

(*æt*) *Cynetan* 939 BCS 734

Chenete 1086 DB, *Kenete* 1220 AD iv, *Kenet* 1227 FF, 1242 Fees

Estkenette 1267 Abbr, 1268 *Ass*, *Estkynet(e)* 1332 *SR*, 1383 Pat, *East Kynnet* t. Eliz WM xxi, *Kynnet* 1670 Aubrey

The place is on the river Kennet (*supra* 8). *East* to distinguish from West Kennett *supra* 294.

LANGDEAN (CIRCLE) (6″). Cf. *Langedeneswyk* 1289 *Ass*, *Langeden* t. Hy 8 *AOMB*. Mr G. M. Young notes that this 'long valley' is mentioned in the bounds of Stanton St Bernard (BCS 600) where the boundary, as it comes down the eastern side of that parish, goes *on longan dene neoðewearde*, i.e. to the bottom of Langdean. He notes further that, in the other versions of this charter (BCS 998, 1053), we have the faulty reading *andlang dene neoþewearde*. The boundary does not go 'along' the valley. It goes up to it and crosses it.

COW DOWN is *Cowdowne* 1570 PembSurv, *v. infra* 430. LURKLEY HILL (6″) is so named in 1794 (*Wilton*).

Marlborough

MARLBOROUGH[1] [mɔ·lbərə]

Merleberge 1086 DB, t. Hy 2 (1314) Ch, 1197 Abbr, 1202 FF, -*berg(a)* 1130, 1158 P *et freq* to 1218 Pat

Marleberg(e) 1091 StOsmund, 1158 RBE, 1227 Fees, -*burgh* 1246 FF, -*berg'* 1249 *Ass et freq* to 1302 Abbr, -*bergh* 1336 Ch

---

[1] Marlborough was extra-hundredal, but may be included in Selkley Hundred for topographical purposes.

Maellesberiense castellum 1140 John of Worcester, *Melle-burga* 1147, *-berga* 1175 France
Mærle beorg c. 1150 (*s.a.* 1110 E) ASC
Marborowe 1485 Pat, *-brughe* 1553 WM xii, *Morrell Burrowe* 1591 WM vi, *Marleberghe al. Marlebroughe* 1596 *FF*, *Marelborowe* 1653 Moulton, *Marebrough* 1749 *FF*

The interpretation of this name is uncertain but the most likely would seem still to be that suggested under Malborough (PN D 307), viz. that it stands for earlier *Mærlanbeorg,* 'hill,' or, in this case, 'barrow of one *Mærla,*' a lost OE name cognate with the recorded OGer *Merila* (Förstemann, PN 1102). Marlborough is not on a hill but in a valley, and there can be little doubt that the **beorg** has reference to the artificial mound of very ancient date which formed the nucleus of the Castle. *Mærla* may have been its sometime owner or the name of someone who had been buried there[1].

Ekwall (DEPN *s.n.* Malborough), on the score of the coincidence involved in assuming a lost personal name being found twice with **beorg,** puts forward tentatively an alternative suggestion, viz. that in both names we have OE *meargealla, mergelle,* 'gentian,' but it should be noted that in the one certain case of that element hitherto found in a place-name, it is still *merghel* in the 14th century (cf. Marldon PN D 516). As to the coincidence there is little in it if **beorg** means barrow in one case and hill in the other, and the coincidence of this rare plant-name being found twice with **beorg** would be almost as great as the coincidence involved in assuming a lost personal name.

MARLBOROUGH STREET-NAMES

BARN ST is *Baronestret* 14th *Bradenstoke* and is probably to be associated with the family of Roger *Baron* (1275 RH). BLOWHORN ST is *Blowhornestreat* 1526 WM xxxvi, (*alias Pylat street*) 1536 ib. xxxviii. BRIDEWELL ST is so named from the old Bridewell, first erected as the town prison in 1787 (H. C. B.). Cf. *supra* 22. BUCK LANE was earlier Elcot Lane, *v.* Elcot *infra* 301. The present name is from the Roebuck Inn. COLDHARBOUR LANE is *Coleherbert lane* 1598 WM xxxviii. It was

---

[1] Association in some way with the recorded *Mærleswegen* (ASC *s.a.* 1067) has been suggested but that name is a very difficult one, being in part at least Scandinavian (NPN 93 f.).

alternatively known as *St Martyns lane* (1565 ib.). The 'cold harbour' is mentioned as *Coleharbour* ib. Cf. *infra* 451. GEORGE LANE is named after the George Inn (H. C. B.). THE GREEN is *la Grene* 1289 *Ass*, *The Grene* 1540 WM xii. HERD ST is *Hurdistrete* 1438, *Hurdilstrete* 1503 *MinAcct*, *Hardestrete* 1533–8 ECP, *Herd street* 1575, *Hurd street* 1672 WM xxxviii. The early forms are too uncertain for any choice between *herd* and *hurdle*. HERMITAGE LANE (lost), so called in 1548 (WM xxxviii), must be another name for *Hyde Lane*. The Hermitage (now a private house) stands in it. We have a reference to it in a record of "John Benton, anchorite of Marlborough presenting my lady with two simnels and holy wax" (LP iv, 2732) (H. C. B.). HIGH ST is *the Highe streat(e)* 1504, 1526 WM xxxvi, *le Highe strete* 1540 *MinAcct*. Cf. *supra* 21. HYDE LANE is so named from Sir Nicholas *Hyde* (ob. 1631), Lord Chief Justice, who lived at Marlborough (H. C. B.). Also called SUN LANE (local) from the Sun Inn. KINGSBURY ST is *Kyngesberystrete* 1438 *MinAcct*. Cf. *Kingesbur'* 1335 ib. and *s.n.* Calne *supra* 256. LONDON RD may be the *regia via* of 1289 (*Ass*). The part outside St Mary's was formerly *Neubury strete* 1334 Pat, *Niweburistret* 1335 *MinAcct*. PORT HILL lies by *Portfield* c. 1840 *TA*, the town open land, *v.* port and cf. Portmeadow in Malmesbury *supra* 52. ST MARTINS ST was earlier *vico de la Newelonde* 1289 *Ass*, *street called Newland* 1565 WM xxxviii. SILVERLESS ST may be *Sylver strete* 1540 WM xii. STONEBRIDGE LANE led to *Stonebridge* 1565 ib. xxxviii. TINPIT LANE was earlier *Baypit Lane*. Cf. *Bay pyttes* 1575 ib. It is near the bay which gives name to Bay Bridge *infra* 303.

Lost names include *Baleystrete* 1327 AD i, *Meidenestrete, Madenestrete* 1335 *MinAcct*, *Bucherrowe* (part of the old market, now demolished) 1548 WM xxxviii, *Deryestreate* 1568 *FF*, cf. Derry Hill *supra* 257.

BARTON FM is *Barton* 1198 Abbr, *Bertone, -a* 1211 RBE, 1224 ClR, *la Berton* 1236 Orig, *Berton de Merleberg* 1249 *Ass*, *Berton Regis* 1316 FA. *v.* beretun. It was the king's manor in DB and continued to be held by the Crown until it passed to the Seymours in the 16th century (H. C. B.). We have similarly a *barton*, no doubt originally a grange of the king's, outside both Gloucester and Bristol.

COW BRIDGE (6″) is *Colebrigge* c. 1300 *Stowe* 798, *Culbrige* 1503 *MinAcct*, *Cowlebridge* 1518 WM xxxvi, *Coolebridge* 1574 ib. xxxviii. The forms are too uncertain for any interpretation, but it is clear that the present form is due to folk-etymology, helped perhaps by its being opposed to a lost *Bulbrigge* (1438 *MinAcct*).

FLEXBURGH[1] (lost)

> *Flexebereg'* 1201 P, *-berg* 13th AD i, *Flexbur'* 1252, *-borgh* 1280 WIpm, *Flexebyr'*, *Flexberg'* 1268, *-burewe* 1279, 1281 *Ass*, *-bury* 1503 *MinAcct*, *Loxbrowe al. Flexbrowe* t. Eliz ChancP
>
> *Flaxburg* 1215 P, *Flaxbarewe* 1263 *For*
>
> *Prior domus Sce Margarete juxta Marlebergh* 1317 Orig, 1327 SR, *Prior Sce Margarete de Flexburgh* 1438 *MinAcct*

'Hill where flax was grown,' *v.* beorg.

ISBURY[2]

> *Everesbyr'* 1249 FF
>
> *Euesbur'* 1257, *Euesebury* 1290, 1331, t. Ed 3, t. Hy 6 *For*
>
> *Evesbury* 13th *Bradenstoke*, t. Ed 2 *For*
>
> *Evenesbur'* 1276 StOsmund
>
> *Enesbury* 1412 Pat, 1413 Inq aqd
>
> *Isbury* 1819 RCH

This is a difficult name. Were it not for the forms *Everesbyr*, *Evenesbur'*, one might well take this name to be a compound of OE efes, 'eaves, border,' and burh. Such a compound would be aptly descriptive of the site of Isbury just on the edge of Savernake Forest where there are still earthworks on the western edge of the old Roman site here[3]. It is difficult however to reject those two forms. One might explain the first as a case of dittography, but that would not explain the second. We seem to have AN interchange between *n* and *r*, as in the forms of Avebury *supra* 293–4. If that is so the interpretation of the name must remain uncertain.

SUMMERFIELD (6″) is *Sumerfeld'* 1202 Cur, 1203 FF, *Somerfelde* 1281 *Ass* (p), possibly with reference to an open space used as summer pasturage. *v.* feld.

BROADLEAZE (6″) is *Broadleas* c. 1840 *TA*. *v.* læs.

---

[1] The site of Flexburgh is unknown. It was a separate holding long after the founding of St Margaret's priory, and the exact interpretation of the phrase in *MinAcct* (1438) is uncertain.

[2] Preserved in ISBURY LANE (6″).

[3] In BCS 677 *efes* seems similarly to be used of the border of Chute Forest.

Mildenhall

MILDENHALL [mainəl]

> *Mildanhald* 803–5 (c. 1200) BCS 324
>
> *Mildenhalle* 1086 DB, *-hal(e)* 1268, 1279 *Ass*, 1297 Cl, (*juxta Marlebergh*) 1305 *FF*
>
> *Mildehale* 1241 Ch, AD ii, 1242 Fees, 1262, *-hall* 1269 Pat, 1282 Ipm
>
> *Midnall* 1539 *Phillipps*, *Mylenoll* t. Eliz WM xxi, *Middenhall* 1675 Ogilby, *Mildenhall oth. Minal* 1760 *Recov*

'*Milda*'s healh or corner of land.'

COCK-A-TROOP COTTAGES (6″)

> *Crokerestrope* 1257 *For*, *Crokkeresthrop* 1282 *Ass*, *Crokeresthorpesend* 1300 WM iv
>
> *Crockerthrop* t. Ed 2 *For*, 1327 *SR* (p), *Crokerethropesende* t. Ed 3 *For*
>
> *Cocketrappe downe* 1578 *Sav*

'þorp or hamlet of the *crocker* or maker of pots.' Cf. Crockerton *supra* 166 and Crockerhill (PN Sx 66). It may be that it takes its name from the numerous sherds turned up by the plough in the neighbouring Black Field, the site of Hoare's *Lower Cunetio* (H. C. B.).

ELCOT MILL (6″) is *Elcot'* 1237 Lib, 1412 Pat, *Ellecote* 1257 *For*, t. Hy 3 *Stowe* 798, 1276 StOsmund, 1286 Ch, *Ele-* 1270 *For*, 1294 *Rental*, 1300 Wm iv, *Elescote extra Marlebergh* 1331 *For*, *Elcote Mill* 1547 Pat. Possibly 'elder tree cot(e),' *v.* ellen.

POULTON (6″)[1] is *Poltone* 1086 DB, *-ton* 1201 Cur, 1242 Fees, 1268 *Ass*, 1316 FA, (*juxta Marleburgh*) 1454 PCC, *Pulton(e)* 1211 RBE, 1227 FF, 1242 Fees, 1249 *Ass*, *Pultun* 1243 Ipm, *Poulten* 1625 WIpm. 'Farm by the pool,' *v.* pol, tun.

SOUND COPSE and BOTTOM are *le Soune* 1384 *FF*, *Sounde* 1443 *MinAcct*, *la Soune* 1487 Pat, *Sound Hill* c. 1840 *TA* (Ramsbury). This is a difficult name. Sound Bottom is a deep-cut, narrow valley. It may possibly be a development of the rare ME *sound*, 'safety, security,' in the sense 'place of safety, shelter.'

---

[1] Cf. Poulton Down (1″).

STITCHCOMBE

> *Stotecome* 1086 DB, *-cumb(a)* 1165 P, 1217 ClR
> *Stutescombe* 1200 Cur (p), 1208 AD i (p), 1316 FA, *-cumb(e)*
>   1228 Cl, 1242 Fees, 1249 *Ass*, 1537 *BodlCh*
> *Studescombe* 1275 RH
> *Stuttescumb* 1281, *-combe* 1289 *Ass*
> *Stotescombe juxta Marleberge* 1282 *Ass*, *Stotescumbe* 1307 *FF*,
>   *-coumbe* 1332 *SR*, *-combe* 1391 *FF*
> *Stichcombe* 1574, *Stytchcomb* 1576 *FF*, *Stuttescombe al.*
>   *Stichcombe* 1626 WIpm

The first element here would seem to be the OE *stūt*, 'gnat,
midge,' used as a personal name. Hence '*Stūt*'s valley,' *v.* cumb.
For the sound development cf. Stuchbury (PN Nth 58).

DEANFIELD BARN[1] (6″), GROVE FM, HILL BARN (6″) and MERE
FM[2] were the homes of Robert *atte Dene* (1327 *SR*), John *atte
Grove* (t. Ed 2 *For*), Adam *atte Hulle* (1327 *SR*), John de *la Mere*
(1279 *Ass*) and John *atte Mere* (1341 NI). *v.* denu, grafa, mere.

DURNSFORD MILL (6″) is perhaps to be associated with the family
of John de *Dunnesford* (1282 WIpm). It is *Durnsford* 1578 *Sav.*

BLACK FIELD is *Blacke fyeld* 1578 *Sav.* EAST CROFT COPSE.
Cf. *Estcroft* 1542 ib. FOLLY COPSE (6″). Cf. *Folly Down* c. 1840
TA and *infra* 451. OXLEAZE COPSE (6″) is *Oxelease* 1637 *Sav.*
v. læs *infra* 438. RABLEY WOOD is *Rabley Wood* 1773 A and D.
SMATCHAM'S COTTAGES (6″) is probably identical with *Maccheham*
1336, *Maccham* 1425 *MinAcct.* The first element may then be
OE *(ge)mæcca*, 'companion.' Addition of initial *s* is common in
dialect. Cf. Pickledean *infra* 306. THICKET COPSE. Cf. *boscus
de Thykett'* 1381 *MinAcct.* WELL GROUND COPSE (6″). Cf. *Well
Ground* c. 1840 *TA.* WERG MILL (6″) is *Wirge* 1577 PCC, *Wary
Mill* 1773 A and D, *Werg Mill* 1820 G. No explanation of this
name can be offered, but it seems to repeat itself in *the Wirgo*
(*TA*) in Milston, a corn-mill. WHITESHARD BOTTOM. Cf. *White
shurde* 1591 WM vi. *v.* sceard, 'gap,' and *infra* 445. There is a
long dyke which crosses this bottom in chalky ground (H. C. B.).
WOODLANDS FM. Cf. *Wodelond* 1403 *MinAcct.*

[1] Cf. *Deneclos* 1427 *MinAcct.*   [2] *Mear Farm* 1773 A and D.

Ogbourne St Andrew and St George

OGBOURNE ST ANDREW, ST GEORGE and MAIZEY[1]

Oceburnan 946–55 (c. 1150) BCS 819

Ocheburne, -borne 1086 DB, *Ocheburna magna et parva* c. 1143 HMC Var vii, *Okeburn* 1208 StOsmund, 1228 Cl, 1242 FF

Occheburna 1133 France, *Ockeburne* c. 1230 SarumCh, 1242 Fees, c. 1250 *Rental*, 1257 Cl, *-borne* 1246 *Kings*, 1252 BM

Ockeburn' Meysy 1242 Fees, *Okkeburne Magna, Parva* 1316 FA, (*Moysy*) ib.

Okeborne Meysy, Prioris, Magna 1268 *Ass*, (*Sci Andr'*) 1289 ib., *North, Parva Okeburne* 1275 RH, *Okeburn Major, Minor* 1291 Tax, *Little Okeburn without Marleberwe* 1296 Ipm, *Okeburne Sci Georgii, Sci Andree* 1332 SR, *Okeborne Seynt George* 1462 Pat

Auquebourne 1390 BM, *Ockborn* t. Eliz WM xxi, *Oakeborne* 1669 *FF*

Oggeburn St George 1449 Pat, *Ogborne Sent George, Sent Androes* 1544 SR

'*Oc(c)a*'s stream,' *v.* **burna**. Cf. *Bynethe Oggendyche* (1292 *Magd*) in the neighbouring parish of Wanborough. The name *Ocea* is on record from Wiltshire in the 9th century. Robert de *Meysey* held a manor here in 1242 (Fees). For the river Og, *v. supra* 9. *Great* and *Little* are applied respectively to Ogbourne St George and St Andrew.

Ogbourne St Andrew

BAY BRIDGE. This name is to be taken together with Baymeadow (Fd) *infra* 498, *water called Baylake* (1547 Pat), *Baywater* (1565 WM xxxviii), *Bay pyttes* (1575 ib.). Mr Brentnall notes that all these names have reference to the *bay* or dam which formed the *King's Great Stew* which lay in the Og between Bay Bridge and Poulton. Frequent mention of it is made in *MinAcct* from 1280 to c. 1400. See *bay* sb.[5] in NED.

---

[1] Ogbourne Maizey is a hamlet in Ogbourne St George parish.

Rockley

> Rochelie 1086 DB, Rokeleya 1155 Templars, Rokel(e) 1222
> ClR, 1258 FF, -ley 1285 FF, la Rokele 1234 Cl (p)
> Roclea t. Hy 1 (1270) Ch, Rocle(e) 1155, 1185 Templars, 1255
> RH, 1273 Ipm, (juxta Marlebergh) 1310 Ass, Roucle 1316 FA
> Rockel' 1242 Fees, -le 1275 RH
> Roukley 1301 Ipm, -le 1332 SR, Rookle 1335 Ipm, Temple-
> rookley 1591 FF, Ruckleyghe 1595 Sadler

'Rooks' clearing or wood,' v. leah. "The rooks are still very
much in evidence and work the district in regular daily com-
panies" (H. C. B.). The Templars held land here from 1155.

Coombe[1], Dean Bottom[2] and Wick Bottom[3] were the homes
of Richard de Coumbe (1332 SR), Hugh de la Dene (1246 Kings)
and Robert de Wika (t. Hy 3 Add). v. cumb, denu, wic.

Castle Fm. The castle is Barbury supra 278. Drove Barn (6″).
Cf. Long, Short Drove c. 1840 TA and infra 429. Middledown
is Middle Down ib. Ogbourne Down is montem de Okeborn'
1289 Ass. Poughcombe (6″) is Pokcombe 1496 Ct, Pookham
c. 1840 TA. Probably 'goblin valley,' v. puca. Smeathe's
Plantation and Ridge. Cf. Smeath c. 1840 TA. Smith
(Section xiii) gives (local) Smeath Ridge. Probably OE smeðe,
'smooth.' It is on the top of the Down. The s is pseudo-
manorial. Temple Bottom. Cf. Temple Bottom Mead ib. and
Temple Fm infra 309.

Ogbourne St George

Herdswick Fm [hesik] is Hessick 1773 A and D, Heswick 1816
Kings, Hessick Barn 1820 G, c. 1840 TA and was the home of
Walter de Hereswyke (1268 Ass). The forms are too late for any
satisfactory interpretation of the name.

Southend is Southend Farm 1841 Devizes and was probably the
home of Gilbert Bisuthe (i.e. 'by south') 1246 Kings.

Moore's Wood is to be associated with the family of William
More (1465 Ct). It is Moores Wood t. Jas 1 ECP.

---

[1] Combe Hill 1773 A and D.   [2] Dean Bottom 1820 G.
[3] pastura de Wik 1282 Kings.

BYTHAM FM [bitəm] is *Bitham* 1820 G. *v.* **bytme** *infra* 425.
CHANTRY MEADOW (6″) is *The Chantry Meadow* c. 1840 *TA*.
CHURCH HILL is *Chirchehyll* 1496 *Ct*. COWCROFT FM (6″) is
Cowcrofte 1561 *DuLa*, *Cow Crate Farm* 1816 *Kings*, *v.* croft
infra 427–8. FOX LYNCH (6″) is so named c. 1840 (*TA*). *v.* hlinc
infra 436. POOR'S FURZE (6″) is so named ib. ROUND HILL
DOWNS. Cf. *Rowndhill* 1559 Pat, *Rounde hill* 1606 *LRMB*.
RUSHMORE POND (6″) is *Ryschmere* 1290 *For*. *v.* rysc, mere.
WESTFIELD is *le Westfeld* 1465 *Ct*. WHITEFIELD is *Whytefeld*
1268 *Ass*, *Witefelde* t. Hy 3 *Add*, *Whightfeld* 1561 *DuLa*. *v.* feld.
WOOLMER FM [uˑmər] is *Wolvemere* 1339 *For*, *Wolfmere* 1348
Cor (p). 'Wolves' pool,' *v.* mere. YIELDING COPSE. Cf. *Ylden*
1496 *Ct*, *Yeldons hedge corner* 1591 WM vi.

West Overton[1]

WEST OVERTON

> *Uferan tune, Oferan tunes land* 939 BCS 734
> *æt Ofærtune* 949 (c. 1150) BCS 875, *Ovretone* 1086 DB,
>   *Ouertun'* 1165 P, *-ton(e)* 1255 RH, 1279 *FF*, 1291 Tax,
>   (*Fifhide, Abbatisse*) 1316 FA, (*Abbesse*) 1524 *SR*, (*East,
>   West*) 1682 *Recov*
> *Uverton* 1242 Fees, *-tun* c. 1250 *Rental*, *Uverton Abbisse* 1263
>   *For*
> *Westovertone* 1275 RH

'Upper farm,' *v.* ufera, tun. Cf. Overton (Ha), (*to*) *uferatune*,
uferantun 909 (12th) BCS 625, *Uverton* 1158, *Overton* 1167 P.

BOREHAM WOOD is *Borham* 1249 *Ass*, t. Hy 3 *Stowe* 798, (*bosc.
de*) t. Ed 2 *For, foresta de Burham* 1268 *Ass*, t. Hy 3 *Stowe* 798,
t. Ed 3 *For, Bourham, Boureham haga* t. Ed 1, *Boureham* t. Ed 2
ib. The persistent *u* and *ou* in the early forms and the topography
suggest that this cannot be identical with Boreham Wood (PN
Herts 74), for the vowel there is clearly an original *o* and the
wood lies high, whereas the site of Boreham would seem to have
been in the valley. The first element may therefore be OE

---

[1] West Overton parish includes the tithing of *East* Overton which has a
different history. BCS 734 gives the bounds of *East* Overton, BCS 875 of
West Overton. *West* Overton is Overton *Abbatisse* and was held by the Abbess
of Wilton, *East* Overton belonged to the Abbey of St Swithin's, Winchester
(H. C. B.). Cf. *Ouertun Prioris* (1167 P).

(*ge*)*būr*, 'peasant,' and the whole name mean 'peasants' homestead,' *v.* (ge)bur *infra* 424 and ham.

FOSBURY COTTAGES (6″) is *Forstesbyria* t. Hy 2 (1270) Ch, *-beria* 1178 BM, *Forstelberia* t. John Dugd ii, *Forstebir'* 1225 ClR, *Forstesbur'* 1242 Fees, *Forstesbury* 1289 *Ass*, *Forestesbury* 1366 Pat, *Fortesbury* 1570 PembSurv, *Fortisbury al. Fossebury* 1654 *Recov*. 'The hill-burh.' Cf. Furzehill *supra* 245.

HURSLEY BOTTOM is (*on*) *hyrsleage* 939 BCS 734, (*on*) *ers leage* 972 (13th) ib. 1285, *lez bottom de Hurseley* 1570 PembSurv, *Husley Bottom* 1818 O.S. We may compare the forms given by Ekwall (DEPN) for Hursley (Ha), *Hurselye* 1171 Winton and others. These suggest the possibility of an OE *hyrs*, 'mare' (cf. Holthausen 185, *s.v.*), cognate with ON *hryssa*, 'mare.' Hence 'mare-clearing,' *v.* leah. See further *Studies*[2] 65.

LOCKERIDGE is *Locherige* 1086 DB, *Lokeruga* 1142, *Lokerugge* 1155–69 Templars *et freq* to 1332 *SR*, with variant spellings *-krigge, -rygge, Locrugge* 1185 Templars. *Lokerigga jvxta Marleberges, Lokerigges extra Marleburghe* c. 1280 Winton. Possibly for OE *loc*(*a*)*-hrycg*, 'ridge marked by enclosure(s),' *v.* loc(a), hrycg.

PICKLEDEAN (6″) is *pytteldene* 939 BCS 734, *Pykkeldean* 1570 PembSurv, *Piggledean* 1815 O.S., *Speckledean* 1820 G. The first element is OE *pyttel*, 'mouse-hawk,' cf. *Studies*[2] 91. Hence 'hawk-valley.' Interchange of [t] and [k] is common. For *sp* cf. Smatcham *supra* 302.

PUMPHREY WOOD is to be associated with the family of Edward *Pumphrey* (1794 *Wilton*), a tenant in Overton. The earlier name was *Cheecheangles* 1542 *Sav*, *Chichangles wood* 1794 *Wilton*, *Chick Changles Wood* 1818 O.S., identified by Mr G. M. Young, with *scyt hangran* 939 BCS 734. hangra appears elsewhere as ME *hangel* (cf. Barnacle (PN Wa 101) and Hangleton (PN Sx 168, 289)) so that there is no difficulty about the identification, even in name. The first element may be OE **scīete*, **scȳte*, 'nook, corner,' hence 'corner wood.' Cf. Shute (PN D 184).

WOOLS GROVE (6″) is *Wolveseyegrove, Wulfsiesgrove, Wulsiesgrove* t. Ed 2 *For*, *Wolciesgrove* 1333 Pat, *Wolles Grove* 1570 PembSurv. '*Wulfsige*'s grove,' *v.* grafa.

DEAN[1] and HEATH COTTAGES[2] (6″) were probably the homes of John *atte Dene* (1332 *SR*) and Ralph *atte Hethe* (1385 *NewColl*). *v.* denu, 'valley.'

BAYARDO FM (6″) is named after a race-horse (G. M. Y.). BITHAM BARROW (6″). Cf. **bytme** *infra* 425. BREACH COTTAGES (6″). Cf. **bræc** *infra* 423. DOWN BARN is so named in 1820 (G). Cf. *Down furlong* 1794 *Wilton*. GREY WETHERS are *The Grey Wethers* 1721 WM xi. A nickname for the sarsen stones here. HENLEY WOOD (6″) is *Hendley* 1570 PembSurv. Probably '(at the) high clearing,' *v.* heah, leah. HILL BARN (6″). Cf. *Hylhouse* ib. LITTLE WOOD (6″) is *Lytlewood* 1542 *Sav*, 1570 PembSurv. PICKRUDGE (6″) is *Pickrudge wood* 1794 *Wilton*. SHAW FM is *Schaga* 1165 P, *Saghe* 1229 StOsmund, *Schages* 1242 Fees, *Shagh* 1279 *Ass*, *Shawe* 1316 FA, (*juxta Savernak*) 1386 *Ass*. *v.* sceaga, 'wood, copse.' SPYE PARK is so called in 1820 (G). WEST OVERTON DOWN. Cf. *super montem de Overton* 1348 *Cor*. WEST WOOD is *Westwode* 1337 Pat. WHITE HILL is *Whithill* 1570 PembSurv.

Preshute

PRESHUTE ['preʃuˑt]

Prestcheta 1185 P, -*chet* c. 1220 HMC Var 1, 1247 Pat (p)

Preschet(e) 1223 SarumCh, 1232 HMC Var 1, 1272 FF

Presteshethe 1249 *Ass*

Preschut(e) 1252 SarumCh, 1268 *Ass*, *Preshut* 1329 Pat, 1614 FF

Prestchut(e) 1279, 1281, 1289 *Ass*, 1290 *For*, 1297 Pat, 1338, 1404 Pat, *Prestshute juxta Marlebergh* 1312 *Ass*, *Prestcheut*, -*chuyt* t. Ed 2 *For*, *Presthut* 1428 FA

Prestechut 14th Bradenstoke, 1331 *Stowe* 925, -*chuyt* 1381 MinAcct

Pershute 1321 Pat, 1322 Ipm, *Perschuyt* 1385 Cl

Presshett 1530, 1568 *Recov*, *Presshatte* 1553 WM i, *Presshyatt* 1553 Pat, *Pres(h)ate* t. Eliz WM xxi

This name is not an easy one. The forms make it clear that the second element is *chete, chute* rather than *schete, schute*. One might, as Ekwall notes (DEPN), suggest that the second element

---

[1] *Lockeridge Dane* 1773 A and D. Cf. *Deaneclos* 1570 PembSurv.
[2] Cf. *Ye heath vel Abbes Wood* ib., i.e. 'abbess,' *v. supra* 305 n.

was another example of Chute (*supra* 12) and that the whole name means '*Chute* belonging to a priest.' More probably, as Ekwall himself suggests, we have OE *cīete*, 'cottage, cell.' The word is in common use in OE, especially in association with monks and anchorites and is probably found also in the unidentified place (*on*) *cygean cytan* (BCS 870) in the bounds of Knoyle, and may well be the first element in Chitterne *supra* 163. Hence 'priest's cottage(s).'

CLATFORD is *Clatford* 1086 DB, 1204 ClR, 1229 StOsmund, 1242 Fees *et passim*, *Clacford Monachorum* 1166 P, *Clafort* t. Hy 2 (1328) Ch, *Clateford* 1289 *Ass*, *Clatford Prioris*, *Clatford Parke* 1622 ParReg. 'Ford where the water-lily (OE *clāte*) grows.' Cf. Claverton (So), *Clatfordtun* c. 1000 (12th) ASWills. There was an alien priory here, a cell of the abbey of St Victor en Caux, France (Jones 207).

GRANHAM FM is *Grendon* t. Ed 1, 1290, t. Ed 2 *For*, 14th Bradenstoke, *Grandoncopice* 1503 *MinAcct*, *Granham* 1773 A and D. 'Green hill,' *v.* dun.

MANTON is *Manetune* 1086 DB, *Maniton* 1229 StOsmund, 1242 Fees, 1249, 1275 RH, *Maninton* 1249 *Ass*, 1257 *For*, -*yn*- 1289 *Ass*, 1300 Ipm, *Manniton* 1265 Misc, *Manyngton* 1281 *Ass*, *Manton* 1259 Ipm, 1428 FA. '*Manna*'s farm,' *v.* ingtun. Cf. Manningford *infra* 320.

STANMORE BARN (6″) is *Stanmer* 1738 *FF*, *Stanmoor* c. 1840 *TA*, and was the home of Richard de *Stanmere* (1327 *SR*). 'Stony pool,' *v.* stan, mere. Cf. Stanmer (PN Sx 312) and Stanmore Copse *supra* 267.

STONE'S WOOD (6″) is to be associated with the family of Margaret *Stone* (1667 ParReg).

BARROW COTTAGES (6″). Cf. *Barrow Piece* c. 1840 *TA*. There is a tumulus here. CONEY BURY (6″) is *Cunney Bury* 1773 A and D, i.e. 'rabbit-burrow.' DEVIL'S DEN is an ancient burial chamber. FOXBURY COPSE (6″) is *Foxberry* c. 1840 *TA*. GLORY ANN BARN is *Glory Ann* 1773 A and D. ROUGH DOWN is *Rugedon* 1201 Cur (p), *Rowedone* 1270 *For*, *Rughedune* 1335 *MinAcct*, *Row Down* 1773 A and D, *v.* ruh, dun. SHARPRIDGE

is *Sharpridge Barn* 1818 O.S. SHOULDER OF MUTTON PLANTA-
TION (6″). Cf. *infra* 455. TEMPLE FM is *Templerookley* 1591
FF. The Templars already owned Rockley (*supra* 304) in
1155. WICK DOWN. Cf. *montem vocatum Wyke* 1570 PembSurv
and wic.

Winterbourne Bassett and Monkton

WINTERBOURNE BASSETT and MONKTON
> *Wintreborne, -burne* 950 (15th) BCS 886, 1086 DB, *-burn(a)*
> 1114 France, 1198 BM, 1220 FF, *Winterborn* 1196 ib.
> *Winterburne Monachorum* 1249 *Ass*, (*Monacor'*) 1275 RH,
> *Moneke Wynterburn* 1251 FF, *Wynterburne Abbatis Glas-
> ton'* 1267 Abbr, *Monekenewynterburne* 1281 *Ass*
> *Wynterburn' Basset* 1249 *Ass*
> *Monketon* 1348 *Cor*, *Mounkton* 1544, *Monkton* 1571 *SR*

Winterbourne must be the name of the upper part of the
river Kennet, *v. supra* 8. Winterbourne Monkton was held by
Glastonbury Abbey (DB). Winterbourne Bassett, which Alan
Basset received from his uncle Walter de Dunstanville, was
confirmed to him by Richard i in 1194 (BM). Cf. Wootton
Bassett *supra* 272.

Winterbourne Bassett

RABSON FM is *Wintreborne* 1086 DB, *Northwinterburna* t. Hy 2
(1270) Ch, *North Wynterburn* 1178 BM, *Abbedeston* 1242 Fees,
Rabbedeston(e) 1275 RH, 1316, 1428 FA, *Rabboteston* 1279 *Ass*,
Rabbodesdon 1332, *Robston* 1544 *SR*, *Northwynterborne al.
Rabeston* 1588, *Rabson* 1719 *Recov*, *Rapson* 1773 A and D.
According to Jones (242) this is the DB manor held by the
Abbess of Amesbury. *Abbedeston* would seem to stand for
earlier *Abbedesseton* and the forms with initial *r* must be
explained as coming from ME *at ther Abbedeston*, 'at the Abbess-
farm or manor.' For the forms cf. Rivar *infra* 355.

RICHARDSON (6″) is *Ricardeston(e)* 1242 Fees, 1245 WM xvi,
1255 RH, 1316 FA, *Richardeston, -y-* 1249, 1370 *Ass*, *Richardston
al. Ricarston* 1561 *FF*, *Rickersons* 1818 O.S. This is a post-
Conquest tun-formation. In 1168 (P) we have mention of

Winterburn' Ric' fil. Hug' and in 1189 (GlastInq) one *Ricardus* held land in *Winterburna*. Hence 'Richard's farm,' v. tun. *Richard* is an OFr personal name of Germanic origin. Rickeston, found twice in Pembrokeshire, has the same history (NCPNW 28, 71).

DROCK PIECE. See under Rockmoor Pond *infra* 340. GRIPPS COTTAGES (6″). Cf. *The Gripes* 1773 A and D, 1818 O.S., *Pasture Grips* c. 1840 *TA* and grip *infra* 452. 'Small water channel.' LAMBOURNE GROUND (6″). Cf. *Lampourneway* 1570 PembSurv. WHYR FM [wəˑr] is *The Wire* 1773 A and D, *The Whyr, Wher Farm* 1820 G.

Winterbourne Monkton

HACKPEN HILL

> (*on*) *hacan penne* 939 BCS 734
> (*super*) *Hakepen* 1245 WM xvi, *Hakepenn(e)* 1275 RH, 1372, 1454 *Winton, Hackpen, Hacpendowne* 1570 PembSurv, *Hackpinn Downes* 1695 NQ viii

This is not an easy name. Some of the difficulties arise from the problem already discussed under Pen Hill *supra* 34, viz. whether **penn** here represents the Old Celtic word for a hill or the English **penn**, 'enclosure.' The probabilities are in favour of the hill-interpretation. The first reference comes from the Overton charter (BCS 734). The boundary passes *oþ þæne herpoð on hacan penne*. Since *penne* is in the dative it would seem that this must be translated 'to the *herepæð* on Hackpen,' and though it is impossible to trace the bounds of Overton exactly, we are certainly not far from the south end of Hackpen Hill at this point in the boundaries as given in the charter. In the next two references we have again the phrase *super Hakepen(n)* and this confirms the suggestion that *Hakepen* must have been the name of the hill itself. If that is so, the first part of the name should probably be associated with OE *haca*, 'hook,' the reference being to the projecting end of the hill running off Monkton Down. This interpretation is consistent with the idea, suggested under Pen Hill *supra* 34, that the word *penn* was so far anglicised that you could compound it with an English element. For such a compound we have a parallel in Hackpen Barton (PN D 538), taking its name from the hill called *hacapenn* (now Hackpen Hill) which thrusts itself forward prominently into the valley of the Culm (BCS 724). Cf. PN D 612, n. 1. See Addenda *supra* xl.

WEST FIELD BARN (6″). Cf. *le Westfeld* 1364 *Ct.* WINDMILL HILL is so named in 1773 (A and D). It is probably *Wyndmulle-hulle* 1334 WIpm.

XXVII. STUDFOLD HUNDRED

Stotfalde, -a hundred 1086 ExonDB, *hundred de Stotfald* 1156, *Stodfoldehdr* 1167, 1168 P, *Stodfold* 1249 *Ass*, 1255 RH, *-felde* 1316 FA. 'Horse or stud enclosure,' v. stott, stod, falod. The hundred is now merged in that of Swanborough *infra* 317. The meeting-place was at Foxley Corner on Lydeway *infra* 316–7. It may have been so called from some ancient enclosure here, v. stodfald and cf. IPN 150–2.

Allington

ALLINGTON

Adelingtone 1086 DB, *Athelinetona* (sic) 1242 Gloucester
    Cartulary
Alingeton 1196 Cur, 1198 Abbr *et freq* to 1316 *FF*, with
    variant spelling *Alynge-, Alungeton* 1242 Fees, *Alinggeton*
    1312 Pat
Alington 1275 RH, 1285 Ch, 1316 FA, *Alyngton juxta*
    Allecanynges 1341 *FF, Alyngton in Canyngmershe* 1394
    GDR

Perhaps, as suggested by Ekwall (DEPN), from OE *æþelinga-tun*, 'tun of the princes,' cf. Athelney (So), earlier *Æþelinga eigg* (ASC). For *Canyngmershe*, v. *supra* 249–50.

CHILD'S FM (6″) is to be associated with the family of Martha *Childe* (1674 ParReg).

THE GOG (6″) is by a small stream and is doubtless the word *gog* noted *infra* 452.

All Cannings[1]

St Ann's Hill (Tan Hill (6")) is *S. Anns Hill* 1610 S, *St Annes or St Anns Hill* 1773 A and D. The famous Tan Hill Fair was held on Aug. 6, the Feast of St Anne. The church of All Cannings is dedicated to that saint.

Chandler's Lane (6") and Clifford's Hill are to be associated with the families of William *Chanlor* (1585 ParReg) and Phillippe *Clifford* (1611 ib.). The latter is *Clifford Hills* 1773 A and D.

All Cannings Down. Cf. *les Dounes de Canynges* 1362 *For.* South Fm. Cf. *Southe Alcannyng* 1620 *FF, South Farm* 1773 A and D. Woodway Bridge. Cf. *Woodway* c. 1840 *TA.*

Chirton

Chirton

> *Ceritone* 1086 DB, *Cheriton(a)* 1242 Fees, 1259 FF, *Cheryton* 1279, 1281 *Ass, Chereton* 1324 FA
>
> *Cherint'* 1196 Cur
>
> *Chireton(e), -y-* 1211 RBE, 1242 Fees, 1307 *Extent*
>
> *Chiriton* 1230, 1245 Cl, 1237 FF, *Chyri-* 1279, 1289 *Ass,* 1286 Cl
>
> *Chirinton* 1249 FF, 1253 Cl, *Chyrin-* 1249, *Chyryn-* 1268 *Ass*
>
> *Churiton(e)* 1286 Ipm, 1289 *Ass, Churyggethon* 1332 *SR*
>
> *Churughton* 1316 FA, 1325 Pat, *Churghton* 1322 Ipm, 1341 NI
>
> *Chirghton* 1349 *FF, Chirughton, -y-* 1373 Pat, 1375 Inq aqd, *Shirghton* 1428 FA, *Cherghton* 1481 IpmR
>
> *Chereweton* 1412 FA, *Cheryngton* 1593 *FF*

'Farm by or belonging to the church,' *v.* cirice, tun. Cf. Cherrington (PN Wa 279).

Conock is *Cunet* 1211 RBE, *Kunek* 1242 Fees, *Cunnuc* c. 1250 *Rental, Conek* 1268, *-ok* 1279 *Ass, -eke* 1316 FA, *Kyneke* 1278 *Ass, Connok* 1372 BM, *Conke* 1522 *SR,* 1527 *Ct.* It is probable that this is a British place-name. The forms suggest a derivative in *-āco-* of *cuno-*, 'high' (cf. Chrest 44), but there is no ap-

---

[1] For the parish name, *v. supra* 249–50.

preciable hill here. The word is also on record as a personal name, and is so found in Ploegonec (Brittany, cf. Chrest 200) and in Boconnoc and Tregunnick (Co), but this does not seem a possible explanation here, since the element is found uncompounded from the earliest records.

Etchilhampton

ETCHILHAMPTON [æʃəltən *olim* æʃliŋtən]

(i) *Echesatingetone, Ecesatingetone* 1086 DB, *Hechesetingeton* 1206 ChR

(ii) *Echehamt', Ehelhamton'* 1196 Cur, *Hechelhamt'* 1228 Cl
Echelhampton 1236 FF *et passim* to 1332 *SR*, with variant spelling *-hamton, Hechelhamtona* 1242 Fees
Ashlington al. Echilhampton 1622, *Echilhampton al. Ashington* 1647 Recov, *Ashlington* 1773 A and D
Itchelhampton t. Eliz WM xxi, *Edghillhampton* 1675 Ogilby

This is a difficult name. In the *TA* the place is grouped with All Cannings and it may be suggested that Etchilhampton is really an offshoot of All Cannings which is doubtless the older and more important of the two places. The element (*i*)*ecels*, a lost OE word denoting 'addition, something added, additional land taken into cultivation,' has been discussed under Nechells (PN Wa 30) and is found in various parts of the country, and like most words in *-els* shows a tendency later to drop the final *s*. It may be suggested as a possibility that Etchilhampton was an (*i*)*ecels* to All Cannings. No explanation of the DB form can be offered, it would seem to have the same first element.

TINKFIELD FM (6″) is *Fing Field Barn* 1773 *Devizes, Tinkfield* c. 1840 *TA*. This lies just west of Etchilhampton Hill, the meeting-place for the Hundred of Cannings (cf. *supra* 249). This suggests that the first element is the Old English *þing*, 'assembly,' used elsewhere in hundred and other names; cf. Tingrith Hundred (PN BedsHu 134) and Fingest (PN Bk 176) where we have the same confusion of initial *th* and *f* and Anglo-Norman *t*. Cf. also perhaps Tinghale (PN Sx 92).

ETCHILHAMPTON HILL is *Ashlington Hill* 1725 *Devizes*, 1744 Act.

Patney

<small>PATNEY</small>

(*æt*) *Peatanige*, (*to*) *Peattanige*, (*to*) *Pittanige* 963 (c. 1150) BCS 1118, (*æt*) *Peattaniggi* 1049–52 (c. 1150) KCD 949

Pateney(*e*) 1171 WintonCart, 1242 Cl, 1255 RH, 1279 *Ass*, 1300 Ch, -*eia* 1205 Pap, -*ie* 1275 RH, -*y* 1280 Abbr, -*ay* 1281 QW, *Pattenei* 1243 Pap

Peteneia 1230 Ch, *Peteny* 1242 Fees, *Pettenye* 1249 *Ass*, *Peteneye* c. 1250 *Rental*

Patney 1284 Ch

'*Peatta*'s well-watered land,' *v. eg.*

NOTE. *Churche lane*, *Tyllyes lane* 1570 PembSurv.

HAIL BRIDGE (6″). Cf. *terra voc. Hayle* 1570 PembSurv. There is a small stream here and it is possible that we have another example of the stream-name *Hail* found in PN BedsHu 7–8. LIMBER STONE BRIDGE (6″). Cf. *Lymberstone meade* 1561 *Corpus*, *Lymberstone*, *Lymerstone* 1570 PembSurv.

Stert

<small>STERT</small> [stə'rt]

Sterte 1086 DB, 1199 P, 1242 Fees, *Stertes* 1197 P, *la Sterte* 1258 Ipm

Stuerte 1196 ClR

Storte ib., 1283 Ch

Stoerte 1189 GlastInq, 1268 *Ass*, 1329, 1334, 1388 Pat

Sturtes 1211 RBE, *Sturte* 1268 *Ass*, 1333 Cl

Steorte juxta Echelhampton 1304 *Ass*, *Steorte* 1314 Cl, 1356 Ipm

Steurte 1311, 1390 Pat, 1333 Misc

v. steort, 'tail, point of land.' The above spellings are attempts to represent a sound [ɶ], the equivalent of ModFr *eu*, ModGer *ö*. This sound is not found in ME except in a dialectal development of OE *eo*. It is common in MidCornish, as in Breton, where it is variously represented in medieval documents by *eo*, *oe*, *eu*, *ue* by English scribes. Thus the MidCornish form of OCorn *mor*, 'great,' appears as *moer*, *meor*, *muer*, *meur*, *mur*.

FULLAWAY FM (6″) is *Foleweye* 1327 *SR* (p), *Fulle-* 1403, 1515 *NewColl*, *-way* 1384 NQ iv, *Fulwey* 1403 *NewColl*, *Fulwaye* 1564 *FF*, *Fulloway al. Fullway* 1695 *Recov*. Probably 'dirty way,' *v.* ful.

HATFIELD FM was the home of John de *Hetfeld* (1321 *Ass*) and William *atte Hethfeld* (1327 *SR*). 'Heath or waste land.' Cf. *Hetefeldesbrygge* 1403, *Hattefeld* 1515 *NewColl*.

HOOD'S FM is to be associated with the family of John *Howdde* (1571 *SR*) and John *Hood* (1735 ParReg). It is *Whoods* 1616 *NewColl*.

Urchfont

URCHFONT [ʌʃənt, ərʃənt]

> *Ierchesfonte* 1086 DB
> *Erchesfont(e)* 1175 P *et freq* to 1332 *SR*, *Earchfount* 1605 *FF*
> *Erkesfonte* 1175 P
> *Archesfunte* 1179 P, *-font* 1376 Pat, *Archefount* 1426 *Ass*
> *Urichesfunte* 1242 Fees, *Urchesfunte* 1289 *Ass*
> *Orchesfunte* 1259 FF, *Orcheffunte* 1428 FA
> *Archfounte al. Urshent* 1564 *FF*, *Urchefount al. Urshent* 1611,
> *Urshent al. Erchfont* 1695 *Recov*

This is a difficult name. Ekwall (DEPN) suggests that the first element is a lost OE personal name *Eohric*, corresponding to ON *Iórekr*. Hence '*Eohric*'s spring,' *v.* funta.

NOTE. CRATE LANE (6″). *v. infra* 427–8.

CROOKWOOD FM is *wood of Crouk*', *Croukwod(e)* 1383, 1395, *Crowkwode* 1460 NQ iv. The place from which the wood took its name is referred to as *Cruk*' 1268, 1274, 1289 *Ass*, *Crouk* 1332 *SR* (p). Cf. also *aqua de Crouke* 1240 SarumCh. This is probably a Celtic place-name from a British word corresponding to MidCornish *cruc*, Welsh *crug*, 'hill, mound.' We do not know the site of the *cruk* from which the wood and stream took their name. There is no conspicuous hill or mound just by the farm.

EASTCOTT is *Estcota* 1167, 1178 P, *Escote juxta Erchesfunte* 1298 *Ass*, *Estcote by Erchesfonte* 1327 Banco, *Escott* 1640 WIpm. 'East cot(e).'

REDHORN HILL takes its name from the stone once known as *Red Hone* which is to be found on the crest of the hill (BM 691.1). *Red Hone* is mentioned in several Acts dealing with the repair of the Turnpike (e.g. 1756, 1784) and it is clear that the name *Redhorn* is a corruption of it, first found in *Redhorn Turnpike* 1812 RCH, by the present REDHORN PLANTATION (6″). *Red hone* is 'red stone' from OE *hān*, 'stone, rock,' the boundary-stone probably having been distinguished as such by some artificial colouring. Cf. *readan hanæ* (BCS 705) in the bounds of Enford, *readan hane* (ib. 756) in those of Swallowcliffe, *rede hane* (ib. 708) in those of Tarrant (Do) and *readanhane* (ib. 801) in those of Blewbury (Berks). The old name is still used locally.

WEDHAMPTON [wediŋtən] is *Wedhampton* 1249 *Ass et freq*, *Wede-* 1274, *Weyd-* 1289 *Ass*, *Woedhampton* 1341 *Cor*, *Wedehamton* 1547 *SR*, *Weddington* 1773 *A and D*. A compound of OE *wēod*, 'weed,' and hamtun, with reference to a weed-grown farm. *Wedehamford* (1570 PembSurv) in Patney must have been close by.

WICKHAM GREEN (6″). Cf. *Wicham* 1237 Ch, *Wykeham leyes* 1460, *Wykehamcliff* 1480, *Wycombe grene* 1549 NQ iv. *v.* wicham. The exact significance of this compound is obscure, cf. EPN *s.v.*

MARSH FM [1], UPHILL FM [2] and WELL HO (all 6″) were the homes of Laurence *in ye Mersch* (1327 *SR*), Thomas de *Uppehull* (1249 *Ass*) and John *atte Welle* (1327 *SR*).

FRANKLIN'S FM (6″) is to be associated with the family of Roger *le Fraunkeleyn* (1281 *Ass*). It is *Frankland Farm* 1773 *A and D*.

BREACH HANGING. Cf. *Northerbreche* 1460 NQ iv. *v.* bræc. CREEPING SHORD (6″) is so named c. 1840 (*TA*). *v. infra* 445. CUCKOO'S CORNER. Cf. *Cuckoo Park* ib. FOLLY WOOD (6″). Cf. *infra* 451. FOXLEY CORNER is *Foxle juxta Erchesfonte* 1342 GDR. *v.* leah. GOOSEHOLE PLANTATION (6″). Cf. *Goosehill* c. 1840 *TA*. It is a hill rather than a hole. THE GREEN (6″) is *the Grene* 1582 NQ iv. KINGSTON WOOD (6″) is *Kingstones Wood*

---

[1] *The Marshe* 1400 NQ iv.   [2] *Uphulle* 1296 *Ass.*

c. 1840 *TA*. LITTLE HILL is *Lytell hill* t. Eliz *LRMB*. LYDEWAY
is *Lyde way* 1515 *NewColl*, *Lide Way* 1773 A and D. Cf. *Lyde*
1403 *NewColl*, *Lydecrofte* 1460 NQ iv, *Lydehunt* 1563 *NewColl*.
It is called *Portway* in *TA* and leads to Devizes (cf. *supra* 16).
OAKFRITH WOOD is *Okfrygh* 1460, *Okesfrith* 1487 NQ iv, *Oake-
frythe* 1542 ib. v. 'Oak wood,' *v.* fyrhðe. PENNING DOWN is so
named in 1820 (G). *v. infra* 453. RUDDLEBATS HANGING (6″)
is *Ridelflat* 1384, *Rudelfate* 1460, *Rudelsfate* 1487, *Rydell Batt
Hoke* 1520 NQ iv. TOWNSEND. Cf. *Townesend close* 1621
NewColl. WEST WOOD (6″) is so named c. 1840 (*TA*).

XXVIII. SWANBOROUGH HUNDRED

Swaneberga hundred 1086 ExonDB, *Suanesbergahðr* 1167 P,
Swaneberge 1196 Cur, -*borge* 1198 Abbr, *Swanebergh* 1227 Fees,
-*berwe* 1249 Ass, -*burwe* 1305 Ass, *hundred of Swannebergh alias
Stodfold alias Rughbergh* 1476 Pat. The meeting-place was at
Swanborough Tump in Manningford Abbots *infra* 320. For
Stodfold, cf. Studfold Hundred *supra* 311.

Alton Barnes and Priors

ALTON BARNES and PRIORS

 Aweltun 825 (c. 1150) BCS 390, *Auuiltone* 1086 DB, *Awelton*
  1155–60 StOsmund, 1205 Pap, 1242 Fees, 1268, (*Berners*)
  1282 Ass

 Awltone, Aultone 1086 DB, *Aulton* 1189 BM, (*Prioris*) 1199 P,
  (*prioris Winton'*) 1249 Ass, (*Berners*) 1258 FF, (*Berner*)
  1285 FF, 1297 Pat, (*Bernes*) 1316 FA, *Priores Aulton* 1321
  Ass, (*by Wilcote*) 1392 Pat, (*Barones*) 1512 *NewColl*

 Alton Barnas 1524 SR

'Farm by the spring or stream source,' *v.* æwielle, tun. In the
bounds of Alton the spring is referred to as *westmæstan æwylle*
(BCS 390). Alton Priors belonged to the priory of St Swithin's,
Winchester. *Barnes* clearly goes back to a holding by a member
of the *Berners* family, but no record of such has been found.

Alton Barnes

MASLEN'S FM and NEATE'S FM (both 6″) are to be associated with the families of John *Maslen* (1778 ParReg) and Hugh *Neate* (1624 *SR*).

Alton Priors

ADAM'S GRAVE is to be identified with the *Wodnesbeorge* of 825 (BCS 390). '*Woden*'s barrow,' cf. Wansdyke *supra* 17.

RED SHORE (6″) is *Reddscherd* 1570 PembSurv and is the *read geat* of the Alton Charter (BCS 390). geat and sceard (*v. infra* 432, 445) alike denote a gap, here the gap in Wansdyke made by the Ridge-way. *red* from the brownish-gold colour of the soil of the dyke as revealed in the gap. For this meaning of *red* in OE cf. PN Nth 26, n. 1. geat is similarly used of a gap in Wansdyke in *woddesgeat* in the same charter, where it is used of the gap made by the Alton-Lockeridge road (H. C. B.).

TAWSMEAD FM is (*to*) *tæsan mæde* 825 (c. 1150) BCS 390. For this name see *Tasworth supra* 259.

WORKWAY DROVE (6″). Cf. *Warckewee* 1272 WIpm, *Warekweye* 1276 SarumCh, *Warkweye* 1485 Pat, t. Ed 3 *For, Workway* 1773 A and D. From OE (*ge*)*weorc-weg*, 'way or road by the stronghold.' The reference is to the camp on Knap Hill.

EAST FIELD is so named in 1820 (G). GOLDEN BALL HILL is so named in 1773 (A and D). It takes its name from the brilliant yellow of *Helianthemum vulgare* in flower, which covers the top of the hill (E. H. G.). KNAP HILL is *The Knap Hill* 1773 A and D. *v.* cnæpp. WALKERS HILL is so named ib. The property passed by marriage to Clement *Walker* (d. 1801) (Aubrey 43).

Beechingstoke

BEECHINGSTOKE

Stoke 941 (14th) BCS 769, 1260 Misc, 1275 RH, 1281 *Ass*,
    1316 FA, *Stokes in Kanyngemershe* 13th Shaston
Bichenestoch 1086 DB, *Bychinstok* 1268, *Bichenestok(e)* 1289
    Ass, 1303 *FF, Bicch-* 1304 Sarum, *Bych-* 1327 Banco, *Bichen-
    stok* 1327 *Ass, Bichyn-* 1403 Pat, *Bychyngstoke* 1431 ib.

Bechynstoke 1513 *FF*, *Be(c)chingstoke* t. Eliz WM xxi
Beauchamp Stoke 1819 RCH

v. stoc, 'settlement.' Beechingstoke lies on the south-eastern edge of the great 'Cannings Marsh' *supra* 249–50. The later distinguishing prefix looks like the OE *bicca*, 'bitch' (gen. pl. *biccena*), perhaps a nickname of reproach. Cf. Beechen Cliff in Bath (So), *Biccheneclyve* 1259 *FF*, *-clive* 1260 Bath Cartulary.

BOTTLE FM (6″) is *botan wælle* 892 (13th) BCS 567, *botan wylle* 934 (14th) ib. 699, *Botenwelle* 942 (14th) BCS 769, *Botewell(e)* 1332 *SR* (p), 1341 NI (p), *Bottewelle* 1394 *GDR*, *Botwell* 1513 *FF*, *Bottle Mead* c. 1840 *TA*. '*Bota*'s spring or stream,' *v.* wielle.

PUCK SHIPTON is *Pukeshepene* 1303, 1342 *FF*, *Pukshepene* 1327 *Ass*, 1412 FA, *Puckshepene* 1347 *FF*, *Pukeshepyn* 1368 Cl, *Poukshupene* 1397 IpmR, *Pokeshippon or Pokeshepon* 1495 Ipm, *Pockshipton* 1553 *FF*. The name is a compound of puca, 'puck, goblin,' and scipen, 'cattle-shed,' *infra* 446.

BROAD STREET is so named in 1773 (A and D).

Charlton

CHARLTON

Cherlentona t. Hy 2 BM, *Cherlinton* 1198 Abbr
Cherleton ib. *et freq* to 1332 *SR*, (*juxta Upavene*) 1325 *FF*
Churleton next Upavon 1302 Ipm
Charleton by Uphaven 1368 Cl
Chorleton 1559 *Recov*

'Farm of the *churls* or free peasants,' *v.* ceorl, tun. *By Upavon* to distinguish it from Charlton near Malmesbury *supra* 55.

CLEEVE HILL is so named in 1820 (G), *v.* clif. COOMBE is so named c. 1840 (*TA*).

Huish

HUISH

Iwis 1086 DB, *Hiwis* 1162 P, 1198 Fees, *Hywis* ib., 1242 ib., *Hywisse* 1268, *Hywych'* 1279 *Ass*, *Huwes* 1291 Tax, *Hywysch* 1293 Ipm, *Hywysshe* 1331 Stowe 925, *Hewishe* 1629 *SR*

v. hiwisc. It denotes a holding of land on which a household is settled.

HILL BARN (6″). 400 yards west-south-west of this is an earth-work which is referred to in the phrase *boscus de Hulwerk* (1257 *For*) and *boscus de Hywish qui vocatur Hulwork* (1270 ib.). On the west side is Gopher Wood (*infra*) which must be the woodland referred to. Other examples of this term in Wiltshire are *Hulwerc* in Pewsham (1189 WM xvi), *Hulwerk* in Tockenham (1540 *MinAcct*).

GOPHER WOOD [*vulgo* koufər] is *Coffers Wood* c. 1840 *TA*, *Coffer Wood* c. 1885 6″ O.S.

Manningford Abbots, Bohun and Bruce

MANNINGFORD ABBOTS, BOHUN and BRUCE

 Maning(a)ford 987 (16th) LibHyda
 Maneforde, Maniford 1086 DB
 Manningeford 1212 Fees, *-ige-* 1227 FF, *Maningeford* 1218
  SarumCh, 1242 Fees, 1249 *Ass*, 1263 *For*, *Maningford(ia)*
  1230 Bracton, 1243 StNicholas
 Parva Maningford, Maningford Petri 1275 RH
 Manyngeford Breuse 1279, *Manyngford Breouse* 1289,
  Maniggeford Brehuse 1289 *Ass*, *Manyngford Brewes* 1314
  Sarum, (*Brewose*) 1398 Pat
 Manyngeford Bon 1279, 1281 *Ass*, *Maningford Boun* 1316
  FA, (*Bohun*) 1321 *Ass*, 1420 *FF*, *Manningford Boundes*
  1571 *SR*
 Manyngford Abbatis 1289 *Ass*, *Manningford Abbottes* 1571 *SR*

'Ford of the people of *Manna*,' *v.* ing. The ford is that on the Avon by the mill in Manningford Bruce. *Abbots* from the Abbot of Hyde, Winchester. *Bohun*, etc. from the family of John de *Boun* (1263 *For*). *Bruce* from the family of *Breuse* (1279 *Ass*), *Breuose* (1289 ib.), *Brewosa* (1304 Sarum). *Petri* perhaps from the holding of Herbert fil. *Petri* in 1242 (Fees).

Manningford Abbots

SWANBOROUGH TUMP (6″) is *Swanabeorh* 987 (15th) LibHyda. 'Barrow of the peasants,' *v.* swan, beorh. The Hundred meeting-place, *v. supra* 317. For *Tump*, *v. infra* 476.

MILL FM was the home of Thomas *oth Mulle* (1348 *Cor*).

THE BUTTS (6″) is *The Buttes* 1558 *DuLa*, probably with reference to archery butts. Cf. *infra* 425.

Manningford Bohun

BOTTLESFORD is *Bottewelleford* 1348 *Cor*, *Botewells Forde* 1591 WM vi, i.e. '*Botwell*('s) ford,' from Bottle *supra* 319, near by.

SMALLBROOK COPSE (6″) is *Small Brook Coppice* c. 1840 *TA*. WOOD BRIDGE is *Wodebrigge* 1434 IpmR, *Wodburge mede* 1558 *DuLa*. For *burge*, *v*. Introd. xxi.

Manningford Bruce

FRITH WOOD[1] is *Frith Coppice* c. 1840 *TA*. *v*. fyrhðe. THE HOLD (6″). Cf. *Hold House, Garden* and *Orchard* ib. MOUNT PLEASANT (6″). Cf. *infra* 455.

Marden

MARDEN

  Mercdene 941 (14th) BCS 769, *Mercdena* 1170 P
  Merh dæne 963 (c. 1150) ib. 1118
  Meresdene 1086 DB, *Mereden(e)* 1211 RBE, 1229 Cl, 1242 Fees
  Mergdena 1167, 1169 P
  Merden(e) 1242 Fees, 1275 RH, 1406 Pat
  Mereghedene 1280 WIpm, *Merghdene* 1291 Tax, *Merghedene* 1304, 1305 *Ass*, 1306 Sarum, 1318 *FF*, 1341 NI, *Myrgheden* 1359 Ipm
  Merewedene 1298 *Ass*, *Merwheden* 1322 Pat, *Merweden(e)* t. Ed 2, 1332 *SR*, 1334 *Ass*, t. Ed 3 *For*, 1362 Ipm, 1412 FA

The early forms suggest the possibility of a compound of OE mearc and denu, hence 'boundary valley,' but the form *merh dæne* comes from a better cartulary than the others and agrees better with the later developments. The probabilities are therefore that the first element is the OE *mærg, merg,*

---

[1] FRITH COPSE (6″).

mærh, mearh, 'marrow, fat,' and that the whole name denotes a fertile valley. For the use of this word in place-names cf. Merrow (PN Sr 142).

MARDEN MILL was the home of John *atte Mulle* (1327 *SR*). It is *Marden Mill* 1606 Sess.

HINDERWAY PLANTATION (6″) is *Hinder Way* 1780 *Devizes*. THE MOORS (6″) is *Moores* 1760 ib.

North Newnton

NORTH NEWNTON

norþ niwetune 892 (13th) BCS 567, *Newetone* 1086 DB, *Neuton* 1222 FF, *Norþneuton* 1242 Fees, *Neweton juxta Uphaven* 1356 *FF*

Nywantun 934 (c. 1300) BCS 699, *Newenton* 1212 Fees, 1268 *Ass*, *Nywynton* 1332 *SR*, *Newington* 1571 ib.

'New farm,' *v.* tun, with long hesitation between inflected and uninflected forms of the adjective. *North* in contrast to South Newton by Wilton *supra* 228.

CUTTENHAM FM is *Cottenham* 1315 *Wilton*, *Codenham, Cotonham* 1499 NQ viii, *Cottenham* 1570 PembSurv. Perhaps '*Cotta*'s ham(m).'

GORES is *lez Goores* 1570 PembSurv, *Gore* 1773 A and D and is identical with (*on ðone*) *gæran* 892 (13th) BCS 567. *v.* gara, 'gore, angle,' etc. The boundary makes a succession of right-angled bends here.

HILCOTT is *Hulcot(e)* 1196 Cur, 1198 Abbr, 1289 *Ass et passim* to 1639 *Sadler, -kot*' 1242 Fees, *Hulecot(e)* 1236 Cl, 1241 FF, 1268, 1289 *Ass*, 1327 Banco, *Hulle-* 1249 *Ass*, *Hilcote* 1522 *SR*, 1526 Ct, *Hilcott al. Hulcott* 1668 *Recov*. The name would seem to be identical with Hulcote (PN Nth 98), the first element being the OE *hulu*, 'shed, hovel.' The name may have been given to some very small dwelling or else to a place of shelter.

WILDS FM (6″) is to be associated with the family of Jonas *Wild* (c. 1840 *TA*).

BUTTS FM. Cf. *Butt Close* c. 1840 *TA* and *infra* 425. CATS BRAIN (6″) is *Catsbrain* ib. *v. infra* 425.

Rushall

RUSHALL

Rusteselve (bis) 1086 DB

Rusteshala, -e 1160 P, 1196 Cur *et passim* to 1332 *SR, -hall'*
1207 FineR, *Rosteshale* 1281, 1289 *Ass*, 1285 Cl, *Rusteshell*
1285 Pat

Rosshall 1416 Pat, *Russhale* 1430 *FF*, 1443 Pat, *Russall* 1535
VE, 1575 *Peramb, Rushall al. Rustehall* 1627 *Recov, Rustall*
1778 *Sadler*

Names with *rust* as a first element are found elsewhere. We
may note *Rusteuuellæ* (BCS 260), now Rusthall (KPN 75–6),
Rustington (PN Sx 172) and a lost Kentish *rustingdenn* (BCS
459). The first named may contain the common word *rust*,
'rust,' but the others more probably contain a personal name
identical with it. OGer names *Rust* and *Rusto* are on record
(Förstemann, PN 1286). Hence '*Rust*'s nook of land,' *v.* healh.

FRANCE FM (6″) is said to be so called because whichever way
you wish to get to it you have to go 'over the water' (School).
OLD CLEEVE is *The Cleeve* c. 1840 *TA, v.* clif *infra* 426. RUSHALL
DROVE (6″) is *le Drove* 1284 AD vi, *v.* draf *infra* 429. SLAY
BARROW (6″) is *Sley Barrow* 1773 A and D, doubtless taking its
name from the neighbouring Slay Down *infra* 329.

Stanton St Bernard

STANTON ST BERNARD

Stantun 903 (13th) BCS 600, (*æt*) *Stantune* 957 (13th) ib. 998
Stantone 1086 DB, 1268 *Ass, Stauntone* 1275 RH
Staunton Fits Herbard 1402 FA
Staunton Barnarde 1553 *Phillipps, Stanton Barnard* 1572
FF

'Stone-farm,' *v.* stan, tun. One *Erebertus* held the manor in
1242 (Fees). The *Fits Herbard* of FA must have been a member
of his family. No explanation of the *Barnard* addition has been
found. To that unexplained addition an unauthorised *saint* has
been prefixed.

HARESTON DOWN (6″) probably takes its name from the *gemerstan* or *maerstan* in the boundaries of Stanton St Bernard (BCS 600, 998, 1053). *v.* (ge)mære. Hareston may stand for the more usual *Hoarstone* from OE *hārstān*, 'boundary-stone.'

THORN HILL is (*on*) *þorn dune* 903 (13th) BCS 600, 960 (13th) ib. 1053, *þorn dun* 957 (13th) ib. 998.

ENGLANDS BRIDGE (6″). Cf. *Yngelandes* c. 1570 *Wilton*. MILK HILL is *Melkhulle, Melkehylle* 1425 *MinAcct*, *Mylkehill, Melke Downe* 1570 PembSurv, with reference to a hill which gave good pasturage.

Upavon

UPAVON

   Oppavrene 1086 DB
   Upeavena 1172 P, *Uppehavene* 1268 *Ass*
   Uphavene 1176 P, 1198 Abbr, *Huphavene* 1202 Cur, 1203
      Bracton, *Upavene* 1211 RBE, c. 1230 SarumCh, *Uphaven*
      t. Eliz WM xxi

('Settlement) further up the river Avon' (*supra* 1), in distinction from Netheravon *infra* 331.

NOTE. *Cokeslane, Shamelplace* 1488 *MinAcct*. The latter is from OE *scamol*, 'bench, shambles.'

WIDDINGTON FM is *Wydyndene* 1331 *MinAcct*, *Withendene* 1488 *DuLa, Weddington* 1773 A and D. Possibly a compound of OE *wiðegn*, 'withy,' as in Wiggen Hall (PN Herts 106–7), and denu, 'valley.'

TOWN END (6″) is *Townsend* c. 1840 *TA* and was probably the home of William *atte Tounesende* (1348 *Cor*).

BENGER'S BARN (6″) is to be associated with the family of Robert *Benger* (1547 *SR*). Cf. Sutton Benger *supra* 74.

BAKE BARN (6″). *v. infra* 450. CASTERLEY CAMP is *Casterley* 1773 A and D, *Catterley* (sic) *Banks* c. 1840 *TA*. COLLEGE FM (6″) belongs to King's College, Cambridge. Cf. *College Down* ib. UPAVON DOWN. Cf. *pastura del Doune* 1397 *DuLa, le Downe* t. Hy 8 *AOMB*.

Wilcot

WILCOT

> (æt) *Wilcotum* 940 BCS 748, *Wilcote* 1086 DB, 1189 WM xvi
> *et freq* to 1341 NI
> *Wylecote* 1268 *Ass*, 1291 Tax, 1297 *FF*, 1327 *SR*, *Wile-* 1275
> RH, 1289 *Ass*
> *Welcot(e)* 1279, 1281, 1289 ib.

Probably 'cottages by the spring,' *v.* wielle, cot(e). The OE
form is from the dative plural *cotum*.

DRAYCOT FITZ PAYNE

> *Draicote* 1086 DB, *Dray-* 1289 *Ass*, 1316 FA, 1327 *SR*,
> *Draicot Rogeri filii Pagani* 1300 *For*, *Dracott* 1571 *SR*

'Cot(e) by the steep ascent,' *v.* dræg and *supra* 69. The place
lies just below a very steep hill. Margery *Fizpayn* held the
manor in 1327 (*SR*).

MAIZLEY COPPICE (6″) is *meosleage* 934 (13th) BCS 748. 'Moss
clearing or wood,' *v.* leah.

OARE

> (æt þam) *oran* 934 BCS 699, *Ore* 1229 StOsmund, 1232 Ch
> *et freq* to 1332 *SR*, (*juxta Draycote*) 1281 *Ass*, *Oare* 1428
> FA
> *Oure* 1440 *FF*, *Hower* 1518–29 ECP, *Oore* 1571 *SR*, *Woore*
> 1585 WM xxi, 1680 *Recov*, *Owre oth. Oare* 1800 ib.

v. ora, 'bank, slope,' etc. The place lies below a steep hill.
The full name of the tithing of Oare as given in the grant setting
forth its bounds (BCS 699) was *Motenesora*, the first element
being apparently a personal name.

RAINSCOMBE HO is *Rammescumbe* 1227 FF, 1280 *FF*, *Remes-*
1227 FF, 1339 *For*, *Rames-* 1234 Cl, *Remmes-* t. Hy 3 *Stowe* 798,
Remescombe 1570 PembSurv, *Ranscombe Abbesse* 1581 *FF*,
Rainscombe al. Abbess Wood al. Burnt Oak 16th *Deed*, *Rambscombe* 1735 *Sadler*. Probably OE *hræfnes cumb*, 'raven's valley.'
Alternatively *Hræfn* may here be a personal name, a nickname
from the bird. By it was *hremnes geat* (BCS 748) in the bounds

of Pewsey. This is perhaps in favour of the personal name. It belonged to the *Abbess* of Wilton.

EAST (6″) and WEST STOWELL is *Stawelle* 1176 P (p), 1202 Cur (p), *Stowelle* 13th *Bradenstoke*, 1229 StOsmund, 1249 *Ass*, *Eststowelle* 1327 *SR*, *Weststouwelle* 1392 Pat. Probably 'spring' or 'stream with *steened* channel,' i.e. with an edging of sarsen, *v.* stan, wielle. Cf. Stowford *supra* 124.

BRISTOW BRIDGE is to be associated with the family of William *Bristowe* c. 1840 *TA*.

CASTLE BARN (6″). Cf. *Castle Ground* c. 1840 *TA*. CHINA COTTAGES (6″) *olim Cheney's* (Sykes). FURZE COPPICE (6″). Cf. *Furze Lodge* ib. GIANT'S GRAVE is the name of an entrenchment north-east of Oare. HARE STREET (6″). Cf. *Hare Street Common* 1773 A and D and *supra* 87. HATFIELD HO (6″) is *Hedfeld* 13th AD iv, *campo de Hethfeld* 1281 *Ass*, *Hatfeld* 1807 *Devizes*. 'Heath or waste land,' *v.* feld. LADIES BRIDGE (6″). Named after Lady and Miss Wroughton of Wilcot Manor (Sykes). LOIN COPSE (6″). Cf. *Loins Meadow* c. 1840 *TA*. PICKED HILL (6″) is so named c. 1840 (*TA*). Cf. *infra* 443.

Wilsford

WILSFORD

> *Wifeles ford* 892 (13th) BCS 567, 934 (14th) ib. 699. *Wifleford* 1275 RH
> *Wivlesford* 1086 DB, *Wiuelesford* 1185 P *et freq* to 1332 *SR*, with variant spellings *Wyv-*, *Wiv-*
> *Wylesford* 1292 Ipm, *Willesford* 1316 FA

'*Wifel*'s ford.' Cf. the same name *infra* 372, and (L), *Wivelesforde* 1086 DB, and *Wifilingfalod* (BCS 677) in the bounds of Ham, *Wifelesham* (ib. 1067) in those of Burbage and *Wiveleshangre* (t. Ed 1 *Lacock*) in Lacock. The ford was at the north-east corner of the parish where Beechingstoke and North Newnton meet Wilsford.

BROADBURY BANKS. Cf. *Broadbury Camp* 1820 G. ELL BARROW is *montem de Ellebergh* 1348 *Cor*, *Ellborrowe* 1591 WM iv, *v.* beorg and *infra* 423. There is a long barrow here.

Woodborough

WOODBOROUGH

Wideberghe 1208 Cur, 1242 Fees
Wodeberg c. 1220 *AD*, -*berge* 1249 *Ass*, -*bore* 1278 Ipm,
 -*burgh* 1279 *Ass*, -*berwe* 1299 Cl, -*bergh* 1318 *FF*, -*borgh*
 1344 Ipm
Wudeberg(h) 1241 Cl, 1257 FF, 1289 *Ass*
Wodbergh 1339 *FF*, -*berwe* 1398 IpmR
Woodborowe 1594, -*broughe* 1647 *FF*

'Wood hill,' *v.* beorg.

FORD WOOD (6″) was near the home of Adam de *la Forde* (1327
Banco). STANFORD (6″) may have been the home of John de
Stanford (1279 *Ct*). Cf. *Stanfordsend* 1725 *FF*.

BREMHILL WOOD. Cf. *Bremhills* c. 1840 *TA*. Probably from
brēmel, 'bramble,' *infra* 424. HONEY STREET is so named in
1773 (A and D), a name given to the Ridgeway as it crosses
Pewsey Vale. Probably so called because it was a muddy
road. HURST'S FM. Cf. *High, Furze, Stone, Middle, South Hurst*
(fields) c. 1840 *TA*. LAMBPIT COPSE (6″). Cf. *Lambpit Ground*
ib. THE SANDS. Cf. *Sand Ground* ib. WOODBOROUGH HILL is
so named in 1773 (A and D).

XXIX. ELSTUB HUNDRED

Alestabe hundred, Eilestebba, Ailestebba 1086 ExonDB, *Lalestebba*
1130, *Ellestubbahдr* 1167, 1168 P, *Ellestubbe* 1196 Cur, 1255 RH,
-*stube* 1198 Abbr, *Elestubbe* 1227 Fees, *Hundred de Elnestub* 1249
Ass. 'Elder-tree stump.' The meeting-place of the Hundred was
in Enford in a field called *Elstub*, the field immediately south-east
of New Town and north-west of Fifield. This identification is
due to Enford School, and the School notes that there is much
elder there still.

Enford

ENFORD

> *Enedford* 934 (c. 1150) BCS 765, 1290 WintonCart, 1309
> Sarum, 1321 *FF*, *-forde* 1086 DB, *Enedeford* 1205 Pap,
> *Enet-* 1242 Fees, *Endford* 1376 *FF*
> *Eneford* 1200 Cur, 1249 Pat, 1252 Cl
> *Enford* 1345 *Ass*

'Duck ford.' The first element is OE *ened*, 'duck.'

CHISENBURY

> *Chesigeberie* 1086 DB, *Chesingbiria* 1202 FF, *Chesingebiria*
> 1211 RBE, *Chesingebyre* 1230 SarumCh, *-bir'* 1250 *Rental,
> Chesingbir' Prioris, manor of Chesingbur' voc. Folye, villa de
> Chesingebir' qui dicitur la Folye* 1275 RH, *Chessburia* 1285
> BM, *West-, Estchesyngebur'* 1289 *Ass*
> *Chisingburi* 1202 FF, *Chisingebiry* 1211 RBE, *-bur* 1227 Ch,
> *-bir'* 1252 FF, *Chysyngbury* 1304 *Ass, Westchisingbury* 1313
> *FF*
> *Chisenbury de la Folly* 1544–53 ECP, *Chisonbury Dallyfolly*
> 1689 *Recov*
> *Chusynbury* t. Ed 1 *Edington, Chusseburia* 1285 BM, *West-
> chusyngebury* 1289 *FF, Chusyngbury* 1304 *Ass, Chusinggebury*
> 1320, *Est Chussyngbury* 1376 *FF*

This is probably from OE *cisingabyrig* (dat.), 'burh of the
dwellers on the cis or gravel.' The sub-soil here is gravelly
(WM xlvi, 7) and Chisenbury Camp, an old earthwork, stands
near by. This is called *Chisenbury Trendle*, i.e. 'circle,' in 1812
(RCH). According to Hoare (16–17) East Chisenbury or
Chisenbury Priors belonged to the Priory of Ogbourne (W).
Already in 1202 (FF) Roger de *la Folie* held the manor of
West Chisenbury or Chisenbury Folly.

COMPTON is *Contone* 1086 DB, *Cumpton* 1256 Cl, *Compton juxta
Eneford* 1298 *Ass*, 1330 Ipm. 'Farm in the combe or valley,'
v. cumb, tun.

FIFIELD is *Fifide* 1230, *Fiffhide* 1279 Pat, *Est Fifhide* 1297 *FF,
Parva Fifhide juxta Eneford* 1310 *Ass, Langefifhide* 1362 *FF,*

Fifhide juxta Enford 1397 IpmR. 'Five hides.' It may represent the 5 hides held by *William* in Enford in 1086 (DB). *East* perhaps in relation to Fyfield *supra* 295. See Addenda *supra* xl.

SLAY DOWN. Cf. *la Slee* 1212 FF and Slay Barrow *supra* 323. Ekwall (DEPN *s.n.* Sleningford) suggests the possibility of a lost OE **slēa*, cognate with Norw *slaa*, 'grass-grown slope,' cf. *slaa* f. 2 (Torp). Such a word would suit this site well, as also The Slay *infra* 357, but for the latter we have no early forms. It is perhaps also the first element in the unexplained Slebech (NCPNW 41).

BADEN BARN, BADEN'S CLUMP and DREWEATT'S BARN (all 6″) are to be associated with the families of Andrew *Baden* (c. 1840 *TA*) and Thomas *Dreweatt* (ib.).

BAKE BARN (6″) is *Bake Farm* 1820 G. *v. infra* 450. COOMBE is *Cumba, -e* 1230 Pat, 1275 RH, *Coombe by Fitelton* 1330 Ipm, *(juxta Enedford)* 1345 *Ass. v.* cumb. COOMBE HILL is *Combe Hill* 1773 A and D. LIDBURY CAMP is *Ledbury camp* 18th *Map.* LITTLECOTT is *Litlecote* 1198 FF, *(juxta Eneford)* 1304 *Ass*, *Luttelcot* 1255 RH (p). *v.* cot(e). LONGSTREET is *Langestret* 1249 *Ass*, *Longstrete* 1412 FA. NEW TOWN is so named in 1773 (A and D). PINTAIL WOOD (6″). Cf. *The Pintail* c. 1840 *TA*, so called from its shape. TWIN BARROWS is so named 1773 (A and D). WATER DEAN BOTTOM. Cf. *Waterdeane* 1591 WM vi. *v.* denu.

Everleigh

EVERLEIGH

> *Eburleagh, Eburleah* 704 (c. 1125) BCS 108
>
> *Everlais* (sic) t. Hy 1 (1318) Ch, *-lay* 1172 P, *-legh* 1249 *Ass et passim*, with variant spellings *-le, -leye, Everelegh* 1281, *Est Everlee* 1306 *Ass*, *(West)* 1347 FF, *Myddell Everley* 1563 ib.

'Wild boar clearing or wood,' from OE *eofor*, 'boar', and leah. West Everley must be the present Lower Everley.

NOTE. *Sarumweie, Pewsey weie* 1591 WM vi. Everleigh lay on the old Marlborough-Salisbury road (H. C. B.).

COMBE COTTAGES (6″). Cf. *le Combe* 1662 *Sav.* COW DOWN is *le Cow Downe* ib. Cf. *infra* 430. EVERLEIGH ASHES. Cf. *Everley*

bosc' t. Ed 2 *For, Everley Ashes* c. 1840 *TA*. EVERLEIGH BARROWS
(6″) are *twigbeorgas* 940 BCS 748, *Two Barrows* 1591 WM vi.
GORE DOWN (6″) is *Gore Downe* 1553 *DuLa, Gourdon Balle* 1591
WM vi. *v.* gara. For *balle, v. infra* 422. LINDEN COPSE (6″) is
Ling Down Coppice c. 1840 *TA v.* Addenda *supra* xl. MILKING
BUSHES and WINDMILL COTTAGES (both 6″) are so named ib.

Fittleton

FITTLETON

> *Viteletone* 1086 DB, *Fitletone* 1211 RBE, *Fiteletune* 1250
> *Rental, -ton* 1301 Ipm, *Fiteleston* 1368 Pat
>
> *Fitelton* 13th AD ii, 1235 Fees *et passim* to 1394 BM, with
> variant spellings *Fytel-, Fithel-* 1242 Fees, *Fitil-* 1303 Cl,
> *Phitel-* 1324 FF, *Pheytil-* 1380 Pat
>
> *Fetelton* 1220 FineR
>
> *Fitlington* 1233 Cl, *Fitlington, Fitelinton, Fithelinton* 1243 ib.
>
> *Futelton* 1275 RH
>
> *Fydelton* 1354 Ipm, *Fidel-* 1433 IpmR, *Fiddleton* 1645 WM
> xix, 1725 *Sadler*

'*Fitela*'s farm,' *v.* tun, ingtun. The same personal name is
found in *on fitelan slædes crundæl* 934 BCS 705 in the bounds of
Enford near by (*v. supra* 328). Probably the same man gave
name to the tun and the slæd. It is probably only a coincidence
that the manor was held TRE by one *Vitel*. See the discussion
of Lat *Vitalis*, OFr *Vitel* (Feilitzen 405–6).

HAXTON

> *Hakenestan* 1172 P
>
> *Hacnestone* 1211 RBE
>
> *Hakenestone* 1212 ClR, 1226–8 Fees, 1331 Ipm, *-ston* 1239 Ch,
> 1249, 1268 *Ass*, 1275 RH, 1289 Abbr, 1298 FF, 1327
> Banco, 1365 BM, 1382 IpmR
>
> *Hakeleston* 1268, 1289 *Ass*, 1368 Pat, 1403 IpmR, *Hackelston*
> 1367, *Hacleston* 1490 Ipm
>
> *Hackeston* 1576 FF

Possibly '*Hacun*'s stone,' the name being of comparatively
late origin and containing the Anglo-Scand personal name
Hacun, Hacon. It is on record from Wiltshire.

BEACH'S BARN is *Beeches Farm* 1773 A and D and is to be associated with the family of Richard *atte Beche* (1332 *SR*) and Robert de *la Beche* (1346 *Ass*)[1], i.e. 'at the beech.' It may be that *s* is pseudo-manorial, and that the name is really local in origin.

THE WARREN (6″) is so named c. 1840 (*TA*).

Netheravon

NETHERAVON

Nigravre, Nigra avra 1086 DB
Nederauena 1149–53 AC, *Nedheravena* 1158 HMC Var i,
    Neðerauena 1173, 1176 P, *Netheraven* 1212 ClR
Niterehavene 1211 RBE, *Netherhaven* 1493 *Sadler*, t. Eliz
    WM xxi, 1675 Ogilby
Nutheravene 1226 StOsmund, 1249, 1345 *Ass*

'(Settlement) further down the Avon,' in distinction from Upavon *supra* 324, *v.* neoðere.

BLACKBALL FIRS (6″). Cf. *Black Ball* c. 1840 *TA* and *infra* 422. COURT FM (6″). Cf. *Court Ground* ib. THE FOLLY (6″). Cf. *infra* 451. GREAT LYNCH. Cf. *Lintch* c. 1840 *TA*. *v.* hlinc *infra* 436. NEWFOUNDLAND FM is so named in 1820 (G) and is in a remote corner of the parish, *v. infra* 455. ROBIN HOOD BALL (6″) is *Robin Wood Ball* (sic) 1773 A and D. *v. infra* 422. The reference is possibly to the tumulus here. WEXLAND FM is *Waxland* 1820 G. Cf. Wexcombe *infra* 347.

XXX. KINWARDSTONE HUNDRED

Cheneuuarestan hundred 1086 ExonDB, *Chenewardestan hdr* 1130, *Kanewardistan* 1174, *Kene-* 1175, *Kinewardstan* 1181, *Kinewarestan* 1186, *Kyne-* 1187 P, *Kinwarestan* 1196 Cur, *Kynewardeston* 1255, *Kene-* 1275 RH, *Kynewerston* 1324 FA, *Kynwarston* 1522 SR. '*Cyneweard*'s stone.' The site of the meeting-place was at or near Kinwardstone Fm *infra* 338.

---

[1] Very early references apparently to the Hicks-Beach family.

Bedwyn

GREAT and LITTLE BEDWYN

(*æt*) *Bedewindan* c. 880 (c. 1000) BCS 553, c. 1000 JEGPh xxxiii, 344 *Bedewinde*, (*in*) *Bedewindan* 778 ib. 225, *Bed(e)uuindan* (acc.) 968 (c. 1225) ib. 1213, *Bedeuuinde* c. 1016 (c. 1225) KCD 1312, *Bedewin(e)*, *a* 1042–66, *Bedewind* 1066–87 Coins *Bedvine*, *-vinde* 1086 DB, *Bedewinde* 1091 StOsmund *et passim* to 1317 Cl, with variant spellings *-wynd(e)*, *Est-* 1154 RBE, 1156, *Bedewinða* 1198 P, *Bidewind'* 1235 Cl, *Cheping-bedewynde* 1276 *Ass*, *Chippingbedewynde* 1279 *GDR*, *Bed-wynd* 1472–85 ECP

Est Bedewyn 1437 IpmR, *Bedewyn* 1438 Pat, *Bedwyn Abbotes* 1502 ECP, *Grete-, Lyttelbedwyn* 1547 *SR*, *East Bedwyne al. Lyttle Bedwyne* 1633 WIpm, *Bidwing* 1653 PCC, *Great Beden* 1655 ParReg

Bedwyn is derived by Ekblom (PN W *s.n.*) and by Ekwall (DEPN) from an OE form of dialectal *bedwine*, *bedwind*, 'wild clematis,' with reference to a place where this plant or some similar one abounded. Already, however, in OE times Bedwyn is found as a stream-name (*v. supra* 1) and it may be that the stream-name gave origin to the place-name and not *vice versa*. If, as seems more likely, the name is pre-English in origin, it might be a compound of British **betuā*, 'birch' (Welsh *bedw*), and **vindā*, 'white' (Welsh *gwen*, fem.).

NOTE. *Chepyngstrete* 1443 AD ii, i.e. 'market-street.'

Great Bedwyn

BRAIL FM, BEDWYN BRAIL is (*in*) *bruilliis regis de Bedewinde* 1231 Cl, *in bruyllis* 1279 *Ass*, *in bruwell* 1290 *For*, *The Broyl of Bede-wynd* 1294 Ipm, *la Bruel* t. Ed 2, *Bruwell' de Bedewynde* 1330 *For*, *The Broyl* 1331 Cl, *lez Broyle* 1570 PembSurv, *Brail Wood* 1819 RCH. This is a common forest term for a park or wood stocked with deer or other beasts of the chase and enclosed as a rule with a wall or hedge. See more fully PN Sx 70–1, *s.n.* Broyle.

CROFTON is *Crostone* (sic) 1086 DB, *Croftun'* 1166 P, *-ton* 1249 *Ass et freq*, *Crofton Brayboef* 1418 Cl, *Croughton* 1650 *Recov*. 'Farm with or by a *croft*,' *v*. tun. Cf. Crofton (Ha), *Crofton(e)* 1086 DB, 1242 Fees. William *Brayboef* held the manor in 1316 (FA).

HACHET LANE (6″) is to be connected with *la Hachiett'* t. Ed 1, *Hacheʒate* 1362, *la Hachghate* t. Ed 3 *For*, *Hattchet felde* 1637 *Sav*. 'Hatch gate,' with reference probably to a gate leading into the forest. *v*. hæcc and geat *infra* 433.

HARDING FM is (*in*) *haran dene* 778 BCS 225, *Haredone* 1086 DB, *Haredena* 1130 P, *-den(e)* 1235 Fees, 1270 *For*, *Harenden* 1281, *Hardene* 1289 *Ass*, *Over, Nether Harden* 1337 FF, *Harding al. Harden* 1626 WIpm. 'Boundary valley,' *v*. har, denu. The Anglo-Saxon form occurs as a boundary-mark in an OE charter.

HAW WOOD is *bosc. de Howe, Hawewode* t. Ed 2 *For*, *Houwode* 1331 *Stowe* 925, *Houwode* 14th *Bradenstoke*, *Howood* 1649 *SarumD and C*. The wood is on a spur of land and the name would seem to go back to OE hoh. Later, as a wood name, there was confusion with ME *hawe*, 'hedge, enclosure,' *v*. haga.

STOKKE HO is *Stocke* 1229 StOsmund, *villa de Stok* 1235 SarumCh, *Stokke* 1252 FF, 1313 Ipm, 1332 *SR, Stoke* 1281 *Ass*, (*juxta Bedewen*) 1485 IpmR. Probably OE stocc, 'stock, stump.' There is a 13th-century effigy of Adam de *Stokke* in Great Bedwyn church (E. H. G.).

TOTTENHAM HO and PARK are *Toppeham* 1264 *Devizes, Toppenham* t. Ed 2, 1362 *For*, 1331 *Stowe* 925, 14th *Bradenstoke, Topenham Hyll* t. Ed 6 WM xv, *Totnam lodge* 1582 WM xiv, *Tottnam Parke alias Totenhais Parke* 1626 WIpm, *Tocknam Parke* 1685 AubreyNH. '*Toppa*'s ham(m).' For the personal name *Topp*, of which this name must be the weak form, cf. Topsham (PN D 454) and Toppinghoe (PN Ess 289).

FROGMORE FM[1] and HILL BARN were the homes of William de *Froggemere* (1249 *Ass*) and Thomas *atte Hylle* (1281 ib.).

BLOXHAM COPSE and BRONSDON'S COPSE (6″) are to be associated

---

[1] *Frogmore copice* c. 1570 *Wilton*.

with the families of Thomas de *Bloxham* (1289 *Ass*) (from Bloxham (O)) and Richard *Brunsdon* (1690 ParReg).

BRIMLEY COPSE (6″) is *Brimley* 1587 *Rental*. CASTLE COPSE is so named in 1697 (*Wilton*). There are some entrenchments here (H. C. B.). DODSDOWN is *Doddysdowne* 1551 Pat, *Doddesdowne* 1637 *Sav*. Near by may have been *Dodescroft* 1281 *Ass*. LANGFIELD COPSE. Cf. *Langfeilde* 1578 *Sav*. SHAWGROVE COPSE (6″). Cf. *Shawe woode* 1542 ib. v. sceaga, 'copse.'

Little Bedwyn

BURRIDGE HEATH is *Burwode* 1161 RBE, (*bosc. de*) t. Ed 2 *For*, *Burwuda, Burewuda* 1195 P, *-wode* 1257 *For*, *Boroods heathe par*. *Little Bedwene* 1604, *Burwoods Heath* 1660 PCC, *Birds Heath* 1812 RCH, *Birge Heath* 1820 G. 'Wood by the burh or camp,' cf. Burwood (PN Sr 96), though it is not clear to what camp reference is made. The sound [dz] has been confused with [dʒ] and then spelled *dge*.

CHISBURY

> *Cheseberie* 1086 DB, *Chessebure* 1247 SarumCh, *-byr'* 1268 *Ass*, *-bur'* 1275 RH, *-bury* 1279 BM, 1284 *FF*, 1292 Cl, *Cheesbury* 1819 RCH
>
> *Chisseberia* 1166 P, *-ber'* 1210 Cur, *-bur* 1210 FF, 1249 *Ass*, *-byr'* 1261, *-bury* 1282 Cl, *Chyssebyr'* 1268 *Ass*
>
> *Chussebur'* 1257 *For*, *-buria* 1285 BM, *-bury* t. Ed 2 *For*, 1316 FA, *-buri* 1332 SR, *-bury* 1408 IpmR

The sub-soil here is gravelly (WM xlvi, 7), but the persistent *ss* here suggests that the first element cannot be cis, 'gravel,' as in Chisenbury *supra* 328. Rather it must be the OE personal name *Cissa*, hence 'Cissa's burh.' There is an ancient earthwork here. In a medieval history of Abingdon Abbey (*Chronicon Monasterii de Abingdon* ii, 268) there is a story to the effect that in the days of *Kinuinus*, king of the West Saxons, there was a certain noble, *Cyssa* by name, who was *regulus* in a district which included Wiltshire and the greater part of Berkshire. He was called *regulus* because his *dominium* included the episcopal see of Malmesbury, but the metropolis of his kingdom was *Bedeuuinde*, i.e. Bedwyn, and in the south part of that *urbs* he built a castellum which was named *Cyssebui* (sic) after him. This story does not belong to the older stratum of Abingdon tradition, and has no historical value (Stenton, *Early History of the Abbey of Abingdon* 1, 2, 13). That does not however prevent us from believing in a sometime possessor of Chisbury named *Cissa*. Cf. *Cissanhamm* (KCD 658) in Westwood. It should be added that the camp itself is certainly far older than the West Saxon period (cf. Crawford in WM xli, 281) and lies west-south-west of Little Bedwyn and north of Great Bedwyn.

GATE CLOSE (6″) is, as Crawford has noted (WM xli, 294), so called from *Pedlar's Gate* (1773 A and D) which was at the junction of the parishes of Little Bedwyn, Froxfield and Shalbourne and was by the ...*nes geat* of the Little Bedwyn charter (BCS 225).

HENSET (lost)[1]

> *Henseta* 1165 P, *-sete* 1211 RBE, 1249 *Ass*, 1290 *For*, *Henset* 1553 *AddCh*
> *Hynsete* 1249 *Ass et freq* to 1443 AD ii, *-sett* 1483 AD i, 1495 *FF*, *-sute* 1279, 1281, *-shute* 1281 *Ass*, *-shete* 1415 *FF*
> *Hunset* 1274 *Ass*
> *Hynesete* 1290 *FF*, 1349 Ipm, 1408 IpmR

The forms are impossible to interpret, especially in view of our ignorance of the exact site of the place.

HORSEHALL HILL. Cf. *Horselget* 778 BCS 225, *on hors heal gæt* 968 (c. 1225) ib. 1213, *Horsehulsfeld* 1362 *For*, *Horsell Hill* 1773 A and D. 'Horse-nook,' *v.* healh.

PUTHALL FM

> *puttan.ealh* 778 BCS 225
> *Putehala* 1175, *Putte-* 1178, 1196 P, *Putehal(e)* 1201 Cur, *Puttehale* 1229 Pat, 1257 *For*, 1325 Cl, 1331 *Stowe* 925
> *Pittehala* 1177 P
> *Puttenhall* 1260 FF, *Pottenhale* 1306 *AD*, 1327 *SR*, *Puttenhale* 1321 *Ass*, 1324 *Misc*, 1327 Banco
> *Puttel(l)* 1674 *Recov*, 1736 ParReg

---

[1] These forms apply to a holding in Little Bedwyn. It had a tithing-man who according to the Pembroke Survey did service in the Hundred of Kinwardstone (H. C. B.).

'*Putta*'s angle or corner of land,' v. healh. Cf. Puttenham (PN Sr 209). Ekwall (*Studies*[2], 91–2) would take some of these names to be derived from an unrecorded OE *putta*, 'hawk.'

TIMBRIDGE FM is *Tymerigg'* 1229 StOsmund, -*rugg*(*e*) 1255 RH, (*by Borbach*) 1305 Ipm, -*rige* 1263, -*rygge* t. Ed 2 *For*, 1311 *FF*, *Tymberigge* 1274 *Ass* (p), *Tymeruggedoune* 1305 Ipm, *Tymeriggesdoune* 1331 *For*. Possibly 'timber ridge,' i.e. a ridge hill which provided timber, as suggested by the 1274 form.

BONNING'S COPSE (6″), COBHAM FRITH[1] and PARLOW FM[2] are probably to be associated with the families of Ralph *Bonyng* (t. Ed 2 *For*), John de *Cobbeham* (ib.) (which probably came from Cobham (K)) and William *Parlere* (1338 Inq aqd, 1426 *Ass*).

BELMORE COPSE (6″) is possibly *Bylkemore* t. Ed 2 *For*, 1374 *Ass* (p). BURNTMILL LOCK (6″). Cf. *Burnt Mill Field* c. 1840 *TA*. THE DELL (6″). Cf. *Upper, Lower Dell, Dell Coppice* ib. v. dell. FORE BRIDGE (6″). Cf. *Fore Bridge Meadow* ib. HORSELEAZE WOOD (6″). Cf. *Horse Leaze* ib. v. infra 438. JOCKEY GREEN is so named from an inn, *The Horse and Jockey* 1773 A and D. KNOWLE FM is (*la*) *Knolle* 1290 *FF*, 1311 Ipm, (*juxta Chissebury*) 1395 IpmR, v. cnoll, 'hillock.' LAWN BORDER (6″). Cf. *The Lawn* c. 1840 *TA* and launde infra 440. LITTLE FRITH. Cf. *Frithwode* 1257 *For*, *Lytleffrith* 1542 *Sav*. v. fyrhðe, 'wooded country.' LITTLEWORTH is *Little Worth* 1773 A and D. v. infra 455. LOWER FM is so named ib.

Burbage

BURBAGE

Burhbece, (*andlang*) *burgbeces* 961 (c. 1225) BCS 1067, *Burhbec* c. 1000 (c. 1225) KCD 1312

(*wið*) *byr bæces* 968 (c. 1225) BCS 1213, (*wið*) *burhbeces* 968 (c. 1250) ib.

Buberge (sic) 1086 DB

Burbetc(*e*), -*bed* 1086 DB, *Burbecha* 1139 SarumCh, -*bech*(*e*) 1158 HMC Var i *et freq* to 1227 Ch

---

[1] *Cobhamfrith* 1542 *Sav*. v. fyrhðe, 'wooded country.'
[2] Cf. *Parler Feilde, Deane* 1633 WIpm.

Burbach(e) 1177 SarumCh, 1211 RBE, 1242 Fees, 1249 *Ass*,
1286 Ipm, *Burbachesauvage* 1321 Cl

Burebech(e) t. Hy 3 *Stowe* 798, 1246 Orig, *-bach(e)* 1246 Cl,
1262 FF

Borebache 1229 StOsmund, 1242 Fees, *Borbache* 1286 *FF*,
1296 Ipm

Burgbeche 1249 *Ass*, *Burghbache Sauvage* 1314, *Burghbach*
1352 Cl

Bourbache 1262 FF, 1332 *SR*, 1339 Ipm, *Boure-* 1339 *FF*

Burbage 1353 *FF*, *Berbage* 1503 Pat, *Burbidge*, *Burbadge* 1585
WM xxi, *Burbatch* 1646 *FF*

The first and third forms refer to a place called Burbage,
the second is found in the bounds of Burbage as set forth in
the Abingdon Cartulary, the fourth and fifth in the bounds of
Bedwyn in the same cartulary. The first element in the name
is clearly burh. There is no burh here now. Professor Ekwall
suggests that the reference may be to the *eorðburh* mentioned
just before *byrbæces* in BCS 1213, but Grundy (ii, 78) identifies
that almost certainly with Godsbury (*infra* 346), and it is a far
cry from Godsbury to Burbage. Traces of the burh may however survive in the name *Burghstrete* sometimes applied to the
road along which Burbage lies[1]. The second element is probably
bæce, bece, 'stream.' The boundary of Burbage and of Bedwyn
(which must then have included part of Easton) at the points
indicated in BCS 1067 and 1213 runs (respectively) down and
up a small stream in a slight depression, and this is doubtless
the bæce. In EPN the second element was taken to be bæc,
'ridge,' but Professor Ekwall notes the difficulty that the
boundary runs along the valley and not along the prominent
ridge on which Burbage itself lies. Burbage (Lei) has the same
forms as this Burbage but is on the top of a prominent hill
and we should probably still associate that with bæc. There
are two Burbages in Db. The forms in PN Db (*s.n.*) really
refer to Burbage in Padley and not to Burbage on Wye. It
lies by a stream. The Pipe Roll form in DEPN is from a
personal name and may refer to either.

---

[1] *Ex inf.* Mr H. C. Brentnall.

BOWDEN FM is *Bowden* t. Ed 6 WM xv, *Bowden otherwise Bowden Fitzwarrens* 1626 WIpm. Cf. *Bowedonesgrove* 1257 *For*. It stands on a rounded hill so possibly we have a compound of *boga*, 'curve, bow,' and dun as in the numerous Devon examples of Bowden (PN D 37).

DURLEY is *Durnley* 1229 StOsmund, *-leg'*, *Durnelyghe* 1264 *Devizes*, *Durle* 1235 Fees, *-leye* 1279, (*juxta Burbache*) 1306 *Ass*, *Derley*, *Dirlay* 1278, 1279 Cl, *Dorlegh*, *Dyerlegh* t. Ed 2 *For*, *Durelee* 1360 BPR. A compound of OE dierne, 'secret, hidden,' etc., and leah.

EASTCOURT (6″) and WESTCOURT are *Estcote* 1257 *For* (p), *Westcote* 1264 *Devizes*, *Wescote* 1446 *MinAcct*, *Westcourtes* 1529–32 ECP, *Wescott* 1668 *Recov*. 'East and west cottages,' *v.* cot(e).

KINWARDSTONE FM is *Kynewardeston* 1282, 1296 Ipm, *Kynewarston* t. Ed 3 *For*, *Kinwarston* t. Eliz WM xxi. The site of the Hundred meeting-place, *v. supra* 331.

LADYWELL COPSE (6″) is *Ladelwlle*, *Ladewlle* 1264 *Devizes*, *Ladelwell pound* t. Ed 6 WM xv, *Ladywell otherwise Ladellwell* 1626 WIpm, *Ladiwell al. Ladewell* 1703 *Recov*. The first element would seem to be the common word *ladle* (OE *hlædel*, ME *ladel*), perhaps with reference to some instrument for raising the water from the well.

PENCELEY (*TA*) is *Pendes clif* 921 (14th) BCS 635 in the bounds of Collingbourne Kingston and *penderes clif* 968 (c. 1225) ib. 1213 in the bounds of Burbage, surviving in the names of half a dozen fields immediately south-west of Southgrove Fm. '*Pendhere*'s slope,' *v.* clif, with common dropping of final *f* as in the colloquial 'Hockley in the Hole' for Hockliffe (PN BedsHu 126).

SEYMOUR POND (6″) is *Suthmere* 1259 *For*, *Sirmore Pond* 1773 A and D. 'South pool,' *v.* mere. It is at the south end of the village.

MARR GREEN[1] and STEEP GREEN[2] were probably the homes of Robert *atte Mere* (1257 *For*) and Alan *atte Stubbe* (1264 *Devizes*). *v.* mere and stybb, 'stump.' The pool is Seymour Pond *supra*.

---

[1] *Margreene* 1662 Sav, *Marr Green or Short Heath* 1773 A and D.

[2] Cf. *Stibmarshe* 1613, *Stibbe Marsh* 1626 Recov, *Steep Green* 1773 A and D, *Stibb Green* c. 1840 *TA* and 6″ O.S.

COLD PARK (6″) is *Cold Parks* c. 1840 *TA*. EARL'S HEATH (6″) is *Arlesheathe* t. Mary *Phillipps, Earles Heathe* 1626 WIpm. EAST SANDS (6″) is *Easte Sande* 1540 WM xii, *le East Send* 1662 *Sav*. GOLDENLANDS FM. Cf. *Golden Lands* (fields) c. 1840 *TA*. HAREPATH FM (6″) is *Harepatch Common* 1773 A and D, *Harepath* 1820 G. It is on the Devizes road, *v.* herepæð *infra* 435. SOUTHGROVE FM is *Sudgrava* 1170 P, *Sugrave* 1222 Pat, *Suthgrave* 1270 *For, Southgrove* 1625 Ipm. *v.* græfe, 'copse' and *infra* 432–3.

Buttermere

BUTTERMERE

> *Buttermere* 863 (12th) BCS 508, (*æt*) *Buter mere* 931 ib. 677, *Bwtermæræ* t. Wm 1 BM, *Butremare* 1086 DB, *-mere* ib., 1199 FF, 1249 *Ass*, 1259 Cl
> *Buttermere* 12th BCS 508, 1268, *-mare* 1276 *Ass*
> *Botermere* 1276, 1278 *FF*, 1308 Sarum, *Botur-* 1440 Pat

Literally 'butter mere or pond,' *v.* mere. The reason for the name is not certain. It probably has reference to the colour of the water as in *buterw(y)elle* (KCD 813) and Butter Hill (Fd) in Hankerton *infra* 462.

HENLEY is *henna leah* 961 BCS 677, *Henle* t. Hy 3 *For, -legh* 1276 StOsmund, *-ley* 1597 *FF, Hendlye* 1666 *Recov*. In BCS 677, 1080 we have mention also of *henna dene, henne dene* in the bounds common to Buttermere and Hurstbourne. 'Clearing and valley of the hens,' *v.* denu, leah.

ROCKMOOR DOWN, ROCKMOOR POND (6″). This is *þrocmere* 863 (c. 1150) BCS 508, 961 (c. 1250) ib. 1080, *þorcmere, þorocmere* 961 (c. 1225) ib. 1080, *Trokkemere* 1410 *Peramb, Rockmoor* c. 1840 *TA*. This name probably repeats itself in the first part of Throckmorton (PN Wo 169). Ekwall (DEPN *s.n.* Throckenholt) calls attention to OE *þroc*, 'table, timber on which the ploughshare is fixed,' which, in the form *drock*, was still used in the 18th century in Gloucestershire of part of the plough (EDD *s.v.*). See further *s.n.* Throcking (PN Herts 187) where reference is made to Drockbridge (Ha), *þrocbriggæ* BCS 393 and Throckley (PN NbDu 196).

drock is also used in Wiltshire and in Gloucestershire,

Berkshire and Somerset of a covered drain, a small watercourse, a ditch, a flat stone across a ditch, and there can be little doubt that we have it in one or other of these senses in Drock Piece in Winterbourne Bassett (*supra* 310) and in field-names The Drocks in Westbury, Drock Bottom in Huish, Drock Piece in Alton Barnes.

BELVEDERE WOOD (6″) is *Belvidere Wood* c. 1840 *TA*. It lies high with a fine view. MOORDOWN FM. Cf. *Moore downe* 1748 *FF*. SHEEPLESS HILL is *Sheepleys Hill* c. 1840 *TA*. *v*. læs, 'pasture.' TOWN FM is so named (ib.). It is just by the village, *v*. tun. WHITE FM is so named in 1773 (A and D).

Chilton Foliat

CHILTON FOLIAT

> *Cilletone* 1086 DB, *Chilton(e)* 1155 RBE, 1166 P *et passim*, (*Foliot*) 1227 Ch, (*Tieys*) 1332 Ch, *Cilton Roberti Foliot* 1167 P

Probably '*Cilla*'s farm,' *v*. tun. Henry *Tyes* had succeeded the Foliots at Chilton by 1300 (Boarstall 312).

CHILTON MARSH (6″). Cf. *le Mersshe* 1553 *AddCh*, *Chilton Marsh* 1732 *Recov*. HITCHEN COPSE (6″). Cf. *Huchinhedge* 1553 *AddCh*. SOLEY is *Salley* 1468 IpmR, *Soley* 1573 *FF*, 1637 WIpm, *Solye* 1589 *FF*, *Souley* 1591, *Sowley* 1619 PCC. The first element is probably sol, 'miry pool.'

Chute and Chute Forest

CHUTE and CHUTE FOREST[1]

> Early references to the village of Chute are *Cett'* 1235 Cl, *Chuth (vill')* 1268 *Ass*, *Cheut* t. Ed 2, *hamelett' de Cheut* t. Ed 3 *For*, *vill. de Cheut* 1289 *Ass*, *Chut* 1307 *FF*, *Chuet* 1312 Cl, *Chewte* 1553 *AddCh*. All other forms refer to the forest from which the village and parish took their names, *v*. *supra* 12.

BIDDESDEN HO

> *Bedesdene* 901 (15th) BCS 597, 1086 DB, *Beddesden* 1272 FF

[1] A modern parish formed from Chute in 1875. It represents roughly the area of Chute Forest after disafforestation (H. C. B.).

Budesden(e) 1257 *For*, 1289 *Ass*, -*dis*- 1286 Ch, *Buddesden(e)* 1297 Pat, 1332 *SR*, 1345 Pat, 1428 FA, 1535 VE, *Biddeston* 1738 *Sadler*

Biddesden lies in a valley which may have been named *byd* from OE *byd*, 'tub, vessel,' noted under Bydemill Brook *supra* 4. To this OE denu, 'valley,' may have been added later when the element was no longer understood.

CONHOLT HO is *Covenholt(e)* 1257 *For*, 1279, 1281 *Ass*, 1332 *SR*, 1355 Ipm, 1570 PembSurv, *Coveholt* 1257, 1270 *For*, *Cuveholt* 1289 *Ass*, *Covenholtesdych* t. Ed 3 *For*, *Conholde* 1590 NQ vii, *Conholt al. Covenholt* 1633 *Recov*. 'Cofa's wood,' *v*. holt. Cf. Coventry (PN Wa 160). *v*. Addenda *supra* xli.

SHAW FM is *Scage* 1086 DB[1], *Shawe* 1257 *For*, *Shaghe* 1332 *SR* (p), *Shawe juxta Chuyt* 1294 *FF*. 'Wood or copse,' *v*. sceaga.

STANDEN is (*in*) *standene* 778 BCS 225, 961 (c. 1225) ib. 1080, 1086 DB, 1165 P, 1199 RBE, 1242 Fees, -*done* 1086 DB, *North-standen*' 1275 RH, *Suthstaunden* 1289 *Ass*, *Grenestaunden* 1300 *For*, *Staunden Chaworthe* 1316 FA. 'Stony valley,' *v*. denu. There are sarsens here. Hugh de *Standene* held the manor of *Standene* from Patricius de *Chaurces* (1242 Fees). *Chaworth* is a late corruption of this name. (For the widely variant forms of this family name see more fully Fees, Index 135.)

BUTLERSFIELD, BUTLER'S ROW, COOPERS ACRE and SOPER'S BARN[2] (all 6″) are to be associated with the families of Henry *Butler* (c. 1840 *TA*), John *Couper* (1430 *MinAcct*) and Henry *le Sopere* t. Ed 2 *For*.

ASHMORE POND (6″) is *Aschmere* 1307 Pat. *v*. mere, 'pool.' BANKS HILL is so named c. 1840 (*TA*). BREACH LANE (6″). Cf. *Breches* 1548 Pat. *v*. bræc. CADLEY is *Caddeleg*' 1249 *Ass*. See Cadley Fm *supra* 244. CATHANGER WOOD (6″) is *Cathangere* t. Ed 3 *For*. '(Wild) cat slope,' *v*. hangra. CHESSAMS COPSE (6″) is *Chasoms Coppice* c. 1840 TA. CROFT HANGER (6″) is *The*

---

[1] This is probably the right identification. Jones (231) notes that *Scage* was in Amesbury Hundred and held by Robert fil. Geroldi who had possessions in this neighbourhood. Shaw Fm is less than a mile from the border of Ludgershall parish in Amesbury Hundred.

[2] Cf. *Soapers Bottom* 1773 A and D.

Croft Hanger ib. DEAN FM is *le Dene* 1270 *For*, *v*. denu, 'valley.'
FLINTY is *Flingley* 1773 A and D. FLINT LANE (6″) is close by.
GAMMONS FM. Cf. *Gamons Fields al. Gamons Closes* t. Jas 1
ECP. HACKNEY PLANTATION (6″). Cf. *Hackly fielde* 1606 *DuLa*.
HIGHLAND COPSE (6″) is *Highlands* c. 1840 *TA*. HONEY BOTTOM
is so named in 1773 (A and D). Probably 'sticky,' 'muddy.'
HOOKWOOD ROW (6″) is *Hocwode* 1257 *For*. LADIES LAWN is so
named c. 1840 (*TA*). See *infra* 440. LIMMER COPSE is *Limmer
Coppice* ib. LITTLE DOWN is *Litledowne* 1553 *DuLa*. LODGE
COPSE (6″) is *le Logge coppys* c. 1490 ib. LONG BOTTOM is so
named c. 1840 (*TA*). MANKHORN ROUND (6″) is *Mankhorn Long
Ground* ib. MOUNT COWDOWN. Cf. *infra* 430. NEW ZEALAND.
This farm is in a remote corner of the parish, *v. infra* 455.
OXHANGER WOOD (6″) is *The Oxhanger* c. 1840 *TA*, *v*. hangra.
REDHOUSE FM is *Red House Farm* ib. SHEEPHOUSE COPSE (6″).
Cf. *Sheephouse Ground* ib. THICKET PLANTATION (6″) is *Thicket*
(ib.). WELL BOTTOM and Ho. Cf. *Wellhouse Meadow* ib. THE
WILDERNESS is so named ib.

Collingbourne Ducis and Kingston

COLLINGBOURNE DUCIS and KINGSTON

> *Colengaburnam* 903 (14th) BCS 602, *at Colingburne*, (*of*)
> *Collengaburnan* 921 (14th) ib. 635, (*æt*) *Collinga burnan* 931
> ib. 678
> *Colingeburne* 1086 DB, 1166, 1170 P *et freq* to 1257 Ch,
> -*burna* 1086 ExonDB
> *Coleburna* 1086 DB
> *Collingeburn(e)* 1199 FF, 1200 Cur, *Koll-* 1249 FF
> *Colingburn' Comitis* 1256 Cl, *Colingeburn Comit*. 1291 Tax,
> *Colyngbourne ducis* 1507 NQ i, *Colyngborne Duk'* 1524 *SR*,
> *Collingbourne Duche* 1587 NQ vii
> *Abbotes Colingburne* 1268, *Colyngeborn Abbatis* 1289 *Ass*
> *Colyngeborn Valence* ib., *Colyngbourn Valaunce* 1469 Pat
> *Colingeburne Kingeston* 1306, *Colyngborne Kyngston* 1372 FF
> *Colyngborne strete* 1509 *DuLa*, *Cullingborn* 1675 Ogilby

Collingbourne was originally the name of the upper part of
the Bourne river (*v. supra* 2). The meaning is probably 'stream
of *Col(l)a*'s people,' *v*. ing, burna. See also Coldridge *infra* 344

and cf. Collingtree (PN Nth 145) and Collaton (PN D 307, 527). *Comitis* and *Ducis* from the holding of the Earls (later Dukes) of Lancaster (1275 RH); *Abbotes* from the holding of the Abbot of St Peter's Winchester (DB); *Valence* from the holding of the family of William de Valence (1253 Cl); *Kingston* from the King's holding (DB). For *strete* cf. Hawk Street *supra* 254.

Collingbourne Ducis

OLD HAT BARROW is identical in site with (*on*) *bradanbeorg* of BCS 635. 'Wide barrow,' *v.* brad, beorg. It is *Three Knightes Burrow* in 1591 (*Map*), perhaps from three parishes meeting here.

SIDBURY HILL [*vulgo* ʃedbəri] is *Shidbury, Chydebur'* 1325 *Cor, Sydbury hyll* 1571 *DuLa, Shudburie, Shudburrowe hill* 1591 WM vi, *Chidbury* 1812 RCH. *v.* burh. There is an old 'camp' here. The first element is uncertain but it may be the lost OE *scydd* discussed in PN Sx 132 *s.n.* Gunshot, the source of ModEng *shed*. Cf. further Paulshott, Puckshot and Denshott (PN Sr 167, 206, 298), *Sheddon* (PN Ess 344). The reference is perhaps to sheds which at one time stood on the site of the camp.

CRAWLBOYS FM[1] and HERON'S COPSE are to be associated with the families of Peter *Crouleboys* (1279 *Ass*), *Croyleboys* (1289 ib.), *Croillebois* (1332 SR) and William *Heron* (1553 *DuLa*).

BLACKMORE DOWN is *Blakemore* 1468 *MinAcct*. CADLEY. Cf. *Cadley Field* c. 1840 *TA* and *supra* 244. COLDHARBOUR COPSE (6″). *v. infra* 451. COW DOWN is *Cowdown* 1553 *DuLa*. HOUGO-MONT FM is so named c. 1840 (*TA*) and is doubtless reminiscent of the battle of Waterloo. LECKFORD BOTTOM (6″). Cf. *Lecke-forde* 1553 *DuLa*. OXDOWN COPSE (6″). Cf. *Ox Down* c. 1840 *TA*. STERT COPSE. Cf. *grava voc' Sterte* t. Ed 2 *For*. *v.* grafa, steort, 'tail.' WELL HO is *Wellehous* 1430 *MinAcct*. WEST HILL is so named in 1773 (A and D). WHITE DITCH (6″). Cf. *White Ditch Field* c. 1840 *TA*. WICKHEATH COPSE is *Wike heth* 1553 *DuLa*. *v.* wic *supra* 25. WIDGERLEY DOWN. Cf. *Wiggele* 1257 *For*. Perhaps '*Wicga*'s leah.'

[1] *Croileboys* 1433 *Phillipps, Croylboys* 1556 *Recov*.

Collingbourne Kingston

AUGHTON [ɔˑtən] is *Colyngborne Afton* 1346 *Ass*, *Affeton* 1469 Pat, *Afton* 1593, *Aughton* 1676 *FF*. '*Æffe*'s farm,' *v.* tun. This is no doubt the *Æffe* to whom Wulfgar left land at Collingbourne in 931 (BCS 678).

BRUNTON

Burhampton 1257 *For*, 1469 Pat, *Colingburne Burhampton* 1310, (*Burghampton*) 1345, (*Bourhampton*) 1346, (*Borhampton*) 1351 *Ass*, *Boramton* 1529 *FF*
Collingborne Brunton 1569, *Brounton* 1602 *FF*, *Burumpton* 1612 *Recov*
Burrington al. Brunton 1674 *Recov*

'hamtun by the burh,' though it is not clear to what burh reference is made.

COLDRIDGE WOOD. Cf. *Colrigge* 1257, *bosc. de Colerygge* t. Ed 1 *For*. In the will of Aetheling Aethelstan (*Anglo-Saxon Wills* 56 ff.) mention is made of *Colungahrycg*. There is no indication where it is, but as the will covers property in neighbouring parts of Hampshire the probability is that *Colrigge* is a reduced form of *Colungahrycg*. Hence 'ridge of the people of *Cola*.' See further *infra* 368 n. 1 and cf. DB *Coleburna* for Collingbourne *supra* 342 and *Colebourne* under Bourne R. *supra* 2.

SUNTON

Southampton 1268, *Colyngburne Suthampton* 1312 *Ass*, *Colyngborn Southampton* 1445 *Phillipps*, (*Southamton*) 1447 *FF*, *Collyngborne Southton* 1547 *SR*, *Collingborne Sowthtowne* 1553 *AddCh*
Sunton 1575 *FF*, *Collingborne Sutton al. Sunton* 1584 *Recov*

'The south hamtun' in contrast to Brunton (*supra*) to the north.

TINKER'S BARN (6″) is to be associated with the family of Geoffrey *le Tinekere* (1257 *For*).

COLLINGBOURNE WOOD is *boscus de Colingburne* 1241 *FF*. CROW DOWN CLUMP is *Crow Down Ring* c. 1840 *TA*. FAIROAK COPSE (6″). Cf. *Fair Oaks* ib. GRUB GROUND (6″) is so named ib.

HARE DOWN (6″). Cf. *Hare Sleight Down* ib. For *sleight*, *v. infra* 454. HEATH COPSE (6″). Cf. *Heath al. East Downe* 1637 WIpm. HIGHFIELD LODGE. Cf. *Heghfelde* 1279 *Ass*, *v.* feld, 'open space.' HILL BARN. Cf. *The Hill* c. 1840 *TA*. HOG DOWN is *Hoggindon* 1250 AD ii, *Hoggendon* 1257 Ch, *Hogdon* 1773 A and D. Cf. *Hoggendoune* 1632 *EcclCom* in Redlynch. LYNDEN DOWN is *Lent Doune* 1553 *DuLa*. Cf. *Lyntedon* 1330 Ipm in Fittleton, *Lentdown* 1603 DKR xxxviii. MERRYLAWN COPSE (6″) is *Moorey Lawn* c. 1840 *TA*. See *infra* 440. OAKETY COPSE (6″). Cf. *Oakety* ib. OLDLANDS BARN (6″) is *Olands* (sic) 1627 WIpm. RAG COPSE. Cf. *The Ragg, Ragg Ground* c. 1840 *TA* and *infra* 453. THE SCRUBS (6″). Cf. *Scrub Ground, Scrub Coppice* ib. and Shrub Ho *supra* 78. SNAIL DOWN is *Snayle doune* 1553 *DuLa*. SUMMER DOWN is *Somerdowne* ib. THORNHILL DOWN is *Collingborne Thornhill* 1626 WIpm. WAGLANDS FM (6″) is *Waglins* c. 1840 *TA*. WATERLANE COPSE (6″). Cf. *Water Lane* ib. WHITELANE COPSE (6″) is *White or Chalk Lane Coppice* ib.

Easton

EASTON

Estone 1086 DB, -*ton(e)* 1175 P, 1198 Abbr, (*by Merleberge*) 1241 Ch, (*Prioris*) 1268 *Ass*, (*juxta Burbache*) 1324 *FF*, *Estton* 1281 *Ass*

Aston 1242 FF, Fees, 1282 Ipm

Eastone 1522 *SR*

'East farm,' *v.* tun. Perhaps so named because east of Milton. Commonly known as Easton *Royal*, probably because the east half of the parish was in the King's forest of Savernake (H. C. B.). There was a small house of Austin Canons here, hence *Prioris* (G. M. Y.).

FALSTONE POND [vɔlstən][1] (6″) is *Falestone* t. Hy 3 Ipm, *Faleston* 1259 *For*, *Falstane* t. Ed 3 ib., *Ballstone Pond* 1773 A and D. This was a forest boundary-mark, so the second element is no doubt stan, 'stone.' The first may be OE *fealu*, 'yellowish, fallow.' Cf. Falstone (PN NbDu 80). Grundy (i, 219) suggests that this may be identical with *Wylberhtes stan* (BCS 635) in the bounds of Collingbourne Kingston.

---

[1] *Volstone Pond* (School).

GODSBURY[1] is *Guthredesburg* 921 (14th) BCS 635, *Godsbury* 1773 A and D. '*Gūðred*'s burh.' See Addenda *supra* xli.

BREACH COTTAGES (6″). Cf. *la Breche* 1249 *Ass*, *Breach Farm* 1820 G. *v.* bræc. CONYGRE FM is *Coneygarth Farm* ib. *v. infra* 427. HILL BARN (6″). Cf. *Hill feild* 1662 *Sav*.

Froxfield

FROXFIELD

> *Forscanfeld* 804 (c. 1200) BCS 324
> *Frossefeld* 1166 P, *Froxe-* 1212 Cur, 1268 *Ass*, 1341 NI, *Frox-*
>   1242 Fees, 1289 *Ass*, *Froxfeld* 1604 WM xxii
> *Vroxfeld* 1297 Ipm, *Throxfeld* 1377 Cl

The stream here is called *Forsca burna* in 778 (BCS 225), i.e. 'frogs' stream,' *v.* forsc. If the form *Forscanfeld* is to be stressed, Ekwall (DEPN *s.n.*) is perhaps correct in taking the first element to be the gen. sg. of OE *forsce*, a stream-name denoting one that is frequented by frogs, rather than an error for *forsca-feld*, 'frogs' open space.' Cf. 'Frogmead (*TA*) in the parish and Introd. xxi.

HUGDITCH is *Hokeddych* 1385 *AD*, *la Hokededych* 1445 AD vi. 'Hooked or curved or bent ditch,' *v.* dic.

FRITH COPSE was near the home of John *atte Frithe* (1332 *SR*, 1341 NI). *v.* fyrhðe, 'woodland.'

ALMSHOUSE COPSE is *Almshouse Coppice* c. 1840 *TA*. HARROW FM is *the Harrow* 1820 G[2]. OAK HILL is *Hochulle* 1257 *For*, *Hokhull* 1268 WIpm, *Okhull* t. Ed 3 *For*, *Ockhulle* 1331 *Stowe* 798, *Okyll* 1468 *MinAcct*. Probably 'hook-hill.' There is a projecting hill here, *v.* hoc. RUDGE is *le Rigge* 1241 Ch, *la Rugge* t. Ed 3 AD i, 1345, *Rygge* 1386 *Ass*, *Rydge al. Rudge* 1639 *Recov*. Self-explanatory. See also Introd. xx. TRINDLEDOWN COPSE (6″) is *Trindle Coppice* c. 1840 *TA*. Probably from OE *trendel*, 'circle.'

---

[1] Properly applies to Crowdown Clump in Collingbourne Kingston, the burh has reference to (the faint traces of) a circular earthwork here. Cf. WM xlii, 592.

[2] Cross Fm 1773 A and D. See Addenda *supra* xli.

Grafton

GRAFTON

Graftone, Grastone 1086 DB, *-ton(a)* 1130, 1186 P *et passim,*
   Est-, West- 1198 Fees, 1275 RH, 1279 *Ass*
Greftone 1211 RBE, *Gratton* 1675 Ogilby
'Farm by the grove,' *v.* graf, tun.

MARTEN is *Martone, Mertone* 1086 DB, *-ton(e)* 1187 P *et freq* to
1428 FA, (*juxta Wexcombe*) 1312 *FF,* (*juxta Schaldeburne*) 1409
Ass, Mereton 1200 P, 1227 Ch. Probably identical in origin
with Martin *infra* 402. The place is near the parish boundary.

WEXCOMBE

West Cumbe 1155 RBE, *Westcumba, -e* 1156, 1158, 1172 P,
   c. 1200 RBE, 1202 P, 1255 RH, 1275 Ch
Wexcumbe 1167 P, 1211 RBE, 1235 Cl, 1296 Ipm, 1331
   Stowe 925, 1332 *SR, Wex Cumba* 1173 P, *Waxcombe* 1426
   Ass
Wexecumbe 1201 Cur, 1275 Cl, 1281 *Ass*

It is difficult to be sure of the interpretation of this name,
seeing that the early forms are so evenly balanced between *west*
and *wex,* but on the old principle of choosing the harder of two
readings it is clear that there is more likelihood that *wex* occasionally gave place to *west* than that *west* has developed to *wex.*
If so, the name must be interpreted as 'wax-valley,' from the
presence of bees in the valley. For a similar compound cf.
Waxholme (PN ERY 29) where reference is also made to
Wexham (Bk) as explained in PN Sx, Pt. I, xli.

WILTON

Wulton 1227 Ch, 1259 FF, 1386 *Ass, -tona* 1230 Bracton,
   -tun 1270 For, *-tone* 1307 Ipm, *Woultone* 1327 *SR*
Wolton(e) 1289 *Ass,* 1290 For, 1332 *SR,* t. Ed 3 For, (*juxta*
   Bedewynde) 1403 IpmR
Wilton 1402 FA, *-y-* 1428 ib., *Wilton al. Wolton* 1574 *FF*

The first element is perhaps OE *wull,* 'wool,' as in Woolwich
(K) (DEPN *s.n.*), referring to a farm where wool was prepared
or kept, *v.* tun. The full series of forms given here do not support

the suggestion in DEPN (*s.n.*) that this is a compound of OE wiell, wyll, 'spring.'

WOLF HALL is *Ulfela* 1086 DB, *Wulfhala* 1180 P, *-hale* 1289 *Ass*, *Wlfhale* 1242 Fees, *Wolfhale* 1249 *Ass*, 1294 *FF*, *Wolphal* 1324 FA, *Wulfall* 1522 *SR*, *Woulfehall* 1616 *FF*. 'Corner or piece of land frequented by wolves,' *v.* healh.

BATT'S BARN (6″) and PIPER'S BARN are to be associated with the families of John *Batt* (1587 WM xlv) and Rafe *Pyper* (1522 *SR*).

CULVERSLEAZE COPSE (6″). *v.* culfre and læs *infra* 428, 438. FAIR-MILE DOWN. Cf. *Fair Mile* 1773 A and D. FOLLY BARN (6″). Cf. *infra* 451. FREE WARREN is *Freewarren* 1773 A and D. PICCADILLY (6″), a nickname for remote cross-roads, cf. *infra* 455. SUDDEN FM is *The Soden Park* t. Ed 6 WM xv, *Suddon Parke otherwise Home parke* 1626 WIpm, *Suddon al. Holme al. Wolfhall* 1671 *Recov*, *Southing* 1773 A and D. TOW BARROW is so named ib.

Ham

HAM

> (*æt*) *Hamme* 931 BCS 677, 1229 Cl *et freq* to 1363 Pat, (*juxta Shaldebourne*) 1342 *GDR*, *Hame* 1086 DB, *Hama* 1166 P, *Hampne* 14th *Bradenstoke*
>
> *v.* hamm, 'enclosure,' etc.

DOWNS (6″) is *Hanger Down* c. 1840 *TA* and the Hanger is identical with the *hangra* in *bofan hangran* (BCS 677) which must have been applied to the whole slope of Ham Hill.

HAMSPRAY HO. Cf. *Spraye* t. Hy 3 *For*, 1276 StOsmund, 1287 *FF*, 1367 *For*, *Spray* 1257 ib. The name goes back to OE *spræg*, 'brushwood' etc., discussed in PN D 208, *s.n.* Sprytown. Cf. Lower Spray in Inkpen over the county border in Berkshire.

PIDGITT FD[1] (*TA*) is *pyddes geat* 931 BCS 677, 'the gate or gap of *Pyddi*,' a name not on record but allied to the recorded *Puda*, *v.* geat.

---

[1] The field lies just south of Inwood Copse on the parish boundary.

HAM HILL. Cf. *Hulmede* 1249 FF. HOGLAND'S COPSE (6″). Cf. *Hog Lands* c. 1840 *TA*. INLANDS COPSE (6″). Cf. *Inlands Field* ib. *v. infra* 439. INWOOD COPSE (6″). Cf. *infra* 459.

Milton Lilborne

MILTON LILBORNE

> *Mideltone* 1086 DB, *Middelton* 1198 Fees, 1236 FF
> *Mydilton Lillebon* 1249 *Ass*, (*Lyllebon*) 1271 FF
> *Milton Lilborn* 1412 FA

'Middle farm,' *v.* tun. Perhaps so named because midway between Pewsey and Easton. William de *Lilebone* held the manor in 1236 (FF), Walter *Lyllebon* in 1278 (*FF*) and William de *Insula Bona* in 1316 (FA). The family came from Lillebonne (Seine Inf.)

NOTE. CLAY LANE. Cf. *East, West Cley* 1628 WIpm. *Cowringlane* ib.

CLENCH is *Clenchia* n.d. AD i, *Clenche* 1289 *Ass*, 1314 *FF*, *Cleynche* 1330 Ipm, 1371 Pat, 1372 IpmR, *Clynche* 1572, 1596 *FF* and gave name to Roger Godale *atte Clenche* (1257 *For*), John de *la Clenche* (1275 RH) and Thomas de *Clenche* (1327 Banco). Clench was no doubt originally a hill-name, as suggested by Ekwall (DEPN), related to the dialect *clench, clunch,* 'lump, mass.' The farm itself lies in a depression but is at the foot of a big rounded hill which lies on its eastern side. Cf. *Clinghill supra* 254, *Clynchehill* (1570 PembSurv) in Ramsbury.

FYFIELD is *Fifide* 1230 Pat, *Fifhide* 1236 FF, (*juxta Middelton*) 1317 *FF*. 'Five hides,' cf. Fifield *supra* 328.

MILKHOUSE WATER is *Mullecote* 1236 FF, *Milecote* 1257, *Mulecote* 1270 *For*, *Melecote* 1289, *Mulecotes juxta Middelton* 1310 *Ass*, *Midelton cum Mulecote* 1327 SR. 'Cottages by the mill,' *v.* myln, cot(e). The modern form is due to folk-etymology, *milcots* passing easily into *milk house*.

TOTTERIDGE FM

> *Tetherigg(e)* 1199 FF, 1257 *For*, *Tederigge* 1205 Cur
> *Teterige* 1211 RBE, *-rigge* 1282 AD vi, *-rugge* t. Ed 3, *-rygge* 1383 AD i, 1495 *FF*, 1513 *AD*

Toteryg 1315 Ipm, *Toderygge* 1362 *For*
Tyterygge 1545 *FF*
Totteridge t. Jas 1 ECP

The interpretation of this name is not easy but the early forms suggest a compound of an OE *tyte* and **hrycg**. OE *tyte* would be allied to *tote*, 'look-out,' now *toot*, LGer *tūte*, Du *tuit*, used of a snout and various other things that project or thrust themselves forward. Here we have a small ridge projecting into the river valley. Hence perhaps 'projecting ridge.'

HAVERING HO (6″) is to be associated with the family of Richard de *Haverynge* (t. Ed 2 *For*) which may have come from Havering-atte-Bower (cf. PN Ess 111). Cf. *Haveringisheth* 1503 *MinAcct*, *Haveringes lane* 1626, *Milton Havering* 1632 WIpm. Earlier known as *Kingesheth*, a holding in Savernake Forest (H. C. B.).

BROOMSGROVE FM. Cf. *Bromesgrove* 1542 *Sav*. GIANT'S GRAVE is *The Giants Grave* 1804 WM xxix. A long barrow. LITTLE ANN is so named in 1773 (A and D)[1]. LITTLE SALISBURY is *New Town or Little Salisbury* ib. A nickname for a new hamlet. Cf. Little London (PN Sx 255). MILTON HILL FM. Cf. *The Hill Ground* c. 1840 *TA*. NEW MILL is so named in 1773 (A and D).

Pewsey

PEWSEY

(*æt*) *Pefesigge* c. 880 (c. 1000) BCS 553
Pevesige 940 ib. 748, *Pevesie, -ei* 1086 DB, *-ia* 1156, 1177 P, *-i* 1254 Pap, *-eye* 1261 FF *et freq* to 1316 FA, with variant spelling *Peues-*, *Peuesy* 1324 Cl
Pusye 1378 Cl, *Pewse* 1524 SR

'*Pefe*'s well-watered land,' *v*. eg. *Pefe* is not on record, but the same personal name, in an extended form *Pefen*, would seem to be found in Pevensey and Pensfold (PN Sx 443, 160).

AVEBRICK FM and HAYBROOK HO (6″) are to be identified with *Abricks* c. 1840 *TA* and probably take their name from *Ebban*

---

[1] The School notes that a neighbouring field is Little Land Coppice (*TA*), now LITTLE ANN COPSE (6″), and suggests with much probability that *Little Ann* was originally a corruption of *Little Land*.

broc (BCS 748) in the bounds of Pewsey. The stream is now called FORD BROOK (6"). There may be yet a third form of the name in *Hayburnham*, a field-name in Wilcot, found in an 18th-century map and located at the headwaters of *Ebban broc* (Sykes).

KEPNAL (6") is *Kepehull* 1275 RH (p), *Keppenhull* 1289 *Ass* (p), *Kepenhull(e)* 1327 *SR* (p), t. Ed 3 *For*, 1341 NI (p), *Kepunhull(e)* c. 1330, t. Hy 4 *For*, *Kepenulle* 1331 *Stowe* 925, *Kepnell* 1522 *SR*. This name must remain an unsolved problem.

MARTINSELL HILL[1] is *Mattelesore* 1257 *For*, 1300 *Stowe*, *Matteles-* 1280 *FF*, *Matlesore* 1302 Pat, *Matels-* 1339 *For*, *Matteleshora* 1370 Ipm, *Martinshall hill* 1549 WM xiii.

The second element in this name is clearly ora, 'bank.' The first element must be associated with the OE name for the camp which stands on the top of it, the *Mætelmesburg* of the Pewsey charter (BCS 784). The full name for the *ora* was doubtless *Mætelmesora*, i.e. '*Mæþelhelm*'s bank.' The development of the name may have been affected by the neighbourhood of *motenesora* (see under Oare *supra* 325) which really forms part of the same ridge as it curves round to the west.

SHARCOTT is *Shervecot'* 1249 FF, *Sherfcot(e)* 1279, 1281 *Ass*, 1339 *For*, *Shurf-* 1289 *Ass*, t. Ed 2 *For*, *Schorf-* 1327 *SR*, *Shercott* 1602 *FF*, 1799 *Sadler*. It would seem that the first element here is OE *sceorf* noted in PN Sx *s.n.* Hodshrove, but the sense 'steep slope' does not suit the site. The slope is a very gentle one. Equally difficult of application would be Wallenberg's suggestion (KPN 123) that it may mean 'cutting, incision, score.'

KNOWLE was the home of Robert de *la Knoll* (1201 Cur) and is *Cnolle* 1249 *Ass*. v. cnoll, 'round hill.'

BOUVERIE HALL (6") takes its name from Canon Bouverie, rector c. 1900 (G. M. Y.). WINTER'S PENNING is to be associated with the family of George *Winter* (c. 1840 *TA*). For *Penning*, *v. infra* 453. Found also in SHARCOTT PENNING (6").

---

[1] Locally always known simply as Martinsell (H. C. B.).

ANVILL'S FM. Cf. *Anvills Ground* c. 1840 *TA*. BALL HO (6″).
Cf. *Ball Field* and *Meadow* ib. and *infra* 422. BROAD FIELD
COTTAGES (6″). Cf. *Broad Field* ib. BUCKLEAZE FM (6″) is
Bucklies 1609 *Longford*. DENNY SUTTON HIPEND is (*le*) *Hypende*
1568 *Sav*, *Denny Sutton Hipend* 1775 *Act*, *Heap End* 1816 O.S.
The name is descriptive of the end of the hill here. HARE STREET
COPSE (6″) is *Hare Street Coppice* c. 1840 *TA*. It is by Hare
Street *supra* 87. THE HASSOCKS (6″) is *Hassocks Wood* ib.
v. hassock *infra* 452. INLANDS COPSE (6″). Cf. *Inlands* ib. and
infra 439. KING'S CORNER (6″) is so named in 1820 (G). It
marks the turn of the Forest boundary (H. C. B.). KNAPP (6″) is
so named in 1662 (*Sav*). *v.* cnæpp, 'hill.' PEWSEY DOWN and
HILL. Cf. *montem de Peuesy* 1279 *Ass*, *Peusedowne* 1332 AD iv,
Downe Pewsey 1585 WM xxi. PICCADILLY (6″) stands at cross-
roads, cf. *infra* 455. RAFFIN (6″). Cf. *Rafin meadow* c. 1840 *TA*.
SOUTHCOTT is *Suthcote* 1249 *Ass*, *South-* 1553 *AddCh*, *v.* cot(e).
SUNNYHILL FM is so named in 1820 (G). SWAN (6″). Cf. *Swan
Mead* and *Piece* c. 1840 *TA*.

North and South Savernake

These are modern parishes formed from extra-parochial portions
of the old forest (*supra* 15).

North Savernake

BROWN'S FM (6″) is *Brown Farm* 1773 A and D. FURZE COPPICE.
Cf. *Fuzzey Coppice Hill* ib. It represents the medieval assart of
Isbury *supra* 300 (H. C. B.). GORE COPSE (6″). Cf. *the Gore*
1578 *Sav*. *v.* gara. It is the *Stolkesgore or Scotsgore* of 1300 *For*.
HIGH TREES FM. Cf. *The High Trees* c. 1840 *TA*. LEVETTS FM
(6″) is so named in 1820 (G). PANTAWICK (6″) is *Ponter Wyke*
1490 *For*, *Ponterwyke, Punterwyke* 1542 *Sav*, *Pentewick* 1773
A and D. Smith (209) notes that Ralf *Panter* represented the
neighbouring borough of Great Bedwyn in 1426. *v.* wic.
POSTERN HILL. Cf. *Postern Gate* 1576 WM xxxviii, *waie called
Posternget* 1565 ib. xxxi. TANCOAT LANE (6″) is *Tankard Lane*
1773 A and D.

South Savernake

SAVERNAKE LODGE, formerly BAGDEN LODGE, is *Baggeden'* 1290, t. Ed 2, 1362 *For*, *Bagden* 1542 *Sav*, *Bagden Lodge* 1786 *Map*. Not far off must have been *baggan geat* 778 BCS 225, *bacgan geat* 968 (12th) BCS 1213. 'Bacga's gate and valley,' *v.* denu.

BRAYDON HOOK is (*to*) *bræcdene geate* 968 (c. 1225) BCS 1213, *caput de Brayden* 1257, *Braiden'* 1259 *For*, *Braedone* 1272 WIpm, *Braydene* 1290 *For*, 1331 *Stowe* 925, 1370 Ipm, *Braydeneshok* 1331 *Stowe* 925, *-houke* t. Ed 3, *Braieden'* 1339 *For*, *viam de Braye*, *puteum de Braydene* 14th *Bradenstoke*, *Braydens hook* 1542 *Sav*. 'Valley in which there is land broken up for cultivation.' *v.* bræc *infra* 423. For this development an exact parallel may be found in the history of Theydon (PN Ess 82). The earliest form of that name occurs in a 13th-century cartulary of Waltham Abbey, in a charter of Edward the Confessor. Kemble printed it as *þecdene*, Thorpe (followed by Ekwall in DEPN) as *þetdene*, but examination of the MS shows that, though *e* and *t* are hard to distinguish in this handwriting, the probabilities are all in favour of *c*. See further Addenda *supra* xxxvi.

BRIMSLADE FM is *Brumslap* t. Ed 1, t. Ed 3 *For*, *Bromessclape* 14th *Bradenstoke*, *Bromslape* t. Ed 3 *For*, *Brymslade al. Brymslade Parke* 1626 WIpm. A compound of OE brom, 'broom,' and slæp, 'slippery place,' etc. The modern form is corrupt.

RAM ALLEY is so named in 1773 (A and D). Crawford (WM xli, 287–8) shows that the place is just by *igfeld* of the great Bedwyn charter (BCS 1213) and *igfled* (sic) of the Burbage charter (ib. 1067) and from this draws the very likely inference that *Eilly* (1275 RH) in Kinwardstone Hundred is to be identified with Alley and goes back to *igleah*, descriptive of the woodland on the isolated hogsback of land just to the west, here described as an ieg or 'island.' For a possible parallel cf. *Iley Oak supra* 154.

HILL BARN was the home of Wm *atte Hulle* (t. Ed 2 *For*).

TARRANT'S FM is to be associated with the family of William *Tarrant* (1676 WM xlv). It is so called in 1820 (G).

APSHILL COPSE. Cf. *Apshullemed'* t. Ed 2, *Apshullcroft* 1362 *For*. 'Aspen hill,' *v.* æps, croft. ASHLADE is *Asshelade* t. Ed 1, *Ashslad* 1331 *For*. The second element is probably slæd. BRICK HILL COPSE (6″). Cf. *infra* 36. CADLEY. Cf. *Cadley Meadow* c. 1840 *TA* and *supra* 244. CROOKS COPSE is *Crooks Coppice* c. 1840 *TA*. HAT GATE. Cf. *le Hacche gate* 14th *Bradenstoke*. KINGSTONES FM. Cf. *Kyngesdoune* t. Ed 3 *For*, *Kingston meade* 1637 *Sav*. 'King's down.' LEIGH HILL [lai] is *la Leye* t. Ed 2 *For*, *Leigh Hill* 1773 A and D, *v.* leah. LUTON LYE (6″) is *Lewdons lye, Lewdens ley* 1542 *Sav*. SAVERNAKE PARK is *Greate Parke of Savernake* 1609 WM xxii. THE WARREN is so named c. 1840 (*TA*).

Shalbourne

SHALBOURNE

Scealdeburnan 955 (14th) BCS 912

S(c)aldeburne 1086 DB, *Scaldi-* 1198 Abbr, *Shaldeborne* 1202 FF *et passim* to 1428 FA, with variant spellings *Sch-* and *-b(o)urne*, *Scaudiburna* 1211 RBE, *-de-* 1214 Cur

Chaldeburne 1375 Cl, *Chauburne* 1540 L

Shalburne 1494 Ipm, *Shawborne* 1547 FF, 1599 *Recov*

'Shallow stream,' *v.* scealde, burna.

ASHLEY DOWN (6″) and HAM ASHLEY COPSE (6″). Cf. *Scortasscheleye* 1331 *Stowe*, *Asshele* t. Ed 2, *Scorte Aschele* t. Ed 3 *For*. '(Short) ash clearing or wood,' *v.* leah. Close by was the *greatan æsc* of the Ham charter (BCS 67).

BAGSHOT

Bechesgete 1086 DB, *-ieta* 1130 P, *Bekesgate* 1289 *Ass*, 13th AD i

Bukesgate t. Ed 2, *Bockesgate* t. Ed 3, 1339 *For*, *Boghkes-* 14th *Bradenstoke*

Basshette 1525 *SR*, *Bagshott* 1684 *Recov*, *Bagshot* 1819 RCH

Probably from OE *Beoccesgeat*, '(forest)-gate of *Beocc*.' Professor Ekwall notes *Beoccesheal* (BCS 1213) in the bounds of Redwyn two miles to the west, named probably from the same man. *Beocca* is on record from Wilts.

BOTLEY HILL (6″) is *Bottele* t. Ed 1, t. Ed 3 *For, bosc. de Bottele* 1331 *Stowe* 925, *Botteleye* 1349 *Ass.* '*Botta*'s clearing or wood,' *v.* leah.

RIVAR [rɑivə] is (*on tha*) *yfre* 931 BCS 677, *Ryver* 1609 *Recov*, *Ryever* 1773 A and D. *v.* yfer, 'slope,' *infra* 450, the modern form going back to ME *at ther evre (ivre)* as in River (PN Sx 123) and River Hill in Binstead (Ha), *la Uvere* 1298 *For, del Evre* 1375 ib. (p). Rivar lies just below a very steep hill-side.

STYPE WOOD is *boscus de la Stupe* 1257 *For*, 1268 *Ass, la Stupe* t. Ed 2, *boscus voc. Stupe* 1362 *For.* The name is probably identical in origin with Steep (Ha), (*la*) *Stupe* c. 1200 Winton, 1316 FA, *la Stiepe* 1230, *Stype* 1233 Selborne, *le Stepe* 1255 HMC Var iv in Herriard (Ha) and *la Stupe* 1270 Selborne in Selborne (ib.), from OE **stīepe*, 'steep place,' from *stēap*, 'steep.' Cf. also *la Blakestupe* (1257 *For*) in Bedwyn.

WELL HO was the home of Robert *atte Welle* (1327 *SR*).

KINGSTONE'S COPSE (6″), NOON'S FM, ORAMS FM (6″), PEARCE'S FM and POLESDONS FM are to be associated with the families of Anthony *Kingston* (c. 1840 *TA*), John *Noon* (1547 *SR*), Thomas *Oram* (c. 1840 *TA*), Catherine *Pearce* (ib.) and William de *Polysdone* (1289 *Ass*), de *Pollesdene* (t. Ed 2 *For*) which may have come from Polesden (PN Sr 100).

BACON'S FM (6″) is *Forstesbury Baconis* 1331 *For, Bacons* 1451 *FF.* See Fosbury *infra* 356. COWLEAZE COPPICE (6″) is so named c. 1840 (*TA*). FOLLY FM is *the Folly* 1773 A and D. *v. infra* 451. GALLOWOOD is so named c. 1840 (*TA*). THE HASSOCKS (6″) is *Hassocks* ib. Cf. *infra* 452. HILLCROFT (6″) is *Hill Croft Ground* ib. HUNGRY LODGE (6″) is a derogatory name. *v. infra* 455. NEWTOWN is *Neweton'* 1234 Cl, *New Town* 1773 A and D. OXENWOOD FM is *Oxenewod(e)* 1257 *For*, 1275 RH. ROPEWIND FM (6″), SLOPE END (6″) and SMAY DOWN. Cf. *Ropewind Mead, Slope End, Smay Down* c. 1840 *TA.* STARVEALL FM is a term of reproach for poor land. *v. infra* 455. WEST-COURT (6″) is *Westcourt* 1452 Pat, *Shalborn Westcorte* t. Eliz ChancP. 'West court,' probably in the sense 'manor.'

Tidcombe

TIDCOMBE

Titicome 1086 DB, *Titecumbe* 1197 P *et freq* to 1332 *SR*, with variant spellings *Tyte-* and *-combe*, *Tytecumbe Husee* 1282 *Ass*

Tydecumbe 1249 FF, 1275 RH, 1279 *Ass*, 1291 Tax, 1316 FA, *Tidecombe* 1286 Ipm, *Tiddecombe* t. Hy 8 *AOMB*

Titcombe al. Tidcombe 1748 *Recov*, *Titcomb* 1812 RCH

Probably, as suggested by Ekwall (DEPN *s.n.*), '*Titta*'s valley' (*v.* cumb), with the same personal name which is found in *Tittandun* BCS 667 (Wo). Hubert *Husee* held the manor in 1282 (*Ass*).

FOSBURY HO

Fostesberge, Fistesberie 1086 DB, *Forstebyri* 1268 *Ass*, *-bury* t. Ed 2 *For*, *Upforstebury* 1229 StOsmund, 1331 *Stowe* 925, t. Ed 3 *For*, *Forstesbery* 1270 *For*, *Westeforstesbyr'* 1289 *Ass* *Forestebur'* 1290, *-bury* t. Ed 2 *For*, *Westforestbury* 1368 Pat *Fossebury* t. Hy 8 *AOMB*, *Fostbury* 1721 *FF*

Identical in origin with Fosbury *supra* 306. *West* Fosbury is probably Bacon's *supra* 355. Why *Up* Fosbury is not clear. It is lower than Bacon's by 100 ft. (H. C. B.).

HIPPENSCOMBE

Heppingcumb' 1231, *Heppingescumb'* 1255, *-gis-* 1261 Cl *Huppanghescumb'* 1257 Cl, *Huppingescumbe* 1257 *For*, 1259 FF, 1275 RH, *Huppengescomb* 1276 StOsmund, *Huppingges-cumbe* 1289 *Ass*, *Huppyngescombe* 1307 Pat, 1331 *Stowe* 925, t. Ed 3 *For* *Hippingescumbe* 1292 Cl, *Ippingescombe* 1371 Ipm

Ekwall (DEPN) hazards the suggestion that the first element here may be the north country *hippings*, 'stepping-stones,' but form and topography alike are against this—Hippenscombe lies in a waterless bottom. The name is a difficult one. Perhaps we should associate it with the name Hipley in Hambledon (Ha), *Huppeleg* 1249, 1270 *FF*, *-le(gh)* 1272, 1314 *Ass*, 1341 *For*, 1343 Pat, *Hippleye* 1256 *Ass*, 1320 Ch, *-le* 1281 Abbr, 1317 Pat, *Hyppeley* 1469 *FF*. Both names alike suggest an OE pet-name

Hyppa, with derivative *Hypping*. *Hyppa* might be a pet-form for OE *Hygebeorht*, cf. OGer *Huppo* (Förstemann, PN 936). If so, the name means '*Hypping*'s valley.'

OAKHILL WOOD is *Ocholt* 1259 *For*, *Ockolt* 1259 FF, *bosc. de Ockholte* 1331 *Stowe* 925. 'Oak wood,' v. **ac**, **holt**, with later corruption.

SCOT'S POOR is *Scott Poor* 1773 A and D, *Scots Poor* 1812 RCH. It is by the *stæt* (sic) *geat* of the Great Bedwyn charter (BCS 1213), a name which Crawford notes as surviving in the *Street Gate* of an Estate map of 1825. Further record of it is found in *streteyate* (1259 FF) in Tidcombe and *Streetgate Down* in the Collingbourne Kingston Tithe Award. It lies on the old Roman road commonly known as Chute Causeway.

BLACK BUSHES (6") is so named c. 1840 (*TA*). BLACKDOWN BARN. Cf. *Blakedone* t. Ed 1 *For*, *Blakden* c. 1490 *DuLa*, *Blackdonlaund* 1562 *Sav*. See *infra* 440. BLACKLANDS ROW (6") is *Blackland* 1637 ib. BULPITT'S COPSE (6") is *Bull Pitts Coppice* c. 1840 (*TA*). CLEVES COPSE is *Cleeve Coppice* ib. v. **clif**. CONEYGRE COPSE (6") is *Coneygre Coppice* ib. v. *infra* 427. EAST DOWN is *Eastdowne* 1662 *Sav*. HAYDOWN HILL. Cf. *Haydon Hill Castle* 1773 A and D. HOLLYGRES PLANTATION (6"). Cf. *Holly Gres Field* c. 1840 *TA*. KNOLLS DOWN (6"). Cf. *Knollesgate* 1331 *Stowe* 925, *Knollghate* t. Ed 3 *For*. v. **cnoll**. NEWFIELD COTTAGES (6"). Cf. *New Field* c. 1840 *TA*. SILVER DOWN is so named c. 1840 (*TA*). THE SLAY. Cf. *supra* 329. TUMMER COPSE and ROW (6"). Cf. *Tummer Mead* ib. There is a pool here, v. **mere**. WARREN COTTAGES (6"). Cf. *the Warren* c. 1840 *TA*.

Wootton Rivers

WOOTTON RIVERS

Wdutun 804 (c. 1150) BCS 324
Otone 1086 DB, *Wotton(a)* 1212 *Cur*, 1242 *Fees*, (*juxta Savernak*) 1331 *FF*, (*Ryver*) 1428 FA, *Otten Rivers* 1743 ParReg
Wutton 1222 FF, (*Ryveyrs*) 1371 Pat

'Farm by the wood,' v. **tun**. Walter de *Riperia* held the manor in 1212 (*Cur*), William de *la Rivere* in 1222 (FF).

FLITWICK (6″) was the home of Ralph de *Flytwyke* (1345 *Ass*). This would seem to be a compound of OE (*ge*)*flit*, 'dispute,' and **wic**. Hence, perhaps, 'farm in disputed ownership.'

HEATHY CLOSE (6″) is so named in 1820 (G). EAST and WEST WICK FMS are *Wike* 1201 Cur (p), *Westwyk*, *Wyke* 1229 StOsmund, *Estwyk* 1268 *Ass*. *v*. **wic** and *supra* 25.

XXXI. AMESBURY HUNDRED

Hundred de Am(*m*)*resberie*, *Ambresberia* 1086 ExonDB, *Ambres-beri hdr* 1159 P. *v*. Amesbury *infra*.

Allington

ALLINGTON

> *Aldinton*(*a*), -*y*- t. Hy 2 (1270) Ch, 1178 BM *et freq* to 1332 SR, (*juxta Neweton*) 1289 *Ass*
>
> *Aldington*, -*y*- 1242 FF, 1268 *Ass*, (*juxta Ambresbir'*) 1279, 1281, 1305 ib., 1325 Pat, *in villa de Aldyngton et non in villa de Aldynton* 1426 *Ass*
>
> *Aldington oth. Allington* 1769 Recov

'*Ealda*'s farm,' *v*. **ingtun**. Cf. Aldbourne *supra* 291–2. Cf. Allington in Stoneham (Ha), *Aldinton* 1186, 1188 P, *Aldington* 13th AD i. In the Assize Roll form of 1426 we have an attempt to assert the correctness of the form *Aldyngton* as against *Aldynton*.

WYNDHAM'S FM (6″) is to be associated with the family of Walter *Wyndham* (c. 1840 *TA*).

ALLINGTONDOWN BARN. Cf. *The Down, East Down* c. 1840 *TA*.

Amesbury

AMESBURY

> (*æt*) *Ambresbyrig* c. 880 (c. 1000) BCS 553, c. 1000 Saints, *Amberesburg* 858 (c. 1150) BCS 495, (*æt*) *Ambresbirig* 955 (15th) ib. 912, *Ambresburch* 932 (14th) ib. 691, *Hambres-buruh* 972 (14th) ib. 1286

Amblesberie, Ambresberie, Ambresberiæ 1086 DB, *Ambresbiria* 1130 P *et passim* to 1384 Cl, with variant spellings -*biri*, -*beri*, -*buri*, -*bury*, -*bir'*, *Amberesbur'* c. 1200 AD iv, *Aumbresberia* 1231 Bracton, *Aumbrebiry* 1241, *Ambrebiry* 1265 Pat, *Estambrebur'* 1289 *Ass*, *Magna Ambresbury* 1321 FF, *Ambresburi Priorisse* 1332 *SR*, *Ammersbury* 1349 Pat, *Ambersbury* 1380 ib., *Greate Ambresburye* 1547 *SR*

Almesberie 1434 BM, *Awmesbury* 1444 Pat, *Amysbury* 1524 *SR*, *Amsburye* 1614 *FF*, *Ambsbury* 1614, *Amesbury alias Ambresbury* 1703 *Recov*

It is impossible to go beyond the suggestion made *s.nn.* Ombersley (PN Wo 268) and Ambersham (PN Sx 97–8), viz. that we have to do with a personal name *Ambre*, *Aembre* cognate with the recorded OGer *Ambri.* Hence possibly '*Ambre*'s burh.' This chances to accord with Geoffrey of Monmouth's speculation (viii, 9) '*in monte ambrii qui ut ferunt fundator eiusdem olim extiteret.*' *Priorisse* from the nunnery here.

NOTE. LYNCHETTS RD. Cf. *The Lynchets* c. 1840 *TA* and *infra* 453.

COUNTESS is *Ambresbur' Comitis* 1327 *SR*, *Contessecourt* 1365 *DuLa*, *Countasyscourt* 1401 FA, *Contescourt* 1409 Cl. Cf. also *the Countesse feild* 1650 *ParlSurv*, representing the manor of Amesbury held in 1332 (*SR*) by Alice de Lacy, Countess of Lincoln.

EARL'S FARM DOWN is *Haradon Hill* 1610 S, 1695 M, 1773 A and D. This is possibly another example of hearg and dun, 'heathen temple down'; cf. Harrowden (PN Nth 125, PN BedsHu 91) and possibly Harrow Hill (PN Sx 165). Cf. also Waden *supra* 295.

RATFYN

Rotefeld(e) (sic) 1086 DB

Rotefen 1115 StOsmund, 1158 HMC Var i, 1372 Pat, -*fan* c. 1250 *Rental, Rocefen* (sic) 1178 BM, *Rotefene* 1230 SarumCh

Rothefen t. Hy 2 (1270) Ch, 1249 *Ass*, 1305 Sarum, 1327 *SR*, Pat, -*ven* 1332 *SR*, *Rothfen* 1407 Pat, 1535 VE

Botenfen (sic) t. John Dugd ii

Roffen 1428 FA, *Rothfenne al. Ratfenne* 1560 *FF*, *Radfyn* 1812 RCH

Possibly '*Hrōpa*'s fen or marsh,' *v.* **fenn**. Persistent medial *e* hardly allows of our taking the first element to be OE *roþ*, 'clearing,' noted in PN Herts 165, *s.n.* Roe Green.

STONEHENGE

> *Stanenges* c. 1130 HH, *Stanheng* 12th Geoffrey of Monmouth, *Stanhenge* c. 1200 Lay, *Stanhenges* 13th AnnMon
> *Stonheng* c. 1250 Lay, *Stonheng* (v.ll. *þe stonheng, stonhenge*) 1297 RG, *Stonehenge* 1610 S
> *the stone hengles* (v.l. *stonehenges*) 1470 Hardyng, *Chronicle the stonege* 1547 Boord (*v.* NED)[1], *Stonage* 1668 Pepys

This is a difficult name. So far as the form is concerned it is clear that the *g* must go back to OE *cg*. That alone will explain the modern [hendʒ] or the earlier and more popular [edʒ] pronunciation. It is clear also that the modern pronunciation [stoun'hendʒ] is an artificial one which has replaced earlier [stɔnidʒ] in which the stress was in its natural position on the first syllable and the stressed vowel was shortened before the consonant-group *nh*.

The first element is clearly OE *stān*, 'stone,' but the second is uncertain. The most natural association is with the common word *hinge*, first recorded from the 14th century in the form *henge*, but going back very probably to a far earlier date and probably to OE *hencg*. The name would have then to be explained by imagining that the main thought in the minds of those who first applied the name to the monument was that the imposts in the trilithons 'hinged' on the uprights. That does not seem however entirely satisfactory.

An alternative suggestion has been made that the second element is really OE *hen(c)gen*, used frequently in OE of an instrument first for hanging, and then for torture generally. The gaunt framework of the trilithons might well be imagined to resemble a series of great gallows or torture-racks. From the formal point of view there would be no great difficulty, for final *en* would, as in so many other words (e.g. *clew* from OE *cliewen*, *maid* from OE *mægden*), be early lost, leaving final *henge*.

---

[1] This quotation is from the NED which gives further examples showing how the name *Stonehenge* in this colloquial form came to be used as a common noun denoting any ancient monument made of huge stones.

The form *hengle* in Hardyng is interesting. It is a word found more than once in ME in the sense 'hinge.' The person who used it probably interpreted the name in the sense 'stone-hinge(s).' See Addenda *supra* xli.

WEST AMESBURY is *Westamberesbir'* 1232 *Lacock, West A(u)mbresbury* 1236 FF, 1324 *FF, Westamsbury alias Littleamsbury* 1662 NQ vii.

COLD HARBOUR (6″). *v. infra* 451. CONEYBURY HILL (6″). Cf. *le Conynger* 1382 IpmR, *le Conyngar* 1503 Ipm, *Coneybury Hill* 1773 A and D. *v. infra* 427. EARLSCOURT FM (6″). Cf. *Earles Farme* 1634 *Longleat, Earles Feild* 1650 *ParlSurv.* FOLLY BOTTOM (6″). Cf. *Folly Garden* c. 1840 *TA* and *infra* 451. GREY BRIDGE (6″) is *Greybrugge* 1365 *DuLa.* HAM HATCHES (6″). Cf. *Ham Close* c. 1840 *TA.* LITTLEFIELD (6″) is *Little Field* ib. OLDDOWN BARN (6″). Cf. *la Doune* 1365 *DuLa, Oldoune* 1518 Hoare. THE PENNINGS. *v. infra* 453. RED HO FM is *Red House Farm* 1809 Hoare. SEVEN BARROWS is so named in 1773 (A and D). TUMBLING BAY (6″) is *The Tumling bay* (sic) 1676 Sess. This term is used (NED *s.v.*) of an outfall from a river or canal. This field lies by the Avon.

Boscombe

BOSCOMBE

  Boscumbe 1086 DB, *-cumba, -e* t. Hy 2 (1270) Ch, 1170–5 NQ i, 1178 BM *et passim*, with variant spelling *-comb(e)*
  Bescumba t. Hy 2 (1270) Ch, *Bascumbe* c. 1180 BM
  Borrescumb' 1256 Cl, *Borscumbe* 1275 RH, 1281, 1306 *Ass,* *-combe* 1327 Banco, 1332 *SR, Borescumbe* 1302 *Ass, -combe* 1364 Cl, 1535 VE, *Borscome* 1537 PCC

The first element may be the OE word **bors*, postulated for Boasley (PN D 174), denoting something of a spiky or bristly nature. Cf. *Borsle* (1362 *Cor*) in Trowbridge and Boseleys in Bromham *infra* 492. The name would have reference to a combe or valley overgrown with such plants. *v.* **cumb.**

BOSCOMBE DOWN WEST. Cf. *Westdowne* t. Eliz *LRMB.*

Bulford

BULFORD

Bultesford t. Hy 2 (1270) Ch, *-tis-* 1178 BM, 1286 Ch
Bulteford t. Hy 2 (1270) ib., 1249, 1268, 1279, 1289 *Ass*, 1255
 RH, 1381 IpmR, *Bolteford* 1275 RH, 1428 FA
Boltiford 1227 FF, *Bulting-* 1249, 1268 *Ass*, *Bulti-* ib.
Bulterford 1332 *SR*
Bultford 1341 NI, (*juxta Amesbury*) 1383 *FF*, 1541 Dugd ii,
 Bulford alias Bultford t. Jas 1 ECP

This is a difficult name. Ekwall may be right in his suggestion that the first element is to be associated with OE *bulut*, 'ragged robin,' the first element being either **bulutig*, an adjectival derivative, descriptive of a ford with ragged robin growing by it, or OE *bulut-īeg*, 'ragged robin island.' The river here is divided into more than one stream. A possible parallel is Boulti-brooke (Radnorshire) for which Charles (NCPNW 174) gives late forms *Bowltibrook, Boultibrooke* (16th, 18th).

MELSOME'S DOWN FM is to be associated with the family of George *Melsome* (c. 1840 *TA*) which probably came from Melksham *supra* 128.

BEACON HILL is so named in 1773 (A and D). BULFORD DOWN. Cf. *lez Downes* t. Jas 1 *LRMB*. BULFORD FIELD. Cf. *Myddel-, North-, South-, Westfeild* t. Eliz ib. LONG BARROW is *Longeborowe* t. Jas 1 ib. SEYMOUR FM (6″) is so named in 1773 (A and D). The *Seymour* family were living in the parish in the 18th century (Hoare 44). SLING PLANTATION. Cf. *le Slinge* t. Jas 1 *LRMB* and *infra* 454. It is a long narrow strip of woodland.

Cholderton

CHOLDERTON

Celdretone 1086 DB, 1170–5 NQ i, *Cheldretona* c. 1180 BM,
 Cheldritune 1270 *For*
Celdrintone 1086 DB, *Cheldrintona* 1174 P, *Cheldrington*
 t. Hy 2 (1270) Ch *et freq* to 1324 Ipm, *-inge-* 1203 Cur,
 Cheldrenton 1242 Fees, *Chelryngton* 1289 *Ass*, *Chelderington*
 1297 Pat

Childreton 1170–5 NQ i, *Chyldrinton* 1268 *Ass*, *Childrȳrton*
   (sic) 1335 Ch
Chaldrinton c. 1280 HMC Hastings, *Chaldrynton* 1316 FA,
   -ing- 1341 NI, 1348 Pat, 1428 FA, *-ing-* 1472 Pat,
   Chauldrington 1557 *Rental*, *Chalderton* 1676 *FF*
Choldrington 1656 ib., *Challerton*, *Chelterton* 1675 Ogilby,
   Cholderton oth. *Choldrington* 1764 *Recov*

There can be little doubt that this name is an ingtun-
derivative of some OE name in *Cēol-*, probably *Cēolðrȳð*.

DEVILS DITCH[1], DOWN BARN, HILLS COPSE and SCOTLAND (all
6ʺ) are *Devils Ditch, Down Piece, Hills Piece, Scotland* c. 1840
TA. The last is on the parish boundary. Cf. *infra* 454–5.
MOUNT PLEASANT FM (6ʺ). Cf. *infra* 455.

Durnford

DURNFORD

Darneford, Diarneford 1086 DB
Durneford 1158 StOsmund, 1163 SarumCh *et freq* to 1474
   Trop, (*Parva*) 1322, (*Moche*) 1412, (*Litell*) 1474 ib.
Derneford(e) 1158 HMC Var i *et freq* to 1316 FA, (*Magna*)
   1270 FF, (*Parva*) 1286 *FF*
Deorneford 1220 SarumCh, 1332 *SR*, (*More*) 1341 NI,
   Dornford 1606 *FF*

'Secret or hidden ford,' *v.* dierne. Cf. Durnaford in St Ive
(Co), *Durneford* 1175 (1348) Pat. Durnford Magna was also
known as *Hungerford* Durnford from its tenure by the *Hungerford* family (Hoare 121). Evelyn calls it *Darneford Magna*.
LITTLE DURNFORD is a hamlet in the extreme south of the
parish.

AVON FM (6ʺ) is *æt Afene* 962 BCS 1083[2], *Avena* c. 1190
SarumCh, *Aven(e)* 1249, (*juxta villam Veteris Sar'*) 1310 *Ass*,
(*juxta Vetus Sar'*) 1330 *FF*, the tenement taking its name from
the river *supra* 1. Distinguished from Avon in Bremhill
supra 87 as near *Old Sarum*.

---

[1] Called simply DITCH on 1ʺ map.
[2] For the identification see *infra* 371.

NETTON

> *Netetune* 1242 Fees, *Netteton juxta Derneford* 1305 *Ass,*
> *Netton* 1310 Cl, *Neton within Salterton* 1342 Ipm
> *Natton(e)* 1289 *Ass*, 1323 Cl
> *Suthneton* 1428 FA

'Farm of the neat or cattle' (from OE *nēata* tun). Cf. Netton (PN D 258). *South* probably in relation to Net Down *supra* 236.

SALTERTON is *Saltertun* 1199 P, -*ton(e)* 1298 Ipm, 1310 Cl, 1393 IpmR, *Saltre-* 1289 *Ass*, *Salterne* 1332 *SR*, *Psalterton* 1641 NQ vii. This is from OE *sealtera-tūn*, 'salt-workers' farm.' Cf. Woodbury Salterton (PN D 602). It is difficult to conceive what the salters were doing here with their *salterne* or salt-houses.

NEWTOWN is *Nyweton* 1289 *Ass*, *Nywentone* 1327 *SR*, *New Towne* 1650 *ParlSurv*, and was the home of Henry *atte Nywe-toune* (1309 WIpm). *v.* tun.

LONGHEDGE FM is so named c. 1840 (*TA*). OGBURY CAMP is *downe called Oakebery* 1649 *SarumD and C, Ogbury Ring or Camp* 1773 A and D. *v.* burh. There is a 'camp' here. SOUTH FM (6″) is no doubt the *Southend Farm* of c. 1840 (*TA*).

DURRINGTON[1]

Durrington

> *Derintone* 1086 DB, -*ton* c. 1160 StOsmund, 1179 P, -*ing-*
> 1281 QW, 1365 Pat, -*yng-* 1388 Cl, 1432 *FF*
> *Durenton(a)* 1178 BM, t. Hy 2 (1270) Ch, -*in-* 1190 P *et freq*
> to 1332 *SR*, with variant spelling -*yn-*, (*juxta Ambresbury*)
> 1319 *FF*, *Duryngton* 1291 Tax, 1398 Cl, *Durryngton* 1522
> *SR*
> *Dorington* 1281 *Ass*, *Doerinton* 1284 *FF*
> *Diryngton* 1389, 1399 Pat, *Dir(r)ington* 1675 Ogilby
> *Hinedurintone* t. Hy 2 (1270) Ch, *Hindorinton* t. John Dugd ii,
> *Hyndurinton* 1268, -*derinton* 1268 *Ass*, *Kingderinton* (sic)
> 1286 Ch, *Indurynton* 1299 Inq aqd, -*in-* 1301 Pat, *Hyn-*
> *dryngton* 1447 IpmR, *Duryngton al. Drunton al. Hyn-*
> *duryngton* 1572, *Hendurington* 1602 *FF*

[1] In 1360 (*WinchColl*) we have reference to *Fourtenebargh*, almost certainly the group of barrows on Durrington Down, north of Fargo Road, which still seem to number fourteen.

'*Dēora*'s farm,' *v.* ingtun. *Hindurrington* seems to be a name for a lost place in the parish, from OE higna, 'monastic or other household.' Cf. Hindon *supra* 191. It probably represented the holding of the nuns of Amesbury (cf. 1270 Ch).

NOTE. FARGO ROAD leads to the western edge of the parish where, in Winterbourne Stoke, there is a field called *Fargo* (*infra* 490). By it lies FARGO PLANTATION in Amesbury.

HACKTHORN (6″) is *le Hakthorn* 1360, *Hackethorn* 1617 *WinchColl*. It may be that there was in OE a compound *haca-þorn*, 'hook-thorn,' corresponding to the Dutch *haakedorn*. Cf. also Hackthorn (L), *Hagetorne* 1086 DB, *Hacatorn, Hachatorna, Hache-torna* c. 1116 Lindsey Survey.

COLIN'S FM and PINCKNEY'S FM (both 6″) are to be associated with the families of William *Collins* (1810 ParReg) and Anne *Pinckney* (1617 *WinchColl*).

CUCKOO STONE (6″) is *Cuckhold Stone* 1790 WM xxxi, one of the few sarsen stones on the Plain outside Stonehenge (H. C. B.). DURRINGTON BRIDGE is so named in 1606 (Sess). DURRINGTON DOWN. Cf. *le Downe* 1617 *WinchColl*, *Durrington Down* 1685 DKR xxxix. DURRINGTON WALLS. Cf. *Longwall* 1790 WM xxxi, *Long Walls* 1812 RCH. An old entrenchment. LARK HILL is *Larkehull* 1360, *-hill* 1617 *WinchColl*. PACKWAY RD (6″) is *Packway* 1790 WM xxxi. WILTWAY (local) is so named (ib.). The old way to Wilton.

Figheldean

FIGHELDEAN [fɑi(ə)ldi·n, *olim* fikəldi·n]

> *Fisgledene* 1086 DB, *Ficheldene* 1115 StOsmund, *-dena* 1139, *Fykel-* 1157 SarumCh, 1158 StOsmund, *Fikel-* 1197 P, 1205 Cur, 1211 RBE, 1227 Ch, 1235 Fees, 1263 Pat, *Ficledene* 1272 Ipm, *Fickledean* 1742 FF
>
> *Figelden* 1227 FF, *Fighelden(e)* 1229 Pat *et freq* to 1321 Ipm, with variant spelling *Fygh-, Fyhel-* 1286 Ipm, *Fighil-* 1310 Ch, *Fyeldean* 1572 FF, *Figgledon* 1641 NQ vii
>
> *Figheldean al. Fickledean* 1616 Recov
>
> *Feildeane al. Fighledeane* 1640 ib., *Feilden* 1645 WM xix, *Filedean* 1718 Recov

'*Fygla*'s valley,' *v.* denu, with the same personal name which is found in Fillongley (PN Wa 82), Fylingdales (PN NRY 116) and Fillingham (L), DB *Figelingeham.* For the form *Fickledean v. supra* 226.

ABLINGTON is *Alboldintone* 1086 DB, *Abblington* 1226 FF, *Ablinton* 1227 Ch, *Eblinton* 1249 *Ass*, 1252 Ch, *Ablyntone* 1351 *Ass.* Probably '*Ealdbeald*'s farm,' *v.* ingtun.

ALTON is *Eltone* 1086 DB, *Alletona* t. Hy 2 (1270) Ch, t. Hy 2 BM, *Aleton(e)* t. John Dugd ii, 1242 Fees, 1268 *Ass et freq* to 1341 NI, *Aletune* 1242 Fees, *Aleton juxta Fygheldene* 1320 FF, *Alton* 1468 ib. '*Ælla*'s farm,' *v.* tun.

CHOULSTON is *Chelestanestone* 1086 DB, *-a* t. Hy 2 (1270) Ch, *Chelstanton* t. John Dugd ii, *Chelseston* 1286 Ch, *Cholleston* 1332, *Cholston* 1525 SR, *Choleston* 1619 *Recov.* '*Cēolstān*'s farm,' *v.* tun.

KNIGHTON FM is *Wenistetone* (sic) 1086 DB, *Knytheton* t. Hy 2 (1270) Ch, *Knyghteton* 1332 *SR*, (*juxta Ambresbury*) 1337 FF. 'Farm of the "knights" or serving men,' *v.* cniht, tun. The initial *w* in the DB form must be a scribal blunder. The *s* is a common Norman-French representation of the OE *h* sound.

SYRENCOT HO [sirənkʌt, *olim* sisənkət]

> *Sexhamcote* 1227 FF, *Sexamecot* 1242 Fees, *Sexhampcote* 1327, 1332 *SR*, 1394 *Ass*, 1412 FA, *Sexhamcott* 1639 FF *Sirencott* 1637 *Phillipps, Cicencutt* 1773 A and D, *Sissingcutt otherwise Syrencot* 1803 *Recov*

Possibly 'cottages with (or by) six homesteads,' a name of the same type as the Sevenhampton discussed *supra* 107–8.

BARROW CLUMP (tumulus) is *Cicencutt Barrow* 1773 A and D. BOURNE BOTTOM. Cf. *Borne meadow* 1591 WM vi. The 'bottom' or valley down which runs Nine Mile River *supra* 9. CLIFFEND (6″). Cf. *The Clift* (sic) 1790 WM xxxi and clif *infra* 426. FIGHELDEAN BRIDGE (6″) is *Feildhen* (sic) *bridge* 1649 *SarumD and C.* GALLOWS BARROW is so named in 1704 (*Wilton*). GUNVILLE COTTAGES (6″). Cf. *Gunwell House* 1773 A and D.

Ludgershall

LUDGERSHALL [lʌgərʃɔ·l]

Litlegarsele 1086 DB, *Lutlegreshale* 1279, *-halle* 1281 *Ass*,
   Lutelegrashale 1281 QW, *Lutergarshale* 1287 Cl
Lotegarsal 1135–53 (1268) Ch, *Lotegareshal(e)* 1203 PatR,
   -hall 1294, *-garshale* 1254 Cl, 1274 Pat, 1294 *Rental*, 1318
   Cl, *-gereshale* 1264 Pat, *-gers-* 1279, *-gres-* 1279, 1281, 1289
   Ass, 1291, 1294 *MinAcct*
Ludkereshala c. 1150 FW
Lutegareshal(e) 1166 P *et freq* to 1249 *Ass*, *-hole* 1175 France,
   -gars- 1198 Abbr *et freq* to 1321 *Ass*, *-garis-* 1234 Cl, *-gers-*
   1255 RH, 1257 *For*, 1260 Cl, 1268 *Ass*, *-geres-* 1292 Pat,
   -gras- 1281 QW, 1289 *Ass*, *-gres-* ib., *Lutgershale* 1290 Cl,
   1332 Pat
Luttegarishal 1234, *-gares-* 1235, 1255 Cl, *Luttegershale* 1261,
   -gars- 1267 Pat, 1305 Cl, 1327 Banco
Lodegareshale 1384 Pat, *Ludgarshale* 1422 FF, *Ludgereshall*
   1453 Pat, *Ludgasall* 1519 AD ii, *Ludgursale* 1535 VE
Lurgarsale 1529 AD vi, *Luggershaull* c. 1540 L, *Lurgushall*
   1577 *FF*, *Lurgesall* t. Eliz WM xxi, *Lurgshall* 1675
   Ogilby

The significance of this name has been dealt with twice before
in the volumes of the Survey, once under Ludgershall (PN Bk
104–6) and again under Lurgashall (PN Sx 111). Early forms
made it clear that they were identical in origin with Ludgershall
(W) and also with Luggarshall in Owlpen (Gl) for which we have
early forms *Lutegareshale* 1220 Gloucester Corporation Records,
1272 *FF*, 1413 *MinAcct*, *Lutegareshall* t. Hy 3 Dugdale (*sub*
Bradenstoke), *Lotegareshale* 1230 Bristol, Glouc. Soc. Trans.
xxii[1], and a lost *Lotegoreshale* 1293 AD ii in Saffron Walden
(Ess).

If we examine all the forms of these names as recorded under
these references, we find that there is one genuine OE form, viz.
(*æt*) *Lutegaresheale* 1015 Wills, and that in a document of which

---

[1] Forms given by Mr F. T. S. Houghton.

there are two contemporary texts[1]. The genuineness of the *u* of the OE form agrees with the later history of all the names in question. There, alike in Wiltshire, Gloucestershire, Buckinghamshire and Sussex, we have *u* (with occasional *o*) in the ME forms, never *e* and only once *i*, with the exception of the form *Litlegarsele* in DB for the Wiltshire name. This makes it impossible to take OE *lȳtel*, 'little,' as the first element as does Ekwall (DEPN). The general development of *lytel* in Wiltshire, as elsewhere, is quite different. The DB form must be explained as an error due to confusion with that word, and is indeed certainly such if OE *Lutegaresheale* is to be identified with this place. The OE *u*-vowel similarly must make us reject attempts at association with OE *hlyte*, 'lot,' and explanation of the name as from *hlytegærshealh*, 'nook of land where pasturage is assigned by lot,' though doubtless at some later stage in its history there may have been association of the middle part of the word with ME *gers*, *gres*, *gras*, 'grass.'

The OE form and the earliest ME forms alike must therefore still be taken, as was suggested in the previous volumes of the Survey (*loc. cit.*) as a compound of an OE personal name *Lut(e)gār*, found also in *Lutgaresberi*, the old name for Montacute (So). For the possibility of such a name see Ludgershall (Bk) *loc. cit.*

The only difficulty involved in this explanation is the occurrence four or five times over of this personal name *Lut(e)gar* with *healh* as against once with *burh*. It may be noted, however, that the *gærshealh* explanation is from that point of view just as difficult. No other examples of *gærshealh* have been noted. If it really was a common compound, why should it never be on record by itself but always be compounded with *lytel* or *hlyte*, still more improbably with an unexplained *lute*, which, as we have seen, is the true OE form of the first element?

NOTE. WINCHESTER STREET is so named in 1515 (AD i). In the same document we find also *le Baklane*, *Churchwey*, the High Cross, Market Cross, *le Shamelles*, i.e. 'butchers' stalls.'

[1] Unluckily we cannot be sure with which of these places it should be identified. In the will of Aeþelstan the Aeþeling it stands between Bygrave (Herts) and a hitherto unidentified *Colungahrycg*. In PN Bk (*loc. cit.*) on the strength of proximity to Bygrave, the Buckinghamshire identification was chosen, but if *Colungahrycg* is Coldridge *supra* 344, then *Lutegaresheale* is almost certainly Ludgershall (W), for Coldridge Wood is on the northern boundary of Ludgershall parish.

BRICKKILN ROW (6″). Cf. *Brickkiln Ground* c. 1840 *TA.*
BUSHYDOWN COPSE, CHAPEL COPSE and NEWDROVE PLANTATION
(all 6″) are *Bushy Down Coppice, Chapel Coppice, the New Drove*
ib. *v. infra* 429. SHOULDER OF MUTTON COPSE (6″). Cf.
Shoulder of Mutton ib. and *infra* 455. SLIMBERSLADE (6″) is so
named ib. SOUTH PARK is (*in*) *Suthparco* 1291 *MinAcct, South-
park* t. Ed 3 *For.* WINDMILLHILL DOWN. Cf. *Wind Mill Hill*
1773 A and D.

Milston

MILSTON

Mildestone 1086 DB *et passim* to 1428 FA, with variant
spelling -*ton*, (*Gogeon*) 1401 IpmR, *Mildistona* 1178 BM
Midleston 1203 Cur, 1242 Fees, 1296 Ipm, *Mideleston*
1262 ib., *Middestone* 1212 RBE, *Middleston* 1226 Pat
Milleston 1309 ib., 1346 *Ass*, *Mulleston* 1330 Ipm, *Mylston*
1468, *Melston alias Myldeston* 1541 *FF*, *Millson* t. Jas 1 ECP
Milston cum Brigmilston 1826 Hoare

Ekwall (DEPN) suggests that this is from OE *midlesta tun*,
'midmost tun.' This is possible from the point of view of form
(cf. *Mildestwic* (DB) for Middlewich (Ch) and various examples
of Middleton found in DB in the form *Milde*(*n*)*tone*), but it is
difficult to say in relation to what other settlements this is
'midmost.'

BRIGMERSTON

Brismartone 1086 DB, *Brihtmarestun* 12th AD ii, *Brigge-
mares-* t. Hy 2 (1270) Ch, *Brithmarston* 1178 BM, *Brict-
mareston* 1204 Cur, *Bryhtmerston* 1273 Ipm, *Brichtmeres-*
1279 *Ass*, *Brightmerston* 1279 Cl, 1282 *FF*, 1428 FA
Briggemareston t. Hy 2 (1270) Ch, *Brig*(*g*)*emarston* 1273 Ipm,
1294 Ch, *Bryghtmerston al. Brygmarston* 1541 *FF*, *Brigmilston* 1812 RCH
Brikmerston 1412 FA, *Bryckmeston* 1524 *SR*, *Breymaston*
1641 NQ vii

The place takes its name from *Brismar* who held the manor
TRE. *Brismar* is the Norman-French spelling of the OE
personal name *Beorhtmǣr, Brihtmǣr.*

SILK HILL is so named in 1773 (A and D).

Newton Tony

NEWTON TONY

> *Newentone* 1086 DB, *-ton* t. John Dugd ii, *Newynton* 1268
> *Ass*, *Nywen-* 1316 FA, *Newenton Tony* 1338, (*Touny*) 1363 Cl
> *Niwetona, -e* t. Hy 2 (1270) Ch *et freq*, with variant spelling
> *Newe-, Neuton juxta Cheldrington* 1281 *Ass*, (*by Ambresbury*)
> 1297 Pat, *Nywetone Tony* 1332 *SR*, *Newetontony* 1347 Ch

'New farm,' *v.* tun and Introd. xxi. Ralph de *Toenye* held the manor in 1254 (Ipm). The family came from Tosny (dept. Eure) (Tengvik 115)

CLEVE HILL (6″) is so named c. 1650 (WM xxxi) and was probably by the home of Richard de *Clive* (1327 *SR*). *v.* clif, 'slope.'

BEAUMONT'S PLANTATION (6″) is to be associated with the family of Roger *Beamont* (1616 ParReg).

FURZE CROFT, THE GROVE, RUBBINGHOUSE FURZE FURLONG (all 6″), TOWER HILL PLANTATION[1] and THE VERGE (6″) appear as *Furze Croft, the Grove Wood, Rubbing Horse Furze Furlong, Tower Hill Plantation, the Verge* c. 1840 *TA*. The Verge is by the parish boundary. PIT WALK (6″). Cf. *Pit Fd* ib. WILBURY Ho. Cf. *Wilbury Hill* 1773 A and D. There are traces of a camp to the west of the house (H. C. B.).

North Tidworth

NORTH TIDWORTH[2] [tedwəθ]

> (*æt*) *Tudanwyrðe* 10th (14th) ASWills
> *Todew(o)rde, Todowrde* 1086 DB, *Todeworthe* 1211 RBE,
> *Todeworth Husee* 1300 For, *Northtodeworth* 1313 FF
> *Tudeworda* t. Hy 2 (1270) Ch, *-wrdia* 1166 RBE, *-wurda* 1186
> P *et freq* to 1316 FA, with variant spelling *-worth, Thudewrda*
> 1178 BM, *Tudeswurda* 1190 P, *Northtudewrthe* 1280 Ipm
> *Tuddewurth* 1235 Cl, *Toddeworth* 1273 FF
> *North Tydworth* 1724 Recov

---

[1] Tower Hill is in Hampshire.
[2] South Tidworth is in Hampshire just over the county border. It has a similar run of early spellings.

'*Tuda*'s farmstead,' *v.* worþ. For the modern vowel, *v.* Introd. xx. Matthew *Huse* had a holding here in 1242 (Fees).

PERHAM DOWN is to be associated with the family of John de *Perham* (1281 *Ass*) and Robert *Perham* (1357 *GDR*). It is *Perham Down* c. 1840 *TA*.

CHALKPIT HILL and GASON HILL (6″) are *Chalk Pit Hill* and *Garson Hill* c. 1840 *TA*, *v. infra* 432. CLARENDON HILL and PICKPIT HILL are *Clarendon Hill* and *Pickpitt Hill* 1773 A and D. THE PENNINGS is *New*, *Old Penning* c. 1840 *TA*. Cf. *infra* 453.

XXXII. UNDERDITCH HUNDRED

Windredic 1086 DB, *Wynderdich* 1255 RH
Wundredic 1191 P, *Wunderdiche* 1255 RH
Wonderdych 1249 *Ass*, 1402 FA, *-dich* 1274 Ipm, 1275 RH, 1289, *-dir-* 1289 *Ass*, *Wondredych* 1346 FF

The ditch from which the Hundred takes its name is said by Hoare (133) to run across a valley to the south of Little Durnford and to ascend the down between that place and Stratford (-sub-Castle) and to adjoin the boundary between the Hundreds of Amesbury and Underditch. In BCS 1083 we have a grant of land at a place called *Afene* and in the bounds of that land we have mention of a *windryðedic*. This must be Avon Fm in Durnford (*supra* 363) and *windryðedic* must be an early form for Underditch. There can be little doubt that the dic took its name from its one-time owner, a woman bearing the name *Wynðrȳð*. The name is not actually found, but both elements are common in OE names and the corresponding OGer *Vundrud* is on record (Förstemann PN 1664).

Stratford-sub-Castle

STRATFORD-SUB-CASTLE

Stratford(*e*) 1091 StOsmund, 1120 SarumCh *et passim*, (*subtus castrum Veteris Sarum*) 1397 IpmR, (*under Castell*) 1541 FF, (*neare Sarum*) 1646 Sess, (*under the Castle*) 1651 FF

'Ford where the (Roman) road crosses,' *v.* stræt. The road is the ancient Port Way. *Under the Castle* with reference to Old Sarum.

OLD SARUM. The forms quoted under Salisbury *supra* 18, before c. 1200, normally refer to this site. Already however in 1187 the two sites of Salisbury were sufficiently recognised for mention to be made in the Pipe Roll of that year of *Vetus Saresbir'*. Later references are (*in*) *Veteri Sar'* 1227 SarumCh, *Burgus Vet' Sar'* 1275 RH, *Burgus Veteris Sarisburie* 1316 FA, *Old Saresbury* 1429 Pat, *Olde Salysbery, the olde castell of Sar'* 1524 *SR, the Olde Castell of Sarum* 1540 NQ vii, *Olde Sarum* 1581 AD v, *Old Salisbury* 1687 *Recov.* The present name is an artificial one, *v.* Salisbury *supra* 18. The north ditch is referred to as *ealdan burhdic* in 972 (BCS 1286) in the bounds of part of Stratford-sub-Castle.

DEAN'S FM (6″) is to be associated with the family of John *Deane* (1604 NQ vii). It is probably *Stratford Deane* (1571 *SR*).

NORTH HILL DOWN. Cf. *North Hill Farm* 1773 A and D.

Wilsford

WILSFORD

> *Wiflesford(e)* 1086 DB, *Wyveleford* t. Hy 2 (1270) Ch, *Wivelesford* c. 1200 HMC Var i, *Wylesford* 1279, *Wyfleford* 1281 *Ass, Willesford* 1425 *FF*
> *Vivelesford* 1231 Ch

'*Wifel*'s ford.' Identical in origin with Wilsford *supra* 326.

LAKE is *Lak(e)* 1289 *Ass,* 1316 FA, 1325 Pat, 1332 *SR,* 1409 *FF.* This is OE lacu, 'streamlet.' There is no stream here except the Avon, but the name may have referred to one of the little branches of the main stream just to the south.

NORMANTON is *Normanton* 1332 *SR et passim, Normanton alias Normington* 1635 *Recov.* The forms are too late to do much with. It may be that this is a late *tun*-formation from some 12th- or 13th-century owner *Norman* or *Northman.* The name cannot be of the same origin as the Danelaw Normantons which are Norse settlements as distinct from Danish, cf. Mawer, *PN and History* 20–1.

HAM PLANTATION (6"). Cf. *Ham feilde* 1649 *SarumD and C.*
v. hamm. ROX HILL is *Rockeshulle* 1227 FF, *Rocks Hill* 1773
A and D. THE SLING (6"). Cf. *Upper, Lower Sling* c. 1840 *TA.*
v. infra 454. It is a long narrow strip of woodland. STARVEALL
PLANTATION (6"). Cf. *infra* 455. WESTFIELD FM (6"). Cf. *West
feild* 1649 *SarumD and C.*

Woodford

WOODFORD

> (*to þæm ealdan*) *wuduforda* 972 (13th) BCS 1286
> *Wodeford* 1120 SarumCh *et passim* to 1332 *SR*, with variant
>   spelling *Wude-*, (*Maior*) c. 1250 *Rental, Netherwodeford*
>   1279 *FF*, (*Magna, Parva*) 1289 *Ass*, (*Minor*) 1332 *SR*,
>   *Litelwodeford* 1422 *FF*, *Upwodford* 1524, *Grete, Lytle Wood-
>   ford* 1525 *SR*

Self-explanatory. At the present day we have Woodford
proper and Upper and Lower Woodford. *v.* neoðera.

HEALE HO

> *Helis* t. Hy 2 (1270) Ch, *Heele* 1279, 1281 *Ass*, 1582 *FF*
> *Hale* 1236 FF, 1268 *Ass*, 1315 *AD*, 1324 *FF*
> *Hyle* 1289 *Ass*, 1305, 1313 *AD*, 1316 *FF*, 1332 *SR*, 1444
>   IpmR, (*by Wodeford*) 1304, 1363, *Hile* 1305, *Hyell* 1531 *AD*
> *Heley* 1547 Pat
> *Heyle* 1560 BM, 1585 *FF*, *Heale al. Heyle* 1653 *Recov*
> *Hayle, Heale, Heele* t. Eliz WM xxi

There can be no doubt that this is the same name as the
common Hale, with variant form Hele, discussed in PN D 46,
s.n. Hele. Cf. *la Hele* (14th AD v) in Lacock and *le Hele* (1243
SarumCh) in Alderbury. It is from the dat. sg. of healh, 'nook,
corner,' which is apt as a description of land in the well-marked
bend of the Avon here. The forms *Hyle*, etc. show an early
raising of *e* to *i* (*y*).

HOOKLANDS (6") is *Hookland* c. 1840 *TA* and was probably the
home of John atte *Hook* (sic) 1348 *Cor. v.* hoc.

BORELAND HILL and SMITHEN DOWN are both so named in 1773
(A and D).

XXXIII. ALDERBURY HUNDRED

Alwareberia, Aluuartberia hundred 1086 ExonDB, with a similar run of early spellings to Alderbury.

Alderbury

Alderbury

(*to*) *Æþelware byrig*   972 (14th) BCS 1286, *Ædeluuaraburh* 976 (12th) Hist. Monast. de Abingdon, *Athelwarabyrig* 10th Swithin

Alwaresberie   1086 DB

Alwarberie ib., *-biri* 1109–20 StOsmund, *-beria* 1158 HMC Var i, *-byr'* 1249 *Ass*, *-buri* 1257 Ipm, *-bury* 1394 *Ass*, *Alewarbir'* 1198 Fees

Alwardberia 1139 SarumCh, *-beri* 1179 P, *-bury*, *-i* 1291 Tax *et freq* to 1535 VE

Alwardeberie 1190 StOsmund, *-bir'* 1212 Cur, *-byr'* 1255 RH, 1256 FF, *-buri*, *-y* 1257 Ipm, 1316, 1324 FA, 1356 Pat, *Alwardesburi* 1288 Ipm

Ailwardesberie 1195 P, *Aylwardebur'* 1250 Fees, *Aylwardesbyr'* 1279 *Ass*

Alwaldesbir' 1196 P

Aldwardbiria 1211 RBE, *-bury* 1356 *FF*, *Aldwarbur'* 1249 *Ass*, *-bury* 1316 Pat

Alrebury 1341 Ch, *Aldersbury* 1531, *Alderburye al. Alwardeburye* 1574 *FF*, *Alwarbury al. Alderbury* 1649 *Recov*

'**burh** belonging to a woman named *Æþelwaru*.' The development of forms with *d* may have been helped by the fact that *Alward* held five hides here in DB (Jones 56). ALWARD HOUSE (6″) is presumably an antiquarian reminder of this.

Ivy Church

Monasterium Hederosum 1109–20 StOsmund, *Capella Ederosa* 1155 RBE, *Monasterio Ederoso* 1224 SarumCh, 1231 Cl, 1249 *Ass*, *monastery of Hederose* 1250 WIpm, *domus ederose* 1404 *Ass*

Ivychirche, Ivi- 1327, *-churche* 1370 Pat, 1465 Cl, *-cherche* 1394 *Ass*, *Ivechurch(e)* 1341 Ch, Pat, *Yvechurche* 1461 *Ct*, *Iveschurch* t. Hy 8 *Rental*

Priorat' de Ederos al. Iveschurch 1536 *MinAcct*, *Ederos al.
Ivechurche* 1541 LP

'Ivy-covered church.' Cf. Ivychurch (PN K 479).

TREASURER'S DEAN (6″). Cf. *Treasurers Copps* 1650 *ParlSurv*.
These lands, belonging to the Dean and Chapter of Salisbury,
were appropriated to the support of the Treasurer of that church
(Hoare 4). Cf. *Tresereresgrove* (13th *For*) in Grovely.

WHADDON is *Watedene* 1086 DB, 1242 Fees, *Hwatedena* 1109–
20 StOsmund, *Watden'* 1242 Fees, 1270 *For*, *Waddene* 1273
Ipm, *Whaddene* 1274 Cl, *Whatden* 1279 *Ass*, *Whadden' juxta
Grimstede* 1329 HMC Var i, *Whaddon* 1332 *SR*. 'Valley where
wheat was grown,' *v.* hwæte, denu.

SHOOTEND is *Alderbury Shoot* 1650 *ParlSurv*, *Shoot End* 1773
A and D, and was no doubt the home of John *atte Shete* (1348
Cor). *v.* sceat, 'corner.' It is in a projecting corner of the
parish.

CASTLE HILL (6″) is so named in 1790 (*Longford*). COMMON
PLANTATION. Cf. *Alderbury Common* 1650 *ParlSurv*. THE
LYNCHETS (6″). *v. infra* 453. NORTHFIELD (6″) is *North Field*
1790 *Longford*. NYTHEFIELD WOOD (6″). Cf. *Nythe Field, Nythe
Mead* c. 1840 *TA*. *v.* Nythe *supra* 284. OAKRIDGE COPSE (6″) is
Oakridge Coppice 1790 *Longford*. RUDGHAMS COPPICE and
LITTLE RIDGHAMS COPPICE (both 6″). Cf. *Rudgehams* ib.
SPELTS COPSE (6″) is *Spelts* 1650 *ParlSurv*. WINDWHISTLE FM
is so named in 1812 (*Longford*). A common nickname for an
exposed or windy site.

Clarendon

CLARENDON PARK

Clarendun 1072 (12th) Round, *Feudal England*, *Clarendona*
1130 P, *-donam* t. Hy 2 (1434) Pat, *-dun'* 1204, *-don* 1207
Cur *et passim*

Clarindon(e) 1115 StOsmund, 1275 RH, 1279 *Ass*, *-yn-* 1327
Misc

Claryngdon 1315 Cl, 1433 Pat, 1451 IpmR, *Clarringdon*
t. Eliz *For*

For further spellings *v.* Clarendon Forest *supra* 12. Ekwall (DEPN) is probably right in interpreting this as 'clover-grown hill,' from OE *cæfren-dūn.* Cf. Clardon *supra* 39. Claverdon (PN Wa 206) which appears as *Claredon* in 1316 (FA), while the *v* is regularly lost in such names as Clarborough (Nt) and Clarewood (Nb), but not as early as in this name.

CHESEL (1820 G) is *Chisele* 1319, *Cheselegh* 1343 *MinAcct, Chissell Hill* 1650 *ParlSurv.* This would seem to be a compound of OE cis, 'gravel,' and leah, or the first element may be ceosol with similar meaning. It is an example of one of those names in which final *le(gh)* has been reduced to syllabic *l.* Cf. Keevil *supra* 142.

DOGKENNEL FM. Cf. *house called the Dogge Kennell* 1650 *ParlSurv, Dog Kennel* 1773 A and D. This farm- or house-name has been found in other English counties, but it is seldom that forms earlier than the 18th or 19th century are available. It was probably originally a nickname given to some very small or insignificant dwelling or hovel.

ASHLEY HILL. Cf. *Asshelee* t. Ed 2, *Asshelehull* 1362 *For.* 'Ash clearing or wood,' *v.* leah. BEECHY DEAN COPSE is *Beechey Deane Copice* 1650 *ParlSurv.* BRICKKILN FM and COPPICE (6″). Cf. *Brickilne Cockroad* and *Copice* ib. Cf. *infra* 427. CANON COPSE (6″) is *Cannon Copice* ib. Cf. *Canonesweye* 1322 WIpm. CARVEREL COPSE is *Caverell Copice* 1650 *ParlSurv* and is possibly the *Culverhill copis* of 1488 *For,* i.e. 'dove-hill,' *v.* culfre. CATT'S GROVE (6″) is *Cattesgrove* 1319 *MinAcct,* 1331 *For.* '(Wild) cat grove.' CRENDLE BOTTOM COPPICE (6″) is probably *Margaret of Crandon Copice* 1650 *ParlSurv* and is possibly *Grounden copice* 1477 Hoare. FAIROAK COPSE (6″) is *Feyrecokcopice* (sic) 1477 Hoare, *copes called Feyre oke* 1568 *For.* FUSSELL'S LODGE is *Fussells Lodge* 1650 *ParlSurv.* GILBERT'S COPSE (6″) is *Gylberdis copice* 1477 Hoare. GRIMSDITCH COPSE (6″) is *Grimmsditch Copice* 1650 *ParlSurv.* Cf. *supra* 15. HENDON COPSE (6″) is *Hendon Copice* ib. HOLE FM is *The Hole Farm* c. 1840 *TA.* HOME COPSE (6″) is *Home Copice* 1650 *ParlSurv.* HUNT'S COPSE (6″). Cf. *Hunts Lodge, Hunts Division* ib. KING MANOR HILL. Cf. *Kings Maner* 1610 S. Clarendon Forest was always a royal possession. LONG COPSE is *Long Copice* 1650 *ParlSurv.*

NETLEY COPSE (6″) is *Netley Copice* ib. PETER'S FINGER is so named in 1773 (A and D). PICKET SAINFOIN (6″) from the grass of that name. For the first element *v. infra* 443. QUEEN MANOR is *Quens* (sic) *Lodge* 1610 S, *lodge called the Queenes Manour* 1650 ParlSurv. RANGER'S LODGE is *Rangers lodge* ib. THE SLIP (6″), a long narrow strip of woodland, cf. *infra* 455. WARNER'S COPSE (6″) is *Warnerscopice* 1477 Hoare, *Warner Copice* 1650 ParlSurv, i.e. 'the warner's or warrener's copse.'

West Dean

WEST DEAN

 (æt) *Deone* c. 880 (c. 1000) BCS 553, 1275 RH, 1279 *Ass*, 1282 Ipm, 1324 FA, 1328 *FF*, 1332 *SR*, *Deon* 1341 NI, *Westdeone* 1345, 1351 Ipm

 Duene 1086 DB, 1315 Ipm, *West Duene* 1319 Inq aqd, *Westduene* 1324 Pat

 Dune 1242 Fees, 1263 Ipm, 1291 Tax, 1316 FA, *Westdune* 1270 Ipm

 Dene 1275 RH, 1282 Ipm, *Westden* 1275 Cl, -*dene* 1279 *Ass*, -*deene* 1310 Ipm, *Westedene* 1401 IpmR, *Deene* 1467 Pat, *Dean* 1547 *SR*

 Doene 1289 *Ass*, 1428 FA, *Westdoene* 1297 Pat, 1327 *Ass*

This is a difficult name. Ekwall (*Studies*[1] 65) would explain it as deriving from an unrecorded *deonu*, a variant of denu, 'valley,' with *u*-mutation. *West* to distinguish from the adjacent East Dean (Ha).

BENTLEY WOOD

 Bentelleswod' t. Hy 2 (1270) Ch, *Bentleswuda* 1178 BM, *Bentleswode* 1270 *For*

 Bentelwoda t. Hy 2 (1270) Ch, -*wode* 1255 RH, t. Hy 3 *Stowe* 798, 1279, 1289 *Ass*, t. Ed 2 *For*, *Bentelewde* t. John Dugd ii, *Bentlewude* 1227 FF, -*wod(e)* 1227 StNicholas, 1257, 1279 *For*

 Bentewud' 1224 ClR, *Benetleg* 1227 Ch

This name goes back to an OE beonet and leah, 'clearing where bent grass grew,' to which wudu was early added. Hence 'wood by a place called *Bentley*,' with occasional genitival form in the first element.

HIGHWOOD COPSE (6″) is *Haywode* 1279, 1281, 1289 *Ass, Hey-*
t. Ed 2 *For*, 1324 Cl. The modern form seems to be corrupt.
The first element would seem to be OE (ge)hæg, 'enclosure,'
etc. Hence 'enclosed or preserved wood,' cf. Heywood *supra*
149.

BARNRIDGE COPSE is *Bardenrigge* 1365 *DuLa*. BEECHWOOD
COPSE and CHURCHWAY COPSE (both 6″) are *Beechwood Coppice,
Churchway Coppice* c. 1840 *TA*. COALPITS COPSE is *Coalpits
Coppice* 1840 WM xxiii. DEAN COPSE is *Dean Wood* ib. FINE
WOOD (6″) is so named ib. HAWKS GROVE is *Hawksgrove Coppice*
c. 1840 *TA*. HOOPING OAK COPSE (6″) is *Hooping Oak Coppice*
1840 WM xxiii. HOWE FM is *la Howe* 1362 *For, la Hoo* 1398
IpmR. 'Hill spur,' *v.* hoh. MAPLEWAY DEAN (6″) is so named
in 1840 (WM xxiii). PEGSBROOK COPSE (6″). Cf. *Peykesbrouk*
1348 WIpm. PICKED COPSE is *Picked Coppice* c. 1840 *TA*, so
named from its shape *v. infra* 443. PRIOR'S COPSE (6″) is
Preyereswode t. Ed 2 *For*. REDMAN'S GORE (6″) is *Redman Gore
Coppice* 1840 WM xxiii. REDRIDGE COPSE (6″). Cf. *la Ryderugge*
t. Ed 2 *For*. SMOKEWAY COPSE (6″) is *Smokeway Coppice* c. 1840
TA. WITMARSH BOTTOM (1820 G) is (*le*) *Whytemersshe* 1331 *For*,
1348 *Cor*.

Farley and Pitton

FARLEY

> *Farlege* 1086 DB, *Ferleg'* 1198 Fees, 1231 Cl, *Farle(y)gh
> juxta Pitton* 1285 FF, (*juxta Claryndon*) 1351 *Ass*
> *Fernelega* 1109–20 StOsmund, *Fernlee* 1185 Templars, -*leye*
> t. Ed 3, *Farnlee* 1257, -*leg'* 1263 *For*

'Fern or bracken clearing or wood,' *v.* fearn, leah.

PITTON

> *Putenton'* 1165 P, *Putteton* 1267 WIpm
> *Putton(e)* 1198 Fees, 1211 RBE *et passim* to 1402 FA, (*juxta
> Farlegh*) 1310 *Ass*
> *Putton alias Pitton* 1726 Recov

'*Putta*'s farm' or 'hawk's farm,' *v.* tun and Puthall *supra*
335–6. For the modern vowel, *v.* Introd. xx.

BOURNE HILL (6″) was near the home of Ralph *atte Bourne* (1327
SR). It is *Bourne Hills* c. 1840 *TA*. *v.* burna.

BIGG'S COPSE, LITTLE MILES COPPICE, NEWMAN'S FM, TAYLOR'S FM and WHITE'S COMMON (all 6″) are to be associated with the families of Richard *Biggs* (1641 NQ vii), John *Miles* (c. 1840 *TA*), Leonard *Newman* (1596 NQ vii), Thomas *Taylor* (1734 ParReg) and Robert *White* (1641 NQ vii).

ADAMS'S MERE (6″). Cf. *Adamesgore* 1227 SarumCh. *v.* **gara**.
BLACKMOOR COPSE (6″). Cf. *Blackmore* 1649 *SarumD and C.*
COLD HARBOUR (6″) is *Coldharbour* c. 1840 *TA*. See *infra* 451.
PICCADILLY CLUMP (6″) is in a far corner of the parish, cf. *infra* 455.

East and West Grimstead

EAST and WEST GRIMSTEAD[1]

> *Gremestede* 1086 DB, 1201 Cur, 1242 Fees, 1272, 1281 *Ass*, -*steda* 1164 P, *Gremsted(e)* 1263 *For*, 1270 Ipm, 1281 *Ass*, 1307, 1327 *Extent*
> *Gramestede* 1086 DB
> *Grenestede,* -*a* 1160 RBE (p), 1167, 1190, *Grenstede* 1198 P
> *Grimesteda,* -*e* 1186 ib., 1200 Cur, 1208 Abbr, 1211 RBE (p), 1235 Fees, 1236 FF, *Gryme-* t. Ed 1 *For*, *Grimstede* 1194 RBE (p), 1199 P, 1213 ClR, *Westgrimstede* 1249 *Ass, Est, West Grimsted'* 1263 *For*
> *Grinestede* 1211 RBE (p), *Gryn-* 1281 *Ass, Istgrinstede* 1324 Ipm, *Grynstide* t. Eliz WM xxi
> *Grimmestede* 1251 WIpm, *Grimmisted* 1257 Cl

Ekwall (DEPN) is probably right in taking this name to be a reduction of OE *grēnehāmstede,* 'green homestead.' For a similar reduction cf. the history of Palmstead (KPN 41), *Perhamstede* BCS 176, *Permestede* 1226 *Ass*.

NIGHTWOOD COPSE is *Knyghtwode* t. Ed 3, t. Eliz *For*, *Knight Wood* c. 1840 *TA*. 'Wood of the "knights" or serving men,' *v.* **cniht** and cf. Knightwood in North Baddesley (Ha), *Knyghtwode* t. Ed 2 *For*.

BUTTER FURLONG FM, FURZY CLOSE COPSE, GALLOW HAYES, HAZEL HILL WOOD and THICKET COPSE (all 6″) appear as *Butter*

---

[1] Formerly two parishes, now united (Kelly).

Furlong (field), *Furzy Close, Gallows Hayes Coppice, Hazel Hill Coppice* and *Thicket Coppice* c. 1840 *TA*. REDLYNCH PLANTATION (6″) is *Redlynch* 1812 *Longford*. Cf. Redlynch *infra* 395. WHITEHOUSE FM is *White House Farm* 1820 G.

Idmiston

IDMISTON

> (*at*) *Idemestone* 947, 948 (14th) BCS 829, 867, 970 (15th) ib. 1259, *-tona* 1189 GlastInq, *-ton(e)* 1230 FF *et freq* to 1316 FA, with variant spellings *Yd-* and *-mis-, Idemistonam* 1189 GlastInq, *Ydomeston* 1268 *Ass*, *Ydmeston* 1428 FA
> *Idemereston* 1268 FF, *Idmerston* 1675 Ogilby
> *Edemeston* 1305 *Ass*, *Edmeston* 1312 WIpm

The would-be OE forms for this name are found in late ME transcripts and the form *Idemereston* may well be more correct than any of the others. If so, the first element is an OE personal name **Idmær*. *Idhild* is on record. Hence '*Idmær*'s farm,' *v*. tun.

BIRDLIME FM. Cf. *chapel of Burdlyme al. Burdlymes in Idmyston* 1554 Pat, *Porton al. Byrdlyme* 1560 *FF, Burdlins* c. 1840 *TA*. It marks the site of the chapel of Porton, founded by Lucia *Burgelon* c. 1323 (WM xxxv, 538). Later spellings are *Burglem, Birdlyme* (ib.), the later and modern forms of the name being corruptions due to popular etymology.

GOMELDON [gʌməldən]

> *Gomeledona* 1189 GlastInq, *-don(e)* 1275 RH, 1281, 1302 *Ass*, 1311 Ipm, 1312, *Gomeldon* 1279 *Ass*, 1316 Trop, *Gomelesdon* 1289 *Ass*
> *Gumelesdon* 1230 FF, *Gumeledun'* 1263 *For, Gumeldon* 1279 *Ass*
> *Gombledon, Gombleton* t. Eliz WM xxi, *Gombeldon* 1617 *FF, Gumbleton* 1658 BM

The forms now available render untenable Ekwall's suggestion (DEPN) of an OE personal name *Gamela* as the source of the first element. The form must be *Gumela*, presumably a derivative of the personal name *Guma* found in Gumber (PN Sx 97) and Gomshall (PN Sr 248). Hence '*Gumela*'s hill,' *v*. dun.

PORTON

   Portone 1086 DB, *-tun'* 1199 P, *-ton(e)*, *-a* 1232 FF, 1236,
     1242 Fees

   Poertone 1086 DB, *-ton(a)* 12th AD iv, 1225 ClR

   Pourton(e) 1160, 1181 P, 1160 RBE, 1198 Fees, 1207 Cur,
     1272 FF, 1316 FA, (*juxta Gomeledon*) 1312 *Ass*

   Powertone 1211 RBE (p)

   Pouereton 1268, *Pouerton* 1281 *Ass*, 1409 Cl, *Poure-* 1397
     IpmR

   Poreton 1545 LP

This name would seem to be identical in origin with Poorton
(PN Do 242) with the same first element occurring also in
Powerstock (ib. 240), one mile from Poorton. In all these names
alike we have, from DB onwards, forms *Powr-*, *Pover-*, *Pour-*,
Povre-, *Por-*, *Poer-*. Ekwall (*Studies*[2] 21 and DEPN) notes that
one or other of the Dorset places is called *Power* in a 12th-century
MS of a grant by Egbert and rightly suggests that we have the
same first element in Porton also. He suggests that this may be
an old river-name, referring in this case to the Bourne.

CHURCH FM (6″) and DOWN BARN were probably the homes of
John de *Ecclesia* (1235–61 GlastRl) and Ralph *atte Dounende*
(1345 *Ass*).

BLAKE'S FIRS and BONAKER'S FM (both 6″) are to be associated
with the families of Johan *Blake* (1583 ParReg) and William
Bonaker (c. 1840 *TA*).

GOMELDON DOWN is (*super*) *Gomelhamdoun* 1321 *Ass*. This
suggests that *Gumela* gave his name to a ham as well as to a dun.
Cf. Gomeldon *supra* 380. HALE FM (6″). Cf. *Halfurlong* 1518
Hoare. IDMISTON DOWN. Cf. *montem de Edemeston* 1305 *Ass*.

Laverstock

LAVERSTOCK [*olim* laʳrstok]

   Lavvrecestoches, *Lavertestoche* 1086 DB, *Laverkstok'* 1198
     Fees, *Laverekestoke* 1211 RBE, *Laverkestok* 1221 Pat, 1236,
     1242 Fees, 1249 *Ass*, 1250 Ipm

Laverstok 1255 RH, 1316 FA
Larkestok 1310 *FF*, (*juxta Sar'*) 1311 Orig, *Laverstocke al.*
    Larstocke 1634 WIpm, *Laystock* 1675 Ogilby

'**stoc** frequented by larks' (OE *læwerce*). Cf. Laverstock (Ha),
DB *Lavrochestoche*, Larkstoke in Admington (Gl), *Lauerkestoke*
1227 *FF* and a lost place of that name in Langley (PN Bk 241 n.).
See Addenda *supra* xli.

FORD is *Winterburneford(a)* 1189 GlastInq, 1270 *For*, *Wynter-*
bournefo(u)rde 1325 *FF*, 1372 Ipm, *Wynterbournes Forde* t. Hy 7
Hoare, *Ford* 1605, *Foord* 1711 *Recov*. The ford was over the
river Bourne, formerly *Winterbourne*, v. *supra* 2.

MILFORD[1] is *Meleford* 1086 DB, 1196 Cur, 1249 FF, t. Ed 3 *For*,
Muleford 1236 Fees, 1249 *Ass*, (*Pychard*) 1268 *Ass*, *Mileford*
1280 Orig, *Mulleford* 1303 *Ass*, *Meleford juxta Sar'* 1321 ib.,
Mulleford Richard 1354 Ipm, *Melford Richard* 1368 Pat, *Milford*
Richarde 1533–8 ECP, *Mivord* 1675 Ogilby. 'Ford by the
mill.' *Richard* fil. Petri held the manor in 1198 (Fees).

MUMWORTH (lost)[2]

    Mummeworth 1250 Ipm, 1279 *Ass*, *Mommeworth* t. Hy 3
        Stowe 798, 1356, (*pontem de*) t. Ed 3 *For*, *Mommeworth*
        1493 Ipm
    Munworth 1533–8 ECP, *Mom-* 1535 VE, *Mommordes myll*
        t. Eliz *DuLa*, *Monworth* 1672 *Rental*, *Mumworth* 1829
        Recov

Most names in *worth* are compounded with a personal name
and we are probably right here in assuming a lost OE name
Mumma, perhaps a pet form of an OE name in *Mund-* or
-mund. Hence' *Mumma*'s enclosure,' v. worþ. Professor Bruce
Dickins notes ModIcelandic *Mummi* for *Guðmundur*.

BURROUGH'S HILL and HATCHES BRIDGE (6") are to be associated
with the families of John *Burrough* (1729 ParReg) and William
de *Hache* (1279 *Ass*). In the latter the *s* may be pseudo-manorial,
v. hæcc, 'gate,' etc.

    [1] Originally in Laverstock. Most of the district is now included within
the bounds of the City of Salisbury.
    [2] It was by the present Dairy House Bridge, on the Southampton Road
(Hoare 219).

BISHOPSDOWN FM. Cf. *Busshopsdown* 1592 DKR xxxviii. COCKEY DOWN (6″) is so named c. 1840 *TA*. ENDE BURGH (6″) is *Andborrowe* 1649 *SarumD and C*. LAVERSTOCK DOWN is *Laverstock Downe* 1650 *ParlSurv*. ST THOMAS'S BRIDGE is *Thomas Beketes Bridge* c. 1540 L, *St Thomas Bridge feilde* 1650 *ParlSurv*.

Melchet Park[1]

MELCHET COURT and PARK. Cf. *Melchet park* 1348 Cl, *Melchard Parke* 1654 ParReg (Whiteparish), *Milchett* 1812 RCH. This was formerly a small extra-parochial district, preserving the name of the old Melchet Forest, *v. supra* 14.

Plaitford

PLAITFORD[1] [plætfəd]

> *Pleiteford* 1086 DB, 1391 AD iii, *Pleitesford* n.d. ib. iv, *Pleyteford* 1263 *For et freq* to 1348 Cl, *Pleyt-* 1289 *Ass*
> *Playteford* 1275 RH, 1289 *Ass et freq* to 1495 Ipm, *Playtfourth* 1484 Pat
> *Pleteford* 1333 Ipm, 1338 *GDR*, *Pledeford* 1338 Pat
> *Platford* 1610 Speed, 1671 *For*, 1695 Gough

This is a difficult name. Ekwall (DEPN) suggests that the first element is OE **pleget*, 'playing,' hence 'ford by which games were held.'

Winterbourne Dauntsey, Earls and Gunner

WINTERBOURNE DAUNTSEY, EARLS and GUNNER

> *Wintreburne* 1086 DB, *Winterburn'* 1198 Fees, 1227 FF
> *Winterburn(e) Comitis Sar'* 1198 P, *(le Cunte)* 1250 WIpm, *Wynterborn' Comitis* 1298 Sarum, *Heorleswynterbourne* 1324 FA, *Eurles-* 1324, *Erles-* 1401 Pat, *Winterbourne Errells* 1553 Phillipps
> *Winterburn Gonor* 1267 Pat, *Wynterburne Gunnore* 1268, *Gonnore Wintresburne* 1268 Ass, *Winterburn' Gonnore* 1275 RH, *Winterborne Gonner* 1585 WM xxi

---

[1] Transferred to Hampshire in 1895.

Wynterburne Dauntesie 1268 *Ass, Winterburn' Daunteseye*
1275 RH, 1316 FA, *Winterborne Dansey* 1641 NQ vii
Wynterburne Chyreburgh 1277 *FF, Wynterborne Cherborgh*
1332 *SR, Winterburne Cherberwe* 1332 Cl

Winterbourne was the old name for the river Bourne (*supra* 2). *Dauntsey* from the family of Roger *Danteseye* (1242 Fees). *Earls* from the *Earls* of Salisbury. *Gunner* from *Gunnora* de la Mare, the lady who held the manor in 1249 (Ipm). Winterbourne *Cherburgh* was an early alternative name for Winterbourne Gunner, from the family of John de *Cherenburgh* (1227 FF), de *Cherburgh* (1242 Fees).

Winterbourne Dauntsey

CLARKE'S BARN (6″) is to be associated with the family of Edward *Clarke* (1547 *SR*).

FIGSBURY RING is *Frippesbury* 1695 M, *Fripsbury* 1721 WM xi, *Clorus's Camp or Figbury Ring* 1773 A and D, *v.* burh. There is a 'camp' here. WINTERBOURNE DOWN is *Winterbourne Downe* 1650 *ParlSurv.*

Winterbourne Earls

HURDCOTT [həˑrkət] is *Herdicote* 1086 DB, *Herde-* 1268 *Ass,* 1371 Pat, *Herdcote* 1316 FA, *Hurdecote juxta Eurleswynterbourne* 1325 *FF, Hurdecote* 1332 *SR,* 1402 FA, *Hurkett* 1606 Sess. 'cot(e) of the herdsmen.' Cf. Hurdcott *supra* 212.

EARLSWOOD (6″) is *Erleswode* t. Ed 2 *For.* SOUTH CROFT (6″) is so named c. 1840 (*TA*).

Winterbourne Gunner

WATERSIDE HO (6″) was perhaps the home of Richard *atte Watere* (1364 *DuLa*).

HORSE BARROW. Cf. *Horse Barrow Field* c. 1840 *TA*. THORNY DOWN is *la Thornydoune* t. Ed 2 *For, Thorn Down* 1773 A and D.

Winterslow

WINTERSLOW

> *Wintreslev, -lei* 1086 DB, *Wintereslawe* t. Hy 2 (1270) Ch, 1215 ClR, 1230, 1234, *-lewe* 1235 Cl, *Wyntreslawa* 1178 BM, *-lawe* 1198 Fees, *-lau* 1201 BM, *-lowe* 1301 FF, 1302 Ipm, *-lewe* 1327 Banco, *Winterslewam* 1189 GlastInq, *-lewe* 1202 FF, *-lawe* 1236 FF, 1242 Fees, *Wyntereslewe* 1255 RH, 1268 *Ass*, 1279 Cl, *-lawe* 1302 Ipm, *-leuwe* 1305 *Ass*, *-lowe* 1322 Ch

> *Winterlawa* 1166 P, *-lawe* 1212–17 RBE

> *West Winterslewe* 1263 For, *Westwynterlewe* 1334 Cl, *Wyntres-lewe Uppinton* 1351 *Ass*

'*Winter*'s mound or burial place,' v. hlæw. An exact parallel is *Wintres hlæw* 940 (c. 1225) BCS 761 in the bounds of Garford (Berks). At the present day we have East, West and Middle Winterslow. The last was formerly Middleton (*v. infra*). The manor of East Winterslow is now Roche Court *infra*. *Uppington* presumably refers to East Winterslow, the highest of the three. For the form *lew*, v. Introd. xx.

HOUND WOOD is *Hundewude* 1275 Ipm, *-wode* 1279, 1331, *Hundwode* t. Ed 2 *For*, 1337 Pat. 'Wood of the dogs or hounds' (OE *hunda wudu*).

MIDDLE WINTERSLOW was earlier *Wynterslewe Middelton* 1345 *Ass*, *Midelton* 1347 FF, *Meddelton* 1425 GDR, later *Midle-winterslewe* 1397 IpmR. 'Middle farm,' v. tun.

ROCHE COURT is *Estwinterslewe* 1257 *For*, *Estwintrelowe* 1279 Cl, *Wynterslowe Eston* 1361 BM, *Wyntreslowe alias Rithiscourt* (sic) 1485 Pat, *East Winterslowe alias Roche Courte* 1632 WIpm. The later name derives from the family of John de *Roches* who held the manor in 1397 (IpmR).

COOPER'S FM (6″) is to be associated with the family of Robard *Coper* (1580 WM xxxvi).

CHICKARD (6″) is *Chickwood* 1713 *Recov*. DUNSTABLE POND. Cf. *Dunstable Croft* c. 1840 *TA*. EASTON DOWN. v. Roche Court *supra*. HARE WARREN (6″) is so named c. 1840 (*TA*).

LIVERY FM is so named in 1773 (A and D). LOPCOMBE CORNER.
Cf. *Lobecombe* 1342 *GDR*, *Lobcombe Corner* 1772 Act, *Lapcombe
Corner or Coniger Hill* 1773 A and D. *v.* cumb and *infra* 427.
RAMSHILL COPSE (6″). Cf. *Rameshull* 1362 *For*, 1365 *DuLa*,
Ramsell Barn 1808 O.S. and Ramsbury *supra* 287. RICHWELL-
STED COPSE (6″) is *Rickwellsted* (sic) *Coppice* c. 1840 *TA*.
SHRIPPLE (6″) is *Shripple* 1714 ParReg, *Shraple* 1820 G.

XXXIV. FRUSTFIELD HUNDRED

Frystesfeld 968 (14th) Wilton Register, *Fristesfeld* 1086
    ExonDB, *Firstesfeld* 1207 Cur, *Fyrstfelde* 1544 LP
Ferstesfeld, -felt hundred 1086 ExonDB, 1316 FA
Fortesfeld Abbatisse 1166 P
Furstesfeldhdr 1167, 1168 P, 1249, 1289 *Ass*
Frestesfelde 1196 Cur, 1198 Abbr
Furstefeld 1255 RH, *Furstfeld* 1402 FA, *Frustfelde* 1544 LP

In 944 King Edmund granted to his *minister* Wulfgar three
hides at a place called *æt Fyrstesfelda*. In the Wilton Register
(11) there is a variant form of the boundaries of an estate of
the same name and extent which was granted by King Edgar
to Wilton Abbey in 968. The name of this estate is clearly to
be identified with the name of Frustfield Hundred, though the
Hundred itself must have included other lands beside those
mentioned in the grant, for the Hundred is assessed at 11 hides
in the ExonDB. The exact site of the estate is unknown. The
first element must be OE *fyr(e)st* used in the sense 'leader,
prince,' as in the cognate German *Fürst*. Hence 'prince's open
country,' *v.* feld.

Landford

LANDFORD

Langeford 1086 DB, 1198 Fees, 1257 Ipm, 1327, 1332 *SR*
Laneford 1242 Fees, 1255 RH *et passim* to 1439 WM xiii,
    Loneford 1412 FA
Landeford 1295 Pat, *Lante-* 1486–93 ECP, *Land-* 1594 *FF*
Lanford 1525 *SR*, 1567 Recov
Landford alias Langford 1676 ib.

It is difficult to say whether the first element is *lang*, 'long,' or *lanu*, 'lane.' The majority of early spellings favour the latter alternative and the stream here is so small that the passage across it could not have been a very long one. The *d* is a much later insertion.

EARLDOMS FM and THE EARLDOMS (6″). Cf. *Earledon* 1551 Pat, *Thirledome* 1553 Hoare, *boscus voc. lez Erledome* 1570 PembSurv, *le Erledoms* 1577 Recov, *Erledoune* 1625 WIpm. It is so called because granted to the earl of Pembroke in the first year of his earldom (Hoare 66).

BRIDGE FM (6″) was the home of William *atte Brugge* (1332 *SR*).

WITTERNS HILL FM (6″) is *Whitehornes Hill* 1637 WIpm, *Whitonsell* 1773 A and D, and is to be associated with the family of Richard *Whytehorne* (1348 *Cor*).

BAGFIELD COPSE is probably *copic' voc. Baggpoole* 1570 Pemb-Surv. BARNSELL COPSE (6″). Cf. *Barneshill* ib. BROOM PARK (6″) is so named c. 1840 (*TA*). DAFFY ROW (6″) is so named ib. FULFORD'S COPSE (6″). Cf. *Fulfords meade* 1686 *Longford*. GLAZIER'S COPSE is *copic' voc. Glasyers* 1570 PembSurv. GREAT FIELD COPSE (6″). Cf. *Great Field* c. 1840 *TA*. HOMAN'S COPSE (6″) is *Homeing coppice* c. 1570 *Wilton*. THE MOOR (6″) is *le More* 1563 *Longford*. *v*. mor. PEAKS COPSE is *copic' voc. Peeks* 1570 PembSurv, *Peakes* c. 1570 *Wilton*. PUGPITS COPSE (6″) is *Puck-pits* 1661 *Longford*. Cf. *Puckmead* ib. and *infra* 444. SHARP HEARN WOOD (6″) is *Sharp Hearn Coppice* c. 1840 *TA*. *v*. hyrne, 'corner.' There is a well-marked corner of land between two streams here. THE SLINGS (6″) is so named ib. A narrow strip of woodland. *v. infra* 455. STAPENS COPSE (6″) is *wood called Stappeton* c. 1570 *Wilton*. STOCKLANE FM (6″). Cf. *Stock close* c. 1840 *TA*. *v*. stocc, 'stump.' WHITEHOUSE FM (6″) is *White-howse* 1637 WIpm. WICKETSGREEN FM (6″). Cf. *Wickets Green* 1820 G. WOODFALLS FM (6″) is *Wolfall* 1570 PembSurv, *Wollfall copice* c. 1570 *Wilton*.

Whiteparish

WHITEPARISH

la *Whytechyrche* 1278, *Wytechirche* 1281 *Ass*, *Whitchirche* 1289 FF, *Whytechirche, Whytcherche* 1289 *Ass*

Whyteparosshe ib., *la Whiteparosse* 1301 *FF*, *la Whiteperesshe* 1305 *Ass*, *la Whyteparyshe* t. Ed 2 *For*, *la Whiteparisshe* 1324 Pat, *Whiteparys* 1359 Ipm, *Whiteparoch* 1414 Pat, *Whyte Perysshe* 1553 WM xii

Album Monasterium 1298 Sarum, *in Albo monasterio* 1428 FA *Whitparishe* t. Eliz WM xxi

The earlier name must have referred to the colour of the original church here. Cf. Whitchurch (PN D 247–8). The use of the same epithet for the later parish is strange.

NOTE. MILES LANE is to be associated with the family of Richard *Miles* (1673 ParReg).

ABBOTSTONE (6″)

Abbedeston 1249 *Ass*, 1256 FF, *Abboteston* 1279, *Abbodeston* 1289 *Ass*, 1316 FA, 1348 Cl, *Abbotestone juxta Estgryme-stede* 1394 *Ass*

Abbesseton 1322 *FF*, 1332 *SR*, *Abbassetone* 1339 Ipm

Abbeston 1405 *FF*, 1412 FA, *Abstone* 1529 *Rental*

Abbassetone was held in 1339 (Ipm) of the Abbess of Wilton and it is clear that this name, like Rabson *supra* 309, must stand for ME *abbedesse-ton*, 'abbess farm.'

ALDERSTONE FM

Aldereston' 1166 P, 1390 Pat, *Aldreston* 1289 *Ass*, 1316 FA

Aldredeston 1227 Pat, 1249 *Ass*, 1255 RH, 1315 Cl, 1344 *FF*, *Aldrydeston* 1334 *Ass*

Aderediston 1272 Pat

This is a late tun-name. It represents the holding of one hide in Frustfield (*Ferstesfeld* 1086 ExonDB) by *Aldred* (TRE and TRW). Aldred is the OE personal name *Ealdred*. For Frustfield, *v. supra* 386.

BLAXWELL FM (6″) is *Blakeswell(e)* 1242 P, 1263 *For*, *Blakareswell* 1306 Ipm, *Blakereswelle* t. Ed 2 *For*, 1348 *Cor*, 1359 Ipm, t. Ed 3, 1362 *For*, *Blackerswell* 1576 Hoare, *Blackswells* 1623 WIpm. The names *Blacre*, *Blacer*, *Blakere* are on record from the 11th century and one or other of them (if they are really different names) probably forms the first element in this place-name. The history of the personal name is uncertain, cf. Feilitzen 203 n. 1. '*Blacer*'s spring,' *v.* wielle.

BRICKWORTH Ho is *Brycore* 1255 FF, t. Ed 2 *For*, *Bricore* 1268 *Ass*, FF, 1315 *FF*, t. Ed 3 *For*, *Brikore* 1268, 1281 *Ass*, (*boscus de*) 1270 *For*, *Brecor* 1523, *-corr* 1561 *FF*, *Brickworth* 1738 *Recov*. The original second element was **ora**, 'slope, bank,' etc., with later corruption as in Galsworthy (PN D 88). The first element might be a Celtic word related to Welsh *brig*, 'top, summit' (from **brik-*). Cf. Brickhill (PN Bk 30). Brickworth is on a hill-slope and *Brik* may have been the British name for the well-marked hill just to the north-west of 'The Pepperbox.' More probably *Bryc*, *Bric* is from earlier *Birc*, *Byrc* and the first element should be associated with OE *beorc*, 'birch-tree.' Under Brigstock (PN Nth 158–9) evidence is given for such a meta-thesised form. If so, this name would be identical in form and possibly in site also with *Beorchore* 1007 (c. 1200) KCD 1303, a place described in the days of Ethelred 2 as a *novum oppidum* and hitherto unidentified.

COWESFIELD Ho

    Colesfeld 1086 DB
    Couenefeld 1166 P
    Cuuelesfeld 1166, 1197 ib., *Cuveles-* 1198, 1236 Fees, 1220
        FF, 1249 *Ass*, *Cuflesfeld* 1257 *For*, *Covelesfeld* 1268 *Ass*,
        1306 Sarum, *Couuelesfeld Loveras* 1337 Ch
    Culesfeld 1255 RH, *Coulesfeld*, *Est-* 1279 *Ass*, (*Loveras*),
        (*Sturmy*, *Spylman*) 1402 FA, *Cowesfeld* 1504–15 ECP

'*Cufel*'s open land,' *v*. **feld**. Cf. East Coulston *supra* 140. Geoffrey de *Luveraz* and Geoffrey *Esturmy* held manors in 1198 (Fees), Walter *Loverace* in 1268 (*Ass*), John *Luveraz* in 1279 (ib.). *Cuuelestone* 1086 DB (held TRW by Ricardus *Sturmid*), *Coleston* 1272 Pat (held by *Loveraz* and *Spileman*) must have been an alternative name for the place. *v*. **tun**.

IVORY COPSE (6″). Cf. *Ryvere* 1397 IpmR, *la Yevere in hundredo de Frustesfeld* 1412 FA, *Yver* 1430 *FF*, *Uverey* 1456 IpmR, *le Ryver* 1526 Ct, *Every Coppice* 1637 WIpm. 'At the bank or steep slope,' *v*. Rivar *supra* 355 and **yfer** *infra* 450.

MEAN WOOD is *Menewode* 1270, t. Ed 2, t. Ed 3, *Manewode* t. Ed 2 *For*. 'Common or boundary wood,' *v*. (ge)**mæne**. The wood lies near the county boundary.

WHELPLEY (6″) is *Welplega* 1166 P, *Walpleia* 1196 Cur, 1198 Abbr, *Welpele* 1200 Cur, *-leg'* 1225 Pat, *-leye* 1242 Fees, 1255 RH, *Whelpeleg'* 1275 *FF*, *-le* 1321 *Ass*, *-legh* 1322 *FF*, 1332 *SR*. Perhaps 'clearing or wood of the cubs or whelps' (OE *hwelp*). But the first element might be a personal name, a nickname from the animal name. Cf. Whelpington (Nb).

BARNCROFT[1], HANGHILL WOOD and PITGARDEN COPSE (all 6″) were probably the homes of Hugh *atte Berne* (1327 *SR*), William *atte Hangre* (1331 WIpm) and Roger *atte Putte* (1281 *Ass*). *v.* bern, hangra, 'slope,' and pytt.

ARNOLD'S COPSE, HASLETTS ROW, HAYTER'S WOOD (all 6″), MORRISHOLT FM[2], ROWDEN'S FM (6″), SANSOME'S FM, SUTTONS, TESTWOOD COPSE[3], THORNS COPSE (all 6″), TITCHBORNE FM, WHITE'S FM and YOUNG'S FM (both 6″) are to be associated with the families of Herbert *Ernald* (1289 *Ass*), Roger *Hasslet* (1678 ParReg), Richard *Hayter* (1692 ib.), John *Morys* (1524 *SR*) and William *Morrys* (1567 ParReg), Mary *Rowden* (1736 ib.), William *Sawnsham* (1547 *SR*) and Richard *Sanson* (1569 ParReg), William *Sutton* (1764 ib.), Richard de *Testewod* (1316 FA) and John de *Terstewode* (1341 NI) (which came from Testwood (Ha)), John *Thorne* (1614 ParReg), Thomas *Tychborne* (1589 ib.), John *White* (1561 ib.) and Thomas *Yowng* of Downton (1525 *SR*).

ASH HILL COMMON. Cf. *Ash Hill Field* c. 1840 *TA*. BROXMORE Ho is *Brockesmor* 1331 WIpm, *Broxmore* 1697 *Recov*. 'Marshy spot of the badger' or 'of a man named *Brocc*.' *v.* brocc, mor. CHADWELL FM (6″) is *Chadewelle* 1268 *Ass*, *Chaldewelle* 1341 *Cor*, *Chadwell* 1570 Hoare. 'Cold spring,' *v.* wielle. Cf. Chadwell (PN Ess 91). CHALKPIT FM (6″). The 'Chalk Pit' is mentioned c. 1840 (*TA*). CLAPGATE COPSE and CONEYGRE ROW (both 6″). Cf. *Clapgate Coppice, Coneygre* ib. and *infra* 451, 427. DEANHILL FM. Cf. *Deane hill close* 1637 WIpm. Near West Dean *supra* 377. GASTON COPSE (6″) is *Garstons* 1661 *Longford*, *Gaston* c. 1840 *TA*. *v. infra* 432. GATMORE COPSE. Cf. *Cotmor* 1331 WIpm. Probably from OE gat, ME got(e), 'goat.' GILLS

---

[1] *Barn Croft* c. 1840 *TA*. [2] *v.* holt, 'wood.'
[3] *Testewood* 1540 WM xii.

HOLE (6″) is *Gill Hole* 1773 A and D. GOLDEN'S FM (6″). Cf. *Goldens croft* 1661 *Longford*. HARESTOCK is so named in 1576 (Hoare). HASSOCK BEECHES (6″) is *Assock Breaches* (sic) c. 1840 *TA*. *v.* hassock *infra* 452. HERMITAGE WOOD (6″) is *Hermit Wood* ib. HOLMERE COTTAGES (6″). Cf. *Holemeres furlong* 13th AD ii. THE HOP GARDENS (6″). Cf. *infra* 452. HUNDRED ACRE COPSE (6″). Cf. *Hundred Acres* c. 1840 *TA*. An ironical name for a field containing 3 roods, 9 poles. Cf. *infra* 455. MOOR FM (6″) is *la More* 1311 *FF*, *Moure* 1394 *Ass. v.* mor, 'marshy land.' MOUNT COPSE and NEWSLADE COPSE (both 6″) are *Mount Ground, New Slade Coppice* c. 1840 *TA. v.* slæd, 'flat valley.' NEWTON is *Neuton juxta Whitcherch* 1289, *Neweton juxta villam de Albo Monasterio* 1310 *Ass. v.* tun. POPPLEHILL (6″) is *Poplar Hill* c. 1840 *TA*. REDHILLS is *Redhills* 1730 *Longford*, *Red Hill* 1773 A and D. SANDLAND COPSE, SHERWOOD COPSE, SHORT-LANDS ROW and STONY DEAN COPSE (all 6″) appear as *Sandlands Drove, Sherwood Mead, Shortlands Row* and *Stony Dean Coppice* c. 1840 *TA*. STREET FM (6″) is so named in 1809 (Hoare). WARREN'S COPSE (6″) is *Warren Coppice* c. 1840 *TA*. WHIPSHILL COPSE (6″) is *Wyppeshull* 1485 Pat. WORTHY HASSOCK COPSE (6″). Cf. *Worthy Field, Worthy Hassock* c. 1840 *TA* and hassock *infra* 452.

No Man's Land

NO MAN'S LAND

This is a very small extra-parochial district on the Hampshire border between the parishes of Landford and Bramshaw (Ha). It is not marked by name in A and D, and the earliest reference to the place which has been found is *Nomans Land, an extra parochial place* (1817 ParReg, Whiteparish).

XXXV. DOWNTON HUNDRED

Duntona, Dontone hundred 1086 ExonDB, *Duntonhdr* 1167 P. *v.* Downton *infra* 394. The Hundred meeting-place may well have been in Downton and it has been identified with the site of the present MOOT HO in Downton where there is a mound. The earliest reference to the mound that has been noted is in the phrase *in quodam loco voc. la Mote in decenn' de Dounton* (1348 *Cor*). Recent archaeological investigations suggest, however, that this mound is of Norman origin, and if that is the case it becomes impossible to take the mound itself to be the meeting-place of a Hundred going back to Saxon times. Cf. WM xliii, 380.

Bishopstone

BISHOPSTONE[1]

> *Bissopeston* 1166, 1190 P, *Bysschopestone* 13th WintonCart, *Byssupeston* 1249, *Byscopeston* 1268 *Ass*, *Busshopeston(e)* 1399 Cl, 1406 Trop
> *Ebleburn Bissopiston* 1244 Pat, *Ebbelesbourne Episcopi* 1310 Sarum, *Eblesbourn Episcopi alias Bisshopeston* 1349 Pat

'The bishop's farm,' *v.* tun. The manor belonged from very early days to the Bishop of Winchester. The name is no doubt a comparatively late tun-formation, the estate and parish having been formed from Ebbesborne.

CROUCHESTON

> *Crocheston* 1249 *Ass*, *-ton* 1329 Ipm
> *Crucheston(e)* 1279, 1281 *Ass*, 1329 Ipm, *Cruscheston juxta Bisshopeston* 1288 FF, 1289 *Ass*
> *Crukeston* 1289 *Ass*
> *Croucheston* 1332 SR, 1428 FA
> *Cryucheston* 1374 FF
> *Cruston al. Churcheston* 1562, *Crouston* 1579 Recov, *Crowston* 1637 *Phillipps*

This name, like the two following ones, may well be a late tun-formation. Since no family *Crouche* has been found in any records relating to the parish, it may be that OE tun or early ME ton has been added to Celtic *cruc*, 'hill, mound.' Cf. Crookwood *supra* 315.

FAULSTON

> *Fallerstone* 1275 RH, *Falleston* 1543 SR
> *Fallerdeston* 1305 *Ass*, 1422 IpmR, *Fallard-* 1309 FF, 1326 Pat, 1329 Ipm, *Falard-* 1332 SR, 1429 FF, *Fallerdson or Fallson* 1773 A and D

---

[1] A detached part of the Hundred.

'*Fallard*'s farm,' *v.* tun. As this personal name is of French origin, the name must be a post-Conquest tun-formation.

FLAMSTON FM (6″)

    Flambardeston(e) 1227 FF, 1281 *Ass*, 1304 *FF*, 1332 *SR*
    Flamberdeston(e) 1227 FF, 1279 *Ass*, 1428 FA
    Flamberstone 1275 RH
    Flambeston 1543 *SR*, *Flambston* 1565 *FF*, *Flampson* 1624
      Recov

This is a late tun-formation. Walter *Flambard* is mentioned in 1202 (Cur) in connection with Ebbesborne, and Walter, son of Robert *Flambard*, held Flamston in 1227 (FF). *Flambard* (well known as the surname of William Rufus's minister) is a Norman personal name of Germanic origin.

NETTON FM is *Nettun* 1227 FF, *-tone* 1332 *SR*, *Netteton* 1249, 1289 *Ass*. Probably identical with Netton *supra* 364.

THROOPE FM (6″) and HILL [tru·p] is *Thrope* 1289 *Ass*, *Throp* 1327, *Throup* 1332 *SR*, *Throwpe* 1570 PembSurv. *v.* þorp, 'village.' It is probably identical with *Ebblesburnthorpe* (1289 Abbr), 'the hamlet dependent on Ebbesborne.'

MILL HO, THE PITS and TOWNSEND FM (6″) were the homes of Thomas *atte Mulle* (1327 *SR*), Robert *atte Putte* (1332 ib.) and William *atte Tounesende* (ib.).

BARROW HO (6″) is *Barwe, Berewe* 1224, 1227 FF. *v.* beorg, 'hill, barrow.' DOWN BARN. Cf. *le Downe* 1489 *Ct*, *Bushoppston Downe* 1570 PembSurv.

Bodenham and Nunton

BODENHAM [bɔd(ə)nəm]

    Boterham 1209 PRWinton
    Boteham 1249 *Ass*, *Botenham* 1260 FF, 1268, 1289, 1345,
      1370 *Ass*, (*pontem de*) t. Ed 3 *For*, *Botnam* 1480 ECP
    Buteham 1249 *Ass*
    Botteham 1255 RH (p), *Bottenham* 1327, 1332 *SR*, 1335
      Extent, 1343 *MinAcct*, 1345 Ipm, 1630 *Recov*
    Bodenham 1695 *Recov*

'*Botta*'s ham(m).'

NUNTON

> *Nunton*(*a*) 1209 PRWinton, *Nunton* 1289 *Ass*, *Nonton* 1365 *GDR*
>
> *Nonyhampton, Nonynton* 1281 *Ass*
>
> *Nounton* 1327, 1332 *SR*, 1474 *EcclCom*, *Nowneton, Nownton* 1524 *SR*, *Naunton* 1565 *FF*

Probably '*Nunna*'s farm,' *v.* ingtun, with an alternative form *Nunninghamtun*.

CLEARBURY RING is *Clereburu* 1632 *EcclCom, Clearbury Ring* 1773 A and D. DOWN FM. Cf. *les Downes* 1632 *EcclCom*. RADNOR HALL. The manor of Bodenham belongs to the Earl of Radnor.

Downton

DOWNTON

> *Duntun* 672 (12th) BCS 27, 826 (12th) ib. 391, (*in*) *Duntune* 948 ib. 862, *Duntune* 955 (15th) ib. 912, *æt Duntune* 997 (12th) KCD 599
>
> *Duntone* 1086 DB, 1159, *Duneton* 1198 P, *Donton* 1290 Pap, *Dounton* 1327 Pat, 1332 *SR*, (*Est*) 1376 *FF, Estdounton* 1433 *FF, Est Downton* 1547 *SR, Eastedowneton* 1585 *FF, Dunkton or Dounton* 1675 Ogilby

'Farm by the down-land,' *v.* dun, tun.

NOTE. *Northstrete, Churchlane* 1425, 1551 *WinchColl, Salt Lane, Watership Lane* 1738 *Longford*. This last is from OE *wæterscipe*, 'body of water, water channel, conduit,' cf. PN Herts 127.

BARFORD PARK is *Bereford* 1086 DB, 1227 *FF et freq* to 1332 *SR*, (*juxta Dunton*) 1282 *Ass*, *Berford juxta Dounton* 1412 FA, *Barford* 1567 *FF*. See Barford St Martin *supra* 212.

FOBWELL (lost) is (*to*) *fobban wylle* 672 (12th) BCS 27, 948 ib. 862, *Fobbewelle* 1289 *Ass*, 1341 *Cor*, 1362, 1368 *For, Fobwell* 1300 *Stowe* 798, 1338 *GDR*. '*Fobba*'s spring,' *v.* wielle. Cf. Fovant *supra* 214.

WALTON (lost) is *Walton*(*e*) 1211 RBE, 1523 *SR*, 1632 *EcclCom, Waletone* 1332 *SR*, (*Weeke and*) *Walton* 1738 *Longford, Wick and Walton Tithing* c. 1840 *TA*. As Downton was an important place in OE times, it is likely that this is OE *wēala tūn*, 'farm of the serfs,' *v.* **wealh, tun.** Other compounds of OE *wealh, weala* in Wiltshire are *Walecote* (13th RegMalm) near Malmesbury, *Waledich* (1289 *Ass*) in Avebury. The name is now lost, but the last references suggest that it may have been near Wick *infra*.

WICK is *Wicha* 1166 P, *Wyke* 1268, 1279 *Ass*, *Weke* 1524 *SR*, (*juxta Newcourt*) 1585 WM xxi, *Weeke* 1642 *SR*. *v.* **wic** and *supra* 25.

DOWNTON MILL was probably the home of David *atte Mulle* (1402 *WinchColl*). It is *molendin' de Dunton* 1268 *Ass*.

BOTLEY'S FM (6"). Cf. *Bottleleaze* 1661 *Longford* and **læs** *infra* 438. FAIRFIELD HO (6"). Cf. *Fairfield* c. 1840 *TA*. LONG CLOSE is so named in 1720 (*Longford*). MOOT HO. *v.* Downton Hundred *supra* 391–2. NEW COURT DOWN is *New Court Down* ib. NEW COURT FM is *Newcourte* 1569 PCC. NORTH FIELD COPSE (6"). Cf. *le Northfeild* 1632 *EcclCom*.

Redlynch

REDLYNCH[1]
> *Radelynch(e)* 1282, 1289, 1345 *Ass*, 1334 *WinchColl et freq* to
>   1402 *WinchColl, Radeling* 1470 IpmR, *Radlyngys* 1490,
>   *Radlynche* 1589 *FF*
> *Redlynche* 1567 ib., -*linch* 1607 WM xxix

'The red ridge or rising ground,' *v.* **read, hlinc.** For -*ling*, -*lyngys* cf. Standlynch *infra* 397.

HAMPTWORTH
> *Hampteworth* 1220 Ipm, c. 1266 Winton *et freq* to 1428 FA
> *Hamtewurth* 1227 FF, c. 1286 Winton
> *Hanteworth* 1268, 1289 *Ass*, 1323 Cl
> *Hampteth* 1662 ParReg (Whiteparish)

Ekwall (DEPN) suggests that the name may go back to an original *hamtun-worþ*, but it is very difficult to accept his further suggestion that this is elliptical for *Hamtunscir-worþ*, i.e. 'farm on the Hampshire (border).' No parallel for such a formation can be adduced and it does not seem to be a likely one.

---

[1] A parish formed from Downton in 1895.

PENSWORTH FMS

> *Pendeleswurth* 1227 FF, *-wrth* 1268, *-worth* 1289, 1345 *Ass*,
> 1327, 1332 *SR*, *Pendleswurth* 1249 *Ass*, 1266 Winton,
> *Penlesworth* 1383 *WinchColl*
>
> *Pensworth al. Pendlesworth* 1720 *Recov*

'*Pendel's* farm,' *v.* worþ. *Pendel* would be an *l*-derivative of the well-evidenced OE personal name *Penda*.

COLE'S COPSE (6″), FRANCHISE'S WOOD[1], GOGG'S BARN (6″), LOCK'S FM[2], PIPERSWEIGHT WOOD (6″), TINNEY'S FIRS and TUCKER'S HAT (6″) are to be associated with the families of Barnaby *Cole* (1642 *SR*), John *le Frensshe* (t. Ed 2 *For*) and William *le Frensshe* (1343 *MinAcct*), Ralph *Gogge* (1327 *SR*), William *Lokke* (1469 *WinchColl*), Henry *Piperwhit* (1327 *SR*), William *Tinney* (c. 1840 *TA*) and George *Tucker* (ib.).

APPSY COPSE (6″) is *Apsey Coppice* 1678 Hoare. BATTENS HILL (6″) is *Batteshulle* 1425 *WinchColl*. Cf. Battscroft *infra* 398. BISHOPS WOOD (6″). Cf. *Bysshopesdene* 1402 ib. The manor of Downton belonged to the Bishop of Winchester. BLACKBUSH COPSE (6″) is *Blackbush Coppice* 1678 Hoare. THE BOG (6″). Cf. *Bog Meadow* c. 1840 *TA*. BOHEMIA is so named in 1820 (G). It is in a remote corner of the parish. Cf. *infra* 455. BROOM HILL WOOD (6″). Cf. *Broom Hill* 1674 *Longford*. BURY HILL (6″). Cf. *Berydowne* 1563 ib. GROVE FM (6″). Cf. *Grove Field* and *Mead* c. 1840 *TA*. KING'S COPSE (6″). Cf. *Kyngesfeld* 1383 *WinchColl*. LANGLEY WOOD is *Langelee* 1345 *Ass*, 1430 *FF*, *Langley Wood* 1660 *Recov*. 'Long leah' or 'wood.' LINCHET'S (sic) COPSE (6″). Cf. *The Linchetts* c. 1840 *TA* and *infra* 453. LODGE COPSE (6″) is *Lodge Coppice* ib. LOOSEHANGER COPSE. Cf. *Losehanger Park* 1684 ParReg, *Looshanger* 1686 *Longford*, *Lushinger Park* 1773 A and D. The second element is hangra, 'hillside'; the first is perhaps hlose, 'pigsty.' MILKHILLS FM (6″) is *Mylkehill* 1563 *Longford*. MOOR COPSE (6″). Cf. *The Moor* c. 1840 *TA*. MOUNT PLEASANT (6″). *v. infra* 455. NEW-HOUSE is *New House* 1773 A and D. OUT WOOD (6″) is so named in 1720 (*Longford*). Cf. *infra* 450. PEAKED WOOD and PIMLICO FIRS (both 6″) are *Picked Wood, Pimlico* c. 1840 *TA*. For the

---

[1] *French Wood* 1773 A and D, *Franchises Common* and *Wood* c. 1840 *TA*.
[2] Cf. *Lokkeshill* 1526 *WinchColl*.

first name, *v. infra* 443. The second is no doubt a nickname from the London place-name. POPPLEHILL COPSE (6″). Cf. *Poppel Hill* ib. QUAR HILL (6″). Cf. *infra* 445. RADNOR FIRS (6″) is named from the Earls of *Radnor*. RAMBRIDGE COPSE (6″) is *Rambridge Coppice* 1678 Hoare. SHEARWOOD COPSE (6″) is *Sherwood Coppice* c. 1840 *TA*. STREET'S COPSE (6″). Cf. *Streets Close* c. 1840 *TA*. STUDLANDS COTTAGE is *Studland* 1677 *Longford*. SUNT COPSE (6″) is *Sunt Coppice* 1678 Hoare. See sunt *infra* 448. It lies low. WELLS COPSE (6″). Cf. *Wells croft* 1503 *WinchColl*. WINDYEATS FM. Cf. *Wynnyatesbush* 1671 *For*. 'Wind-gap(s),' *v.* geat.

Standlynch

STANDLYNCH

> *Staninges* (sic) 1086 DB
> *Stanlinc'* 1198 Fees, *-linche, -y-* 1209 PRWinton, 1268 FF, 1332 *SR*, 1388 BM, *North Stanlynch* 1398 Bodl, *Staunelynch* 1508 Pat, *Standlinch* 1558–79 ECP, *Standleech* 1641 NQ vii
> *Stanlinghe* 1249, *-linge* 1268 *Ass*, 1275 RH, *-lynghe* 1311 Ipm, *Standlynche al. Standlynge* 1605 *Recov*
> *Stallynch* 1361 BM, 1400 *BodlCh*

'Stony hill or slope,' *v.* hlinc. Cf. Stallenge Thorne (PN D 534) and Stanlidge Pond in Minstead (Ha), *Stanlynche* 1490 *For*.

CHARLTON is *Cherlet(on)* 1209 PRWinton, 1266 Winton, 1316 FA, *Churleton* 1279, 1281 *Ass*, *Cheorlton* 1332 *SR*, *Charleton by Dounton* 1358 Pat, *Charelton* 1524 *SR*. 'Farm of the *churls* or free peasants,' *v.* ceorl, tun.

PRIVETT FM (6″). Cf. *bosco de Prevet* 1268 *Ass*, *boscus de Pryvet* t. Ed 3 *For*, *Privatt wood* 1632 *EcclCom*. Probably from the plant name. Cf. *Privetheye* (14th AD ii) in Wootton Bassett.

WITHERINGTON FM

> *Widetone* 1086 DB
> *Widintona, Widentona* 1209 PRWinton
> *Wythiton* 1255 RH (p), *Wythyton* 1397, *Whithiton* 1456 IpmR, *Withyton* 1474 *EcclCom*, *Withiton* 1567 FF
> *Wythetun'* 1270 *For*, *Wytheton* 1327, 1332 *SR*, 1349 *FF*, 1393 Cl, *(juxta Dounton)* 1375 IpmR
> *Wydinton* 1279, 1281, *Wyditon* 1289, *Wydenton* 1289 *Ass*

Withington 1632 *EcclCom*, *Wethrington* 1675 Ogilby, *Whither-ington* 1773 A and D

Apparently 'farm by the withies' (OE *wiðegn*), *v.* tun. The place lies low by the Avon marshes.

BATTSCROFT COPSE[1] and COLES'S BURY (both 6″) are to be associated with the families of William *Bat* (1388 *WinchColl*) and Nicholas *Cole* (1327 *SR*). The *Bat* family may also have given name to Battens Hill *supra* 396.

THE PENNINGS (6″) is *The Penning* c. 1840 *TA. v. infra* 453. STANDLYNCH BRIDGE (6″) is *Stanlynchbrigge* 1382 Works. TRAFALGAR HO. This was originally the manor house of Standlynch. The estate was bought by the King and Parliament to commemorate the services of Lord Nelson and given to his brother the first Earl Nelson (Hoare, Addenda 71).

Woodfalls

WOODFALLS[2]

Wudefolde 1258 FF, -*faude* 1275 RH (p), *Wodefald*, -*faud* 1268 *Ass et freq* to 1400 IpmR, with variant spelling *Wude*-, *Wodefeld* 1289, 1327 FF, 1316 FA (p), *Wodefolde juxta Duntone* 1309, *North Wodefeld* 1368 FF, *Wodfolde beside Dounton* 1495 Ipm, *Wudfoldshutte* 1508 *EcclCom*

North Woodwolles 1595 NQ vii

Woodfall 1721 Recov

'Fold by the wood,' *v.* fal(o)d. For -*shutte*, *v.* Shootend *supra* 375.

MORGAN'S VALE. This is a modern residential district. The site is marked as *Morgans Bottom*, i.e. '*Morgan*'s valley' in 1820 (G) and c. 1840 (*TA*). The surname *Morgan* has not been noted in connection with Downton but is found in Salisbury and adjacent parishes from the 16th to the 19th century (PCC, ParReg).

CHURCH CLOSE COPSE (6″). Cf. *Church Close* c. 1840 *TA*. KITE CROFT (6″) is *Kutecrofte* 1383, *Kete-* 1425, *Kyttecroft* 1551

---

[1] *Battescrofte* 1319 Bodl. *v.* croft.
[2] A parish formed from Downton in 1914.

WinchColl. v. croft and OE *cȳte,* 'kite.' LODGE FM is *Lodge farme* 1638 *Longford.* PACCOMBE FM (6″) is *Packham* ib., *Packam* 1773 A and D. PARADISE COPSE (6″). Cf. *Paradise* c. 1840 *TA* and *infra* 453. PARK ASHES (6″) is *Park Ashes Coppice* ib. RIDGE FM (6″). Cf. *The Ridge* 1720 *Longford.* SLAB LANE (6″). Cf. *Slab Ground* c. 1840 *TA.* STEWARDS ROW (6″). Cf. *Stewards Dean* ib.

XXXVI. DAMERHAM HUNDRED

Damrehā hundred, Domerhā hundred 1086 ExonDB. *v.* Damerham *infra* 400. The Hundred consisted of two detached parts, the parish of Compton Chamberlayne and the parishes of Damerham and Martin, now in Hampshire. Later known as South Damerham Hundred in contrast to the artificially created Hundred of North Damerham, *v. supra* 65 n. 1.

Compton Chamberlayne

COMPTON CHAMBERLAYNE

Contone 1086 DB, *Cumpton* 1208, 1234 FF, 1249 *Ass*
Compton Chamberleyne 1316 FA

'Farm in the combe or valley,' *v.* cumb, tun. Robert *Camerarius* held the manor in 1208 (FF), Geoffrey *le Chaumberleng* in 1234 (ib.).

NAISHES FM was probably the home of John *atte Nasshe* (1348 *Cor*), from ME *atten ashe,* 'at the ash.'

DICKETTS (6″) is to be associated with the family of John *Duckett* (sic) (1642 *SR*).

BREACH FM (6″). Cf. *la Breche* 1328 WIpm and *infra* 423. COMPTON DOWN and WOOD. Cf. *Dounforlong* ib., *boscus de Compton* 1257 *For.* COMPTON IVERS (6″) is *la Vuere* (sic) 1328 WIpm. 'Steep slope or bank,' *v.* Rivar *supra* 355. HOLLY HEAD COPSE and WURS COPSE (both 6″) are *Holley Head Coppice* and *Wurs Coppice* c. 1840 *TA.* LONG FOLLY (6″). *v. infra* 451.

Damerham

DAMERHAM[1]

> (*æt*) *Domrahamme* c. 880 (c. 1000) BCS 553, (*at*) *Domerham*
> c. 945 (14th) ib. 817, (*æt*) *Domerhame* c. 1100 ASC (D) *s.a.*
> 946, (*æt*) *Domarhame* 10th ASWills
>
> *Dobreham* 1086 DB, *Domerham* 1186 P, 1189 GlastInq *et
> passim* to 1428 FA, *Dumeram* 1202 Cur, *Domereham* 1237
> Pap, *Parva Domerham* 1242 Fees, *Parva Domberham* 1296
> WIpm, *Domerham* 1586 *Sadler*
>
> *Damerham* 1231 Pap, (*alias Domerham*) 1564 *Recov*, *Damerum*
> 1675 Ogilby

The name would seem to go back to OE *dōmera hamm*,
'**hamm** or enclosure of the judges,' but the circumstances under
which such a name could have arisen are completely obscure.

NORTH and SOUTH ALLENFORD FMS. Cf. *Elyngford*[2], *Alyngforde*
1518 Hoare, *Alyngford* 1540 LP, 1570 PembSurv. The stream
here is now known as Allen River, but as no early references to
it have been noted, it may well be a late back-formation from
the place-name.

BOULSBURY FM is *Baltesberg*, *Baulesberg* 1189 GlastInq, *Bolesbergh* 1225 SR (all p), *Boelesburg'* 1279 GDR, *Boles-*, *Bolisburghe*
1297 Hoare, *Bolesbergh* 1334 *Ass*, 1342 *GDR*, -*borghe* 1518
Hoare, *Bollesbrugh* 1540 LP, *Ballesborough* 1570 PembSurv.
The early forms are not sufficiently consistent with one another
for any satisfactory suggestion to be possible. The second element is **beorg**, 'hill' or 'barrow.'

DRAKE NORTH (6") is *drakenhorde* 940–6 (15th) BCS 817,
Drakenworthe 1518, *Drakenorth Coppice* 1539 Hoare, *Drake-
north al. Drakenworth* 1540 LP. 'Dragon hoard or treasure.'
The name preserves some ancient legend.

HIGHWOOD COPSE and HIGH HAYWOOD COPSE (both 6") are
Haywod' c. 1250 GlastRl, *Hay-*, *Haiwode* 1324, 1333, *Hyehay-
wode* 1518, *Highhaye Wodde* 1539 Hoare. Identical with Heywood *supra* 149.

---

[1] Transferred to Hampshire in 1895.
[2] GrundyH (70) gives a 14th-century form *Elingford*.

HUCKLE COPSE (6″) is *Huchwell* 1189 GlastInq, *Huchewila* 1225 *SR* (p), *Hukawell'* c. 1250 GlastRl, *Hukewelle* 1332 *SR* (p), *Huckewelle, Howkewylle* 1518, *Huckull Grove* 1539 Hoare. '*Hucca*'s spring or well,' *v.* wielle. Cf. Hucking (PN K 219), Hockley (PN Wa 294).

KNOLL FM and DOWN. Cf. *knolle* 946 (15th) BCS 817, *la Cnolle* 1256 *Ass*, *Knolleslade* 1518 Hoare. *v.* cnoll, 'hill,' and slæd.

LOPSHILL is *Lospushale* 946 (15th) BCS 817, *Luppishale* 13th Hoare, *Loppeshal(e)* 1249 *Ass*, 1315 Ipm, 1317 Cl, 1428 FA, *Luppes-* 1289 *Ass*, *Lopes-* 1460 IpmR, *Lopsale* 1518 Hoare, *Lopseal* 1773 A and D. This name must remain an unsolved problem. The original second element was healh.

RYVERS COPSE (6″) is *le Ryver, la Ewre, Ewreshole* 1518 Hoare and was the home of Adam de *la Ryvere* (1312 *Ass*), de *la Rivere* (1332 *SR*). Another example of OE yfer, 'slope,' etc. (*infra* 450), with the ME development noted under Rivar *supra* 355.

STAPLETON FM is *Stapelham* 1189 GlastInq, 1225 *SR* (p), 1249 *Ass et freq* to 1332 *SR*, *-pil-* 1297, *-hame, Stapulhamesyate* 1518 Hoare. A compound of OE stapol, 'post, pillar, staple,' and ham or hamm. For *yate*, *v.* geat.

WIGMORE COPSE (6″) is *Widemere* 946 (15th) BCS 817, *Wydemere* 1518, *Widmer* 1539 Hoare, *Wigmore Coppice* c. 1840 *TA*. 'Wide pool' or 'withy pool,' *v.* mere.

HYDE FM was the home of Elias de *la Hide* (1242 Fees). It is the *hide of lospushale* of BCS 817 and may well be the *1 hide in Dobreham*' mentioned separately in DB, *v.* hid.

ASHRIDGE COPSE is *Assheredge Coppice* 1545 LP. BAGLAND PLANTATION (6″) is *Baggelonde* 1518 Hoare. BALL HILL COPSE (6″). Cf. *la Balle* ib., *Ball Field* c. 1840 *TA* and *infra* 422. BIDDLESGATE COPSE (6″) is *Byddelgates* 1570 PembSurv and takes its name from Biddlesgate Fm in Cranborne (Do). For the history of that name *v.* PN Do 100. BLACKHEATH DOWN. Cf. *Blackehethe* 1518 Hoare. BOARDENGATES COPSE (6″). Cf. *Boardengate Meadow* c. 1840 *TA*. BREACH COPSE (6″). Cf. *la Breache, Estbreache* 13th, 1518 Hoare and bræc *infra* 423.

CHANNEL HILL FM (6″) is *Chandle Hill* c. 1840 *TA* and may be identical with *Chaldeenehull* 1518 Hoare. Perhaps 'cold valley,' *v.* ceald, denu. COLT GREEN COPSE (6″) is *Collegrene* ib., *Colt Green* c. 1840 *TA.* CORNPIT FM may have been near *Cornedale* 1518 Hoare. CROCKERS COPSE (6″). Cf. *Crockers* ib. DAMERHAM MILL (6″). Cf. *Lytylmylle, Millefurlong* ib. ELEVEN CROSS, ENDLESS COPSE and FURZE CLOSE (all 6″) are so named c. 1840 (*TA*). GOULD'S COPSE (6″) is *Golders Coppice* 1539 Hoare. Cf. *Golderiscrofte* 1518 ib. HOLM HILL (6″) is *Home Hill* c. 1840 *TA.* KINGLAND COPSE (6″). Cf. *Kynglonde, Kyngesbarghe* 1518 Hoare. *v.* beorg. THE MARSH is *la Mershe, Oldemershe* 1518 Hoare. SINKHOLE COPSE (6″) is *Sinkhole Coppice* c. 1840 *TA.* SOUTH END is *Southeende* 1518 Hoare. WEST PARK. Cf. *Parkefelde, Parkeshurne* ib. *v.* hyrne, 'corner.' WHITE LEAZE COPSE (6″). Cf. *White Leaze* c. 1840 *TA.* WOOLENS COPSE (6″) is *Woolens Coppice* ib. and may be near the *Wolonde* of 1518 (Hoare), i.e. 'crooked land,' *v.* woh and cf. Woollensbrook (PN Herts 212–13). YEW TREE COPSE (6″) is *Yew Tree Coppice* c. 1840 *TA.* The yew may be referred to in *la Ewe, la Yowe, Yewenede* 1518 Hoare.

Martin

MARTIN[1]

> *Merton(e)* 946 (14th) BCS 817 *et freq* to 1428 FA, *Est-* 1483 Pat, *West-* 1518 Hoare, *Merton al. Martin* 1756 FF
> *Meretun* 1225 SR, *-ton* 1227 Ch, 1237 Pap (p)
> *Merten* 1316 FA, *Mertyn* 1491 Ipm

'Farm at the boundary,' *v.* (ge)mære. The place is on the borders of Hampshire and Wiltshire. EAST MARTIN is a hamlet to the east of Martin, which must be the *Westmertone* of 1518 (Hoare).

BLAGDON HILL is *Blakedounesdich* 1237, *Blakedon(e)* 1279 *Ass*, 1281 Hoare, *Blackedoneweye* 1518 Hoare. 'Dark hill,' *v.* blæc, dun. The ditch is Bokerly Dyke.

TIDPIT is *Tudeputte* 1242 Fees, 1289 *Ass*, 1300, 1307 Ipm, *Todeputte juxta Domerham* 1255 Hoare, *Tudeput next Merton*

---

[1] Transferred to Hampshire in 1895.

1345 Misc, *Todputte* 1518 Hoare, *Tytpit* 1570 PembSurv, *Tippet or Tidpit* 1773 A and D. '*Tuda*'s pit or hollow,' *v.* **pytt.** For the modern vowel cf. Tidworth *supra* 370 and Introd. xx.

TOYD FM is *Tohyde* 13th Hoare, *Twyd* 1255 Misc (p), *Twohide* 1518 Hoare, *Towhide* 1540 LP, *Twoyde, Twoyd, Twyde* 1570 PembSurv, *Twyde* 1642 WIpm, *Tweed* 1675 Ogilby. 'Two hides,' *v.* hid and cf. Tinhead, Fifield *supra* 141, 207. As Martin is not mentioned in DB we cannot trace the history of this measure of land.

BUSTARD MANOR (6″) is *Bustard Farm* 1567 Hoare. KITES NEST FM. Cf. *Kites Nest* c. 1840 *TA.* LONG BARROW (6″) is *Langbaroghe* 1518 Hoare. MARTIN DOWN is *mons vocatus la Downe* 1570 PembSurv. MARTIN DROVE END. Cf. *Droveende, Drovefurlong* 1518 Hoare and *infra* 429. PARADISE. Cf. *infra* 453. SWEETAPPLES FM (6″). Cf. *Sweetapple Field* c. 1840 *TA.* TALK'S FM (6″) is *Tulkes* 1570 PembSurv, *Talks Mead* c. 1840 *TA.* TOWNSEND LANE (6″). Cf. *infra* 449.

THE ELEMENTS, APART FROM PERSONAL NAMES, FOUND IN WILTSHIRE PLACE-NAMES

This list includes all elements used in uncompounded place-names or in the second part of compounded place-names. Most words found as the first elements of place-names are also included if they are of historical or linguistic interest. Under each element the examples are arranged in three categories, (a) uncompounded elements and those in which the first element is a significant word and not a personal name, (b) those in which the first element is a personal name, (c) those in which the character of the first element is uncertain. Where no statement is made it may be assumed that the examples belong to type (a). Elements which are not included in the *Chief Elements used in English Place-Names* are distinguished by an (n) after them. The list is confined with few exceptions to names for which there is evidence before 1500.

ac Brownockhill, Fairoak, Gospel Oak, Shire Rack.
æcer Amour-, Ballick-, Bean-, Black-, Goat-acre.
ærn Chitterne (?), Colerne, Potterne, Washern (?).
æsc Ashley (4), Ashmore, Ashton (3), Axford (?), Naish, Naishes, Nash, Portash.
æþeling (n) Allington (?). **æwielle** Alton. **æwielm** Ewen.
amore (n) Amouracre. **anstig** Ansty. **apulder** Appledoe.
bæce, bece Beckhampton, Burbage.
bæþ (n) Bathampton. **bake,** ModE (n) Bake (several).
balle, ME Ball Down, Black Ball, (b) Burdens Ball.
bay, ME (n) Bay Bridge. **bearu** Barrow (2).
beaw (n) Bewley. **bedd** (n) Honeybed. **beg** Baydon (?).
begeondan (n) Yarnbrook. **benc** (n) Kate's Bench.
beo Bincknoll.
beofor Beversbrook. **beonet** Bentham, Bentley.
beorg Barrow (2), Berryfield, (a) Bishoper, Brokenborough, Cocklebury, Ell Barrow, Everley Barrows, *Flexborough*, Larborough, Long Barrow (2), *Rowborough*, Row-, Swan-, Wanborough, White Barrow, Woodborough, (b) *Bedborough*, Bowls Barrow, *Brenchesbergh*, Marlborough (?), Neale's Barrow, (c) Boulsbury, Ende Burgh, Kill Barrow, Silbury.
bere Barford (2). **beretun** Barton (2).
berewic Berwick (4). **bern** Barncroft, Barns Hill.
bicca (n) Beechingstoke (?).

biscop Bishoper, Bishopstone (2), Bishopstrow, Bushton.

boc Beach's. boga (n) Bowden (?).

*bors (n) Boscombe. box Box.

bræc Brache, Bratton, Braydon Hook, Breach (11), Breaches.

brandiron, ModE (n) Brandier.

bremel Bremhill, Bremilham.

broc Brockhurst, Brook (8), Broughton, (a) Berry-, Bevers-, Brog-, By-, Gang-brook, Gauze Brook, Hol- (2), Hollybrook, Lid Brook, Mill-, North-, South-, Small- (2), Swans-, West- (2), Yarn-brook, (b) Avebrick, Widbrook, (c) Pegsbrook.

brocc Brocklees. brom Broome, Southbroom.

brycg Bridge (4), (a) Boyton, Bradford, Cow (2), Fox, Gang, Grey and Harnham Bridge, *Kingsbridge*, Lacock Bridge, Long Bridge, Long-, Neigh-, Rey-bridge, Semington Bridge, Stanbridge, Standlynch Bridge, Stock-, Trow-, Whitebridge, Wood Bridge (2), Woodbridge, (b) Back Bridge, (c) Edge Bridge, Honeybridge.

bufan Bowood. bugge, ME (n) Bugley, Bugmore (?).

bulut, *bulutig (n) Bulford (?). bur Bowerhill.

(ge)bur (n) Boreham.

burh Berry, Boreham (in Warminster), Brunton, Burbage, Burderop, Burridge, Bury (2), Burytown, (a) Broad-, Chisle,-Fos- (2), Hazel-, Mem-, Mistle-, Old-bury, Pomeroy, Rings-, Salis-, Sid-, Spels-, West-, Whits-, Winkel-bury, (b) Alder-, Ames-, Bad-, Bar-, Bud-, Chis-, Ebs-, Gods-, Heytes-, Malmes-, Rams-, Tis-, Yates-bury, (c) Ave-, Bag-, Battles-, Bil-, Bux-, Chisen-, Clear-, Clitch-, Figs-, Is-, Lid-, Lug-, Og-, Scratch-, Wils-, Yarn-bury.

burhtun Bourton (2), Burton (4).

burna Bourne (3), Bournelake, (a) *Garesbourne*, Gauze Brook, Hag-, Med-, Mel-, Mil-, Range-, Rod- (2), Sam- (2), Shalbourn(e), Whit-, Winter-bourne (3), Woburn, (b) Aldbourne, *Cadeborne*, Ebbesborne, Ogbourne, (c) Colling-, Ingel-bourne.

butere Buttermere. butte, ME (n) Butts.

byd (n) Byde, Bydemill (5), Beardwell, Biddesden (?).

bymere (n) Bemerton.

castel, ME (n) Castle (2).

catt Cathanger, Catts Grove, Kate's Bench.

cawel (n) *Cawdon* (?). ce(a)for Cheverden.

ceald Calcote, Chadwell, Chalcot, Chaldicotts, Chalfield, Challymead, Coldcot (?). cealf Choulden.

ceapmann (n) Chapmanslade. ceaster Chislebury.

*ceolc (n) Chalke. ceorl Charl-cote, -ton (4).

ceosol Chisledon. chapele, ME (n) Chapel (2).

chase, ME (n) Aldbourne Chase. cicen (n) Chicksgrove (?).

ciete (n) Chitterne (?), Preshute.   cietel Chettles (?).
*cigel (n) Chilmark.   cild Chilhampton, Chilton (?).
cirice Ivy Church, Whitchurch.
cis *Chesel* (?), Chisenbury.   *clacc (n) Clack.
*clæfren (n) Clarendon (?).   clæg Clay (3).
clate Clattingar, Clatford, Cloatley.
clenche, ME (n) Clench, Clinghill (?).
clere, ME (n) Clears, Clear Wood.
clif Cleeve (4), Cleve, Clyffe (2), Avoncliff, Rams Cliff, Swallowcliffe, White-, Worm-cliff, (b) Baycliff, *Penceley*.
*clopp (n) Clapcote.   clos, ME Bearclose.
cnæpp Knapp (4).   cniht Knighton (3), Night Wood.
cnoll Knoll (3), Knolls, Knowle (3), Bincknoll.
cnugel (n) Knoyle.   *cocc (n) Cockhill.
coccel (n) Cocklebury (?).   cokel, ME (n) Cocklebury (?).
cockrode, ME (n) Cock Road, Cockroad.
cofa Cove.   coniger, ME (n) Coneybury.
coppe, ME Copehill.   corf (n) Corton.
cot(e) Coate (2), Costow, Cote, Cotmarsh, Cuttice, (a) Calcote, Chalcot, Chaldicotts, Charl-, Clap-cote, Cold-, Dray-cot (3), Eastcott, *Eastcott*, Eastcourt (2), Elcot, Foscote, Hil-, Hurd-cott (2), Littlecote, Littlecott (2), Littlecourt, Milkhouse, Murcott, Nethercote, *Nethercott*, Sharcott, Shorncote, Smith-cot, Southcott, Syren-, Wal-cot, *Westcott*, Westcourt, Wilcot, (b) Calcutt, Earls Court, Uffcott, Westlecott.
court ME, (n) Old and Queen Court.
crawe Cranhill (?).   cristelmæl Christian Malford.
crockere, ME (n) Cock-a-troop.
croft Croft, Crofton, Ben-, Burys-, Cow-, Cratch-croft, East Croft, Housecroft, Kite Croft, New-, Row-, South-, Wood-croft, (b) Ad-, Batts-, Pax-croft, (c) Harris Croft.
crouche Crouch's (2).
cu Cole Park, Conrish, Cowage (2), Cow Bridge, Cowcroft, *Cowfold*.
cul (n) Colerne (?).
cumb Coombe (15), Coombe's, Compton (3), Ash-, Bos-, Bur-combe, Castle and East Combe, El-, Gat-, Hal-, Har-, Hol-, Little-, Mala-, Man-combe, Markham, Mar-, Mer-, Pough-, Pres-combe, Roakham, *Rowcombe*, Swan-, Thorn-, Wex-, Wit-, Wood-combe, (b) Catcomb, Chet-, Hippens-, Luc-, Stitch-, Tid-combe, (c) Al-, Au-, Bel-, Bid-, Bush-, Don-, El-, Hit-, Lop-, Mes-, Rains-, Rans-, West-, Win-combe.
cwead (n) Quidhampton (2).   cwylle (n) Quelfurlong.
cyf, cyfel (n) Keevil (?).

cyning *Kingsbridge*, Kings-down (2), -field, -mead, -ston (2), Kington (?).

cyta Kite Croft.

dell Dalwood (?).

denu Danes, Dean (6), Deanfield, Denmead, Biddesden (?), Braydon, Brazen, *Cawdon*, Cheverden, Chisledon, Fresden, Harding, Haredene, Hazeldon, Langdean, Langden, Long Dean (2), Marden (2), Oxen-, Pickle-dean, Standen, Stone-down, Surrendell, Uddens, Whaddon, Widdington, (b) Bag-den, Figheldean.

deor Derriads, Totterdale (?).

dic Ditchampton, Ditteridge, Great Ditch, Grims Ditch (2), Hugditch, Row Ditch, Vernditch, Wansdyke, Whittonditch, (b) *Underditch*.

dierne Durley, Durnford. **domere** (n) Damerham.

draca (n) Drake North. **dræg** Draycot (3).

draf (n) Drove, Droveway.

dun Donhead, Down (4), Downton, Chitterne and Pewsey Down, Baydon, Blackdown, Blagdon, Bowden (2), Choulden, Clar-, Claren-don, Cleverton, *Elyngdon*, Garsdon, Granham, Hay-, Hen-don, High Down, Hindon, Hog Down, Honey-, Hunger-down, Hydon, Kingsdown (2), Moredon, Red Down, Rough Down (2), Rowden, Sheldon, Swindon, Thorn Hill, Thorny Down, Waden, Whaddon, *Whorwellsdown*, (b) Arn Hill (?), Blunsdon, Brims Down, Chaddington, Gomeldon, Hannington, Lowden, Mannington (?), (c) Dods-, Ebb-down, Edington, Lynden, Rowden.

dyncge (n) Dunge.

ea Ray, Eaton, Minety (?), Neigh Bridge, Reybridge.

ears (n) Ashgrove.

ecels (n) Etchilhampton, Nichills (?).

efes Isbury (?). **efn** (n) Even Swindon.

eg Iford, *Iley*, Forty (2), (b) Dauntsey, Lutsey, Oaksey, Patney, Pewsey, (c) Eisey (?).

ende Townsend (3), Town and West End. **ened** Enford.

eofor Everley. **eþe** (n) Edington (?).

fæstærn (n) Vasterne.

falod Cole Park, *Cowfold*, *Stodfold*, Stotfield, Woodfalls.

fealu Falstone. **fearn** Vernditch.

feld Field, Field's, Ashton-, Berry-, Brad-field, Castlefields, Chal-, Frox-field, *Frustfield*, Hat- (2), High- (2), Kings-, Lang-field, Rowde and South Field, Summer-, West- (2), White-, Wick-, Yarn-field, (b) Cowes-, Wink-field, (c) Bay-fields, Bearfield.

fenn Venn, (b) Ratfyn. **fersc** Fresden. **fiergen** Ferne (?).

fleax *Flexborough*.   flies (n) Flisteridge (?).
(ge)flit (n) Flitwick.
ford Ford (4), Ax-, Bar- (2), Biss-, Black-, Bottles-, Brad-, Brit-, Bul-, Christian Mal-, Clat-, Dept-, Durn-, En-, I-, Land-, Lang- (2), Maid-, Mil-, Plait-, Quemer-, Rat-, Slaughter-, Somer- (2), Stan-, Staple-, Sto-, Stow- (2), Strat- (2), Stur-, Wish-, Wood-ford (2), (b) Cod-, Dod-, Manning-, Ug-, Wils-ford (2), (c) Allenford, Catharine Ford, Henfords, Leck-Swains-ford.
*forst (n) Fosbury (2), Furze Hill.   forð (n) Forty.
fox Foscote, Fox-ham, -hangers, -hill, -ley (2), -more.
funta (a) Teffont, (b) Fovant, Urchfont.
furlang (a) Quelfurlong.   fyr(e)st (n) *Frustfield*.
fyrhðe Freegrove, Freeth, Frieth, Frith (3), Oakfrith.
gærstun Gaston (2), Gaston's.
gara Gore (3), Gores (2), Ashgoe.
gat Gastard, Gatcombe, Goatacre.
geard Derriads, Hopyard, Wormwood, (b) Bridzor.
geat Yatton, Deepets, Durlett, Highgate, Hachet, Hat Gate, Newgate, Watergates, (c) Bagshot.
græfe Grove, An-, Ash-, Bla-, Hay-, Not-, Shorten-, Thorn-grove, (c) Chicksgrove.
grafa Grafton, Grove (12), Grovehill, (a) Catts Grove, South-grove, (b) Woolsgrove, (c) Broomsgrove.
grange, ME (n) Grange.
grene Green, Church Green and Nettleton Green.
*grieten (n) Grittenham.   gripe, ME (n) Grip.
grund, grynde (n) Groundwell.
haca (n) Hackpen (?), Hagbourne.
hæcc Hatch (2), Hatches, Hachet.
(ge)hæg Hayes, Hays, Haygrove, Heywood (2), Highwood (2), Bushayes, Cuttice, Hillays, King-, Rook-hay, Southey, Sundays, Trussenhayes, Witcha, (b) *Kings Hay*, (c) Land-hayes, Tokes.
hæme Badbury Wick, *Chechemetorn*, Ditchampton, Liddington Wick.
hæþ Hatfield (2), Heath, Black Heath (2), Burntheath, Corsley, Earls and Wick Heath.
hætt Hatt.   haga Haugh.   ham (a) Corsham.
hamm Ham (6), Damer-, Gritten-ham, (b) Chippen-, Ingles-ham, (c) *Dutman's*.
ham or hamm Bent-, Bore-, Bremil-, Brom-, Dryn-, Fox-, Gritten-, Harn-, Hart-ham, Hyam, Lack-, Lang-, Lyne-, Newn-, Pews-ham, Stapleton, Stock-, Summer-, Thorn-, Up-, Whet-, Widden-ham, (b) Bald-, Belling-, Boden-,

Caden-, Cutten-, Hornings-ham, Lucknam, *Moxhams*, Tocken-, Totten-ham, *Wittenham*, (c) Bon-, Dock-, Col-, Melks-ham, Melsome.

hamstede Grimstead.

hamtun Hampton (?), Bat-, Beck-hampton, Brunton, Chil-, Etchil-, Nether-, Quid-hampton (2), Serrington, Seven-hampton, Sevington, Sunton, Uppington, Wedhampton.

han (n) Redhorn.

hanginde, ME (n) *Hangingblunsdon*, Hanging Langford, *Hangingstoke*.

hangra Hanger, Birc-, Cat-hanger, *Chichangles*, Clattingar, Foxhangers, Loose-hanger, (b) *Chadlanger*.

har Harcombe.　**hara** Haredene, Harnham (?).

hassuc Haxmore.　**heafod** Donhead, Seend Head.

healh Hayle (?), Heale, Crom-, Horse-, Midge-hall, Thrash-nells, Wolf Hall, Wraxall (2), (b) Ludgers-, Milden-, Rus-hall, (c) Lopshill, Puthall.

heall Hall.　**hecg** (n) Swatnage.　**hencg** (n) Stonehenge (?).

henep, hænep (n) Hamshill (?).　**heort** Hartham, Hartley.

heuedlinges, ME (n) Huntenhill

hid Hyde (2), Bulidge, *Fifhide*, Fifield (2), Fyfield (2), Tinhead, Toyd, (b) Tilshead.

hielde (c) Beacon Hill (?).　**hierde** Hurdcott (2).

hiewet (n) Hewetts.

higna Hindon, *Hindurrington*, Hinton.

hiwisc Huish, (b) Hardenhuish.　**hlædel** (n) Ladywell (?).

hlaw, hlæw Rudloe, (b) Winterslow, (c) Chedglow, Dunley.

hliep-geat (n) Lypiatt, Lyppiatt, *Lippet*.

hlinc Lynch (3), Redlynch, Standlynch.

hlype Lipe.　**hoc** Hook (2), Hooklands, Hookwood.

hocede (n) Hugditch.　**hoh** Haw, Howe (2).

holh Holbrook (2), Holloway.

holt Holt (2), (a) Hazeland, Oakhill, Sparcells, (b) Conholt, Poulshot.

hord Drake North.　**horn** Horn Wood.

hreod Rowde, Rodbourne (2), Rodmead.

hrycg Ridge (3), Rudge, Rudloe, Ash-, Barn-, Brem-, Cold-, Ditte-, East-, Eu-, Fliste-ridge, Great Ridge, Hawk-, Locke-, Nor-, Red-, Rhotte-, Sand-, South-, Stor-, Timb-, Totte-, Wheat-ridge, (b) Cutte-, Mar-ridge, (c) Pockeridge.

huluc (n) Hilcott.　**hund** Hound Wood.

hus Housecroft, Moor-, Wood-house (2).

hwelp (n) Whelpley.　**hwyrfel** *Whorwellsdown*.

hyll Hill (12), Apshill (2), Barnsell, Bemer-, Ber-hills (2), Breach, Brimble, Buck, Callow, Charlock and Church Hill (3),

Clay-, Cling-, Cock-, Cope-, Cran-hill, Dockle, East Hill, Farnell, Fernhill, Fowley, Fox-, Furze-, Green- (6), Hag-, Hams-hill, Horse Hill, Hunten-, Kite-hill, Lark, Little, Mappledore, Middle (4) and Milk Hill, Milk Hills, Nash, Oak and Red Hill, Roug-, Round-hill (2), Rye and Sand Hill, Sedgehill, Spin Hill, Spirt-, Stoke-, Stone-, Thorn-hill (4), Thornhills, Toothill, Uphill, Waite and West Hill, White- (3), Wid-hill, Wind Hill, Woodhill, (b) *Mousehill*, Patcombe Hill, Paven Hill (?), Pudnell, Snodshill, (c) Battens and Caen Hill, Godsell, Kepnal, Lickhill, Limpers and Lus Hill, Peckingell, Ramshill (2), Rox Hill, Totterdale, Whipshill.

hyrne Hern, Washern (?).   **hyrs** (n) Hursley (?).

hyrst Hurst (3), Chilvester, Raesters, Ravenshurst.

iggoð Nythe, Nythefield.

ing Filands (?), Stapling (?).

ing(a) Aldbourne, Arn Hill, Coldridge, Collingbourne, Deverells Wood, Manningford.

ingas Cannings.

*****ingtun** (b) Abling-, Alder-, Alling- (3), Bulking-, Cholder-, Cor-, Durring-, Fidding-, Fittle-, Grittle-, Hanker-, Hedding-, Hilmar-, Hilper-, Homing-, Hullaving-, Kilming-, Laving-, Lucking-, Nettle-, Nun-, Tythering-, Tyther-ton.

*****inhoc** (n) Ennix, Ennox, Innox.   **iw** Euridge, Uddens.

lacu Lake, Bournelake.   *****lacuc** (n) Lacock (?).

(ge)lad Cricklade.   **(ge)læt** (n) Longleat.

læfer Larborough, Larmer.

land Black-land, -lands (2), Eng-, In-lands, Kingland, Lamp-, New- (3), No-, Old-lands (3), Rag-, Red-land, Redlands, Studland, West-, Wink-, Wood-lands (5), Woolens, (b) Pink Lane, (c) Bagland, Englands (2).

launde, ME Lawn (2).   **leac** Lackham (?).

leactun Latton.

leah Lea, Leigh (8), Ley, Lye, Lyes, Lyemarsh, Alley (?), Ashley (6), Ashleigh, Bent-, Bew-, Boak-, Brad- (2), Brim-ley, Brocklees, *Chesel* (?), Cloat-, Cors-, Cran-ley, Danes Lye, Dur-, Ever-ley, Farleigh, Far-, Fox-ley (2), Grovely, Hart-, Hen- (3), Hurs-ley, *Iley*, Keevil, Langley (4), Lilly, Lin-, Maiz-ley, Medleys, Mor-, Net-, Nor-, Oak-ley, Penleigh, Rock-, Row- (2), Russ-, Sem-ley, Sewell, Ship-, So-ley, Southleigh, Stan-, Start-, Stock- (2), Stud- (4), Swin-, Swind-, Thing-, Twat-, Whelp-, Whist-, Whit-ley (2), Whidleys, Woolley, (b) Billhay, Bot-, Cad-, Luck-ley, *Selkley*, Tink-, Widger-, Willes-, Wins-ley, (c) Bug-, Chat-, Frankleigh, Keasley, Pimperleaze.

lin Lyneham.   **lind** Lynes.   **loc**(a) Lockeridge.

logge, ME (n) Lodge Copse. lusþorn (n) Lus Hill (?).

(ge)mæcca (n) Smatchams (?).

mæd Medbourne, Berry Mead, Broad- (3), Chally-, Den-mead, Hill and Ivy Mead, Kings-, Long-, Lot-mead, North Meadow, Pit Meads, Rod-, Round-, Taws-, Wal-, West-mead, (c) Boys Meadow.

mægþe (n) Maidford.

(ge)mæne Mancombe, Manwood, Mean Wood.

(ge)mære Markham, Marten, Martin, Mercombe.

maiden, ME (n) Maddington, Maiden Bradley.

mapel Maples. mapuldor Malacombe, Mappledore.

mearc Chilmark. mearh (n) Marden.

mere Marr, Mere (2), Ashmore, Buttermere, Frogmore (2), Holmere, Larmer, Rockmoor, Rushmore (2), Seymour, Stan-, Wig-more, Woolmer, Woolmore, (b) Dudgemore, Imber, (c) Bridmore.

mersc Marsh (13), Marshwood, Marston (4), Cot-, Hey-, In-marsh, Little Marsh, Outmarsh, West Marsh, West-, White-marsh (2), *Witmarsh*, (b) *Canningmarsh*, (c) Craysmarsh.

midlest(a) (n) Milston (?). minte Mynte, Minety (?).

mor Moor (6), Moors (2), Moorhouse, Moorshall, Moredon, Morley, Murcott, Alder-, Berry-moor, Blackmore (2), Broadmoor, Fox-, Gat-, Hax-more, Highmoor, Little Moor, Nethermore, Roughmoor, (c) Bel-, Brox-, Bug-, Pips-more, Prickmoor, Ruddle-, Stor-more.

morgen-giefu (n) Mooray.

myln Melbourne, Milbourne, Milford, Milkhouse, Mill (21), Mills, Byde, Crabb, Home, North and West Mill, Windmill Hill (2).

mynster Warminster.

næss Neston (?). neat Net Down (?), Netton (2), Notton.

neoðere Netheravon, Nethercote.

ora Nowers, Oare, Barker's, Brickworth, Wardour, (b) Martin-sell.

orceard Orchard.

paroche, ME (n) Whiteparish. penn v. supra 34.

pic (n) Pickwick.

pikede, ME (n) Peaks Wood, Pickett Furlong, Picket Wood.

pil (n) Pile. pirige Perry, Purton.

plane, ME (n) Salisbury Plain.

*pleget (n) Plaitford (?). plume Pomeroy (?).

pol Pole's, Pool, Poulton, (a) Horsepool, -pools, (c) Gutch Pool.

pond, ME Pond. port Westport, Portway.

preost Prescombe, Preston (2).

puca Poughcombe (?), Puck Shipton, Pugpits.

pund, ME (n) Pound (9).   pryfet (n) Privett.

purley, ME (n) Parley, Purleigh.   *putta (n) Puthall (?).

pytt Pitt (3), Pits, Pitgarden, Pitlands, Pit Meads, Pythouse, (a) Clay Pit, Har-, Frog-pit, Pugpits, (b) Tidpit.

pyttel (n) Pickledean.

quabbe, ME (n) Quobbs, Quobwell.

ræw Row, Seend Row, Siderow, White Row, Woodrow.

ragge, ME (n) Rag, Ragland, Dutchy Rag.

rippel (n) Ripples.

riþ *Horsley Upright Gate*, Seagry, (b) Abberd.

rymed (n) Roundway.   rysc Rushmore.

*sænde (n) Seend.

sand Sambourne, Sandhayes, Sandridge, Sands (3).

sceacere (n) Sugar Hill.

sceaga Shave, Shaw (5), Shawgrove, *Freshaw*, Moorshall, Woodshaw.

sceald Shalbourne.   sceard Red Shore, Whiteshard.

scearn Sherrington.   *sceorf (n) Sharcott.

*sceot (n) White Sheet (2) (?).   *sciete (n) Shootend, Shute (2).

scipen Puck Shipton.   scir-gerefa Shrewton.

scora (n) Sherston.   *scydd (n) Sidbury (?).

scylf Sheldon.   scytere Short Street.

sealh Selwood, Zeals.   sealtere (n) Salterton.

secg Seagry, Sedgehill.   sele Silbury (?).

shrubbe, ME Shrub.

slæd Slade, Slade's (2), Slads, Ashlade, Chapmanslade, (b) Paxlet, (c) Heronslade.

slæp Brimslade, *Horsley Upright Gate* (?).

slah-þorn (n) Slaughterford.   *slea (n) Slay Down.

*smeðett (n) Smithwick.   snæp (n) Snape, Snapes.

sperte, ME (n) Spirthill.   splot (n) Splatts.

spora (n) (c) Gasper (?).   spræg (n) Spray, Sprays.

spring (n) Spring Head.   *stæfer (n) Staverton.

stan Standlynch, Stan-ford, -ley (2), -more, -ton (3), Broad-, Fal-, Hail-stone, Sherston, (b) Haxton, Kinward-, Powten-stone, (c) Limber Stone.

stapol Staple, Staple-ford, -ton.   stearc (n) Startley.

stede *Chapelstede*, Hursted, Nursteed, Plaster, Wicksted.

steort Stert (3), Stert's, Gastard.

*stiepe (n) Steep, Stype Wood.

stiepel (n) Steeple Ashton, Langford, and *Lavington*.

stoc Stockton, (a) Erlestoke, Limpley, Purton and Winter-bourne Stoke, Stoke Farthing, Beechingstoke, Braden-, Laver-stock, (b) Baver-, Od-stock.

stocc Stock, Stockbridge, Stockham, Stock Street and Wood, Stokke.

stod *Studfold*, Studley (4).　**stow** Costow.

stræt Stratford (2), Stratton, Street (2), *Eastmanstreet*, Long, Nether, Old, Rook and Short Street, (b) Hawk Street (?).

strod Stroud (2).　**stubb** Stub, *Elstub*.　*stybb (n) Steep.

sumor Somerford (2), Summerham.　*sunt, ME (n) Sunt.

sur (n) Surrendell.　**swan** Swanborough.

swin Swincombe, Swindon, Swinley.

tæse (n) Tawsmead, *Tesworth*.　*teo (n) Teffont (?).

þiccett (n) Thicket.　**þing** Thingley (?), Tinkfield.

þorn Hackthorn, Thickthorn (2).

þorp, þrop Throop, Thrup, (a) Burderop, Cock-a-troop, Eastrip, Eastrop, Hilldrop, Westrop (2), (b) Restrop.

þroc (n) Rockmoor.　**þyrel** Durlett.

þyrelung (n) Turleigh (?).

tote (n) Totterdale (?).

treow Trowbridge, Bishopstrow, Pantry Bridge.

trousen, ME (n) Trussenhayes (?).

tun Townleaze, Abbotstone, Addes-, Al-, Ash- (3), Bemer-ton, Bishopstone (2), Boreham, Bratton, Broad Town, Brough-, Bush-, Charl- (4), Chir-, Comp- (3), Cors-, Cor-, Crof-, Ditchamp-, Down-, Easter-, Eas-ton (6), Easton Town, East Town, Ea-, Fisher- (2), Graf-, Hin- (3), Hor-, Kings- (2), King- (3), Knigh- (3), Len-, Lidding-, Little-ton (3), Little Town, Madding-, Mars-ton (3), Marten, Martin, Middleton, *Middleton*, Mil- (2), Mils-, Monk- (2), Nes-, Net- (2), Nettle-, Newn- (2), New-ton (3), Newtown (2), Norrington, Nor- (3), Not-, Over-ton, Park Town, Poul-, Pres-, Pur-, Salter-, Seming-, Seving-, Sherring-, Shrew-, Stan- (3), Staver-, Stock-, Stour-, Strat-, Sut- (3), Up-ton (3), *Walton*, Wessing-, Wil- (2), Withering-, Woodmin-, Woot- (2), Wor-, Wrough-, Yat-ton, (b) Afton, Alderstone, Al-, Alvedis-, Asser-, Bap-, Bayn-ton, Biddestone, Boy-, Brigmers-, Brix-, Bup-, Chil-, Cholder-, Chouls-, Couls-, Dil-, Din-, Els-, Fauls-, Flams-ton, Fugglestone, Gurston, Hodson, Homan-, Idmis-, Man-, Orches-, Pit-ton, Richardson, Rolleston, Thoulstone, Up-, Wolver-ton, (c) Calstone, Chapper-, Chil-, Crocker-, Crouches-, Norman-, Por-ton, Rixon, Sloperton.

twicene Touching (?).　**tyte** (n) Totteridge (?).

ufera Overton.　**uppe** Upavon, Upham.

wad Whaddon, Woodhill.　**wæd** *Ayleswade*.

wænn (n) Wanborough.　**(ge)wæsc** Shipways, Washerne.

waite, ME (n) Waite Hill.

warren, ME (n) Aldbourne Warren.

wealh Walcot, Wallen, Walmead, *Walton* (?).

weard Wardour. **weax** (n) Wexcombe.

weg Broad-, Cart-, Fulla-, High-, Hollo-way (3), Holloway's, King-, Lyde-, Port-, Ridge-way, Ridge Way, Roundway, Trow Lane, Wash-, West-way, White Way, Workway, (c) Collo-, Shift-way.

weod (n) Wedhampton. **weoh** (n) Waden.

(ge)weorc *Hilwark*, Workway.

wic Wick (23), *Wick*, Wick-heath, -sted, Wyke (2), (a) Conrish, Cowage (2), Flit-, Pick-, South-wick, (b) Chadden-, Fowls-, Herds-, Panta-, Wads-wick, (c) Lottage.

wice Whitsbury (?), Wishford. **wicham** Wickham.

wielle Well (4), Well Head, Wellhouse, Wilcot, Ash-, Beard-, Black-well, Bottle, Bride-, Chad-, East-, Ground-, Hol-well, Kettle, Lady-, Lud-, Oak-, Quob-well, Smith's Well, Sto- (2), Sweet-well, Wash-, West-wells, (b) Blax-, Crud-, Cumber-well, *Fobwell*, Godswell, Huckle, Loxwell, Nabals, Tiswell, (c) Colwell, Coppershell, Emwell.

wingeard Winyard.

winter Winkelbury, Winterbourne (3 series).

wisce Whistley. **wiðegn** (n) Widdenham (?).

wiðegn Witherington.

wiðig Widey's, Wigmore (?), Witherington.

woh Woburn, Woolens (?).

worþ Hampt-, High-, Little-worth, (b) At-, Brink-worth, *Cadworth*, Chel- (2), Dun-worth, *Mumworth*, Pens-, Sop-worth, *Tesworth*, Tid-, Wink-worth, (c) Pertwood.

worþig Worthy. **wrocc** (n) Wraxall (2).

wudu Wood (2), Woodborough, Woodbridge (2), Woodfalls, Woodford, Woodsend, Woodshaw, Wootton (2), Bentley and Bower Wood, Bowood, Burridge, Char-, Charl-wood, Clear Wood, Crook-, Cro-, Dal-wood, Deverells Wood, Earlswood, Fairwood, Haw Wood, Hey- (2), High-wood (3), Hill-, Hook-wood, Horn Wood, Horwood, Hound Wood, Inwood (2), Man-, Marsh-wood, Mean Wood, Night-, North-, Nor-wood, Nor Wood, Oxenwood, Peaks and Round Wood, Selwood, Southward, South and Stock Wood, Thick-, West-wood (4), Whitewood (2), Wollard, (c) Cakewood, Mans and Silk Wood.

wudumann (n) Woodminton.

wulf Wolf Hall, Woolley, Woolmer, Woolmore.

wull (n) Wilton (?). **wyrm** Wormhill, Wormwood.

yfer Ivers (4), Ivory, Rivar, Ryvers, Brockhurst, Brokerswood, Long Iver (2).

CELTIC NAMES

A. *Hill-names or compounds of such.* Brickworth (?), Conkwell, Conock, Cricklade, Crook Hill (?), Crookwood, Crouch Hill, Hackpen (?), Knook, Lydiard, Pen(n) (*supra* 34), Tollard.

B. *Wood- or forest-names.* Braydon, Chicklade (?), Chitterne (?), Chittoe, Chute, Melchet, *Penchet*, Savernake.

C. *River-names or compounds of such.* Avon (2), Bedwyn (?), Biss, Calne, *Colne*, Corsley, Corston, Deverill, Fonthill, Gauze Brook, Idover, Kennet, Lynt, Nadder, Pew, Sem, *Semenet*, Stour, Thames, Weaverne, Were (?), Wylye, Yarnfield (?).

D. *Miscellaneous.* Cherhill, Cheverell, Fosse Way, Icknield Way, Kemble, Membury (?), Pertwood (?), Pimperleaze, Porton (?), Quemerford, Salisbury.

FRENCH NAMES

Brail, Brittox, Clears, Devizes.

NOTES ON THE DISTRIBUTION OF THESE ELEMENTS

A few notes on the distribution of certain place-name elements may be given. The significance of this distribution depends to a considerable extent upon a comparison of the distribution in other counties, more especially in neighbouring and adjacent counties. The counties adjacent to Wiltshire are Gloucestershire, Oxfordshire, Berkshire, Hampshire, Dorset and Somerset. For Gloucestershire and Hampshire we have very full collections of material. For Dorset we have Dr Fägersten's book on *The Place Names of Dorset* (1933). For the other three counties the material is at present confined for the most part to forms from printed documents.

ærn. There are four examples, all of which are DB manors.
beorg is common. It is nearly always used of a barrow rather than of a hill. Only three are names of DB manors.
beretun and berewic are both alike rare.
bræc is common and characteristic but, except for Bratton, it is only found in minor names.
broc and burna are about equally common. The latter is generally used of a larger stream than broc. Two in broc are DB manors, ten in burna.

burh. The proportion of names in this element is higher than in most counties because of the large number which have reference to ancient camps and the like which are so common in the east and south-east of the county. Fifteen are names of DB manors. (See distribution map at end.)

burhtun. Three of the examples are in close association with the *burhs* of Malmesbury, Mere and Warminster and may be 'settlements by the burh.' The others would seem to be examples of *burhtun* in its more usual sense of fortified settlement. None are DB manors.

ceaster is unknown except for one example, a strange thing in a county so full of ancient camps.

cote is fairly common but, except for four examples, is confined to the north and more especially the north-east of the county. This agrees with its total absence in Dorset and its frequency in Gloucestershire, Berkshire and Hampshire. Thirteen are DB manors.

cumb is common, twice as common as **denu**. It is most frequent on the Somerset and Dorset border. **denu** is very rare in Dorset and Somerset. **dell** is found once. Eight in **cumb** are DB manors, six in **denu**.

Of the terms **dun, hrycg** and **hyll**, **hrycg** is the least popular, **dun** is roughly twice as common and **hyll** three times so. The names of eight DB manors end in **dun**, two in **hrycg** and three in **hyll**.

falod is very rare, four of the five examples being found in the compounds 'cow-fold' and 'stud-fold.' It is unknown in Dorset and Somerset.

feld. Of the forty-five or more examples, some twenty only are old and have reference to open land as against woodland. The compounds with North, South, etc. generally have reference to the open fields of the township. Six are DB manors.

ford. It is interesting to note that of some fifty examples twenty-five are names of DB manors.

(ge)hæg is almost confined to the west and south-west of the county, linking on with the common use of this term in Dorset and Somerset. None are DB manors.

ham and **hamm.** In this county as elsewhere it is very difficult to distinguish names in **ham**, 'homestead,' from those in **hamm** and again to distinguish those in which **hamm** denotes an enclosure and those in which it denotes a river-meadow. One would have expected that the ancient town of Chippenham would be a **ham** but the earliest forms make it clear beyond question that it is really a **hamm**, the settlement being so called because it lies in a big bend of the Avon. Of the **ham(m)** names some eleven are names of DB manors. It is interesting to note that ham(m) is, except for Bodenham, Damerham, Harnham, Stapleton and the lost *Dutman's*, practically confined to the north of the county and there is found chiefly in the Devizes, Trowbridge, Chippenham, Calne area. (See distribution map at end.)

hamstede is only found once (in the south-east of the county) and then it is the name of a DB manor.

hamtun is more common than usual. It is not found in the south-west of the county. There is an important group along the valleys of the Wylye and the Nadder. Only two are DB manors.

healh is not common. Five are DB manors. It is equally rare in Dorset.

hid. Of the eleven examples, four are names of DB manors and three, though the names are later than DB, may be identified with manors in DB.

hiwisc. The two examples are names of DB manors.

hoh is very rare. It is equally rare in Dorset and Somerset but more common in Hampshire.

ingas. There is only one example and that a DB manor.

ingtun is common but not so common as in Dorset, Hampshire and Somerset. Eighteen out of twenty-three are DB manors. (See distribution map.)

leah is very common, rather more common than in Somerset and Gloucester, twice as common as in Dorset, but only half as common as in Hampshire. The distribution map shows how it is commonest in the old forest areas of Braydon, Chippenham, Melksham, Pewsham, Savernake, Chute, Clarendon, Melchet, Grovely and Selwood. Salisbury Plain and the high land on the Berkshire border have none of these names. Thirteen are names of DB manors.

Of the two terms ora and ofer denoting a bank, ora is found several times but ofer seems to be unknown.

stede is found but rarely. None are names of DB manors.

stoc is found seven times as the name of a DB manor.

þrop, þorp is found mainly in the north of the county, and is thus adjacent to the names in this element which are found in Gloucestershire and Berkshire. There is one isolated example in the south of the county. This agrees with its great rarity in Somerset and its absence in Dorset.

tun is very common, the commonest of all elements. It is rather more common than in Hampshire, but not as common as in Dorset and Somerset. Some seventy-eight, roughly one-half of the whole number, are DB manors. A good many contain the name of their holder in post DB times, but such names are not quite so common as in Dorset and Devon. They include (*a*) Abbotstone, Addeston, Bishopstone (2), Bushton, Kingston (2), Maddington, Monkton (2), Rabson, Shrewton, (*b*) Bupton, Crockerton (?), Croucheston (?), Elston, Faulstone, Flamston, Gurston, Homanton, Normanton (?), Richardson, Rixon (?), Rolleston. Alderstone, Brigmerston and Brixton derive from the holder TRE.

wic is very common as added to parish names, some twenty-five examples in all. Only two are names of DB manors. It is more common than in Dorset and Hampshire but equally common in Somerset. In agreement with this, the distribution shows that it is very rare in the south-west of the county.

worð is about as common as in Hampshire and Gloucestershire, rather more so than in Dorset and Somerset (including in Somerset the names in **worðig**). It is unknown in the Salisbury Plain area. Ten out of the sixteen examples are names of DB manors.

PERSONAL NAMES COMPOUNDED IN WILTSHIRE PLACE-NAMES

Names not found in independent use are marked with a single asterisk if they can be inferred from evidence other than that of the place-name in question. Such names may be regarded as hardly less certain than those which have no asterisk. Those for which no such evidence can be found are marked with a double asterisk.

A. Old English

Abba (Abberd), *Æffe* (f) (Aughton), *Ægel (*Ayleswade*), *Ælfgeat* (Alvediston (?)), *Ælla, -e* (Alcombe, Allington, Alton), *Æschere* (Asserton), *Æþelwaru* (f) (Alderbury), *Ætta* (Atworth), *Babba* (Bapton, Baverstock), *Bacga* (Back Bridge, Bagden (?)), *Badda* (Badbury), *Bǣga (Baynton), *Bǣgloc* (Baycliff), *Bealda* (Baldham), *Beorhtmǣr* (Brigmerston), *Beorhtric* (Brixton), *Bera (Barbury), *Bīedin (Biddestone), *Billa (Bilhay), *Billing* (Bellingham), *Blacer* (Blaxwell), *Blunt (Blunsdon), *Bodel (Bowls Barrow), *Boia* (Boyton), *Botta* (Bodenham, Botley), *Brænci (Branch), *Brocc (Broxmore), *Brynca* (Brinkworth), *Brȳni* (Brims Down), *Bucge* (f) (Bugley), *Budda* (Budbury), *Bulca (Bulkington), *Cada* (Cadenham, *Cadworth*, Cat Brook, Cadley, Catcomb), *Can(n)a* (Cannings), *Ceadela (Chaddenwick, *Chadlanger*), *Ceatta* (Chaddington, Chetcombe), *Cēol* (Chelworth), *Cēolla* (Chelworth), *Cēolðrȳð* (f) (Cholderton), *Cēolstān* (Choulston), *Cilla* (Chilton (2)), *Cippa (Chippenham), *Cissa* (Chisbury), *Cnabba (Nabals), *Coda*, *Codda (Codford),

*Cofa (Conholt), Cola (Calcutt), *Colla (Collingbourne (?)),
*Corta (Corton), *Cosa, *Cossa (Corsham), Cotta (Cuttenham),
Crēoda (Crudwell), Cūda (Cutteridge), *Cufel (Coulston, Cowes-
field), Cumbra (Cumberwell), *Cȳfa (Keevil (?)), Cynegār
(Kings Hay), Cynehelm (Kilmington), Cyneweard (Kinward-
stone), Dēora (Durrington), Dodda (Dodford), *Dōmgeat
(Dauntsey), Dudd (Dudgemore), Dunna (Dinton, Doncombe,
Dunworth), *Dutta (Dutman's), Ealda (Aldbourne, Allington),
Ealdbeald (Ablington), Ealdhere (Alderton), Ealdred (Alder-
stone), *Eard, Eardwulf (Earls Court), *Earna (Arn Hill Down
(?)), Ebba (Avebrick), *Ebbel (Ebbsborne), *Eohric (Urchfont
(?)), Ēða (Edington (?)), Fitela (Fittleton), *Fobba (Fobwell,
Fovant), Fugel (Fugglestone, Fowlswick), *Fygla (Figheldean),
Gēat (Yatesbury (?)), God (Godsell), *Grytel (Grittleton),
*Gumela (Gomeldon), Gūðred (Godsbury), Hana (Hannington),
*Haneca (Hankerton), *Hēahðryð (Heytesbury), Heddi (Hed-
dington), Helmheard (Hilmarton), Heregeard (Hardenhuish),
*Hodd (Hodson), *Horning (Horningsham (?)), Hræfn (Rains-
combe (?), Ramsbury, Ramshill), *Hrōþa (Ratfyn), *Hucca
(Huckle), *Humma (Homington), Hūna (Honeybridge (?)),
Hūn(d)lāf (Hullavington), *Hylpric (Hilperton), *Idmǣr (Idmis-
ton), Imma (Imber),* Ingen, -in (Inglesham), *Ippi (Ebsbury),
Lāfa (Lavington), Lēofa (Luccombe), Locc (Loxwell), Locca,
Lucca (Lucknam), Lolla (Lowden), *Luca, Lucca (Luckington,
Luckley), *Lusthere (Lushill (?)), *Lutt (Lutsey), *Mǣssa (Mar-
ridge), Mæþelhelm (Martinsell), Manna (Manton, Manningford),
**Mehha (Mannington (?)), Milda (Mildenhall), *Mocc (Mox-
hams), Moll (Mousehill), *Mumma (Mumworth), *Nēðel
(Nettleton (?)), Nunna (Nunton), Oca, Occa (Ogbourne), Oda,
Odda (Odstock), Ordric (Orcheston), *Padeca (Patcombe),
*Pæccel (Paxcroft), *Pæcci (Paxlet), *Pættel (Battlesbury (?)),
*Peatta (Patney), *Pefe (Paven Hill (?), Pewsey), *Pendel
(Pensworth), Pendhere (Penceley), Pinca (Pink Lane (?)), Puda
(Pudnell), *Punt (Powtenstone), Putta (Puthall (?), Pitton),
*Rust (Rushall), *Seolca (Silk Wood, Selkley), *Snodd (Snods-
hill), *Soppa (Sopworth), *Stūt (Stitchcombe), Swēta (Swat-
nage (?)), Þeodwulf (Tilshead), *Tīedre (Tytherton, Ty-
therington), *Tilluc (Tinkley), *Tysse (Tisbury), Titta
(Tidcombe), Toca, Tocca (Tockenham), *Toppa (Tottenham),
Tota (Twatley (?)), Tuda (Tidworth, Tidpit), Ubba (Upton),
*Ucga (Ugford), Uffa (Uffcott), *Wæddi (Wadswick), *Wicel
(Westlecott), Wicga (Widbrook, Widgerley), *Wifel (Willesley,
Wilsford (2)), Wina (Winkfield), Wine (Winsley), *Wineca
(Winkworth), Winter (Winterslow), *Wocc (Oaksey), Wulfhere
(Wolverton), Wulfsige (Wools Grove), Wynðryð (f) (Underditch).

B. Anglo-Scandinavian

Hacun (Haxton), *Þolf* (Thoulstone).

C. Celtic

Maildub (Malmesbury).

D. French or Continental

Fallard (Faulston), *Flambard* (Flamston), *Gerard* (Gurston), *Ricard* (Richardson), *Rolf* (Rolleston).

E. Miscellaneous

Elias (Elston), *Huckman* (Hugmanton).

FEUDAL AND MANORIAL NAMES

Manorial holder's name added: Alton Barnes and Priors, Ashton Gifford and Keynes, Avebury Trusloe, Berwick Bassett, Broughton Giffard, Calstone Wellington, Chilton Foliat, Clevancy, Clyffe Pypard, Collingbourne Ducis, Compton Bassett and Chamberlayne, Coombe Bissett, Draycot Cerne, Fitzpayne and Foliat, Easton Grey and Piercy, Ebbesborne Wake, Fifield Bavant, Fisherton Anger and De la Mere, Fonthill Bishop and Giffard, Langley Burrell, Leigh Delamere, Littleton Drew and Pannell, Lydiard Millicent and Tregoze, Manningford Abbots, Bohun and Bruce, Marston Meysey, Milton Lilborne, Newton Tony, Norton Bavant and Ferris, Ogbourne Maizey, Pool Keynes, Rodbourne Cheney, Somerford Keynes, Stanton St Bernard and St Quintin, Stoke Farthing, Stratford Tony, Sutton Benger and Mandeville, Teffont Evias, Tollard Royal, Tytherton Lucas, Upton Lovel and Scudamore, Winterbourne Bassett, Dauntsey, Earls and Gunner, Wootton Bassett and Rivers, Yatton Keynell.

In the following names the manorial addition alone remains as the place-name: Cottles, Fitzurse, Kellaways, Pinkney (*olim* Cottles Atworth, Langley Fitzurse, Tytherington Kellaways, Sherston Pinkney).

Manorial holder's name prefixed: Bishop's Cannings, Maiden Bradley, *Maiden Winterbourne* (now Maddington), Erlestoke. Note also Bishopstone (2), Kingston Deverill, Monkton Deverill, Monkton.

Other manorial additions occur in early documents, but are now lost, e.g. Chisenbury *de la Folie*, Collingbourne *Valence*, Hampton *Turville*, *Nun* Eaton).

Other manorial names include: Abingdon Court, Amberleaze, Birdlime, Countess, Crawlboys, Earldoms, Havering Ho, Hungerford, Mount Sorrel, Roche Court, Warneford Place.

Miscellaneous additions: All Cannings, Beechingstoke, Bower and Broad Chalke, Broad Blunsdon and Hinton, Castle Combe and Eaton, Hanging Langford, Limpley Stoke, Market Lavington, Monkton Farleigh, Long Newnton, Rood Ashton, Steeple Ashton and Langford, Water Eaton. Added to the place-name we have: Collingbourne Kingston, Stratford-sub-Castle, Sutton Veny, Teffont Magna, Winterbourne Monkton. Parishes of the same name are distinguished as Great (Broad), Little (e.g. Cheverell, Somerford), or by the dedication of the church (e.g. Berwick, Blunsdon, Codford, Donhead, Kington, Ogbourne, Orcheston). Other additions found in medieval documents are now lost, e.g. *Childe Cnoel*, *Cold Berwick*, *Gilden Ashton*, *Hanging Stoke*, *Steeple Lavington*, *Temple Rockley*. For their interpretation consult references in Index.

FIELD AND MINOR NAMES

(a) *Field and minor names arranged under the forms of their elements, mainly as recorded in EPN. For* (n), *v. supra* 404.

ac. We may note *anlipian æc* (dat.) (BCS 748), 'solitary oak,' *la Loweoke* (t. Ed 2), *Fayroke* (1390), *Coppydoke* (1430), i.e. 'pollarded,' *la Mereoke* (1406), 'boundary oak,' from OE (ge)mære.

ād (n), 'pile or heap of ashes,' is twice found in personal names, e.g. in Walter *atte Node* (1327) in East Knoyle.

æcer. We have fields of every size from two to sixteen acres (except thirteen and fourteen), the commonest being five and ten. We may note *Thrymacres* (1261) from OE *þrēom* (dat. pl.), *Noefacres* (1261), i.e. 'nine,' *Endleveacrys* (1379), and we have also fields of twenty and forty acres. Their shape or size are recorded in *Langacres* (1328), *Brodeaker* (1232), *le Wouakere* (t. Hy 3) from *woh*, 'crooked,' *le Shirpakere* (1279), the common *Pykedeacre* (1348) or *Pickedacre* (1616) (*infra* 443), *Taylydaker* (1585), *Stertaker* (t. Hy 3), from *steort*, 'tail,' *Garbradakeres* (1176), i.e. of the breadth of a gore, *Balledacre* (1341), describing ground which is bare or has been broken into small clods (cf. NED *s.v.*); crops in *la Ryeaker* (13th), *la Bereacre* (1293), from bere, 'barley,' *Flexaker* (1570), *Lynacre* (1331) from lin, 'flax'; soil in *Chelcacre, Moracre* (t. Hy 3), *le Goryacre* (1300) from gor, 'mud,' *Stonyacre* (1329), *Salteakers* (1570); colour in *rubra acra* (1235), *Greneaker* (1430), *Whiteacre* (1409); *la guldene acre* (13th) may refer to colour or to the richness of the crops. We have reference to situation in *Brokacre* (13th), *Sladacre* (13th), *v.* slæd, *Bacheacre* (1395) (cf. Burbage *supra* 337), *Deneacre* (t. Hy 3), *Lyncheacre* (1369), *v.* hlinc, *Weyacre* (1269), *Vordrofacre* (1341), *v.* draf *infra* 429, *le Herpethackere* (1297), *v.* herepæð *infra* 435; to animals, etc. in *Hundacre* (1328), *Conyacre* (1422), more than one *Voxacres* (1374), *Gosacre* (t. Hy 3), *Hurtesacre* (13th) from heort, 'stag.' Descriptive are *Pryttyackres* (1278), *Gidiacre* (t. Hy 3), *Oldakyr* (1473), *Sweetacre* (1612). OE *hēafod-æcer*, 'strip of land lying at the head of a field,' is found several times, the earliest being *Hevedaker* (1203), and we may also note *Tweyhevedacres* (1328). We probably have reference to charitable uses in *Almesaker* (1270), *Levediacre* (1327) from 'Our Lady,' *Lampeacre* (1630) and *Preestesacre* (t. Hy 8). The reeve must have had a special interest in *Refeacres* (13th) and *le Reeveacre* (1626). Only rarely do we have reference to an individual owner as in *Simundes acre* (1224), *Martines acre* (1273). *Doleacres* (13th) must have been shared (*v.* dal).

OE æspe, æps appears alike as *asp* and *apse* in modern field-names as in *Asptree, Aspbed, Aps Close, Apsehay.*

æwielm (n), 'spring,' is found several times as in *la Ewelme* (1240) and *Smalewelme* (1279).

apulder is found several times in boundary-marks, qualified by woh, 'crooked,' in *wogan apoldran* (BCS 477), by har, 'gray,' in *haran apoldre* (ib. 748), by swete in *swete apuldre* (ib. 1030).

balke, ME (n), so common in other areas, has only been noted twice, in *Rowe balk* (1638), 'rough balk.'

balle, ME (n) is common and is doubtless used for the most part in the sense noted in Hoare's *Hundred of Westbury* (54, note b), viz. "a landmark of earth set up as a boundary mark," a meaning not recorded in NED. The earliest examples are *Loverdesballe* (1232 Lacock), *Knyghtebal* (t. Hy 3 Edington), *Cripelesballe* (1300 Stowe 798) (from OE crypel, 'burrow') and *Kyppyngesballe* (1341) from a personal name. Cf. Sandy Balls in Fordingbridge (Ha), *Sondyballes* 1488 Ipm. *Ball(e), The Balle(s)*, etc. are common in the 16th century.

banke, ME. We may note *Northbanke* (t. Hy 3 Edington) in Lavington, a much earlier use of the term in southern England than any recorded in NED. It is occasionally found later as in *Linch bank* (1591).

bedd (n) is common in *Withibed* (BCS 752). Note also *le leuer bedde* (KCD 632) from *læfer*, 'wild yellow iris,' *Nettelbedd* (1591). Later we have Leek Beds Field, Aspbed (*TA*).

benc (n) is found in *Gretebenche* (1232 *Lacock*) in Calne, *Benchacre* (1235 WM xxxiii) in Longbridge Deverill, *Hoke-benche* (1439 ib. iii) in Cheverell, *Benechehurst* (1509 *MinAcct*) in Aldbourne, *Benchefurlonge* (1570 *Add*) in Bremhill, *Benche lane* (1592 *Add*) in Bromham and *Myddle benche* (ib.) in Brem-hill and in Kate's Bench Clump *supra* 172. It is curiously restricted in the area in which it is found, and it is unlucky that in one case only do we know the site to which it is applied. In Kate's Bench it lies at the top of a gently sloping hill which rises from five to seven hundred feet. We must take it that in this area OE *benc* was used in something the same way as the Anglo-Scandinavian loan-word *banke*. In modern field-names we have Bench Piece in Seend. In *copicium voc. Benchedmapel* (1348 *For*) in Clarendon Forest we have an unexplained derivative of this word.

beorg, as in the major names, clearly refers in the great majority of cases to a barrow rather than to a hill. Several examples of 'broken' barrows have been noted as in *brocenan-beorh* (BCS 934) and it is probable that the numerous 'rough' barrows, as in *rugan beorh* (ib. 508) have similar references to barrows that have been despoiled. *finbeorh* (ib. 992) is a 'heap' barrow (cf. Finbury PN Wa 182). *Wegilbergh* (1377) is from OE *hweogol*, 'wheel.' We have reference to the soil of which it is made in *sand beorh* (BCS 699), *Stanigan beorh* (ib. 1030), *Groteneberwe* (1341) (cf. Grittenham *supra* 66); to its size or shape or colour in *lang beorh* (11th), *greatan beorhge* (KCD 778), *Bradenberghe* (1310), *grenanbyorh* (BCS 598); to the animals, etc. which frequented it in *eferbeorh* (11th) from *eofor*, 'boar,' *gosabeorg* (BCS 956), *ernebergh* (ib. 867) from *earn*, 'eagle.' In *Abbenbeorg* (BCS 500), *Brouning bergh* (ib. 867), *Ludanbeorh* (ib. 1004), *Oswaldes bergh* (ib. 677), *Wommanborw* (1422) we have references to the occupant or owner of the barrow. We find groups of barrows in *Twamberghes* (1360), *seofon beorgas* (BCS 1285) and a solitary one in *enlippanberwe* (ib. 904) from OE *ānlīepig*, 'solitary.' **beorg**, 'hill,' is most probable in *Wacche-berewe* (1317) and *Galowes barowe* (1570). *wadbeorge* (BCS 225) from OE **wad**, 'woad,' would seem to be a hill rather than a barrow and so probably is *wudu beorch* (ib. 27) and *cealdan beorge* (ib. 948).

bræc, 'land newly taken into cultivation,' is common, as in *Brache* (1212), *la Breche* (1236), *Brodebreche* (1227), *Langebreche* (t. Ed 1), *la Holebreche, le Netherebreche, le Hokydbreche* (1454),

Zelwebrech (14th), i.e. 'yellow,' *Sandebreche* (c. 1300), *Whetebreche* (1512), *Barlichbreche* (1407), *Wythebreche* (t. Hy 8), *Vernibrech* (1301), i.e. 'bracken-grown,' *la Surebreche* (13th), *Cattesbreche* (1356). It is one of the commonest of all elements in modern Wiltshire field-names, generally in the form *Breach*, *the Breach*, but we have also *the Breaches*, *the Brache*.

brædu (n), 'breadth, broad strip,' is found very rarely as in *Stikebrede* (1488), *Longe brede* (1623).

bremel, 'bramble(s),' is common in Wiltshire field-names in the forms *Brimble*, *Brimhill*, *Bremhill*. Cf. Bremhill *supra* 86.

broc is common, as in the major names. Among the commonest compounds are *Holebrok* (1227), *smalanbroc* (BCS 477), *mare broc* (KCD 641), *merebroc* (1232), *markbrok* (BCS 1127), from **(ge)mære** and **mearc**, denoting boundary brooks.

brode, ME (n), 'broad strip of land,' is found on occasion as in *Short Brode* (1446), *le Brode* (1540).

brycg. We have noted three examples of *Stanbrygge* (13th) as against five of *Wude bricg* (BCS 1093) and one of the 'brushwood causeway' type represented by *Rissin bridge* (t. Ed 6), from OE *hrīsen*, 'made of brushwood,' fully discussed under Risebridge (PN Ess 119). *la Voutbrigge* (1341 *Cor*) in Chippenham must be used of a bridge with vaulted structure and carries back the word *vault* some 50 years (cf. NED *s.v.*). Occasionally the bridge is associated with a person as in *Ailwardesbrugge* (1365), *Hanelotesbrugge* (1279). Fairly common is the metathesised form *burge* as in *Broken burge* (1590), *Shortburge* (1650). See Introd. xxi.

(ge)bur (n). A number of minor names in Wiltshire would seem to contain this OE word denoting a peasant, a husbandman, a *boor*. OE *(ge)būr-land* survives in *Burelond* (1273) and Boor Lands in Ogbourne St George. Note also *Burelinche* (1224) from **hlinc**, *Bourhersshe* (1397) from **ersc**, *le Bourefeld* (1415), *Burleazue* (t. Jas 1) from **læs** and cf. Bower Chalke *supra* 203-4. It may be that in some of these compounds we have OE **bur**, 'dwelling,' as in *Goggeboure* (1397), 'marsh-dwelling,' *v.* **gog** *infra* 452. Cf. *Radulf atte Boure* (1397).

burh is as common in the minor as in the major names with reference to ancient earthworks and the like. Commonest of all are the 'earth-burhs' as in *eorðbyrig* (BCS 600), *Orthbury* (13th), *Orebiry* (t. Hy 3), *Erthbery* (id.), *Erdbur'* (1415), and the 'old burhs' as in *ealdan burh* (BCS 1053), *la Hialdebir'* (1205) and *Oldebury* (1412). *Forthbery* (1406) and *la Vorthbury* (1522) in Colerne, suggests that the word *for(e)bury* noted in PN Ess 596 and PN Herts 296 as denoting land in front of a *bury* or manor house, may sometimes be a compound of *forth* rather than *fore*. Cf. also *Forbury* (1518) in Damerham.

Berry and *Bury* are very common in modern field-names such as *Berry Mead*, *Bury Croft*. Generally they are so called because near the manor house, but occasionally they take their name from a neighbouring earthwork.

burna is common as in the major names. We may note *rithe burne* (KCD 632), a reduplicative compound of rið, 'streamlet,' *Brokesburn* (1232), a parallel to Broxbourne (PN Herts 219) with a similar *Cattesburne* (1232) and two examples of *Lorteburn* (1232), 'dirty stream.' Cf. Hogs Mill River (PN Sr 4). *Enedeburne* (1279) is a parallel to Enford *supra* 328.

butte, ME (n) is fairly common in the plural form as in *Buttes* (1220), *Shorte* and *Longe buttes* (1289), *Brode-*, *Letelbuttes* (1393). It usually has reference to strips of land abutting on a boundary, often at right angles to the other ridges in the field, but in such a name as *Robinhood butts* (1649), it clearly has reference to the village archery butts.

buttuc (n) has been noted several times as in *le Buttokes* (1328), *les Buttekes* (1422), *le Sortebuttokes* (13th), *Collebottekes* (1438), *The Bottok* (1558). *buttucas* is found once in an OE charter (cf. PN Nth 26 n.l.) and seems there to be used of rounded slopes resembling buttocks, and it is probable that that is the sense in which it is used in most, if not all, the above examples. Cf. Ashgrove *supra* 208, and *Whitears* (1738 *Longford*) in Downton. *Short-buttocks* suggests, however, the possibility that *buttok* may sometimes be a diminutive of the term *butt(e)* *supra*.

byrgels (n), 'burial-place,' is, as one would expect, found again and again in the OE charters of a county so full of ancient burial-places as Wiltshire. Occasionally one has the simple noun as in (*to*) ðære burgilsan (BCS 600), or *byrgels* in association with a man's name as in *Hoces byrgels* (ib. 1213), *Ealhæræs byrgelse* (ib. 948), but the great majority make reference to the heathen character of the burial-place as in *hæþenan byrgels* (ib. 1030), *haþenum byrgelsum* (ib. 917). Only one example of its survival into the ME period has been noted, in *Hetheneburyelse* (1374), and only one possible example of its survival as a field-name (*infra* 491).

bysc gives rise to a number of late but picturesque names such as *Barlegged Bush* (1608), *Beggars Bush* (1649), *Pissingebushe* (1590), *Welfarebushe* (1370).

bytme (n), 'bottom,' is occasionally found as in *Holebutme* (1328), *Bittom* (1690). In printed documents it is often mistranscribed as in *le Butine* (1302). Survives in the modern *Bittoms*, *the Bittoms*, *Bithams*, *Bitham Close*, *Bittam Close*.

cattesbraȝen, ME (n), 'catsbrain,' is found several times in this county. We may note *Catesbragen* (13th StNicholas) in Broad Chalke, *Cattesbrain* (1518 Hoare) in Idmiston, *Cates-*

bruyne furlong (1608 NQ) in Chisledon, *Catbraine* (1608 WM) in Somerford. It refers to coarse soil consisting of rough clay mixed with stones. Cf. Catsbrain (PN Bk 127), Catsbrane in South Stoke (O), *Catesbrayn* (1366 Eyns), and PN BedsHu 297, PN Sr 367, PN Wa 338. The reason for the name is obscure.

causey, ME (n) is occasionally found as in *Parkerescausey* (1346) and *Causweye* (1623).

ceart, cert, 'rough common,' seems to be found once in *Chertehulle* (13th RegMalm) in Malmesbury. Hitherto it has not been noted outside Kent and Surrey.

ceastel and stanceastel are occasionally found. Grundy (*Essays and Studies* viii, 43 ff.) has discussed the use of these terms in OE charters. It is a loan-word from Lat *castellum* and Grundy shows that in more than one instance in the Anglo-Saxon charters the word is associated with Roman sites not necessarily of a military character[1]. Fragments of early walls have been found on the sites of the *stanceastla* in the Ham charter (BCS 677). We may note also *Stanchestle* (c. 1300 *Malm*) in Brokenborough, *Chastles* (1317 NQ viii) in Alderton, *le Chastle* (c. 1400 *Malm*) in Malmesbury, *Chestlefield* (1634 WIpm) in Semington, *Chestell* (1638 *Kings*) in Homington, *Chesteldeene* (1518 Hoare) in Damerham. *Chestles Fd* (*TA*) in Rolleston is near the site of an ancient village and there is a *Chestles* (*TA*) in Nettleton by Westfield Fm. It may be that other fields such as *Chessell, Cheswell, Chesells, Cheswells*, really go back to *chestle*.

ceorl, 'free peasant, churl,' is occasionally found as in *ceorle-cumb* (BCS 390), *Cherlewyk* (1281), *Charleham* (1558).

clif is common as in *Stanclyf* (BCS 458), *Stonycliff* (1311), *Redeclive* (13th), *Michel Clyve* (1253), *Bovetheclyve* (1360), i.e. 'above the cliff,' *Forthclyf* (1341), probably one which juts out, *Beveresclive* (1257), *Notteclive* (1288) from OE *hnott*, 'bare,' and several with personal names as in *wulfheres clif* (BCS 477), *Reyneresclive* (1263). Often it denotes little more than a slope. Survives in *the Cleve, Cleeve(s)* and also, fairly commonly, as *Clift*.

close, ME (n) is common but generally late. We may note *le Brodeclose* (1297), *Homclos* (1432), *Pykedclose* (1570) and *Picked close* (1634), cf. *infra* 443, *Shering close* (t. Ed 6), *Hawkeing close* (1633), *Faggot close* (1627), *Football close* (1629), *Smalbonesclos* (1353), *Wicked close* (1629), *Newbride close* (1637), *Doveclos* (1381), *Kyte close* (1638).

---

[1] It is very doubtful if Grundy is right in postulating another word *cistel* from Lat. *cistella*. *cestil* and *cystel* in OE probably both go back to earlier *cæstil* from *castellum*.

cnæpp and cnoll are fairly common as in *le Knappes* (t. Ed 2), *Goldknappe* (1570), *Grenecnolle* (1323). *Weredeknolle* (1331) in Clarendon is possibly land which had to render certain services of defence, cf. *werian land* in B.T. The variant cnyll, discussed in PN Sx 169 *s.n.* Knell, is found in *Knylle forlong* (1393 StNicholas).

cockrode, ME, is found in the form *la Cockrode* (1374 *For*) and is common in modern field-names in the forms *Cockroad*, *Cockroads*, *Cock Road*. As noted by Charles (NCPNW 300) it is an alternative word for a *cockshoot*, where woodcock are caught in nets.

coninger, ME (n), 'rabbit warren,' appears in a variety of forms as in *le Conynger* (1383), *lez Conyger* (1570), *le Connyngarth* (1503), *le Conyngary* (1570), *The Conigree* (1641). Modern forms are *Connigre*, *Connegre*, *Conygre*, *Conegree*, *Congreve*, *Conegars*, *Coneygarth*, *Coney Gore*.

coppede, ME (n), 'peaked, rounded, pollarded,' is found in *Coppydoke* (1430). It appears in various reduced forms in modern field-names as in *Copthorn*, *Copythorn*, *Coppit Mead*, *Coppit Close*, *Coppit Nowers*, *Copid Ash*.

cotsetla (n), 'cottager,' is frequent in the minor names of this county. The *cotsetla* held his cottage in return for certain services rendered to his lord, the main one being that he worked for his lord on the Monday in each week throughout the year (see Liebermann, *A.S. Gesetze* II, ii, 559). Straton (WM xxxii, 305) notes that in the Pembroke Survey we find survivals of this tenure in semi-servile tenants who are called *cotsetlers* (and the like), who held about five acres of land with their cottages and had to work for the manor farm one day a week (see further *infra* 440). Examples are *Cotsettlemede* (1270 *Magd*) in Wanborough, *past. voc. Cotsetles* (1282 *MinAcct*) in Edington, *Cotsetleham* (t. Ed 1 *Lacock*) in Calne, *Cotsetle* (1325 Pat) in Hilperton, *Cotsetelelond* (1363 *NewColl*) in Colerne, *Cotsetlelond* (1374 *WinchColl*) in Durrington, *Cossetelfeld* (1570 PembSurv) in Ramsbury, *Cossettle* (t. Jas 1 *Ct*) in Corsham, *Corsickle* (1641 WIpm) in Liddington and *Cossicle* (1844 *Merton*) in Stratton St Margaret. A Hampshire parallel is Costicles Enclosure in Colbury, *Cotseteles* 1331, *Cossakles* 1595, *Costicles* 1671 *For*.

croft, 'small enclosure,' is very common. We have reference to things growing there in *Bencroft* (1360), *Filethicroft* (1251) from OE filiðe, 'hay,' *Heycroft* (13th), *Lincrofte* (13th), from lin, 'flax,' *Ryecroft* (1331), *la Medecrofte* (1278), *Grascroft* (1224), *le Rischcroft* (t. Hy 3), *le Ferncrofte* (1341), *Thistelcroft* (1406), *Versicroft* (1362), i.e. 'furzy'; to the soil in *Sandcroft* (1370), *Chalkcroft* (1448) and *Vennecroft* (1397) from fenn, 'marsh';

to the shape in *Goredcroft* (1406), *Hornecroft* (t. Hy 3), *Pykecroft* (1457); to the animals, etc. feeding or found there in numerous examples of *Chalvecroft* (t. Hy 3), *Calvescroft* (1327), *la Schipe-crofte* (1327), *Horscroft* (1265), *Gosecroft* (1327), *Hoggecroft* (1439), *Harecroft* (1281), *Sparrowcroft* (1409), *Wolvecroft* (1485), *Brochescroft* (1383) from brocc, 'badger'; to the building to which it is attached in *Berncroft* (1291), *Colverhouscroft* (1270), i.e. 'dovecot,' *Halcroft* (13th), *Courtecroft* (t. Hy 4). Sometimes we have descriptive epithets as in *Bradecrofte* (1224), *Aldecrofte* (t. Ed 1), *Newecroft* (1373), *Grenecrofte* (1406), *Crokedcroft* (1362), *Schortecroft* (t. Hy 3), *Wildecroft* (1327), *Goldenecroft* (1224), *Dedecrofte* (t. Hy 3), *Blakecroft* (1518) and *Whytecrofte* (13th), *Ruecrofte* (1204) from ruh, 'rough,' *Opencroftes* (1550), perhaps in contrast to *Hacchcroft* (1402), i.e. one that is provided with a hæcc or gate. In *Marlyngcroft* (1383) and *Dungcroft* (1555) we have reference to the treatment of the soil. There is reference to the rent in *Pennicroft* (1517), to the time of occupation in *Sumercrofte* (1245), to the in-farm in *Homcroft* (13th), to the beneficiary holder in *Churchcroftes* (1360), *Frerescroft* (1348), to a *morgen-giefu*, i.e. a morning bridal gift, in *Morwywecroft* (1363) (cf. Mooray *supra* 186), and occasionally to individual holders as in *Semannescroft* (1265), *Petitescroft* (t. Hy 3), *Smewynescroft* (13th), *Wulsiescroft* (1227) and *Clobbecroft* (1245) held by Walter *Clobbe*. *Manecrofte* (t. Hy 3) and *Menecroft* (1382) were held in common, deriving from OE *(ge)mǣne*, 'common.' In modern field-names it appears in the form *crot*, *crat(t)*, *crate*, as well as the normal *croft*. EDD notes the Wiltshire pronunciation [kra·t]. *Crate* is similarly found in So (GrundySo 93).

crundel, generally used of a quarry or a chalk pit, is common in the OE charters, as in *scealdan crundle* (BCS 635), from sceald, 'shallow,' *lytlan crundelle* (ib. 756), *durnen crundel* (ib. 477), from dyrne, 'secret,' *cealc crundel* (11th), i.e. 'chalk,' *thry crundelas* (BCS 27). *Morðcrundel* (ib. 1268) was the scene of some forgotten murder. Only rarely does the word survive till later days, as in *Crondelle* (1518) and *The Crundyll* (1623).

culfre, 'dove, pigeon,' is common in such compounds as *Culverhay(es)*, *Culver Leaze*, *Culverwell*, *Culver Close*.

cumb is as common in the minor as it is in the major names. We have reference to the soil in *stancumb* (BCS 757), *Cleycombe* (1377); to shape or size in *mycelan* and *smalan cumbe* (BCS 477), *widan cum* (ib. 595), *Holewecumb* (1312); to things growing there in *brembel cumb* (BCS 757), *cærscumb* (ib. 948) from cærse, 'cress,' *fileðcumb* (ib. 1067) from filiðe, 'hay,' *higcumb* (ib. 27), i.e. 'hay combe,' *Vernecumbe* (t. Hy 3), *Thornecombe* (1331); to animals or birds found there in *sceapa cumb* (BCS 832), *wulf-cumb* (ib. 588), *Foxcombe* (1373), *Horscomb* (1357), *Ywecumb* (1333), *Neatcumbe* (1234) from neat, 'cattle,' *Swynecumb* (t. Hy 3), *Glydecumbe* (1253) from *glida*, 'kite,' *Ernescumbe* (1199) from *earn*, 'eagle,' *wrokcumb* (BCS 717) from *wrocc*, 'buzzard' (cf. Wraxall *supra* 113), *crawancumb* (ib. 508), *Goscombe* (1430). Sometimes we have reference to a person as in *Alwoldescumb* (1249).

dæl, 'valley,' is occasionally found as in *Shorvedale* (1227) (cf. Sharcott *supra* 351) and *lasse dale*, 'smaller valley' (BCS 586).

dæl (n), 'part,' in the compound *feorðandæl*, 'quarter,' is found in *Wheteferendelles* (c. 1300), 'quarter sown with wheat.' It probably survives in *Farthingdale* in Kington St Michael.

dal, 'portion or share of land,' especially of the common field, is occasionally found as in *la Withydole* (14th), *Suredole* (1400), *Shortdole* and *Longdole* (t. Ed 6), *Longe doles* (1603), *Ditchdoles* (1680). *Dolmede* (1249) must be meadow-land divided into *doles*. In *dolemannes beorh* (KCD 655), *Dalemannesforlong* (1240) we must have reference to a village official who was responsible for arranging these *doles*.

(ge)delf is common in the compound (*le*) *Standelf* (c. 1300), 'quarry.' In modern field-names it sometimes takes the form *Standhill, Stanhill*.

denu, 'valley,' is common in the minor as in the major names.

dic, 'ditch, dyke,' is very common indeed as one might expect in a county so full of ancient earthworks and the like. With a descriptive epithet we have *Depedych* (1348), *greatandic* (BCS 1071), *Langediche* (t. Hy 3), *ealdandic* (BCS 782) (several examples), *fulandic* (ib. 987), *rugan dic* (ib. 699), 'rough ditch' (several examples), *scortan dyc* (ib. 921), *Wytediche* (1267), *wogan dic* (BCS 479), 'crooked' from *woh*, *folcesdic* (ib.), *Meredich* (13th), 'boundary' from OE (ge)*mære*, *mylendic* (BCS 469), 'mill-ditch,' *la Waterdiche* (1257). Some have the name of the owner before them as in *Aldefrythesdich* (1259), *Ealcheres dic* (BCS 477).

draf (n), '*drove*,' for cattle or sheep is common, much commoner than in counties hitherto treated, except perhaps Huntingdonshire where it has reference to the fen-droves. We may note *andlang drafæ* (BCS 705), 'along the drove,' *ultra Dravam* (1212), 'beyond the drove,' *Bradedrave* (1220), *la Drove* (1277) and *la Fordrove* (1570).

dun, as was to be expected, is as common among the minor as among the major names. We have several examples of *beorh dun* (BCS 49), bringing before us a typical Wiltshire landscape—

a barrow-strewn down. Equally characteristic are *clænan dun* (ib. 917) and *smeðandune* (ib. 748). References to the animals feeding there are common, as in *Lambedoun* (1348), *Oxedoune* (1329), *Rotheresdune* (1273), *Chelvedune* (958); less common are references to crops as in *Otedoune* (1341), *Whaddon* (1463), *Rydone* (13th). One of the commonest of all compounds in later days is *cow-down* as evidenced by such phrases as "The western end of the *cowe doune* of the mannor" (1591 PembSurv) and "The parish *cowdowne*" (1723 *Kings*) in Brixton Deverill. Cf. also "cow commons, called *cow downs*" as quoted in EDD from Wiltshire in the early 19th century.

ea, 'river,' is found in a few field-names such as *Emead*, *Yeamead*, *Raymead*. For *Yeamead* cf. the common Devonshire stream-name *Yeo* (PN D Pt I, xxxiii), for *Raymead* cf. Reybridge *supra* 103.

edisc. A few examples of this word, denoting 'small field, aftermath pasture,' have been noted as in *Tatan edisc* (BCS 27), with a personal name, *hides edisc* (ib. 672), apparently a genitival compound with *hid*, 'hide of land,' hence 'pasture belonging to the hide,' *le Edische* (1403), *Edisshe feild* (1566).

emnett (n), from earlier *efnet*, 'level ground,' is found in *Emnet* (1522) in Colerne and probably also in *Emelet* (1227) in Chittoe and, with affixed article, in *Nemnet* (1397) in Colerne, and *Lemnette* (1250) in Alvediston.

ende is very rare, Wiltshire in this respect offering a great contrast to such counties as Hertfordshire and Essex and (in a less degree) to such counties as Devon, Surrey and Warwickshire.

ersc, 'stubble land,' is very rare. We may note *Walershe* (1292), *Bourhershe* (1397), probably from bur, 'peasant.'

ett (n). This collective suffix is rare in Wiltshire and has only been noted in one early example of *le Thornet* (1503) and two examples of *haselette*, 'hazel-thicket,' one in Savernake (1248 Ch) and the other in Winterbourne Gunner (1364 *Ct*). The latter example very probably gave name to the *Hazlitt* family. Among modern field-names we have *Shrubbitts, Bushets, Rushetts*.

It is also used (cf. PN Ess 578–9) to form nouns from adjectives, cf. Roughett and Smithwick *supra* 56, 247. Another such derivative (*The*) *langet*(*t*)[1] is found in a group of field-names confined to the north and north-west of the county and is used there of fields which are long and narrow. Sometimes it takes the form *langate*. Cf. GrundyGl 17.

---

[1] This word is wrongly taken as a form of *landshard* in NED *s.v.*

falod, 'fold,' is as rare in the minor as it is in the major names. We may note *wifiling falod* (BCS 677), probably from the personal name *Wifel* (cf. *supra* 326) and *Derefold* (1503), *la Wodfolde* (1446).

feld is as common in the field and minor names as in the major names. Among the more technical terms are *le Portfelde* (1438) in Marlborough, the 'town' open field, *le Tounfelde* (c. 1450), *le Innefeldes* (1451), *Homefeild* (1583), *Cossetelfeld* (1570) (*v.* cotsetla *supra* 427). *Tenauntry Feildes* (1630), *Tenantry Feild* (1697) have reference to the old common or open-field husbandry of parts of a manor occupied by tenants, as distinct from the lord's demesne. *Þunresfeld* (BCS 469), 'field of *Þunor*,' may be a relic of heathenism.

fenn is very rare. We may note *le Fenne* (1261).

fleot is used of a small stream in various field and minor names in Wiltshire, appearing later in the form *Fleet*.

furh, 'furrow,' is fairly common as in *weter furh* (BCS 477), *mær furh* (ib. 757) (from (ge)mære, 'boundary'), *ealdan furh* (ib. 704), *Wetefur* (1341) (probably 'wheat furrow'), *brode furgh* (BCS 752), *Frogge furrowe* (1626).

furlang as a name for a division of the common field is very common indeed. We have several examples of *Portfurlang*, i.e. belonging to the town, from 1243 on, and of *Tounforlong* (in similar relation to the village or hamlet) from 1234 on. *Twyforlong* (1341) must be a double furlong. We have reference to its site or soil in compounds with *Dene* (13th), *Slad* (1277), *Quab* (13th) (i.e. 'marsh'), *Mor* (1227), *Sand* (13th), *Stan* (1348), *Strod* (1356) (i.e. 'marsh'), *Mersh* (1260), *Flint* (1265); to size or shape in *Brodefurlong* (1261), *Langeuorlange* (BCS 672), *Scorteforlang* (t. Ed 1), *Mochelforlong* (1445), *Wohefurlang* (1212) (from woh, 'crooked'), *Goridefurlong* (1365), *Pyked furlonge* (1558), *Wydeforlong* (13th); to crops or other vegetation in *Berefurlonge* (1224) (from bere, 'barley'), *Benforlong*, *Riforlong* (1265), *Pusforlong* (13th) (i.e. 'pease'), *hegforlong* (BCS 922), *Barlyfurlong* (1503), *Witheforlong* (1323), *Thornfurlong* (1333), *Rixforlong* (t. Ed 1) (from rysc, 'rush'), *Gorsteforlong* (13th), *Myntefurlong* (1518), *Papifurlang* (1227) (i.e. 'poppy'); to animals or birds in *Bulleforlong* (1455), *Cou-*, *Shep-forlong* (1327), *Stotforlong* (1333), *Craneforlong* (1227), *Colverforlong* (13th), *Dokforlong* (1336). Very rarely have we any reference to the owner or occupier as in *Elstanforlong* (1281), *Presteforlong* (13th). In modern field-names it occasionally appears as *Furland*, sometimes given by the schools as *Firland* or, with dialectal *v*, as *Verland*.

fyrhðe, 'wood,' is common as in the major names. Examples

are *la Fridhe* (1256), *le Frithe* (1312), *Newfrith* (1362), *le Gret frythe* (1536), *Coufryght* (1460). Survives as *the Freath*. The form *Thrift*, so common in some parts of the country, does not seem to be found in Wiltshire.

gærstun, 'grass-enclosure, paddock,' is very common indeed as in *Garston* (1204), *la Garstone* (13th), *le Garseton* (1323), *Heigarston* (13th), *The Gaston* (1553), *le Hanginggarston* (14th), *Cleygarstone* (13th), *hors gærstun* (BCS 757). In such compounds as *Otegerstone* (13th), *Pease Gaston* (1586) it has clearly come to mean nothing more than 'small enclosure, paddock.' Modern forms include *The Garcons*, *Gasson(s)*, *Garstons*, *Gastons*, *Gaskins*, *Gascoignes*, *Gayson*, *Garson*.

gafol (n), 'payment, tax,' is found in *Gavilhacche* (1375), *Gaveldone* (1460). Cf. *s.n.* Galleywood (PN Ess 234).

gara, 'gore, triangular piece of ground,' is common as in *la Gare* (1241), *la Gore* (1269). More precise references to its shape are found in *hokedan garan* (BCS 917), *scearpan garan* (KCD 687). We may note also *Olde gore* (13th), *Forsakenegore* (1327), *gemænan garan* (BCS 542) (from (ge)mæne, 'held in common'), *Outegore* (1328), *le Haywardesgore* (1345), *flitgaran* (BCS 705) (from *flit*, 'strife,' used of disputed land), *le Fursgore* (1348), *Medgore* (13th), *Stonygore* (1362), *Wolvegore* (1331). Occasionally it is compounded with a personal name as in *leofheres garan* (10th).

gardin, ME (n) is occasionally found as in *Oldegardyn* (1439), *Southgarden* (1489), *le Saffron garden* (1536), *Hopgarden* (1634).

geat, 'gate, gap,' is common. It is often compounded with a personal name as in *leofsiges get* (BCS 985), *Titferðesgeat* (ib. 734). Some of these names are ambiguous—*hundesgeat* and *hremnesgeat* (ib. 748) may have reference to the animal or bird or to persons nicknamed from such. *crypel geat* (ib. 699) has reference to a low opening in a fence through which sheep can pass from one field to another (*v. cripplegate* in EDD). Other compounds are *dyrnan geat* (BCS 677) (from dyrne, 'hidden'), *wide geat* (ib. 705), *horsgeat* (ib. 611), *streteyate* (1259), *Burghȝate* (1327), *Droveyate* (1354).

graf(a), 'grove, copse,' and **græfe** with the same sense, are common. The latter is often difficult to distinguish from **græf**, 'pit,' but the probabilities are that the latter is only rarely present. From graf(a) we have *schortegrove* (1257), *le Brodegrove* (1271), *Hanegrove* (1275), perhaps from *hana*, 'cock,' *Cokgrove* (1343), *Okegrove* (1327), *Shepegrove* (1438), *le Whomegrove* (1500), i.e. home-grove, *Kingesgrove* (1211), with occasional compounds with a personal name as in *Alverychesgrove* (1382). Early examples are *haran grafan* (BCS 1213) (from har, 'grey') and *ellen grafan* (ib. 748) (from ellen, 'elder-tree'). From græfe or græf we have *Kinges grave* (1203), *Corsgrave* (cf. Corston *supra* 50), *Alfredthesgrave* (1248), *Perciesgrave* (13th). *Hasel-grave* (1275) must be from græfe. Confusion of græfe and grafa is common as in The Grove in Lydiard Millicent *supra* 37 and PN Herts 244.

hæcc, 'gate,' is occasionally found as in *la Hecche* (1257), *Gavilhacche* (1375) (from gafol, 'tribute'), *Est-*, *Westheche* (1375). *The Hatchet* derives from the OE *hæcc-geat*, 'hatch-gate.' Cf. *hæcc geat* (KCD 739) in Hannington and PN Ess 580.

(ge)hæg, 'woodland enclosure,' is common as in *la Heghe* (1281), *le Nywehey* (1460), *Oldeheye* (1400), *Aldeheye* (1422), *Grenehey* (1406), *Meneheye* (1241) (from (ge)mæne, 'common'), *Privetheye* (14th), *Hetheneheye* (1279) ('overgrown with heath'), *Rokehay* (1453), *Snytehey* (1399) (from snyte, 'snipe'), *Colverhey* (1283) (common) (from culfre, 'wood-pigeon'), *Oxeheye* (1331), *Raheie* (BCS 922) (from ra, 'roe'), *Colteshey* (1460), *Chalfhey* (1451), *Puriheye* (1332) (from pirige, 'pear-tree'), *Maderhey* (1390) and frequent compounds with personal names as in *Howeleshey* (1241), *Peggeshey* (1330), *Semannesheye* (1347).

hæð is occasionally found as in *Blakehethe* (13th), *Kokeshethe* (13th), *Bluntesheth* (1293), *Alsieshethe* (c. 1400), the two latter being derived from personal names.

ham and hamm are as usual very difficult to differentiate even if one has forms going back to the OE period. Thus in the bounds of Burbage and Bedwyn respectively (BCS 1067 and 1213) the same piece of land is referred to as *bidan ham* and *bydan hamm*. Examples of *hamm* in ME and Early ModE are fairly common, and here no doubt the names go back to OE hamm and the name is to be interpreted either as having reference to a strip of ground by a river or to a small enclosure. We may note *la Hamme* (1249), *les Hammes* (1627), *Stonihamme* (1270), *Langehamme* (1370), *sidan hamme* (BCS 757) (from sid, 'wide'), *Brodehamme* (1445), *haywardes hamme* (BCS 922), *Personeshamme* (1291) (doubtless a piece of glebe-land), *Savageshamme* (1300), *Palmereshamme* (1341), *Horsehamme* (1591), *le Folehamme* (13th). *Sakenehamme* (1278) is doubtless a piece of land about which there has been a dispute, from OE sacan, 'to bring a suit.' In many other cases though we have no early forms in *hamm* as distinct from *ham*, the probabilities are all in favour of hamm. Such are *Chercheham* (1245), *Refham* (1327) and *Revesham* (1420), *le Parsonsham* (1422), *Cotsetleham* (t. Ed 1) (*v.* cotsetla *supra* 427), *Haywardes-hame* (13th), *Comenham* (1570), *Charleham* (1558) (from ceorla (gen. pl.), 'free peasants'), *Parsonage Ham* (1608). *Dockyham* (1638) was probably one grown over with *dock*, *Threhurnedham*

(1373) was a three-cornered one. It is very common in modern field-names such as *the Ham, Long Hams*.

ham appears as a first element in many field-names, developing later to *home* and is there descriptive of a field which is in the immediate neighbourhood of an estate or mansion. The earliest example is Home Fd in Hankerton (*Homfeld* c. 1300 *Malmesbury*), the next is *Homecroft* (1503). In later field-names we have compounds with *close, croft, field, grove, hanging, hill, laynes, leaze*.

hamsteall is rare. Two examples have been noted: *le Hamstall* or *Hamsteed* (1632) and Homestall in Wootton Rivers.

hamstede has been noted once in *Hamsteede* (1667) in Chippenham.

hangra, 'slope,' is fairly common. In *clophangra* (BCS 508) the first element probably denotes a hill. We may note also *Appellhangere* (t. Hy 3), *Haselhangere* (1259), *Apshanger* (1300), *Treuhangre* (1420) in which we clearly have reference to wooded slopes, a common later sense. On the other hand the original sense 'slope' is preserved in *le Flexhangere* (t. Ed 1) from fleax, 'flax.'

heafod, 'head-land, unploughed land at the end of the arable where the plough turns,' is occasionally found, both in the singular and in the plural, as in *linkes havede* (BCS 500), *le Medeheden* (1453), *le Mead hades* (1558). It is used in a similar sense in the compounds *Heved aker* (1203), *Tweyheved acre* (1328). In modern field-names we have *the Headen, the Heddon, Hades*, all plural forms. We also find the compound *andhēafod* in OE as in (be ðam) *andheafdan* (BCS 689).

healf (n) is found several times in Wiltshire but has so far not been noted elsewhere in the course of the Survey, except in *Langehalve* (1275 AD i) in Breamore (Ha). The chief examples are terr. voc. *Hundhalve* (1301), *Ryghalve* (1341) (from ryge, 'rye'), *Thornhalve* (1353), *Langehalve* (1371), *Culputtehalve* (1375) (probably from col-pytt, 'charcoal pit'), *Brodehalven* (1383), *Sherdhalve* (1393) (from sceard *infra* 445), *Fyvehalf* (1518) (perhaps the common expression for four and a half), meadow called *Tething* (i.e. 'tithing') *Halfe* (1630). The exact sense is uncertain and it may not have the same sense in all the compounds. In the last two examples it probably stands for half-(acre). In some it may have the sense 'side, part.' Later examples are *Three Halves, Seven Halves*.

healh, 'nook, corner,' is somewhat rare. It appears in the form *le Hale* (1224), but also as *le Hele* (1243) in Alderbury, *la Hele* (14th) in Lacock, *le Hele* (1243) in Alderbury, *le Hele* (1528) in Damerham. Cf. s.n. Heale *supra* 373. Note also *Vernhale*

(13th) (from **fearn**, 'bracken'), and occasional compounds with a personal name such as *baldwineshealh* (BCS 225).

hecge (n) is occasionally found as in *ruwan hecgan* (BCS 677), i.e. rough hedge, *beowan hammes hecgan* (ib.), *Blakehegge* (1331), *la Quenehegge* (1312), *Medehegge* (1406), *Coldehegge* (1420), *Roberhegge* (1518).

hechinge, ME (n). A common Wiltshire field-name element. The earliest examples noted are *la Hechinge* (1232 *Lacock*) in Lacock, *le Heyching* (1360 *WinchColl*) in Durrington, *le Hicchynge* (1489 *Ct*) in Fittleton, *Pewsey hitching* (1609 *Longford*), *Hitchinge* (1611 WIpm) in Stanton Fitzwarren, *The Hitchen* (1638 WM xxx) in Chisledon, *The Hitchin* (1649 *SarumD and C*) in Cricklade. This must be the word *hitching*, recorded in the EDD from Oxfordshire, as used of "part of a field ploughed and sown during the year in which the rest of the field lies fallow" and is to be associated with the word *hitch* used in Oxfordshire, Berkshire and Wiltshire of the changing of crops in an open or common field, and the term *hitchland* or *hookland* used of "a portion of the best land in a common field, reserved for vetches, potatoes, etc., instead of lying fallow for two years" (WiltsGloss *s.v.* *hookland*). The ultimate history of the word is obscure. Kennett in his *Parochial Antiquities* (*s.v.*), from which the EDD reference comes, speaks of this land as being sometimes 'fenced' off, and in the discussion of Innage (PN Wa 45–6) the editors were inclined to associate these words with OE *hæcce, hecce*, 'fence, rails,' rather than 'hook.' The Wiltshire alternation between *hookland* and *hitchland* suggests, however, that the association should rather be with *hoc* and *inhok* (*infra* 436, 438). In modern field-names we have the forms *Hitching*, *Hitchen, Hitchin, Hitchens, Hitchings*. Cf. Hitching (GrundySo 86), Hitchen, Hitching (GrundyGl 16).

herepæð is frequently used in OE charters of an 'army road.' It survives later as *Harepath*. Grundy (GrundyH 90) notes that *herepæð* in the English and Latin versions respectively of BCS 635 is rendered *lawpath* and *legalis semita*. See further his article *passim*. **hereweg* is not on record from OE but survives in Hareways Fields *infra* 510. For **herestræt** cf. Hare Street Fm *supra* 87.

hid, 'hide,' is occasionally found as in *le Hyde* (1440), *le Halvehyde* (1258).

hielde, 'slope,' has been noted in *la Hulde* (1227), *le Hulde* (13th), *le Hylde* (1509).

hiwisc, 'measure of land on which a household is settled,' is found in *la Wytehiwisshe* (t. Ed 2), *Oxehuish, Long huishe, Broad huishe* (1636). Modern *Yewish*.

hlaw, hlæw is commoner in names found in the OE charters than in later documents. In OE we have the form *hlaw* in *beaceshlawe* (BCS 917), *hlæw* in *lortan hlæwe* (ib. 705), *posseshlæwe* (ib. 756), *hlew* in *fontanhlewe* (ib. 469), *eangyð ehlew* (ib. 1004). *lew* is found in ME *Wolvingeslewe* (13th), *low* (from hlaw) in *Couleslowe* (1310) and *Lullowe* (1383). *v.* Introd. xx.

hlinc is very common and a characteristic Wiltshire element. Primarily denoting 'a bank, rising ground, steep slope, escarpment,' it developed various technical senses such as "terraces a few yards wide on the escarpment of the downs, the remains of ancient earthworks, narrow ledges along the steep face of the down, probably made by sheep feeding there, a raised turf bank dividing or bounding a field, a strip of greensward dividing two pieces of arable land in a common field" (WiltsGloss *s.v.* *linch*). The boundary sense is clear in *mærhlinc* (BCS 757), *land score hlinc* (ib. 597). Reference to size or shape is common as in *wogan hlinc* (ib. 477) from woh, 'crooked,' *Longelinche* (1224), *Gretelynche* (1328); to its surface in *ruwan hlincæ* (BCS 390) from ruh, 'rough,' and *Smethelinge* (13th); to soil in *stan hlinc* (BCS 757), *stenihte hlinc* (ib. 477), *Stonyelynch* (13th), *Drytlynch* (1341) from dryt, 'dirt,' *Grotelinche* (1341) from greot, 'gravel,' *meos hlinc* (BCS 677) from meos, 'moss.' Among other compounds we may note (*a*) *grenan hlinc* (987), *hwitan hlinces* (BCS 1213), *Blacklinge* (1594), (*b*) *deor hlinc* (BCS 795), *hafoc hlinc* (ib. 1004), *Foxlynche* (1350), *Wormlynche* (1318), (*c*) *ðorn hlinc* (BCS 1071), *Privet lynche* (1289), *Leslinche* (1335) from læs, 'pasture,' *Puselinche* (1327) from peose, 'pease,' *Esterheillinge*, *Westerheylinge* (1240), possibly 'the more easterly and the more westerly hay-linch.' Compounds with personal names are occasionally found as in *wines hlinc* (BCS 795), *Chelewyneslynche* (1518), *Uggedeslinche* (1276). It commonly survives in the form Linch, Lynch, occasionally as *link*. See also *linchet infra* 453.

hlot (n) is fairly common, but late, as a term for land assigned by lot as in *le Lott* (1540), *Littlelott* (1570), *les Lottes* (1637). It is very common in *TA* in the compound *Lotmead*. An early example is *Lott meade* (t. Ed 6).

hlypgeat (n), 'leap-gate,' is fairly common. See under Lypiatt Fm *supra* 96.

hoc, 'hook, bend, projecting corner,' is occasionally found as in *Combeshoke* (1348), *le Hooke* (1558). It may also represent land taken into temporary cultivation (cf. inhok *infra* 438 and GrundyGl 16, GrundySo 237–8).

hoh, 'hill,' is as rare in the minor as in the major names. We may note *le Howe* (1297), *le Blakehooge* (1327) and, possibly, *Personeshouwe* (1348), i.e. 'parson's hill.'

holh, 'hollow,' is common in the OE charters, especially in the plural form, as in *catthola* (BCS 477), *hwitanhola* (ib. 748), *oteres hole* (ib. 782).

holmr. One example of ME **holm,** 'water meadow,' has been noted in *Longeholme* (1393) in Harnham.

holt, 'wood,' is occasionally found as in *Boghholte* (1289), perhaps containing *bog,* 'bough,' *Brockeholt* (1570) and *Hestanesholt* (1300) from a personal name.

hrycg, 'ridge,' is as common in the minor as in the major names. It survives in *Long Rudges, Rudge Leaze, Rudges, the Ridge.*

hryding, 'clearing,' is occasionally found as in *Rudinges* (13th), *Westrudyng* (1487), *Newe Rydinge* (1570).

huluc (n), 'hovel,' is found several times compounded with **stede,** 'site,' as in *Hulkestede* (1232 *Lacock*) in Chitterne, *Holkestede* (1341 *Rental*) in Broad Hinton, (1460 ib.) in Semington, (c. 1460 ib.) in Steeple Ashton. Note also *Swineholke* (t. Ed 1 *Lacock*) in Lacock, *Hulkehille* (1536 *MinAcct*) in Maiden Bradley.

hus. *le Culverhouse* (1264), 'dove-cot,' *Stokhus* (1335), 'timber-house,' *Preosteshous* (1347), *le Bachouse* (1402), 'bake-house,' may be noted. Note also Daye House and Day House *supra* 217, 282, i.e. 'dairy-house.'

hyll is as common among the minor and field-names as in the major names. We may note a few of them: *Pleyhill* (BCS 635), *Blerianhylle* (ib.) from *blerig,* 'bald,' presumably used of a bare hill, *Grotehull* (1360) from **greot,** 'gravel,' *Popylhill* (1496), cf. *popple-stone,* 'pebble' (WiltsGloss), *Mylkehulle* (1269) from its good pasturage, *Torhull* (1295), a repetitive compound of the Celtic loan-word **torr,** 'rock, rocky peak,' *Isnehulle* (1328), apparently from *īsen,* 'iron.' *Stroutehulle* (1348) from OE *strūt,* 'strife,' probably was on some boundary (cf. Studborough, PN Nth 29) and so was *Menhulle* (14th) from *(ge)mǣne,* 'common.' *Chesthull* (1449) in Winterbourne Stoke may contain ME *cheste,* 'strife' (cf. Chesland *supra* 125) or, in this area of ancient burials, it may contain OE *ciest,* 'chest, coffin' (cf. *s.n.* Chestham, PN Sx 216). *Velethulle* (1397) probably derives from OE *fyllet, fiellet,* 'place cleared by felling,' surviving in Gloucestershire *fellet, vellet* (EDD and PN Ess lvi, *s.n.* Filham). *Tothulle* (BCS 922), 'look-out hill,' is an early example of a well-known compound.

hyrne, 'corner,' is occasionally found as in *Medhurne* (1310), *Blyndehurne* (1518), *The Hurne* (1635). It survives in *Hern, the Hurn.*

hyrst, 'wood, wooded hill,' is not very common. *hunighyrst* (BCS 469) is presumably one where bees swarmed. *Durhurst* (1270) is from **deor,** 'animal, deer.'

inhecche, ME (n), used in the same sense as *inhok infra*, is found in *Innedge, Innidge* in Aldbourne (t. Jas 1 *LRMB*).

inhok, ME (n). Examples of this element, fully discussed under Innox Mill *supra* 134, are common in field-names. We may note *le Hinhoc* (13th WM xxxiii) in Lacock, *Northynnoke* (1428 Aubrey) in Kington St Michael, *le Inhok(e)* (1495 *Ct*) in Zeals, (1522 *NewColl*) in Colerne, *Inocks* (1549 WM xliv) in Clyffe Pipard, *Innock Corner* (1588 WM xxxiv) in North Wraxall, *Hinnex* (t. Jas 1 *Ct*) in Corsham, *Innox* (1634 Ipm) in Semington. It survives as *Inhooks, Innocks, Innox, Innicks, Innex, Enocks, Enox, Enock, Hinnocks, Ninnicks*. Found also in So, Gl with the same variety of forms.

Compounds of in(n) with land, mæd, mor and wudu are in common use to denote fields, etc. attached to the home-estate (cf. NED *s.v. inland*). *inland* sometimes appears as *England*.

lacu, used of a slow-moving sluggish stream, is common in this county. In OE charters we may note *bromlace* (BCS 600), *blacan lace* (ib. 699), *foslace* (ib. 788) (from *fos*, 'ditch'), *æsclace* (ib. 1093), *rishlak* (ib. 904), *ealdan lake* (KCD 778). Other examples are *Redelake* (1224), *Smalelake* (1249), *Foullelake* (13th), *Fernelake* (1341), *Pullelake* (1278) (from pull, 'pool'). Compounds with a personal name are occasionally found as in *Gurdaneslake* (1348), *Waltereslake* (1419). Found in modern field-names as *Lake*.

læs, læswe (dat.), 'pasture,' is perhaps the commonest of all field-name elements in Wiltshire. Reference to the animals feeding there is common as in *Coulese* (1347) and *Cowenlese* (1327), *Oxenlese* (1383) and *Oxelese* (c. 1400), *Rotherlese* (1446) and *Rutherlease* (1564) (from hryðer, 'cattle'), *Horse leaze* (1439), *Sheepe lease* (1603), *Lamblees* (1540). *Sumerlese* (t. Ed 1) is common. *le Inleaze* (1609) stands in contrast to *le Utterleys* (1563). *le Towne lese* (1515) must have been by the 'town' or village (*v.* tun). *Nightlees* (1563) must have reference to pasture-land where the cattle are left out at night. Compounds with a personal name are very rare as in *Edytheslese* (1453). Very common indeed in modern field-names in the form *Leaze*. Among the commonest compounds are Cow Leaze, Ox Leaze, Larks Leaze, Fatting Leaze. *Leazowes* and *Leazeways* are variants deriving from the OE dat. sg. *læswe*, later *leasowe*. Occasionally *leaze* appears now in the form *leys*. But some examples of *leaze* go back to earlier *ley, leyes*. Cf. leah *infra* 440. Curious compounds are those with cultivated plant-names including *Bean Leaze* (3), *Pease Leaze, Oat Leaze* (3), *Wheat Leaze* (2). Possibly these go back to earlier *leys* or they may refer to grass-lands which were later cultivated.

lain, ME (n) is common and characteristic of Wiltshire. We may note *Lainmede* (13th), *Leynecroft* (1503), *le Personage leynes* and *Bakonsleyn* (1540), *Hillelayn* (1542), *le Innerleynes* (1563), *Breach laynes*, *Gorelaynes* and *le leynes* (1570), *The Layns* (t. Jas 1), *Millaynes*, *East Laynes* and *Muncton Laynes* (1626), *Rush laynes* (1638), *Ground called Leynes* (1641), *the Laines* (1706). The exact sense of the term is unknown. It has been discussed in PN Wo 391, PN Sx 310 *s.n.* Tenant Lain and PN K 354 *s.n.* Rolvenden Layne. Probably it denotes land which is periodically allowed to lie fallow by being sown in regular *laines* or divisions. See further *lain* (EDD and NED) and discussion by Wallenberg (PN K *loc. cit.*). Surviving in *the Laynes*, *the Lines*, *Loin(s)* and perhaps *Lion(s)*.

land is very common indeed and is doubtless often used in the technical sense 'strip of land in an open field,' as in *Fourteene land* (1662), the very common *Wowlond* (1289), *Wowelond* (13th), *Woghelond* (1302), *Wooland* (1612) from **woh**, 'crooked,' *Croked land* (1603), *Brodelonde* (1240), *Smalelond* (13th), *Langeland* (1220), *Shortelonde* (13th), *Hevedlond* (t. Ed 1), where the plough turned. We have reference to the soil in *Sandilande* and *Cleyelande* (13th), *la Cleytelonde* (14th) from *clǣgiht*, 'clayey,' *le Stonylonde* (1315), *Blakelond* (t. Hy 3), *Whitelonde* (1328), *Sourlande* (1427); to the period or state of cultivation in numerous examples of *Aldelonde*, *Oldelonde* and *Eldelonde* (13th), with occasional *Newelond* (1357), *Dead Land* (1558), *Wyldland* (1442); to its being taken into cultivation in *le Brechlonde* (13th) (*v.* **bræc** *supra* 423); to crops in *Barlicheland* (1227), *Otlond* (1310), *Wetelande* (1227), *la Benelonde* (1347), *Ryland* (1428), *la Rienelond* (1335) from *rygen*, 'covered with rye,' *Pislond* (1328), *Flexlond* (1397); to vegetation in *Fernylond* (1240), *Netelilonde* (1290), *Redelond* (1224), *Thornelond* (1518), *Clenelond* (1269), *Roulond* (1269), *Papyland* (1448); to animals or birds in *Bollelond* (1350), *Horslond* (1363), *Calvelond* (1348), *Goselond* (1397), *Dokelond* (1258); to the shape of the 'land' in *Gorelonde* (1393), *la Garedelonde* (1240), and *la Goredelond* (t. Hy 3), *Pykedelond* (1335) and *Pikydlond* (1518); to situation or outline in *Denlond* (1297), *Floudelonde* (1328), *la Sculflond* (t. Hy 3) (from **scylf**, 'shelf'), *Lynchelond* (1393) (from **hlinc**, 'hill'), *Hollelonde* (1265), *Brokenlond* (1357), *le Hangindelonde* (1270), *Sunderlande* (1468), *Sounderlond* (1406) and *Synderland* (t. Jas 1) (from *sundor* 'apart'). *le Innelonde* (c. 1300), *la Inlond* (1350), *Inlond* (1460) are common, and such lands formed part of the home estate. Note further *Tenpoundworthelond* (1336). We have reference to the owner or occupier in *Erleslond* (1397), *Presteslond* (1348), *Revelandes* (1397), *Hinelande* (10th) from OE **higna**, 'monks';

cotsetelelond (1363) (*v.* cotsetla *supra* 427); to the lack of such in *Nomanneslond* (1518).

One common compound of land is *Monday-land*. We may note *Mondaylonde* (1346 *Add*) in Castle Combe, *Mundaylond* (1447 *Merton*) in Highworth, *Mondaislonde* (1468 *MinAcct*) in Trowbridge, *Mondailonde* (1488 *DuLa*) in Oaksey, *Mondaylond* (1566 *Add*) in Bremhill, also 'tenement and garden called *Mundies thing*' (1556 WM xxx) in Castle Combe. In one or two cases this may be a compound with the personal name *Monday* or *Munday*, but there can be little doubt that it usually refers to land held by the tenure of giving the first day of the week to the service of one's lord (cf. cotsetla *supra* 427). Such holders were called *Lundinarii* or *Monday men*. Reference is made to such in the Lacock cartulary and elsewhere (cf. WM xxxii, 305, 315).

landscearu (n), 'boundary, landmark,' is common in OE charters as in *wyrhtena landscare* (BCS 795) from *wyrhtena* (gen. pl. of *wyrhta*, 'wright'), *eatstanes landscare* (ib. 985) (from a personal name), *Landeschore* (1227), *la Landschere* (1241), *Lanshare Lane* (1495), *la Landshere* (1566). Modern *Landshare*.

launde, ME, 'open space, glade,' is occasionally found as in *le Launde* (1420), *Laundecopice* (1477), *Drakelawnde* (1483). Commonly survives in the form *Lawn*.

leah is as common among the minor and field-names as in the major. It appears normally as *-ley*. There are a good many examples of modern names in *-leaze* which go back to 17th- and 18th-century *-ley(s)* and in one case, viz. Broadleaze in Calne, the name seems to go back to *Brodelye* (1232 *Lacock*).

mæd is very common indeed. We have reference to size or shape in *miclanmed* (BCS 469), *Brodemed* (13th), *Smalmede* (1249), *la Langemede* (1341), *Ryngmede* (1338), *Goremede* (1453) (from *gara*), *Pyked mead* (1563), *Picked meade* (1649); to soil or the character of the countryside in *Steanemeade* (1626), *Ven meade* (1630) (from *fenn*), *Lawndmede* (1473) (from launde, 'open country'), *Hardemed* (1373), *Smethemed* (1227); to the creatures feeding there in *Ruthermede* (1323) (from hryðer, 'cattle'), *Exemede* (1383) (from *exen*, 'oxen'), *Calfmede* (t. Hy 4), *Haresmed* (1425), *Dokemede* (1397), *Cranemede* (1341), *Colvermede* (1399), *Swanemed* (1350), though this is ambiguous as the first element might be from *swān*, 'peasant'; to plants or trees growing there in *segmede* (BCS 921), *Wythymede* (1491), *Ryxemede* (1460) (from rysc, 'rush'), *Garsmede* (1281), *Reodemede* (1447), *Thachmeed* (1377), *Salʒmed* (1224) (from sealh, 'willow'), *Apuldurmede* (1362), *Birchinmede* (1535), *Wychmede* (1224); to situation in *Combemede* (1351), *Hulmede* (1273), *Hulymede*, *Holemed* (13th), *Clyvemede* (1466), *Dounemede* (1447), *Suthmede*

(1232), *Estmede* (1357); to presence or absence of water in *Rounyngmeade* (1570), *Dryemed* (1381), *Spirts meade* (1599). We have reference to the owner, holder or beneficiary holder in *Kinggesmede* (1277), *Eorlesmede* (1382), *Shreeves meade* (1632), *Prestmede* (1383), *Chauntry meade* (1558), *Lordesmede* (1509) and several examples of *Ladymede* (1281), *Mannemed* (14th), *Childer-mead* (1603), *Baldewenemede*, *Vincentesmede* (1471), *Aylyvemede* (1341) (from OE *Æþelgifu*), *Radgaresmede* (1309), *Huginesmed* (1269). More technical are *Portmede* (1365) in Bishopstrow, 'the common town-meadow,' *le tounmede* (13th), 'farm-meadow,' *Akermannemed* (1341), *Cotsettlemede* (1270) (cf. cotsetla *supra* 427), *Heywardesmede* (1224), *le Rhevesmede* (1315), numerous examples from 1242 on of *Dolmede, le Dolemed, le Doolemed*, 'mead held by shares,' of *Lottmeade* from t. Ed 6, 'meadowland assigned by lot,' of *Sondermede, Sowndurmede, Syndremeade*, 'separate meadowland,' from 1463 on, and of (*la*) *Inmede*, 'home farm meadow,' from 1283 on. We may note also *Menmeade* (t. Ed 6) and *Meane meade* (1606), 'meadowland held in common,' from (*ge*)*mæne*, 'common,' *Lam*(*m*)*as meade* (1574) (cf. *infra* 452), and *Tythe mede* (t. Jas 1).

(ge)mæne (n), 'common,' is a common element in such compounds as *gemænan garan* (BCS 390), *Menhulle* (14th), *Meneheye* (1241), *Menewode* (1328), *Meane meade* (1606), *Meane goore* (1651). Modern names probably containing this element, for they lie on parish boundaries, are *Mann Leys, Mandown, Manland*(*s*), *Manleys, Manbreach, Menyett*.

(ge)mænscipe (n), 'community,' gives rise to *Manship* on the boundary of West Ashton.

(ge)mære, 'boundary,' is common in the OE charters and later as in *Wulvruneimere* (1525), *Tornetrowe meere* (1650). Modern compounds are *Mere Ash, Merfield, Merrell, Mere Lands, Meer Meadow, Meerman Field*, all on parish boundaries.

mere is very common, specially in the Old English charters. We may note a few of the more interesting examples there and elsewhere: *þyrran mæræ* (BCS 508), from *þyrre*, 'dry,' *Hyne mere* (1279), 'monks' mere,' from higna, *grendlesmere* (BCS 677) in Ham, probably so named from the monster Grendel, but in actual fact not at all a romantic mere, *Padmere* (1430) and *Froggemere* (1409), from the toad and the frog respectively, *Rowremere* (1403), from OE *hragra*, 'heron' (cf. Raughmere, PN Sx 51).

mersc is common, as in the major names. We may note *Portmarshe* (1538) in Calne, the 'town' marsh, *Smethemers* (1307) and *le Rowemerse* (13th), *Walemerse* (1245) in Dilton, 'serfs' marsh' (*v.* wealh), *Cornmersh* (1374).

mor is common, as in the major names. We may note *Scinneresmore* (1224), 'wizard's marsh,' and *Madmannamore* (t. Hy 3), 'meadmen's or (possibly) madmen's marsh,' *Dikedemore* (1245), *Grutemore* (1267), from greot, 'gravel,' *Snytemore* (c. 1300) from *snyte*, 'snipe,' *Nuthermore* (1327), 'lower moor.'

myln is common. We may note *Portmelne* (1219) in Marlborough, 'town mill,' *Tunmulle* (13th), *Mahewesmelne* (1269) from the personal name *Mayhew*, *Isomberdesmylle* (1540), *mill called Stangrist* (c. 1300), *la Toukyngmulle* (1338) in Horningsham carrying back the word *tucking-mill* some 130 years earlier than NED.

myrig (n), 'pleasant,' is occasionally found as in *Muryhulle* (1439), *Meryfyld* (1465), *Muryfelde* (1518).

nattok, ME (n) has been noted three times in early Wiltshire material: *nattok* (13th RegMalm) in Malmesbury, (c. 1400 *Malm*) in Kemble, and *le Nattok* (1445 *Eton*) in Hullavington, surviving in the form Nadhooks (*infra* 464). This word, of unknown origin and meaning, has been discussed in previous volumes (cf. PN Nth lii, 277, PN Sr xlv, 364, PN Ess 586).

nest (n) is fairly common as in *Swanesneste* (1329), *Crowes neste* (1594), *Gose neste* (t. Jas 1), *Brocknest* (1609), i.e. 'badger-nest,' *Longgnest* (1649) and later *Duck's Nest, Kite's Nest, Cuckoo's Nest*.

ofer, 'bank,' is very rare as in *Northovere* (1374).

ora, 'border, bank,' is more common as in *lind oran* (BCS 917) from lind, 'lime-tree,' *Padenore* (1227), *Owere* (1518), *The Ore* (1635). It survives as *Oar, Wor, (the) Woor*, and seems to be commonly used of a field by the bank of a stream, but can refer to other banks also. In *Nowers* we have affixed *n* from earlier *atten ore*.

orceard is occasionally found as in *ordceard* (BCS 755), *le Oldeorchard* (1360).

pæð is common in the OE charters as in *sticelan pað* (BCS 588), 'steep path,' *lambapæð* (ib. 734), *holan paþe* (ib. 756), *stodpeð* (ib. 1004) from *stōd*, 'stud,' *smalan pæð* (BCS 832), *grene pað* (KCD 778). In post-Conquest documents we have *le Swonespathe* (1374) from swan, 'peasant,' *le Horspath* (1485) and *Prestespath* (1535). Sometimes the word is compounded with a personal name as in *cuðhardespæð* (BCS 1213).

parke. We may note *Hompark* (1291) and *Whome parke* (1558).

pearroc, 'small enclosure,' is found in *Perrok* (t. Hy 3) and *Collins Parrock* (1629). *parrock* is still in use in Wiltshire.

pece, ME (n), 'piece,' is in fairly common but late use as in *Cornerpece, Tomlynspece, Hedpeces* (1570), *le Hangingepece* (1590), *Hookepece* (1619), *Ringes peece* (1641).

penn, 'pen, enclosure,' is found in *la pinne vel penne* (BCS 796), *Stretpen* (13th), *Calfepanne* (1518), *Neates penne* (1591) from neat, 'cattle.' It is fairly common in later field-names as in *The Penn, the Cowpens, Oxpens, Cuckoo Pen*.

penok, pinnok, ME (n), apparently a diminutive of penn *supra*, is found in *Penok* (t. Hy 3 *Edington*) in Lavington, *Pynnok* (1341 *Rental*) in West Ashton, *Pynnokes* (1397 Trop) in Broughton, *Pynnocke* (1491 *Ct*) in West Ashton, *Pynhok* (1500 Pat) in Corsley. It survives in two or three modern examples of fields called *Pinnock(s)*.

pightel, ME, 'small field, enclosure,' so common elsewhere, has only been noted once and that in the modern name *The Pightle* in Aldbourne. Equally rare is its nasalised variant **pingle**. We have noted *Pyngellis* (1503 *MinAcct*) in Highworth and the modern *Pingles* in Brinkworth.

pikede, ME, is very common in the ModEng form *picked* in such field-names as Picked *Acre, Bit, Close, Common, Corner, Crate, Field, Five Acres, Furlong, Ground, Ham(s), Heath, Hill, Hoe, Hyde, Lains, Leaze, Marsh, Mead, Piece*. A variant form is *picket(t)* as in *Picket(t)* Close, Furlong, Mead. Occasionally it retains the form *piked* as in *Piked* Crate, Down, Ground, Hoe. More often it appears as *peaked* as in Peaked Breach, Close, Croft, Field, Furland, Furlong, Gore, Mead, Meadow, Patch. It denotes an area with sharp corners or angles. *peaked* seems as a rule to go back to earlier *piked* rather than to be a fresh derivative from *peak* as distinct from *pike*.

pil (n), 'stake,' is found in *le Pyle* (1341), *la Pile* (1535).

place, ME (n), is found in *Loggeplace* and *Pyryplace* (1338), *Amyseplace* (1391) and *Prytesplace* (1513) from personal names and *Galowesplace* (1558).

plæsc, 'shallow pool,' is found occasionally in the forms *plash, plaish*. We probably have a diminutive of this in *Plashet* (*TA*) in East Knoyle and *Plasketts* (*TA*) in Bemerton, both in low-lying land, and *Medowplasshet* (1549). *Plaskett* (*TA*) in Chute is, however, on high ground though there is a pond at the bottom of the field. Possibly this is the word *plashet*, 'fence of living wood,' discussed in PN Ess 488–9 *s.n.* Pleshey. For the *k*-form cf. *s.n.* skilling *infra* 454.

platt. See plott *infra* 444.

plegstow, 'place of play,' where village sports and the like were held, is common in Wiltshire. We may note *Ric. atte Pleistowe* (1333) in Bishops Cannings, *Nich. atte Pleistowe* (1327) in Wilcot, *Will atte Pleystowe* (1333) in Tidcombe, *Robert atte Pleystoue* (1333) in Calne, *William atte Pleistow* (1327) in Winterbourne Stoke, *Pleystouaker* (1311) in Homington. A common alternative is **plegstede** as in *Pleistude* (1278) in Highworth, *Thomas atte Pleistede* (1333) in Castle Combe, *Nich. atte Pleistede* (1333) in Kington St Michael. We may also note *Playshott* (1598) in Knoyle, *Playestock* (1594) in Whitsbury, *Pleyhill* (BCS 635) in Collingbourne, *Pleystrete* (1278) in Maiden Bradley. Note also modern *Play Mead*. **plegstow** appears in modern field-names as *Plaisters, Plaisterers*.

plek, ME (n), 'small piece or plot of ground,' is occasionally found as in *The Plecks* (1650, 1676). See further PN Sr 217, PN Wa 331.

plott, ME (n) is occasionally found as in *Penyplotte* (1397), *Honyplott* (1401), *le Garden plotte* (1540), *Tounynge plott* (1561), *Rogers plott* (1650). Occasionally found later in such forms as *Platt, Rush Plat, Mead Plat, Plat Bush*.

pludd, ME (n), 'pool, puddle,' is found in the surname *atte Pludde* (1363) and in *Chauncelers pludde* (1567) in Mere. The word belongs definitely to the west and south-west (cf. refs. in NED) and survives in Somersetshire *plud*, 'the swampy surface of a wet field.'

pol is common as in *le blake pole* (BCS 458), *hyssa pol* (ib. 595) (deriving possibly from OE *hysse*, 'tendril,' cf. DEPN *s.n.* Hurstbourne), *henne pole* (KCD 632), *brytta pol* (ib. 778) ('Britons' pool'), *Pukpole* (1232) ('goblin pool'), *Padepole* (1243) ('toad-pool'), *Stakepole* (1289), *Hornpoule* (1341), *Cornerpol* (1422), *Cleypoll* (1553). The most interesting is, however, *Nikerpole* (1272 *For*) which gave name to Henry de *Nykerpole* (1333 SR) and *Nicapoolescroft* (1578) in Mildenhall. This is from OE *nicor*, 'water-monster' (cf. *Nikerpoll* in PN Sx 562). It is not always easy to distinguish it from **pull**, 'pool,' cf. *le Horspull* (t. Ed 3 *Rental*) in Edington which is *le Horspole* (1358 Pat).

ponde, ME, is occasionally found as *la Horsponde* (1283), carrying the compound back some 400 years earlier than the NED.

port, 'town,' is common as in *Portmelne* (1219) in Marlborough, *Portmede* (1365) in Bishopstrow, *Portfurlange* (1243) in Alderbury. In *Portmannesethe* (13th) we have reference to a *port-man* or burgess (cf. NED *s.v.*). There are also several examples of *port-way*, denoting a road to a town, and one of *port-street*.

puca, 'goblin,' is common in field-names as in *Pukpole* (1232 Lacock). Later we have *Pookcroft, Puck Hay, Pockeridge*.

pull, 'pool,' and **pyll**, 'small stream,' are not easy to distinguish in Wiltshire, at least in ME. The latter should normally appear as *pill* in ModEng. *la Pulle* (13th) and *Pokepulle* (1528), 'goblin pool,' may be noted.

pund (n), 'enclosure, pound,' is found in *North punde* (1486).

pundfald (n), 'pinfold,' is found several times as in *la Pound-fald* (13th), *Pundfold* (1300), *Punfald* (1422).

pytt is common. We have descriptive adjectives in *hwitan pyt* and *blacan pyt* (BCS 479) and possibly in *Redeput* (1348), though this may contain hreod, 'reed'; reference to things found there in *chelc pyt* (BCS 1216), *Stanputte* (1224), *Torfputtes* (1348), *la Clayput* (1348), *le Marlengputte* (1348) (many examples), *Lampet* (1328) ('loam-pit'), *Lymepyttes* (1509), *Mamepitt* (1551) (probably for *malmepit*, from OE *mealm*, a mixture of sand and chalk). *wulf pyttan* (BCS 917) are clearly pits used for snaring wolves; the reason for the compound *Oxeneputte* (t. Hy 3) is not so obvious. *Pukeputte* (13th) is a goblin pit, and numerous are the examples of compounds with a personal name as in *Prattesputt* (1348), *Dodesput* (1278). *Possession pitt* (1650) is mysterious.

quabbe, ME (n), 'boggy place,' is found in *le Quabbe* (13th) and modern dialectal *quob*.

quarre, ME (n), 'quarry,' is fairly common. Cf. Quarr (Wt), *Quarraria* c. 1150 BM. Common in modern field-names such as *Quar(r) Close, Ground, Leaze, Piece, Quarland, Tile Quar Ground*. See Quar sb.[2] (NED).

ræw, 'row,' is found in such names as *hlinc ræwe* (BCS 782), *le Stanrewe* (13th), *la Rewe* (1309). Generally becomes *row* but occasionally *rew*. Cf. Introd. xx.

rakke, rekke, ME (n) is common in modern field-names in the form *rack* as in *Rack Close, Hill* and *Mead, Racklands, Racks*. The only early example that has been noted is Rack Close *infra* 482, going back to the 15th century. Its sense is uncertain and more than one word may be involved. There is a dialect word *rack* used in Wiltshire of a narrow track or pathway and also of a boundary.

sceard, 'notch, gap,' is common and characteristic of Wiltshire. It is used of a gap in a hedge, a narrow passage between walls or houses (WiltsGloss *s.v. shard, shord, sheard*). Used also of a gap in a dyke, cf. Shepherds' Shore *supra* 251 and *Dichsherd* (1269). The colour of the soil revealed in the gap gives rise to such in *þeth wite scerd* (sic) (BCS 962), *le Redesherde* (1362 For). The surname *atte Notescherde* (1333 *SR*) in Roundway, perhaps containing as its first element OE *hnott*, 'bald, shaved,' with reference to the baring of the hill-side. The commonest of all compounds however is one with OE *wægn*, 'waggon,' found in such names as *wanserde* (13th StNicholas) in Broad Chalke, *le Wansherde* (13th Bradenstoke) in Chitterne, *Wansherd* (1224 FF) in Lavington, *Wenschirde* (t. Hy 3 *Edington*) in Edington, *Wenscherd* (1310 Ipm) in Yatesbury, *Wayneschard* (13th Trop) in Codford, *Whansherde* (1383 *MinAcct*) in Britford, *Weynsherde* (c. 1400 *Malm*) in Malmesbury. There can be little doubt that this has reference to waggon-roads making their way up the downs through some 'gash' or 'gap' in the hill, though it may in some cases be simply a 'gap' in a hedge or dyke, through which a waggon could make its way. *Shard* and *Shord* are similarly used in So and Gl (GrundySo 239, Gl 18).

scipen, 'sheep-shed, cattle-shed,' is found in *le Rede Shupene* (1304 Pat) in Pewsham, *Cowshippen* (1616 DKR xxxviii) in Chippenham and *Shependoune* (1550 Pat), *Shepton Down* (1629 WIpm) in Edington.

slæd is as common in the minor as in the major names. It denotes a shallow valley or depression and usually survives in the form *slade*.

smoke, ME (n) is found as an element in various field-names, usually with æcer or *acre* as the second element. We may note the following early examples: *Smocaker* (c. 1220 *Magd*) in Hilmarton, *la Smokacre, Smokfurlang* (1276 StNicholas) in Broad Chalke, *le Smochacre* (13th *Bradenstoke*) in Overton, *Smokehalfacre* (c. 1310 *Malm*) in Hankerton, *Smokeacre* (c. 1500 ECP iii) in Calne, id. *alias Reveacre* (1518 Hoare) in Idmiston, *Smokeclose* (t. Jas 1 *LRMB*) in Southwick, *Smokeacre* (1635 WIpm) in Boyton, *Smoakacre* (1725 WM xlvi) in Broad Town. Cf. *Smokacres* (1326 AD vi in Andover (Ha)). The term *smoke-acre* is noted by Canon Goddard in WAM (xlvi, 368) as used (t. Chas 1) of land in Codford, and he rightly associates it with the term *smoke-silver* and *smoke-penny*, used of taxes paid to ministers of divers parishes (Pat 4 Ed 6) in lieu of tithewood, but used also of the money paid to the sheriff for holding certain lands. The tax was probably so called because it was a householder's tax and *smoke-acre*, etc. were names attached to lands held by such payments. In later days it often appears in the form *smock* as in *Smock Furlong, Smock Land, Smock Acre*.

snæp (n), 'boggy land,' is found occasionally in the form *snap*, *snape* and is recorded in So, Do and D as a dialect word.

splot (n), 'patch of land,' is found in *la Grenesplotte* (1317 WM viii), *William atte Splotte* (1327 SR), *Moresplot* (1277 *Rental*), *la Splotte* (1373 *Ct*), *le Splottes* (1397 *Ct*), *Homesplott* (1667 Recov), *Milsplat* (1721 ib.).

stæppe (n), 'step,' has been noted in *les Stappes* (1380) and *bridge called Steppe* (1300).

stapol, 'pillar, post,' is occasionally found as in *stænenan stapole* (BCS 782), *la Stapele* (1227), *Pykstapel* (1279).

stede, 'place, site,' is common as in *ealdan treowstede* (BCS 477), *Okestede* (1463), *Chiricstede* (BCS 1285), *Hulkestede* (1232) and *Holkestede* (1400) (*v.* huluc *supra* 437), *Pleistude* (1278) (cf. plegstow *supra* 443), *Shepstede* (1310), *Lewestede* (1448) (from hleo, 'shelter'), *Litelstede* (1485), *Millstede* (1513). *scelcesstede* (BCS 469) is a compound of *scealc*, 'servant.'

steort, 'tail of land,' is common in the minor as in the major names. Often used in the plural as in *Sterts, Stearts, Stirts*.

sticce (n) is fairly common. The earliest example is *sticche, clenan sticche* (BCS 1127). Others are *Forlangesticche* (13th), *Delstiche* and *Stielstiche* (1204) (from *stigel*, 'path'), *Hayward-sticche* (t. Hy 3), *Sulstiche, Goddingistiche* (1235), *Shortestiche* (1243), *Bukstiche* (1256), *Gosestiche* (1277), *Akermannestiche* (13th), *Puttelestyche* (1306) (from *pyttel*, 'mouse-hawk'), *The Stycchies* (1393), *Eststyche* (1473), *Stitche* (1603), *Catstitch* (1727). The uniform *i*-vowel makes it impossible to derive these forms from the common OE *stycce*, 'piece,' for that must in Wiltshire have given some ME forms in *stucche*. Rather it must go back to an OE *sticce*. There is a dialectal *stitch* denoting 'a ridge or balk of land,' especially a strip of ploughed land between two water furrows (*v. stitch* sb.[3] in NED), but the early forms of this have *steche* rather than *stiche* and, so far as our knowledge goes, this is definitely an East Anglian term. For the present therefore the interpretation of this word must remain an unsolved problem. Equally difficult is what seems to be the derivative EModE stitching found in *Stitchinge* (1570), *Stiching* and *Overstitchings* (1629–30), *Stitchings* (1682) and *Long Stitchings* (1725).

stigel is found in a number of compounds. It is difficult to know if it means 'small path' or 'stile' as we now understand it. We may note *Welkestile* (1227), perhaps one used by walkers, *milesstile* (1260), a compound of *mile*, and *crockerenstyle* (1518), one used by potters.

*strigel (n) is found once in the name *le Strizele* which survives as Strills, in Bratton, *infra* 479. This would seem to be identical with Ger *striegel* (OHG *strigil*), French *étrille*, a loan word from Lat *strigilis*, 'curry-comb.' It may be that the word was a loan-word in OE also and is here applied to the shape of the field. The outlines of the field resemble a curry-comb and the curved site at least is certainly old.

strod is found in the common *Bolstrod* (1364), 'bull-marsh.' So also later *Stroud(s)*.

stybb, 'stump,' is common in boundary-marks. We may note *Apeldorestob* (BCS 458), *thornstib* (ib. 598), *ellernestubbe* (ibi 672) (from ellern, 'elder'), *þe elde stobbe* (ib. 750), *ellenstub* (ib. 788), *crowenthornisstibbe* (ib. 904), *ellenstybbe* (ib. 917), *ællenstybbæ* (ib. 948), *Withenstubbe* (13th) (from *wiðegn*, 'withy').

sundor (n), 'separate, apart,' is found in a few minor names in Wiltshire. It is applied as a rule to pieces of land on the border of the parish. Cf. Cindrum *infra* 462 and note also *Sunderhill, Cinder Leaze* among modern field-names. Cf. *Syndermead* (GrundySo 160).

sunt, ME (n), 'marshy ground,' first noted in PN Sx 201 and further discussed in PN D Pt 2, x, is found in the personal name William *atte Sonte* (1333 *SR*) in Berwick Bassett. Mr G. M. Young (PN Nth xlvii) noted for us that in documents relating to Somerford Keynes, land in that parish is alternatively known as *Pillesmore* and *Pyllesunt* in 1328 and 1364.

sweora (n), 'neck, col,' is occasionally found as in *le Swere* (13th), *le Swyre* (1328), *la Swere* (1397).

taile, ME (n) is found in *Goretaile* (1377).

tenement, ME (n) is found in *Hikkestenement* (1363).

þorn is common, especially in boundary-marks as in *greatan þorn* (BCS 477), *eald thorn* (11th), *culuer þorn* (BCS 672) and *hafuc þornæ* (ib. 948), named from the wood-pigeon and the hawk respectively, *fegeran þorne* (KCD 632) from *fæger*, 'fair.' The use of thorn-trees as boundary-marks gives rise to the numerous compounds with har, descriptive first of a grey stone or thornbush and then by sense transference, of a boundary-stone or thornbush as in *haran þorn* (KCD 778) and later *Horthorneforlong* (1348), *Hoorethornes close* (1570), *Whore Thornes* (1587). *wroht þorne* (BCS 748) is compounded with *wrōht*, 'accusation, strife,' and probably has reference to some boundary dispute. We may also note *Applethorne* (13th), *Blakethorne* (ib.), *Calvesthorne* (1248), *Houndesthorne* (13th), *Coppethorne* (1331) and *Copped Thorne* (1671) with reference to thornbushes that have been cut, *le Housthornes* (1348) and the curious *Resting thorne* (1606), which is perhaps ironical.

þorp. Two unidentified examples have been noted—*Thrup* (t. Hy 3) in Warminster and *Edbaldesthrop* (1348) in Ramsbury.

þwang (n), 'thong, strip,' is found several times as in *Thwanges* (1241), *The Thwange* (1253), *le Twange* (1281), *le Longe Twange* (1289), *le Twang* (1341), *le Twanges* (1360). It survives in such field-names as *Long Thong*.

þyrne, 'thorn bush,' is occasionally found as in *rugan þyrnan*, *brembel þyrnan* (11th), *le Blakethurne* (13th), *la Horethurne* (1331), 'boundary thorn.' *v.* þorn *supra*.

torr seems occasionally to be used as in *la torre* (BCS 458) in Dauntsey and *Torhulle* (1295 StNicholas) in Broad Hinton.

trenche, ME (n), noted in PN Wo 143 as a term for a track through a forest, is found in *Randolvestrenche* (1343) and *the upper trench* (1650) in Clarendon Forest.

tun, 'farm, hamlet, settlement,' is common in such compounds as *la Tounmede* (13th), *Tounforlong* (1234), *Tunmulle* (13th) and in later field-names such as *Town Leaze* and the very common *Townsend*. *town* need not imply anything larger than a village or hamlet.

twicene (n), 'cross-roads,' is found occasionally. It appears in the forms *Twitchen* and (possibly) *Twitchell*.

tyning (n), 'fencing,' is characteristic but late as in *The Tinning* (1608 Lewis) in North Wraxall, *Tyning* (t. Jas 1 Ct) in Corsham, *New Tyning* (1640 WIpm) in Bradford on Avon. Cf. Tyning in Radstock (So), *la Tunyng* 1278 Ass and GrundyGl 19, So 241.

weg is very common. We have reference to its size in *bradan weg* (10th), *smalanweges* (BCS 1216); to its antiquity in *ealdanweg* (ib. 1053); to its sloping character in *healdan weg* (ib. 783) (from *heald*, 'sloping'), *Haldeweye* (1269) and *lytlan hyldeweg* (10th) (from hielde, 'slope'). 'Hollow' ways are common as in *ealdan hole weg* (BCS 970), *Eldeholewey* (1227). Boundary roads and paths are common as in *mearcwege* (BCS 1067) and *le Mereweye* (KCD 584), *Greene mereway* (1641). The purpose of the way is indicated in *Droveweye* (1393), *Bereweye* (13th) and *higwege* (KCD 641) to carry barley and hay respectively, *Lichwey* (1270) for a funeral procession (from *lic*, 'corpse'); its destination in *cyricweg* (10th), *wuduweg* (10th), *burhweye* (ib. 672), *Fordewey* (1289), *wylle weg* (ib. 595), *le Waterweye* (1343). We have reference to the soil in *stan weie* (KCD 641), *stanihtan weg* (10th), *Sandweie* (KCD 632), *Greneway* (1269) and *hwitanweg* (BCS 756). *stiȝelweye* (BCS 717) suggests a way which is only a narrow path, *Pyleway* (1323) must be marked by stakes (OE *pīl*) and so must *stuperdewey* (1373). The latter would seem to be a derivative of OE *stūpere*, 'post, prop,' and denote a road either marked by or made with posts or props. *stappeweye* (1335) would seem to be one with steps, *Twiseledeweye* (13th) was 'forked' (from OE twisla) and *Ryngweye* (1327) was circular. We have reference to the users of the road in *weale weg* (BCS 1067), 'Britons' or serfs' road,' *le Salterweye* (1327), *Chepmanneweie* (1224), *Irmongerweye* (13th), *Prestwey* (1570), *Packway* (1791), and to the payment of toll in *Tholeweie* (1227). Occasionally the first element is a personal name as in *Lyvyldeweye* (1348) from OE *Lēofhild* (f.) and *Luttesweye* (13th).

wer, 'weir,' has been noted several times as in *clif were* (BCS 752), *mylen ware* (ib. 1030), *Plumwere* (13th), *Vysshwere* (1327) and *le Fysshwere* (1356).

weyour, ME (n), 'pond, dam,' has been noted once in *The Weiere* (1630).

wic. A few additional examples have been noted including *Wodewyke* (13th), *Cherlewyk* (1281), *Couewyk* (1327), *le Wyke* (1330), *Eldewyk* (1362), *Wodewardwyke* (1383). In modern field-names we find *Cowitch* (cf. Cowage *supra* 269).

wiell(e) is very common. We may note *Maydenewelle* (1260) and three or four associated with saints' names: *Seyntedythwelle* (1409), *Sidefollewelle* (t. Ric 2) from St Sidefull, said to be buried in Exeter (cf. Exeter St Sidwells, PN D 437), *Keyneswell* (1587) from St Keyne, and perhaps *Petreswelle* (1279). *Hurdlingwell* (1397) is presumably a well protected by *hurdles*, but the noun *hurdling* has not hitherto been recorded.

wisc, 'damp meadow, marsh,' is occasionally found as in *ceab wisc* (BCS 782), *Bikewisse* (t. Hy 3), *Wikewissh* (1336). Cf. modern *Wish Mead*.

worþ, 'enclosure,' is occasionally found as in *la Worthe* (1283), *le Worthe* (1485), *Riworthe* (1247), *Wyteworth* (13th), *Estworthe* (1419).

worþig, 'enclosure,' is found in *Worthy* (t. Hy 3) in Maiden Bradley, *campo uocata Worthy* (1357 *GDR*), now Worthy Mead in Malmesbury (though this may alternatively be a complimentary nickname) and in *la Worthy* (1518) in Idmiston. It is found in a few modern field-names such as *Great Worthy*.

wudu is very common. We may note *Mortuus boscus* (1227), i.e. 'dead wood,' *Bremlewud* (1241), from **bremel,** 'bramble,' *Inwode* (1269) and *Homewode* (1353) as against *Outwode* (1333), *Menewode* (1328) from *(ge)mǣne,* 'common.'

yfer[1], 'bank, edge, escarpment,' is characteristic of the county doubtless because of the steep escarpments of the chalk downs, though it is used of other banks also. It is commonest in the form *Ivers* as in Burcombe, Compton, and Sutton Ivers, with reference to the steep rise of the downs above those places. Sometimes it appears in the form *Ivory*.

(b) Some of the more common elements in field and minor names either not found or of very rare occurrence in records earlier than the 16th century.

bake, beak. The vb. *beak* (WM xxvi, 89) is used in Wiltshire in the sense 'to chop up with a mattock the rough surface of land to be reclaimed, afterwards burning the parings' and the sb. *beak* is similarly used of ploughed land thus reclaimed. This word in the form *beak*, but still more commonly in the form *bake*

---

[1] This is the correct form rather than *yfre* as given in EPN.

is very frequent in Wiltshire field-names. The compound **burn-beak** (very often in the form **burn-bake**) is similarly used (*op. cit.* 95) in the sense 'to reclaim land by paring and burning the surface before cultivation.' It appears occasionally in the corrupt form *burnbrake*.

barton, 'farm-yard, rick-yard,' is in common use locally (E. H. G.), but is not often found in early records. We may note Pig Barton, Cow Barton. It occasionally takes the form *barken*.

bell is common with *Acre, Close, Croft, Lands, Lawn, Leaze, Meadow.* Doubtless it often denotes fields so called because they provided the endowment for the church bells, but some may derive from inns of that name. This is certainly the case with *Bell Living* in Imber *infra* 482.

burgess is found in a number of field-names, generally in association with ancient boroughs as in Burgess Ground in Cricklade, Burgess Mead in Malmesbury and Westbury, Burgess Piece in Ludgershall, but occasionally elsewhere, as in Burgess Meadow in Durrington. Note *Burgess Bargain* (1677).

clap-gate, a swing gate shutting on either of two posts, is fairly common.

clapper, 'rabbit-burrow,' is occasionally found as in *Clapper Piece, Clapper Close.*

cold harbour is a common term of reproach for buildings or places which by reason of their situation, soil, etc. give no satisfaction to their users or occupiers. For a full discussion of this name, which is usually of quite late origin, *v.* PN Sr 406–10.

drift and **drift-way** are common terms for a cattle path or lane.

dring, drung are used of a narrow passage or lane. Cf. WM xlvi, 492–3 for the former.

folly is common in minor names whether in the name The Folly or in such compounds as Folly Barn, Copse, Cottages, Farm (several), Plantation, Row and Wood. For none of them have we any early authority, the earliest being some four or five examples recorded in 1773 (A and D) as *The Folly*. The use of the term *folly* in place-names has been discussed in an Appendix to PN Wa (382–5) and, in rather fuller revised form, in *Romania* (lxii, 378–85)[1]. There it is shown that the original use of Folly in place-names was undoubtedly as a nickname for some form of human folly, amusement or pleasure, and that there was no foundation for the theory that *la Folie* in French place-names was a dialectal form of *la feuillée*, used of some shelter made of foliage and the like. The history of most of the Wiltshire examples

---

[1] After the publication of this article there appeared in NoB (xxv, 130–73) an independent study of these names by Karl Michaelsson which after exhaustive examination of the evidence came to much the same conclusion.

of *folly* is that they similarly are examples of this or that kind of human folly, etc. It should be noted however that in southern England, especially in Hampshire, Berkshire and Wiltshire, *folly* is often applied to copses, plantations and the like. Some of these may be examples of human folly, but that can hardly be true of all. This extension of the term still presents a problem in semantics (*op. cit.* 384–5).

friday is occasionally found in field and minor names, especially in the compound *Friday St.* Note also *Frydaysham* (t. Jas 1) and *Frydayesgate* (1603) in Ashton Keynes. Here we may have to do with a personal name. It is probably a nickname of inauspicious omen. Cf. fully PN Sr 410–11.

gog, 'bog, quagmire,' is occasionally found as in *The Gog, Gog Ground, Gogmire.* 'A boggy place called the Gogges' (Aubrey NH 25).

goss, goss(e)y are common for *gorse, gorsy.*

grip, 'trench, water-channel' (NED sb.²), is found perhaps in one or two minor names. Its application in Grip Wood (*supra* 119) is obscure, unless it refers to the channel of the Avon there.

ground, 'a piece of land enclosed for agricultural purposes,' common in west and south-west England, is common in Wiltshire. It is tending to be replaced by *field.* Examples are *Church Ground, Picked Ground, Rushy Ground, Windmill Ground, Spittle Ground.* The earliest example noted is *Copped Ground* (1608).

hassock is occasionally found in minor and field-names, sometimes in the plural form. It is generally and primarily used of the tall-growing grass which forms regular hassocks or stools in wet open woods or boggy fields, but when it is associated, as it is in two or three cases, with words denoting woodland, it may have the sense 'wooded shaw, small wood,' as recorded from Berkshire and Sussex in EDD.

hop-garden, hop-yard are both used of a piece of land once devoted to the cultivation of hops. The latter is much the more common of the two. No hops are now grown in Wilts, but the tradition remains in many places.

kitchen is used in compounds with *close, field, furlong, mead,* probably to denote fields in specially domestic use.

lagger is occasionally found. It is a West Country term denoting a long narrow strip of land or copse. Cf. GrundyGl 17.

lammas is very common in field-names such as Lammas *Ham, Land, Leaze, Field* and *Ground,* and has reference to certain lands under particular cultivation till harvest which reverted to common pasturage at Lammastide (August 1st) and remained as such till the following spring.

linchet, lynchet(t) and (occasionally) linchard are fairly common in Wiltshire. The history of this word, used in something the same way as *linch* itself (cf. hlinc *supra* 436) is obscure. No early examples of its use have been noted. It is applied to a balk of green land between two pieces of ploughed land and (more often) to a terrace cut out of the slope in the face of a chalk down.

living is occasionally found, used of a farm or tenement. For its full technical sense in Wiltshire and Dorset cf. *living* sb. (EDD) and Slade's Fm *supra* 84.

night-leaze is found two or three times, with a pseudo-historical variant *Knights Leaze*. It would seem to denote pasture into which the cattle were turned at night.

paradise is common, but no example earlier than 1540 (*Paradice*) has been noted. It is probably used simply as a complimentary nickname.

parlour is found occasionally, as in *Parlour Close, Green Parlour*. It is probably a name of the nickname type.

patch is common as in *the Patch, Clay Patch, Clover Patch, Sour Patch*.

penning, 'enclosure for cattle,' a derivative of penn *supra* 443, is very common and characteristic. No examples have been noted earlier than *The Penninge* (1609), *le Penninge* (1651).

plock-pits, used of a pit for wood sawn into logs, has been noted twice.

pudding is common in names descriptive of sticky soil and the like as in *Pudding Close, Mead, Lands, Lane*, etc.

purley, purlieu, is found several times in Wiltshire in ancient forest-areas. It denotes specially a piece of land on the edge or fringe of a forest, especially land which by a new perambulation (OFr *puralee*) had been partially disafforested, but it is also used of border-land in general. *purley* is an anglicised form of the original French term and *purlieu* a re-gallicising of the pseudo-English *purley*. In modern field-names it appears variously as (*the*) *Purley*, (*the*) *Purlieu*, *Purleigh*. No example has been noted earlier than the 17th century. For a full discussion of the name *v*. NED *s.v. purlieu*.

rag is used in Wiltshire of a small piece of woodland as in the phrase "There is also a parcell of *Ragge* of woode there" (1591 WM vi, 200) and in the woodland names *le Ragge* (1567 *Ct*), *Poachers Ragg* (WM xl, 125), *Bisshopsragg* (1542 *Sav*) and *the Great Ragg* (1733 *Map*). We may note also Rag Wood in Bossington (Ha), *the Raggs* 1611 DKR xxxix. It survives in *the Rag(g)*, *the Raggs*, *Rag Acre* and *Mead, Raglands*.

rainbow is found occasionally. It may refer to land which is ploughed *rainbow*, i.e. parallel to the sides of a curving field (PN Ess 600).

roundabout generally has reference to a field with a clump of trees in the middle (cf. PN Wa 336).

scotland is found occasionally in minor names in Wiltshire. The places may be so called because subject to the payment of some *scot* (cf. Scotland, PN Sx 238, PN D 212, PN Nth 117, PN Sr 206, 222). It is possible that the name may also be given as a nickname to some remote farm or field. Scotland Hill and Scotland *supra* 75, 140 are so situated.

several(s) is used of land held in separate ownership as in *Burdens Several, Gills Several, Severals*.

sid(e)ling is used of a field which runs along an edge. Cf. *sidlingweg* (BCS 957) and *Sidling* (GrundySo 205).

skilling is found in a few field-names, Skilling Close in Norton, Cherry Orchard Skilling in Luckington, Skilling Ground in Rowde and probably Skillam Mead in Brokenborough, all from *TA*. There is also a *Skillings* on Bradley Fm in Holt (1826, 1829 *Deed*). All these contain the dialectal *skelling, skilling*, etc., recorded *s.v. skeeling* in EDD. It denotes a shed, outhouse, and seems to correspond to the north-country *shealing*. Initial *sk* is curious and is found in this word in Berks, Do, Gl, Ha, He, Sr, Sx, Wt. Cf. PN D Pt. 1, xxxv for parallels. See Introd. xxi.

sleight, with occasional variant *slait*, is very common as used of a sheep walk or pasture. Cf. "a sheep *sleight* or sheep pasture" (1702 *Longleat*), but no early examples of it have been found. In EDD it is taken to be identical with *slait* (Ha), *slate* (Gl, So), used in the same sense and associated with slæd, 'valley,' because the word *slade* is recorded as being used of a sheep-walk, a bare flat space on the top of a hill. Persistent final *t* makes it very difficult to believe in this association, and the semantic association is equally difficult. The persistent *gh* and the diphthongs *ei, ai* point rather to a lost OE **sleht*, the cognate of ON slétta, 'level place,' NCy *sleet*. This word is on record in other Germanic languages, Goth *slaíhts*, OHG, MLG *sleht*, OSax *slicht*, the original idea being something that is level or has been levelled, and this would fit the sense admirably. Outside the county one ME form has been noted in Dorset. Fägersten (PN Do 111) gives ME *atte Sleyste* (1333 *SR*) as the source of Sleight in Corfe Mullen. The form *sleight* is also found in Somerset and Gloucestershire. Cf. GrundySo 235, GrundyGl 19.

sling is commonly used of a long narrow strip of ground. Cf. sling (PN Wa 336).

slob is used of a muddy piece of ground as in *Slob* and *Slob Leaze*.

string(s) is commonly used of a long narrow strip of land, often woodland, especially in a valley by a stream.

swathe is occasionally used, probably as a measure of grass-land.

t(w)ink, 'chaffinch,' is found in *Twink Leaze* and *Tinkmarsh*.

(c) Miscellaneous field-names.

Among miscellaneous minor and field-names we may note: *virgata voc. Debonere et Colde* (1518), heap of stones called *Deade Mann* (1651), (*apud*) *Dedwomanne* (1518), *the Dottes* (1591), *messuage called Dromedoryes* (1633), *Eight Mennes Parte* (1630), *le Goldhord* (t. Hy 3), *le Halfmoone* (1590), *vico voc. Hockerill* (1670), cf. Hockerill (PN Herts 202–3), *ground called Longhope* (1753), *Mynstrelfurlong* (1518), *le Stelepeare furlong* (t. Jas 1), *Stoppehole* (1453), *past. voc. Tenne Pence* (1608), *Wayshepaylemarshe* (1581), *acra voc. Whitehorse* (1570). The mysterious Whewes (PN Sr 269) repeats itself in *claus voc. Wewes* (1546) in Wootton Bassett and *The Weawe* (1638) in Chippenham.

For many we have no early forms at all. This is specially true of names of the nickname type:

Sometimes they are complimentary as in *Butter Leaze* and *Meadow, Eden Garden, Fill Tubs, Golden Ground, Park, Stitch* and *Valley, Good Acre, Helps Well, Ketch Hares, Largess, Lucky, Mount Pleasant* (several), *Pound of Butter*.

More often they are uncomplimentary as in *Bad Mead, Barebone(s), Beastly Furlong, Beggar Hay, Beggars, Beggars Bush* (several), *Hill, Patch* and *Tyning, Breakheart, Cain Ground, Devils Bed, Dairy* and *Mead, Difficulty, Famish Beggar, Hunger-down, Hunger Hill* (several), *Hungry Hill, Knawbone, Labour in Vain, Leathern Hill, Little Profit, Little Worth* (several), *Losing All, Lousy Mead, Lowsy Marsh, Nicks Hole, Paupers, Pickpocket, Pinch Gut, Pinch Poor, Poor Mans Pasture, Rotten Furlong, Rotten Row, Sleepy Bottom, Small Gains* (several), *Starve Acre, Starveall* (several), *Starve Croft*.

Nicknames from shape are *Broad Ribs, Buttocks* (several) (cf. *supra* 425), *the Harp, Long Harp, the Heart, the Leg, Leg of Mutton, Shoulder of Mutton* (several), *the Slip* (several).

Nicknames for remote fields are *Botany Bay, Jericho, New England, Pennsylvania, California, Quebec, Worlds End*.

Ironical are such names as *The City, Little London, Little Salisbury, Hundred Acres* (for some very small field), *Piccadilly*.

Many field-names have reference to ownership or occupation as in *Burgess Mead, Ground*, etc. (cf. *supra* 451), *Reeves Acre, Close, Cowleaze, Croft, Field, Hay, Hill, Mead* and *Orchard, Shreves Mead, Parsons Acre, Ground*, etc., *Parsonage Acre, Ham* and *Ground*, etc., with reference to glebe land.

Lands in disputed ownership bear such names as *No Mans Land* (several), *No Mans Ball, Whose Land*.

Lands used for charitable purposes have such names as *Alms Piece, Chapel Mead, Chantry Ground, Church Leys*.

Among the commonest references to crops are the numerous examples of *French Grass Fd* and *Rye Grass Fd*.

References to the labour needed are perhaps found in *Boy Piece, Old Mens Mead, Four Days Mead, Three Mens Hays*.

(*d*) *Field-names, arranged under hundreds and parishes. The basis is in each case the Tithe Award for the parish, where such exists. The names in the Award, so far as we have early forms for them, are given first. These are followed by those names for which we have no early forms, but which can be explained by reference to the glossary of elements found in the field and minor names (supra 421–56). After these, material received from the Schools is given so far as it supplements or further elucidates the material found in the TA, with the same method of comment as for the TA names.*

Highworth Hundred

CASTLE EATON. Bawstead[1] (*Over, Nether Borsted* 1552 *FF, Bosted* 1556 Pat, *Borestead* 1669 *Sadler. v.* burhstede, 'site of a burh,' but no traces of such are now to be found). South Ham (cf. *les hammes* 1627 WIpm and William *atte Hamme* 1277 *Rental. v.* hamm). North and South Linget (*Little, Lower Longet*(*t*) 1639 WIpm, *v. supra* 430). New Takein is probably self-explanatory. For Coney Gore, Lawnd Marsh, Long Lion, Long Pudding, *v. supra* 427, 440, 439, 453. The School adds Long Forty (*supra* 43) and Normead (*Northmeade* 1627 WIpm) and gives Costards and Curls for *Castars* and *Courls* (*TA*).

HANNINGTON. For Picked Ground *v. supra* 443.

HIGHWORTH and SOUTH MARSTON. Badbrook, now *Badgebrook* (School). Bridge Mead (cf. Alan *atte Brugge* 1333 *SR*). Cow Leaze (*Cowsleese* 1641 WIpm). Dead Pits (*Dodesput* 1278 *Ct*,

---

[1] Now known as Bowstead (School)..

Dydpytt 1572 *WinchColl, Didpitt al. Dudpitt* 1640 WIpm). Duns Elm (id. 1773 A and D). Ford Ducks (*Foredox* 1641 WIpm). The Ham (*The Hammes* ib. *v.* hamm) lies low by the river. Hitchings Ground (*Hitchinge* 1542 *WinchColl. v. supra* 435). The Laines (cf. *le personage leyns* 1540 *Rental, ground called Leynes* 1641 WIpm. *v. supra* 439). Long Marsh (*Langhemershe* 1341 *Cor*). Maggot Hill (id. 1773 A and D). The Marsh (cf. Thomas *atte Mersshe* 1329 *Ass*). Mockney (cf. *Mokenhulle juxta Highworthe* 1312 *FF, Mokenhull(e)* 1513 ib., 1676 *Recov.* 'Mocca's hill'). Mockney lies low and must be his marshland, *v.* eg. Mundays Field, Upper, Lower Mundays (*Mundaylond* 1447 Moulton, *Maundefeld* 1463 *Ct, Mondaylond* 1512 *Ct. v. supra* 440). Pill Lake (*Pullelake* 1278 *Ct. v.* pyll, 'stream,' and lacu, 'stream'). Rudluck is by a small stream and is probably for *hreod-lacu*, 'reed-stream.' Sheep Cripple (cf. *Crypel geat supra* 432). The Slade (cf. *Sladforlong* 1277 *Rental. v.* slæd). Strickney (*Strikeneye* 1278 *Ct.* A compound of OE styric, 'heifer,' ME *stirk, strik,* in the weak gen. pl., and eg, 'marshland.' Cf. *Strichenestrete* in Exeter (PN D 22)). Stony Crockle (cf. *Crok(e)welle* 1277 *Rental,* 1329 WIpm from *crocc,* 'jug, vessel,' and wielle). West Leaze (*West Leasowe* 1641 ib. *v.* læs). For Cats Brain, Folly Plantation (in Folly Field), Lammas Land, the Langate, Little Lawn, Rag Ground, Smock Furlong, Town Close, *v. supra* 425, 451, 452, 430, 440, 453, 446, 449.

Mr W. H. Gale of Highworth Council Junior School has given much supplementary information, including the following: Biddle (*Budewelle* 1333 AD i, *Bydwell* 1540 *Rental.* Cf. Byde-mill Brook *supra* 4. This spring is the source of one of the feeders of the Colne). Chilleth Meadow (cf. *Chyllade* 1277 *Rental,* the second element being clearly (ge)lad, 'water-course'). Moor Meadow (cf. *Moresplot* ib. and splot *supra* 446). Stowell (id. 1278 *Ct,* doubtless 'stone-spring'). Water Furrows (*le Waterforows* 1540 *Rental*).

Among the modern names there are several examples of *Forty* (cf. *supra* 43), all in low-lying marshy ground, and of Peaked, Picked and Pickett (cf. *supra* 443). *The Butts* has reference to volunteer rifle-butts, *Canada* is reputed to be so nicknamed from good crops grown there, *Cornwall* and *Land's End* are certainly so named from their remote situation, *Starveall Barn* has a bad reputation, *Wiltshire Ham* is the first field over the river from Berkshire, *Pest House Close* is a relic of the plague. *Gorselake* and *Goslake* are from lacu, 'small stream,' and in some documents are reduced to *Goslick*. *Ring Ground* shows relics of an old earthwork.

INGLESHAM. For the Lains, Picked Hams, Small Gains, *v. supra* 439, 443, 455. Meer Leys is on the parish boundary, *v. supra* 441.

MARSTON MEYSEY. Black Gore (*Black Goare* 1763 *Sadler*), *v.* gara. The Layers (*pasture ground called the Leyre* 1635 WIpm). The sense is not certain, but it is probable that *leyr* (from OE *leger*) is here used of a place for animals to lie down in. We are familiar with it as used of wild animals, but it is used also in dialect of a place for domestic animals. Cf. *lair* sb.[1], 4 (NED). Woodcock (1763 *Sadler*). For the Butts, Coneygree, the Garcons, Green Leys, the Hitching, Laines, the Pleck, Purley, the Slades, *v. supra* 425, 427, 432, 438, 435, 439, 444, 451, 446. Purley is on the county boundary.

STANTON FITZWARREN. Bean Lands (*la Benelonde* 1347 AD i). Horshill or Hossil Lane (*Horswell'* 1245 WM xvi). Leaden Hill (*Lodenhulle* (sic) 1277 *Rental*). Sand Hills and Hitching (cf. *Sandpittes, Hitchinge* 1641 WIpm, *v. supra* 435). For Picked Mead, Quar Ground and Walnut Crate, *v. supra* 443, 445, 427–8.

STRATTON ST MARGARET. In an estate map of 1844 (*Merton*) we have Breach Meadow (cf. *Esturebreche* 1261 AD vi and *v.* bræc). Cossicle is from *cotsetla*, *v. supra* 427. Harnells (*Harehull* 1261 AD vi, *Harnhull* 1278 *Ct.* Either 'hare(s) hill' or 'boundary hill,' *v.* har). Old Berries (*Oldebury* 1412, 1447 *Merton.* 'Old burh or camp'). For Long Gore, *v. supra* 432.

Scipe Hundred

BLUNSDON. Barn Fd (*Barn close* 1626 WIpm). Little Marsh (cf. *The Marsh* 1636 WIpm). For Breach Meadow, Dole Acre, the Langett, Picked Fd, Pinch Gut, Starveall, String, *v. supra* 423, 429, 430, 443, 455, ib., ib.

RODBOURNE CHENEY. Bremhill Acre (*Brimhill* 1733 *Map.* *v. supra* 424). Dole Mead (*Dowle meade* ib. *v.* dal). Drove Way (cf. *la Drove* 1277 *Rental*, *v.* draf). Home Close (id. 1641 WIpm). New Mead (cf. *Pitles newe meed* ib.). Broad Way, Filks and Haddington are *bradan weg, filican slæd* and *headdan dune* 943 (c. 1150) BCS 788. For Burnbake, Folly Ground, Gore Mead, Horse Leys, Langate, the Lynch, Picked Corner, Pig Lains, Twenty Swaths, *v. supra* 450, 451, 432, 438, 430, 436, 443, 439, 455.

Staple Hundred

LYDIARD MILLICENT. Great, Little Horsy (*Horsheye* 13th *Bradenstoke. v.* (ge)hæg). Upper, Lower Marsh (cf. *North, South Marrish* 1649 WM xl). Great, Little Moor (*Little Moor* ib.). Shelfinch (*Shilfinch al. Shynelinche* 1632 WIpm). Will Croft (*Wolcrofte* 13th *Bradenstoke*). For the Breach, Cock Roads, the Langett[1], Little Worth, Picked Ground, Pudding Close, *v. supra* 423, 427, 430, 455, 443, 453.

PURTON. Bean Hill (*Bynehill* 1630 WIpm, *Bean Hill* 1744 *Map*). Berk Fd (1744 *Map*). Brook Mead (*Brookmeade* 1630 WIpm). Calves Close (*Calfe close* ib.). Cob Hill (*Cobhill* ib.). Upper, Lower Down (cf. *Downe way* ib.). Ford Mead (cf. John *atte Forde* 1333 *SR*). Gutter Mead (cf. *Three Gutters* 1649 WM xl). Hay Laines (*Hay Lain* 1744 *Map. v. supra* 439). Hurn (*Hurne* 1630, *The Hoorne* 1641 WIpm. Cf. William *atte Hurne* 1398 *Ct. v.* hyrne). Mallords (may be *Malford* 1632 WIpm). Marsh Furlong (*Machfurlonge* (sic) 1638 ib.). Meer Stone (*Mere Stones* 1744 *Map*. 'Boundary stones'). Old Land (*le Oldelond* 1398 *Ct*). Pitsworth (*Pikesworth* 1503 *MinAcct*). Plecks (*The Plecks* 1650 *ParlSurv. v. supra* 444). Puck Pit (*Pokkeput* 1398 *Ct.* 'Goblin pit or hollow.' *Pukeburne* 1257 *For* may have been near by). Rag Mead (cf. *The Ragg* 1649 WM xl and *supra* 453). Shillings (1744 *Map*). Shooters Hill (may be *Shooterclyffe* 1630 WIpm). Water Furlong (1632 ib.). Well Mead (cf. Adam de *Puteo* 1272 *Ass*, i.e. 'of the well'). West Mead (*West meade* 1641 WIpm). Windmill Hill (*Wyndemyll Hyll* 1515 WM xxxiii). For Brandiers, Burn Bake, Coneygre, Dole Mead, the Folly, Horse Leys, Langett, Pennings, Picked Close, Pirton and Robins Laines, *v. supra* 62, 450, 427, 429, 451, 438, 430, 453, 443, 439.

Cricklade Hundred

CRICKLADE. Arkells (*Ackehulle* c. 1350 *Bradenstoke*). Bean Moor (*Benmores* 1649 WM xl). Broad Croft (*Brodecroft* t. Hy 4 *Ct*). Burslade (*Boroghslade* 1331 *For, Barslade* 1650 *ParlSurv. v.* burh, slæd, taking its name from the camp on Bury Hill *supra* 39). Culver Hay (*Culverhey* 1649 *SarumD and C.* 'Dove enclosure'). Double Days (*Double Daies* 1636 WIpm). Hill Close (1650 *ParlSurv*). Hitching Ground (now *Itchen*) (*The Hitchin* 1649 *SarumD and C, Hitchin feild* 1650 *ParlSurv. v. supra* 435). Kite Close (*Kyte close* 1633 WIpm). Lady Mead (*Lady-*

---

[1] *Langcott* (School).

mede t. Hy 4 *Ct*). Pitt Close (*Pett close* 1650 *ParlSurv*). Powells Croft (now *Pauls Croft*) (*Paulescroft* t. Hy 4 *Ct*). Redlands (*Read landes* 1650 *ParlSurv*, lying low and containing hreod, 'reed'). Rudgeway Piece (*Ridgway* ib. *v. supra* 17). Great, Little Sales (*The Sales* ib.). Spittle Ground (now *Spittal's*) (*field called Spittle* 1630 WIpm, doubtless from some hospital). Stoney Hurst (*Stony Hurst* 1591 WM vi. *v.* hyrst). Water Furlong (*Waterfurlong* t. Hy 4 *Ct*, *Walter furlong* 1630 WIpm). For Brimhill, Butts Ham, Folly Ground, Idovers, Lammas Ham, Picked Furlong, Great and Little Purlieu (now *Purely*), *v. supra* 424, 425, 457, 2-4, 452, 443, 453.

From the School we have Stockum Lake (*Stokenlake* t. Hy 4 *Ct*), an old name for Key R. (*supra* 8), 'sluggish stream marked by stumps.' Also two examples of Langate, apparently for *Langett* (*supra* 430), for by them there are long narrow fields. Trenders Great, Middle and Small Ground lie on a rounded hill and probably go back to OE *trendel*, 'circle.' Small and Big Meers are on the parish boundary (*v.* (ge)mære *supra* 441).

LATTON. The School gives Gastons, the Hams (river meadows), the Lake (with a small stream), Big Severals, *v. supra* 432-3, 454. Also Swan's Neck, so called from its shape.

LEIGH. The School gives Blackmoor (*Blackmore* 1680 *Devizes*); Deadlands (ib.), noted as wet land; The Pickets (a field with sharp angles, cf. *supra* 443); the Poor's Platt (*supra* 443) which at the time of the Enclosure Award (1767) was apportioned for the benefit of the poor of the parish.

Malmesbury Hundred

MALMESBURY. Breach (cf. *le Netherebreche* 13th RegMalm and *supra* 423). Broad Field (*Bradefeld* ib.). Charr Mead (may be *Chalmede* t. Jas 1 *LRMB*, *Charlmead* 1650 *ParlSurv*). Chesle Brook (cf. *le Chastle* 13th RegMalm and ceastel *supra* 426). Church Hays (*Church Heyes* 1608 NQ viii). Clyatts (*Cleygate* 956 (14th) BCS 922, *Clyetts* 1763 *Sadler*). Dodding Hill (cf. *Doddingesdone* 13th ib.). Gaston (*Garstone* 1553 NQ vii, *Gaston* 1632 WIpm. *v. supra* 432). Upper, Lower Grove (cf. *la Grove, la Grofcrofte* 13th RegMalm). The Ham (*Hamme* 1628 WIpm. *v. supra* 433). Home Close (1627 ib.). Kemboro Field (*Kyngberewe* 13th RegMalm, *Kemborough fielde* 1627 WIpm. *v.* beorg, 'barrow'). Lock Share (*le Loksherde* 13th RegMalm. *v. supra* 445). Long Croft (*Langecrofte* ib.). Long Meadow (*Longmeade* 1669 *Recov*). Lot Mead (*Lottmeade* ib.). Great, Little Lynch (cf. *Long Linche* 1650 *ParlSurv.* *v. supra* 436). Newlands (*Newlandes hill* 1547 Pat). Priest Lands (*Prestlandes* ib. Cf. *Prestemed, Prestecroft* 13th RegMalm). Quar Close (cf. *Quarr-pittes* 1628 WIpm. *v. supra* 445). Sheffield (*Shelfield* 1628 WIpm, *Shilfeilde* 1640 ib.). Shuttlebourne (*Schotelesbure* 13th RegMalm, *Shutelborewe* 1334 *Ass*). Turtle Bridge (*Turtillbrigge* 1526 *MinAcct*). Worthy Mead (*campo vocato Worthy* 1357 *GDR. v.* worþig *supra* 450). Yet Ground is a derivative of geat, 'gate, gap.' For the Butts, Hitching, Home Close, Hunger-down, Picked Leaze[1], Rush Plat, Scotlands, Starveall, Stibbs, the Tining, Withy Slad, *v. supra* 425, 435, 434, 455, 443, 444, 454, 455, 447, 449, 446. Still Stays would seem to be a nickname for a field whose character never changes.

Rodbourne and Corston School gives Chartnams (*Chalken Ham TA*), Mosses (*Morses* ib.) and notes that Withy Slad (*TA*) is very wet ground. It also gives Coarse Heath (*Course Heath TA*) at the head of one of the feeders of Gauze Brook, cf. *supra* 7. It adds Ham Gassons, Red Skillen Ground (*supra* 432, 454) and Scrape-bone (nothing ever obtained from this field).

Chedglow Hundred

ASHLEY. Rowdens (*Rowdowns hedge* 1591 WM iv). For Coneygre, the Headen, Holly Bush Tyning, the Lains, Long Thong, Picked Piece, the Slait, Town Leaze, *v. supra* 427, 434, 449, 439, 448, 443, 446, 449.

BROKENBOROUGH. Buckthorn (*Bubbethorne* 956 (14th) BCS 922, c. 1300 *Malm*. '*Bubba*'s thorn tree'). Cugmoors (*Coggemore* ib.). Gastons (*la Garstone* ib. *v. supra* 432). Mill Hill and Mead (cf. Alice *atte Mulle* 1333 *SR*). Pear Tree Leaze (cf. *ad pirum* 956 (14th) BCS 922). Shurn Hill may be *Scherneberewe* 13th RegMalm, from OE scearn, 'dung.' For Butt Slades, Coneygre, Hitching, the Langet, Little Worth, Picked Lands, Pudding Mead, Skillam Mead, the Tinings, *v. supra* 425, 427, 435, 430, 455, 443, 455, 454, 449.

CHARLTON. Coneygres (*le Conynger* 1535 VE. *v. supra* 427). Gingles Leaze (cf. *Gingells* 1677 NQ vii). Gods Croft is former Glebe Land (School). Little Worth is stony, poor ground (ib.). Smock Tail may perhaps be associated with smoke *supra* 446. School gives it as *Smock Tile*. For Upper and Lower Breach, Cold Harbour, Gossy Hill, Knaps, the Lagger, Lowsy, the Lynch, Picked Leaze, Upper and Lower Purleigh, the Rag,

---

[1] Picket Leaze (School).

v. supra 423, 451, 452, 427, 455, 436, 443, 453, ib. The Purleighs are on the outskirts of Braydon Forest (School).

The School adds Poor Ground (poor land), Under Acre (a tiny field), Lord Andover's Stall (a stall there is reputed to have been built in order to provide Lord Andover with a vote) and Idovers (*supra* 3).

CRUDWELL. Amen Corner is probably to be associated with the beating of the bounds. Angrove Meadow (*Hanegrove* 1275 *Magd*). The Butts (*the Bottes* 1356 ib. *v. supra* 425). Church Field (*Churchcrofte* 1300 Archaeologia xxxvii). Cindrum (*Sunderhamme* 974 (14th) KCD 584, *in loco qui appellatur Sunder* 901 (14th) BCS 586. 'Separate enclosure,' *v. supra* 448). Clay Croft (id. t. Ed 6 *DuLa*). Dirt Hanger (*Durtanger* ib. *v.* hangra). Dropping Well (*Drupwelle* c. 1300 *Malm*). Grove Ridge (*Grauerugge* 956 (14th) BCS 922. *v.* grafa). Hickmoor (*Hykemeres stream* 974 (14th) KCD 584, *Ykemere* 13th RegMalm, *Hickmore* t. Ed 6 *DuLa*. The second element is mere, 'pool'). Honey Ham Close (*Honnyham* ib.). Horse Croft (*Horscroft* ib.). Inlands (*Inlonde* 974 (14th) KCD 584, *Inlondesweye* 1356 *Magd*. *v. supra* 438). Lilly Field (*Lylley feild* t. Ed 6 *DuLa* may be the *suthe Linleye* of 1300 (Archaeologia xxxvii). 'Flax-clearing,' *v.* leah). Great, Little Paradise (*le great Paradice* t. Ed 6 *DuLa*. Cf. *supra* 455). Penny Ham Fd (*Pennyhams* ib.). Ramwell (ib.). Ridingwell (*cf. Rydinge feild* ib. and hryding *supra* 437). The Stirts (*Stert* ib. *v. supra* 447). For Coneygree, Grass Idover and Idover, Hitching Fd, Home Laynes, Pinkmarsh, Puck Hay, Reves Hay, the Tining, *v. supra* 427, 3, 435, 439, 55, 444, 456, 449.

GARSDON. Church Leaze (*Over Churchleys* 1677 NQ vii. *v. supra* 438). Cowleaze (*Cow Leyes* ib.). Fatting Leaze[1] (*Flattingleyes* (sic) ib.). Heath's Mead (cf. Richard *atte Hethe* 1333 *SR*). Long Mead (*Longemeade* 1677 NQ vii). Ludwell Leaze (*Ludewel* 13th RegMalm. 'Loud spring'). Neap Hill (*Nepehill* 1535 VE, *Neaphill mead* 1677 NQ vii, from OE *nǣp*, 'turnip'). For Breach, Coneygre, Gossey Hill, Mondays Hill and Mead, Parrock, Quar Leaze, Crucks Worthy and Great Worthy, *v. supra* 423, 427, 452, 440, 442, 445, 450. The School reports local forms as follows: Cunygre (*Coneygre TA*); Fletcher's Ground (*Flatchers* ib.); Munday Hills (*Mondays Hill* ib.); Wick's Mead (*Weeks Mead* ib.).

HANKERTON. Barrel Piece (may be *Berewelle* c. 1300 *Malm*. 'Barley-spring'). Butter Hill (may be *Boterewelle* 13th RegMalm. Cf. Buttermere *supra* 339). Home Fd (*Homfeld* c. 1300

---

[1] Fat and Leaze (School).

Malm). Inn Mead (*le Inmede* ib. *v. supra* 438). Oatlands (cf. *Otegarstone* ib. *v. supra* 432). For the Breaches, Cock Road, the Garstons, Hatchett Piece, Idover, the Langet, Great and Little Purlieu, Quarr Piece, Rainbow Hill, Sheepburge, *v. supra* 423, 427, 432, 433, 3, 430, 453, 445, 454, 424.

Lea. Bean Hay (*Benhay* 1774 *Wilton*). Chinswell (*Chincell* ib.)· Gogmore lies low by a stream, cf. *supra* 452. Knole Hill (cf. William *atte Knolle* 1333 *SR*). Long Mead (*Longemed* 1437 *MinAcct*). Man Breach is on the boundary, *v.* (ge)mæne and bræc *supra* 441, 423. Nearn Hill (*Nurnell* 1788 *Map, Nurn Hill* 1807 ib.). Rush Croft[1] and Wood Croft (*le Ryschcroft, Wodecroft* 1437 *MinAcct*). For Great Breach, Conygre, Great and Little Goss, the Penn[2], Picked Leaze, *v. supra* 423, 427, 452, 443, ib. The School adds Nott Hill and Nut Hill (*Nothill TA*), Vernal (*Fernehill* 1677 NQ vii).

Long Newnton. For the Breach, Coneygre, Lagger, Long Thong Tyning, the Plaish, Strodlands, *v. supra* 423, 427, 452, 448–9, 447, 443.

Oaksey. Base Hay (*Batshey* 1568 *DuLa*). East Mead (*Eastemeade* ib.). Long Mead (*Longe meade* 1591 WM vi). Moor Leaze (*Moorlease* 1730 *Sadler*). Plistrage Fd (*Pistredg* (sic) *corner* 1591 WM vi). Side Ham (*Sidhamme* 1347 *DuLa, Sydeham* 1420 *MinAcct*. 'Wide enclosure,' *v.* sid, hamm). Small Mead (*Smalemede* 1347 *DuLa*). South Fd (*Southfeld* ib.). Stockham (*Stockum bridge* 1591 WM vi). Westwood Fd (*Westwode* 1347 *DuLa*). Wick Ground (cf. *Wikeforlong* 1420 *DuLa, Wick greene* 1591 WM vi. *v. supra* 25). For Conigree, the Heddon, Langett, Linch, Little London, the Sling, the Splatts, *v. supra* 427, 434, 430, 436, 455, 454, 446.

Startley Hundred

Brinkworth. Bridge Mead (cf. John *atte Brugge* 1333 *SR*). Broad Mead (*Broadmead* 1633 WIpm). Church Croft (*Churchecroft* 1357 *GDR*). Crowcum (*Crookham Lane* 1816 O.S.). Hamster Mead derives from *hamster*, the name of a species of rodent. This is taken in NED to be a loan word from German, but Hamsterley (Du), *Hamsterlege* 1242 *Ass*, suggests that the word may also be native English. Lip Gate Mead (cf. Thomas *atte Lupezate* 1333 *SR. v. supra* 96). Lyncroft (*Lincrofte* 13th RegMalm. 'Flax croft'). Water Hills (cf. John de *Watterehulle*

---

[1] Russ Croft (School).
[2] By a stream and therefore 'enclosure' and not 'hill.'

1333 *SR*). Windmill Field (*Windmill leaze* 1637 WIpm). For Breach, Copid Ash, the Folly, Gog Ground, Home Mead, Hungry Hill, Great and Little Idovers, Knaps, Lot Mead, Ore, Paradise, Pingels, Purlieu[1], Rag, Roundabouts, *v. supra* 423, 427, 451, 452, 434, 455, 3, 427, 441, 442, 455, 443, 453, ib., 454. The School adds Brickhill (near Old Clay Pit), doubtless for *Brickkiln*, cf. *supra* 36; Van Diemens in a remote corner of the parish, cf. *supra* 455; Lagger, a marshy field, cf. *supra* 452.

CHRISTIAN MALFORD. Chillison (*Chel(e)wardesham* 1232 Ch, 13th *Bradenstoke*. '*Cēolweard*'s ham(m)'). North Mead (*Northmede* 1232 Ch). For Breaches, Butts, Church Leys, Picked Leaze, Pullens Gassons, Starve Acre, *v. supra* 423, 425, 438, 443, 432, 455.

DRAYCOT CERNE and STANTON ST QUINTIN. For the Breach, Home Mead, Picked Leaze, Sheep Sleight, *v. supra* 423, 434, 443, 454.

FOXLEY. For Connegre, Kingslate, Pockeridge, Starve All, *v. supra* 427, 446, 97, 455.

HULLAVINGTON. Aspenny (may be *Apshanger* c. 1300 *Malm*. 'Aspen slope,' *v.* hangra). Bean Leaze (1753 *Eton*). Broad Mead (*Broadmeade* 1599 *Devizes*). Chowell Mead (*Cholwell* 1753 *Eton*, i.e. 'cold spring'). Cow Leaze (*Coweleaz* 1583 AD v). Deadlands (*Dead land* 1558 *Eton*, i.e. 'worn-out land'). Dean Mead (cf. *la Dene* c. 1350 *Bradenstoke*. *v.* denu). Double Bush (1753 *Eton*). Down Furlong[2] (*Dun furlong* ib.). Fullbrooks (*Fulbroke* 1558 ib.). Gassons (*le Garston* 1445 ib. *v. supra* 432). Hay Furlong (*Heiforlong* c. 1350 *Bradenstoke*). Inhooks (*Little Innocks* 1753 *Eton*. *v. supra* 134). Little Mead (*Little mede* 1549 NQ iv). Long Hammer (1753 *Eton*). Meerway (*Merewey* c. 1350 *Bradenstoke*. 'Boundary way'). Nadhooks (*le Nattok* 1445, *Nattocks* 1753 *Eton*. Cf. *supra* 442). Nethercotts (*Nethercote* 1558 ib.). Tile Pits (*Tilepitts* 1753 ib.). Water Furrows (ib.). West Fd (*Westfeild* 1583 AD v). For the Cleve, Cock Road, Conygre, Elm Leys, the Leys, Linchcroft, Picked Piece, Town Leaze, the Tyning, *v. supra* 426, 427, ib., 438, ib., 436, 443, 449, ib. The Grip is by a small stream, *supra* 452. The School gives the local pronunciation of Nadhooks as *Narrocks*. Unluckily there is nothing distinctive in its topography which will help in determining the meaning of this obscure but frequently recurring element. The School adds

---

[1] Purley, Purleaze (School), all on the edge of Braydon Forest.
[2] Dunfurling (School).

Moormead (1753 *Devizes*); Ryelands (*Rylands* 1599 ib.), and gives Roughleaze (*Ruffleaze TA*) and the Ryvy (possibly for *Ryefield* ib.).

NORTON. For Gossey Mead, Hunger Down, the Lynch, Picked Mead, Skilling Close, Tyning, *v. supra* 452, 455, 436, 443, 454, 449.

SEAGRY. Alder Ham (*Alderham* 1706 WM xliii). Clay Corner (1648 ib.). Copy Thorn (*Copped Thorne Furlong* 1677 ib. xxxi. 'Pollarded thorn tree'). Cow Leaze (*Cowleze* 1648 ib. xliii). The Grove (ib.). Knapps (ib., *Napps* 1705 ib. *v.* cnæpp). The Legger Hill (*The Lagger* 1648 ib. *v. supra* 452). Mill Furlong (ib.). The Moors (*Mores* ib.). North Fd (*Northfeild* ib.). Shadwell (1608 ib. xxxi. Probably 'shallow spring' from sceald, 'shallow'). Sheep Fd (*Sheep feild* 1648 ib. xliii). For Brimble, Gasson, Goss Croft, Lynch, Slate, Star Leys, Stitches, Worthies, *v. supra* 424, 432, 452, 436, 446, 438, 447, 450. Goss Croft is for *Gorse Croft*.

LITTLE SOMERFORD. Breaches (*le Breche* 1451 *MinAcct. v. supra* 423). Cow Meadow (cf. *le Cowlese* ib.). Ferny Leaze (*Fearney lease* 1695 NQ ii). Stock Mead (*Stokemede* 1451 *MinAcct*). For Nurnhills cf. Nearn Hill *supra* 463. For Englands Pen, Worthies, *v. supra* 443, 450.

SUTTON BENGER. Long Lands (*Longelonde* 1289 *Ass*). Pucksey (1604 *Longford*). Stearts, Steart (*la Sterte* 1269 Aubrey. *v. supra* 447). For Picked Heath, Swaynes Leys, *v. supra* 443, 438.

Dunlow Hundred

ALDERTON. Bacon Hill (*Bagenhulleslade* 1317 NQ viii. '*Bacga*'s hill,' with slæd). Brokenbrow is probably for *Brokenbeorg*, 'broken barrow.' Early Mead may be *Arleg*' 1249 FF. Eastmans Wells (*Estmound(es)welle* 1357 NQ viii. '*Eastmund*'s spring.' Cf. estmondestone (BCS 921) in Brokenborough). Holbrook (*Holebrok* 1317 NQ viii. *v.* holh). Little Mead (*Lytelmede* 1357 ib.). Normans may be *Normer furlong* ib. It is on the northern edge of the parish, *v.* (ge)mære. Purchell (*Perchehulle* ib.). For Great Tyning, *v. supra* 449.

EASTON GREY. Bove Town is above the village, *v.* tun *supra* 449. Cloud Hill (*Clowd hyll* 1545 DeedsEnrolled. Cf. Clouds *supra* 176). The Grove (cf. *Estonesgrove* 1348 *Cor*). Long Mead (*Longe meade* 1627 WIpm). Racks (cf. *Lyttell Racke* 1545

DeedsEnrolled, le Great, Lytle racke 1556 *FF. v. supra* 445). Wadding Hill (*Waddon* 1545 *DeedsEnrolled*). For Breaches, Broad Leys, Coneygre, Folly Leaze, Sheep Sleights, Wheat Linch, *v. supra* 423, 438, 427, 451, 454, 436.

LITTLETON DREW. For Blind, Carr and Millway Tyning, the Folly, the Idover, Innocks, the Laynes, *v. supra* 449, 451, 3, 134, 439.

LUCKINGTON. For Cherry Orchard Skilling, Down Breach, Fill Tubs, the Folly, Gassons Mead, Grass Lippiatt, Long Rudges, Picked Ground, Tyning, *v. supra* 454, 423, 455, 451, 432, 96, 437, 443, 449.

Thorngrove Hundred

CASTLE COMBE. Broad Mead (*Brodemede* 1422 *Add*). Bull Mead (*Bullmede* 1513 ib.). Gassons (*le Gaston* ib. *v. supra* 432). The Grove (ib.). Henley (*Henley hill* 1422 ib., probably 'high clearing'). Hill House Wood (cf. *Hilhous* 1346 *AddCh*). Long Lands (*Longlandes* 1513 *Add*). Mill Ground (cf. *Millestede, le Millehamme* 1422 ib. *v.* hamm). Shalley (*Schaldelegh* 1346 *AddCh*. The first element is *scealde*, 'shallow'). For Cleves, Elves Tyning, the Hatchet, the Leys, the Ridings, Sheep Sleights, Stirts, *v. supra* 426, 449, 433, 438, 437, 454, 447.

GRITTLETON. Acmore (*Ackmore* 1615 WM xxii). Adderalls (*Adrills* 1666 ib. xliv). Broad Mead (*Broadmead* 1625 ib.). Butts Leaze (cf. *The Butts* 1622 ib. and *supra* 425). Clayett Mead (*Cleyate* 940 (14th) BCS 750, *Clayett* 1615 WM xxii. 'Clay-gate,' from clæg and geat). Drung Shortlands (cf. *The Drung* 1783 WM xliii and *supra* 451). Fishlands (*Fishland* 1623 WM xxii). Greenway Tyning (cf. *The Greenway* 1631 ib. xliv and *supra* 449). Holden (*holedene* 940 (14th) BCS 750, *Houlding Bottom* 1623 WM xxii, *Holden leaze* 1696 ib. xliv. 'Hollow valley'). Lapwell (1615 WM xlii). New Leaze (1625 ib.). Netherford (*Etherford* 1726 ib. xliv). Sand Pits (*Sandpitts* 1636 ib.). Smallmeads (*Smallmead* 1631 ib.). Southfield (*Southfeilde* 1623 ib.). Stone Hill (*Stonehill furlong* 1696 ib.). Town Fields (*Townefield* 1741 ib.). Twizzle Ash (*Twisle Ash* 1623 ib. xxii. *v.* twisla, 'fork'). For Cold Harbour, Conegars, Dayhouse Fd, Hitchings, Home Close, Idover, Ox Leys, Purley, Quar Leaze, Rag Acre, *v. supra* 451, 427, 437, 435, 434, 3, 438, 453, 445, 453.

WEST KINGTON. North Field (*Northefylde* 1585 *AOMB*). Rough Down (*Row Down* 1773 A and D). Stirts (*la Sterte* 1269

Aubrey. *v.* **steort**). West Fd (*Westfylde* 1585 *AOMB*). For Beggars Tyning, Butts Leaze, Connigre, the Freath, the Gores, Great and Little Hern, Lynches, Play Mead, Quar Piece, Slait, Stitchens, *v. supra* 449, 425, 427, 431, 432, 437, 436, 444, 445, 454, 447.

NETTLETON. Berry Croft (*Burycrofte* 1562 *AddCh*. It lies by Burton *supra* 81). Long Furlong (*Langforlang* 944 (14th) BCS 800). Great, Little Marsh (cf. *Mershefurlong* 1562 *AddCh*). For Brimble Hay, Chestles, Gore Tyning, Hitchings[1], the Hurn[1], Pinch Poor, Quarr Close, *v. supra* 424, 426, 432, 435, 437, 455, 445. Clack Mead is just by the highest ground in the neighbourhood and is probably another example of the word noted under Clack *supra* 271. Sunderhill[1] is on the parish boundary (cf. *supra* 448).

The School gives Cadnum for *Cadman TA*, Tuckers Nap for *Tuckers Knap TA* and adds Jenny Verland (cf. *supra* 431).

Chippenham Hundred

BIDDESTONE and SLAUGHTERFORD. Ass Furlong (*Awse furlong* 1631 WIpm). Barrow Hill (cf. *Barrowes* ib.). Binsey (*Bynsey* ib.). Gastons (*Gastons furlong* 1641 WIpm. *v. supra* 432). North Fd (*The North field* ib.). Slade Piece (cf. *Slade furlong* 1631 ib. *v.* **slæd**). Stock Bridge (*Stockbridge meade* 1641 ib.). Uptons (*Upton* ib.). Wattledge (*Wadlynch close* ib., i.e. 'woad hlinc'). For Breeches, Clanville, Hill Garston, Innex, Picked Leaze and Marsh, Lowsy Marsh, the Plash, Standhills, Starveall, *v. supra* 423, 70, 432, 438, 443, 455, 443, 429, 455. There is a quarry by Standhills.

The School adds Downalls (*Downhills TA*); Gibbs Horn (*Gibsham* ib.); Normoor (*North Moor* ib.); Ruins (*Rowens* ib.); Shally (*Shellow* ib.); Slimridge (*Slimbridge* ib.); Watershaw (*Watershawe* ib.). It also adds the Bye and Bye Piece, with a remarkable curve in the latter, probably from OE *byge*, 'curve,' cf. PN D 194, 221; two or three fields called Heaves, where there are old barrows; the Laggar(d), a long field; Ridgeway, on the Chippenham-Biddestone road; Sand and Tile Quarr, names of old quarries.

BOX. Ally Croft (*Alley croft* 1630 *Devizes*). Barn Close (*Barne close* 1623 WIpm). Bollings Leaze (cf. *Bollens Mill* 1677 NQ viii). Blackley Fd (*Blacklie* 1630 *Devizes*). Broad Leigh (*Bradeley* 1623 WIpm). Chalk Leaze (*Chalkelees* 1549 NQ iv).

---

[1] Hitchens, Ern, Sun Drills (School).

Chapel Fd (*Chappelfield* 1623 WIpm). Charlands (*Charlandes* 1630 *Devizes*). Cold Harbour (*Coulde Harbor* ib. *v. supra* 451). Coney Garth[1] (*Coniger wall* 1623 WIpm. *v. supra* 427). Craw Leaze (ib.). Culver Hayes (*Culverhaie* ib. 'Dove enclosure'). Fogham (*Foggome* 14th Trop, *Vaggome* 1348 *Cor*, *Foggam* 1465 Trop, *Foggham* 1630 *Devizes*. Perhaps '*hamm* with *fog*-pasture'). Grove Mead (cf. *le Grove* 1623 WIpm). Haw Leaze (*Haw lies* 1630 *Devizes*). Holbrooks (*Holbroke* 1623 WIpm). Hunting Croft (*Huntinge crofte* ib.). Lady Croft (1630 ib.). Lippiatts (*Lipyeate* ib. *v. supra* 96). Long Mead (*Longe mead* ib.). Ludwells (*Ludwell* 1559 *FF*. 'Loud spring'). Mutton Leaze (*Mutton ley* 1630 *Devizes*). Newlands (*Newlandes* 1629 WIpm). Oat Leaze (*Oate lese* 1630 *Devizes*). Overstitch (*Overstitchings* 1629 WIpm. *v. supra* 447). Quarr Close (*le Quarr close* 1623 ib. *v. supra* 445). Rack Close[2] (*Racke, Recke* ib., *Racke slates* 1630 *Devizes. v. supra* 445). Sharpcroft (1559 *FF*). Stankley (*Stanckleys* 1623 WIpm). Stitchens (*Stiching* 1630 *Devizes. v. supra* 447). Swinleys (*Swine leyes* ib. *v.* læs). Warleaze[2] (*Worlese* ib. Cf. **ora** *supra* 442. It lies by Box Brook). Well Springs (ib.). Wick Fd (cf. Clement de *Wyke* 1333 *SR*. It is *Weeke* 1629 WIpm. *v. supra* 25). For Bar Yates, Broom Tyning, Cleeves, Headlands, Lagger Meadow, Sheep Sleights, Skilling, Great Slob, Waterstitch, *v. supra* 432, 449, 426, 434, 452, 454, ib., 455, 447.

The School, in a very full survey made by Mr H. A. Druett and Mr Swan, has noted further names found in *TA* and in the Survey of 1630: Holli(e)s (*Holleyes* 1630); Old Lyons (*Olyne* ib.); The Sty (*Stey Feild* ib.); Tinklands (*Tincknams* ib.); Toghill (*Tug Hill* ib.); Waincroft (*Wan Croft* ib.); Weirhayes (*Weuere hayes* ib., *Weavers Hayes* c. 1840). It is not near By Brook or Weavern. The School also notes modern forms Carbin, Gassons, Hanley, Sheep Slade, Stickle Hill, Water Witch for *TA Corbham, Garston, Hankley, Sheep Sleight, Stickley Hill, Water Stitch*.

BREMHILL. Elder Wells (*Ellenwell* 1592 *Add. v.* ellen, 'elder'). Long Mead (*Longmede* 1564 ib.). Mill Ham (*Myllehams* 1570 ib. *v.* hamm). Old Fd (*Oldefeild* ib.). Oxen Leaze (*Oxeleaze* 1592 ib.). Well Close (*Welclose* 1564 ib.). In the *EnclA* (1775) we have Balls Ground (cf. *Balls greene* 1592 *Add*); Cleeves (cf. *le Clif* 937 (14th) BCS 716); Cow Leys (*Cowlease* 1564 *Add*); Dole Mead (*Dolemeade* 1592 ib. *v. supra* 429). For Hanging Breach, Lains, Starve Croft, *v. supra* 423, 439, 455. Sideland Ground runs along the side of a hill and probably stands for earlier *sidling* (*supra* 454).

---

[1] Coneygore (School).   [2] Rat Close, Worleaze (School).

CHIPPENHAM. Abdons (*Abden* 1671 BorRec). Ayres (*The Eyres* 1373 Trop). Bayden (cf. Cristina de *Beydon* 1333 *SR*, whose family perhaps came from Baydon *supra* 285). Blackwell (*Blackwellham* 1695 BorRec). Borne Leaze (cf. *le Burne* 1281 Trop). Breach (*le Breche* ib. *v. supra* 423). The Butts (*The Butt* 1675 BorRec. *v. supra* 425). Claypoles (*Cleypoll* 1553 *Devizes*). Downhams (*Dounham* 1245 WM xvi). East Fd (*Estfeld* c. 1300 *Stowe*). Fairfoot Hill (may be *Fayreforde* 1512 *Ct*). Gaston Mead (*The Gassons* 1714 NQ vi. *v. supra* 432). Henryes (may be identical with *Henreþe, Henrichfurlonge* 13th RegMalm. 'Hen-stream,' *v.* riþ). Hill Close (1549 NQ iv). Kings Brook Mead (cf. *Kings brooke hill* 1605 BorRec). Mancroft (*Manecrofte* t. Hy 3 BM. 'Common croft,' *v.* (ge)mæne). It is on the parish boundary. Matford (*Matfordescroft* t. Ed 3 *AD*). Moor Mead (*Mooremead* 1685 *Add*. Cf. *la More* 1245 WM xvi. *v.* mor). North Croft (*Northe Crofte* 1549 NQ iv). Pitts Leaze (cf. Agnes *atte Putte* 1333 *SR*). Poltingham (*Powltingham* 1685 *Add*). Ruding (*Rydeings* 1666 NQ v. *v.* hryding). Salters Ham (cf. *Salters croft* 1605 BorRec). Stowells Mead (cf. Nicholas de *Stowelle* 1333 *SR*. 'Stone-spring'). Vernal (*Vernhale* c. 1400 *Malm*. 'Bracken nook'). Water Meadow and Wood (cf. Sibil *ate Watere* and Walter *atte Wode* 1333 *SR*). For Beggars Patch, Bell Leaze, Coneygre, Fleet Fd, Inhooks, Littleworth, No Mans Land, Picked Leaze and Down, Poor Tining, Port Mead, Rudgy Fd, Sheep Sleight, Smock Furlong, *v. supra* 455, 451, 427, 431, 438, 455, 456, 443, 449, 444, 437, 454, 446. Ray Mead is by the Avon, cf. Reybridge *supra* 103. Lowden School adds Skillen Field, cf. *supra* 454.

COLERNE. Alders Grove may be *Alverychesgrove* 1382 *NewColl*. 'Ælfric's grove'). Annaslade (*Alaynesslade* 1363 ib. 'Alan's slæd'). Ashley Fd (*Aysschle* 1397 ib.). Bag Mead (*Bagmedes* t. Jas 1 *LRMB*. Cf. *Baggelane* 1397 *NewColl*). Buttocks (*Buttokes* 1522 ib. *v. supra* 425). Chowell (*Chaldewell* 1363 ib. 'Cold spring'). Cleaves (*la Clyve* 1382 ib. *v.* clif). Coombes Piece (*Combeswode* 1406 ib., *The Combes* t. Jas 1 *LRMB*). Great and Little Crutch (*la Crouche* 1397 *NewColl*. 'Cross'). Down Fd (*Downefeild* t. Jas 1 *LRMB*). Gaston Piece (*Garston* 1382 *NewColl*. *v. supra* 432). The Ham (*le Hamme* 1522 ib.). Home Close (1712 *Ct*). Hurdwell (*Herdewell* 1382, *Hurdewelle* 1397 *NewColl*. Cf. Hurdcott *supra* 212). Innex (*Muchele Ynhok* 1397, *le Inhoke* 1522 *NewColl, Innock* t. Jas 1 *LRMB*. *v. supra* 438). Kidley (*Kitley* 1608 Lewis). Little Down (*Lyteldoune* 1406 *NewColl*). Long Furlong (*Longefurlong* 13th RegMalm). Upper, Lower Marsh (*Marshe* t. Jas 1 *LRMB*). Monks Meadow (cf. *Monekestyle* 1382 *NewColl*. *v.* stigel, 'ascent'). Querne Acre (*Querneacres* 1363 ib., from cweorn, 'hand-mill'). Townsend (cf. Thomas *atte Tounesende* 1333 *SR*). Wallingford Mead (*Warlingfords* t. Jas 1 *LRMB*). Weavern Meadow is by By Brook *supra* 4. Will Robin (*Wild Robins* 1712 *Ct*). Wood Lucks (*Woodlocks* ib.). For Bithams, Breaches, the Hitchings, Linchett, Losing All Fd, the Lynch, Lyppiatt, the Rag, Sheep Sleight, Starveall, *v. supra* 425, 423, 435, 453, 455, 436, 96, 453, 454, 455.

CORSHAM. Cottles Fd (may be *Cossettle* t. Jas 1 *Ct*. *v. supra* 427). Dodsill (*Dodeshulle* 1373 Trop. '*Dodd*'s hill'). Ducks Leaze, Edge Down, Harp and Cross Fd, Hinnocks, Leggar Ground, Great and Little Tyning, Wet Mead are *Ducks Leaze, Edge Down, le Harpe, Hinnex coppice, le Legger, le Tyning, Wettmead* t. Jas 1 *Ct*. *v. supra* 438. Gastons and How Mead (*la Garston, Houmede* 1351 *MinAcct*. *v.* hoh and *supra* 432). Prestley (cf. *Priesthill* 1644 *Recov*). Widmore (*Widemore* t. Hy 3 *AD*). For Beggars Hill, Burnbake, Conygre, Culver Leaze, Famish Beggar, the Lake, Penning, Picked Mead, Purleigh, Quar Ground, Roundabout, Scotland, Small Gains, Long Swathe, *v. supra* 455, 451, 427, 438, 455, 438, 453, 443, 453, 445, 454, ib., 455, ib. Scotland is on the extreme edge of the parish. Worleaze lies on a sloping bank, *v.* ora *supra* 442. The School gives the following modern forms: Bread Croft, Catsel, Cowleys, Foxells, Fussells, Ley, Quarry Ground for *Broad Croft, Catswell, Cowleaze, Fox Hills, Fossil Hill, Lye, Quar Ground* (*TA*).

HARDENHUISH. Bull Mead (*Bulls mead* 1640 WIpm). Laines Mead (cf. *Layne Hills* ib. and *supra* 439). Old Borrows (*la Hialdebir'* 1205 ClR, *Oldberye* 1638 WIpm. *v.* burh). Ridings Mead, Long Ridings (*Rydinges* 1640 WIpm. *v.* hryding). For Gastons Mead and Hungerdown, *v. supra* 432, 455.

KINGTON ST MICHAEL and KINGTON LANGLEY. Barberland (may derive from the *beuerbourne* of BCS 751. 'Beaver stream'). Bittles Spring (cf. *Bydellwell* 1517 WM iv). Byde Mill (*Bidemell* c. 1260 Aubrey. *v. supra* 4). Chapel Fd (cf. *Chapel Hay* 1670 Aubrey, on the site of a chapel pulled down in 1640). Coles Ham (*Goldshame* 1290 WM iv). Conegre (cf. *coppice called Cunnygrove* 1582 NQ vii). Culverwell (1517 WM iv. 'Pigeon spring'). Emead (*on þe ya* BCS 751. 'On the river' (OE ea)). Enox Piece (cf. *Northynnokes* 1428 Aubrey and *supra* 438). Everetts (1783 Act). Gingells (from the family of *Gengell*, cf. Robert *Gengel* 1273 Aubrey). Holdings (cf. *holandene* BCS 751, i.e. 'hollow valley'). Lay Croft (1783 Act). Lipyeat (*of þan lypʒate* BCS 751. *v. supra* 96). Mansell (*Manshill* 1783 Act). Matt Close (ib.). The Moors (cf. *Moremeade* 1428 ib.). Oakford (*to acford* BCS 751). Pegler's Pasture (*Peglars* 1783 Act). Great, Little Slait (cf. *Upper, Lower Sleights* 1706 WM xliv. *v. supra* 454). Staverland (may be by *stanforde* BCS 751. Cf. Staffords *infra* 496). Tweenwoods (*Twinwood* 1783 Act). Vernall (*Vernolls great Downe* 1642 WIpm, *Vern knoll* 1670 Aubrey. Probably 'fern knoll'). Wood Leaze (1706 WM xliv). For Farthingdale, Hungry Hill, Oak Riddings, Old Gaston, Ridings, Tining, Worthy, *v. supra* 429, 455, 437, 432, 437, 449, 450.

Kington Langley School adds Longlands (*Longelonde* 1289 *Ass*), and records Cowleys, Dry Leaves and Longleaves for *Cowleaze* (*TA*), *Dry Leaze* and *Long Leaze*.

LACOCK. Ashleys (*Asseleye* 1232 Lacock, *Aissheley* 1540 *MinAcct*. *v.* leah). Bean Acre (1767 Act). Broad Mead (ib.). Cockleys (*Cockeleye* 1232 *Lacock*). Cow Leaze (1767 Act). Dean Hill (*Denehill* 1642 WIpm). Fatting Leaze (*Fattingelease* 1540 *MinAcct*). Flax Leaze (*Flexlegh* 1308 NQ iii, *Flexleys* 1536 *MinAcct*). Goodley Hill (*Godelegh* ib., *Goodeleys* 1536 *MinAcct*, *Godley Hill* 1767 Act). Hobbs (ib.). Luckhorn (*Luckehorne* 1540 *MinAcct*, *Luke-* 1642 WIpm. *v.* horn). Mill Ham (*le Melehamme* 1308 NQ iii. *v.* hamm). Normead (*Normede* 1536 *MinAcct*). Ox Leaze (1767 Act). Pensdown (*Pensedone* 1308 NQ iii, *Pennesdoune* 1642 WIpm. There is a small isolated hill here and we may have another example of penn, 'hill,' cf. Pen Hill *supra* 33). Pond Mead and Rail Mead (1767 Act). Strick Leaze (*Stricklye* ib., probably from *strik* for *stirk*, 'heifer'). Thickets (*Thicketts alias Thekett meade* 1536 *MinAcct*). White Cross (1767 Act). Winterwell (*Wynterwelle* 1308 NQ iii, referring to intermittent spring). Withy Hayes (*Wythyheyes* 1540 *MinAcct*). In 1767 (Act) we have Innex (*le Hinhoc* 13th WM xxxiii. *v. supra* 438). Inn Lands (*le Inlonde* ib. *v. supra* 439). Sowbury (*Sothebury* 14th AD v, *Southbery* 1540 *MinAcct*). For Lawns, Piccadilly, Pinch Gut, Roundabout, Shoulder of Mutton, *v. supra* 440, 455, ib., 454, 455. Hackpin is curious. It lies low and can have nothing to do with Hackpen *supra* 310. It may be a compound of haca and penn, 'enclosure with a hook.'

LANGLEY BURRELL. Black Pool (*Blakpole* 1281 Trop). Lains Mead (cf. *The Layns* t. Jas 1 ECP and *supra* 439). Pencroft may be *Penicroft* 1240 Aubrey, *Pennicroft* 1517 WM iv, so called from its rent. For Butts, the Fleet, Gastons, Herne Close, the

Lawns, Picked Leaze, Roundabouts, Sheep Sleight, Smoke Ground, Sterts, *v. supra* 425, 431, 432, 437, 440, 443, 454, ib., 446, 447. No Man's Land is a detached field of Chippenham parish.

LEIGH DELAMERE. Binnell (*bien hylle* 1043 (c. 1250) KCD 767. 'Bees hill'). Marsh (*le Merssh* 1512 *Ct*). *Bydwell* (1512 *Ct*) is the *byde wil* of KCD 767. For Hitchin, Mere Pits, Picked Mead, Poor Mans Pasture, Quarr Leaze, Starveall, Tining, *v. supra* 435, 441, 443, 455, 445, 455, 449.

PEWSHAM. For Great and Little Ball, Bennetts and Panns Pew, the Bittoms, Cold Harbour, Emmetts Rag, Picked Leaze, Upper and Lower Raggs, Small Gains, *v. supra* 422, 14, 425, 451, 453, 443, 453, 455. Fleet is by a tiny feeder of the Avon, *v.* fleot *supra* 431.

SHERSTON. Blackwell Hill (cf. *Blackwell mead* 1670 NQ vii). Bracey Moor (*Brasemoore* ib.). Breach (*le Breche* 13th *Malm.* *v. supra* 423). Buslers (*Burslegh* 1335 Ipm. *v.* leah). Craymore (*Cramer* 1672 NQ vii). East Fd (*Eastfeild* ib.). Filmoor (*Filmoore* 1640 WIpm). Gallow Hill (1563 NQ vi). Garsons (cf. *Gaston feild* 1674 NQ vii and *supra* 432). The Ham (*le Ham* 13th RegMalm, *Hammes* 1335 Ipm. *v.* hamm). Hinchell (*Hench hill* 1677 NQ vi). Hornshill (1640 WIpm). Hydes Mead (cf. *Hyde house close* ib.). Lot Mead (cf. *le Lot* 1670 NQ vii). Noble Cross (ib.). Oat Furlong (ib.). Old Leaze (1640 WIpm). Paternoster (*close called Pater noster* 1677 NQ vii. Cf. PN Sr 107). Pock Ridge (*Poukeryche* c. 1300 *Malm.* 'Goblin ridge'). Purnell Hill (*Perne hill* 1674 NQ vii. Cf. *Purndene* 13th *Malm*). Querns Piece (*Quernes peice* 1640 WIpm). Rough Leaze (1670 NQ vii). Southmore (*Southmoor* ib.). Thorn Gate (*Thorne gate* ib.). Wabley (*Wabbeleye* 13th RegMalm). Windmill Fd (*Windmill feild* 1670 NQ vii). For Clanvill, Conegree, Hitchins, Lucky, Picked Piece, Pinnocks Gate, Rudge Leaze, Slait, Tile Quar Fd, Tyning, Little Worthy, *v. supra* 70, 427, 435, 455, 443, ib., 437, 454, 445, 449, 450. Merways is on the Luckington boundary, *v.* (ge)mære *supra* 441. Woe Hill Fd is by an isolated hill of irregular shape, *v.* woh, 'crooked.' Blackwell, Hobbs Leaze, Southmore (*TA*) now appear as *Brackrell, Obb's Close, Soumor* (School).

SOPWORTH. Roughborough (*Rowborrow* 1672 NQ vii. *v. supra* 423). For Black Ridings, Picked Piece, Short Butts, Tynings, *v. supra* 437, 443, 425, 449.

NORTH WRAXALL. Broadlands (*Broade lands* 1608 Lewis). Cold Crate (*Coldcroft, Coulecroft* ib. *v. supra* 427–8). Great and Little Ham (cf. *Hamacre* ib.). Innicks (*Innock* ib. *v. supra* 438). Lawn Tyning (cf. *The Laund* ib. and *supra* 440, 449). The Moor (cf. *Moore hill* ib.). New Tyning (cf. *The Tinning* ib. and *supra* 449). For Townsend, *v. supra* ib. The Batch is at the head of a long valley down which flows a feeder of By Brook. Cf. *supra* 428. Salisbury Plain is on the high open ground by the cross-roads at the School.

YATTON KEYNELL. Bull Mead (*Bullmead leaze* 1638 WIpm). Sheep Sleights (cf. *Sleights* 1706 WM xliv. *v. supra* 454). Stockbridge (*Stockburg* 1638 WIpm, *v.* Introd. xxi). For Cold Harbour, Conegre, Hunger Hill, Picked Acre, Rudgy Lands, Rudgeway, Storts Bush, Great Tining, *v. supra* 451, 427, 455, 443, 437, 17, 447, 449. Cold Harbour (two examples) are on high exposed land, Conegre is now known as *Congler*, Hunger Hill is noted as poor land, Quarr Hill is by an old quarry (*supra* 445), Rudgeway is the long track parallel to Cromhall Lane running from Grove Lane to Easton Piercy.

Bradford Hundred

ATWORTH. Burridge (*Bourigge* 1353 Trop). Chapits (*Chapit* 1640 WIpm). The Hales (*Hales* 1642 ib. *v.* healh). Hooks Mead (*Hokes* 1649 WM xli). Leys Fd (*Leesfeild* ib.). Moor Leaze (cf. *le More* 1453 *MinAcct*). North Croft (*le Northcrofte* 1548 Pat). Stitchings (*Stichinges* 1611 WM xli. *v. supra* 447). For Brimble Croft, Conigre, Fill Barns, Hamstich, Penning, *v. supra* 424, 427, 455, 449, 453.

The School adds: Cradle Field (from its shape); Fur Ground (in a remote part of the parish, cf. Furleaze *supra* 71); Hop Yard; Luke Stone (on the parish boundary, perhaps associated with verses from St Luke in the beating of the bounds), and notes that in Whirley Hole (*TA*) there is a hole where, in winter, the water whirls round. It gives Heales (*Hales TA*, cf. *supra* 373), Purditch (*Purdick TA*) and Silleaze (*Silleage TA*).

BRADFORD ON AVON. Barn Close (*Barne close* 1636 WIpm). Broadmead (*Broade meade* ib.). Clay Fd (cf. *Clailande* 1204 FF). Cole Croft (*Colecroft* 1332 AD i). Coombs Leaze (*Coombs* 1687 WM xliii). French Grass Fd (*French Grass Tyning* 1710 ib. iv. *v. supra* 449). Gaskins (may be *Garston* 1204 FF. *v. supra* 432). Hareknap (*Hare Kanpper, Hare Knapp* 1640 WIpm. 'Hare hill'). Hollands Mead (*Holland* 1453 *MinAcct*). Home

Mead (*Homemead* 1637 WIpm). Kings Cross Tyning (cf. *Kings Cross* 1583 WM xiii and *supra* 449). Marsh Croft (1649 WM xli). Moon Hedge (*Moonehedge* 1720 ib. xliii). Muchell Mead (*Muchelmed* 13th *Shaston*. 'Big meadow'). Pound Close (1649 WM xli). Ray Mead (*Reymeade ground* 1640 WIpm, cf. Reybridge *supra* 103). Sterts (*Stertes* ib. *v.* steort). Stone Hill (*Stonehill* 1589 WM xii). Well Ground (cf. William de *Puteo* 1289 *Ass*). Winterleys (*winderlæh* 1001 (c. 1250) KCD 658, *Winderleaze* 1632 WIpm). Yea Mead (*Eamead* ib. *v.* ea, 'water.' It lies by the Avon). For Beggars Bush, Cold Harbour, the Halves, Hawkshord, Innocks Mead, Great and Little Loins, Picked Close, Shoulder of Mutton, Smoke Acre, Spy Park, Great Tyning, *v. supra* 455, 451, 434, 445, 438, 439, 443, 455, 446, 252, 449. Spronke would seem to be from OE *spranca*, 'shoot, sprout,' preserved in dialectal *spronk*, 'stump of a tree,' hitherto only recorded from Kent, Sussex and Surrey (NED *s.v.*).

BROUGHTON GIFFORD. Chessells (*Chessel* 1558 WM vi, *Chesselfreth* 1642 WIpm. *v.* fyrhðe). Great Mead (*Mochell meade* 1641 ib. *v.* micel, 'great'). Green Way (cf. *Greene mereway* 1642 ib. *v. supra* 449). Ox Leaze (*Oxelease* 1641 ib.).

MONKTON FARLEIGH. Marycroft is on the north border of the parish and the first element may be OE (ge)mære, 'boundary,' cf. Mary Brook (PN Wo 13). White Cross Mead (*Wyttecrosse* 1453 *MinAcct*). Whitsales may be *Wycchesole* 1485 *Ct*. 'Pool (*v.* sol) where wych-elm grows.' For Cold Harbour, Coneygree, Pennsylvania, Plaisterers, Plock Pits, Starveall, Tyning, *v. supra* 451, 427, 455, 443, 453, 455, 449. Pennsylvania is in a remote corner of the parish.

HOLT. Dudleys (*Dodelegh* 1353 Trop, *Duddelegh* 1351, *-ley* 1386 FF. '*Dudda*'s clearing or wood,' *v.* leah). Holes Hill (*Holes* 1546 WM iii). Green Ham now *Grinham* (*Greneham* 1432 *MinAcct*). Hatchleys (*Hatchleaze* 1670 *Map*). Lousley (*Lowsley* 1546 WM iii). Midlings is in the middle of the parish. Park Mead (cf. *The Park* 1546 WM iii). Side Leys (*Sideleaze* 1766 *Deed*, from sid, 'broad'). For the Breach, Great Slait, the Tyning, *v. supra* 423, 454, 449. Hucksters is locally pronounced *Uxchers*. Modern field-names[1] include Burn Beake Ground, the Gaston (pron. *Gassen*), *v. supra* 451, 432. For Skilling Bradleys, *v. supra* 454. It is a field containing a cowshed. The Drung is the name of a narrow passage in the village (*supra* 451). Home Croft and How Croft (1770) or Hawcroft (1900) are locally pronounced *Unkerd* and *Awkerd* respectively.

[1] *Ex inf.* Mr J. H. Pafford.

LIMPLEY STOKE. For the Folly, Narrow Drung, Plaisters, Rough Breach, Smock Land, Twink Leaze, Wall Tining, *v. supra* 451, ib., 443, 423, 446, 455, 449. Sheer Croft is on the county boundary and probably derives from scir, 'county.'

WESTWOOD. Clay Furlong (*Cleyfurlong* 1453 *MinAcct*). Elm Hayes (*Elmehay* 1632 WIpm). For Long Tyning, Tiningsfield, Twitchells Meadow, *v. supra* 449.

WINKFIELD. Gore Mead (*Goremede* 1453 *MinAcct. v.* gara, or gor, 'mud'). Grove (cf. William *atte Grove* 1249 *Ass*). Long Foreheads (*Langforyerd* 1453 *MinAcct* may derive from OE forierð, 'headland'). North Hills (*Northyll* ib.). Slough (*le Sloo* 1432 ib., *la Slowe* 1585 *Recov*, from OE slōh, 'slough, mire'). Taggle Mead (*Tanggelmede* 1453 *MinAcct*). For Conigre, Dole Mead, Hitching, Short Platt, the Tining, *v. supra* 427, 429, 435, 444, 449.

WINSLEY. Bittoms lies low by the Avon. *v. supra* 425. Catsditch (*Catstitch* 1727 *Map. v. supra* 447). Cliff Tyning (*le Clyffe* 1453 *MinAcct. v. supra* 449). Conigre (*The Coninger* 1727 *Map. v. supra* 427). Coppety Row (*Coppity Row* ib.). Gillstich (*Gellstitch* ib. *v. supra* 447). The Grove (cf. *Grove Tineing* ib. and *supra* 449). The Ham (ib.). Long Mead (*Langmede* 1453 *MinAcct*). Merfield (*Merefelde* 1341 *Cor, v.* (ge)mære *supra* 441. It lies on the parish boundary). Norwood (1727 *Map*). Pit Close (cf. William *atte Putte* 1333 *SR*). Stapeley (*Stapely* 1727 *Map*). Warnage Mead (ib.). For Breach, Hatchett Piece, Pudding Close, Rowbarrow, Scotland, Waterstitch, *v. supra* 423, 433, 453, 423, 454, 447. The School adds No Man's Land (on the border), Stearts (*supra* 447) and gives Tedge Hill as an alternative for *Tedzell* (*TA*).

SOUTH WRAXALL. Barn Furlong (cf. *Bernstiche* 1445 *Ct* and *supra* 447). Dun Mead (*Donmead* 1583 WM xiii). Ellbridge (ib., probably 'plank-bridge,' from þelbrycg, cf. EPN *s.v.*). Hawkley (*Hanecleye* (sic) t. Ed 1 WM i. 'Hawk clearing or wood'). Timbridge (*Tymmeridge* 1583 WM xiii). For Conigre, Innocks, Lippots Hill, Lynch Bottom, Quar Leaze, Rudges, *v. supra* 427, 438, 96, 436, 445, 437.

Melksham Hundred

BULKINGTON and KEEVIL. Home Close (1626 WIpm). Ox Leaze (*Oxen Leaze* 1706 DKR xlii). Plot Mead (cf. *The Plotts* ib.). For Hitchin Leaze, Peaked Ground, Great and Little Tyning, *v. supra* 435, 443, 449.

ERLESTOKE. The School gives Barley Crate (*supra* 427–8); Clover Loin (probably for lain *supra* 439); Tynin (cf. tyning *supra* 449) and Big and Little Vize, so called because on the road to Devizes, cf. *supra* 242–3.

HILPERTON. Cottles may be *Cotsetle* (1325 *Pat*). *v. supra* 427. Leap Gate (cf. Robert *atte Luppeʒete* 1348 *Cor. v. supra* 96). For Bell Lands, Buckles Balls, Plock Pits, Shoulder of Mutton, Townsend, *v. supra* 451, 422, 453, 455, 449. Townsend is at the east end of the village. Frying Pan (with a long handle-like projection) may be so called from its shape.

MELKSHAM. Broadmead (*Broadmeade* 1642 WM xli). Cadley (*Cadleyes* 1650 *ParlSurv*). Cheswell Ground (*Chestlefeild* 1638 WIpm. *v. supra* 426). Cock Renals (*Cocks Reynolds* 1607 *Sadler*, *Cock Reynoldes* 1638 WIpm). Court Leaze (*Courtley* ib.). Cray Croft (*Crayes* 1607 *Sadler*). Dewpit (*Duports* ib., *Dewport* 1650 *ParlSurv*). Ell Ground is L-shaped. The Grove (1650 *ParlSurv*). Hatch Mead (cf. Richard *atte Hacche* 1333 *SR*. *v.* hæcc). High Leaze (*Hyley* 1640 WIpm). Mill Mead (cf. Richard *atte Mulle* 1333 *SR*). Normead (*Northmead* 1536 *MinAcct*). Rowlands (*Rowland* 1638 WIpm). Rowley (*Inner Rowley* ib.). Sharps Leaze (*Sharps* 1607 *Sadler*). Way Fd (cf. *Waye acre* 1650 *ParlSurv*). White Croft (*Whitecrofte* ib.). Wisneage[1] may be *Winseleaze* 1638 WIpm. For Barelegs, the Beak, Burnbake, Cowitch, Fatting Leaze, the Knapp, Lammas Lands, Leg of Mutton, Little Worth, Paradise, the Penn, Penning[1], Picked Ground, the Tynings, *v. supra* 455, 450, 451, 269, 438, 427, 452, 455, ib., 453, 443, ib., 449, 453. Cinder Leaze lies on the northern edge of the parish (*v.* sundor *supra* 448).

Forest and Sandridge School notes that fields called Tumps (cf. *TA*) have many knolls. It gives Eldermore for *Aldermoor TA*, Casleaze for *Calves Leaze* ib. and Ox Leaves for *Ox Leaze* ib.

Melksham St Michaels School gives Long Conigres (cf. *supra* 427), Lagger (a long field, cf. *supra* 452) and the nickname Catch-me-can, and gives Cyricks for *Cynicks TA*. Pease Bridge is far from any stream and is probably for *Pease Breach*, cf. *supra* 423.

POULSHOT. Wall End (*Wallings* 1638 WIpm). Wood Leaze (*Woodleazes* ib.). For Breach, Butts, In Mead, Long Lawns, Nine Halves, Withy Knapp, *v. supra* 423, 425, 438, 440, 434, 427. Hundred Acres (3 roods, 38 perches) is ironical.

---

[1] Wismeaze, Pennons (School).

SEEND. For Breach, Chassell, the Clears, Coneygre, Enocks Mead, Gaston, Upper and Lower Gore, the Halves, In Moor, New Tyning, Picked Mead, Pips Lains, *v. supra* 423, 426, 156, 427, 438, 432, ib., 434, 438, 449, 443, 439. Hundred Acres (2 roods, 14 perches) is ironical. Bench Piece[1] lies on a slope, cf. **benc** *supra* 423. The School adds Butts, Lains, Lammas Patch, Sand Field (*Sandfeild* 1639 NQ iii), Town Ground (in the village), cf. *supra* 425, 439, 452, 449.

STAVERTON. Sour Croft (*Sowercroft* 1553 *DuLa*). Townsend Leaze (cf. William *atte Tounesende* 1333 *SR* and *supra* 449). For Breach, Butts, Cock Road, Lot Mead, Pig Barton, *v. supra* 423, 425, 427, 436, 451.

TROWBRIDGE. Ash Leaze (*Assheleys* 1649 WM xli). Bird Leaze (*Bridlease* 1571 WM xv). Down Hays (*Downe heys* 1553 *DuLa*). Goose Acre (*Goseacre* t. Ed 4 ib.). Ham Mead (*Ham meade* 1671 WM xv. Cf. *Hamecrofte* 1488 *DuLa*). Hill Croft (*Hillcrofte* 1612 ib.). Long Mead (*Longemede* 1468 *MinAcct*). Manleys is on the parish boundary, cf. (ge)mæne *supra* 441. Mill Mead (*Millemede* 1488 *DuLa*). Pavey Mead (*Pavymede* t. Ed 4 ib.). Whitticks (*Whittock* 1553 ib.). For Brandires, Home Close, Lousy Mead, Roundabout, Shoulder of Mutton, Slob, Tyning, *v. supra* 62, 434, 455, 454, 455, ib., 449.

Whorwellsdown Hundred

STEEPLE ASHTON and GREAT HINTON. Bar Furlong (*Barefurlong* t. Hy 8 *Rental*). Binland (*Benlond* 1341 ib. 'Bean land'). Broadmead (*Brodemed* t. Hy 8 ib.). Clays, Clay Close (*The Cley* 1627 WIpm). Culliver (*Culverford* 1476 *Rental*. 'Pigeon ford'). Hawkham (*Haukecombe* t. Hy 4 ib. 'Hawk cumb'). Horselands (*Horslonde* 15th WM xvi). Laydown (*Leydowne* 1550 Pat). Leaseham (*Lessam landes* 1629 WIpm). Long Meadow (*Long-mede* 1491 *Ct*). Moor Croft and Mead (cf. *Morforlong* 1373 *Ct*, *le More* 1491 ib.). Normeads (*Norþmed* 1373 ib.). Oathill (*Otehill* t. Jas 1 *LRMB*). Pinnick (*Pynnok* 1341 *Rental, Pynnocke* 1491 *Ct. v. supra* 447). Slowgrove (*Slagrave* 1257 *For, Slogrove* 1373 *Ct*. 'Sloe thicket'). Windmill Furlong (cf. *Wynmylfeld* t. Hy 8 *Rental*). For Clap Gate Fd, the Lain, Long Thong, Quar Leaze, Shoulder of Mutton, Great and Long Tyning, *v. supra* 451, 439, 448, 445, 455, 449.

---

[1] Bench Peace (School).

WEST ASHTON and SEMINGTON. Bean Hill (*Benhulle* 1341 *Rental*). Biss Mead (*Bissemeade* 1629 WIpm. For the river, *v. supra* 2). Copytrough is no doubt for 'copped (i.e. pollarded) tree.' Cranhill (*Cranhulle* 1341 *Rental*). Crawley (1629 WIpm). Dolls Mead (may be *Doddismede* 1476 *Rental*). The Ham (*hamme* 964 (late) BCS 1127. *v.* hamm). Home Meadow (*Whomemead* t. Jas I *LRMB*). New Leaze (*Newlese* 1460 *Rental*). White Lands (*la Whitelonde* 1341 ib.). For Dole Mead, Frith, Leg of Mutton, Manship, Mizmaze Wood, Picked Leaze and Mead, *v. supra* 429, 431, 455, 441, 23, 443.

NORTH BRADLEY. Appledores (cf. *Apuldurmede* 1362 *Cor. v.* apulder, 'apple-tree'). The Breach (*The Breche* t. Jas I *LRMB. v.* bræc). Mill Mead (cf. Walter *atte Mulle* t. Hy 4 *Rental*). Oaken Close (*Okey close* 1641 WIpm). For Leazeways, Lot Mead, Lottery, Picked Ground, Slob Leaze, Wheel of Fortune, *v. supra* 438, 436, 455, 449, 455, ib. Gally Acre is probably for *Gallow* Acre.

COULSTON and EDINGTON. Adnell (*West Adnell* 1627 WIpm). Breach Knowl (cf. *Estbreche* 1397 *Ct*). Broad Croft (1627 WIpm). Chapel Close takes its name from the old chapelry of Baynton (WM x, 258). The Clays (*la Cleye* t. Hy 3 *Edington*). Feltham (*Fieltham* BCS 1127, probably 'homestead by the place cleared by felling,' cf. PN Ess lvi, *s.n.* Feltham (So)). The Ham (*le Hamme* t. Hy 3 *Edington*). Inn Mead (*Inmede* ib. *v. supra* 438). The Leys (*la Leose* 1367 Pat, *le Leese* 1393 IpmR). Lynch (*la Lynche* 1397 *Ct. v. supra* 436). New Croft (*Nywcroft* ib.). Nor Mead (*Normede* 1540 *MinAcct*). Pigshill (*Pykkeshull* 1283 ib. *v. supra* 96). Sharpcroft (1397 *Ct*). Sheepcroft Mead (*Shepecrofte* 1550 Pat). For Burnbrake (sic), Dring, the Folly, Lynchett, Upper and Lower Oare, Peaked Gore, Penning Mead, Upper and Lower Stitch, the Tyning, *v. supra* 451, ib., ib., 453, 442, 443, 453, 447, 449. Dring is a long narrow field, cf. *supra* 451. Hundred Acres (3 roods) is ironical.

Erlestoke Junior School adds Barton and Tenantry Down, cf. *supra* 431. Upper and Lower Vize Ground lie by the Devizes road and are perhaps named from it (cf. Vize Way for Devizes Way). Mardidge is just by the parish boundary and may stand for OE *mǣr-dic*, 'boundary ditch or dyke.'

SOUTHWICK. Acrefield (*Acrefeild* t. Jas I *LRMB*). Alder Grove (*Aldergrove* 1551 Pat). Dods Mead (cf. *Dodesmere* 1552 *Winch-Coll*). Dole Mead (*Dollmede* t. Jas I *LRMB. v. supra* 441). Moxome (*Mockesham* ib.). Ridge Leaze (*Ridgeley* ib.). Smoke Close (ib. *v. supra* 446). For Burnbrake (sic), the Frith, Green

Parlour, Picked Lands, the Sling, Starve Acre, Stitchings, *v. supra* 451, 431, 455, 449, 454, 455, 447. The Sling is a long narrow strip.

Westbury Hundred

BRATTON, DILTON, HEYWOOD and WESTBURY. Bean Croft (*Byne crofte* t. Jas 1 *LRMB*). Bitham Close (*close called Bottom* 1649 *SarumD and C*). Breach[1] (cf. *Est-, Westbreche* 1375 WIpm and *supra* 423). Broad Mead (*Brodemede* 1249 *Edington*). Bull Croft[1] (*Bulls croft* 1634 *Longleat*). The Conygre (*le Conyger close* 1626 WIpm. *v. supra* 427). Cox Steed (*Cokstede* 1536 *MinAcct, Cocke-* 1545 LP). East Marsh (*Istmersche* 1334 *Edington*). Fairwood (*Fairewood coppice* 1641 WIpm). Fleets (*le Fleete* 1325 NQ ii, *the Fleete* t. Jas 1 *LRMB, v.* fleot *supra* 431. It lies by a tiny stream). The Lines (cf. *East Laynes, Millaynes* 1626 WIpm. *v. supra* 439). Lions Fd (*Lyons feild* ib. *v. supra* 439). The Marsh (*le Marsh* 1634 *Longleat.* Cf. *Brattonmershe* 1491 *Ct*). Marsh Mead (*Marshmede* 1626 WIpm). Palmers (cf. *Palmeresham* 1397 *Ct, Palmers marsh* 1633 WIpm). Petticoat Lane (cf. *Petitescroft* 1325 NQ ii, which might later appear as *Petticroat.* Cf. croft *supra* 427). Pitsomes (*Pytsam* 1626 WIpm). Rough Breach (*Rowbrechis* t. Hy 8 NQ iii. *v.* ruh, bræc). Round Croft (*Rounde croft* t. Jas 1 *LRMB*). Rush Croft (*la Rischcrofte* t. Hy 3 *Edington*). Sand Hills (*Sandhull* 1397 *Ct*). Showells (may be *Sewells* 1638 WIpm, perhaps from OE *scēawels*, 'scarecrow'). Stock Mead (*Stockemede* t. Jas 1 *LRMB. v.* stocc, 'stump'). Strills (*le Striȝele* 1325 NQ ii. *v. supra* 447). Summer Leaze (*Somerlees* t. Jas 1 *LRMB. v.* læs). Withy Mead (*Withiemead* 1634 *Longleat*). Wood Stiles (*Wodestyghele* c. 1300 NQ ii. *v.* stigel, 'ascent'). For Appledores, Barn Tyning, Burgess Mead, Cats Brain[2], Cinder Leaze, the Drocks, Durn Croft, the Folly, Garston, the Gore, Grip Tyning, Knawbone, Labour in vain, Lot Mead, Lousy Oak, Lypyatt Ground, Mundays, No Man's Land, Paradise, Picked Leaze, Pool Breach, Quarr Tyning, the Rag, Sand Shoard, Shrubbits, Slob Ground, Starve Acre, Stitchens, Tyning, Venn Common, *v. supra* 216, 449, 451, 425, 448, 338, 363, 451, 432, ib., 452, 455, ib., 436, 455, 96, 455, 456, 455, 449, 423, 445, 453, 445, 430, 455, ib., 447, 449, 431. Mere Ash (*v.* (ge)mǣre *supra* 441) is on the county boundary. Mann Leaze (*v.* (ge)mǣne *supra* ib.) is on the parish boundary. Twitchens lies by the junction of two foot-paths (*v.* twicene *supra* 449). World's End lies on the parish boundary.

---

[1] Pron. *Britch, Bullkirt* (School).
[2] School notes that this is unkind land, a mixture of heavy clay and stone.

Dilton Marsh School adds: Breech Mead (*v. supra* 423); Dillycuts (*Dillycots TA*); Little Neldar (alders grow here, perhaps from *at then alder*); Mud Parrick (probably dialectal for *paddock*); Whitecroft (pronounced *White kirt*).

Dilton Council School adds the Leg (a long narrow field) and Little Linney. The latter would seem to be the common Devon *linhay*, 'small enclosure.'

Warminster Hundred

BISHOPSTROW. Hilwood (*Hillwood* 1550 Pat). Pit Fd (cf. *Putmad* 1234 *Longleat*). Pucks (cf. *Pukpole* 1232 *Lacock*. 'Goblin pool'). For Butts Close, Moothill, *v. supra* 425, 151. Raymead is by the Wylye, cf. *supra* 430.

NORTON BAVANT. The Gores (*The Gowers* 1609 Hoare, *v. supra* 432). Long Mead (*Longmeade* 1650 *ParlSurv*). North Fd (*Northfeild* t. Jas 1 *LRMB*). West Fd (*West feild* 1609 Hoare). For Burn Bake, Tenantry Ground, *v. supra* 451, 431.

SUTTON VENY. The School gives the following: Hitchcombe (*Hudescombe* 1400 WM xxxvii, '*Hudd*'s valley,' *v.* cumb); Mount Mill (*Mountemulle* ib.); Sand Field (cf. *la Sonde* 1421 *MinAcct*). For the Bake, the Cleeve, Peaked Fd, the Tyning, cf. *supra* 450, 426, 443, 449. Church Acres formerly used to pay candles for (ruined) St Leonard's Church. Fuzzey Common, with clumps of furze.

UPTON SCUDAMORE. Breach (*le Breche* 1362 *Cor*, 1445 *Ct*. *v. supra* 423). Chapel Close is by the site of Norridge Chapel. Cold Castle Tyning (cf. *Colcastell* 1640 *Longleat*. Probably so nicknamed with reference to the Romano-British settlement just to the north). Copthorn Tyning (*Coppedethorne* 1445 *Ct*. 'Pollarded thorn tree'). Ellen Croft (1640 *Longleat*). Lay Croft (*Leycroft* 1640 *Longleat*). Moat Ground (cf. *Moteforlong* 1445 *Ct*). The Moors (*The Moore* 1640 *Longleat*). For Malm Quar Tyning, Mondays Tyning, Play Close, Sand Shord, Smock Acre, Whitshord Tyning, *v. supra* 449, 440, 443, 445, 446, 445.

WARMINSTER. Beast Leaze (*Bestleaze* 1649 *SarumD and C*). Butt Close (*Buttclose* 1612 *Corpus*). Long Croft (*Longecroft* 1581 ib.). Pit Mead (*Pytt meade* 1649 *SarumD and C*. Cf. Edward *atte Putte* 1333 *SR*). For Moothill, *v. supra* 151. The School adds Fernicombe (*Verncumbe* t. Hy 3 *Longleat*); Haygrove (*Heygrove* 1367 *Corpus*); Woodman Mead (*Woodmansmeade* 1581 ib.).

WARMINSTER HUNDRED (DETACHED)

DINTON and TEFFONT. Earthpits (cf. *Earthpitt close* 1690 *Wilton*). Gason (*le Garston* 1322 Hoare, *Garson* 1690 *Wilton*. *v. supra* 432). Mill Mead (*Mylmeade* 1570 PembSurv). Orchard Coppice (cf. Simon *atte Orcharde* 1333 *SR*). Oxen Leaze (*Oxenlease* 1570 PembSurv). Pits Mead (*Pittemeade* ib.). The Woores (*Oars* 1801 *Map*. Cf. ora *supra* 442. The fields are on the bank of the Nadder). In a map of 1801 we have Bitham Wales, cf. *supra* 425. In one of 1844 (*Wilton*) we have, in Dinton, Foul Mead (*Vowlemeade* 1570 *PembSurv*) and, in Teffont, Linterne (*Linthorne* 1690 *Wilton*). Black Horse Fd is so called from the neighbouring inn.

FISHERTON DE LA MERE. For Linches, Paradise, Picked Piece, Town Mead, *v. supra* 436, 455, 443, 449.

Heytesbury Hundred

BOYTON. For Bake, Between the Cleves, Upper and Lower Bitham, Conygar, Friday's Linch, Picked Piece, Tyning, White Sheet, *v. supra* 450, 426, 425, 427, 436, 443, 449, 175.

CHITTERNE. Flax Land (*Flexland* 1711 WM xliii). Kite Hill (may be the *Cuteborwe* of 13th *Bradenstoke* from OE *cȳte*, 'kite.' It is *Kitehill* 1711 WM xliii). Long Lands (*Langelond* 1323 *DeVaux*). Windmill Down (cf. *Wynmulle* ib.). Woohill Fd (*Wohill Field* 1711 WM xlii. 'Crooked hill,' *v.* woh). Wormsey (*Wormseyfeild* ib.). For the Beak, Peaked Tining, *v. supra* 450, 443. The School adds Amen Corner, Beggar's Bush Fd, Gassons, Piccadilly Track, *v. supra* 482, 455, 432, 455.

CODFORD. Cat Pill is by a tiny stream (cf. *supra* 444). Long Ham (*Langham meade* 1632 WIpm). Red Meadow (*Red Meade* ib.). Rushy Mead (cf. *Rushes* ib.). Smock Acre (*Smoake acre* ib., *v. supra* 446). Stardway (*Stanerdewey* 1341 Trop, probably for *Stauerdewey* from the lost OE *stæfer*, 'pole,' etc. noted *s.n.* Staverton (*supra* 133). Perhaps a road marked by or made with poles). Townsend Close (cf. John *atte Tounesende* 1333 *SR*). West Fd (*Westefeld* 1323 *DeVaux*). For Badlinch, Bake Shooting, the Cleeve, Picked Furlong, *v. supra* 436, 450, 426, 443.

BRIXTON DEVERILL. Badbury may be *Babbeborrowe* 1454 *Kings*. '*Babba*'s barrow,' *v.* beorg). Honeycutts (*Hunycutts* 1723 ib.).

Poppy Map (cf. *Papyland* 1448 ib.). West Fd (*Westfeld* 1333 WM xxxvii). In 1746 (*Kings*) we have Tricketts Hill (*Trottekes-hulle* 1282 ib.), deriving from *Trottuc*, a diminutive of *Trott*. For Smoke Land, *v. supra* 446.

HILL DEVERILL. Broad Mead (*le Brodemede* 1337 AD iii). The Thicket (*le Thiket* 1547 Pat). For Coneygar, Picked Close, *v. supra* 427, 443.

LONGBRIDGE DEVERILL. Bellericay (*one close called Bellericary* (sic) 1732 *Longleat*. Cf. PN Ess 146. This would seem to be another example of the mysterious name *Billerica*, recorded from Essex, Kent and Somerset). Blackhill Furlong (*le Blake-hulle* 1315 *Longleat*, *Blakehill* 1547 Pat). Broad Mead (*Bradde-mede* 1235 WM xxxiii). South Ham (cf. *The Ham* ib.). For Rack Close, close called Rainbow, *v. supra* 445, 454.

HEYTESBURY. The School gives Sheep Meadow (cf. *Sheepleaze* t. Jas 1 *SP*), West Meadow (*Westmede* 1453 *MinAcct*) and also Conigre, Garston, Starve Hole, Tynings, cf. *supra* 427, 432, 455, 443.

HORNINGSHAM. Ansty Fd (*Anstye juxta Devrel Langebrigge* 1310, *Anstygh juxta Hornyngesham* 1330 *Ass*. *v*. Ansty *supra* 183. It lies just west of Rye Hill Fm on high ground, but the exact application here is difficult to determine). Clanwell Fd (*Clanwelle* 1341 *Cor*. 'Clean spring'). Kings Croft (*Kyngescroft* 1502 *Longleat*). Little Mead (*Litle meades* 1540 *Add*). Nutbury (*Nutborowe* ib.). Petty Ridge (*Putterigge* t. Hy 3 *Longleat*. Perhaps 'kite ridge.' Cf. Puthall *supra* 335). Rack Close (*Recke-close* 1453 *MinAcct*. *v. supra* 445). Water Mead (cf. *Water-furlong* 1540 *Add*). For Picked Close, *v. supra* 443. Syllabubs Knapp (*TA*) lies next to Dairy Coppice (6″).

IMBER. Bell Living is named from the Bell Inn. There is also a field called Ducks Living. Cf. *supra* 453. Coneygre (cf. *Conigerclose* 1540 *MinAcct* and *supra* 427). For the Bake, Cleve Fd, Great and Little Tyning, *v. supra* 450, 426, 443.

UPTON LOVELL. King Meadow (*Kyngmede* c. 1350 *Bradenstoke*). Mill Meadow (*Milemede* ib.). West Mead (*Westmede* 14th AD iii). For Gaston, Tyning, *v. supra* 432, 449. The School adds Amen Corner, perhaps from the beating of the bounds.

Mere Hundred

MAIDEN BRADLEY. Barn Ground (cf. *Barnebreche* 1467 Trop. *v*. bræc). Broad Mead (*Brademede* c. 1300 *Longleat*, *Brodemede*

t. Hy 8 *AOMB*). Cockstead (*Cokkestede* 1277 Trop). Dry Fd (*Driffeld* 1536 *MinAcct*). Frankham (*Francumb* n.d. Hoare, -*combe* 1536 *MinAcct. v.* cumb). The Hams (*la Hamme* 1277, *Hammes* t. Hy iv HMC xv, a series of small enclosures, right away from water, *v.* hamm). Hucklebreach (*le Hokedbreche* 1336, *Hokebrech* 1407 Trop, *Hucklebridge* 1784 *Map*. 'Hooked or curved bræc'). Mere Fd (cf. Walter *atte Meere* 1352 *MinAcct. v.* (ge)mære *supra* 441. On the parish boundary). Mill Close (cf. John *atte Mulle* 1327 *SR*). Rook Mead (*Rokesmede* 1536 *MinAcct*). Sandy Breach (cf. *Sandwilbreche* 1407 Trop). Well Mead (*Welmede* 1336, *Wylle mede* 1407 Trop). West Ham (*Westham* t. Ric 2 HMC xv, -*hamme* 1536 *MinAcct*). For Gore Marsh, Horse Tyning, Marlands, Picked Land, Rags, Shoulder of Mutton, *v. supra* 432, 449, 441, 443, 453, 455.

The School adds: Mappas, lying in a pass between two hills, which is almost certainly from OFr *malpas*, 'difficult pass,' as in Malpas (Ch); Saffron Garden (near the site of the Priory), the only example noted in Wiltshire; Wants Mead by cross-roads which must go back to ME *wente, wante*. It is by 'Four Wants,' a common term for cross-roads.

It gives Gore's Marsh for *Gore Marsh* (*TA*), but as the field is wedge-shaped, the *TA* form must be the correct one. Homer Gore's Marsh by it corresponds to *Homer Ground* (*TA*) with a small 'hollow mere' here. *hol-mere* frequently becomes *homer*.

MONKTON DEVERILL. Ruddocks Close is *Rudicks* 1740 *Sadler*. For the Lays, Lot Mead, Parrock, *v. supra* 438, 436, 442

EAST KNOYLE. Broad Hayes (*Brodehay* 1609 *Corpus*). Brook Lands (*Bruckland* ib.). Calf Hay (*Calfhays* ib.). The Drove (ib. *v. supra* 429). Leaze Hay (*Leashayes* 1629 DKR xl). Long Hayes (*Longehay* 1567 *Ct*). Penning (*The Penninge* 1609 *Corpus. v. supra* 453). Pond Close (cf. Adam *atte Ponde* 1333 *SR*). For Breaches, Burn Bake, Culverhayes, Innox Ground, the Leg, Picked Ground, Plashet, Rew, Tenantry Down, *v. supra* 423, 451, 433, 438, 455, 443, ib., 445, 431.

WEST KNOYLE. Church Furlong (cf. *le Churchakere* 1297 Trop). Crewley (*Cruly* 1630 WIpm). Green Hayes (*Grynehayes* 1609 *Ct*). Play Acre (cf. *Playshott* 1598 *EcclCom* and *supra* 443–4). Summerleaze (*Sommer lease* 1638 WIpm). Wood Furlong (*Woodfurlonge* 1668 Moulton). For Coneygarth, Quar Closes, the Tining, *v. supra* 427, 445, 449.

MERE and ZEALS. Ball (cf. *Ball more* 1563 *Rental, Balle knappe* 1595 WM xxix. *v.* cnæpp and *supra* 422). Beast Garston

(*Bearsgarston* 1650 *ParlSurv. v. supra* 432). Black Leaze (cf. *Blackley* ib.). Bramble Furlong (*Bremley furlong* 1566 *Ct*). Broad Hays (*Brodehayes* 1563 *Rental*). The Brook (cf. John *atte Brok* 1300 Ipm). Chilpits (1595 WM xxix). Chisletts (1650 *ParlSurv*). Court Close (ib.). Fisherhays (*Fisher Hayes* 1595 WM xxix). Gamlands (*Gamblyn's* 1730 ib.). Ganage (*Gannage* 1595 ib.). Green Hays (*Green Hayes* ib.). Grove Mead (*Grove meade* 1650 *ParlSurv*). Haycroft (*Heycroft* 1563 *Rental*). Hockridges (*Hockerydge* ib.). Horse Croft (*Horscroft* 1300 Ipm). Hurdles (*Hodelgrove* 1394 *GDR*, *Huddelles hearne* 1566 *Ct*, *Hurdles Hearne* 1640 WM xxix, from a personal name *Huddel*). Hurle Scene (*Hurle Seene* ib.). Lambrooks (*Lambrok* 1563 *Rental*). Liance Fd (*Lyense* 1595 WM xxix). Long Mead (*Long meade* 1650 *ParlSurv*). Marsh Mead (cf. William *atte Mersshe* 1333 *SR*). Mere Mead (*Meer meade* 1640 WM xxix). The Moor (*le More* 1567 *Ct*). Moot Fd may have been the meeting-place for the Hundred of Mere *supra* 172. It lies between Barrow Street and Lyemarsh Fm. Naplocks (*Knaplock* 1563 *Rental*). North Fd (*Northfeild* 1609 *Ct*). Park Mead (*Parrocke meade* 1585 WM xxix). Pease Hill (1650 *ParlSurv*). Pithayes (*Pithey* ib.). Ridge Common (cf. *le Rudge* 1609 *Ct*). Rowley (1563 *Rental*. 'Rough clearing'). Sniggs Mead (*Snygge mede* 1420 *Longleat*. *snig* is an old name for the eel, recorded from 1483 in NED). South Mead (*South meade* 1585 WM xxix). Star Mead (*Starr meade* 1650 *ParlSurv*). Stedham (*Stodeham* 1567 *Ct*, *Stedham* 1595 WM xxix). Water Mead (*Water medowe* 1585 ib.). Whatley (John de *Whatelegh* 1333 *SR*, *Wheatly* 1595 WM xxix). Widenham (*Widdynham* 1495 *Ct*. 'Withy ham(m)'). For Barebones, Burn Bake, Bushy Frith, Butts Ground, Clapp Gate, Frith Ground, Garston, Halves, Leg, Oar, Paradise, Pinnocks, *v. supra* 455, 451, 431, 425, 451, 431, 432, 434, 455, 442, 455, 443.

Stourton. For Bell Lawn, Breach Hill, Cock Road, Gascoignes, Innock, *v. supra* 451, 440, 423, 427, 432, 438.

Dunworth Hundred

Chicklade. For Beak, Penning, Starve Acre, *v. supra* 450, 453, 455.

Chilmark. Barn Hill (*Baren hill* 1632 *Wilton*). Broadland (*Brodeland* 1570 PembSurv). Broad Leaze (1693 *Wilton*). Clay Bush and Hill (*Claybushe, Cleyhill* 1570 PembSurv). Crook Ground (cf. *Crookes* ib.). Fowlers Meadow (cf. *Fowles Moor*

1632 *Wilton*). Frontley (*Fronttnell* 1570 PembSurv). Long
Mead (*Longe mede* ib.). New Leaze (*New lease* ib.). Odney (ib.).
Pudding Mead (*Podinge mede close* ib., referring to a sticky
meadow). Sandy Close (*Sandyclose* ib.). Trenleaze (*Trenley* ib.,
Trendlies 1632 *Wilton*, probably from OE *trendel*, 'circle,' with
reference to the outlines of the hill). Westmead (*la Westmede*
c. 1270 ib.). For Burnbake, Eden Garden, Starve Acre, Three
Halves, *v. supra* 451, 455, ib., 434. Menyett lies where the old
road from Chilmark to Chicksgrove cuts the Chilmark-Tisbury
boundary. 'Common gate,' *v.* (ge)mæne, geat *supra* 441.

DONHEAD ST ANDREW. Barn Close (1704 Hoare). Coppit
Nowers (*Copped Nowers* 1677 ib. *v. supra* 442. It lies on a
rounded bank). Holloway Close (*holeweg* 956 (14th) BCS 970).
Madgrove (*Madde Grove* 1544 LP). Nighvers (*Nyvers* 1608
Hoare. It lies on a steep hill, *v.* yfer *supra* 450, with affixed *n*
from *atten yvre, v.* æt). White Sheet Close (*White Sheet* ib.).
For Burnbake, Leg Close, Pecked Close, Pleck Close, *v. supra*
451, 456, 443, 444. The School records Halves which must
correspond to *Great* and *Little Have* (sic) (*TA*), *v. supra* 434;
Heaven Close (*Haven Close* ib.); Pound Lane, the site of the
pound for both Donhead parishes.

DONHEAD ST MARY. Amor Mead (1677 Hoare. Cf. *Amouracre*
supra 136). Black Furlong (1608 ib.). Bratch Close (*Brache* ib.
v. supra 423). Cholden Close (*Chelvedune* 956 (14th) BCS 970.
'Calves' hill'). Clay Piece (cf. *Cleys* 1608 Hoare). Pond Close
(id. ib.). For Bittam Close, Congreve Meadow, Culver Hays,
Ice Gasson Close, Pecked Close, Slat Furlong, Small Gains,
Yate Close, *v. supra* 425, 427, 433, 432, 443, 454, 455, 432.
Holy Oak Close is near the parish boundary and the oak may
have been so called from association with the beating of
the bounds. Portway Close is on the road to Melbury, *v.*
supra 16.

FONTHILL BISHOP. The Marsh (cf. John *atte Mersshe* 1362 *Cor*).
Pit Furlong (cf. *Pytteclose* 1467 *MinAcct*). For Cleve, Gaston,
v. supra 426, 432.

FONTHILL GIFFARD. Park Mead (cf. *le Parke* 1373 AD ii). For
Birch Balls, Cock Road Coppice, Down Linch, Stun Lawn, *v.*
supra 422, 427, 436, 440.

SEDGEHILL. Butter Stakes (*Butterstakes* 1558 FF). Sharp Hay
(*Sharpe hayes* ib.). For Crate Lane, Enoch, Freaths, Home
Leaze, Platt, Pleck, Sweet Halves, *v. supra* 427–8, 438, 431, 434,
443, 444, 434.

SWALLOWCLIFFE. London Elm (*London elme close* 1649 WM xli). Picked Close (1737 *Wilton. v. supra* 443). Quarry Hill (cf. *Quarr acre* ib. and *supra* 445). Range Hill and Rookley (ib.). For Starve Acre, *v. supra* 455. Harwood Coppice is on the parish boundary and contains OE har, descriptive of a boundary mark.

TISBURY and WARDOUR. Broad Mead (*Brodemede* 1382 *Harl*). Chantry Close (*Chuntre closes* (sic) t. Hy 8 Hoare, the endowment of some ancient chantry). Chapel Mead and Hays (cf. *Chappell close* ib.). Church Mead (ib.). Dodden Fd[1] (*Doddone* 1373 AD ii). Fords Mead (cf. John *atte Forde* 1333 *SR*). Gossel (*Gosewille* 1382 *Harl*. 'Goose spring'). Little Mead (*Litelmed* ib.). Marsh Close (cf. *le Mersshe* ib.). Orchard Mead (cf. John *atte Norcharde* 1333 *SR*). Park Mead (*Parkmede* 1382 *Harl*). South Croft (*Suthcroft* ib.). For Bratch, Cleve Close, Coppit Mead, Gaston, Hop Garden, Knapp Close, Leg Mead, Long Cratt and Cratt Close, Paradise, Picket Close and Hayes, Pinkwell, *v. supra* 423, 426, 427, 432, 452, 427, 455, 427–8, 455, 443, 55. The School adds The Bakes, Starveacre, *v. supra* 450, 455.

Chalke Hundred

ALVEDISTON. Broad Leaze (*Broadlease* 1640 WIpm). Crawley Fd (cf. John de *Crawele* 1333 *SR*, *Crowley gore* 1618 *Map*. *v.* leah). Culverhays (*Culverheye* 1570 PembSurv. 'Dove enclosure'). Fiddlepit (*Fiddlepitt* 1665 *Wilton*). Great, Little Gaston (*Gaston* 1640 WIpm. *v. supra* 432). Hemphays (*Hempheye* 1570 PembSurv. 'Hemp enclosure'). Long Mead (*Longemede* ib.). Pit Close (cf. Vincent *atte Putte* 1333 *SR*). Sharp Close (*Shap* (sic) *closes* 1640 WIpm). Sheats Close (cf. *Sheates meades* ib.). Whatcombe (*Watecombe* 1570 PembSurv. 'Wheat combe'). For Burnbake, the Leg, Pinkham, *v. supra* 451, 455, 55. The School adds Ashland (*Ashlands* 1665 *Wilton*) and gives Bere Hill for *Barehill* (*TA*).

BERWICK ST JOHN. Goatton (*Goteham* 1570 PembSurv). Michael Mead (*Michelmeade* ib. 'Big mead'). Pincombe (*Pynkecombefeld* ib. *v.* cumb and *supra* 55). Stub Hedge Fd (*Stybbhedge* ib.). Whistly Mead (*Whisteleyfeld* ib., cf. *supra* 246). White Lane (*Whitland* ib.). For Gaston, the Lawn, Lynchards, Picked Mead, Small Gains, *v. supra* 432, 440, 453, 443, 455.

---

[1] *Dodding* (School).

BOWER and BROAD CHALKE. Berry Hill Fd (*Berryhills, Beryhill* 1570 PembSurv). Cleeve (cf. *Muchelclive* 1276 StNicholas), *lez Cleves* 1570 PembSurv. *v.* clif). Court Close (cf. *Westcourte* ib.). Hill Way (cf. *super hullam* 13th, *Hulfurlang* 1276 St. Nicholas). Howgore (*Howgoores* 1570 PembSurv. *v.* gara). Low Fd (*Lowfeld* ib.). South Fd (*la Suthfeld* ib.). West Fd (*Westfeld* ib.). For Peaked Acre, Picked Close, *v. supra* 443.

EBBESBORNE WAKE. For Burnbake, Butts Close, *v. supra* 451, 425. The School adds Black Smaldon (*Blacksmal Down* 1710 *Wilton*); Bunckley Hanging (*Bunckley Hill* ib.); Jervis Combe (1710 *Wilton*); Weatherdon (*Weather Down* ib.). It further records Chadwell (*Chedwell TA*), probably 'cold spring'; the Leg (a long field); Quid Barton, 'dirty barton,' cf. Quidhampton *supra* 226 and barton *supra* 451; Twistle's Way, at the forking of tracks, from OE twisl, 'fork'; two examples of *cratt* (cf. croft *supra* 427-8) and Bush Vurlong (cf. Introd. xxi).

SEMLEY. Well Close (cf. Thomas *atte Welle* 1333 *SR*). For Bottom Leg, Burnbake, Coppit Close, Gayson Hill, Parsons Legs, Wores, *v. supra* 455, 451, 427, 432, 455-6, 442.

TOLLARD ROYAL. Upper, Lower Brach (*The Braches* 1618 *Map. v. supra* 423). Bugdens (*Buckden* ib.). For Gate and Peaked Furland, Half Hide, Halves, Hatchet Piece, Headland, Hop Garden, *v. supra* 443, 431, 435, 433, 434, 432, 452. Manland is on the parish and county boundary, *v.* (ge)mæne. For Long Croft the School gives *Long Crat*, cf. *supra* 427-8.

Cadworth Hundred

BARFORD and BAVERSTOCK. For Sling, *v. supra* 454.

BURCOMBE. Barnwell Fd (*Bernewelle* 1289 *Ass*). Dod Mead (*Dodemeade* 1570 PembSurv). East Fd (*Estfeld* ib.). The Marsh (*lez Marshe* ib.). Oxenham (ib.). Picked Close (*Peaked Close* 1803 *Map. v. supra* 443). South Ham (*Southham* 1705 *Wilton*). West Fd (*Westfeld* 1570 PembSurv). White Croft (1439 WM xiii). For Bake Fd, Cleeve, In Mead, *v. supra* 450, 426, 438.

FOVANT. Broad Mead (*le Brodemede* c. 1240 *Wilton*). Burrow Hill (1689 ib.). Strings Mead (*String meade* ib.). Turnbridge Close (*Turnbridge* ib.). For Burnbake, Louzy Mead, the Sling, Tenantry Fd, *v. supra* 451, 455, 454, 431.

SUTTON MANDEVILLE. Well Mead (cf. Ralph *ad Welle* 1341 *Cor*). For the Leg, Pinnock, *v. supra* 455, 443. The School adds Cratt, *v. supra* 427–8, and gives Picks Close for *Pitts Close TA*.

Cawdon Hundred

BRITFORD. Church Close (1650 *ParlSurv*). Drove (cf. *le Drovewaye* 1323 *DeVaux. v. supra* 429). Kings Mill Fd (*Kingesmulne* t. Ric 2 Hoare). Long Dean (*Longdene* 1323 *DeVaux*. 'Long valley'). Ox Mead (may be *Exemede* 1383 *MinAcct, Ax meade* 1650 *ParlSurv*, from OE *exen*, 'oxen'). Riles (may be *Rihull* 1383 *MinAcct, Riehull* 1535 *Rental, The Ryalls* 1650 *ParlSurv*. 'Rye hill'). Row Barrow (*Roweborgh* 1376 *DeVaux*. 'Rough barrow.' *v. supra* 423). Rushy Meadow (cf. *le Ruysche* 1323 *DeVaux*). Stone Hill (*la Stenyhulle* ib., *Stonyhull* 1535 *Rental*). Woodborough Piece (*Wadbury* 1323 *DeVaux*. The first element may be *wād*, 'woad'). For Paradise, Picked Piece, Sling, *v. supra* 455, 443, 454.

COOMBE BISSETT. East Fd (*le Estefeld* 1323 *DeVaux*). The Ham (cf. *Estham* 1473 *WinchColl*). Lynch (*le Lynche* ib. *v. supra* 436). Old Lands (*Oldelond* 1323 *DeVaux*. 'Worn-out land'). For Bake, Town Mead, *v. supra* 450, 449.

STRATFORD TONY. Ibsbornes (cf. Ebble R. *supra* 7). Warden Hill (*Wardenhull* 1473 *WinchColl*). For the Beak, Butts Croft, the Gore, Linch, *v. supra* 450, 425, 432, 436.

Branch Hundred

BEMERTON. The Plasketts *supra* 443.

LANGFORD. Bell Acre was traditionally used by the Sexton as payment for the bellropes he was called upon to provide (School). Cf. *supra* 451. Broad Mead (*Broadmeade* 1697 *Wilton*). Ham (*Ham* 1570 *PembSurv*). Hunnions (may be *Honyhams* ib. 'Honey hamm'). Mary Croft (*Marycroft* 1697 *Wilton*). The Moor (*lez Moore* 1570 *PembSurv*). For Beake, Brach Furlong, Buttocks, the Butts, Coneygar, Lynch, Old Lains, the Penning, Picked Hill, Pickett Furlong, the Purlieu, Smoke Furlong, Tenantry Down, Three Halves, Town Mead, the Wor, *v. supra* 450, 423, 425, ib., 427, 436, 439, 453, 443, ib., 453, 446, 431, 434, 449, 442. The Wor is on the northern bank of the Wylye. Troy Town is intriguing, now called *Tray Down* (School).

SOUTH NEWTON. Bonhams Mead (*Bonham bushes* 1651 Hoare).
Broad Hams (*Brodehamme* 1445 IpmR. *v. supra* 434). Broad
Mead (*Broadmeade* 1651 Hoare). East Fd (*Estfeld* 1570 Pemb-
Surv). The Hams (cf. *Sevenhams* ib. and Sevington *supra* 107).
Home Fd (*Hoomefeld* ib.). Inn Mead (*Innemeade* ib. *v. supra*
438). Long Ham (*Langenham* 1315 *Wilton, Longham* 1570
PembSurv). Middle Fd (*Middelfeld* ib.). Peaked Close (*Pyked
close* 1570 *Wilton. v. supra* 443). Pin Marsh (*pynding mersc* 943
(13th) BCS 782, *pinding ford* 10th (13th) Wilton Cartulary,
Pynne marshe 1570 PembSurv, from OE *pynding*, 'dam'). Rye
Mead (*Reymeade* c. 1570 *Wilton, Raye meade* 1651 Hoare. Cf.
Reybridge *supra* 103). West Croft (*Westcroft* 1570 PembSurv).
For Burnbake, Hatchet Croft, the Sling, the Stitches, *v. supra*
451, 433, 454, 447.

SHERRINGTON. For the Butts, Coneygar, Lynchet, Picked Mead,
Smoke Acre, Tenantry Down, *v. supra* 425, 427, 453, 443, 446,
431.

STAPLEFORD. West Mead (*Westmede juxta Stapulforde* 1376
Ass). For Beak, Burnbake, the Butts, Cleve, Coneygre, *v. supra*
450, 451, 425, 426, 427.

WILTON. Broad Mead (*Brodemede* 1535 VE). The Marsh (cf.
Estmarsh 1570 PembSurv). Middle Fd (*Middelfeld* ib.). Peaked
Mead (*Pyked meade, Pikedmeade* ib. *v. supra* 443). For Hunger
Hill, Lawn, *v. supra* 455, 440. *v.* Addenda *supra* xli.

Dole Hundred

BERWICK ST JAMES. North Fd (*Northfeld* 1301 Ipm). Pie Marsh
(*Pipe marshe* 1591 WM xvi). South Fd (*Suthfeld* 1301 Ipm).
For Burnbake, the Drove, the Penning, Picked Lands, Smock
Acres, *v. supra* 451, 429, 453, 443, 446.

MADDINGTON. Linch (*Lynche* 1323 DeVaux. *v. supra* 436). For
Beggars Bush, the Cleave, Gaston Piece, the Lawn, Tenantry
Down, *v. supra* 455, 426, 432, 440, 431. The Bury is close by
Bourton Fm *supra* 233.

ORCHESTON ST GEORGE. For Bakeland, Peaked Furlong, *v.
supra* 450, 443.

ORCHESTON ST MARY. Garstones (*Gerston* 1227 Ch. *v. supra*
432). For Burnbake, Conygre, Picked Acre, Shoulder of
Mutton, Three Halves, *v. supra* 451, 427, 443, 455, 434.

ROLLESTON. For Chestles Fd, the Lain, Picked Fd, *v. supra* 426, 439, 443.

SHREWTON. For Path Lynch, Shoulder of Mutton, Town Furlong, *v. supra* 436, 455, 449.

WINTERBOURNE STOKE. Cheswell Fd[1] (may be *Chesthull(e)* 1455, 1488 *MinAcct*. The first element may be OE *ciste*, 'chest, coffin'). Cow Down (1574 WM xxxiv. *v. supra* 430). Droveway (*The Drove* ib. *v. supra* 430). Farm Down (*Ferme downe* 1591 ib. xvi). Ham Fd (*The Hame* 1574 ib. xxxiv. *v.* hamm). Horse Croft (ib.). Hyde Fd (cf. Edith *atte Hide* 1333 *SR*, *Hyde feild* 1574 WM xxxiv). The Marsh (*le Mersshe* 1455 *MinAcct*). Middle Down (1574 WM xxxiv). Midsummer Mead (*Midsomer mead* ib.). Small Mead (ib.). Vicarage Acre (ib.). West Brook Fd (*West brook* ib.). Woolhams Mead (*Woolams* ib.). For Breach Fd, Burn Bake, Lynch, Lynchett, Old Lain, the Penning, Tenantry Down, *v. supra* 423, 451, 436, 453, 439, 453, 431. Fargo is the name of the field in the far north-east corner of the parish (cf. *supra* 365).

Rowborough Regis Hundred

GREAT CHEVERELL. The School gives the Crate, the Folly (*supra* 427, 451), Gaston Field and Ground (*la Garston* 1422 *Ct*, *supra* 432), the Pennings, Tyning, *supra* 453, 449.

EASTERTON. Court Close (*Courte closes* 1591 WM vi). The Downs (cf. *super dunam* 1218 FF). Kings Ground (cf. *Kingesmere* 1227 FF and *Kingiscrofte* 1190 WM vi). For Night Leaze, Sleight, Starve Croft, *v. supra* 438, 454, 455.

MARKET LAVINGTON. Bishops Ground (cf. *Bissopesdich* 1301 *Extent*. The Bishop of Salisbury had a holding in West Lavington (1316 FA)). Breach (*la Breche* 1224 FF. *v. supra* 423). Broad Mead (*Brademede* ib.). Cleeves Close (cf. *le Clif* ib.). Forehill (cf. *Fordune* t. Hy 3 Edington. 'Before the down'). Ham (*Hamme* 1224 FF. *v.* hamm). Hollow Way (*Holeweie* 1227 ib.). Wish Mead (*Wychmede* 1224 ib.). For Burnbake, Cain Ground, Laines, Picked Piece, Tining, *v. supra* 451, 455, 439, 443, 449. Pennsylvania is on the parish boundary, cf. *supra* 455.

WEST LAVINGTON. Bowers Hill (cf. *Burelinche* 1224 FF. *v. supra* 436). Chalk Croft (may be *Chalvecroft* t. Hy 3 Edington.

---

[1] Chessel (School).

'Calves' croft'). Court Close (1542 *LP*). Garstone (*Gerstune* 1227 FF. *v.* gærstun). Lynch (*la Linche* t. Hy 3 *Edington, Linches* 1301 *Extent. v. supra* 436). Mill Fd (cf. Richard *atte Mulle* 1327 *SR*). Vaux Hill Fd (*Foxulle* 1227 FF, *v.* Introd. xxi). West Fd (*Westfeld* 1301 *Extent*). For Burnbake, Laynes, Lynch, Night Leazes, the String, *v. supra* 451, 439, 436, 438, 455.

Rowborough Hundred

DEVIZES and ROUNDWAY. Marsh Mead (cf. *The Mersh* t. Jas 1 *LRMB*). For the Lawn, *v. supra* 440. The School adds Pook's Lane, i.e. 'goblin's lane.'

MARSTON. Horse Leaze (*Horsleas* 1545 AD v). For Penning, Pennsylvania, *v. supra* 453, 455.

POTTERNE. Great, Little Doles (*The Doles* 1545 AD v. Cf. *Dolmede* 1242 SarumCh. *v. supra* 429). Great, Little Flags (*le Flagges* 1626 WIpm). Garston (*la Garston* 1422 *Ct. v. supra* 432). Long Mead (*Longe meade* 1545 AD v). Rudge Mead (cf. *Rigge* 1341 *Cor*). Sprays (cf. Alexander de *Spray* 1333 *SR*). Thorny Croft (*Thornecroft* 1222 FF). For Barebone, Breach, Breakheart, Butterwell, Clay Shord, Coneygre, Cow Barton, Hatchet Piece, Lousy Bench, Monday Mead, New England, Peaked Meadow, Penning, *v. supra* 455, 423, 455, 339, 445, 427, 451, 433, 455, 440, 455, 443, 453. New England is by the parish boundary.

ROWDE. Bullhanger (*Bolhangre* 1342 *GDR, boscus de Bullanger* 1503 *MinAcct. v.* hangra). The Burrells (*The Burials* 1721 *Map*, which may be a survival of OE *byrgels supra* 425). Crawberry (*Croborowe* t. Jas 1 *LRMB*). Dunsbrook (cf. Thomas de *Donesbroke* 1346 *Ass, Dunsbroke* t. Hy 8 *MinAcct*). Goss Hills (*Goswell* 1721 *Map*). The Ham (*Ham* t. Jas 1 *LRMB*). Home Close (ib.). Larkum (*Larkomsley* 1721 *Map*). Pyke Leaze (*Piked Leaze* ib. *v. supra* 443). Raymead (*Raymede* t. Jas 1 *LRMB*. Cf. Reybridge *supra* 103. It is by a stream). Upper, Lower Ridge (*The Rigge* ib.). Slade Furlong (*Slatfurlonge* 1641 WIpm). Swillway (*Swilly* 1721 *Map*. Cf. *Swilles feilde* t. Jas 1 *LRMB*. It is by a stream). Vernicroft (*Veroncroft* 1721 *Map*). For Brimble Furlong, Hitchens, Linchetts, Peaked Ground, Skelling Ground, *v. supra* 424, 435, 453, 443, 453. The School adds Pinnocks (*supra* 443) and gives Cowley's for *Cowleaze TA*.

WORTON. Cockersail Acre may be *Cockestal* 1362 *Cor.* Sow Cotts (*Southcroft or Sowcruds* 1812 *Map*). For Butt Leaze, Coneygre, the Strings, *v. supra* 425, 427, 455.

Cannings Hundred

BISHOP'S CANNINGS. Great, Little Breach (*Breach* 1635 WIpm. *v. supra* 423). Broad Lands (*Broadlands* 1649 *SarumD and C*). Caswells (*Casewell* 1623 *Add*). Chawcroft (may be *Chall crofte* ib.). The Cliffs (*v. supra* 426). Dock Lands (*Docke lande* ib.). Dole Mead and Pits (*le Dolemede* 1351 *DeVaux, Dolepitts* 1661 *Devizes. v.* dal and *supra* 429). Little Mead (*Littlemeade* 1635 WIpm). Lypiates (*Lypyate* 1564 *Add. v. supra* 96). Pikes Acre (*Pyked acre* ib. *v. supra* 443). Quarr Leaze (*The Quarre* 1623 *Add, Quarleys* 1635 WIpm. 'Quarry leaze,' *v. supra* 445). Rough Croft (*Rowcroft* 1377 *MinAcct*). Sand Fm (cf. *The Sands* 1661 *Devizes*). Shipton Piece (may be *Sheepe Down* 1631 WIpm). Stone Acre (*Stony acre* 1564 *Add*). Town Furlong (*Towne furlong* 1661 *Devizes*). Wood Leaze (*Wode lese* 1623 *Add*). For the Butts, the Lains, the Lake, Linchett, Peaked Meadow, the Penning, Starts, Starve Croft, *v. supra* 425, 439, 438, 453, 443, 453, 447, 455. Mere Lands is on the parish boundary, *v.* (ge)mære *supra* 441.

Calne Hundred

BERWICK BASSETT. Farnborough (*Farneborough* 1636 WIpm). Swallows (*Swallowes* ib.). For the Drove, Picked Bit, *v. supra* 429, 443.

BROMHAM. Bawks Hill (*Balkes* 1409 *Ct. v. supra* 422). Boseleys (*Borseley* 1570, *Boresley* 1592 *Add. v.* Boscombe *supra* 361). Broad Mead (*Brodemeade* 1564 ib.). Bushy Leaze (1771 WM xlv). The Castle (cf. *Castell hyll* ib.). Cinder Barrow (*Synderbarrows* 1570 ib. *v. supra* 448). Upper, Lower Clay (*le South, North Cley* 1564 ib.). Coombs (*Combes* ib.). Cow Leaze (*Cowlease* ib.). The Ham (*le Hamme* 1399 *Ct. v.* hamm). Hemscrooch (*Hempcrouche* 1409 ib. *v.* crouche, 'cross'). The Hooks (*le Hoke* ib. *v.* hoc). Kings Elms (1771 WM xlv). Long Mead (1652 ib. xlii). The Lye (*Lye* 1592 *Add. v.* leah). Parsons Mead (cf. *Personeshamme* 1354 *Ct*). Pond Leaze (cf. *Pond Mead* 1652 WM xxxii). Rudlands (*Rydland* 1564 *Add*). Stockwell Close (*Stocwell* 1288, *Stokwellestret* 1354 *Ct.* 'Spring by the stump'). Stony Croft (*Stonycrofte* 1592 ib.). West Fd (*le West-*

feld 1351 AD iv). For Burnbeak, Cockroad, Picked Mead, Roundabouts, Shoulder of Mutton, *v. supra* 451, 427, 443, 454, 455.

CALNE. Blackthorn (*Blakethorn* 1471 WM xxxiv). Boor Down (cf. *Burelond* 1273 Ipm, *Bourefeld* 1527 Marsh and (ge)bur *supra* 424). Brickkiln Ground (*Brickhill* 1754 *Map*. Cf. *supra* 36). Broad Leaze (*Brodelye* 1232 *Lacock*). Castle Fd (*Castilfelde* 1553 Marsh). Chiden Hill (*Chiding Hill* 1725 *Map*). Doodiddle (may be *Dolytelemede* 1370 *Cor*, a nickname of reproach). Froghill (*Froggehull* 1273 Ipm). The Ham (*le Hamme* 1548 Pat). Hankers (may be *Hangerlonde* 1232 *Lacock*. *v.* hangra). Hipping Stone (*Hippingstone Bottom* 1725 *Map*. Possibly identical with the NCy dialectal word for a stepping-stone). Holloways (*Holeweie* 1525 AD i). Honey Garston (*Hunnygarston* 1649 *SarumD and C. v. supra* 432). The Hurst (*Hurst* 1637 WIpm, *v.* hyrst). Latchmoor (*Lachemere* 1273 Ipm. *v.* lache, 'sluggish stream'). Lime Kiln Piece (cf. *Limekilne* 1703 *Map*). Long Acre (cf. *Angereslangaker* 1232 *Lacock*). Menley (is on the parish boundary, *v. supra* 441). Moon Croft (*Monecrofte* 1562 *Add*). Newlands (*Newlande* 1563 BM). Padford (*Pedeford* c. 1300 *Stowe*). Pigeon Close (*Pidgion close* 1695 WM xlvii). Play Close (cf. Robert *atte Pleystowe* 1333 *SR. v. supra* 443). Rack Close (*The Rack Close* 1694 *Devizes. v. supra* 445). Red Moor (*Redmore* 1296 FF, *Radmores* 1471 WM xxxiv). The Ride (*Ride Wood Plantation* 1778 *Map*). Rough Mead (*Rouwemede* 1232 *Lacock. v.* ruh). Round Hill (may be *Roghenhulle* 1358 Ipm. 'Rough hill,' *v.* ruh). Short Croft (*Shortecrofte* 1637 WIpm). Stitchings (cf. *The Stiches* 1649 *SarumD and C. v. supra* 447). Vernalls (*Fernehill* 1555 Pat). Water Mead (*Waturmede* 1471 WM xxxiv). Wenhills, Wen Hill (*Wenhulle* t. Ed 1 *Lacock*, *Weynehyll* 1493, 1500 ECP, *Waynehill* 1555 Marsh; cf. also *Waynfeld* 1548 Pat). For Burnbake, Coneygre, Devils Bed, Doubtful Piece, Innicks, Lynch, Great and Little Oar, Picked Hill, Quarr Ground, Sheep Sleights, *v. supra* 451, 427, 455, ib., 438, 436, 442, 443, 445, 454.

Calstone School adds Hitchings (*supra* 435), North Field (*Northfeld* 1527 Marsh) and shows that Bye Croft (*TA*) is in a sharp bend of the road, cf. *supra* 467.

CHERHILL. For Buttocks Corner, Three Halves, *v. supra* 425, 434. The School adds Pill Land (cf. *supra* 444) by a hollow once filled with water and called Pill Pond.

COMPTON BASSETT. Dean Meadow (cf. *Deneforlong, Denelond* 1304 Ipm). The Marsh (*le Marays* 1274 ib.). Great, Little Pen (*la Penna* 14th AD vi. *v. supra* 334). Trendalls is on a circular hill, from OE *trendel*, 'circle'; cf. The Trundle (PN Sx 54, PN D, Pt. I, liv). White Ditch (*la Whytedich* 1369 *MinAcct*). For Cold Harbour, Rag Mead, *v. supra* 451, 453.

HEDDINGTON. Ball Breaches (may be *Balkebreche* 1232 *Lacock*. *v. supra* 422–3). Blacking Hill Fd (may be *Blakehulle* ib.). Broad Leaze (*Broade lease* 1640 WIpm). Davy Hay (*Davyehay* ib.). The Gore (*The Goare* 1640 *SarumD and C. v.* gara). Hanging Land (cf. *Hangerlonde* 1232 *Lacock*, *v.* hangra). Mobley (*Mabley meade* 1640 WIpm). Notfields (*Notfield, -fould* ib.). Ochre Ridge (*Ockerugge* 1232 *Lacock.* 'Oak ridge' or '*Occa*'s ridge'). Townsends (cf. Walter *atte Tounesende* 1333 *SR*). Well Ground (cf. William *atte Welle* ib.). For the Balls, Bidwell, Cains Ground, Upper and Lower Crate, Hitching Fd, Linches, Picked Leaze, *v. supra* 422, 116, 455, 428, 435, 436, 443. Hundred Acres (20 perches) is ironical.

YATESBURY. Barrow Slade (cf. *Berouforlong* 1304 Ipm. There are two barrows here). Butts Mead (cf. *Bottes* ib.). Garstons Acre (*le Garstone* ib. *v. supra* 432). Head Land (*Hevedlond* 1310 ib. *v. supra* 439). For Lains, Dry Penning, Scotland, Three Halves, *v. supra* 439, 453, 454, 434. The School adds Craat or Craft, *v. supra* 428.

Kingsbridge Hundred

BROAD TOWN and CLYFFE PYPARD. Breach (1549 WM xliv. *v.* bræc). Broad Mead (1762 *Brazenose*). Clay Fd (*Clayfield* 1706 ib.). Cole Croft (*Callcroft* 1549 WM xliv). Cow Leaze (*Cowleys* 1706 *Brazenose*). Hanging Lands (*Hanginge lands* 1626 WIpm). Hatchets (*The Hatchett* 1706 *Brazenose. v. supra* 433). Home Close (*Who(l)me close* 1549 WM xliv). Inlands[1] (*Innlands* 1706 *Brazenose. v. supra* 438). Innox (*Inocks* 1549 WM xliv. *v. supra* 438). Jericho Fd is on the edge of Clyffe Pypard parish, cf. *supra* 455. Kings Croft (*Kingescrofte* t. Hy 8 *AOMB*). Great, Little Marsh (cf. *Two Marsh Meades* 1626 WIpm). Mead Heavens (*Mead Heydens* 1706 *Brazenose*). Mountain Lains (*Monckton lane* 1549 WM xliv, *Muncton laynes* 1626 WIpm. *v. supra* 439). North Leaze (*North leys* 1706 *Brazenose*). Red Lands (*Redlands* ib., i.e. 'reed-lands'). Reeves Mead (cf. *le Reeve acre* 1626 WIpm). Roughlands (*Rolands down* 1549 WM xliv). Sheep Sleight (*The Sleight* 1753 *Map. v. supra* 454). Side Croft[1] may be *Sudcroft* 1626 WIpm. Wheatalls[1] (*Whethulle*

[1] Englands, Seed Croft, Wheat Hills (School).

1370 AD vi, *Whittles* 1742 *Map*. 'Wheat hill'). White Fd (*Whitefield* 1706 *Brazenose*). For Idovers, Lains Mead, Mount Pleasant, Picked Mead, Purley, *v. supra* 3, 439, 455, 443, 453. Hundred Acres (1 rood, 33 poles) is ironical. Canon Goddard adds Cock Walk (a steep path up the Hangings); Harepath (a foot-path up the steep hill, possibly from herepæð *supra* 435); Littleworth (an isolated cottage, cf. *supra* 455); The Purley is a copse on the edge of the parish, cf. *supra* 453; Sideling Wood runs along the escarpment, cf. *supra* 454.

The School reports Black Furland (*Black Furlong TA*), Castle Herrings (*Castle Headings* ib.), Clip (*Clip and Go* ib.), Row Down (*Rough Down* ib.). It adds Inmore and Skilling Ground (cf. *supra* 438, 454) and Quidnell (cf. Quidhampton *supra* 226).

HILMARTON. Black Fd (cf. *Blac forlang* c. 1220 *Magd*). Bourne Fd (cf. *Burnefurlang* ib.). Broad Mead (*le Brodemede* 1512 *Ct*). Gaston Fd[1] (cf. *la Garston* c. 1300 *Bradenstoke*. *v. supra* 432). The Leigh (cf. *Leyforlong* 1345 *Magd*). Long Drove (cf. *Bradedrave* c. 1220, *le Drove* 1345 *Magd*, *le Drovewey* 1512 *Ct*. *v. supra* 429). Moors (*le Moores* 1626 WIpm. *v.* mor). Wood Leaze (*Woodleaze* 1636 WIpm). For the Lains, Lammas Mead, the Nap, Picked Leaze, Sleight, *v. supra* 439, 452, 427, 443, 454. Hundred Acres (2 roods, 11 poles) is ironical.

The School adds Big and Little Dene (cf. *Deneforlong* c. 1220 *Magd*).

LYNEHAM. Cock Mead (*Cockemede* 1540 *MinAcct*). Quarr Close (cf. *Quarr fields* 1666 *Sadler* and *supra* 445). Worrells (*Wyrall* ib.). Pucklechurch is just by the church. Cf. Pucklechurch (PN Gl 124). It is tempting to take this as a nickname, 'goblin's church,' from OE *pucel*, 'goblin.' The name repeats itself in an unidentified field *pecia voc. Pockle church* (1570 PembSurv) in Winterbourne Bassett, not far away.

The School adds: Black Mead (*Blacke mead* 1635 WIpm); Coarse Marsh and the Course (at the head of separate feeders of Cowage Brook, cf. Gauze Brook *supra* 7); Skilling Fd (*supra* 454); Twistle Close (between the junction of two roads, from OE twisl, 'fork') and War (for the more usual *Wor*) recorded as The Ore (1635 WIpm) on the bank of a stream, *supra* 442.

Bradenstoke School adds: Faircraft (*Feyrecrofte* 1540 *MinAcct*); Marlleaze (*Morelese* ib.); Woodleaze (1636 WIpm) and gives *Whorles* for Worrells *supra*.

[1] Gassons (School).

TOCKENHAM. Black Close (cf. *Blakelonde* 13th *Bradenstoke*). Broad Mead (*Brademede* ib.). The Hill (cf. John *atte Hulle* 1333 *SR*). Inwoods (*le Invode* 1331 *MinAcct. v. supra* 450). Laines (cf. *Leynecrofte* 1503 ib. *v. supra* 439). East Ley (*Estlye* 1331 ib.). The Marsh (cf. *Mershdych* 13th *Bradenstoke*). Smallinger (*Smalhangere* ib. 'Narrow slope,' *v.* hangra). West Mead (*Westmede* ib.). For Thong, *v. supra* 448. The School adds The Coombes (*le Combe* 1331 *MinAcct*), Roddle (*Rodhill TA*), Roughits (cf. *supra* 430).

WOOTTON BASSETT. Bittern Pond (*Bittern Ponde* 1714 WM xliv). Broken Lawn (may be *Brokenelond* 1394, *Brokyng land* 1525 AD vi). Brook Mead (*Broke* 1503 *MinAcct*). Darvells (*Derefolde* 1503 *MinAcct.* 'Animal enclosure'). High Meads (*le Hygh mede* 1546 *Ct*). Madcroft (*Litilmedecroft* 1503 *MinAcct*). New Mead (*Newemede* ib.). Orchard (cf. Richard *atte Norchard* 1333 *SR*). Pishill (*Pushulle* 1334 WIpm, *Pesehille* 1503 *MinAcct.* 'Pease hill'). Pitbridge (cf. John *atte Pytte* 1376 ib.). The Pleck (*The Plecke* 1676 WM xliv. *v. supra* 444). Pound Fd (*Poundefolde* 1503 *MinAcct*). Ryelands (*Rylands* 1525 AD vi. *v. supra* 439). Staffords Mead (*Stoford* 1503 *MinAcct. v.* Stowford *supra* 124). For Breach, Burnbake, Gogmire Ground, Idivers, Largess, Lousy Close, Picked Close, Pinnocks, Scotland, Skilling Ground, *v. supra* 423, 451, 452, 3, 455, ib., 443, ib., 454, ib.

Blagrove Hundred

LYDIARD TREGOZE. The Folly (1805 *Map, v. supra* 451). Hazell Close (may be *Hasell hill close* 1638 WIpm). Pill Acre (*le Pyle acre* 1512 *Ct*) lies by a tiny stream and probably derives from pyll *supra* 444. For Cock Road, the Ham, Idovers, Lains, the Pleck, Rag (common), *v. supra* 427, 433, 3, 439, 444, 453. Meer Mead is by the parish boundary, *v.* (ge)mære *supra* 441.

The School adds South Sea and New Zealand, both probably so called because in remote corners of the parish, and gives *Brickhill* for Brick Kiln Mead, *Hatchet* for Hatch Gate and *Plex* for the Pleck, cf. *supra* 36, 433.

SWINDON. For Broad Breach, Court Naps, Great Culvery, Laggers Hill, the Lains, Picked Mead, Sheep Sleight, Small Gains, Upper and Lower String, *v. supra* 423, 427, 433, 452, 439, 443, 454, 455, ib.

WROUGHTON. The Berry (cf. *Berry Meade* 1608 WM xxxvi). The Breach (*la Breche* 1331 WintonCart). Dudman Hades (*Dudman's Hades* 1805 *Map. v. supra* 434). Folly Furlong

(*The Folly* ib. *v. supra* 451). Great, Little Hurst (cf. *Hurst medowe* 1608 WM xxxvi). Ruddles Mead (*hrud wylle* 956 (c. 1150) BCS 948, 'reed-spring,' *v.* hreod, wiell). Sour Fd (*Sour Grounds* 1805 *Map*). Spring Furlong (*Springfurlong* 1659 WM xxxvi). For the Lain, the Parlour, Picked five acres, Snap Fds, *v. supra* 439, 455, 443, 446.

Thornhill Hundred

CHISLEDON. Berricrofts (cf. *Bury marsh* 1619 WM xxi). Bourne Meadow (cf. *Borne forlong* 1608 NQ viii). Close Lake (1641 WIpm). Cossical (*meadow called Corsickle* ib., probably a corruption of earlier *cotsetl*, *v. supra* 427). Fore Mead (*Foremeade* 1641 WIpm). North Close (ib.). The Plain (*The Plaine* ib.). Stertsmarsh (1709 *Sadler*). Great, Little Wexell (*Waxhill* ib. Cf. Wexcombe *supra* 347). For Burnbake, Picked Meadow, *v. supra* 451, 443.

LIDDINGTON. Cowleaze (*Cowleys* 1695 NQ viii). Dial Close (*Dyall close* ib. Cf. PN Sr 368). Island Meadow (*Ilands Mead* 1695 NQ viii). Great, Little Marsh (cf. John *atte Mersshe* 1333 SR). For the Lains, the Lynches, Picked Mead, the Purley, *v. supra* 439, 436, 443, 453.

WANBOROUGH. Upper, Lower Hyde (cf. *le Hyde* 1233 *Magd. v.* hid). For the Frith, the Pills, *v. supra* 431, 444. The Pills is by a small stream.

The School adds Coombe (*Litelcoumbe* 1374 *Magd*, *v.* cumb); Cossickle (cf. *Cotsettlemede* ib. and *supra* 427); Dockham (*Dokham* 1349 WIpm, 'hamm where dock grows'); Wetfurrow (*Weteforw forlong* 1374 Cl); Windmill Piece (cf. *Wyndmulle post* ib.). It also gives The Forty (marshland, cf. *supra* 43), Inmead (*supra* 438); Pickett, Picket Piece, Picket Inlands, Picket Linch (all fields with sharp angles, cf. *supra* 443), Poor Ground (two, used as charitable endowments, cf. *Almesaker* 1270 *Magd*), Starveall (two, poor soil).

Ramsbury Hundred

BAYDON. The School gives Homer Meadow and the Severals (cf. *supra* 483, 454), also the Varton (for Barton *supra* 451).

LITTLE HINTON. Great, Little Hams (*le Ham, Litleham* 1476 *Winton. v. supra* 434). Inn Mead (*le Inmede* 1419 ib. *v. supra* 438). New Leaze (*Neweles* 1476 ib.). For Breach Mead, Peaked Patch, Hither and Far Woor, *v. supra* 423, 443, 442.

RAMSBURY. Cross Mead (*Crossemede* 1570 PembSurv). Dry Meadow (*Drymede* 1425 *MinAcct*). Hams (*les Hames* 1406 *SarumD and C, Netherham* 1570 PembSurv). Home Fd (cf. *Whome Close* 1570 *Wilton*). Puttle Corner (*Pothale* 1456 *FF, Pottel grove* 1570 PembSurv, adjoins Puthall in Bedwyn *supra* 335). Rack Meadow (*Rackmede* ib. *v. supra* 445). Thornham (cf. *Thornehambridge, Thorneham* ib.).

Selkley Hundred

ALDBOURNE. Droveway (1751 *Longleat. v. supra* 429). Green Hill (*Grenehill* 1587 *Rental*). Harts Hook (*Hart hooke* ib. Cf. *Herteslande* 1468 *MinAcct*). Heydown (*Heydon* 1689 WM xlii). New Meadow (*Newmade* 1553 *DuLa*). Rooksbury Fd (*Roksburye* 1509 ib.). Rose Fd (*Rowes feld* 1580 ib., *Rosefield* 1587 WM xlii). Sandridges (*Sandridge* 1587 *Rental, Saundredge yeatt* 1591 WM vi. *v.* geat). Summer Leaze (*Sommer leaze* 1650 *ParlSurv*). West Fd (*Westefeld* t. Ed 4 *DuLa*). Witch Hill (cf. *Highwichell* 1552 WM xxxiii). For Great and Little Hooks, Lynchet, Old Lains, Picked Acre[1], the Pightle, *v. supra* 436, 453, 439, 443, ib.

The School adds: Bottle Copse (so called from its shape); Hundred Acres (a really large field and therefore not ironical); Jacob's Well Hill (where a spring appears after heavy rain); Port Hill (on the Hungerford-Cricklade road, which must have been a Portway, cf. *supra* 16).

AVEBURY. The Drove (cf. *Drove furlonge* 1640 WIpm and *supra* 429). West Fd (*West feilde* t. Jas 1 *LRMB*). Whitelands (1640 WIpm). For Breach, Folly Hill, Penning, *v. supra* 423, 451, 453.

The School adds Canada (distant and cold); Cratts (*supra* 428); Gawson (from *Gasson, v. supra* 432); Big and Little Island (well watered); three fields called Whyr (on the bank of a small stream, probably from ora *supra* 442).

BROAD HINTON. Galworth (*Gallworth* 1706 *Brasenose*). Great, Little Marsh (cf. *le Marsh* 1695 ib.). For Great and Little Breach, the Laines, Little Worth, Picked Ham, Sheep Slait, *v. supra* 423, 439, 455, 443, 454.

EAST KENNETT. For the Penning, *v. supra* 453.

MARLBOROUGH and PRESHUTE. Bay Meadow (*Baihedemede* 1503, *Baymede* 1570 *MinAcct*. Cf. Bay Bridge *supra* 303). Bell Close

---

[1] Picket Land (School).

(1570 *MinAcct*). Broad Mead (*Broade Meade* 1649 WM xli). Castle Mead (*Castellmede* 1540 *MinAcct*). Coursers Gore (*Coursers Goare* 1682 *Sadler*). Culvers Mead (*Culverhousemede* ib. 'Dove house mead'). East Fd (*Estfeld* t. Hy 8 *AOMB*). Harts Mead (*Harte meade* 1570 WM xxxviii). Long Meadow (*Langemede* 1438 *MinAcct*). Moor Mead (cf. *The More* t. Hy 8 ib.). Mundays Mead (*Mundayes Mead* 1714 *Sadler*, cf. *infra* 440). Priors Croft (*le Priors crofte* 1557 *Pat*). Pudmore (*Podemere* 1335 *MinAcct*, *Podemore* 1438 ib.). Rowdown (*Rowdon* 1570 PembSurv). Sheep Down (*Shepedoune* ib.). The Thorns (*le Thornes* ib.). West Fd (*Westfeld* 1553 *Pat*). For Barken Hangings, Clapper Piece, Folly Down, Little London, Portfield, Small Gains, *v. supra* 451, ib., ib., 455, 444, 455. Zulu Land is in the far south-east corner of the parish (School), cf. *supra* 455.

MILDENHALL. Broad Mead (*Brodemede* 1381 *MinAcct*). Cold Hill (*Coldehill* 1578 *Sav*). Cowslip Hill (*Cowslade hyll* ib. *v.* slæd). Frogmore (*Frogg moores* ib.). Nickamoor Fd is probably to be associated with *Nicapooles Croft* (ib.) which must have been by *Nikerpole* (1272 Ipm), the home of Henry de *Nykerpole* (1333 *SR*). This is a pool haunted by water-demons, from OE *nicor* (PN Sx 562 and PN Ess 598–9). The field is by the Kennet. The Pits, Pit Mead (cf. William *atte Putte* 1333 *SR*, *Pyttclose* 1578 *Sav*). Rack Mead (*Rackmede* 1570 Pemb-Surv. *v. supra* 445). Staples (cf. Robert *atte Stapele* 1333 *SR*. *v.* stapol. It is just by the highest point in the neighbourhood which may well have been marked by a stapol or post). For Breach, Burgess Mead, Clapper Piece, Coneygar, the Half, the Lawn, Linchard, the Oar (1779 *EnclA*, 'footway along the *Oare* or *Wore*'), Small Gains, *v. supra* 423, 451, ib., 427, 434, 440, 453, 442, 455.

OGBOURNE ST ANDREW. Berry Mead (cf. *Buryfyld* 1465 *Ct*). Cow Leaze (*le Cowlese* ib.). Crawlings (*Crawlynch* ib., *Crawlings* 1743 *Sadler*. 'Crow-hill,' *v. supra* 436). Great, Little Lynch (*les Lynches* 1496 *Ct*). Woodway Hill (*Woodway Fd* 1778 *EnclA*). For Burnbake Hill, Crate Meadow, Picked Meadow, *v. supra* 451, 428, 443.

OGBOURNE ST GEORGE. Blacklands (*Blackelonde* 1465 *Ct*). Bushy Cowleaze (cf. *le cowlese* ib. "There are many haw-thorn bushes here" (School)). Coneygar, now *Conygre*, (*Coneygere* 1751 *Longleat*. *v. supra* 427). Droveway (ib. *v. supra* 449). Garston Ends (cf. *Horssepolegarston* 1465 *Ct*). Hensell (*Hyneshyll* 1496 ib.). Inkwoods (*Inkwood* 1751 *Longleat*). Motley Corner (*Mottley* ib.).

The School adds Balls Pit (*Ballys pytts* 1496 *Ct*); The Butts *supra* 425); Franklins (*Franklands* c. 1840 *TA*, cf. Franklin's Fm *supra* 316); West Halve (on the west side of the parish, cf. healf *supra* 434); White Hill (1751 *Longleat*). For Boor Lands, Bushets, *v. supra* 424, 430.

WEST OVERTON. The School gives the following: Gasson (*v.* gærstun *supra* 432); Hatchety Hatch (on the edge of the forest, *v.* hæcc *supra* 433); Rowden Mead (1773 A and D) and Samborne Close, giving another name for the Upper Kennet (*supra* 8).

WINTERBOURNE BASSETT. Drove Way (cf. *la Drave* 13th AD vi and *supra* 429). West Fd (*Westfeld* 1570 PembSurv). For Conigar Mead, Sheep Sleight, Snap Mead, Long Wor Fd, *v. supra* 427, 454, 446, 442. The School adds Cowlease (*Cowe lease* 1570 PembSurv); Whettles (*Whetehill* ib.) and Slates, probably for sleight *supra* 454, and gives Grisbag for *Gristbag TA*, probably a nickname of praise.

WINTERBOURNE MONKTON. The School gives Cratts, Brook Verland and Han Verland, cf. *supra* 428, 431.

Studfold Hundred

ALL CANNINGS, ALLINGTON and ETCHILHAMPTON. Farrall (1608 WM xi)[1]. Ford Mead (*le Forde* 1563 *NewColl*). Homer (*Hollmeare* ib. *v. supra* 483). Knights Leaze (*Nightlees* ib. *v. supra* 438). Lains[1] (cf. *le Innerleynes* ib. *v. supra* 439). Old Mead (*Ould meade* 1608 WM xi). Ox Moor (*Oxmoore* ib.). Parsonage Ham (*Parsons hamme* ib.). Peaked Croft (*Pykecroft* 1457 AD iv. *v. supra* 443). Rushy Mead (*Rushmede* 1563 *NewColl*). Stibb Meadow (cf. *Stibbe* 1608 WM xi and *supra* 447. Sunderham Mead (*Syndremede* 1570 PembSurv. *v. supra* 448). Townsend (at the end of the village). Whettons (cf. *Whetton ditch* 1608 WM xi, *Wheaten Ditch* n.d. *Map*). For Amors Mead, the Gore, Hare Path, Herne Ham, Lynchett, Penning, Pudding Mead, Rushetts, *v. supra* 136, 432, 435, 437, 453, ib., ib., 430. Hundred Acres (2 roods, 1 pole) is ironical. All Mixon is probably for *Old Mixern*, i.e. 'manure-house.'

The School adds: Ivies or Nithys, the name of some low-lying marshy fields south-east of All Cannings Bridge. We may probably compare Nythe *supra* 284. Sidehills (*TA*) is recorded as *Zidles*, with local *z* for *s*. The Old Pound is the name of the village green.

---

[1] Farrow, Upper and Lower Loin (School).

CHIRTON. The School gives Knightleys (*Nightleaze* 1570 PembSurv, cf. *supra* 438); The Sands (*Est Sondes* ib.) and Penning (*supra* 453).

PATNEY. The School gives The Clay (cf. *Clayfeild* 1570 PembSurv); Maddocks (*Marrocks* ib., probably 'boundary oaks,' from (ge)mære and ac, as the field is on the parish boundary); Summerlands (cf. *Somerhill* ib.). It also gives Penning (*supra* 453) and Seldom Seen, a nickname for a field in a remote part of the parish.

STERT and URCHFONT. East, West Clay (*le Cleyes* 1563 *NewColl*). Common Mead (cf. *le comen lees* 1515 ib.). Cow Leaze (*le Cowlese* ib.). Crannell (*Cranhill* 1549 NQ ii. 'Crane or heron hill'). The Down (cf. *Downehouse* 1634 NQ vi). East Fd (*Eastfeild* 1563 *NewColl*). Upper, Lower Heath (*Heythball* 1563 ib. *v. supra* 422). Home Close (1626 ib.). Inlands (*Inlond* 1460 NQ iv, *Inneland* 1515 *NewColl*. *v. supra* 438). Lye Croft (*Lyecroft* 1546 NQ v). Maggot Mead (cf. *Magott woodes* 1605 ib.). Moor Mead (cf. *le Moores* 1626 *NewColl*). Orchard Close (cf. *le Orchard* 1563 ib.). Road Mead (may be *Rudmede* ib.). Staple Mead (*Staplemeade* 1605 NQ v. *v.* stapol). Tanners Hole (cf. *tannera hol* BCS 1295, a Kentish charter). Well Ground (cf. *Estwelleacre* 1487 NQ iv). White Croft (*Whytecroft* 1460 ib.). For Grass Breach, Little Profit, Peaked Mead, the Penning, Pink Mead, Quabbs Close, Smoke Acre, *v. supra* 423, 455, 443, 453, 55, 445, 446. The School adds Ham Brook (*the Ham* 1570 PembSurv), by a small brook; Hundred Acres is noted as a very small field (ironical), and Dark Croft (*TA*) becomes *Dark Grat*.

Swanborough Hundred

ALTON BARNES. Broad Well Spring (*bradewelle* 825 BCS 380, *Brodwelbrooke* 1616 *NewColl*. 'Wide spring'). Farm Down (cf. *Fearme Meade* ib.). Home Close (*le Whom close* ib.). The Orchard (*le Orchard* 1563 ib.). For Barken Ground, Barton Field, *v. supra* 451. The School adds Little and Big Ford (*le Forde* 1563 *MinAcct*) and Picket (cf. *Picked acre* 1616 *NewColl* and *supra* 443).

ALTON PRIORS. The School adds Stanchester (cf. *supra* 426).

BEECHINGSTOKE. Gold Hill (*Goldhyll* 1561 *Corpus*). Nouncil (*Nownshill* ib.). Press Land (*Prestland* ib. 'Priests' land'). Sheeplands (*Shepeland* ib.). For Butts Ground, Garson, Picked Ground, *v. supra* 425, 432, 443.

CHARLTON. For Garston, Lammas Mead, Penning, Play Garston, Stert Fd[1], *v. supra* 432, 452, 453, 441, 447. The School adds the Crat or Croft (*supra* 428).

HUISH. For Coneygar, Drock Bottom, Long Half, Picked Fd, Platt, Smokeham, *v. supra* 427, 339, 434, 443, ib., 446.

MANNINGFORD ABBOTS. For the Butts, *v. supra* 425.

MANNINGFORD BOHUN. Court Meadow (cf. *Courte Close* 1558 *DuLa*). Wick Close (cf. *le Wyke* 1330 *MinAcct*. 'Dairy farm,' *v.* wic and *supra* 25). For Lynchet, Picked Wick Close, Townsend, *v. supra* 453, 443, 449.

MANNINGFORD BRUCE. Long Meadow (*Longemed* 1330 *MinAcct*). Moor Fd (cf. *The More* 1558 *DuLa*. *v.* mor). Rusletts is a continuation of the *slæd* noted under Russletts *infra*. For Butts Close, Lains, Town Field, *v. supra* 425, 439, 449.

MARDEN. For Beak Ground, Linch, *v. supra* 450, 436.

NORTH NEWNTON. Broad Doles (*Brodedolles* 1570 PembSurv. *v. supra* 429). Doles (*lez Dooles* ib.). Great, Little Gason (*la Garston* ib. *v. supra* 432). Hill Mead (*Hillemeade* ib.). Nether Hays (*Netherhays* ib. *v.* gehæg). Oatlands (*Ottland* ib.). Pigeon Close (may be *Culverhaies* ib. 'Dove enclosure'). Ranscomb (*Remescombe* 1570 *Wilton*, i.e. 'raven-valley'). Russlett (*riscslæd* 892 (13th) BCS 567, 'rush-valley,' *v.* rysc, slæd). Sheephouse Close (may be *Shippingclose* 1570 PembSurv, *Shepingclos* c. 1570 *Wilton*, from OE *scipen*, 'cow-shed'). War Mead (*Warmeade* 1570 PembSurv). For the Crate, Hitchings Ground, Piked Ground, Sterts, *v. supra* 428, 435, 443, 447.

RUSHALL. Haystock (*Havestok* 1289 AD vi, *Haystock* 1570 PembSurv). For Garston[2], Golden Stitch, the Penning, Tucking Mill[2], *v. supra* 432, 447, 453, 442. Man Mead[2] is on the borders of Rushall and Charlton, *v. supra* 441.

The School adds Duck's Acre from the gift by Lord Palmerston of this field to endow an annual dinner for the threshers of Charlton St Peter in honour of Stephen Duck, the thresher poet who was born here.

STANTON ST BERNARD. Breach Meadow (cf. *lez breach* 1570 PembSurv). Dogland (cf. *Doggelane* ib.). East Mead (*Eastmeade* 1632 *Wilton*). Upper, Lower Fern (cf. *pastura vocata Verne* 1570 PembSurv. *v.* Ferne *supra* 188). Horse Balls (*Horse-*

---

[1] Pron. [sti·ərt] (School).
[2] Gasson, Tucker Mill, Mawn Mead (School).

balles ib. *v. supra* 422). Long Ham (*Longham* 1682 *Wilton*). Mill Ham and Mead (*Mylhams, Milmeade* 1570 PembSurv). The Moor (*The Moore* 1682 *Wilton*). Piles Close (cf. *Pylepeece* 1616 *NewColl*). Splatts Mead (cf. *Splott* 1682 *Wilton. v.* Splatts *supra* 263). Sunder Mead (*Syndermede* 1570 *Wilton*, Pemb-Surv. It lies by the stream forming the parish boundary). White Moor (*Whitmoure* ib.). Whittick (*Wythick* 1632 *Wilton*). For Bake, In Lands, Strouds, Tenantry Down, *v. supra* 450, 438, 447, 431.

UPAVON. Barley Hill (*Balrichulle* (sic) 1289 AD vi). Dock Mead (cf. *Dockemedestorte* ib., *Dokemede* 1397 *DuLa. v.* steort, 'tail, point'). Flower Ditch Fd (*Flower ditch* 1591 WM vi). Ham Fd (cf. *le Hamme* 1289 AD vi and hamm). Hay Mead (*Hieghmede* 1591 WM vi). Mill Ham and Mead (cf. *Mulnehoke, Mulnelond* 1397 *DuLa*). Sheffords Mead (*Shefforde* 1591 WM vi). For Lynch Fd, Lynchet, Newman's Folly, Slay Fd, *v. supra* 436, 453, 456, 329.

WILCOT. Cranmore (1540 *MinAcct*). The Drove (*Ye Drove* 1696 *Devizes. v. supra* 429). For Breaches, Linch, Mundays Close, Nap Ground, Picked Hill, Seven Halves, *v. supra* 423, 436, 438, 427, 443, 434. The Heart is so called from its shape. Portway is the track down Oare Hill, a little to the west of the present road, *v. supra* 16. Name not now used. The School gives Kramers for *Cranmore TA* and Sidelands for *Sidelong Ground TA*, *supra* 454.

WOODBOROUGH. Mill Close and Mead (cf. William *atte Mulle* 1333 *SR*). For Barwick Mead[1], Bremhills, the Lawns, Picked Ground, Strings, Three Halves, *v. supra* 184, 424, 440, 443, 455, 434. The School notes several fields in *Hurst* (*supra* 437), which is somewhat rare in Wiltshire.

Elstub Hundred

ENFORD. For the Drove, Lynch, the Parlour, Penning Close, Plock Pile Mead, Stert, *v. supra* 429, 436, 455, 453, ib., 447.

EVERLEIGH. The Gaston (*le Garston* 1488 *DuLa. v. supra* 432). Upper, Lower Park (cf. *The Parke* 1612 ib.).

FITTLETON. Bullon (may be *Bouledone* 1329 Ipm). Pigeon Close (cf. *Pigeon House close* 1603 DKR xl). For Beak, Cleeve Mead,

---

[1] Barrack Meadows (School).

Crate, Garsons, the Sling, *v. supra* 450, 426, 428, 432, 454. Hundred Acres (28 poles) is ironical. The Sling is a long narrow strip.

NETHERAVON. Corfe Mead (1650 *ParlSurv*). Dykeswater Mead (cf. *The Dike* 1591 WM xvi). Parsonage Mead (1650 *ParlSurv*). Peasehayes (*Peacehayes* ib.). For Breach, Landshare Meadow, Picked Mead, Wiltway, *v. supra* 423, 440, 443, 509. Landshare Meadow is on the Avon which here forms the parish boundary.

Kinwardstone Hundred

GREAT BEDWYN. Bar Fd (cf. John *atte Barre* 1333 *SR*). Clay Pits (*Cleyputte* 1374 *For*). Costar Lands (cf. *Costoo copice* 1570 PembSurv, probably from *cotstōw*, 'cottage-site'). The Heath (cf. John *atte Hethe* 1333 *SR*). Lady Mead (*Ladie meade* 1570 PembSurv). Long Mead (*Uplangemede* 1235 SarumCh). Pound Fd (*Punfalde* 13th *Bradenstoke*, i.e. 'pinfold'). Sands (cf. *le Sandes* 1637 *Sav*). For Burdens Several, Coneygre, Gutter Shord, Picked Corner, Smoke Acre, *v. supra* 454, 427, 445, 443, 446. Lime Kills is dialectal for *Lime Kilns*. Man Lands is on the parish boundary, *v.* (ge)mæne *supra* 441.

LITTLE BEDWYN. Breach Ground (cf. *Breach* 1637 *Sav. v. supra* 423). The Holts (cf. William de *Holt* 1333 *SR*). Home Close (1649 *SarumD and C*). Merrell Down (*Marrell Down* 1633 WIpm). North Fd (*Northefeilde* 1637 *Sav*). Parlour Fd (*Parler field* 1663 WIpm; cf. William *le Parlere* 1337 *For*). For Picked Meadow, *v. supra* 443.

BURBAGE. Drove Close (cf. *Drove copice* 1570 *Wilton, West Drove* 1662 *Sav. v. supra* 429). Hazel Ditch (*Hasildiche* 1570 *Wilton*). Long Mead (*Langemed* 1264 *Devizes*). Lyehill (cf. *le Lyghe* ib. *v.* leah). Monheath (*Manheath* 1635 DKR xli). Pittons Bush (*Peattens Bush* c. 1800 *Map*). Rudmead (*Rodmed* 1264 *Devizes*, from hreod, 'reed'). For Breach Mead, Buttocks, Folly Ground, Pudding Acre, Severals, Sprays, Sterts, *v. supra* 423, 425, 451, 453, 454, 348, 447.

BUTTERMERE. For Clapper Close, Hitchings, Picked Ground, Great and Little Several, *v. supra* 451, 435, 443, 454. Picket Hill (*Picked Hill TA*) goes up to a peak (School). Wood Cotes (*TA*) is *Woodcut* and Raycroft (*TA*) is *Raycut* (School).

CHUTE. Ashridge (cf. John de *Ayschrugge* 1333 *SR*; 'ashes still here' (School)). Lammas Mead (*Lowmas Meade* 1548 Pat. *v. supra* 452). Long Croft (*Langecroft* 1324 Cl). The Marsh (cf.

Marshe yeatt 1591 *DuLa*. *v*. **geat**). Pit Meadow (cf. John *atte Putte* 1341 *Cor*). Wattscroft (may be *Wastcroft* 1606 *DuLa*). For Cockroad, Coneygre, Grey Lains, Hatchets, the Lawn, Lousy Hill, Lynch, Mundays Down, Picked Mead[1], Plasket[1], the Sling, Three Halves, *v. supra* 427, ib., 439, 433, 440, 455, 426, 448, 443, ib., 454, 434. The School gives Bushel Leaze (*Bushy Leaze TA*) with explanatory story of an old woman and her daughter who gathered a bushel while leazing here; Hop Garden (*Hop Lands TA*); Louse Hill (*Lousy Hill TA*). It adds Clumper Ground, noted as heavy clay working into clods; Wentways, between various tracks, probably from ME *wente*, 'path.' Hatchett Lane and Inn derive from one of the 'hatch-gates' into Chute Forest (*supra* 12). Jubilee Clump at the highest point on Chute Causeway was formerly Whistling Ground from its wind-swept position, while Queen's Field was enclosed at the time of the Jubilee.

COLLINGBOURNE DUCIS. Long Meadow (*le Langemede* 14th AD ii). For Hitchings, the Lawn, Pen Fd, Stert Copse, *v. supra* 435, 440, 443, 447.

COLLINGBOURNE KINGSTON. Crooks Mead (cf. *Crooks coppice* 1641 WIpm). Ewe Down (*Iudon* 1241 FF, i.e. 'yew-down'). Garston (cf. *Gaston aker* 1568 *Sav* and *supra* 432). Hawley Fd (*Hawleyfilde* ib.). The Heel (*le Hylde* 1509 *MinAcct*. *v*. **hielde**, 'slope'). Stone Hill (*Stonehill* 1568 *Sav*). For Burgess Meadow, Culverslade, Knapp, Pickett Mead, the Several, Tenantry Fd, Town Croft, Townsend, *v. supra* 451, 428, 446, 427, 443, 454, 431, 449. String Coppice is a long narrow strip, *v. supra* 455. The School adds Presslands (*Prestland* 1650 *ParlSurv*), land belonging to the incumbent of the parish. Ham Meadow (*v*. **hamm**) lies low by the Bourne and so does Raylands (cf. Rey-bridge *supra* 103). For Crat Meadow, *v. supra* 428.

FROXFIELD. Home Close (*Home close alias Holly Close* 1671 *Recov*). For Breach Field, Hatchetts, Lawn Mead, Ninnicks, Severals, *v. supra* 423, 433, 440, 438, 454.

GRAFTON. In the *EnclA* (1792) we have Oxleaze (*Oxlease* 1540 *MinAcct*) and The Park (cf. *Parkefilde* 1573 *Sav*). The School adds Folly Meadow, Gaston, Picked Piece, Severals, Swath, *v. infra* 451, 432, 443, 454, 455.

HAM. For the Breach, Cocks Balls, Lashmore, the Severals, *v. supra* 423, 422, 493, 454.

[1] Pickit Piece, Flashet (School).

MILTON LILBORNE. Chislet Mead (*Childeslade* 1282 Ipm. *v.* slæd). Clay Fd (cf. *East Cley* 1632 WIpm). Down Fd (cf. *East, West Downe* 1628 ib.). Heath Close (cf. *Mylton heathe* 1609 WM xxi). Hitching Acre (cf. *Pewsey hitching* 1609 *Longford* and *supra* 435). Manfield[1] is on the parish boundary, cf. (ge)mæne *supra* 441. New Mead (*la Nywemede* 1272 *Ass*). Pugpits (may be 'goblin pits,' cf. Pugpits *supra* 387). Great, Little Sands (cf. *East Sandes* 1628 WIpm). For Acremans Severalls, Picked Fd, Severals, *v. supra* 454, 443, 454.

The School adds Twivers, the name of two fields where Deane Water joins the Avon, a dialectal variant of *twyford*, 'double ford,' and notes that Cole Croft (*TA*) is locally *Calcot*. It also adds The Packway, a deep-cut boundary lane on the east, and The Drunge (*supra* 451), a narrow valley-way between houses. Wootton Rivers School adds Klondyke (good land).

PEWSEY. Blacknell (1609 *Longford*). Broom Croft (*Broome croft* ib.). The Gore (*The Gores* 1609 *Longford. v.* gara). Long Moor (*Long Moore* ib.). Mill Croft (ib.). For the Cleeve, Garstons, Picked Leaze, *v. supra* 426, 432, 443.

SAVERNAKE. Clay Pit Fd (*Cleyputte* 1374 *For*). Wigmore (*Wygmere* 1362 ib.). For Conygar, the Drang, the Lawn, Peaked Gore, Picked Ground, Rag Fd, Sheep Sleight, Three Halves, *v. supra* 427, 451, 440, 443, ib., 453, 454, 434. The Drang is a long narrow strip, *v. supra* 451.

SHALBOURNE. Bars Bottom (cf. *la Bers* 1302 Pat. *bers* denotes a hedge used to form a deer-enclosure and has been discussed in PN Wo 389, PN Sx Pt. I, xliii). Fernal (*Fernhulle* 1257 *For*). Radnams (*Radenham* 1339 ib.). Rough Lands (*Rowland* 1568 *Sav*). For Cleeves, Gore Mead, Hassocks, Several, Slaight, *v. supra* 426, 432, 452, 454, ib.

TIDCOMBE. For the Freith, the Gores, Lynch, *v. supra* 431, 432, 436. String is a long strip between two large fields, *v. supra* 454.

The School adds Holloways (*Holeweye* 13th *Bradenstoke*); Holt Lands (cf. *Holtebal* ib., the *bal* is perhaps a boundary mark (*supra* 422), as the field is on the parish boundary, and gives *Rudges* for Ridges (*TA*).

WOOTTON RIVERS. Loscombes (*Lossecombe* 1542 *Sav*). Moor (cf. *Weste moore* ib.). For Homestall, Picked Furlong, Rag, *v. supra* 434, 443, 453. The School adds the Breach, *v. supra* 423.

---

[1] *Manvells* (School), *v.* Introd. xxi.

Amesbury Hundred

ALLINGTON. For Inn Mead, Picked Meadow, *v. supra* 438, 443.

AMESBURY. The Cliff (cf. *Clyvemulle* 1365 *DuLa*. *v.* clif, 'slope'). Droveway (cf. *ultra Dravam* 1222 FF. *v. supra* 429). Fleet Mead (*Fletemeade* 1541 Dugd) lies by a back-water of the Avon, *v.* fleot *supra* 431. Fold Meadow (cf. *le Folds* ib.). Northams (*Northam* 1365 *DuLa*, *Northams mead* 1650 *ParlSurv*). Southam Mead (*Sutham* 1222 FF, *Southam feild* 1650 *ParlSurv*. In distinction from Northams *supra* 433. *v.* hamm). Totterdown (1773 A and D). West Fd (*Westfeld* 1222 FF). Witnams (*Wittenham* 1365 *DuLa*, *Whittenam mead* 1650 *ParlSurv*). Woolson Hill (may be connected with *Wolsyngeswelle, Wolsyngeshulle* 1365 *DuLa*, the first element of which seems to be an *-ing* derivative of OE *Wulfsige* (personal name)). For the Bake, Burnbake, Picked Furlong, Well Penning, *v. supra* 450, 451, 443, 453.

BOSCOMBE. Churchill Furlong (*Churchehill* t. Jas 1 *LRMB*). Ash Verlon is probably for *Ash Furlong* (cf. Introd. xxi). For Coneygare, Head Acre, Lousey Bush, Paradise Fd, Picked Mead, Rudge Hill, *v. supra* 427, 422, 455, ib., 443, 437.

BULFORD. Chalk Croft (*Chawcrofte* t. Jas 1 *LRMB*). Great Mead (may be *Michell meade* ib. *v.* micel). Lower Ham (*Netherham* ib. *v.* hamm). Low Fd (*le lowe feilde* ib.). For Old Lains, the Penning, Picked Mead, Pound of Butter, *v. supra* 439, 453, 443, 455.

CHOLDERTON. For Picked Lains, Tenantry Down, *v. supra* 443, 439, 431.

DURNFORD. Earth Pits (cf. *Earthpitte* t. Jas 1 *LRMB* in Bulford). Middle Fd (*Middle feild* 1649 *SarumD and C*). Mill Ham and Meadow (*Mullehammes, Mullemede* 1343 *MinAcct*. *v.* hamm). Peaked Meadow (*Picked meade* 1649 *SarumD and C*. *v. supra* 443). For Conygre, Knapp Croft, Old Bake, *v. supra* 427, ib., 450. Catsbrain (School) is so called from the soil, cf. *supra* 425, while Cocked Hat (ib.) is so called from its shape.

DURRINGTON. Bad Meadow (*Badmeade* 1609 *Devizes*). Berricker (*Berry acre* ib., *Bury* 1649 *SarumD and C*. *v.* burh). Cliff (cf. *Bovetheclyve* 1360 *WinchColl*, i.e. 'above the slope,' *v.* clif). Colts Ham (cf. *Colteshey* 1460 ib. *v.* gehæg). New Leaze (*Neweleaze* 1609 *Devizes*). Oxland Hill (*Oxenlond* 1360 *Winch-*

Coll). Priests Close (*Priestes close* 1650 *ParlSurv*). From a *Survey* of 1790 (WM xxxi) we have The Batch (*le Bache* 1460 *WinchColl. v.* bæc). Borrow Acre (cf. *Borowe furlong* 1609 *Devizes, Burrowe* 1649 *SarumD and C. v.* beorg). Single Dean (*Singledeane* 1609 *Devizes*). Sloven Ball (*Slovens Ball* 1617 *WinchColl. v. supra* 422). Underclift (*Wondreclyf* 1460 ib.). For Burgess Orchard, Burnbake, Green Nap, Mundays Mead, the Penning, the Plaskett, *v. supra* 451, ib., 422, 440, 453, 443.

FIGHELDEAN. Benfield (c. 1704 *Wilton*). Broad Way (1627 WIpm). The Crook (1704 *Wilton*). The Down, Down Bake (cf. *les Dounes* ib. and *supra* 450). The Ham (1650 *ParlSurv*). Lanchet Furlong (1704 *Wilton*). Norden Hill (ib.). Picked Acre (1617 *WinchColl. v. supra* 443). Sheer Barrow (*Sheerbarrow* 1704 *Wilton*). For Bakeland, Butts Close, Down Bake, the Halves, Lammas Land, the Lawns, Linchet, Peaked Meadow, New Penning, Tenantry Down and Penning, *v. supra* 450, 425, 450, 434, 452, 440, 453, 443, 453, 431, 453.

LUDGERSHALL. West Fd (*le Westfeld* 1291 *MinAcct*). Wooldridges (*Wilrugge, Wulrugge* ib.). For Breach, Burgess Piece, Coneygre, Mundays Down, No Man's Ball, Quarland, Shoulder of Mutton, Town Fd, *v. supra* 423, 451, 427, 440, 456, 422, 445, 455, 449. No Man's Ball is on the parish and county boundary.

MILSTON. For Beak, Court Herne, Hitching, the Hyde, the Penning, *v. supra* 450, 437, 435, ib., 453. For the Wirgo, cf. Werg Mill *supra* 302.

NEWTON TONY. Great Broadberry (cf. *Broad Berry Field* 1695 WM xxxi). Church Hill (ib.). For Picked Hyde Fd, *v. supra* 443. The schools add The Loop, the Triangle, new fields east and west respectively of Newton Tony Curve.

NORTH TIDWORTH. For Picked Mead, Several, *v. supra* 443, 454.

Underditch Hundred

STRATFORD-SUB-CASTLE. Castle Fd (*Castlefeild* 1649 *Sarum-D and C*). Marsh Furlong (*Mershforlong* 1351 *Ass, Mercheforlond* 1353 AD iii). Pauls Dean (*Poulisdene* 1420 AD iv, cf. Poulshot *supra* 130). St Johns Fd (*St Joanes feild* 1649 *SarumD and C*). For Ivers Mead, the Pennings, Town Meadow, *v. supra* 450, 453, 449. Ivers Mead lies below steeply rising ground.

WILSFORD. For Dry Cratt, Penning, Stert, *v. supra* 428, 453, 447.

WOODFORD. For Bake, Coneygre, Hassocks Close, Linch Croft, Peaked Fd, *v. supra* 450, 427, 452, 436, 443.

Alderbury Hundred

ALDERBURY. Cock Gore (*Copgoare* 1650 *ParlSurv, Copped Gore* 1814 *Longford. v. supra* 427, 432). Foxberry (*Foxbury* 1650 *ParlSurv*). Home Close (1649 *SarumD and C*). For the Beak, the Lawn, Picked Mead, *v. supra* 450, 440, 443.

WEST DEAN. Bushy Leaze (*Busshey leaze* 1677 WM xxi). Coneygre (*Cunnigere* ib. 'Rabbit warren'). Pit Close (*Pitt close* ib.). For Hatchett, Penning, Tenants Down, *v. supra* 433, 453, 431. The School gives *Kingsil Hill* for Kingshill.

GRIMSTEAD. Brickkiln Common (cf. *Brickilne* 1650 *ParlSurv*). Cock Road (*Cockroad* ib. *v. supra* 428). Whitemarsh Brow (cf. *la Whytemersshe* 1348 *Cor*). For Picked Common, Picket Mead, *v. supra* 443.

IDMISTON. Broad Mead (*Brodemede* 1518 Hoare). Butts (*le Buttes* ib.). Chapel Croft (cf. *Chapelfurlong* ib.). Church Hill (*Churchulle* ib.). The Crate (*la Crofte* ib. *v. supra* 428). The Drove (cf. *Drovelande* ib. and *supra* 429). Hazel Hill (*Hazel-hulle* ib.). Hogdean Bottom (*Hockedeane, Hocdeene* ib.). Horse Barrow Piece (may be *Haresborghe* ib.). Longlands (*Longlonde* ib.). Marsh Fd (cf. *The Marshe* 1637 WIpm). Old Down (*Oldowne* 1518 Hoare). Pit Piece (cf. *Pyttelond* ib.). Ramsell (may be *Rameslade* ib. *v.* slæd). Redlands (*Rudlonde* ib., from hreod, 'reed'). Sweat Hill (*Swetehylle, Swetenehulle* ib.). Turpitt Fd (cf. *Turbutthulle* ib.). Wheat Fd (may be *Whytefoldes* ib.). Wiltway Fd (*Wyltewey* ib., i.e. road to Wilton). For Breeches, Cold Harbour, Coneygar, Gaston Furlong, Lain, Linch, Picked Crate, *v. supra* 423, 451, 427, 432, 439, 443, 428. Hundred Acres (31 poles) is ironical. Sling (cf. *supra* 454) is a strip by the river.

LAVERSTOCK. Swaynes Croft (cf. *Swaynesfeld* 1397 IpmR). For Bake, Picked Meadow, Shoulder of Mutton, *v. supra* 450, 443, 455.

PITTON and FARLEY. Bentcrate (may be *Bynecroft* 1549 *Sarum-D and C. v. supra* 428). Dunley (*Dunly hill* 1640 NQ viii). East Fd (*East feilde* ib.). Howes (*The Howes* 1650 *ParlSurv*). Litch-wells (may be *Lutteswell* 1227 SarumCh, 'Lutt's spring,' cf. Lutsey *supra* 248). Middle Fd (*Middle feild* 1649 *SarumD and C*). North Fd (*Northfeild* ib.). Picked Meadow (*Picked meade* 1636

WIpm. *v. supra* 443). Rodsley (cf. *boscus de Radesle* 1257 *For*, *Roddesle* 1331 *MinAcct*, 1368 *For*). For Cock Road, *v. supra* 427. The Sling is a long narrow field (School). Luce Wood (*TA*) is recorded by the School as *Lucid*, Linterns (ib.) as *Lintons*, Oat Close (ib.) as *Wet Close*.

WINTERBOURNE DAUNTSEY. Smoke Land (cf. *Smocke acre* 1518 Hoare and *supra* 446). For Burnbake, Hatchett Piece, Lynch Fd, *v. supra* 451, 433, 476. The School adds Sling Field and Plantation, a long strip by the road (*supra* 453).

WINTERBOURNE EARLS. Hill Close (1627 WIpm). Honey Mead (*Hony meade* 1649 *SarumD and C*). Hyde Fd (*Hide feild* ib.). Marsh Croft (cf. *The Marshe* 1627 WIpm). Whitmarsh (*White-mersh* 1331 *For*). For Mundays Croft, *v. supra* 440. The School adds Pickett Piece (cf. *Picked Meade* 1627 WIpm, with sharp corners); Ell Field (*TA*) appears as *Ell Crot*, so called from its shape, and many other fields have *crot* for *croft* (cf. *supra* 428).

WINTERBOURNE GUNNER. For Clap Gate, Culver Meadow, *v. supra* 451, 428.

WINTERSLOW. Whiteway (*Whyteweye juxta Wyntereslowe* 1348 *Cor*). Wood Leaze (*le Wodelese* 1362 *For*). For the Bake, Coneygre, Drove, Linchets, Picked Acre, Pickpocket, *v. supra* 450, 427, 429, 453, 443, 455. Wiltshire Bottom is in a detached part of the parish, adjoining Hampshire.

Frustfield Hundred

LANDFORD. For Mundays, *v. supra* 440.

WHITEPARISH. Bidnells (cf. John *atte Bodenhulle* 1333 *SR*, Thomas *atte Budenhulle* 1346 *Ass*). Breach Mead (cf. Nicholas *atte Breche* 1341 *Cor*). French Orchard (cf. *le Frensshey* 1331 WIpm, from (ge)hæg). Hareways (cf. William *atte hereweye* 1289 *Ass*, John *atte Hereweye* 1333 *SR. v. supra* 435). It lies by the Romsey-Salisbury road. Marsh Mead (cf. William *atte Mersshe* 1341 *Cor*). Small Gains (*Small gains* 1709 *Wilton. v. supra* 455). West Fd (*Westfeld* 1331 WIpm). For Bell Croft, Enocks, Gaston, Linchetts, Picked Fd, Hoe and Down, Purlieu Fd, Yewish, *v. supra* 451, 438, 432, 453, 443, 453, 435. The Sling (*supra* 454) is a narrow strip. Sunt Meadow is close by Sunt Copse *supra* 397.

Downton Hundred

BISHOPSTONE. Allicombe Bottom (cf. *Alrecombe* 1328 WIpm. 'Alder combe'). The School adds Bake Ground, Picket Close (*Picked Close* 1634 *Wilton*), *v. supra* 450, 443.

BODENHAM and NUNTON. Marsh Furlong (*Mersfurlang'* 1260 FF). Well Piece (cf. Richard *atte Welle* 1333 *SR*). For Costals, Penning Piece, *v. supra* 427, 453.

DOWNTON and REDLYNCH. Barn Fd (cf. *Berncroft* 1402 *Winch-Coll*). Birchen Coppice (*Birchin Coppice* 1632 *EcclCom*). Hares Spur (*Harespurre* 1686 *Longford*. Cf. Gasper *supra* 181). Hatchet Close (cf. *Hakyate* 1402 *WinchColl. v.* geat and *supra* 433). Home Croft (*Homecroft* 1503 ib.). Merry Croft (*Merry-croft* 1686 *Longford*). Timbury (cf. *Tymberhull* 1503 *WinchColl*, -*hills* 1686 *Longford*). For Burnbake, Conygre, the Doles, Gaston, Lammas Hay, Leg Ground, Oare, Paradise, the Pen, Picked Piece, *v. supra* 451, 427, 429, 432, 452, 455, 442, 455, 443, ib.

Damerham Hundred

COMPTON CHAMBERLAYNE. Barn Fd (cf. *Overberne* 1328 WIpm). Bratch Coppice (cf. *le Breche* ib. and *supra* 423). Brim Lands (*Brembyllonde* ib.). Little Croft (*Lytelecroft* ib.). Stoney Land (*Stanynglond* ib.). Town Mead (cf. *Tounforlong* ib.). Whiteland (*Whitelonde* ib.). For the Beak, Compton Folley, Garston, Picked Park, Starvealls, Tenantry Down, *v. supra* 450, 451, 432, 443, 455, 431.

DAMERHAM[1]. Blackfull Furlong (cf. *Blackepole*). Broad Mead (*Brodemede*). Butts Ground (cf. *lez Buttes*). Chuppers (*Chup-pare*). Culver Hayes (*Culverhay* 1545 *Ct*. 'Dove enclosure'). Hangoak Ground (cf. *Hangyngoke*). Hill Pits (*Helpyttes*). Kings Fd and Mead (cf. *Kyngesdone*). Long Down (*Langdoune*). Upper, Lower Marl (cf. *Merle corner*, *Marlecorner*). Mill Meadow (cf. Thomas *atte Mulle* 1341 *Cor*, *Millefurlong* 1518). Orchard Close (cf. *le Orcharde*, *Oldeorcharde*). Park Fd (*Parke-felde*). Pitlands (*Pyttelonde*). Ryalls (*la Ryall*). Slade Bottom (cf. *Sladisheued* c. 945 (15th) BCS 817, *la Slade* 1518. *v.* slæd). Sour Land (*Souerlonde*). Townsend Meadow (cf. *Townesend-furlong*). Upley (*Upley*, -*lie. v.* leah). White Barrow Fd (cf.

---

[1] The forms, unless otherwise stated, are from a Survey of 1518 (Hoare).

Whytebaroghe). Whatcomb (*Wad(e)combe*). White Hill (cf. *Whethulle, Whetehulle, Wethulle,* 'wheat hill'). White Stile (*Whitestuyle*). For Hughs Ball, the Lawn, *v. supra* 422, 440.

MARTIN[1]. Broad Shard (*Brodesherde. v. supra* 445). Cocknells or Cacknells (*Cakenhulle, Cattenhulle*). Great, Little Dean (cf. *Deen furlong, Lytledeene. v.* denu). Dunny Dole (*Dyny-, Dynne-, Denydole*). Gratton Stitches (*Grotenstichene, Gratenstiche, Gratenhulstiche. v. supra* 447). Heath Close (cf. *le Heeth*). Holloway Fd (*Holeway*). Horseys (cf. Galfr. de *Horseye* 1289 *Ass*). Isserden (*Yseworthedeene, Iswordeene, v.* worþ). Lanhams Meadow (cf. *Lanehame*). Long Furlong (*Longfurlong*). Lynch (*le Lynche* 1545 *Ct. v. supra* 436). Milkway (*Mylkeway, Melkewaie.* Cf. Milk Hill *supra* 324). Play Close (cf. *Pleycrofte*). Pollshard (*Poleshorde. v. supra* 445). Rutland Piece (cf. *Rudde-, Rudlonde, Rudlondende*). Sheep Down (*Shepdowne*). Short Furlong (*Shortefurlong*). Standcroft (*Stane crofte, Standecroftes*). Whitcomb (*Whitcombe, Wydcombe*). For Burnbake, Penning, *v. supra* 451, 453.

[1] The forms, unless otherwise stated, are from a Survey of 1518 (Hoare).

INDEX

OF SOME WORDS OF WHICH THE HISTORY IS ILLUSTRATED IN THIS VOLUME

INDEX

OF PLACE-NAMES IN WILTSHIRE

The primary reference to a place is marked by the use of Clarendon type.

No attempt has been made in this Index to include street-names or, except in the case of certain elements (e.g. yfer, wic), those names which at once suggest the parish in which they are to be found, e.g. Bishopstone Downs and Folly (in Bishopstone).

In grouping names together no distinction has been made (i) between *s* and *'s*, e.g. Batten's Fm and Battens Hill are grouped together under Batten's, (ii) between names written in one or two words, e.g. Cold Harbour and Coldharbour are grouped under Cold Harbour. Parish names are given separately.

INDEX

OF PLACE-NAMES IN COUNTIES OTHER
THAN WILTSHIRE

*[References to place-names in Bk, Beds, Hu, Wo, NRY, Sx, D, Nth, Sr, Ess,
Wa, ERY and Herts are not included, as these have been fully dealt with in
the volumes already issued upon the names of those counties.]*

CAMBRIDGE: PRINTED BY
W. LEWIS, M.A.
AT THE UNIVERSITY PRESS